MICROECONOMICS

Fifth Edition

Edwin G. Dolan
George Mason University

David E. Lindsey
Deputy Director
Division of Monetary Affairs
Board of Governors of the Federal Reserve System

The Dryden Press
Chicago   New York   San Francisco   Philadelphia   Montreal   Toronto   London   Sydney   Tokyo

Acquisitions Editor: Elizabeth Widdicombe
Developmental Editor: Rebecca Ryan
Project Editor: Karen Vertovec
Design Director: Alan Wendt
Production Manager: Barb Bahnsen
Permissions Editor: Doris Milligan/Cindy Lombardo
Director of Editing, Design, and Production: Jane Perkins

Copy Editor: Nancy Maybloom
Indexer: Leoni McVey
Compositor: York Graphic Services, Inc.
Text Type: 10/12 Plantin Light

Library of Congress Cataloging-in-Publication Data

Dolan, Edwin G.
   Microeconomics/Edwin G. Dolan, David E. Lindsey.—5th ed.

   Bibliography: p.
   Includes index.
   1. Microeconomics.   I. Lindsey, David Earl.   II. Title.
HB172.D65   1988   338.5   87-31421
ISBN 0-03-020397-X

Printed in the United States of America
890-032-98765432
Copyright © 1988, 1986, 1983, 1980, 1977 by The Dryden Press,
a division of Holt, Rinehart and Winston, Inc.

Address orders:
111 Fifth Avenue
New York, NY 10003

Address editorial correspondence:
One Salt Creek Lane
Hinsdale, IL 60521

The Dryden Press
Holt, Rinehart and Winston
Saunders College Publishing

Cover Source: Wassily Kandinsky, *Shaking Balancement*, 1925, The Tate
               Gallery, London. Copyright Artists Rights Society,
               Inc., New York/ADAGP 1987.

The Dryden Press Series in Economics

Asch and Seneca
Government and the Marketplace

Breit and Elzinga
The Antitrust Casebook

Breit and Ransom
The Academic Scribblers, *Revised Edition*

Campbell, Campbell, and Dolan
Money, Banking, and Monetary Policy

Dolan and Lindsey
Economics, *Fifth Edition*

Dolan and Lindsey
Macroeconomics, *Fifth Edition*

Dolan and Lindsey
Microeconomics, *Fifth Edition*

Eckert and Leftwich
The Price System and Resource Allocation, *Tenth Edition*

Gardner
Comparative Economic Systems

Hyman
Public Finance: A Contemporary Application of Theory to Policy, *Second Edition*

Johnson and Roberts
Money and Banking: A Market-Oriented Approach, *Third Edition*

Kaufman
The Economics of Labor Markets and Labor Relations

Kidwell and Peterson
Financial Institutions, Markets, and Money, *Third Edition*

Lindsay
Applied Price Theory

Link, Miller, and Bergman
Econograph: Interactive Software for Principles of Economics

Nicholson
Intermediate Microeconomics and Its Application, *Fourth Edition*

Nicholson
Microeconomic Theory: Basic Principles and Extensions, *Third Edition*

Pappas and Hirschey
Fundamentals of Managerial Economics, *Second Edition*

Pappas and Hirschey
Managerial Economics, *Fifth Edition*

Puth
American Economic History, *Second Edition*

Rukstad
Macroeconomic Decision Making in the World Economy: Text and Cases

Welch and Welch
Economics: Theory and Practice, *Second Edition*

Yarbrough and Yarbrough
The World Economy: Trade and Finance

Preface

Change Is the Only Constant

It has been a decade and a half since the authors first collaborated on an economics text. Those years have shown that in economics, change is the only constant.

Since our first effort to set forth the principles of economics for beginning students, economists have gained a better understanding of both the world at large and their own discipline. In macroeconomics, more is known about the dynamics of inflation and disinflation, the role of expectations in shaping economic behavior, and the interaction of the domestic economy with the world economy. In microeconomics, the contributions of public choice theory have lent a new perspective to many policy issues, the work of the modern Austrian school has brought new emphasis to the role of entrepreneurship, and long-established fields of economics such as antitrust policy, human resources, and income distribution have taken on new life.

But the economy has not stood still in the face of economists' improved understanding. Events have continued to pose new questions. Economists still disagree on such matters as the effects of the federal deficit, the proper strategy for monetary policy, the sources of volatility in securities prices and exchange rates, the reasons for differences in men's and women's average pay, and the effects of antipoverty policies, to name just a few areas of controversy.

The rapid pace of change in economic theory and reality makes teaching economics a challenge. Meeting that challenge requires a textbook that changes too. First, the book must bring the latest policy issues and theoretical topics into the classroom and explain them clearly. Second, the book must emphasize the ways of thinking that all economists use to attack new problems, even where they do not ultimately agree. Finally, the book must reflect ongoing innovation in pedagogical techniques so that the complexities of economics are made accessible to the beginning student.

This fifth edition of *Microeconomics* responds to the need for change with these major innovations:

1. **Feature: Focus on entrepreneurship.** A new chapter, Chapter 12, covers theories of entrepreneurship and the market process, including contributions of the modern Austrian school. Coverage of entrepreneurship is not limited to this special chapter, however. The role of entrepreneurship in the market economy is repeatedly stressed when discussing supply and demand, theory of the firm, industrial organization, and microeconomic policy.

   Purpose: To show how the market economy deals with scarcity in a world in which change is a "given" and information is one of the key scarce resources.

   Benefit: Students learn that microeconomics is more than a set of abstract geometrical exercises.

2. **Feature: Public choice economics.** Another new chapter, Chapter 19, covers public choice economics. As with the topic of entrepreneurship, the

influence of public choice theory is not limited to this chapter. Related topics, including theories of rent seeking, externalities, market and government failure, and privatization are developed in Chapter 5, near the start of the course, and in many of the applied micro chapters.

Purpose: To show that basic economic concepts apply to public as well as private choices.

Benefit: Provides a perspective on the strengths and limitations of democratic government in the sphere of economic policy.

3. **Feature: State-of-the-art pedagogy.** Enhanced teaching and learning aids and a new generic organization of boxed cases mean that the fifth edition of *Microeconomics*, like past editions, defines the state of the art in pedagogy.

Purpose: To help students see the forest as well as the trees.

Benefit: Students who understand economics as a way of thinking rather than just a grab bag of models retain more of what they learn in the principles of economics course.

Keeping a textbook like this up to date is not simply a matter of adding new material. Selective pruning is also necessary. In deciding what to eliminate, our overriding aim has been to focus on a few key models and concepts that will unify the student's way of thinking about economics. Input from many reviewers, users, and students has helped us in this task. In some cases, topics have been deleted when they were found repetitive or were used by only a minority of instructors. Other topics, such as farm policy, no longer appear as separate chapters but are grouped with related topics elsewhere.

Edwin G. Dolan and David E. Lindsey have collaborated on every edition of this book. In this edition, Lindsey has returned to the status of full coauthor. His wide knowledge of economic theory and insider's view of the policy process complement Dolan's experience in the classroom and as a government microeconomic analyst. Of course the views expressed in this book are those of the authors and do not necessarily reflect the views of the Board of Governors of the Federal Reserve System or other members of its staff. The following pages outline the approach of this book to the changing world of economics in more detail.

Organization of the Book

The Introductory Chapters

The book begins with a set of chapters that provide an overview of economics and the economy. As a group, these five chapters provide the background that students need to proceed with either a macro-first or micro-first course sequence.

Chapter 1, "What Economics Is All About," focuses on scarcity and choice as the issues that define the discipline of economics. It gives an idea of how economists, as people, think, confront disagreement, and work in academic, business, and government careers. Chapter 2, "Exchange and Production," looks at the central problems of what, how, and for whom that every economy faces. Chapter 3, "Supply and Demand," presents the basic model on which both micro and macro chapters build, stressing reactions to disequilibrium as well as equilibrium. Chapter 4, "The Role of Business: The Firm, Financial Markets, and Corporate Control," looks at current issues, such as takeovers and insider trading, as well as traditional material relating to the organization of the firm. Chapter 5, "The Role of Government: Market Failures, Rent Seeking, and Privatization," uses the concept of market failure to discuss such topics as provision of public goods and control of externalities and uses the concept of rent seeking to explain why government failures also sometimes occur.

Core Chapters and Applications

The central objective in revising the micro chapters of this text has been to blend new perspectives in microeconomics with the traditional core of neoclassical maximizing models. This has meant reorganization of existing material, addition of new material within several chapters, and addition of two new chapters.

Chapter 6, "Applying Supply and Demand," provides new applications of elasticity, including the issue of tax incidence. Chapter 7, "Rational Choice and Consumer Behavior," gives expanded attention to the general notion of rational choice as background for the specific topic of consumer choice. The chapter now also covers the topics of consumer and producer surplus.

The first section of Chapter 9, "Supply under Perfect Competition," has been rewritten to survey the varieties of market structure before examining perfect competition as a special case. Topics in the next two chapters have been regrouped. Regulated natural monopolies are now covered together with other monopoly topics in Chapter 10, "The Theory of Monopoly." Chapter 11, "Industrial Organization, Monopolistic Competition, and Oligopoly," now groups the topics covered in its title plus the subject of cartels.

A distinguishing feature of this text is its emphasis on the role of entrepreneurship in the economy. In this respect, it draws extensively on the modern Austrian theory of entrepreneurship and the market process. The importance of entrepreneurship as a force of change in the economy is developed as a counterpoint to the neoclassical notion of static equilibrium beginning in Chapters 2 through 5 and continuing through all of the chapters. The various threads of the discussion are drawn together in the new Chapter 12, "Entrepreneurship and the Market Process."

The influence of public choice theory can be seen at many points in the text. Chapter 5, which introduces the role of government, raises the notions of rent seeking, government failure, and privatization, all prominent themes of public choice theory. The new Chapter 19, "The Theory of Public Choice," shows how many policy actions taken by government can be understood in terms of the rational behavior of voters and government officials. The influence of the public choice approach can also be seen in a number of the other applied micro chapters. For example, public choice concepts are used to explain the prevalence of protectionist policies in Chapter 20, "International Trade and Trade Policy."

There has been some pruning in the micro chapters. The previously separate chapters on antitrust and regulation have been combined into one. There is no longer a separate chapter on farm policy, although much of this material has been retained in the form of case studies in Chapters 3, 5, and 11. Finally, we have added an abbreviated version of "Careers in Economics" from the *Study Guide* as an appendix to the text.

Pedagogy

Many innovative features of earlier editions of *Microeconomics* have become industry standards. An example is multilevel vocabulary reinforcement, with boldface terms, marginal definitions, and an end-of-book glossary. While others play catch-up, the process of innovation and refinement continues in this new edition of Dolan/Lindsey.

Bracketing

One of the most solidly established techniques of effective pedagogy is that of *bracketing*. Every good classroom lecturer uses bracketing in the form of "Here's what we are going to say; here it is in detail; here is what we just said." The textbook equivalent is chapter preview and review. Sheer volume of preview and review material counts for less than do the care with which the two are tied together and what comes between. Here are the key bracketing techniques used in *Microeconomics:*

- Each chapter opens with a set of *learning objectives* posed in the form of issues to be addressed in the chapter. These are then used in question form to organize the *chapter summary*.

- A list of *key terms from previous chapters* appears at the beginning of each chapter. This is balanced by a list of *newly introduced terms* at the end of the chapter.

- Each chapter begins with a *lead-off case* and ends with a *case for discussion*. The first item in the *problems and topics for discussion* at the end of the chapter asks students to apply what they have learned to issues raised in the lead-off case. The case for discussion is followed by its own set of questions. (Answers to these questions are given in the *Instructor's Manual*.)

Generic Organization of Boxed Cases

Since its first edition, *Microeconomics* has been a leader in the use of case studies as a teaching and learning tool. In addition to the lead-off cases and cases for discussion used to bracket each chapter, numerous *boxed cases* appear within each chapter. An innovative feature of this edition is the organization of these cases into four generic categories, each with a specific purpose:

1. **Economics in the News.** Illustrates an abstract concept raised in the chapter with an actual quoted or paraphrased news item. Example: "Cookie Stores Feel the Bite as Market Shifts" (Chapter 9).

2. **Applying Economic Ideas.** Uses a tool learned in the chapter for solving a problem drawn from real life. Example: "The Opportunity Cost of a College Education" (Chapter 1).

3. **Who Said It? Who Did It?** Highlights the contribution of an economist of the past or present to a key idea discussed in the chapter. Example: "Adam Smith on the Invisible Hand" (Chapter 1).

4. **Perspective.** Takes a look at a controversial issue or adds additional detail to a point raised in the chapter. Example: "The Effect of Advertising on Consumer Perceptions" (Chapter 12).

The Package

A complete support package provides instructors and students with everything they need to teach and learn economics.

Test Bank

Written by Louis Amato and Irvin B. Tucker III, both of the University of North Carolina at Charlotte, in collaboration with Edwin G. Dolan, the *Test Bank* includes more than 2,000 items. The authors have fully class-tested each item, guaranteeing a comprehensive, "teacher-friendly" selection. The *Test Bank* contains the following features.

Number and Type of Questions
The *Test Bank* offers over 1,000 multiple-choice and true/false questions. It also contains many graphical questions.

Distribution of Questions by Chapter

- Each chapter has an appropriate number of questions based on its content and length. This varies from 40 questions for the first, introductory chapter to 120 for some of the core concept chapters.
- Some questions appear in alternate forms to permit reuse.
- Questions are arranged in the approximate order of the chapter coverage of each topic.

Categorization and Coding
All questions are coded according to level of difficulty and cognitive learning type. These are E (easy), M (moderate), D (difficult), DF (definition or fact), SA (simple analysis), and CI (complex interpretation). This allows the instructor to select a spectrum of questions for testing both recall learning and concept comprehension.

Graphing Emphasis
Many questions ask students to work directly on graphs. Questions are formatted to follow the "hands-on" sample items in the *Study Guide*.

Recordkeeping Aid
The *Test Bank* contains marginal recordkeeping space for the instructor to personalize it with the date each question is used and the percentage of students who correctly answer each question.

Additional Exam and Essay Problems
The *Instructor's Manual* contains two exam and essay problems for each chapter with which to supplement tests. Exam and essay problems typically serve as excellent extra-credit test questions for more proficient students. Answers are included.

Computerized Version
The *Computerized Test Bank* (available for the Apple® IIe, IBM® PC, IBM® PC-XT, and mag tape) allows the instructor to create tests tailored to particular

requirements. By using the questions stored on disk, both short quizzes and full-length exams can be quickly and easily constructed.

The *Computerized Test Bank* allows instructors to

- preview questions on the computer screen
- edit publisher-supplied questions and create personalized questions
- select exam questions manually or randomly
- create exam headings and determine the amount of space to be allotted each question
- scramble questions to create multiple versions of the same test
- print exams with answer keys and student answer sheets
- store exams created for future use
- produce partial hard copy of most graphs that appear in the *Test Bank*.

"Sticky-paper" versions of all graphs are also available for placement on the master copy.

Direct Service Hotline

For instructors who have any technical difficulties with the *Computerized Test Bank*, The Dryden Press/TEC offers a direct service number: 516-681-1773, 9 a.m. to 5 p.m. EST.

Instructor's Manual

The *Instructor's Manual* for *Microeconomics* is intended to help new instructors prepare their first principles course and experienced instructors retailor their course to mesh optimally with the text. With these aims in mind, the *Instructor's Manual* includes the following features.

What's Different Here and Why

This section, found at the beginning of each chapter, helps convert the course outline and lecture notes from other texts to *Microeconomics*, fifth edition. Changes from the fourth edition of *Microeconomics* are noted. This section also provides technical information on the theoretical models that underlie the book.

Instructional Objectives

All elements of the *Microeconomics* package—text, *Study Guide*, *Test Bank*, and *Instructor's Manual*—are coordinated by means of specific instructional objectives listed in each chapter of the *Instructor's Manual*. In the text, they are listed for students at the beginning of each chapter. Questions covering every topic on the list of instructional objectives are included in the *Test Bank*.

EconoGraph II

An important element of the *Microeconomics* package is *EconoGraph II*, a computer-aided instruction program featuring interactive graphical exercises and simulations. It consists of nine computer-based lessons divided between micro- and macroeconomic topics. A special section in the corresponding chapters of the *Instructor's Manual* discusses the use of *EconoGraph II*.

Lecture Notes and Suggestions

Each chapter of the *Instructor's Manual* contains a section of lecture notes in outline form. The pages are perforated and three-hole punched to facilitate their integration with the instructor's own lecture notes. The lecture notes cover the optional appendixes as well as the chapters. In addition, they list transparency acetates that are available for use with the text. The use of the transparencies is more fully discussed in a separate transparency guide.

Examination Problems and Essays

Each chapter contains two or three suggestions for examination problems and essays. These are valuable supplements to the multiple-choice and true/false questions contained in the *Test Bank* where the teaching situation permits grading of problems and essays.

Answers to Selected Problems and Topics for Discussion

Answers are given to selected items from the "Problems and Topics for Discussion" sections of the text as well as the "Case for Discussion" sections in each chapter. Items that involve library research or ask questions that pertain to students' personal or community situation are omitted.

Course Planning Guide

In addition to these chapter-by-chapter features, the introductory section of the *Instructor's Manual* contains extensive suggestions on course planning to fit a wide variety of course calendars.

Study Guide

The *Study Guide* for *Microeconomics* provides students with hands-on applications and self-testing opportunities. It reinforces the text and prepares students for exams. The *Study Guide* contains the following features.

Where You're Going

All parts of the *Microeconomics* package are tied together by a numbered set of learning objectives for each chapter. These learning objectives, which also appear in the text and the *Instructor's Manual,* are given in the "Where You're Going" section of each chapter of the *Study Guide*. A list of terms introduced in the chapter is also provided.

Walking Tour

The "Walking Tour" section is a narrative summary of the chapter and incorporates questions on key points. Students work through this material, answering the questions as they go along. Answers to the questions are given in the margins.

Hands On

This section contains graphical and numerical exercises that give students hands-on experience in working with the concepts covered in the chapter. It is particularly helpful to students who require extra work in order to master difficult graphical material. Complete solutions, including graphs, are given at the end of the chapter.

Economics in the News

Each of these sections takes the form of a brief news item with questions that relate the item to concepts covered in the chapter. Answers are found at the end of the chapter. These items are particularly valuable in preparing for essay-type exam questions. This feature is the *Study Guide* version of the case study approach used in the text and links economics to the real world.

Self Test

This section consists of 15 multiple-choice questions, which are similar in structure to those in the *Test Bank* and act as a final checkpoint before an exam. Annotated answers to the self-test items are given at the end of the chapter.

Don't Make This Common Mistake

These are special boxes, strategically placed throughout the *Study Guide*, that caution students against certain common mistakes made by successive generations of economics students. All of these mistakes are easy to avoid if the student is alerted to them.

Careers in Economics

A unique feature of the *Study Guide* is the "Careers in Economics" section. This section, written by Keith Evans of California State University, Northridge, has been updated for the fifth edition. This material should appeal to students considering a major in economics.

EconoGraph II

Created by Charles Link, Jeffrey Miller, and John Bergman of the University of Delaware, *EconoGraph II* is a computer software package for principles of economics. It consists of nine interactive tutorial lessons. These lessons include the topics students find most difficult to master, including

- supply and demand
- money expansion
- AS/AD
- Keynesian cross analysis
- cost functions
- supply under perfect competition
- monopoly.

EconoGraph II is designed for use with IBM PCs with at least 128K of memory, DOS 2.0, and a color graphics card (use with IBM compatibles is possible but not guaranteed). Features include:

1. Intensive instruction in the use of graphs, which are critical in economics.
2. Self-contained 10- to 40-minute lessons.
3. Diagnostic questions and problems in which the computer tells students what they did right or wrong.
4. Graphical manipulations in which students can plot lines and shift curves.
5. Graphs constructed in stages so that each stage can be explained and important aspects highlighted.
6. Self-paced instruction to allow for repetition and review.

GraphPac

A completely new concept in student study aids, *GraphPac* is the first graph note-taking device available to economics students. Each *GraphPac* tablet contains reproductions of all major graphs in the text with additional graph-ruled margins. *GraphPac* allows students to take notes on key graphs without having to sketch transparency acetates, masters, or basic chalkboard drawings. The marginal graph rules provide space for students to reproduce additional graphs drawn by the instructor during a lecture. This is especially useful when the student wants to capture the effect of a shift or change in a basic graph.

GraphPac is free to students upon adoption of the text. It can be ordered by submitting the request number when placing a textbook order.

GraphPac is unique to the fifth edition of *Microeconomics*.

Transparency Acetates

The transparency acetates are two color and computer generated. This provides maximum accuracy and readability. For complete pedagogical consistency, the color used in the graphics matches that in the text. There are more than 160 acetates of graphs from the text. Each transparency has a complete teaching note to help instructors integrate the transparency into their lectures.

Some Words of Thanks

We wish to thank the following people for their help in revising this edition:

Jack Adams, *University of Arkansas*
Charles Bennett, *Gannon University*
Thomas Bonsor, *East Washington University*
David Brasfield, *Murray State University*
Donald Bumpass, *Texas Technical University*
William Carlisle, *University of Utah*
James Clark, *Wichita State University*
Avi Cohen, *York University*
C. M. Condon, *College of Charleston*
James Cover, *University of Alabama*
J. R. Cowart, *Mobile College*
Kenneth DeHaven, *Tri-County Technical College*
Mary Deily, *Texas A&M University*
Howard Elder, *University of Alabama*
Charles Ellard, *Pan American University*
Michael Erickson, *Eastern Illinois University*
Christopher Fiorentino, *West Chester University*
David Fractor, *California State University, Northridge*
Gary Galles, *Pepperdine University*
Lynne Gillette, *Texas A&M University*
Robert Gillette, *Texas A&M University*
Fred Graham, *University of Texas, Arlington*

Harish Gupta, *University of Nebraska*
James Hamilton, *University of Virginia*
Oskar Harmon, *University of Stamford*
Charles Hegji, *Auburn University, Montgomery*
John Holland, *Iona College*
R. James, *James Madison University*
Robert Jerome, *James Madison University*
James Jonish, *Texas Technical University*
Ebrahim Karbassioon, *Eastern Illinois University*
Bruce Kaufman, *Georgia State University*
Calvin Kent, *Baylor University*
James Kyle, *Indiana State University*
Luther Lawson, *University of North Carolina, Wilmington*
Stephen Lile, *Western Kentucky University*
Joseph Lin, *Louisiana State University*
Raymond Lombra, *Pennsylvania State University*
Don Losman, *National Defense University, Washington*
J. L. Love, *Valdosta State College*
David MacPherson, *Pennsylvania State University*
Jay Marchand, *University of Mississippi*
Benjamin Matta, *New Mexico State University*
John Mbaku, *Kennesaw College*

Eugene McKibbin, *Fullerton College*
Shah Mehrabi, *Mary Washington College*
Joseph Mesky, *East Carolina University*
Don Meyer, *Louisiana Tech University*
Steve Meyer, *Francis Marion College*
Jefferson Moore, *Louisiana State University*
J. M. Morgan, *College of Charleston*
John Murdoch, *Northeast Louisiana University*
Kenneth Nowotny, *New Mexico State University*
James O'Neill, *University of Delaware*
Pat Papachristou, *Christian Brothers College*
Carl Pearl, *Cypress College*
Thomas Peterson, *Central Michigan University*
John Piscotta, *Baylor University*
J. M. Pogodzinski, *Georgia State University*
David Rees, *Mesa College*
Michael Rendich, *Westchester Community College*
D. Rogers, *LeMoyne College*

Donald Schaefer, *Washington State University*
Bruce Seaman, *Georgia State University*
Frank Slesnick, *Bellarmine College*
Phillip Smith, *Gainesville Junior College*
Ken Somppi, *Auburn University*
David Spenser, *Brigham Young University*
Henry Thomasson, *Southeastern Louisiana University*
Timothy Tregarthen, *University of Colorado, Colorado Springs*
David Tuerck, *Suffolk University*
Arienne Turner, *Fullerton College*
Steven Ullmann, *University of Miami*
K. T. Varghese, *James Madison University*
Thomas Vernon, *Clarion University of Pennsylvania*
Michael Watts, *Purdue University*
William Weber, *Illinois State University*
Don Williams, *Kent State University*
Eugene Williams, *Northwestern State University*
Ernie Zampelli, *Catholic University of America*

In addition, we would like to thank the staff of The Dryden Press for making this edition possible. They are a truly dedicated, tireless group of professionals.

Edwin G. Dolan
Great Falls, Virginia

David E. Lindsey
Arlington, Virginia

December 1987

About the Authors

Edwin G. Dolan grew up in a small town in Oregon. He attended Earlham College and then Indiana University, earning a B.A. degree from Indiana. After staying at Indiana to earn an M.A. in economics, he completed his Ph.D. at Yale University. Dolan spent the next few years teaching economics at the University of Connecticut, Dartmouth College, and the University of Chicago. He has served as a specialist in transportation regulation, both in the antitrust division of the U.S. Department of Justice and at the Interstate Commerce Commission. For the last ten years, he has taught economics at George Mason University.

David E. Lindsey comes from the university town of West Lafayette, Indiana. He received his B.A. from Earlham College and his Ph.D. from the University of Chicago, where he studied under Milton Friedman. Lindsey taught economics for several years at Ohio State University and Macalester College. He began his long-running collaboration with Dolan on their principles text while at Macalester. Since 1974 he has been on the staff of the Board of Governors of the Federal Reserve System, where he now serves as Deputy Director of the Division of Monetary Affairs.

Contents in Brief

Contents

An Overview of the Market Economy

Part One

1 What Economics Is All About

After reading this chapter, you will understand . . .

- What economics is all about.
- How the need to choose is related to the concept of cost.
- The roles that households, business firms, and government units play in the economy.
- What markets are and how they work.
- Who worries about unemployment, inflation, and economic growth and why.
- Why economists sometimes disagree.
- How ethics and value judgments enter into economics.

How to Cope with a Teacher Shortage

"There's a limit to how much good you're doing serving tea and Coke. I identify more with being a third-grade teacher than I ever did with being a flight attendant." So says Kendall Hagerty, a former American Airlines flight attendant, recently retrained in a program devised by the city of Dallas to meet an acute teacher shortage. In Maine, a lobsterman and a blueberry farmer are among those enrolled in a new mid-career teacher training program. Delaware is converting people with chemical-industry backgrounds into science teachers, and Texas is training laid-off oil geologists.

Teaching economics

The armed forces are particularly ripe for teacher recruiting. Military personnel retire early, get generous pension benefits to supplement a teacher's pay, and are experienced in discipline and leadership. So the University of West Florida now offers teacher training on nearby Navy and Air Force bases, and Arizona State University targets the military in a new mid-career program.

These efforts reflect a shrinking supply of teachers in the face of strong demand. Between 1972 and 1982, enrollment in teacher education programs fell by 50 percent. Women and minority-group members, the traditional groupings from which teachers emerged, now have wider opportunities in higher-paying fields. Also, more teachers are retiring or quitting.

One result of the shortages: After many years of indifferent, even contemptuous treatment in the job market, teachers are being fawned over and catered to by recruiters who scour the country for prospects.

At one job fair, Prince George's County, Maryland, gave away book bags, balloons, and apples to lure teachers to its table, where it told them about all the goodies they would get if they signed on—including a month's free rent and cut-rate car loans.

Bad form, competitors complained. Tough, says a spokesman for the district. "It's a cutthroat market out there. Teachers deserve to be competed for,"

3

he adds. Helped by a recent 21 percent salary raise as well as the balloons, the county was swamped with 4,000 applications for 400 jobs.

Source: Francis C. Brown III, "Recruiting Drive: Shortage of Teachers Prompts Talent Hunt by Education Officials," *The Wall Street Journal,* January 15, 1987, 1. Reprinted by permission of *The Wall Street Journal,* © Dow Jones & Company, Inc. 1987. All Rights Reserved. Photo Source: © Chris Paganelli.

Scarcity
A situation in which there is not enough of a resource to meet all of everyone's wants.

THE balloons and book bags are symptoms of the efforts of Prince George's County officials to cope with a universal economic problem: scarcity. **Scarcity** is a situation in which there is not enough of some resource to meet everyone's wants. In this case, the scarce resource is people. School administrators across the country want people to serve as teachers to educate the children entering their classrooms. But there are not enough people to do everything at once; thus, school administrators are taking actions to attract flight attendants, lobstermen, and oil geologists to change careers. In another situation, the scarce resource might be fresh water. In order to be available for household use, water might have to be diverted from farming. In still another, the scarce resource might be time. In order to find time to devote to studying, hours spent satisfying other wants, such as sports, might have to be cut back. Scarcity is something that is encountered in thousands of forms every day.

Economics
The study of the choices people make and the actions they take in order to make the best use of scarce resources in meeting their wants.

The concept of scarcity is central to economics. In fact, **economics** can be defined as the study of the choices that people make and the actions they take in order to make the best use of scarce resources in meeting their wants. The above example illustrates the actions and choices of two groups of people. First are the school officials who are making choices and taking actions that they hope will attract the teachers they want. Second are the people who are making the choice of whether to devote their limited working years to teaching or to some other career.

In this book, we will meet scarcity in hundreds of situations. As we do so, we will see how the discipline of economics provides a framework for analyzing actions and choices that are directed toward fulfilling people's wants.

Scarcity and Choice

In a world of scarcity, we constantly encounter trade-offs between one goal and another. If we spend more on lunch, we may have less left to spend on dinner. If we live in the country, we may have to commute farther to work. On a national level, if we spend more on defense, other federal programs may have to be cut back. The number of such trade-offs is limitless.

Goods
All things that people value.

Services
The valued acts that people perform for one another.

One trade-off highlighted in the opening article in this chapter is that between goods and services. **Goods** are simply all the things that people value—blueberries, lobsters, oil, or whatever. **Services** are the valued acts that people perform for one another—teaching school, serving meals on an airplane, providing insurance, and so on.

Education is an example of a service. In the long run, getting an education may help you achieve a higher standard of living, but in the short run, it means sacrifice. To finish college—or even high school—you may have to spend your savings, postpone getting a full-time job, or live at home longer than you would like. Further, education entails trade-offs not just for one person but for the economy as a whole. Resources must be devoted to building classrooms rather than factories or airports. Teachers and school staff cannot work at producing other things at the same time. Finally, while students who graduate may eventually contribute more to the economy than they would had they shortened their education, they will contribute less during the time they are in school.

The Production Possibility Frontier

Economists are fond of using graphs to illustrate key concepts. We will use many graphs in this course.[1] As an introduction to the use of graphs in economics, we will use a simple graph to illustrate the concept of scarcity.

The actual U.S. economy is complex. It produces thousands of different goods and services. To facilitate our first illustration of scarcity, we will envision a simpler economy in which just one service is produced, education, and just one good, cars. Exhibit 1.1 shows the trade-offs between education and cars for such an economy. The horizontal axis measures the quantity of education in terms of the number of high school graduates "produced" per year; the vertical axis measures the production of cars. Any combination of education and cars can be shown as a point in the space between the two axes. For example, production in some year of 10 million high school graduates and 5 million cars would be represented by point E.

In drawing this figure, we assume given supplies of the basic inputs known as **factors of production**. There are three of these. **Labor** consists of the productive contributions made by people working with their minds and muscles. **Capital** consists of all the productive inputs created by people, including tools, machinery, structures, and intangible items such as computer programs. **Natural resources** include everything that can be used as a productive input in its natural state, such as farmland, building sites, forests, and mineral deposits. The factors of production used to produce education include labor in the form of teachers and staff; capital in the form of buildings, desks, and computers; and natural resources in the form of building sites and fuel with which to heat buildings. The figure also assumes a certain state of technology for the production of both cars and education.

Exhibit 1.1 shows that even if all factors of production were devoted to education, there would be a limit to the quantity of education that could be produced. To illustrate, suppose that the limit is 20 million graduates per year. The extreme possibility of producing 20 million graduates and nothing else is shown by point A in Exhibit 1.1. As the figure is drawn, the maximum output of cars if no resources whatever are put into education is 18 million, shown by point B. Between these two extremes is a whole range of possible combinations of education and other goods. These intermediate possibilities are shown by points such as C and D, which fall along a smooth curve. This curve is called a **production possibility frontier.** It is called a "frontier" because it is a boundary between the combinations of education and cars that can be produced and those that cannot given the available technology and factors of production.

Points A, B, C, and D, which lie directly on the curve, stand for the combinations of education and cars that can be produced. Combinations inside the

Factors of production
The basic inputs of labor, capital, and natural resources used in producing all goods and services.

Labor
The contributions to production made by people working with their minds and muscles.

Capital
All means of production that are created by people, including tools, industrial equipment, and structures.

Natural resources
Anything that can be used as a productive input in its natural state, such as farmland, building sites, forests, and mineral deposits.

Production possibility frontier
A graph showing the possible combinations of goods that can be produced in an economy given the available factors of production and technology.

---

[1] Readers who would like to review the basic techniques of graphing may refer to the appendix to this chapter.

Exhibit 1.1   Production Possibility Frontier

This figure shows possible outputs of cars and education in a simple economy where these are the only two products. Technologies and the available supplies of factors of production are assumed to be fixed. If all factors are devoted to education, 20 million high school graduates can be "produced" each year (point A). If all factors are devoted to making cars, 18 million cars can be made each year (point B). If the factors are divided between the two products, combinations such as those at points C and D are possible. The curve connecting A, B, C, and D is called a *production possibility frontier*. The slope of the frontier shows the opportunity cost of education in terms of cars. For example, between points C and D, producing an extra graduate requires giving up two cars. Points inside the frontier, such as E, are also possible and can be reached even if not all factors are used or some are used inefficiently. Points outside the frontier, such as F, cannot be reached with the available resources.

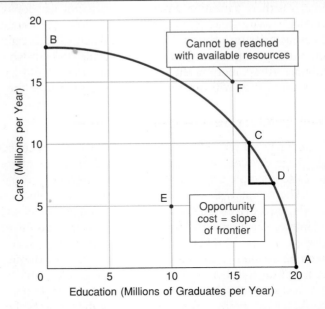

frontier, such as E, are also possible and do not require the full use of all available factors. But a combination represented by a point outside the frontier, such as F, cannot possibly be produced given the scarcity of factors of production and the available technology. It can be produced only if new factors of production become available (say, through growth of the labor force) or if new technologies permit more output per unit of the currently available factors.

Opportunity Cost

At any point along the frontier, there is a trade-off between education and cars. Given the scarcity of factors of production, choosing to produce more of one must mean choosing to produce less of the other. For example, suppose we begin at point C, where 16 million students are graduating from high school each year and 10 million cars are being made. If we want to increase the output of graduates to 18 million per year, we must give up some cars and use the freed-up factors of production to build and staff classrooms. In moving from point C to point D, then, we will be trading off production of 4 million cars for the extra 2 million graduates; that is, over this range of the frontier, each extra graduate will cost us about two cars.

Cost is a central concept in economics. In a world of scarcity, it is rare to get something for nothing. Typically we must bear costs in order to obtain benefits. In ordinary conversation, laypeople tend to use the term *cost* rather loosely; economists, however, are more cautious. The key cost concept in economics is that of **opportunity cost**—the cost of doing something as measured in terms of the value of the lost opportunity to pursue the best alternative activity with the same time or resources. In Exhibit 1.1, opportunity cost is shown by the slope of the production possibility frontier. For example, in moving from point C to point D, we sacrificed two cars for each additional graduate. Thus, in this range of the frontier, the opportunity cost of one graduate is two cars.

Opportunity cost
The cost of a good or service measured in terms of the lost opportunity to pursue the best alternative activity with the same time or resources.

In real life, we cannot refer to a handy book of production possibility frontiers to measure opportunity costs. Often prices stated in dollars and cents give an accurate picture of opportunity costs. For example, if a hamburger costs $3 and a bratwurst $1, we can say that the cost of eating a hamburger is the lost opportunity to eat three bratwursts. In other cases, time is a more appropriate measure of opportunity cost than is money. For example, the cost of spending an hour studying economics is the loss of the opportunity to spend the same hour studying math. In still other cases, such as that discussed in "Applying Economic Ideas 1.1," both time and money are involved in the calculation of opportunity cost.

We will find many applications for the concept of opportunity cost in this course. Economics, after all, is about scarcity and choice. Because time and resources are scarce, we must choose to give up one opportunity in order to take advantage of another many times each day.

What Economists Do

We now know a little about the subject matter of economics: It deals with scarcity and choice. What, however, do economists *do?* It is highly unlikely that they just sit around bemoaning the opportunities they passed up when they entered their chosen profession. In the broadest sense, as we have said, they study the ways in which people deal with the problem of scarcity. But it will be useful, as a preview of this course, to take a closer look. We will begin with the distinction between *microeconomics* and *macroeconomics*.

Microeconomics

The prefix *micro* comes from a Greek word meaning "small." **Microeconomics** is the branch of economics that deals with the choices made by small economic units—households, business firms, and government units.

Microeconomics
The branch of economics that deals with the choices and actions of small economic units—households, business firms, and government units.

Units of Analysis
In economics, a *household* is a group of people who pool their incomes, own property in common, and make economic decisions jointly. People who do not belong to such a group are counted as one-person households. Households supply factors of production and consume the goods and services that are produced.

Business firms are the second basic unit of microeconomic analysis. Firms buy factors of production from households and use them to produce goods and services. Firms come in many shapes and sizes. According to census data, there are more than 16 million business firms in the United States, ranging from small stores and family farms to huge corporations. Chapter 4 discusses the role of business firms in more detail.

Microeconomics also analyzes the actions of *government units* such as Congress, the courts, and regulatory agencies. As we will see throughout this book, units of government have a major impact on the economic lives of firms and households; their decisions, in turn, are affected by events in the economy. Chapter 5 examines the relationship between government and business in the U.S. economy.

APPLYING ECONOMIC IDEAS 1.1

The Opportunity Cost of a College Education

How much does it cost you to go to college? If you are a resident student at a typical four-year private college in the United States, you can answer this question by making up a budget like the one shown in Table A. This can be called a budget of *out-of-pocket costs*, because it includes all the items—and only those items—for which you or your parents actually must pay in a year.

Table A   Budget of Out-of-Pocket Costs

Tuition and fees	$ 5,800
Books and supplies	400
Transportation to and from home	400
Room and board	2,900
Personal expenses	700
Total out-of-pocket costs	$10,200

Your own out-of-pocket costs may be much higher or lower than these averages. Chances are, though, that these are the items that come to mind when you think about the costs of college. As you begin to think like an economist, you may find it useful to recast your college budget in terms of *opportunity costs*. Which of the items in Table A represent opportunities that you have forgone in order to go to college? Are any forgone opportunities missing? To answer these questions, compare Table A with Table B, which shows a budget of opportunity costs.

Table B   Budget of Opportunity Costs

Tuition and fees	$ 5,800
Books and supplies	400
Transportation to and from home	400
Forgone income	8,000
Total opportunity costs	$14,600

Some items are both opportunity costs and out-of-pocket costs. The first three items in Table A show up again in Table B. In order to spend $5,800 on tuition and fees and $400 on books and supplies, you must give up the opportunity to buy other goods and services—say, to buy a car or rent a ski condo. In order to spend $400 getting to and from school, you must pass up the opportunity to travel somewhere else or to spend the money on something other than travel. But not all out-of-pocket costs are also opportunity costs. The last two items in the out-of-pocket budget are examples. By spending $3,600 a year on room, board, and personal expenses during the year, you are not really giving up the opportunity to do something else. Whether or not you were going to college, you would have to eat, live somewhere, and buy clothes. Because these are expenses you would have in any case, they do not count as opportunity costs of going to college.

Finally, there are some items that are opportunity costs without being out-of-pocket costs. Thinking about what you would be doing were you not going to college suggests a major item that must be added to the opportunity cost budget but does not show up at all in the out-of-pocket budget. Had you not decided to go to college, you probably would have taken a job and started earning money soon after leaving high school. As a high school graduate, your earnings would be about $8,000 during the nine months of the school year. (You could work during the summer even if you were attending college.) Because this potential income is something you would have to forgo for the sake of college, it is an opportunity cost even though it would involve no monetary outlay.

Which budget you use depends on the kind of decision you are making. If you have already decided to go to college and are doing your financial planning, the out-of-pocket budget will tell you how much you will have to raise from savings, parents' contributions, and scholarships in order to make ends meet. But if you are making the more basic decision between going to college and taking up a career that does not require a college degree, the opportunity cost of college is what counts.

Markets

Microeconomists are interested not only in the actions of households, firms, and government units but also in how those actions are coordinated. In an economy such as that of the United States, markets play a key role in coordination.

A market is any arrangement that people have for trading with one another. Some markets, such as the New York Stock Exchange, are highly visible and organized. Others, such as the word-of-mouth networks that put teenage baby-sitters in touch with people who need their services, do their work informally and behind the scenes. Whether visible or not, markets play a key role in the job of putting scarce resources to their best uses in meeting people's wants and needs. Markets accomplish this by performing three essential tasks.

The first task is to transmit information. In order to put resources to their best possible uses, the people who make decisions must know which resources are the most scarce and which uses for them are best. Markets transmit information about scarcity and resource values in the form of prices. If a good becomes more scarce, its price is bid up. The rising price signals buyers to cut back on the amount of that good that they buy and alerts producers to find new sources of supply or substitute less costly resources. As a good becomes more abundant, its price tends to fall. The falling price signals users to favor that good over more costly ones.

The second task that markets perform is providing incentives. Knowing the best use for scarce resources is not enough unless people have an incentive to use them in that way. Markets offer many kinds of incentives. Consumers who are well informed and spend their money wisely achieve a higher standard of living with their limited budgets. Workers who stay alert to job opportunities and work where they can be most productive earn the highest possible incomes. Profits motivate business managers to improve production methods and tailor their goods to consumers' needs. The importance of the market as a source of incentives led Adam Smith to call it an "invisible hand" that nudges people into the roles they can play best in the economy (see "Who Said It? Who Did It? 1.1").

The third task of markets is to distribute income. People who supply factors of production—their own labor skills, capital, or natural resources—receive high incomes if they put them to the best possible use. People with fewer skills or resources to sell receive lower incomes, even if they make an equal effort to use what they have wisely. Businesspeople who take risks and guess right make large profits; those who take risks and guess wrong suffer losses. In short, the market distributes income according to the value of each person's contribution to the production process—which is not always in proportion to the effort expended in making that contribution.

The Microeconomist's Job

To say that microeconomists study households, firms, and markets is one way to describe what microeconomists do. But the question can also be answered in terms of what microeconomists do for a living, that is, the kinds of jobs they hold.

Many microeconomists are employed in private firms. For example, an insurance company might hire an economist to study the impact of economic trends on the insurance industry and help design new kinds of insurance policies to meet changing customer needs. An electric utility might employ an economist to help prepare proposals for rate changes. A trade association representing the natural-gas industry might employ an economist to analyze the impact of changes in government regulations. In these examples, the economist is employed by the business as a specialist. In other cases, people trained in microeconomics rise to positions at the firm's general management level.

Market
Any arrangement that people have for trading with one another.

WHO SAID IT? WHO DID IT?   1.1

Adam Smith on the Invisible Hand

Adam Smith was the founder of economics as a distinct field of study. He wrote only one book on the subject—*The Wealth of Nations*, published in 1776. Smith was 53 years old at the time. His friend David Hume found the book such hard going that he doubted many people would read it. But Hume was wrong—people have been reading it for more than 200 years now.

The wealth of nations, in Smith's view, was the result not of accumulating gold or silver, as many of that time

believed, but of ordinary people working and trading in free markets. To Smith, the remarkable thing about the wealth produced by a market economy is that it does not result from any organized plan; rather, it is the unintended outcome of the actions of many people, each of whom is pursuing the incentives the market offers with his or her own interests in mind:

> It is not from the benevolence of the butcher, the brewer, or the baker that we expect our dinner, but from their regard to their own interest. . . . Every individual is continually exerting himself to find out the most advantageous employment for whatever capital he can command. . . . By directing that industry in such a manner as its produce may be of the greatest value, he intends only his own gain, and he is in this, as in many other cases, led by an invisible hand to promote an end which was no part of his intention.[a]

Much of the discipline of economics as it has developed over two centuries consists of elaborations of ideas found in Smith's work. The idea of the "invisible hand" of market incentives that channels people's efforts in directions that are beneficial to their neighbors remains one of the most durable of Smith's contributions.

[a] Adam Smith, *The Wealth of Nations* (1776), Book 1, Chapter 2. Photo source: Library of Congress.

Thousands of microeconomists are employed by government. Government regulation of business is the source of many such jobs. The economists who work for insurance companies, electric utilities, gas companies, and the like find government economists working on the other side of every issue. Government economists often work closely with lawyers in cases involving regulation, equal opportunity, international trade disputes, and other issues. While the lawyer interprets the laws that apply to the case, the economist analyzes the effects on prices, markets, incomes, and jobs.

Finally, many economists work for colleges, universities, and research institutes. Most of them teach either full or part time and devote the rest of their time to research on problems of economic theory. Academic economists do quite a bit of applied research, too. Businesses, law firms, and government agencies often hire them as consultants rather than employing full-time, in-house economists.

The chapters on antitrust law and regulation, labor relations, poverty, the environment, and international trade in this book provide many other examples of the kinds of work microeconomists do.

Macroeconomics
The branch of economics that deals with large-scale economic phenomena, particularly inflation, unemployment, and economic growth.

Macroeconomics

The prefix *macro* comes from a Greek word meaning "large." Thus, **macroeconomics** refers to the study of large-scale economic phenomena, particularly inflation, unemployment, and economic growth. These phenomena result from the combined effects of millions of microeconomic choices made by households, firms, and government units. A review of the performance of the U.S. economy in the years since World War II will serve us as a preview of the subject matter of macroeconomics.

Unemployment

One of the key indicators of an economic system's health is its ability to provide a job for anyone who wants one. The economy's performance in this area is measured by the **unemployment rate**—the percentage of people in the labor force who are not working but are actively looking for work. (People who are not actively looking for work—full-time students, retired people, and so on—are not counted as members of the labor force and thus are not included in the unemployment rate.)

Even in the best of times the unemployment rate does not fall to zero. In a healthy, changing economy, it is normal for a certain number of people to be out of work for a short time when they first enter the labor force or when they have quit jobs in order to look for better ones. There is some disagreement as to what the "normal" or "natural" unemployment level is. A generation ago, it was thought that an unemployment rate of 4 percent was a reasonable goal. Given the structure of today's economy, many economists think that an unemployment rate of 6 to 6.5 percent indicates a healthy job market. We will look at this issue in some detail in later chapters.

Exhibit 1.2 shows the U.S. unemployment record since 1950 with the 4 to 6.5 percent range highlighted for reference. During the 1950s and 1960s, the unemployment rate generally stayed within this range. There were higher rates of unemployment in some years than in others, but these episodes were brief. In the 1970s and 1980s, the performance of the job market deteriorated, even taking into account changing views of the acceptable upper limit for the unemployment rate. In 1975, the rate jumped to 8.3 percent—at that time, the highest since the Great Depression—and in 1982, it averaged nearly 10 percent. From 1975 to 1986, the rate dropped below 6.5 percent in only two years. Macroeconomics explores the reasons for increases in the unemployment rate as well as some proposals for dealing with them.

Inflation

Inflation means a sustained increase in the average level of prices of all goods and services. Price stability—that is, the absence of inflation—is a second major sign of an economy's health. True price stability means no increase at all in the average price level. However, many economists and policymakers find moderate rates—3 percent per year or less—acceptable.

Exhibit 1.3 shows trends in inflation in the United States since 1950. Until the late 1960s, inflation stayed more or less within the safe range. In fact, for the entire century from the Civil War to the mid-1960s, inflation averaged only about 2 percent per year; higher inflation rates occurred mostly in wartime.

The inflation of the late 1960s was related in part to the Vietnam War. During the 1970s, the inflation rate varied widely and stayed above the 3 percent benchmark for the entire decade. Then, in the early 1980s, the inflation rate fell abruptly—far more so than many economists had expected. However, the inflation of the 1970s and the fear of its return have had a lasting impact on the U.S. economy.

Unemployment rate
The percentage of people in the labor force who are not working but are actively looking for work.

Inflation
A sustained increase in the average prices of all goods and services.

Exhibit 1.2   Unemployment in the United States Since 1950

There is no one unemployment rate that is universally accepted as best for the U.S. economy. A zero rate is never reached, because there are always people who are out of work while changing jobs or looking for first jobs. A generation ago, a rate of 4 percent was thought to be a reasonable target, and such rates were sometimes reached in the 1950s and 1960s. Today unemployment rates of 6 or even 6.5 percent are seen as consistent with a healthy economy. In the 1970s and early 1980s, however, there were many years in which unemployment was excessive even by this standard.

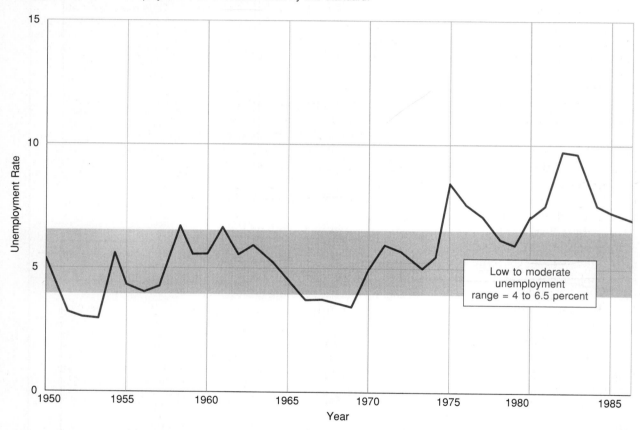

Source: *Economic Report of the President* (Washington, D.C.: Government Printing Office, 1987), Table B-35.

Gross national product (GNP)
A measure of the economy's total output of goods and services.

Economic Growth

Economic growth is a third major sign of economic health. The economy must grow in order to provide jobs for new workers and permit everyone a rising standard of living.

The most often used measure of the economy's total output is **gross national product,** or **GNP.** In order to be meaningful as a measure of economic growth, changes in GNP over time must be adjusted for the effects of inflation. Suppose we want to see how much the U.S. economy grew from 1972 to 1986. In 1972, GNP was about $1,200 billion. In 1986, it was a little over $4,200 billion—3.5 times as high. However, this does not mean that people's standard of living was 3.5 times as high in 1986. Much of the increase in GNP can be explained by

Exhibit 1.3   Inflation in the United States Since 1950

True price stability means no increase at all in the average price level. However, many economists believe that an inflation rate of 3 percent per year or less is acceptable. As the chart shows, such low inflation rates were the rule during the 1950s and early 1960s. Inflation soared in the 1970s and returned to moderate levels in the mid-1980s. In this figure, the inflation rate is measured in terms of the consumer price index, which is a weighted average of the prices of products that consumers typically buy.

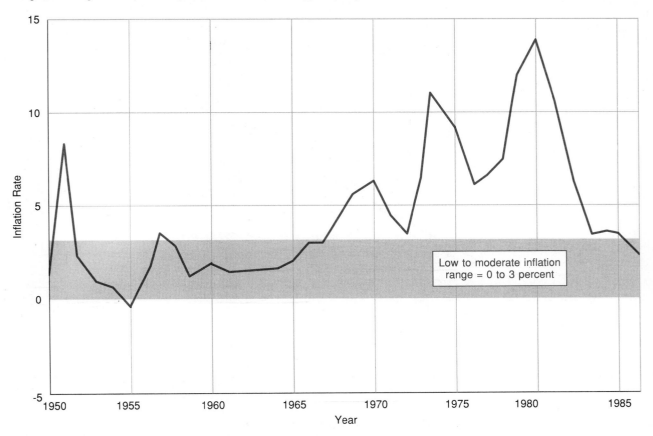

Source: *Economic Report of the President* (Washington, D.C.: Government Printing Office, 1987), Table B-58.

higher prices; in fact, the price level was 2.5 times as high at the end of 1986 as it was in 1972. In order to get an accurate comparison with the 1972 GNP, the 1986 GNP must be divided by 2.5 to account for the change in the price level.

Economists use the term **nominal** to refer to data that have not been adjusted for the effects of inflation. The term **real** is used to refer to data that have been adjusted for inflation. In the above example, we can say that in 1986 *nominal GNP* was $4,200 billion and *real GNP* (relative to 1972) was $1,680 billion ($4,200 billion divided by the more than 2.5-fold increase in prices over the 1972 to 1986 period).

From 1950 to 1986, the growth rate of real GNP in the United States varied around a trend of about 3 percent per year, which most economists consider

Nominal
In economics, a term that refers to data that have not been adjusted for the effects of inflation.

Real
In economics, a term that refers to data that have been adjusted for the effects of inflation.

Exhibit 1.4   Economic Growth in the United States Since 1950

This chart shows the growth of the U.S. economy since 1950. It shows real gross national product for each year (that is, gross national product adjusted for inflation) and a trend line for real-GNP growth over the whole period. A growth rate of 3 percent per year or more is considered healthy. As the figure shows, real GNP sometimes rises above the trend and sometimes falls below it.

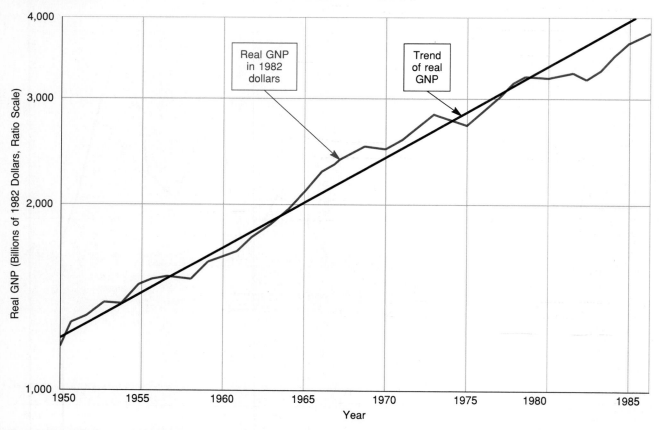

Source: *Economic Report of the President* (Washington, D.C.: Government Printing Office, 1987), Table B-2.

quite satisfactory (see Exhibit 1.4). However, it did not follow this trend smoothly. In some years output fell below the trend, and in others it rose above it. The reasons for these fluctuations in the level of real GNP and for its trend over time are a major focus of macroeconomics.

The goals of full employment, price stability, and economic growth are closely linked. When real output falls, the unemployment rate tends to rise. When real output rises, the rate of inflation sometimes—but not always—tends to speed up. These are two of many linkages among economic phenomena. Macroeconomics studies these linkages in detail, along with others involving interest rates, the money supply, consumption and investment levels, and the international value of the dollar.

The Macroeconomist's Job

Having looked at the subject matter of macroeconomics, we will close with a brief look at some of the jobs held by macroeconomists. Like their micro colleagues, macroeconomists hold jobs in business, government, and academic institutions.

Business macroeconomists are hired to advise managers on the impact of economic trends on their firms. This is often crucial to the firms' survival. Take, for example, the home-building industry. People's ability to buy houses depends on their incomes and on the interest rates at which they can obtain mortgage loans. Firms in every part of the home-building industry—construction, lumber, and other building supplies—can benefit from information on economic trends and policies. As we will see shortly, it is not easy to forecast economic trends. But even when reliable forecasts are impossible, economists can help managers make plans based on a set of "what-if" projections. The example of the housing industry can be extended to others, from consumer goods to banking to transportation. Businesses that do not employ economists often hire consulting firms to advise them on macroeconomic trends.

Government agencies also employ macroeconomists to aid in planning and forecasting. In addition, thousands of economists are employed by government units in charge of macroeconomic policy. The Federal Reserve System, which guides monetary policy, is a major employer of macroeconomists. The U.S. Treasury is another. The Office of Management and Budget and the Council of Economic Advisers, which advise the President, also have large economic staffs. Still other macroeconomists are found in the Congressional Budget Office and on the staffs of congressional committees.

Finally, many macroeconomists are employed by colleges, universities, and research institutes. Like academic microeconomists, they divide their time among teaching, research, and consulting.

Why Economists Sometimes Disagree

George Bernard Shaw once complained that if you took all the economists in the world and laid them end to end, they wouldn't reach a conclusion. Harry Truman begged for a "one-armed economist" because those with two arms kept saying, "On the one hand, . . . and then on the other hand, . . . " But one could argue that economists are no worse than other professionals. Physicists disagree about the origin of the universe. Doctors disagree about treatments for heart disease. Teachers disagree about methods of teaching math. So why are economists singled out for jokes?

The idea that economists can't agree results partly from the fact that disagreement makes the news while agreement doesn't. In fact, economists present a united front on a wide range of issues. For example, one survey found that more than 90 percent of economists concur with the following statements:[2]

---

[2] J. R. Kearl, Clayne L. Pope, Gordon C. Whiting, and Larry T. Wimmer, "A Confusion of Economists?" *American Economic Review* (May 1979): 30. It is worth noting that the survey revealed widespread disagreement on certain other matters, such as the economic power of labor unions and the optimal level of spending for national defense.

- Tariffs and import quotas reduce general economic welfare.

- A ceiling on rents reduces the quantity and quality of housing available.

- Increased government spending or a tax cut is likely to speed recovery from a recession.

But the jokes about disagreement among economists have deeper roots than the newsworthiness of controversy. In the remainder of this chapter, we will discuss some of the chief causes of these disagreements in the contexts of theory versus reality, forecasting, and positive versus normative economics.

Theory and Reality

One reason suggested for economists' disagreements is that they are unrealistic. For example, they are said to make too many simplifying assumptions, such as that people are motivated only by greed, and perform calculations based on information they cannot possibly have.

Indeed, economic theory *is* full of "unrealistic" assumptions. It has to be for the simple reason that economic reality is complex. To take just one example, suppose an economist is asked what effect a tax cut will have on consumers' total spending. There are hundreds of millions of consumers. Their manner of spending depends on their moods, hopes, fears, and health; on the weather; on interest rates, bank regulations, and new products on the market; on wages, fringe benefits, and lottery winnings. The list is endless.

But economists do not try to make a complete list of the things that influence consumer spending. Instead, they try to identify the factors that have the greatest influence and use them as the basis for a theory or—to use an expression favored by economists—a model. A model is an attempted representation of the way in which facts are related. Models can be—and often are—expressed in ordinary English, but they are also often presented in graphical or mathematical form.

Model
A simplified representation of the way in which facts are related.

As an example, consider the question of tax cuts and their effects on consumer spending. One widely accepted economic model says that the change in consumer spending depends on how much the tax cut raises consumers' after-tax incomes and on how long consumers expect the tax cut to remain in effect. In proposing such a model, economists don't deny that other things affect consumer spending; they simply say that of all the things that matter, these two are the most useful. In much the same way, engineers who build model aircraft to be tested in wind tunnels are careful to represent the shape of the wings accurately but do not bother to round out their models with tiny seats equipped with armrests and magazine racks.

Clearly, however, this approach contains the seeds of many disagreements. One economist's model of consumer spending might take only the above two factors into account. Another's might also consider whether the tax cut affects mainly upper-income or middle-income consumers. Which model is better? One approach to testing competing theories is to see which one better fits statistical data from the past relating to the phenomenon in question. But such tests are not always conclusive. Data on past events may be unreliable. One model may better explain the events of one period and the other those of a different one. Before the dispute is resolved, someone else may propose a third theory that challenges both models.

Forecasting

An economic model is considered good if it correctly explains the relationships of two or more key facts. Such models often help us understand past economic events. For example, macroeconomics presents models that provide useful insights into the causes of the Great Depression of the 1930s or the high inflation rates of the late 1970s. But even the best economic models are limited in their ability to help us foretell the future.

At best, economic models allow us to make statements that take the following form: "If A, then B, other things being equal." Most economists would agree with the statement "If income taxes are lowered, consumers will spend more provided that the many other factors that affect spending don't change in the meantime." It is a short step from this type of statement to a **conditional forecast,** which is simply an "if-then" statement about the future. For example, an economist might say that if income tax rates are cut by 10 percent in July 1989, total consumer spending will rise by $100 billion in 1989, $120 billion in 1990, and $145 billion in 1991, other things being equal.

Conditional forecast
A prediction of future economic events, usually stated in the form "If A, then B, other things being equal."

Why are economic forecasts such a source of controversy? One obvious reason is that forecasters are often wrong. They have sometimes missed major turning points in the economy. They also often disagree among themselves. It is not uncommon for one forecaster to predict recession while another predicts continued expansion.

But the problem does not lie entirely with forecasters. Part of it is due to the way forecasts are reported to the public. On television and in the newspapers, forecasts are often reported in the unconditional form "This is how it will be" rather than in the conditional form "If A, then B, other things being equal" that the forecaster intended. In addition, it is not always made clear that even forecasts that are reported as simple numbers are really statements about probabilities. For example, it may be reported that a certain economist has predicted that a tax cut will add $100 billion to consumer spending when the proper way of putting it would be that there is a 90 percent probability that the tax cut will add between $80 billion and $120 billion to spending.

Most economists take the view that forecasts, for all their faults, are a better basis for making business decisions and public policy than whims and guesswork. For example, a maker of building supplies might ask a forecaster, "If the economy grows as much in the second half of the year as it did in the first, how will the demand for new houses be affected?" The answer might be: "A 3 percent rate of economic growth will cause housing demand to rise by somewhat more than 3 percent if interest rates remain the same. However, each percentage point rise in the mortgage interest rate will cause about a 5 percent drop in the demand for housing." Getting an answer like this isn't as good as having a crystal ball, but it is better than nothing.

At the same time, economists caution against overrelying on forecasts. In the 1970s, many forecasters projected higher oil prices throughout the 1980s. Many oil companies, banks, and even national governments got in trouble when they relied too heavily on these forecasts, which turned out to be wrong. This issue of how much government policymakers should rely on forecasts is especially controversial, because so much is at stake when major policy decisions are made.

Positive versus Normative Economics

Economists, as we have seen, sometimes disagree over issues of theory. They disagree even more often when they try their hands at forecasting. But nothing produces as much disagreement as issues of economic policy. Should the government try to prop up the price of wheat and corn? Should automobile imports be restricted? Should taxes be raised in order to cut the federal budget deficit? Questions like these tend to bring economists out of their corners ready to fight.

However, before the sparks start to fly, it is worth noting the chain of reasoning on which policy decisions are based. There are three steps:

1. If policy X is followed, outcome Y will result.

2. Outcome Y is a good (or bad) thing.

3. Therefore, let us adopt (or not adopt) policy X.

Positive economics
The part of economics concerned with statements about facts and the relationships among them.

The first step in this chain of reasoning is a conditional forecast. Forecasts are examples of **positive economics,** that is, the portion of economics that is limited to making statements of fact and relationships among facts.

Disputes are common in positive economics. Economists may disagree over whether facts are accurate, how they are related, and how they are likely to unfold in the future. But these disputes can—at least in principle—be resolved by scientific methods. Repeated measurement, statistical tests of theories, and comparison of forecasts with actual events are a few of the ways in which the area of disagreement on matters of positive economics can be narrowed.

Normative economics
The part of economics devoted to making judgments about which economic policies or conditions are good or bad.

But positive statements of the type "If policy X, then outcome Y" do not tell us whether policy X is desirable. In order to make a policy decision, one must also decide whether outcome Y is good or bad. Statements of the type "Outcome Y is good" are examples of **normative economics**—the part of economics that is devoted to making judgments about which economic policies or outcomes are good and which are bad.

Most economists do not think of themselves as experts in philosophy or ethics. Yet economists who want to influence policy are in a better position to do so if they can point to some general principles on which their views are based. Those who base their opinions of a policy on whim or prejudice are less likely to be listened to than those who speak in terms of well-thought-out values. Calling your opponent a racist or a fascist may win cheers from those who already agree with you and boos from those who are already against you. But name calling is far less likely to win uncommitted people to your side than is an articulate explanation of your reasons for thinking that your opponent's policies will have undesirable outcomes. With this in mind, let us now look at some basic concepts of normative economics.

Efficiency and Fairness

One standard by which economic policies can be judged is *efficiency*. In economics, as elsewhere, this means doing something with a minimum of waste, effort, and expense. (A more precise definition of economic efficiency will be given in Chapter 2.) But a policy that is merely efficient may not be good; other standards must be applied. Among the most important of these is fairness.

Fairness can play two roles in relation to efficiency. First, it may be used to complement efficiency when the choice is between two or more equally efficient policies—for example, those that differ only in terms of which groups of people bear costs or receive benefits. In such a case, we might reason as follows:

1. Policies X and Y are equally efficient, but they will distribute benefits to different groups.

2. The distribution of benefits under policy X is fairer.

3. Therefore, we should follow policy X.

Second, the standard of fairness may be used to override that of efficiency. Many people believe that efficiency should not be pursued at the expense of fairness. If both goals cannot be reached at once, efficiency should be sacrificed in the name of fairness. In such a case, our reasoning might run as follows:

1. Policy X would be inefficient, but it would be more fair than policy Y.

2. Efficiency is desirable, but fairness is more important.

3. Therefore, if there is no policy that is both efficient and fair, choose policy X.

In whatever manner it is used, the standard of fairness plays a major role in policy analysis. However, it also raises a problem that the standard of efficiency does not, namely that fairness means different things to different people. Rational debate on matters of economic policy is difficult when people attach different meanings to the same term and fail to make those meanings clear. With this problem in mind, let's look at two concepts of fairness that often arise in discussions of economic policy.

The Egalitarian Concept of Fairness

One widely held view equates fairness with equitable distribution of income. The phrase "from each according to ability, to each according to need" reflects this viewpoint. This concept of fairness is based on the idea that all people, by virtue of their shared humanity, deserve a portion of the goods and services turned out by the economy.

There are many versions of this concept. Some people believe that all income and wealth should be distributed equally. Others think that people have a right to a "safety net" level of income but that any surplus beyond this may be distributed according to other standards. Still others think there are certain goods, such as health care, food, and education, that should be distributed equally but it is all right for other goods to be distributed unequally.

In policy debates, the egalitarian view of fairness often takes the form "What effect will this policy have on the poor?" Consider the debate over rent control for city apartments. Some people favor ending these controls on the grounds that they discourage new-housing construction and upkeep of existing housing. Others oppose ending rent controls because they believe that higher rents would cause hardship for consumers in the lowest income groups. Chapter 3 will provide an economic analysis of this policy problem.

The Libertarian Concept of Fairness

A second widely held view links fairness to people's right to live their lives according to their own values, free from threats and coercion. This concept of fairness stems from a long tradition in Western political thought, especially the idea of liberty as stated by such philosophers as John Locke and Thomas Jefferson.

The libertarian view of fairness puts economic rights, such as the rights to own property and to make exchanges with others, on a par with the basic rights of free speech, free press, and free worship. From this viewpoint, efforts to promote fairness should stress equality of opportunity. Attempts to redistribute income by placing a penalty on economic success or giving people unequal access to markets are seen as unfair whether or not they lead to equality of income.

In policy debates, proponents of the libertarian point of view often argue that competition and economic freedom lead to a general prosperity that is good for everyone. For example, libertarian economists have led the fight to end regulations protecting business firms from competition. They have argued that when new, small airlines are allowed to compete with larger, more established ones, when savings and loan associations are allowed to compete with banks, and when natural-gas producers are allowed to compete with oil producers in an open market, the firms that best serve the consumer will be the ones to prosper.

Why the Distinction?

Distinguishing between positive and normative economics and among different meanings of normative terms like "fairness" will not settle all policy disputes. Still, viewing policy analysis as a three-step process in which both positive and normative elements play a role makes policy debates more rational in three ways.

First, the distinction between positive and normative analysis makes it clear that there are two kinds of disagreement on policy questions. We can disagree as to whether policy X is good or bad because we disagree on the positive issue of whether it will cause outcome Y, which we both desire. Alternatively, we can agree that policy X will cause outcome Y but disagree on the normative issue of whether Y is a good thing. Once the source of the disagreement is clear, the argument can be more focused.

Second, when positive statements are mixed with normative ones, they may not be judged on their merits. Reactions to value judgments tend to be much stronger than reactions to statements of fact or theory. Consider tax policy. There has been much debate in recent years about the effects of tax cuts and increases on the federal budget deficit, interest rates, and economic growth. Many issues of fact and theory need to be resolved. But economists operating in the positive mode often find it hard to get the attention of policymakers who are distracted by charges and countercharges of "soaking the rich" or "milking the poor."

Third, it is important to make the distinction in order to be aware of the ways in which normative considerations influence the conduct of positive research. At one time it was thought that a "purely" positive economics, completely untainted by normative considerations, could be developed. Within this framework, all disputes could be resolved by reference to objective facts. Today this notion is less widely held; instead, it is recognized that normative considerations influence positive research in several ways. The most significant is simply the selection of the topics that are considered important enough to investigate. Also, normative views are likely to influence the ways in which data are collected, ideas about which facts can be taken as true, and so on.

This book will raise many controversial issues as it tours the subject of economics. For the most part, we will focus on the positive economic theories that bear on these issues, but we will touch on normative considerations as well. However, a textbook can provide no more than a framework for thinking about public issues and policies. Your job will be to blend positive theories and normative judgments within this framework to reach your own conclusions.

Summary

1. **What is economics all about?** *Economics* is the study of the choices people make and the actions they take in order to make the best use of scarce resources in meeting their wants. Resources are said to be *scarce* when people do not have enough of them to meet all their wants. At all times and in all societies, everyone faces the scarcity problem in some form.

2. **How is the need to choose related to the concept of cost?** Because resources are scarce, when people choose to use them in one way, they must forgo the opportunity to use them in another. The cost of doing something, measured in terms of the forgone opportunity to do the next best thing with the same time or resources, is called *opportunity cost.* Opportunity cost can be illustrated by the slope of a *production possibility frontier.*

3. **What roles do households, business firms, and government units play in the economy?** *Microeconomics* is the branch of economics that deals with the choices made by small economic units—households, business firms, and government units. Households supply the basic factors of production, namely labor, capital, and natural resources. Business firms buy the factors of production from households and transform them into goods and services. Government units—including Congress, the courts, regulatory agencies, and others—influence the economic choices made by households and firms. In turn, all of these are influenced by events in the economy.

4. **What are markets, and how do they work?** A *market* is any arrangement people have for trading with one another. Markets play a key role in putting resources to their best uses. In so doing, they perform three tasks. First, they transmit information, in the form of prices, that helps households and firms decide which of the possible ways of using scarce resources are most valuable. Second, they provide incentives, especially in the form of profits. Third, they distribute income according to the value of each person's contribution to the production process.

5. **Who worries about inflation, unemployment, and economic growth, and why?** The branch of economics that studies large-scale economic phenomena, particularly unemployment, inflation, and economic growth, is known as *macroeconomics*. The *unemployment rate* is the percentage of people in the labor force who are actively looking for work but are unable to find it. *Inflation* is a sustained increase in the average price level of all goods and services; it is measured by the consumer price index. Economic growth is measured by the rate of increase in real *gross national prod-*

uct. (The term *real* refers to economic quantities that have been adjusted for inflation. Quantities that have not been adjusted for inflation are known as *nominal* quantities.)

6. **Why do economists sometimes disagree?** Economists, like other professionals, sometimes disagree about how the world works. They construct *models* in an attempt to explain relationships among facts, but they may disagree about which aspects of reality should be emphasized in a given model. They use their models to make *conditional forecasts*, that is, "if-then" statements about the future. But because the future cannot be known with certainty, these forecasts are themselves a source of disagreement. The portion of economics that is devoted to constructing models and making forecasts is known as *positive economics*.

7. **How do ethics and value judgments enter into economics?** The part of economics that is devoted to making judgments about whether economic policies or events are good or bad is called *normative economics*. The concepts of efficiency and fairness are important in such policy decisions. Judging the value of an economic policy requires both a positive analysis of the policy's likely effects and a normative judgment of the desirability of those effects.

Terms for Review

- scarcity
- economics
- goods
- services
- factors of production
- labor
- capital
- natural resources
- production possibility frontier
- opportunity cost
- microeconomics
- market
- macroeconomics
- unemployment rate
- inflation
- gross national product (GNP)
- nominal
- real
- model
- conditional forecast
- positive economics
- normative economics

Questions for Review

1. How are the terms *scarcity* and *economics* related? Can you think of any resources that are not scarce?

2. How can cost be measured in terms of forgone opportunities? Illustrate the concept of opportunity cost with a production possibility frontier.

3. Which of the following are microeconomic issues? Which are macroeconomic issues?
   a. How will an increase in the cigarette tax affect smoking habits?
   b. What caused the rate of inflation to fall so rapidly between 1980 and 1984?
   c. Does a high federal budget deficit tend to slow the rate of real economic growth?
   d. How would quotas on steel imports affect profits and jobs in industries that use steel as an input, such as automobiles and construction?

4. What is a market? What three tasks do markets perform? Describe the arrangements by which people buy and sell houses, football tickets, and haircuts. Are all of these markets?

5. Compare the 1960s and the 1970s in terms of inflation, unemployment, and growth in the U.S. economy. How do the 1980s look by comparison so far?

6. What is an economic model? Why do economists use theories and models instead of limiting themselves to verbal descriptions of economic events? In what ways does the use of models lead to disagreements among economists?

7. Why is it important to distinguish between positive and normative economics? What are the roles of efficiency and fairness in making policy decisions?

Problems and Topics for Discussion

1. **Examining the lead-off case.** A "shortage" means that there is less of something available *at the current market price* than buyers want. (This term will be defined formally in Chapter 3.) On the basis of information given in this case, is Prince George's County facing a teacher shortage? Is there reason to think it was previously facing a teacher shortage? What role do the three functions of markets play in helping to overcome shortages? Is "shortage" a synonym for "scarcity"? Does the fact that after the 21 percent salary increase 4,000 applications were received for 400 jobs mean that there is no longer a teacher shortage?

2. **Scarcity for millionaires.** Suppose you won $1 million in a lottery. Would this remove all problems of scarcity and choice from your life? Would time still be a scarce resource for you? What other things might

still be scarce? Can you imagine anyone who would face no economic problems of any kind?

3. **The production possibility frontier.** A farmer has four fields spread out over a hillside. He can grow either wheat or potatoes in any of the fields, but the low fields are better for potatoes and the high ones are better for wheat. Here are some combinations of wheat and potatoes that he can produce:

Number of Fields Used for Potatoes	Tons of Potatoes	Tons of Wheat
4	1,000	0
3	900	400
2	600	700
1	300	900
0	0	1,000

Use these data to draw a production possibility frontier for wheat and potatoes. What is the opportunity cost of wheat, stated in terms of potatoes, when the farmer converts the highest field into wheat production? What happens to the opportunity cost of wheat as more and more fields are switched to wheat?

4. **The nature of your household.** To what kind of household do you belong? How large is the group of people with whom you pool income and share decision making? Are you a member of a one-person household for some purposes and of a larger household for others? How are economic decisions made in your household?

5. **The market for video games.** After a boom in the early 1980s, the video game industry ran into trouble. Consumer interest in these games leveled off, and competition forced prices and profit margins down. Some firms left the industry; others seriously considered doing so. How does this example illustrate the three functions of markets?

6. **Your role in the market for education.** As a student, you are a buyer in the market for education. What price signals affected your decision to go to college? What market incentives, if any, made you decide as you did? How do you think your education will affect your future position in the distribution of income?

7. **Macroeconomic indicators.** Exhibits 1.2, 1.3, and 1.4 give data on unemployment, inflation, and economic growth, respectively, through the end of 1986. Extend the charts using the most recent available data. For annual data, a good source is the *Economic Report of the President*, published each January or February. For current-year data, check business news sources such as *The Wall Street Journal* or *Business Week*. Two

government publications, the *Survey of Current Business* and the *Federal Reserve Bulletin*, are also useful sources of data. The government releases information on the unemployment rate and the consumer price index each month and information on the growth of real GNP every three months.

8. **Nominal and real salaries.** Professor Alvarez began teaching economics at State University in 1967. In that year, she earned a salary of $9,500. Sixteen years later, her salary had risen to $26,000. Meanwhile the price level had risen to 2.98 times its 1967 value. How much did her real income grow or shrink?

Case for Discussion
Public Policy and Auto Safety

Whether or not the government should require cars to be equipped with airbags has been a matter of debate for years. The following editorial on this subject appeared in Business Week:

Transportation secretary Elizabeth H. Dole will issue by July 11 a final ruling as to whether or not auto manufacturers must start including airbags as required equipment in cars. This issue is hotly controversial, and Secretary Dole will rule on it in a climate of renewed concern over drunk driving. She will probably issue mandatory accident-safety standards that can be met either by airbags or automatic seat belts. If so, this shows a commendable degree of flexibility. What the Secretary should not do is flatly order airbags in all automobiles.

Airbag enthusiasts say the device will save lives. But the safety issue is not airbags vs. nothing at all—in that case, the airbag would win hands down—but airbags vs. the shoulder-lap harness, which is cheaper and less risky. Estimates are that the airbag will add anywhere from $300 to $500 to the cost of a car. Regular seat belts add about $60 to a car's cost, automatic seat belts about twice that. As to the far more important issue of reliability, the airbag is an electronic device subject to failure. The chances that it might not inflate when needed or inflate at the wrong time are small but real, and in either case could produce injury or death. Neither problem arises with seat belts, which are highly effective when used.

The catch, of course, is that only 10 percent to 15 percent of drivers use belts. A state law requiring their use will probably make many people buckle up. Automatic belts are a good idea. Auto makers, insurance companies, and safety organizations should work harder to promote seat belt use. Over time, though, it is likely that the new attack on drunk driving by raising the national drinking age to 21 will save more lives than making airbags mandatory in everybody's car.

Source: "Airbags: A Matter of Choice," p. 160, reprinted from July 16, 1984 issue of *Business Week* by special permission, © 1984 by McGraw-Hill, Inc.

Question
Analyze this editorial in terms of the three steps of policy analysis. Which statements of positive economics are used to support the argument? What normative judgments are made or implied? What role does the standard of efficiency play in the argument? What view of fairness underlies the argument? Is there any way to tell from this editorial?

Appendix to Chapter 1   **Working with Graphs**

How Economists Use Graphs

Students at one well-known college have their own names for each course. They call the astronomy course "Stars," the geology course "Rocks," and the biology course "Frogs." Their name for the economics course is "Graphs and Laughs." This name choice demonstrates two things. First, it shows that the students think the professor has a sense of humor. Second, it shows that in their minds economics is a matter of learning about graphs in the same way that astronomy involves learning about stars, geology about rocks, and biology about frogs.

However, economics is not about graphs; it is about people. It focuses on how people make choices, use resources, and cooperate in their attempts to overcome the universal problem of scarcity. But if economics is not about graphs, why are there so many of them in this book? The answer is that economists use graphs to illustrate their theories of people's economic behavior in order to make those theories more vivid and memorable. Everything that can be said in the form of a graph can also be said in words, but saying something in two different ways is an established learning aid. The purpose of this appendix is to show how to make the best use of this tool.

Pairs of Numbers and Points

The first thing to master is how to use points on a graph to represent pairs of numbers. The table in Exhibit 1A.1 presents five pairs of numbers. The two columns are labeled "x" and "y." The first number in each pair is called the *x value* and the second the *y value*. Each pair of numbers is labeled with a capital letter. Pair A has an x value of 2 and a y value of 3; pair B has an x value of 4 and a y value of 4; and so on.

The diagram in Exhibit 1A.1 contains two lines that meet at the lower left-hand corner; these are called *coordinate axes*. The horizontal axis is marked off into units representing the x value and the vertical axis into units representing the y value. In the space between these axes, each pair of numbers from the table can be shown as a point. For example, point A is found by going two units to the right along the horizontal axis and then three units straight up, parallel to the vertical axis. This represents the x value of 2 and the y value of 3. The other points are located in the same way.

Exhibit 1A.1   Pairs of Numbers and Points

Each lettered pair of numbers in the table corresponds to a lettered point on the graph. The x value of each point corresponds to the horizontal distance of the point from the vertical axis; the y value corresponds to its vertical distance from the horizontal axis.

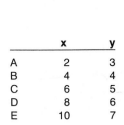

	x	y
A	2	3
B	4	4
C	6	5
D	8	6
E	10	7

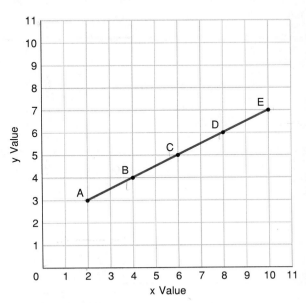

The visual effect of a graph usually can be improved by connecting the points with a line or a curve. By doing so, it can be seen at a glance that as the x value increases, the y value also rises.

Common Economic Graphs

Exhibit 1A.2 shows three typical economic graphs. Each type of graph will appear many times in this book. Part a of Exhibit 1A.2 shows the relationship between the price of a subway token and the number of people who ride the subway each day at any given price. The corresponding table shows that as the price of tokens goes up, fewer people ride the subway. The graph shows the same thing. In economics, when a graph involves both money values and quantities, the vertical axis is usually used to measure the money values (here the price of tokens) and the horizontal axis to measure the quantities (here the number of riders per day).

Part b of Exhibit 1A.2 uses quantities on both axes. Here the purpose is to show the various combinations of milkshakes and hamburgers that can be bought at the local carry-out when milkshakes cost $.50 each, hamburgers cost $.50 each, and the buyer has exactly $2.50 to spend. The table shows that the possibilities are five burgers and no shakes, four burgers and one shake, three burgers and two shakes, and so on. The graph gives a visual representation of this "menu." The points are drawn in and labeled, and a diagonal line is used to

Exhibit 1A.2   Three Typical Economic Graphs

This exhibit shows three graphs typically used in economics. Part a shows the relationship between the price of tokens and the number of riders per day on a city subway system. For a graph that shows the relationship between a price and a quantity, it is conventional to put the price on the vertical axis. Part b shows the possible choices for a person who has $2.50 to spend on lunch and can buy hamburgers at $.50 each or milkshakes at $.50 each. Part c shows how a graph can be used to represent change over time.

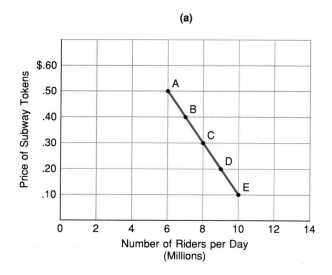

(a)

	Price of Subway Tokens	Number of Riders per Day (Millions)
A	$.50	6
B	.40	7
C	.30	8
D	.20	9
E	.10	10

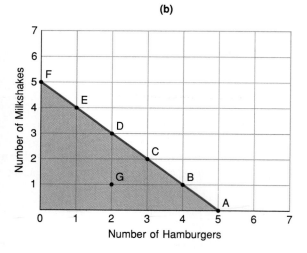

(b)

	Number of Hamburgers	Number of Milkshakes
A	5	0
B	4	1
C	3	2
D	2	3
E	1	4
F	0	5

Year	Unemployment Rate (Nonwhite Males, 16–19 Years Old)
1969	21.4%
1970	25.0
1971	28.9
1972	29.7
1973	26.9
1974	31.6
1975	35.4
1976	35.4
1977	37.0
1978	34.4

Source: Part c is from President's Council of Economic Advisers, *Economic Report of the President* (Washington, D.C.: Government Printing Office, 1979), Table B-30.

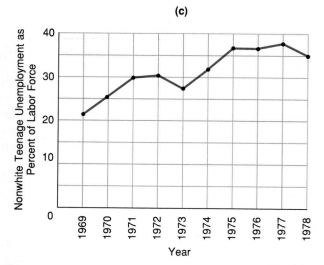

(c)

connect them. If the purchase of parts of hamburgers or milkshakes is allowed, the buyer can choose among all the points along this line (for example, 2.5 burgers and 2.5 shakes). A buyer who wants to have some money left over can buy a lunch shown by a point within the shaded area, such as G (which stands for two burgers and one shake and costs just $1.50). But unless the buyer gets more money, points outside the shaded area cannot be chosen.

Part c of Exhibit 1A.2 shows a third kind of graph that is often used in economics—one that indicates how a magnitude varies over time. This example shows what happened to the unemployment rate of nonwhite teenage males over the years 1969 to 1978. The horizontal axis represents the passage of time; the vertical axis shows the percentage of nonwhite teenage males who were unemployed. Graphs such as this are good for showing trends. Although teenage unemployment has had its ups and downs, the trend in the 1970s was clearly upward.

Slopes

When discussing graphs, it is convenient to describe lines or curves in terms of their slopes. The slope of a straight line between two points is defined as the ratio of the change in the y value to the change in the x value between the points. In Exhibit 1A.3, for example, the slope of the line between points A and B is 2. The y value changes by six units between these two points, whereas the x value changes by only three units. The slope is the ratio 6/3 = 2.

When a line slants downward such as the one between points C and D in Exhibit 1A.3, the x and y values change in opposite directions. Going from point C to point D, the y value changes by −1 (that is, decreases by one unit) and the x value changes by +2 (increases by two units). The slope of this line is the ratio

Exhibit 1A.3 Slopes of Lines

The slope of a straight line drawn between two points is defined as the ratio of the change in the y value to the change in the x value between them. For example, the line between points A and B in this exhibit has a slope of +2, whereas the line between points C and D has a slope of −½.

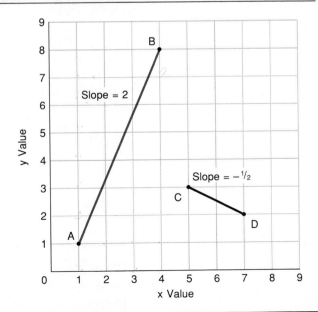

Exhibit 1A.4   Slopes of Curves

The slope of a curve at any given point is defined as the slope of a straight line drawn tangent to the curve at that point. A tangent line is one that just touches the curve without crossing it. In this exhibit, the slope of the curve at point A is 1 and the slope of the curve at point B is −2.

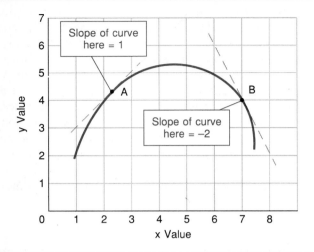

−1/2. A downward-sloping line such as the line between C and D is said to have a *negative slope*.

The slope of a curved line, on the other hand, varies from one point to the next. The slope of a curve at any given point is defined as the slope of a straight line drawn tangent to the curve at that point. (A *tangent* line is one that just touches the curve without crossing it.) In Exhibit 1A.4, the slope of the line at point A is 1 and the slope at point B is −2.

Abstract Graphs

In all the examples given so far, there have been specific numbers for the x and y values. But sometimes we know only the general nature of the relationship between two magnitudes. For example, we might know that when incomes rise, people tend to increase their meat consumption. The increase is rapid at first, but at very high incomes meat consumption levels off. If we want to show such a relationship without worrying about the precise numbers involved, we can draw a graph such as that in Exhibit 1A.5. The vertical axis is the quantity of meat consumed per month, with no specific units. The horizontal axis is income, also with no specific units. The curve, which rises rapidly at first and then levels off, shows the general nature of the relationship between income and meat consumption: When income goes up, meat consumption rises, but not in proportion to the change in income.

We will use many such abstract graphs in this book. In contrast to graphs with numbered axes, which present specific information, these express general principles.

Study Hints

How should you study a chapter that is full of graphs? The first—and most important—rule is to avoid trying to memorize graphs. In every economics class, at least one student comes to the instructor after failing an exam and

Exhibit 1A.5   An Abstract Graph

When we know the general form of an economic relationship but do not know the exact numbers involved, we can draw an abstract graph. Here we know that as people's incomes rise, their consumption of meat increases rapidly at first, then levels off. Because we do not know the exact numbers for meat consumption or income, we have not marked any units on the axes.

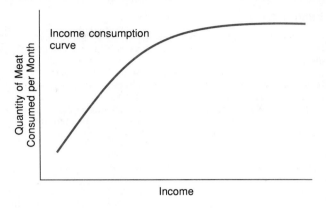

exclaims, "But I learned every one of those graphs! What happened?" The usual reply is that the student should have learned economics instead of memorizing graphs. Following are some hints for working with graphs.

After reading through a chapter that contains several graphs, go back through the graphs one at a time. Cover the caption accompanying each graph, and try to put the graph's picture into words. If you cannot say as much about the graph as the caption does, reread the text. Once you can translate the graph into words, you have won half the battle.

Next, cover each graph and use the caption as a guide. Try to sketch the graph on a piece of scratch paper. If you understand what the words mean and can go back and forth between the caption and the graph, you will find that the two together are much easier to remember than either one separately.

Making Your Own Graphs

For some students, the hardest kind of test question to answer is one that requires an original graph as part of an essay. Here are some hints for making your own graphs:

1. Write down the answer to the question in words. If you cannot, you might as well skip to the next question. Underline the most important quantities in your answer, such as "The larger the *number of students* who attend a college, the lower the *cost per student* of providing them with an education."

2. Decide how you want to label the axes. In our example (Exhibit 1A.6), the vertical axis is labeled "cost per student" and the horizontal axis "number of students."

3. Do you have specific numbers to work with? If so, the next step is to construct a table showing what you know and use it to sketch your graph. If you have no numbers, you must draw an abstract graph. In this case, all you know is that the cost per student goes down when the number of students goes up. Sketch in a downward-sloping line such as the one in Exhibit 1A.6.

4. If your graph involves more than one relationship between quantities, repeat steps 1 through 3 for each relationship you wish to show. When constructing a graph with more than one curve, pay special attention to points at which you think the curves should intersect. (This happens whenever the

Exhibit 1A.6 Constructing a Graph

To construct a graph, first put down in words what you want to say: "The larger the *number of students* at a university, the lower the *cost per student* of providing them with an education." Next, label the coordinate axes. Then, if you have exact numbers to work with, construct a table. Here we have no exact numbers, so we draw an abstract graph that slopes downward to show that cost goes down as the number of students goes up. For graphs with more than one curve, repeat these steps.

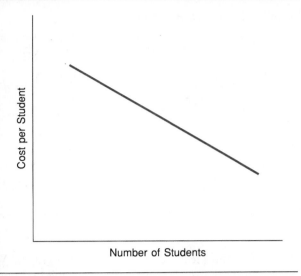

x and y values of the two relationships are equal.) Also note the points at which you think two curves ought to be tangent (which requires that their slopes be equal).

5. When your graph is finished, try to translate it back into words. Does it really say what you want it to?

A Reminder

As you read this book and encounter the various kinds of graphs, turn back to this appendix now and then. Do not memorize graphs as meaningless pictures; if you do, you will get lost. If you can alternate between graphs and words, each one's underlying point will be clearer than if you rely on either one alone. Keep in mind that the primary focus of economics is people and the ways in which they deal with the challenge of scarcity.

2 Exchange and Production

After reading this chapter, you will understand . . .

- The ways it is decided what goods and services the economy is to produce.
- The roles of efficiency, investment, and entrepreneurship in the decision on how goods and services will be produced.
- The impact of positive and normative economics on the decision on for whom goods and services will be produced.
- The principle that guides the division of labor within an economy and among nations.
- How capitalist and socialist economies differ in their approach to the questions of what, how, and for whom.

Before reading this chapter, make sure you know the meaning of . . .

- Factors of production
- Production possibility frontier
- Opportunity costs
- Capital
- Markets
- Positive economics
- Normative economics

Muddy Cars Draw Tickets in Moscow

MOSCOW, USSR. In spring, as the sun comes out, the temperature inches past freezing and the snow begins to melt, is not the time to own a car in the Soviet Union.

The problem is mud. At the end of winter, Russia turns to mud. It leaps from the puddles and melting mounds of dirty snow, coating vehicles that venture past.

Dirty cars, however, are against the law in the Soviet Union. Traffic police, bored on the beat, can wave over a mud-splattered car and either fine the driver as much as 30 rubles (about $45 at the official exchange rate) in some cities, tell him to proceed directly to a car wash, or confiscate his license until the entire car has been inspected for flaws.

Nicks, dents and scratches on the body of a car also are against the law. Drivers of unsightly cars can be fined or have their licenses confiscated. Bald tires, bad paint jobs—even flashy paint jobs—are considered violations of traffic esthetics and reason enough to harass the auto owner.

Car owners here often find themselves between a rock and a hard place. One recounted the following exchange with a huffy traffic policeman:

"You can't drive with tires like that."

"What am I supposed to do? The wait for new tires is 20 months right now."

"That's hardly my problem."

Top on a Soviet driver's list of priorities are spare parts, which are not necessarily here when you need them. One Soviet traveling in Australia used the occasion to buy a camshaft for his Soviet-made car, according to a newspaper report. Foreigners owning Soviet cars here get their spare parts from Finland, and pay import duties on them.

The problem is partly explained by a miscalculation by the Soviet automobile industry, which at one point assumed that the life span of a Soviet car would be seven years. In reality, 31 percent of the 11 million cars on the roads are more than 11 years old, which creates an unplanned strain on the system.

Faced with shortages and poor service, car owners compensate as best they can. Some simply steal what they need, which is why most Soviet drivers remove windshield wipers and side mirrors and lock them up whenever they leave their cars on public streets.

One Soviet driver recalled a road trip through the western Soviet Union on the way back from Eastern Europe. "When someone stole our windshield wipers, we knew we were home again."

Source: Celestine Bohlen, "Muddy Cars Draw Tickets, and Dents Are a Nyet-Nyet," *The Washington Post*, March 17, 1987, A20. Reprinted with permission. Photo Source: © 1987 Phyllis Woloshin.

THE troubles of Moscow's drivers bring us back to the central problem of economics: dealing with scarcity. In this chapter we take a closer look at that problem. We begin with three basic questions that every economic system must answer:

1. *What* should be produced given limited supplies of labor, capital, and natural resources? (How many tires? How much bread? How many airplanes?)

2. *How* should goods and services be produced? (Should tires be made of synthetic or natural rubber? Should they be brought to market by truck, rail, or air? Should the stores that sell them have many clerks using adding machines or fewer clerks aided by computers?)

3. *For whom* should goods and services be produced? (For ordinary people shopping in ordinary stores? For stores that cater to the elite? For export?)

Examining these questions in detail will clarify the economic problem and the tools economists use to understand it.

This chapter has another purpose. Moscow's car situation highlights the questions of what, how, and for whom. But it also shows that different societies deal with the problem of scarcity in different ways. The Soviet economic system answers the questions of what, how, and for whom quite differently than does that of the United States—and these are only two of the world's many economic systems. Although we will deal primarily with the U.S. economy, we must not lose sight of the fact that the basic problems of economics are universal.

The Economic Problem

Scarcity means that we cannot have enough of everything to satisfy all our wants; instead, we must choose. The questions of what, how, and for whom highlight three key choices that must be made in every economy.

What to Produce?

Soviet drivers' search for tires and windshield wipers illustrates the question of what should be produced. If more good tires were produced, they would be more widely available, but there would be an opportunity cost in that the factors of production used to produce the extra tires would be unavailable for use in the production of other goods and services. In Chapter 1, we used a production possibility frontier to illustrate the problem of what to produce using the example of cars and education. The same approach can be used for the choice between tires and bread, guns and butter, and any other alternatives.

The choice of what to produce is sometimes illustrated by Robinson Crusoe's shipwreck on an uninhabited island. Crusoe wakes up hungry in the morning. But what should he eat? He can spend the day fishing and eat poached grouper, or he can spend the day hunting and dine on roast pheasant. If we drew a production possibility frontier illustrating Crusoe's choice between fish and game, we would notice one important aspect of the problem of what to produce: the fact that once the production possibility frontier is reached, more of one good can be produced only at the cost of giving up the opportunity to produce some quantity of another good. But this example skirts another important aspect of the problem—namely that in a modern economy producers and consumers are not interchangeable. The choice of which goods to produce is made by firms, while the choice of which goods to consume is made by households. Thus, there must be some way to tell producers what consumers want.

In Chapter 1, we noted that markets play this signaling role in the U.S. economy. They are the primary channel of communication between firms and households. Firms put goods on the market; consumers tell them yes or no by buying or not buying. This is sometimes called the principle of **consumer sovereignty.** In the Soviet as well as some other economies, markets play a smaller role in communicating consumers' wants to producers. We will return to the question of alternative ways of organizing the economy later in the chapter.

Consumer sovereignty
A system under which consumers determine which goods and services will be produced by means of what they decide to buy or not to buy.

How to Produce?

How goods and services should be produced is a second key question that must be answered in every economy. This too is a question that Crusoe would face on his island. Should he fish with a line or a net? Should he hunt with a gun or snares? Let's look at three aspects of the question of how to produce.

Efficiency in Production

One aspect of the question concerns the choice of the best method of producing a given output with given factor supplies and technology. For example, consider the trade-off between clean air and other consumer goods, represented by the production possibility frontier in Exhibit 2.1. Suppose that we are at point A on this frontier. Starting from there, making the air a little cleaner will require forgoing the opportunity to produce some other goods.

However, there is more than one way to clean up the air. For instance, suppose we want to reduce the pollution from electric power plants. These plants can be made cleaner by either switching to low-sulfur coal or installing stack scrubbers that clean the gases emitted by high-sulfur coal. Which choice is better depends on where the plant is located relative to coal sources, the age of the plant, and so on. If the right choice of technique is made, the economy will slide down the production possibility frontier from A to, say, B. If the wrong choice is made, more other goods will have to be given up in order to attain the same level of clean air. That will leave the economy at a point inside the production possibility frontier, such as C.

Economists say that points lying on the frontier, such as A and B, are characterized by **efficiency in production.** By this they mean that starting from

Efficiency in production
A situation in which it is not possible, given available technology and factors of production, to produce more of one good or service without forgoing the opportunity to produce some of another good or service.

Exhibit 2.1   Efficiency in Production: Cleaning Up the Air

This production possibility frontier shows the trade-off between clean air and other goods. Suppose that we are at point A. Starting from here, the air cannot be made cleaner without some sacrifice of other goods. If efficient pollution control techniques are chosen, the economy can slide down the frontier to another efficient point, such as B. If inefficient techniques are chosen, the economy may end up at a point such as C. Moving from A to C sacrifices more than the amount of other goods necessary for achieving a given increase in clean air.

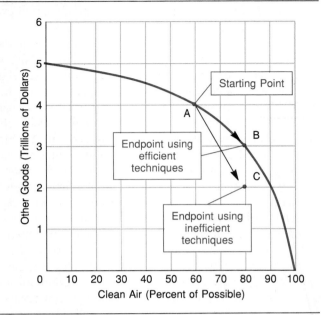

point A or B it is impossible, given the available technology and factors of production, to produce more of one good or service without forgoing the opportunity to produce another good or service. Point C, in contrast, is *inefficient;* that is, it represents an ill-chosen set of pollution control techniques. Starting from that point, it would be possible to have more other goods and services without sacrificing clean air by changing to more appropriate means of control, such as using cheap low-sulfur coal rather than expensive stack scrubbers.

Investment

A production possibility frontier is drawn on the assumptions of given supplies of factors of production and given technologies. The question of how to produce, then, is in part a matter of using the available factors efficiently so that the economy will not fall inside the frontier. If the assumptions are relaxed, the production possibility frontier can be used to illustrate other aspects of the question of how to produce.

Let us return to the case of Robinson Crusoe. The simplest way for Crusoe to catch fish is to stand on the shore and use a hook and line; with this technique, he could catch enough fish to live on. However, he could also use another method: He could stop fishing for a few days and use the time to weave a net and build a boat; then, using the boat and net, he could catch many more fish per hour spent fishing. His new equipment would let him have as many fish as before and give him extra time in which to hunt birds; have more fish and the same number of birds; or have more of both.

Construction of the boat and net is a simple form of investment. **Investment** is the process of accumulating capital. The boat and net are capital because they are durable means of production made by people. The act of building them is an investment by Crusoe just as building a new continuous-casting mill would be an

Investment
The act of increasing the economy's stock of capital, that is, its stock of means of production made by people.

Exhibit 2.2   Expansion of the
Production Possibility Frontier

Production possibility frontiers assume given supplies of
factors of production and a given state of knowledge. In the
short run, the economy can increase the output of capital
goods only by decreasing the output of consumer goods. In
the long run, however, accumulation of capital will expand
the frontier, as shown here. Population growth, discoveries
of new natural resources, and innovation by entrepreneurs
are other things that can cause the frontier to expand.

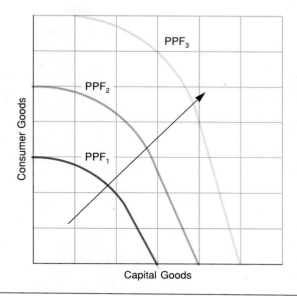

investment by a steel company. Once the investment has been made, the range
of production possibilities expands.

Similarly, the production possibility frontier of a modern economy expands
over time as the result of capital accumulation; this is shown in Exhibit 2.2. In
this version of the production possibility frontier, the vertical axis measures the
output of consumer goods and the horizontal axis measures the output of capital
goods.

In the short run, the economy is confined to movements along a fixed frontier such as PPF_1. Given the factors of production and technology assumed in
drawing this frontier, the economy would have to produce fewer consumer
goods such as cantaloupes and ski vacations in order to produce more capital
goods such as tractors and ski lift equipment. Such a shift in output would be
shown by a movement down and to the right along PPF_1.

Over time, however, increased output of capital goods would increase the
economy's productive capacity. With better farm equipment, more cantaloupes
could be grown per acre of land; with faster ski lifts, the same number of lift
operators could transport more skiers to the top of the mountain. The productive capacity of capital-goods-producing industries could also be increased: Ro-
bots could be used to produce tractors, better machine tools could increase
output of ski lifts, and so on. In the long run, then, accumulation of capital
allows the whole production possibility frontier to shift outward from PPF_1 to
PPF_2 and beyond. As this expansion takes place, the economy can expand along
a path such as that shown by the arrow, on which output of both capital and
consumer goods can be increased.

Capital accumulation is not the only way for the economy to grow. Increased
supplies of other factors of production—for example, labor—would also expand
the frontier. The discovery of new natural resources would do the same thing,

although the depletion of known natural resources would inhibit the expansion. Additional investment—substituting capital for natural resources—would be required in order to overcome this slowdown.

Entrepreneurship

Increasing the quantities of factors of production is one way to expand the production possibility frontier, but it is not the only way. There is still another aspect of the question of how to produce that we have not explored. **Entrepreneurship,** as economists call it, is the process of looking for new possibilities: finding new ways of doing things, being alert to new opportunities, and overcoming old limits. It is a dynamic process that breaks out of the static constraints set by given technology and factor supplies.

In the world of business, entrepreneurship is often linked with the founding of new firms. When a Henry Ford sets out to launch a whole new industry, there are few givens to deal with. New production processes must be invented. The constraints of existing sources of supply must be overcome. Consumers are encouraged to satisfy wants and needs to which they gave little thought before because there were no products that could satisfy them. This kind of exploring and experimenting is the essence of entrepreneurship.

But entrepreneurship is not limited to founding new firms. The manager of a Ford plant may be less of an entrepreneur than the founder, but the manager's work is not entirely routine. Unexpected problems arise that must be solved somehow—often by figuring out a new way of doing things.

Entrepreneurship does not have to mean inventing something, although it sometimes does. It can take other forms as well. It may mean finding a new market for an existing product—for example, convincing people in New England that tacos, long popular in the Southwest, make a quick and tasty lunch. It may mean taking advantage of differences in prices between one market and another—for instance, buying hay at a low price in Pennsylvania, where growing conditions are good in a certain year, and reselling it in Virginia, where a drought has damaged the hay crop.

Consumers can be entrepreneurs too. They do not simply repeat the same patterns of work and leisure every day. They seek variety—new jobs, new foods, new places to visit. Each time you try something new, you are taking a step into the unknown. In this respect, you are playing the role of entrepreneur.

For Whom to Produce?

The final part of the economic problem is the question of for whom goods should be produced. At first, this might seem primarily a normative question, one involving the equitable division of a given quantity of output. Family fights, lawsuits, and even wars have touched on different views of what constitutes a fair distribution of the goods and services an economy produces. However, some basic principles of positive economics apply here too.

Efficiency in Distribution

The positive economics behind "for whom" can best be seen when production has already occurred and there is a fixed supply of goods and services. Suppose that 30 students get on a bus to go to a football game. Bag lunches are handed out. Half the bags contain a ham sandwich and a root beer; the other half contain a tuna sandwich and a cola. What happens when the students open the bags?

Entrepreneurship
The process of looking for new possibilities—making use of new ways of doing things, being alert to new opportunities, and overcoming old limits.

They don't just eat whatever they find—they start trading. Some swap sandwiches; others swap drinks. Maybe there isn't enough of everything to give each person his or her first choice. Nevertheless, the trading makes at least some people better off than they were when they started. Further, no one ends up worse off, because if some don't want to trade, they can always eat what was given to them in the first place.

This example shows that the "for whom" question is partly about efficiency: Starting from any given distribution of goods, the allocation can be improved through trades until it fits people's preferences. So long as it is possible to trade in a way that permits some people to better satisfy their wants without making others worse off, we can say that **efficiency in distribution** can be improved even while the total quantity of goods remains fixed. The federal food stamp program illustrates this principle in action. How many food stamps, if any, a family should get is a subject of debate. But once that question has been settled, each family should be allowed to choose the mix of foods it prefers.

Incentives in Distribution and Overall Economic Efficiency

Efficiency in production and efficiency in distribution are two aspects of the broader concept of economic efficiency. Overall **economic efficiency** means a state of affairs in which it is impossible to satisfy one person's wants more fully by altering either the pattern of production or the pattern of distribution without causing another person's wants to be satisfied less fully.

When this broad notion of economic efficiency is taken into account, the application of positive economics is not restricted to situations in which the total amount of goods is fixed in advance. This is because the rules for distribution are likely to affect the pattern of production. One reason is that the rules for distribution are likely to affect the quantities of labor and other factors of production supplied. Most people earn their incomes by providing labor and other factors of production to business firms. Therefore, when we speak of the system of distribution, we mean the overall system that sets wages, salaries, and returns to the owners of capital. Another reason is that the rules for distribution will affect incentives for entrepreneurship. Some people may work hard to discover new ways of doing things even if they expect no material reward, but that is not true of everyone.

In short, if the system of distribution rewards hard work and careful use of resources, there will be more goods available for distribution. If goods are distributed in a way that is irrelevant to people's efforts and choices, less will be produced. Finally, still less will be produced if the distribution system rewards people for wasting scarce resources.

This is not to say that incentives are the only thing that counts in deciding for whom goods and services should be produced. Almost everyone would agree that fairness should be kept in mind too (although not everyone would concur on the meaning of "fairness"). We will return to the issues of distribution, incentives, and fairness at many points in this book.

Efficiency in distribution
A situation in which it is not possible, by redistributing existing supplies of goods and services, to satisfy one person's wants more fully without causing some other person's wants to be satisfied less fully.

Economic efficiency
A state of affairs in which it is not possible, by changing the pattern of either distribution or production, to satisfy one person's wants more fully without causing some other person's wants to be satisfied less fully.

Exchange and Comparative Advantage

As we have seen, some aspects of the economic problem can be found in a one-person economy such as that of Robinson Crusoe alone on his island. But a one-person economy cannot hold our attention for long. The questions of what, how, and for whom to produce are, in practice, *social* ones—questions concerning the proper way to cooperate in the tasks of production and distribution. In this section, we look at one of the most powerful principles guiding cooperation in production.

Comparative Advantage and Cooperation: An Example

Jim and Bill have agreed to spend their Saturdays helping a local political candidate prepare mailings of campaign literature. There are two steps in preparing a mailing. One consists of stuffing envelopes with several pieces of literature and sealing them; the other is typing address labels and sticking them on the envelopes. The steps can be performed in either order.

Bill has excellent clerical skills; he can stuff 300 envelopes an hour and type 100 labels an hour. Jim is a bit fumble-fingered; he can stuff only 100 envelopes an hour and type only 50 labels an hour.

The first Saturday, they sit down to work at 8:00 a.m. with a list of 1,200 people who are to get that week's mailing. They begin with stuffing. At 400 an hour (100 for Jim and 300 for Bill), this part of the job takes them 3 hours. Then they start typing and sticking on labels. At 150 per hour (50 for Jim and 100 for Bill), the labels take them another 8 hours. At 7:00 p.m.—11 hours after they started—they are done. Hard work, but it was all for a good cause.

On the second Saturday, Jim takes a look at the 1,200 envelopes piled on the table and fears it will be another long day. "Look," he says to Bill, "you're a lot better at this kind of thing than I am. Let me do the stuffing—that's the easy part. Save yourself for the typing, which takes most of the time." At first this strategy looks promising. Since Jim can stuff as quickly as Bill types, they work through the pile at a rate of 100 envelopes per hour. By the end of the day, though, the job has taken them 12 hours—an hour longer than the first week.

The third Saturday rolls around. This time Bill has an idea. "Stuffing those envelopes took you all day last week," he says. "Let me do that part. You start out typing, and when I'm finished stuffing I'll help you finish up the labels." Bill swiftly gets to work, and in four hours he has stuffed the whole pile of envelopes. Meanwhile, Jim, to his embarrassment, has managed to type a paltry 200 labels, and 1,000 remain. But with Bill joining in the typing, they go through the pile at 150 per hour, completing the remaining labels in 6 hours and 40 minutes. They finish at 6:40 p.m. after a total workday of 10 hours and 40 minutes—their best record yet.

It took three weeks for Bill and Jim to find the best pattern of cooperation. Is there a way they could have found it immediately, without the trial and error? There is. The key lies in the notion of opportunity cost. In this case, the opportunity cost of typing one address label is measured by the number of envelopes that could have been stuffed in the same amount of time. Bill can stuff 300 envelopes an hour or type 100 labels an hour; for him, the opportunity cost of typing 1 label is stuffing 3 envelopes. Jim can stuff 100 envelopes an hour or type 50 labels an hour; for him, the opportunity cost of typing 1 label is stuffing only 2 envelopes. The reason the work goes fastest when Jim spends all his time typing is that the opportunity cost of typing is lower for him than it is for Bill.

Because the opportunity cost of typing is less for Jim than for Bill, Jim is said to have a **comparative advantage** in typing. Bill, on the other hand, has a comparative advantage in stuffing. The opportunity cost of stuffing an envelope is one-third of an address label for Bill and one-half of a label for Jim.

Comparative advantage
The ability to produce a good or service at a lower opportunity cost than another person or country.

David Ricardo and the Theory of Comparative Advantage

David Ricardo, the greatest of the classical economists, was born in 1772. His father, a Jewish immigrant, was a member of the London stock exchange. Ricardo's education was rather haphazard, and he entered his father's business at the age of 14. In 1793, he married and went into business on his own. These were years of war and financial turmoil. The young Ricardo developed a reputation for remarkable astuteness and quickly made a large fortune.

In 1799, Ricardo read Adam Smith's *The Wealth of Nations* and developed an interest in political economy (as economics was then called). In 1809, his first writings on economics appeared. These were a series of newspaper articles on "The High Price of Bullion," which appeared the following year as a pamphlet. Several other short works

Art Source: Bettmann Archives

added to his reputation in this area. In 1814, he retired from business to devote all his time to political economy.

Ricardo's major work was *Principles of Political Economy and Taxation*, first published in 1817. This work contains, among other things, a pioneering statement of the principle of comparative advantage as applied to international trade. With a lucid numerical example, Ricardo showed why it is to the mutual advantage of both countries for England to export wool to Portugal and import wine in return even though both products can be produced with less labor in Portugal.

But international trade is only a sidelight of Ricardo's *Principles*. The book covers the whole field of economics as it then existed, beginning with value theory and progressing to a theory of economic growth and evolution. Ricardo held that the economy was growing toward a future "steady state." In this state, economic growth would come to a halt and the wage rate would be reduced to the subsistence level.

Ricardo's book was extremely influential. For more than half a century thereafter, much of economics as written in England was an expansion of or a commentary on Ricardo's work. The most famous economist influenced by Ricardo's theory and method was Karl Marx (see "Who Said It? Who Did It? 2.2"). Although Marx eventually reached conclusions that differed radically from any of Ricardo's views, his starting point was Ricardo's theory of value and method of analyzing economic growth.

The principle to be drawn from this example is that the cost of producing a given output is minimized if each party involved specializes in the task in which he or she has a comparative advantage. It is important to note that the principle of comparative advantage works even when one party (Bill, in this case) is, in an absolute sense, better at everything. It is Jim's typing skill compared to his own stuffing skill that counts, not his typing skill versus Bill's. Although somewhat of a klutz at clerical tasks, Jim contributes more by typing than by stuffing.

International Applications

Wider applications of comparative advantage abound. The first application of this principle was not to the division of labor within a country but to trade among countries (see "Who Said It? Who Did It? 2.1"). The most basic principle of international trade is that two countries can both raise their living standards through a pattern of trade that follows comparative advantage.

Suppose, for example, that in the United States a tractor can be produced with 100 hours of labor and a pair of shoes with 2, while in China the same products require 500 and 5 labor hours, respectively. Can each country gain by trading? Yes—if each follows the principle of comparative advantage.

Who has the comparative advantage in which product? Consider tractors first. Under U.S. conditions, shifting enough labor from shoes to produce 1 more tractor (100 hours) requires giving up the opportunity to produce 50 pairs of shoes. In China, shifting enough labor from shoes to produce 1 more tractor (500 hours) means giving up 100 pairs of shoes. Thus, the opportunity cost of tractors in terms of shoes is lower in the United States than in China. Similarly, shifting enough labor from tractors to make 100 pairs of shoes (200 hours) will require giving up 2 tractors in the United States. In China, shifting enough labor from tractors to shoes to make 100 pairs of shoes (500 hours) will require giving up only 1 tractor. Hence, China has a comparative advantage in shoes.

Next, suppose that initially each country produces 1 million tractors and 100 million pairs of shoes a year. Now each shifts production in the direction of the product in which it has a comparative advantage. The United States adds, say, 100,000 tractors to its output by shifting 10 million labor hours from shoes. Shoe output thus drops by 5 million pairs. Meanwhile, China steps up its shoe output by 7 million pairs by shifting 35 million labor hours from tractor building. Chinese tractor output drops by 70,000.

As a result of these changes, world output of both goods has increased. Tractor output is up 100,000 in the United States and down only 70,000 in China for a net gain of 30,000 tractors. Shoe output is up 7 million pairs in China and down only 5 million pairs in the United States for a net gain of 2 million shoes. Clearly there has been a gain in terms of efficiency in production. But the fruits of the increase in production are not well distributed. The U.S. is awash in tractors but actually has fewer shoes than before even though world shoe output has increased. Similarly, China is flooded with shoes but has fewer tractors even though world tractor output has increased. To draw an analogy with an earlier example, it is as though the person who packed the bag lunches for the bus trip put several cans of soda and no sandwiches in some bags and several sandwiches but no drinks in others.

In order to benefit from the increase in world output made possible by specialization according to comparative advantage, the gains in productive efficiency must be redistributed by trade. The United States must export some of its tractors in exchange for some of China's shoes. Negotiators must get together and strike a bargain that benefits both countries. A possible bargain—one that divides the gain in world production equally between the two countries—is shown in Exhibit 2.3. Under the terms of trade established there, the United States exports 85,000 tractors to China in exchange for 6 million pairs of shoes. This leaves both countries with more of both products than they started with. By means of international trade and comparative advantage, then, there have been gains in both the productive and distributional aspects of economic efficiency.

Market Prices and Comparative Advantage

Much more will be said about the organization of production and international trade in later chapters. The examples given here are highly simplified. Nonetheless, as more details are added to models of trade and production, it will still be true that efficiency gains are realized when the principle of comparative advantage is respected.

Exhibit 2.3   Gains from Trade: An Example

In this example, it is assumed that in the United States it takes 100 hours to build a tractor and 2 hours to make a pair of shoes, while in China it takes 500 and 5 hours, respectively. Before trade, each country is assumed to produce 1 million tractors and 100 million pairs of shoes. The United States then steps up tractor output by 100,000 at the expense of 5 million pairs of shoes. China steps up shoe output by 7 million pairs at the expense of 70,000 tractors. These actions increase total world output of tractors by 30,000 units and total world output of shoes by 2 million pairs. Tractors are then exchanged for shoes, with the United States exporting 85,000 tractors and importing 6 million pairs of shoes. The result, as the following table shows, is that both countries end up with more of both shoes and tractors.

	United States	**China**
A. Before Trade		
Tractors	Produced: 1,000,000 Consumed: 1,000,000	Produced: 1,000,000 Consumed: 1,000,000
Shoes	Produced: 100,000,000 Consumed: 100,000,000	Produced: 100,000,000 Consumed: 100,000,000
B. After Trade		
Tractors	Produced: 1,100,000 Exported: 85,000 ⟶ Consumed: 1,015,000	Produced: 930,000 Imported: 85,000 Consumed: 1,015,000
Shoes	Produced: 95,000,000 Imported: 6,000,000 ⟵ Consumed: 101,000,000	Produced: 107,000,000 Exported: 6,000,000 Consumed: 101,000,000

But this raises a question: How do people know whom to hire for which jobs and from whom to buy various goods and services? The answer is that they depend on information transmitted to them via market prices. In competitive markets, prices tend to reflect opportunity costs. (This is a central concept of microeconomic analysis that will be developed over several chapters.) Comparative advantage requires that one buy where opportunity costs are lowest; for the most part, this simply means buying where prices are lowest. When Bill and Jim compete in the market for clerical services, we can count on Bill to submit the lower bid on stuffing services and Jim the lower bid on typing services.[1] When competing in world markets, China will usually be able to underbid the United States on shoes and the United States will usually be able to underbid China on tractors. Neither labor markets, international markets, nor any other markets work perfectly at all times. But as long as competition tends to keep market prices close to opportunity costs, markets will do a remarkably good job of organizing production and exchange.

_____

[1] What if Bill turns in the lower bid on both typing and stuffing services? This might happen at first, but if it does, Bill will be swamped with work and Jim will have nothing to do. Bill will then tend to raise his rates and Jim to cut his until each gets some of the work. Of course, since Bill is more productive at both tasks, he will probably end up earning a higher income. There is no rule of markets saying that people will earn equal incomes—but that is a story for another chapter.

Economic Systems

The questions of what, how, and for whom are all parts of an economic problem that apply to the economies of the United States, the Soviet Union, Crusoe's island, and all other economies, real or fictional. But although all economies are alike in the problems they face, they differ in the way decisions are made. The U.S. economy, as we have mentioned, relies heavily on markets and the price system to guide decisions. But there are other approaches to decision making. In this section, we make some brief comparisons.

Ownership and Economic Decision Making

To *own* something means to have the right to use it and prevent others from using it. If you own something, you are an economic decision maker. You decide who uses it and how it is used. Because owners are decision makers, ownership of business firms is a key feature of any economic system.

In the United States, most firms are controlled by the people who own the firms' capital, that is, their buildings, production equipment, inventory, and so on. Depending on the exact legal form of ownership, these people may be small-business proprietors, partners, or corporate stockholders. Chapter 4 will discuss these three forms of ownership in more detail. The point here is that whatever the legal details, a system in which control of business firms rests with the owners of capital is called capitalism.

Capitalism
An economic system in which control of business firms rests with the owners of capital.

Not all firms—even in the United States—are owned and controlled by capitalists. For instance, mutually or cooperatively owned firms are owned by the people who work in them or use their services. Examples include mutual insurance companies and savings banks, agricultural and consumer cooperatives, private colleges and universities, and not-for-profit publishers such as the organization that puts out *Consumer Reports*. Other firms are owned by the government, such as the Tennessee Valley Authority, the U.S. Postal Service, and, until recently, Conrail. Mutual, cooperative, and government ownership are all forms of *social* ownership. A system in which social ownership prevails is called socialism.

Socialism
An economic system in which firms are owned and controlled by the people who work in them or by the government acting in their name.

However, in the real world there are no purely capitalist or socialist systems; rather, all existing systems are mixtures of the two forms. In the United States, Canada, Western Europe, and Japan, the newly industrialized countries such as Brazil, South Korea, and Taiwan, and some less developed countries, capitalism prevails. Nevertheless, mutual, cooperative, and government-owned firms exist in all these economies.

In the Soviet Union, Eastern Europe, China, and many other less developed countries, social ownership prevails. The theories on which these economies are based can be traced to the writings of the nineteenth-century economist Karl Marx (see "Who Said It? Who Did It? 2.2"). Following Marx's precepts, almost all industry in these countries is government owned, but some private ownership can be found in farming, retail trade, and services. One country—Yugoslavia—has its own home-grown brand of cooperative ownership and control.

However, our purpose here is not to list the world's economic systems but to show that different forms of ownership place authority for decision making in the hands of different groups of people. Under capitalism, the owners of capital are the managers and entrepreneurs. Under mutual and cooperative ownership,

---

Karl Marx: Economist and Socialist

Karl Marx—German philosopher, revolutionary, and patron saint of socialism—was also a well-known economist. From the age of 31, he lived and worked in London. His thinking was strongly influenced by the British classical school of economics, especially the writings of David Ricardo. But while economists of the classical school were, for the most part, sympathetic to the capitalist system, Marx took the tools of classical economics and turned them against capitalism.

The cornerstone of classical economics was the *labor theory of value*—the doctrine that the values and relative prices of various goods are determined mainly by the number of labor hours that go into their production. For Marx, the labor theory of value was more than a mere description of how prices are determined. He went on to argue that if labor is the source of all value, workers should receive the whole product of their labor. He viewed it as unjust that under capitalism a large part of the product was paid to owners of land and capital in the form of rent, interest payments, and profit—in his terms, "surplus value."

In his massive work *Capital*, Marx tried to show that capitalism was headed for collapse and would be followed by a socialist revolution. All of his life he worked with revolutionary groups to prepare for that day. Following the revolution, he envisioned an economy based on collective ownership and economic planning. He gave the name communism to the highest form of socialism, toward which the revolution would strive and in which the principle of "from each according to his ability, to each according to his need" would govern production and distribution. Today "communism" is used to describe the economic systems of the Soviet Union, Eastern Europe, and other countries that follow Marxist principles, even though these are not pure communism in the Marxist sense of the term.

Marx was not the first socialist, nor are all of today's socialists followers of Marx. Nevertheless, he must be regarded as the most influential thinker in the history of socialism and one of the most important economists of all time.

Photo Source: Library of Congress

---

managers are chosen by workers, consumers, or some other group. Under forms of socialism that feature government ownership, managers are public employees.

Styles of Decision Making

No less important than differences in who makes economic decisions are differences in how those decisions are made. Broadly speaking, there are three styles of decision making: market decision making, regulation, and planning.

Markets

Chapter 1 discussed the role of markets in decision making. Markets perform three tasks: (1) They transmit information on the values of resources to firms and households; (2) they set incentives for workers, traders, and entrepreneurs; and (3) in the process of doing these things, they determine the distribution of income. Beginning with Chapter 3, the remainder of this book will be devoted primarily to the ways in which markets do all three.

Although the role of markets in decision making is greatest in capitalist systems, most socialist economies also use markets. Take cars in the Soviet

Union. Cars are produced by a government-owned firm and sold in a government-owned store. Nevertheless, the choice of what to buy—a car, furniture, airline tickets, or whatever—is a market decision; that is to say, this decision is governed, at least in part, by the prices of available goods. Quite recently the use of markets by Soviet motorists has been extended. Private automobile repair shops, which previously operated "underground," have been allowed to emerge in the public marketplace to compete with inefficient government-run repair shops.

Other socialist countries use markets much more extensively. In Poland, the bulk of the farm sector relies on markets. China uses markets heavily in light industry and services. Hungary and Yugoslavia use market incentives throughout their economies—in fact, systems such as theirs are often called *market socialism*.

Regulation

Regulation
Government intervention in the market for the purpose of influencing the production and distribution of particular goods and services.

No economic system leaves all decisions to the market. Even in the most strongly capitalist systems, the government plays a major role in the decisions of what, how, and for whom. Its activities in this area are known as **regulation.** The U.S. Food and Drug Administration's regulation of prescription drugs affects *what* pharmaceutical firms produce. The Environmental Protection Agency's rules on air and water pollution affect *how* firms produce their outputs. Laws such as the federal minimum wage law and the Davis-Bacon Act determine levels of pay for many workers and thus affect *for whom* goods and services are produced. We will discuss many kinds of regulation in later chapters.

Planning

Economic planning
Systematic government intervention in the economy with the goal of improving coordination, efficiency, and growth.

The governments of many countries go beyond regulation and engage in **economic planning.** This can be defined as systematic intervention in the economy with the goal of improving coordination, efficiency, and growth.

Because planning and regulation differ mainly in degree, there is no sharp line between them. The most comprehensive planning is found in socialist economies such as that of the Soviet Union. There each firm, be it a tire factory, auto-parts plant, or distillery, is required to follow a plan governing its level of output, production methods, sources of supply, and so forth. As the article that opens this chapter illustrates, planning mistakes may take years to correct or never be corrected at all.

Other socialist countries engage in more limited planning. They try to coordinate the work of the largest firms and set a framework for economic growth, but they leave more detailed decisions to each firm's managers. Some countries in which capitalist ownership prevails have tried this style of planning too; France is a notable example. The United States probably has the smallest degree of national economic planning in the world.

Looking Ahead

This is not a book on comparative economics; most of its examples are based on the American economic system. Still, it is worthwhile to keep the variety of economic systems in mind. The basic problems of what, how, and for whom are universal ones that have many possible solutions. Further, even within the U.S. economy, a great many competing forms of ownership and decision-making approaches coexist.

Summary

1. **How is it decided what goods and services the economy is to produce?** Scarcity means that we cannot have enough of everything to satisfy all our wants. Therefore, it must somehow be decided what, among all possible combinations of goods and services, is to be produced. This means that there must be some way for consumers to tell producers what they want. In the U.S. economy, markets are the principal channel through which consumers communicate with producers.

2. **How do efficiency, investment, and entrepreneurship enter into the decision of how goods will be produced?** For given factors of production and technology, the range of goods and services from which an economy can choose can be represented by a production possibility frontier. If production is organized efficiently, the economy will be on its production possibility frontier. In that case, it will be impossible to more fully satisfy one want without less fully satisfying some other. The economy cannot move outside the frontier with a given supply of factors, but investment—that is, the accumulation of additional capital—can expand the frontier. The frontier can also be expanded through entrepreneurship, which is the process of looking for new ways to do things, being alert to new opportunities, and overcoming old limits.

3. **How do positive and normative economics bear on the question of for whom goods will be produced?** The question of for whom goods will be produced is partly a normative question, that is, one of fairness. However, the question has positive aspects as well. For one thing, a given output of goods and services must be efficiently distributed so that one person's wants cannot be better satisfied without less fully satisfying someone else's. For another, positive economics can be used to analyze the way in which the choice of goods distribution will affect incentives and, hence, the quantity and selection of output.

4. **What principle guides the division of labor within an economy and among nations?** When people cooperate in production, efficiency requires that the division of labor follow the principle of comparative advantage. A person who is able to produce a good or service at a lower opportunity cost than someone else is said to have a comparative advantage in producing that good or service. Trade among nations, as well as the division of labor within an economy, will be most efficient when it follows the principle of comparative advantage.

5. **How do capitalist and socialist economies differ in their approaches to the questions of what, how, and for whom?** A capitalist economy is one in which control of business firms rests with owners of the firm's capital. Such economies rely heavily on markets to guide the decisions of what, how, and for whom. A socialist economy is one in which firms are controlled by the people who work in them or by the government acting in the workers' name. Such economies tend to rely more extensively on planning. In practice, all economies use a widely varying mixture of markets, planning, and regulation.

Terms for Review

- consumer sovereignty
- efficiency in production
- investment
- entrepreneurship
- efficiency in distribution
- economic efficiency
- comparative advantage
- capitalism
- socialism
- regulation
- economic planning

Questions for Review

1. In what sense do markets serve as a channel of communication between consumers and producers in a capitalist economy?

2. Under what conditions will an economy operate inside its production possibility frontier? How can the frontier be expanded?

3. Why does the question of for whom to produce raise both normative and positive economic questions?

4. Why can it be said that everyone has a comparative advantage in something even if there is nothing a person can do that someone else cannot do better?

5. Give examples of social forms of ownership in the United States and capitalist forms of ownership in the Soviet Union and Eastern Europe. Give examples of markets, regulation, and economic planning as methods of decision making in various countries.

Problems and Topics for Discussion

1. **Examining the lead-off case.** Compare the situation faced by Soviet and U.S. motorists in terms of the roles of markets, regulation, and planning. What useful purpose, if any, do you think is served by regulations requiring cars to be clean, neatly painted, and so on? Would you favor such a regulation in the United States? Why or why not?

2. **Pollution and growth.** Exhibit 2.2 shows an expanding production possibility frontier. Relabel the horizontal axis of this figure so that it represents "clean air" as in Exhibit 2.1. If the economy followed the path of the arrow in the diagram, it would be possible to enjoy both more material goods and cleaner air. Yet, at least in some locations, the air has become dirtier as output of other goods has expanded over time. Does this mean that the production possibility frontier is not expanding as shown in the exhibit? Does it mean that growth must be stopped if we want to keep the air from getting dirtier? Or does it mean that during the expansion the economy is following a different path than the one shown in the exhibit? Illustrate your answer with a diagram. Discuss the issue of clean air versus other goods in an expanding economy from the viewpoint of both positive and normative economics.

3. **Efficiency and the production possibility frontier.** Turn back to problem 3 from Chapter 1. Note that the accompanying table assumes that the farmer switches his highest field first from potatoes to wheat. What would happen if instead he grew potatoes in the three highest fields and wheat in the two lowest? How would that point be represented in relation to the production possibility frontier? How would you describe such a situation? Now compare the opportunity cost of producing wheat in the top field with that in the bottom field. Which field has a comparative advantage in producing wheat? Which has a comparative advantage in producing potatoes? In using the highest fields first for wheat, is the farmer following the principle of comparative advantage? Why or why not?

4. **Comparative advantage.** Suppose you learned that the great pianist Vladimir Horowitz was also an amazing typist. Knowing this, would it surprise you to discover that he hired a secretary to type his correspondence even though he could do the job more quickly himself? How does this relate to comparative advantage?

5. **International trade.** In the United States, a car can be produced with 200 labor hours, while a ton of rice requires 20 labor hours. In Japan, it takes 150 labor hours to make a car and 50 labor hours to grow a ton of rice. Which country has a comparative advantage in cars? In rice? Show that both countries can have both more cars and more rice by trading at a rate of five tons of rice per car. If trade that follows the principle of comparative advantage is beneficial to both parties, why do you think the United States limits the import of Japanese cars while Japan restricts the import of U.S. rice? Discuss.

6. **Efficiency in distribution and the food stamp program.** The federal food stamp program leaves low-income families free to choose their preferred mix of foods. However, instead it could give them a ticket book with so many bread coupons, so many milk coupons, so many meat coupons, and so on. Which plan do you think would be more efficient for a given cost to the government? Would it be still more efficient if low-income families were allowed to trade their food stamps for cash? (Such trading does happen, but it is restricted by law.) Or perhaps low-income families should be given cash in the first place and allowed to spend it on whatever they want. Discuss this issue, taking both positive and normative economics into account.

Chinese peasant farmers

Case for Discussion
Growing Rich in Wenjiang County

Wu Xiangtin, a farmer in Wenjiang County, is growing rich—at least by Chinese standards—off the so-called "responsibility system." This is a program in which plots of land have been turned over to farmers for up to 15 years to use in producing goods for consumer markets. Wu earns about $15 a day by selling the eggs produced by his 200 chickens. Last year, he claims, his total income was about 10,000 yuan, or roughly $4,800.

The newly affluent Wu has purchased a new house, a new chicken coop, and a TV set. His next project is to raise rabbits, ducks, and geese. He notes that duck and goose eggs command higher prices than chicken eggs.

Wu's projects are typical of the entrepreneurial energy that was bottled up by Chairman Mao's policies. In 1966, at the start of the Cultural Revolution (a campaign to shape Chinese society along more purely socialist lines), Wu was working as a veterinarian at a nearby commune. The political turmoil made it impossible for him to remain at that job, so he began raising pigs. Local socialist activists, known as Red Guards, denounced him as an "exploiter" and warned,

"You will be taking the capitalist road if you raise ducks or chickens."

Wu becomes indignant at the suggestion that the Communist party might someday take away his chickens. "It's the policy of the party," he says. "The party will never take away my 10,000 yuan."

Maybe not. For the time being, local party officials, far from denouncing Wu, are showing him off to foreign visitors as a success story of the new China. Moreover, they say that because of the responsibility system, the average income of the 1,300 people in Wu's production brigade has more than doubled since 1978.

But there are problems that could hinder further change. The most obvious is inequality of income, which could trigger a backlash. Take Wu's neighbor, Li Xiaochuan, who lives in a cramped and dirty house. Li has only four pigs, six chickens, and an income about one-tenth of Wu's. At some point, he and other poor peasants may come to resent their "rich" neighbor and seek a return to what they see as more egalitarian policies.

Source: David Ignatius, "China's Capitalistic Road Is Uphill from Here," *The Wall Street Journal,* May 4, 1984, p. 30. Reprinted by permission of *The Wall Street Journal,* © Dow Jones & Company, Inc. 1984. All Rights Reserved. Photo Source: Reuters/Bettmann Newsphotos.

Questions

1. In what ways does Wu fit the definition of an entrepreneur?

2. How does this story illustrate the three functions of markets? How does it illustrate the use of markets in a socialist society?

3. What examples are given in this story of the what, how, and for whom decisions that every economy faces?

4. Discuss the tension between the Maoist belief that pure socialism should strive for equality above all and the desire of China's current leaders to make the economy more efficient and productive.

Suggestions for Further Reading

Defoe, Daniel. *The Adventures of Robinson Crusoe.* London, 1719.

The examples used in this chapter are only fancifully related to this classic novel. However, try reading it with an eye to understanding the economic problems faced by Crusoe and, later, by Crusoe and Friday together.

Goodman, John C., and Edwin G. Dolan. *The Economics of Public Policy,* 3d ed. St. Paul, Minn.: West, 1985.

Chapter 2 uses the issue of the military draft versus the volunteer army to illustrate the concepts of opportunity cost and

the production possibility frontier. Chapter 3 compares the U.S. and British methods of deciding who receives medical treatment.

Wiles, P. J. D. *Economic Institutions Compared.* New York: Wiley, 1977.

This book compares the methods used by different economic systems to solve the problems they all face. Chapter 6, which deals with cooperatives, communities, and communes, is of particular interest.

3 Supply and Demand

After reading this chapter, you will understand . . .

- How the price of a good or service affects the quantity demanded by buyers.
- Other market conditions that affect demand.
- How the quantities of goods and services that producers supply are affected by prices and other market conditions.
- How supply and demand interact to determine the market price of a good or service.
- Why market prices and quantities change in response to changes in a variety of market conditions.
- How price supports and price ceilings affect the operations of markets.

Before reading this chapter, make sure you know the meaning of . . .

- Markets and their functions (Chapters 1 and 2)
- Real and nominal values (Chapter 1)
- Opportunity cost (Chapter 1)
- Comparative advantage (Chapter 2)
- Entrepreneurship (Chapter 2)

Are the Fakes Real or the Real Ones Fake?

Marylou Whitney—Mrs. Cornelius Vanderbilt Whitney—is well aware that there are a lot of fake diamonds around these days. She wears them much of the time.

"I'm delighted with fake jewelry," says Whitney, who can certainly afford the real thing. She explains: "I would like to wear real, but it isn't safe." And when she does wear real, she says, she passes it off as fake, saying that she is amused "that people who don't have the real thing pretend their fakes are real, and people like me pretend the real is fake."

A cubic zirconia can easily pass for a diamond.

Marylou Whitney's fakes and many others are CZs, made from a substance called cubic zirconia. CZs have about the same refractive index (brilliance) as diamonds and more light-dispersion (fire) than the real thing. They can be very convincing. In 1983 reporter John Stossel of the TV show "20/20" embarrassed the jewelry industry by taking a CZ and a $50,000 diamond to New York's jewelers' row. Half the jewelers he visited thought the CZ was a diamond.

But there is one big difference between diamonds and CZs: price. CZs sell for $15 to $150 a carat, compared to $2,000 to $20,000 a carat for diamonds. Why? Supply and demand, of course. About 200 million carats of CZs are made every year, compared to about 9 million carats of jewelry-quality diamonds. And although CZs are pretty, there is no demand for them for nonjewelry uses. CZs are too soft to make cutting tools, and they are no help in laser technology. So if you want to sparkle like a Whitney, CZs could be your best friend.

Source: Joan Kron, "If Diamonds Can Be a Girl's Best Friend, CZs Are Good Pals," *The Wall Street Journal*, June 15, 1984, p. 30. Reprinted by permission of *The Wall Street Journal*, © Dow Jones & Company, Inc. 1984. All Rights Reserved. Photo Source: © 1987 Phyllis Woloshin.

As we have seen, a key function of markets is that of transmitting information in the form of prices. Prices give buyers and sellers signals regarding the opportunity costs of goods and services. Buyers' and sellers' responses to these signals, in turn, determine what is produced, how it is produced, and for whom it is produced.

The role of prices is so central to the functioning of a market economy that the field of microeconomics is sometimes referred to as "price theory." This chapter introduces the theory of prices. The centerpiece of the chapter is a set of tools that show how supply and demand affect the prices of CZs, chicken, dental services, beef, and just about everything else. Once these tools are clearly understood, it becomes difficult to pick up the business page of a newspaper without noticing "supply" and "demand" between the lines of every story.

Demand

Just a few years ago, compact disk players carried price tags of $1,000 and up. At that price, they were a plaything for the rich audiophile—the person who just had to have the best available sound even if it cost the equivalent of a Caribbean vacation. Today discounters sell CD players for as little as $100, and that same flawless sound can be heard booming out of dormitory windows on any campus in the country. Is it surprising that when the price fell more CD players were sold? Hardly—it was simply the law of demand in action.

Law of demand
The principle that, other things being equal, the quantity of a good demanded by buyers tends to rise as the price of the good falls and to fall as its price rises.

The law of demand can be stated formally as follows: In any market, other things being equal, the quantity of a good or service that buyers demand tends to rise as its price falls and to fall as its price rises. We expect this to happen for two reasons. First, if the price of one good falls while the prices of other goods stay the same, people are likely to substitute the cheaper good for goods they would have bought otherwise. (When chicken is on sale and beef is not, people have chicken for dinner more often.) Second, when the price of one good falls while incomes and other prices stay the same, people feel a little richer. They use their added buying power to buy a bit more of many things, including a little more of the good whose price went down. In many cases, as we will see, these two factors combine to boost sales of goods whose prices fall and cut sales of goods whose prices rise.

Behind the Law of Demand

While the formal law of demand satisfies common sense, three of its elements are worth clarifying.

Quantity Demanded

It is important to understand what is meant by *quantity demanded*. This is the quantity that buyers are willing and able to buy over a given period, such as a month or a year. Quantity demanded is not the same thing as quantity wanted or needed. I might *want* a Porsche, but the last time I checked, the sticker price was over $40,000. At that price I would have to give up too much else to buy one, so I choose not to. The quantity of Porsches I demand at the going price is zero.

On the other hand, I might *need* dental surgery to avoid losing my teeth. But suppose I am poor. If I cannot pay for the surgery or find a benefactor to pay my way, I am out of luck. The quantity of dental surgery I demand therefore is zero, however great my need.

Other Things Being Equal

The phrase *other things being equal* means that a change in the price of a product is only one of a number of things that affect the quantity people are willing to buy. If real incomes go up, people are likely to buy more of many goods even if their prices do not drop. If tastes change, people will buy more of some goods and less of others even if prices do not change. Other factors can affect demand even when prices remain fixed.

For example, "other things being equal" means that the prices of other goods are assumed to remain the same as buyers respond to a change in the price of any one good. As economists put it, *relative prices* are what count.

It is important to distinguish between changes in relative prices and changes in nominal prices—the number of dollars actually paid per unit—during periods of inflation. If the price of eggs goes up 10 percent at the same time that consumers' nominal incomes and the prices of muffins, butter, and all other goods rise by 10 percent, we should not expect any change in the quantity of eggs demanded. The opportunity cost of buying eggs does not change in this situation. As before, buying a dozen eggs means giving up the opportunity to buy three muffins, a jar and a half of jam, or whatever. The law of demand does not apply to this situation because other things are not equal as the price of eggs climbs.

During a period of inflation, the relative price of a good may fall even though its nominal price is going up. For example, from 1974 to 1978, the nominal price of gasoline rose, but at a less rapid rate than the rate of inflation. People responded to the lower relative price of gasoline by buying more. In 1979 and 1980, the nominal price of gasoline went up faster than the prices of other goods. People responded to the increase in the relative price by buying less.

The Demand Curve

The law of demand states a relationship between the quantity of a good that people intend to buy, other things being equal, and the price of that good. This one-to-one relationship can be shown in a table or a graph, as in Exhibit 3.1.

Look at the table that forms part a of the exhibit. The first line shows that when the price of chicken is $.64 a pound, the quantity demanded per year is 1.4 billion pounds. Reading down the table, we see that as the price falls, the quantity demanded rises. At $.60 per pound, buyers plan to purchase 1.5 billion pounds per year; at $.56, they plan to buy 1.6 billion pounds; and so on.

Part b of Exhibit 3.1 presents the same information in graphic form. The graph is called a demand curve for chicken. Suppose we want to use the demand curve to find out what quantity of chicken will be demanded at a price of $.40 per pound. Starting at $.40 on the vertical axis, we move across, as shown by the arrow, until we reach the demand curve at point A. Continuing to follow the arrow, we drop down to the horizontal axis. Reading from the scale on that axis, we see that the quantity demanded at $.40 per pound is 2 billion pounds per year. This is the quantity demanded in line A of the table in part a.

Demand curve
A graphic representation of the relationship between the price of a good and the quantity of it that buyers demand.

Movements along the Demand Curve

The effect of a change in the price of chicken, other things being equal, can be shown as a movement from one point to another along the demand curve for chicken. Suppose the price drops from $.40 to $.20 per pound. In the process,

Exhibit 3.1   A Demand Curve for Chicken

Parts a and b show the quantity of chicken demanded at various prices. For example, at a price of $.40 per pound, buyers are willing and able to purchase 2 billion pounds of chicken per year. This price-quantity combination is shown by line A in part a and point A in part b.

(a)	
Price of Chicken (Dollars per Pound)	Quantity of Chicken Demanded (Billions of Pounds per Year)
.64	1.4
.60	1.5
.56	1.6
.52	1.7
.48	1.8
.44	1.9
A .40	2.0
.36	2.1
.32	2.2
.28	2.3
.24	2.4
B .20	2.5
.16	2.6

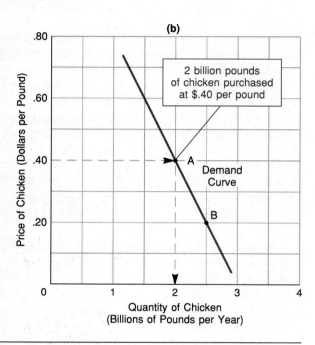

the quantity that buyers plan to purchase rises. The point corresponding to the quantity demanded at the new, lower price is point B (corresponding to line B of the table). Because the quantity demanded increases as the price decreases, the demand curve has a negative slope.

Economists speak of a movement along a demand curve as a **change in quantity demanded.** Such a movement represents buyers' reaction to a change in the price of the good in question, other things being equal.

Change in quantity demanded
A change in the quantity of a good that buyers are willing and able to purchase that results from a change in the good's price, other things being equal; a movement from one point to another along a demand curve.

Shifts in the Demand Curve

Demand curves such as the one in Exhibit 3.1 are always drawn on an "other things being equal" basis. They assume that as the price of chicken changes other factors, such as consumers' incomes, consumers' tastes, and the prices of other goods, remain fixed. If any of these other factors changes, the quantity of chicken that consumers are willing and able to buy will change even if there is no change in the price of chicken. We must then draw a new demand curve. The new curve, like the old one, will have a negative slope, following the law of demand, but it will be shifted to the right or the left.

Change in demand
A change in the quantity of a good that buyers are willing and able to purchase that results from a change in some condition other than the price of that good; a shift in the demand curve.

Economists speak of a shift in the demand curve as a **change in demand.** Such a shift represents a change in buyers' plans caused by some factor other than the price of the good in question. Several sources of changes in demand are worth looking at. Among the most important are changes in the prices of other goods, changes in consumers' incomes, changes in expectations, and changes in tastes.

Changes in the Prices of Other Goods

The demand for a good may be affected by changes in the prices of related goods as well as by changes in the price of the good in question. Exhibit 3.2 shows demand curves for lettuce and cabbage, either of which can be used to make salad. People's decisions about whether to eat tossed salad or cole slaw depend on the prices of both lettuce and cabbage.

Suppose that the price of lettuce starts out at \$.70 a pound and then rises to \$1.00 a pound. The effect of this change is shown in part a of Exhibit 3.2 as a movement along the lettuce demand curve from point A to point B. With the price of lettuce higher than before, consumers will tend to buy more cabbage than they would otherwise (part b). Now suppose the price of cabbage is \$.50 a pound. Before the price of lettuce went up, consumers would have bought 20 million pounds of cabbage a week (point A' on cabbage demand curve D_1). After the price of lettuce has gone up, they will buy 26 million pounds of cabbage a week at the same price (point B' on cabbage demand curve D_2). Thus, an

Exhibit 3.2   Effects of an Increase in the Price of Lettuce on the Demand for Cabbage

An increase in the price of lettuce from \$.70 to \$1.00 per pound, other things being equal, results in a movement from point A to point B on the lettuce demand curve. This is called a decrease in the quantity of lettuce demanded. With the price of cabbage unchanged at \$.50 per pound, consumers will substitute cabbage for lettuce. This will cause an increase in the demand for cabbage, which is shown as a shift in the cabbage demand curve from D_1 to D_2.

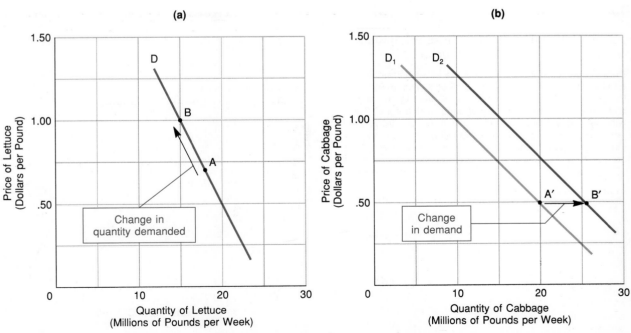

increase in the price of lettuce causes a *movement along* the lettuce demand curve and, at the same time, a *shift* in the cabbage demand curve.

People tend to buy more cabbage when the price of lettuce goes up because they use one in place of the other in their salads. Economists call such pairs of goods **substitutes** because an increase in the price of one causes an increase in the demand for the other—a rightward shift in the demand curve. In effect, when the price of lettuce goes up, the opportunity cost of cabbage—that is, the amount of lettuce consumers must give up in order to buy a given amount of cabbage—falls.

Consumers react differently to price changes when two goods tend to be used together. One example is tires and gasoline. When the price of gasoline goes up, people drive less; thus, they buy fewer tires even if there is no change in their price. An increase in the price of gasoline hence causes a movement along the gasoline demand curve and a simultaneous leftward shift in the tire demand curve. Pairs of goods that are related in this way are known as **complements.** In effect, when the price of gasoline goes up, the opportunity cost of using tires—including the amount that must be spent on gasoline to drive a given distance—rises.

Changes in Consumer Income

Another key factor affecting the demand for a good is consumer income. When their incomes rise, people tend to buy larger quantities of many goods, assuming that their prices do not change.

Exhibit 3.3 shows the effect of a rise in consumer income on the demand for chicken. Demand curve D_1 is the same as that shown in Exhibit 3.1. According to this curve, the quantity demanded at a price of $.40 per pound is 2 billion pounds and the quantity demanded at $.20 per pound is 2.5 billion pounds.

Substitutes
A pair of goods for which an increase in the price of one causes an increase in demand for the other.

Complements
A pair of goods for which an increase in the price of one results in a decrease in demand for the other.

Exhibit 3.3   Effect of an Increase in Consumer Income on the Demand for Chicken

Demand curve D_1 in this graph is the same as that shown in Exhibit 3.1. It assumes a given level of consumer income. If their incomes increase, consumers will want to buy more chicken at any given price, other things being equal. This will shift the demand curve to the right to, say, D_2. At $.40 per pound, the quantity demanded will be 3 billion pounds (B) rather than 2 billion (A); at $.20 per pound, the quantity demanded will be 3.5 billion pounds (D) instead of 2.5 billion (C); and so on.

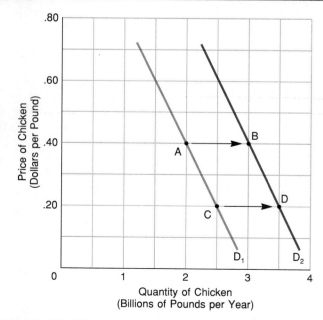

Consumer income was one of the items covered by the "other-things-being-equal" condition when this demand curve was drawn.

Suppose, however, that consumer incomes rise. With higher incomes, people will want to eat more protein than before, including chicken, at any given price. Suppose that consumers are now willing to buy 3 billion pounds of chicken instead of 2 billion at a price of $.40 per pound. This change is shown as a move from point A to point B in Exhibit 3.3. Given the new, higher income, even more chicken would be bought if the price were $.20. Instead of 2.5 billion pounds, as shown by D_1, buyers now might plan to purchase 3.5 billion pounds. This corresponds to a move from point C to point D.

In both cases, the effects of a change in consumer income at a given price are shown by a movement off the original demand curve, D_1. Points B and D are on a new demand curve, D_2. Thus, the increase in income has shifted the demand curve for chicken to the right. If the price of chicken later changes while income remains at the new, higher level, the effects will appear as movements along the new demand curve.

In sum, there is a demand curve for every possible income level. Each represents a one-to-one relationship between price and quantity demanded *given* the assumed income level.

In the above example, we assumed that an increase in income would cause an increase in the demand for chicken. Experience shows that this is what normally happens. Economists therefore call chicken a **normal good,** meaning that when consumers' incomes rise, other things being equal, people will buy more of it.

There are some goods, however, of which people will buy less if their incomes rise, other things being equal. For example, your classmates with higher incomes are likely to go out for pizza more often than those with lower incomes; this implies that the demand for dorm food falls as income rises. Similarly, people who do their cooking at home tend to buy less flour when their incomes rise and buy more baked goods instead. People tend to buy fewer shoe repair services when their incomes rise; instead, they buy new shoes. Also, they tend to ride intercity buses less often, since they would rather fly or drive. Goods such as dorm food, flour, shoe repair services, and intercity bus travel are called **inferior goods.** When consumers' incomes rise, the demand curve for an inferior good shifts to the left instead of to the right.

Changes in Expectations

Changes in buyers' expectations are a third factor that can shift demand curves. If people expect the price of a good to rise relative to the prices of other goods or expect the opportunity cost of acquiring the good to increase in some other way, they will step up their rate of purchase before the change takes place.

In a classic case of this type, consumers rushed to buy cars in December 1986 before a new tax law went into effect. After January 1987, car buyers expected to be unable to deduct the sales tax on a new car from their federal income taxes. Depending on the state and the car's price, the change in tax treatment could easily have equaled a price increase of $200 to $300. After running well above normal in December, new-car sales fell in January. Because more cars were sold in December than would have been sold at the same price had consumers not expected the tax law to change, buyers' behavior in December could be properly interpreted as a temporary rightward shift in the demand curve for cars.

Normal good
A good for which an increase in consumer income results in an increase in demand.

Inferior good
A good for which an increase in consumer income results in a decrease in demand.

Changes in Tastes

Changes in tastes are a fourth source of changes in demand. Sometimes these happen rapidly, as is the case in such areas as popular music, clothing styles, and fast foods. The demand curves for these goods and services shift often. In other cases, changes in tastes take longer to occur but are more permanent. For example, in recent years consumers have been more health conscious than in the past; as a result, they have reduced their demand for high-cholesterol foods such as beef, eggs, and whole milk. Such changes can disrupt whole industries, as "Economics in the News 3.1" indicates.

Supply

We now turn from the demand side of the market to the supply side. As in the case of demand, we can construct a one-to-one relationship between the price of a good and the quantity of it that sellers intend to offer for sale. Exhibit 3.4 shows such a relationship for the chicken market.

Supply curve
A graphic representation of the relationship between the price of a good and the quantity of it supplied.

The upward-sloping curve in Exhibit 3.4 is called a **supply curve** for chicken. Like demand curves, supply curves are based on an "other-things-being-equal" condition. The supply curve for chicken shows how producers

---

ECONOMICS IN THE NEWS 3.1

Consumer Switch to Chicken Brings Change to Beef Industry

GREELEY, COLORADO. Rhonda Miller is building a better steak.

Donning rubber boots, a white coat and a hard hat in Monfort of Colorado Inc.'s chilly packing plant, she mixes up a secret recipe of shredded beef and seaweed extract and pushes it through a stainless steel extruder to make logs of meat.

After the meat binds together in a cooler, she slices it into perfectly shaped, lean strip steaks and seals them in individual packages. "My husband loves these because they're so convenient," says Miller, the company's research director.

The new, tender steak is a radical departure from the unpopular, fatty chuck roasts that roll down conveyor belts

at Monfort's plants. Cattlemen are praying that the refabricated steak and other new, easy-to-fix Monfort products will halt the decline in the cattle business.

But beef has lost its central place on the American dinner plate, forcing a wrenching shrinkage in the nation's cattle herds to a 23-year low. Consumers, who have eaten more chicken each year for two decades, are clearly indicating that many of them have begun to prefer it to beef. One reason is the way the chicken industry has quickly capitalized on chicken's more healthful image, which it acquired when many medical researchers began warning that consumption of too much red meat could contribute to heart disease, strokes, and possibly cancer.

Desperately seeking to avoid being trampled further, some beef packers are struggling to go beyond their traditional cost-cutting to create new products to win back consumers. At stake is the economic survival of packers, Midwestern farm feedlots and hundreds of small communities dependent on livestock sales. Cowboys are being forced off the range, and millions of acres of Western grasslands are lying idle.

Exhibit 3.4   A Supply Curve for Chicken

Parts a and b of this exhibit show the quantity of chicken supplied at various prices. As the price rises, the quantity supplied increases, other things being equal. The higher price gives farmers an incentive to raise more chickens, but the rising opportunity cost of doing so limits the supply produced in response to any given price increase.

(a)

Price of Chicken (Dollars per Pound)		Quantity of Chicken Supplied (Billions of Pounds per Year)
	.64	2.6
	.60	2.5
	.56	2.4
	.52	2.3
	.48	2.2
	.44	2.1
A	.40	2.0
	.36	1.9
	.32	1.8
	.28	1.7
	.24	1.6
B	.20	1.5
	.16	1.4

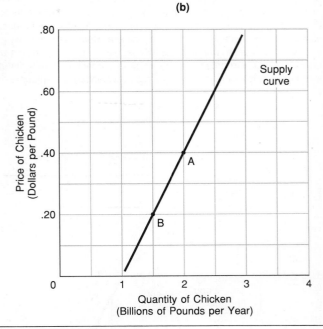

(b)

change their plans in response to a change in the price of chicken assuming that there are no changes in the prices of other goods, in production techniques, in input prices, or in any other relevant factors.

Movements along the Supply Curve

Why does the supply curve have a positive slope? Why do sellers, other things being equal, plan to supply more chicken when the price that prevails in the market is higher than they will be when the prevailing market price is lower? Microeconomics courses give a detailed discussion of what lies behind the supply curve, but a preliminary answer, based on the concept of opportunity cost, can be given here.

Part a of Exhibit 3.5 shows a production possibility frontier for chicken in an imaginary rural county. Here the most attractive alternative to raising chickens is growing tomatoes. The production possibility frontier, like those we have seen earlier, is a curve that becomes steeper as the quantity of chicken produced increases. This happens because not all farms or farmers are alike. Some, because of the nature of their land or skills, have a comparative advantage in raising chickens. As we saw in Chapter 2, this means that they can raise chickens at a relatively low opportunity cost, measured in terms of the quantity of tomatoes they would otherwise be able to grow. Other farmers have a comparative advantage in growing tomatoes. For them the opportunity cost of raising chickens is comparatively high.

Exhibit 3.5   Opportunity Cost and
the Supply of Chicken

Part a of this exhibit shows a production possibility frontier for chicken and tomatoes in a hypothetical rural county. The slope of the frontier at any point shows the opportunity cost of producing an additional pound of chicken measured in terms of the quantity of tomatoes that could have been produced using the same factors of production. The frontier curves because some operators have a comparative advantage in producing tomatoes and others a comparative advantage in producing chicken. Because the curve gets steeper as more chicken is produced, the opportunity cost rises, as shown in part b. The supply curve slopes upward because in order to shift factors of production from tomatoes to chicken, an incentive—in the form of a higher price—is needed to overcome the rising opportunity cost of chicken.

(a)

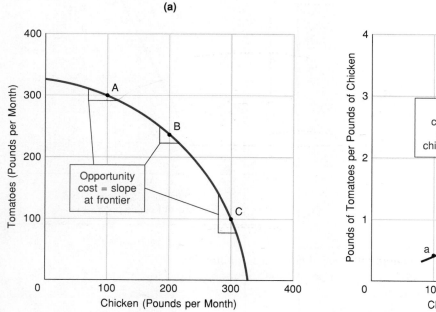

(b)

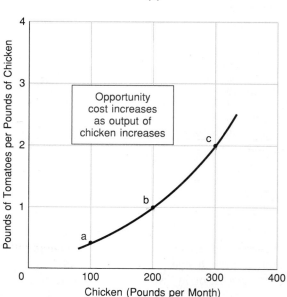

When chicken farming is introduced in the county, those operators with a comparative advantage in raising chickens are the first to enter the market. At point A on the frontier, for example, the opportunity cost of an additional pound of chicken, shown by the slope of the frontier, is about a half-pound of tomatoes. As chicken output rises, farmers further along the frontier are drawn into the market. At point B, the opportunity cost has risen to one pound of tomatoes per pound of chicken. To increase output still more, even those who are comparatively best at growing tomatoes will have to switch to chickens. Thus, at point C the opportunity cost of chickens has risen to two pounds of tomatoes.

Part b of Exhibit 3.5 graphs the opportunity cost of producing an additional pound of chicken beyond the quantity already being produced. The height of each point (a, b, and c) on the opportunity cost curve of part b corresponds to the slope of the frontier (at points A, B, and C) in part a. Now we can see why the supply curve has a positive slope: The price of chicken must rise (in this case, relative to the price of tomatoes) in order to provide the incentive needed to draw in factors of production whose comparative advantages lie less and less strongly in the direction of chicken raising.

Shifts in the Supply Curve

As in the case of demand, the effects of a change in the price of chicken, other things being equal, can be shown as a movement along the supply curve for chicken. This is called a **change in quantity supplied.** A change in some factor other than the price of chicken can be shown as a shift in the supply curve. This is referred to as a **change in supply.** Four sources of change in supply are worth noting. Each is related to the notion that the supply curve reflects the opportunity cost of producing the good or service in question.

Technological Change

A supply curve is drawn on the basis of a particular production technique. From time to time, changes in technology reduce opportunity costs of production. Producers will then plan to sell more of the good than before at any given price. Exhibit 3.6 shows how such an event would affect the chicken supply curve. Supply curve S_1 is the same as the one shown in Exhibit 3.4. According to S_1, farmers will plan to supply 2 billion pounds per year at a price of $.40 per pound (point A).

Now suppose that new factory-farming techniques reduced the quantity of labor used in raising chickens. In terms of Exhibit 3.5, the technological change would stretch the production possibility frontier to the right; its intercept with the horizontal axis would move to the right but its vertical intercept would not change. The opportunity cost, which is indicated by the slope of the curve, would be lower for each given quantity of chicken. Using the new techniques, farmers would be willing to supply more chicken than before at any given price. They might, for example, be willing to supply 2.6 billion pounds of chicken at $.40 per pound (point B). The move from A to B would be part of a shift in the entire supply curve from S_1 to S_2. Once the new techniques were established, an increase or decrease in the price of chicken, other things being equal, would result in a movement along the new supply curve.

Change in quantity supplied
A change in the quantity of a good that producers are willing and able to sell that results from a change in the good's price, other things being equal; a movement along a supply curve.

Change in supply
A change in the quantity of a good that producers are willing and able to sell that results from a change in some condition other than the good's price; a shift in the supply curve.

Exhibit 3.6   Shifts in the Supply Curve for Chicken

Several kinds of changes can cause the supply of chicken to increase or decrease. For example, a new production method that lowers costs will shift the curve to the right from S_1 to S_2. An increase in the price of inputs, other things being equal, will shift the curve to the left from S_1 to S_3. Changes in sellers' expectations or in the prices of competing goods can also cause the supply curve to shift.

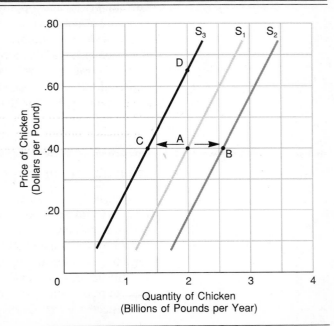

Changes in Input Prices

Changes in input prices are a second item that can cause supply curves to shift. An increase in input prices, other things being equal, raises the opportunity cost of producing the good in question and, hence, tends to reduce the quantity of it that producers plan to supply at a given price. Refer again to Exhibit 3.6. Suppose that starting from point A on supply curve S_1, the price of chicken feed increases and no other, offsetting changes occur. Now, instead of supplying 2 billion pounds of chicken at $.40 per pound, farmers will supply, say, just 1.4 billion pounds at that price (point C). The move from A to C is part of a leftward shift in the supply curve, from S_1 to S_3.

If the price of feed remains at the new level, changes in the price of chicken will cause movements along the new supply curve. For example, farmers could be induced to supply the original quantity of chicken—2 billion bushels—if the price rose enough to cover the increased cost of feed. As you can see in Exhibit 3.6, that would require the price to rise to $.64 per pound (point D).

Changes in Prices of Other Goods

Changes in the prices of other products can also produce a shift in the chicken supply curve. Suppose that the price of tomatoes rises while the price of chicken stays at $.40. If this happens, the opportunity cost of raising chickens, in terms of forgone tomato profits, increases even though there is no change in the opportunity cost measured in physical quantities. The change in the price of tomatoes thus gives farmers—even some who have only a weak comparative advantage in tomatoes—an incentive to shift from chickens to tomatoes. The effect of an increase in the price of tomatoes can thus be shown as a leftward shift in the chicken supply curve.

Changes in Expectations

Changes in expectations can cause supply curves to shift in much the same way that they cause demand curves to shift. Again we can use farming as an example. At planting time, a farmer's selection of crops is influenced not so much by current prices and opportunity costs as by the prices and opportunity costs expected at harvest time. Long-term expectations also affect supply. Each crop requires special equipment and know-how. We have just seen that an increase in the price of tomatoes gives farmers an incentive to shift from chicken to tomatoes. The incentive will be stronger if the increase in the price of tomatoes is expected to be long-lasting. If it is, farmers are more likely to buy the special equipment needed for that crop.

Interaction of Supply and Demand

As we have seen, markets transmit information, in the form of prices, to people who buy and sell goods and services. Taking these prices into account, along with other knowledge they may have, buyers and sellers make their plans. As shown by the demand and supply curves, buyers and sellers plan to buy or sell certain quantities at any given price.

In each market, many buyers and sellers make different plans. When they meet to trade, some of them may be unable to carry out their plans according to the expected terms. Perhaps the total quantity that buyers plan to purchase is greater than the total quantity suppliers are willing to sell at the given price. In that case, some would-be buyers must change their plans. Or perhaps planned sales exceed planned purchases at the given price. In that case, some would-be sellers will be unable to carry out their plans.

Sometimes no one is surprised: The total quantity buyers plan to purchase exactly matches the total quantity producers plan to sell. When buyers' and sellers' plans mesh when they meet in the marketplace, no one needs to change plans. Under these conditions, the market is said to be in **equilibrium.**

Market Equilibrium

Supply and demand curves, which reflect buyers' and sellers' plans, can be used to give a graphical demonstration of market equilibrium. Exhibit 3.7 uses the same supply and demand curves as before, but this time both are drawn on the same diagram. If the quantity of planned sales at each price is compared with the quantity of planned purchases at that price (either the table or the graph can be used to make the comparison), it can be seen that there is only one price at which the two sets of plans mesh. This price—$.40 per pound—is the equilibrium price. If all buyers and sellers make their plans with the expectation of a price of $.40, no one will be surprised and no plans will have to be changed.

Shortages

But what will happen if, for some reason, buyers and sellers see a price of chicken other than $.40 a pound and make their plans accordingly? Suppose, for example, that they base their plans on a price of $.20. Exhibit 3.7 shows that at a price of $.20, buyers will plan to purchase chicken at a rate of 2.5 billion pounds per year but farmers will plan to supply only 1.5 billion pounds. When the quantity demanded exceeds the quantity supplied, as in this example, the difference is an **excess quantity demanded** or, more simply, a **shortage.** In Exhibit 3.7, the shortage is 1 billion pounds of chicken per year when the price is $.20 per pound.

Shortages and Inventories
In most markets, the first sign of a shortage is a drop in **inventories,** that is, in the stocks of the good that have been produced and are waiting to be sold or used. Sellers plan to hold a certain quantity of goods in inventory to allow for minor changes in demand. When they see inventories dropping below the planned level, they change their plans. Some may try to rebuild their inventories by increasing their output, if they produce the good themselves, or by ordering more from the producer. Some sellers may take advantage of the strong demand for their product to raise its price. Many sellers will do a little of both. If sellers do not take the initiative, buyers will—they will offer to pay more if sellers will supply more. Whatever the details, the result will be an upward movement along the supply curve as price and quantity increase.

As the shortage puts upward pressure on price, buyers will change their plans too. Moving up and to the left along their demand curve, they will cut back on their planned purchases. As both buyers and sellers change their plans, the market moves toward equilibrium. When the price reaches $.40 per pound, both the shortage and the pressure to change plans will disappear.

Equilibrium
A condition in which buyers' and sellers' plans exactly mesh in the marketplace so that the quantity supplied exactly equals the quantity demanded at a given price.

Excess quantity demanded (shortage)
A condition in which the quantity of a good demanded at a given price exceeds the quantity supplied.

Inventory
Stocks of a finished good awaiting sale or use.

Exhibit 3.7   Equilibrium in the Chicken Market

Parts a and b of this exhibit show the same supply and demand curves for chicken presented earlier. The demand curve shows how much buyers plan to purchase at a given price. The supply curve shows how much producers plan to sell at a given price. At only one price—$.40 per pound—do buyers' and sellers' plans exactly match: the equilibrium price. A higher price causes a surplus of chicken and puts downward pressure on price. A lower price causes a shortage and puts upward pressure on price.

(a)

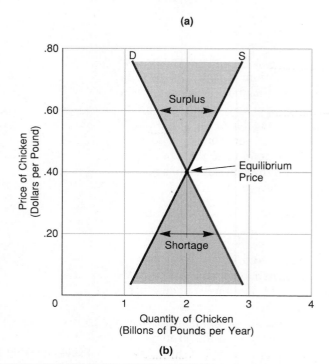

Quantity of Chicken
(Billons of Pounds per Year)

(b)

Price per Pound (1)	Quantity Supplied (Billions of Pounds) (2)	Quantity Demanded (Billions of Pounds) (3)	Shortage (Billions of Pounds) (4)	Surplus (Billions of Pounds) (5)	Direction of Pressure on Price (6)
.64	2.6	1.4	—	1.2	Downward
.60	2.5	1.5	—	1.0	Downward
.56	2.4	1.6	—	0.8	Downward
.52	2.3	1.7	—	0.6	Downward
.48	2.2	1.8	—	0.4	Downward
.44	2.1	1.9	—	0.2	Downward
.40	2.0	2.0	—	—	Equilibrium
.36	1.9	2.1	0.2	—	Upward
.32	1.8	2.2	0.4	—	Upward
.28	1.7	2.3	0.6	—	Upward
.24	1.6	2.4	0.8	—	Upward
.20	1.5	2.5	1.0	—	Upward
.16	1.4	2.6	1.2	—	Upward

Shortages and Queues

In the markets for most goods, sellers have inventories of goods ready to be sold. There are exceptions, however. Inventories are not possible in markets for services—haircuts, tax preparation, lawn care, and the like. Also, some goods, such as custom-built houses and machine tools tailored to a specialized need, are not held in inventories. Sellers in these markets do not begin production until they have a contract with a buyer.

In markets in which there are no inventories, the sign of a shortage is a "queue" of buyers. The queue may take the form of a line of people waiting to be served or a list of names in an order book. The queue is a sign that buyers would like to purchase the good at a faster rate than producers have planned to supply it. However, some plans cannot be carried out—at least not right away. Buyers are served on a first-come, first-served basis.

The formation of a queue of buyers has much the same effect on the market as a fall in inventories. Sellers react by increasing their rate of output, raising their prices, or both. Buyers react to the rising price by reducing the quantity they plan to purchase. The result is a movement up and to the right along the supply curve and, at the same time, up and to the left along the demand curve until equilibrium is reached.

Surpluses

Now suppose that for some reason buyers and sellers see a price of chicken that is higher than the equilibrium price—say, $.60 per pound—and base their plans accordingly. Exhibit 3.7 shows that farmers will plan to supply 2.5 billion pounds of chicken per year at $.60, but their customers will plan to buy only 1.5 billion pounds. When the quantity supplied exceeds the quantity demanded, there is an **excess quantity supplied,** or a **surplus.** As Exhibit 3.7 shows, the surplus of chicken at a price of $.60 per pound is 1 billion pounds per year.

Excess quantity supplied (surplus)
A condition in which the quantity of a good supplied at a given price exceeds the quantity demanded.

Surpluses and Inventories

When there is a surplus of a product, sellers will be unable to sell all they had hoped at the planned price. As a result, their inventories will begin to grow beyond the level they had planned to hold in preparation for normal changes in demand. Sellers will react to the inventory buildup by changing their plans. Some will cut back their output. Others will cut their prices in order to reduce their extra stock. Still others will do a little of both. The result of these changes in plans will be a movement down and to the left along the supply curve.

As unplanned inventory buildup puts downward pressure on the price, buyers change their plans too. Finding that chicken costs less than they had expected, they buy more of it. This is shown as a movement down and to the right along the demand curve. As this happens, the market will be restored to equilibrium.

Surpluses and Queues

In markets in which there are no inventories, surpluses lead to the formation of queues of sellers looking for customers. Taxi queues at airports are a case in point. At least at some times of the day, the fare for taxi service from the airport to downtown is more than enough to attract a number of taxis equal to the demand. In some cities, drivers who are far back in the queue try to attract riders with offers of cut-rate fares. More often, though, there are rules against fare cutting. The queue then grows until a surge of business shortens it again.

Changes in Market Conditions

On a graph, equilibrium looks like an easy target. In real life, however, it is a moving target. Market conditions—all the items that lie behind the other-things-being-equal contingency—change frequently. When they do, both buyers and sellers must revise their plans as the point of equilibrium shifts.

Response to a Shift in Demand

Let's first consider a market's response to a shift in demand. The decline in demand for beef described in "Economics in the News 3.1" (page 58) provides a good example. Exhibit 3.8 interprets this case in terms of the supply and demand model. As the figure is drawn, the market initially is in equilibrium at E_1. There the price is $.50 per pound (quoted on a live-weight basis as at stockyard auctions) and the quantity produced is 25 billion pounds per year. Now the changed dietary habits of U.S. consumers cause the demand curve to shift to the left from D_1 to D_2. This is a *shift* in the demand curve, because it is caused by a change in tastes—one of the things covered by the other-things-being-equal assumption that lies behind the curve. What will happen next?

If the price does not change—that is, if it remains at $.50 per pound—there will be a surplus of beef. The supply curve indicates that at that price, ranchers will plan to produce 25 billion pounds per year. However, according to the new demand curve, D_2, consumers will no longer buy that much beef at $.50 per pound. Instead, given their new tastes, they will buy only 15 billion pounds at that price.

However, the price does *not* stay at $.50. As soon as the demand curve begins to shift and the surplus starts to develop, beef inventories rise above their planned levels, putting downward pressure on the price. As the price falls, ranchers revise their plans. They move down and to the left along their supply curve, reducing the quantity supplied as the price drops. This is a *movement*

Exhibit 3.8   Effects of a Decrease in Demand for Beef

This exhibit shows the effects of a decrease in demand for beef caused by a shift in tastes away from high-cholesterol foods. Initially the market is in equilibrium at E_1. The change in tastes causes a shift in the demand curve. At the original equilibrium price of $.50 per pound, there is a temporary surplus of beef. This causes inventories to start to rise and puts downward pressure on the price. As the price falls, producers move down along their supply curve, as shown by the arrow, to a new equilibrium at E_2. There both the price and quantity of beef are lower than before the shift in demand.

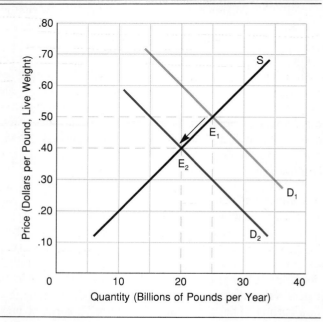

along the supply curve, not a shift, because the ranchers are responding to a change in the price of beef. Nothing has happened, as far as we know, to change the other-things-being-equal conditions, such as technology, input prices, and so on. Thus, nothing has happened to cause the supply curve to shift.

As ranchers move down along their supply curve in the direction shown by the arrow in Exhibit 3.8, they eventually reach point E_2, where their plans again mesh with those of consumers. At this point, the price has fallen to $.40 per pound and production to 20 million pounds. Although health-conscious consumers would not have bought that much beef at the old price, they will do so at the new, lower price. E_2 is thus the new equilibrium.

Entrepreneurship and Equilibrium

If producers reacted passively to changes in market conditions, this would be the end of the story. As "Economics in the News 3.1" relates, however, cattle producers are not passive folks. They are not happy with the change in market conditions, so they fight back. Rhonda Miller, for example, fought back by trying to invent a better steak that would be both lean and tender. Other examples of new beef products are precooked London broil, premixed meatloaf, and pastrami packed in individual foil pouches. These are *entrepreneurial* responses to the decline in demand for beef. By developing new products and creating new opportunities, beef industry entrepreneurs hope to change consumer tastes back in favor of beef. If successful, they will push the demand curve back to the right. As demand rises, the price will rise and producers will be able to move back up along their supply curve.

The constant activity of entrepreneurs keeps economics from being a ho-hum exercise in curve pushing. Supply and demand analysis gives us a way to describe what entrepreneurs are trying to do. In this case, they are attempting to stimulate demand by developing new beef products. In another case, they might be trying to push costs down, thus shifting the supply curve. Supply and demand analysis also gives us a way to make conditional predictions of markets' reactions to changes brought about by entrepreneurs in the same way that it allows us to predict changes effected by forces beyond their control. In this case, the reaction to a shift of the demand curve back to the right would be more beef produced and a higher price. But supply and demand analysis cannot predict exactly what entrepreneurs will try next or whether they will succeed. The only thing we can be certain about in a market economy is that the future will bring surprises—new ways of doing things that no one has ever thought of before.

Applications of Supply and Demand

In the study of economics—both macro and micro—we will encounter a great many applications of supply and demand. While each situation is unique, each to some extent draws on ideas developed in this chapter. This section gives only an inkling of the possible range of applications.

Changing Market Conditions: The Case of Dentists

The examples given so far in this chapter concern markets for goods, but the same tools apply to markets for services. In this case, we look at the market for dental services. As "Economics in the News 3.2" tells us, this market has under-

ECONOMICS IN THE NEWS   3.2

What's Good for America Isn't Necessarily Good for the Dentists

When Dr. Murray Helfman set up his practice 25 years ago, fortune seemed to smile on him. Dentistry, which began as a sideline for barbers, had become a respected profession. Rich-dentist jokes were the rage. By the early 1970s dentists' incomes were finally approaching those of physicians.

But after a quarter-century in practice, Helfman, who lives in Rochester, New York, is hardly a rich man. He doesn't drive a Mercedes and owns no country home. If his wife didn't help out by managing his office, he would have trouble making ends meet. He moans: "I have three kids in college and a house that I couldn't afford to live in if I hadn't bought it 13 years ago."

The American Dental Association claims the average dentist nets $59,530 a year, but that average covers a lot of grief. Adjusted for inflation, this figure has been shrinking since it peaked some dozen years ago. Dentists' real net incomes are no higher now, on average, than they were in the early 1960s.

The problems are particularly intense among younger practitioners. Older dentists went into business when demand was rising and entry costs were relatively low, but consider the obstacles that confront a dentist starting out in the world. Four years in a decent dental school can easily cost $50,000. And unless Daddy is affluent, that's all debt.

Then try to set up a practice. The expenses are astronomical. Operating room equipment will run about $24,000; office supplies and reception area, $10,000; a modern X-ray machine, $5,000. Add the incidentals, and today, an average office costs something like $60,000.

In all this, the federal bureaucracy has, as usual, done the wrong things. In the late 1960s federal officials decided Americans were getting inadequate dental care, and the government began spending to encourage dental education. Old dental schools expanded, while new ones opened. The result was too many dentists.

On top of this, there are fewer patients coming through the door. Are Americans neglecting their teeth? Hardly. The basic difficulty is simple. Cavity-filling has always been the bread-and-butter business for most dentists. But cavities are going the way of smallpox and polio in the United States. Tooth decay has declined by about 50 percent since the mid-1960s. According to the ADA, one out of three people of college age has never had a cavity. Army dentists, who see a cross section of society, used to tell horror stories about mouths full of rotten teeth. Now they see lots of cavity-free mouths. The reason for this? Better nutrition, for one thing. And fluoridation of drinking water is an even bigger factor.

For many dentists, then, the dream of affluence is fading. Instead of a BMW, a Toyota. Instead of striving for wealth, many young dentists now settle for the security of salaried dentistry. Says Dr. Thomas Ciuchta, a 20-year-old Temple University School of Dentistry graduate: "I see friends who have their own practices sitting idle two days a week with their expenses building up. I like the security of knowing exactly what I'm making."

Ciuchta gets his regular paycheck from a clinic called Dentalworks located in the Hess's department store in Allentown, Pennsylvania. At such facilities, which are often franchises owned by nondentists, 40-hour weeks, including Saturdays, are the rule and starting salaries are often under $30,000.

Source: Richard Greene, "What's Good for America Isn't Necessarily Good for the Dentists," *Forbes*, August 13, 1984, 79–84.

---

gone major changes in recent years. Let's see how this story looks when told in terms of the supply and demand model.

A Shift in Supply

According to the news item in "Economics in the News 3.2," the late 1960s saw government encouragement of dental school expansion. The effect can be represented as a rightward shift of the supply curve for dentists as shown in part a of Exhibit 3.9. The supply curve shifts because students were willing to fill the new vacancies in dental schools and thus add to the supply of dental services *given* dentists' prevailing earnings—$40,000 per year in 1967 dollars, as the figure is

Exhibit 3.9   Changing Conditions in the
Market for Dental Services

This exhibit shows the impact on the market for dental services of two changes in market
conditions. Part a shows the effect of government efforts to increase the number of students
going to dental school. This action shifts the supply curve to the right and, by itself, would
move the market from E_1 to E_2. At the same time this government policy is increasing the
supply of dentists, however, improvements in dental health are reducing the demand for
their services. The effect of the improvement in dental health is shown as a shift in the
demand curve in part b. Taking the changes in both educational policy and dental health
into account, the market moves to a new equilibrium at E_3, where S_2 and D_2 intersect. Had
the demand shift occurred with no change in policy regarding dental schools, the market
would have moved to E_4, where D_2 intersects S_1.

(a)

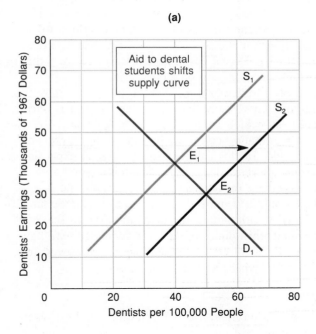

(b)

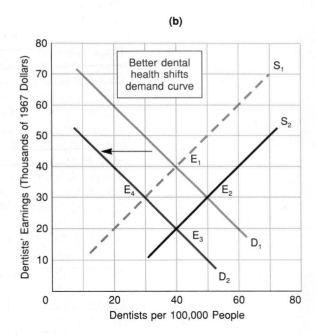

drawn. By itself the expansion of dental schools would have been sufficient to
create a surplus of dentists. The surplus would have put downward pressure on
dentists' earnings. As earnings fell, other things being equal, the market would
have reached a new equilibrium at E_2, where supply curve S_2 intersects demand
curve D_1.

Compare part a of Exhibit 3.9 with Exhibit 3.8. In Exhibit 3.8, which shows
the market for beef, a fall in price is caused by a shift in the demand curve. The

market moves along its supply curve to a point at which both the equilibrium price and quantity are lower. In part a of Exhibit 3.9, the fall in dentists' earnings is caused by a shift in the supply curve. The market moves along demand curve D_1 to point E_2, where the equilibrium price is lower and the equilibrium quantity is greater.

Adding a Shift in Demand

If the world were run for the convenience of economics professors and their students, things would happen one at a time. A market would be hit with either a shift in demand or a shift in supply, thus keeping diagrams tidy. But reality is far less cooperative. In the case of dental services, as "Economics in the News 3.2" makes clear, the expansion of dental schools was only part of the story. In addition, at the same time dental schools were expanding, there was an improvement in dental health that acted on the demand side of the market. Because people were suffering fewer cavities, they tended to make fewer visits to the dentist at any given price. This improvement in dental health can be represented by a leftward shift in the demand curve as shown in part b of Exhibit 3.9. This shift in the demand curve increased the surplus of dentists and added to the downward pressure on price. Together the two changes in market conditions moved the equilibrium point to E_3. Dental earnings fell by more than they would have as a result of dental school expansion alone.

Exhibit 3.9 shows that supply and demand analysis can be applied to complex changes in market conditions where more than one thing happens at once. The key to considering such cases—which are common in the real world—is to break things down into those forces that act on the supply side of the market and those that act on the demand side. In this case, the dental school expansion shifted the supply curve because more students were then willing and able to train to become dentists at any given earnings level. With no change in the incidence of cavities, this alone would have moved the market to E_2. At the same time, the improvement in dental health shifted the demand curve to the left. Had dental schools not expanded, this alone would have depressed earnings, moving the market to E_4, where S_1 intersects D_2. Taken together, however, the two shifts moved the market to E_3, where S_2 and D_2 intersect.

Entrepreneurial Reactions

Before leaving the market for dental services, it is worth noting that here, as in the case of the market for beef, there were entrepreneurial responses to changing market conditions. Dentists did not react passively, simply dropping their prices and continuing the same old style of solo practice. Instead, they tried to attract new customers by such means as setting up dental clinics in shopping centers. These "doc-in-a-box" clinics have attracted many patients who never—or rarely—made the effort to make appointments in traditional dental offices. The innovations in dental services moderated the decline in demand caused by fluoridation, better nutrition, and so on.

Price Supports: The Market for Milk

In our earlier example of the market for beef, a decrease in demand caused a surplus, which in turn caused the price to drop until the surplus was eliminated. Markets are not always left free to respond to prices in this manner, however. A case in point is the market for milk.

Exhibit 3.10 shows the market for milk in terms of supply and demand curves. Suppose that initially the market is in equilibrium at point E_1. The wholesale price of milk is $13 per hundredweight, and production is 110 million hundredweight per year. A trend in taste away from high-cholesterol foods—the same trend that hit the market for beef—then shifts the demand curve for milk to the left. As in the case of beef, the result is a surplus, as shown by the arrow in Exhibit 3.10.

Here, however, the similarity between the beef and milk markets ends. In the beef market prices are free to fall in response to a surplus, but in the milk market they are not. Instead, an elaborate set of government controls and subsidies sets a support price for milk. As the exhibit is drawn, the government agrees to pay $13 per hundredweight for all milk that cannot be sold at that price on the open market. With the demand curve in position D_1, there is no surplus; thus, the government need not buy any milk. But with the demand curve in position D_2, there is a surplus of 40 million hundredweight per year. Under the price support law, the government must buy this surplus and store it in the form of cheese, butter, and other products with long shelf lives. Over the years, the government has accumulated vast stores of such products at a cost of billions of dollars. Dairy farmers have been happy to sell the extra milk, but the cost to consumers and taxpayers has been high.

Without price supports, the shift in demand would cause the price of milk to fall to the new equilibrium price of $10 per hundredweight. But when price supports are applied to a product at a level higher than the equilibrium price, the result is a lasting surplus condition. This happens because the support price sends conflicting messages to consumers and producers. To consumers the $13 price says, "Milk is scarce. Its opportunity cost is high. Hold your consumption down." To producers it says, "All is well. Incentives are unchanged. Feel free to continue using scarce factors to produce milk." A drop in the price to $10 would send a different set of messages. Consumers would hear, "Milk is cheaper and

Exhibit 3.10 Price Supports for Milk

Suppose that initially the market for milk is in equilibrium at E_1. A shift in tastes away from high-cholesterol foods then shifts the demand curve to D_2. If the price were free to fall, there would be a temporary surplus that would push the price down to a new equilibrium at $10 per hundredweight. In practice, the government maintains a system of price supports for milk at a level shown here as $13 per hundredweight. Because the price cannot fall, the surplus is permanent. The government must buy the surplus milk, in the form of butter and cheese, in order to keep the price from falling.

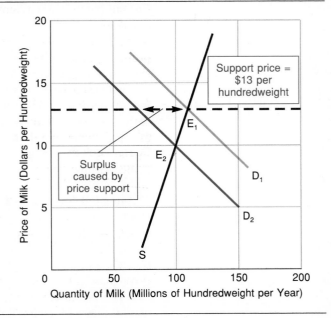

more abundant. Although it is not cholesterol free, you might consider drinking more of it." Producers would hear, "The milk market isn't what it once was. Look at your opportunity costs. Is there perhaps some better use for your labor, capital, and natural resources?"

From time to time, the government has tried to eliminate the milk surplus by shifting the supply curve to the left so that it would intersect the demand curve at the support price. In recent years, for example, dairy farmers have been encouraged to sell their cows for beef, thus reducing the size of their herds. But these programs have failed to eliminate the milk surplus. The chief reason has been dairy farmers' entrepreneurial response to the high price of milk. In particular, the government's efforts to cut herd size have been largely offset by increased output per cow as a result of genetic improvement and better farm management practices. Thus, the government's vast stocks of butter and cheese continue to grow.

Price Ceilings: The Case of Rent Control

In the milk market, the government maintains a support price that is above the equilibrium price. In other markets, a price ceiling that is below the equilibrium price is maintained. An example of this type of market intervention is rent control in housing markets.

Rent control in one form or another exists in several major U.S. cities, including New York, Washington, D.C., San Francisco, and Los Angeles. The controls vary across cities, but the essential common feature—at least for some categories of apartments—is that maximum rents are established by law. In all cases, the purpose is to aid tenants by preventing landlords from charging "unreasonably" high rents. What is unreasonably high is determined by the relative political strengths of landlords and tenants rather than by supply and demand.

Intended Effects

Exhibit 3.11 interprets the effects of rent control in terms of supply and demand. For simplicity, it is assumed that the rental housing stock consists of units of equal size and rental value. Part a of the figure shows the effects of rent control in the short run. Here the short run means a period of time that is too short to permit significant increases or decreases in the stock of rental housing; thus, the short-run supply curve is a vertical line.

Under the conditions shown, the equilibrium rent per standard housing unit is $500 per month on each of the 100,000 units in the city. A rent ceiling of $250 is then imposed. This results in a gain to tenants of $250 per unit per month, or $25 million per month in total, and an equal loss to landlords. This sum is shown by the shaded rectangle. The benefit to tenants at the expense of landlords is the principal intended consequence of rent control.

Unintended Short-Run Effects

Rent control, like many government policies, has unintended as well as intended effects. In the short run, when the stock of apartments is fixed, the unintended consequences stem from the apartment shortage created by the controls. The shortage occurs because the quantity demanded is greater at the lower ceiling price than at the higher equilibrium price.

The increased quantity demanded has several sources. First, people who would otherwise own a house or condominium may now want to rent. Second,

Exhibit 3.11   Effects of Rent Control

Part a shows the short-run effects of rent control. In the short run, the supply of rental apartments is considered to be fixed. The equilibrium rent is $500 per month. A rent ceiling of $250 per month is then put into effect. One possible outcome is that landlords will charge disguised rent increases, raising the true price back to $500 per month. If such disguised increases are prohibited, there will be a shortage of 50,000 units at the ceiling price. Part b shows the long-run effects when there is time to adjust the number of units in response to the price. If the ceiling price is enforced, landlords move down their supply curve to E_2. The shortage then becomes even more severe than in the short run.

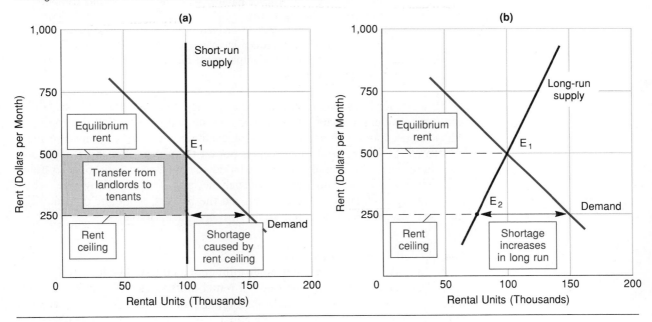

people who would otherwise live in noncontrolled suburbs may now seek rental units in the city. Third, each tenant may want more space, which means a demand for more of the standardized units shown in Exhibit 3.11.

The shortage creates a problem for both landlords and tenants: How will the limited supply of apartments be rationed among those who want them? Both landlords and tenants devise a number of creative—or, as an economist would say, entrepreneurial—responses.

One response on the part of landlords is to seek disguised rent increases. These may take the form of large, nonrefundable "key deposits" or security deposits. Alternatively, they may take the form of selling old, used furniture or drapes at high prices as a condition for renting apartments. Finally, certain maintenance or security services for which landlords might otherwise have paid may be transferred to tenants.

Tenants too may get into the act. When they decide to move, they may sublet their apartments to other tenants rather than give up their leases. Now it is the tenant who collects the key money or sells the old drapes to the subtenant. The original tenant may have moved to a distant city but maintains a bank account and a post office box for use in paying the rent. The subtenant is instructed to play the role of a "guest" if the landlord telephones. The charade may get very elaborate and go on for decades in cities such as New York, where rent control is a long-established tradition.

Rent control advocates view these responses as cheating and often try to outlaw them. If prohibitions are enforced, the landlord will face many applicants for each vacant apartment. In that case, the landlord must decide to whom to give the apartment. In his book *Rent Control: The Perennial Folly*, Charles W. Baird describes the effects in these terms:

> People with unconventional life styles will be told to look elsewhere. Families without children will be favored over families with children. Tenants without pets will be favored over tenants with pets. . . . Families whose heads have histories of steady employment will be favored over families whose heads are just beginning employment or frequently change jobs. Landlords know from experience that people with steady employment histories tend to be more dependable in paying their bills.

If a landlord has two applicants for a vacancy who are alike as far as family and job considerations are concerned, he or she will tend to pick the applicant whose noneconomic characteristics—for example, race or religion—are most appealing. The other applicants will be put on the waiting list and sent to look elsewhere. People who make decisions based solely on economic considerations are often accused of being crass, materialistic, and uncaring. However, when people are forbidden to make decisions on the basis of economic criteria, they may well use other criteria that are even more uncharitable.[1]

Unintended Long-Run Effects

In the long run, rent control has other unintended effects. The long run in this case means enough time for the stock of rental units to grow through construction of new units or shrink through abandonment of old ones or their conversion to condominiums. Other things being equal, the higher the rent, the greater the rate of construction, and the lower the rent, the greater the rate of abandonment and/or conversion. This is reflected in the positively sloped long-run supply curve in part b of Exhibit 3.11.

If rent controls are enforced so that there are no disguised charges, the stock of rental units shrinks and the market moves from E_1 to E_2. At E_2, the unintended effects that appeared in the short run become more pronounced. The number of people subject to housing discrimination increases relative to the short-run case. The number of people potentially subject to discrimination equals the difference between the number of units available and the number sought by renters. Graphically, this is the horizontal gap between the supply and demand curves at the ceiling price. In the short run, there was a shortage of 50,000 units; in the long run, this increases to 75,000 units.

Rent controls are often defended as being beneficial to the poor. But when all of the unintended effects of rent control are taken into account, it seems questionable whether poor families really benefit. In cases where disguised rent increases are possible, the true cost of rental housing is not really decreased. Further, it is hard to believe that landlords' tendency to discriminate against minority group members, single-parent families, and tenants with irregular

---

[1] Charles W. Baird, *Rent Control: The Perennial Folly* (Washington, D.C.: The Cato Institute, 1980), 60–61.

work histories will benefit the poor. The most likely beneficiaries of rent control are stable, middle-class families who work at the same jobs and live in the same apartments for long periods.

Looking Ahead

As the great economist Alfred Marshall once put it, nearly all of the major economics problems have a "kernel" that reflects the workings of supply and demand (see "Who Said It? Who Did It? 3.1"). This chapter covered the basics of the supply and demand model and illustrated it with some applications. Many more applications will be found in both the macro- and microeconomics courses. In macroeconomics, the supply and demand model is applied to financial markets, labor markets, and the problem of determining the rates of inflation and real output for the economy as a whole. In microeconomics, the model is applied to product markets, factor markets, and policy issues ranging from pollution to farm policy to international trade.

A detailed look at the underpinnings of the model in the microeconomics course will show that the model fits some kinds of markets more closely than

---

WHO SAID IT? WHO DID IT? 3.1

Alfred Marshall on Supply and Demand

Alfred Marshall, considered by many the greatest economist of his day, was born in London in 1842. His father was a Bank of England cashier who hoped the boy would enter the ministry. Young Marshall had other ideas, however. He turned down a theological scholarship at Oxford to study mathematics. He received an M.A. in mathematics from Cambridge in 1865.

While at Cambridge, he joined a philosophical discussion group. There he became interested in promoting the broad development of the human mind. He was soon told, however, that the harsh realities of economics would prevent his ideas from being carried out. Britain's productive resources, it was said, could never allow the masses sufficient leisure for education. This disillusioning episode appears to have triggered Marshall's fascination with economics.

Photo Source: The Granger Collection, New York.

At the time, British economics was dominated by the classical school founded by Smith and Ricardo. Marshall had great respect for the classical writers. Initially he saw his own work as a simple application of his mathematical training to strengthen and systematize the classical system. Before long, however, he was breaking new ground and developing a system of his own. By 1890, when he brought out his famous *Principles of Economics*, he had laid the foundation of what we now call the *neoclassical* school.

In an attempt to explain the essence of his approach, Marshall included this passage in the second edition of *Principles:*

> In spite of a great variety in detail, nearly all the chief problems of economics agree in that they have a kernel of the same kind. This kernel is an inquiry as to the balancing of two opposed classes of motives, the one consisting of desires to acquire certain new goods, and thus satisfy wants; while the other consists of desires to avoid certain efforts or retain certain immediate enjoyment . . . in other words, it is an inquiry into the balancing of the forces of demand and supply.

Marshall's influence on economics—at least in the English-speaking world—was enormous. His *Principles* was the leading text for decades, and today's student can still learn much from reading it. As a professor at Cambridge, Marshall taught a great many of the next generation's leading economists. Today his neoclassical school continues to dominate the profession. It has received many challenges but so far has weathered them all.

others. The fit is best for markets in which there are many producers and many customers, the goods sold by one producer are much like those sold by others, and all sellers and buyers have good information on market conditions. Markets for farm commodities, such as wheat and corn, and financial markets, such as the New York Stock Exchange, are examples that meet these standards. However, even in markets that do not display all of these features, the fit is often close enough to enable the supply and demand model to provide useful insights into what is going on. Thus, the supply and demand model serves a precise analytical function in some cases (for example, the supply of and demand for wheat) and a broader, metaphorical function in others (such as the supply of and demand for clean air). It is this flexibility that makes the model one of the most useful items in the economist's tool kit.

Summary

1. **How does the price of a good or service affect the quantity of it that buyers demand?** According to the *law of demand*, in any market, other things being equal, the quantity of a good that buyers demand tends to rise as the price falls and to fall as the price rises. For any given market, the law of demand sets up a one-to-one relationship between price and quantity demanded. This relationship can be shown by a downward-sloping *demand curve*.

2. **How do other market conditions affect demand?** A change in any of the items covered by the other-things-being-equal clause of the law of demand causes a shift in the demand curve, known as a *change in demand*. Examples include changes in the prices of goods that are *substitutes* or *complements* of the given good; changes in consumer incomes; changes in expectations; and changes in tastes.

3. **How are the quantities of goods and services supplied by producers affected by prices and other market conditions?** In most markets, an increase in the price of a good will increase the quantity that producers are willing to supply. This relationship can be shown as an upward-sloping *supply curve*. The higher price gives producers an incentive to supply more, but rising opportunity costs set a limit on the amount they will supply at any given price. A change in any of the items covered by the other-things-being-equal assumption underlying the supply curve will shift the curve. Examples include changes in technology, in input prices, in the prices of other goods that could be produced with the same factors of production, and in expectations.

4. **How do supply and demand interact to determine the market price of a good or service?** In a market with an upward-sloping supply curve and a downward-sloping demand curve, there is only one price at which the quantity that producers plan to supply will exactly match the quantity that buyers plan to purchase. This is known as the *equilibrium price*. At any higher price there will be a *surplus* and at any lower price a *shortage*.

5. **Why do market prices and quantities change in response to changes in a variety of market conditions?** A change in any market condition that shifts the supply or demand curve will change the equilibrium price and quantity in that market. For example, the demand curve may shift to the right as the result of a change in consumers' incomes. This causes a shortage at the old price, and the price begins to rise. As the price rises, suppliers move up along the supply curve to a new equilibrium. Alternatively, better technology may shift the supply curve to the right. In that case, there is a surplus at the old price and the price starts to fall. As it does, buyers will move down along their demand curve to a new equilibrium.

6. **How do price supports and price ceilings affect the operation of markets?** A price support prevents the market price from falling when the demand curve shifts to the left or the supply curve shifts to the right. The result is a permanent surplus. The government may have to buy and store the surplus to maintain the price, as in the case of milk. A price ceiling prevents the price from rising to its equilibrium level. The result is a permanent shortage. The total quantity supplied will be less than buyers would like to purchase at the ceiling price or even at the equilibrium price.

Terms for Review

- law of demand
- demand curve
- change in quantity demanded
- change in demand
- substitutes
- complements
- normal good
- inferior good
- supply curve
- change in quantity supplied
- change in supply
- equilibrium
- excess quantity demanded (shortage)
- inventory
- excess quantity supplied (surplus)

Questions for Review

1. How does the concept of demand differ from the concepts of want and need?

2. What conditions are covered by the "other-things-being-equal" clause in the law of demand? What effect does a change in any of these conditions have on buyers' plans?

3. Using an example from agriculture or industry, explain why we normally expect the supply curve for a good to slope upward. Give examples, other than those used in the text, of events that can cause a supply curve to shift.

4. How do inventories put upward or downward pressure on prices when markets are not in equilibrium? How is equilibrium restored in markets in which there are no inventories of finished goods?

5. Describe each of the following in terms of shifts in or movements along supply and demand curves: (a) a market's reaction to a shift in supply; (b) a market's reaction to a shift in demand.

6. Will a price support that is lower than the equilibrium price lead to a surplus, a shortage, or neither? What about a price ceiling that is higher than the equilibrium price?

Problems and Topics for Discussion

1. **Examining the lead-off case.** Make a sketch of the markets for CZs and diamonds. You know the approximate equilibrium price and quantity from the opening case in this chapter, but you must guess at the slopes of the demand and supply curves. Do you think the demand curves for these goods slope downward in the usual way? Why or why not? Do you think the supply curves slope upward? Why or why not?

Now suppose there is a breakthrough in mining technology that lowers the cost of producing natural diamonds. Use your diagram to show what will happen in the diamond market. Will the supply curve shift? Will the demand curve shift? Will the new equilibrium price be higher or lower than the original price? What about the new equilibrium quantity? What will happen in the CZ market? Will the supply curve, the demand curve, or both shift? In which direction will the equilibrium price and quantity of CZs move?

2. **A shifting demand curve.** A vending machine company has studied the demand for soft drinks sold in cans from machines. Consumers in the firm's territory will buy about 2,000 cans of soda at a price of $.50 on a 70-degree day. For each $.05 rise in price, the quantity sold falls by 200 cans per day; for each 5-degree rise in the temperature, the quantity sold rises by 150 cans per day. The same relationships hold for decreases in price or temperature. Using this information, draw a set of curves showing the demand for soft drinks on days when the temperature is 60, 70, and 85 degrees.

3. **Demand and the relative price of motor fuel.** In 1979 and 1980, the nominal price of motor fuel rose more rapidly than the general price level, pushing up the relative price of motor fuel. As we would expect, the quantity sold decreased. In 1981 and 1982, the relative price leveled off and then began to fall; however, the quantity sold did not increase but continued to fall. Which one or more of the following hypotheses do you think best explains the behavior of motor fuel sales in 1981 and 1982? Illustrate each hypothesis with supply and demand curves.

   a. In the 1970s, the demand curve had the usual downward slope. However, in 1981 and 1982, the demand curve shifted to an unusual upward-sloping position.

   b. The demand curve sloped downward throughout the period. However, the recession of 1981 and 1982 reduced consumers' real incomes and shifted the demand curve.

   c. The demand curve has a downward slope at all times, but the shape depends partly on how long consumers have to adjust to a change in prices. Over a short period, the demand curve is fairly steep because few adjustments can be made. Over the long term, it has a somewhat flatter slope because further adjustments, such as buying more fuel-efficient cars or moving closer to work, can be made. Thus, the decreases in fuel sales in 1981 and 1982 were delayed reactions to the 1979 and 1980 price increases.

4. **Shortages, price controls, and queues.** In 1974 and again in 1979, shortages in the world oil market caused long lines of motorists to form at gas stations in the United States but not in European countries. Do you think this had anything to do with the fact that the United States had price controls on gasoline but European countries did not? Back up your reasoning with supply and demand curves.

5. **Eliminating queues through flexible pricing.** You are a member of the Metropolitan Taxi Commission, which sets taxi fares for your city. You have been told that long lines of taxis form at the airport during off-peak hours. At rush hours, on the other hand, few taxis are available and there are long lines of passengers waiting for cabs. It is proposed that taxi fares from the airport to downtown be cut by 10 percent during off-peak hours and raised by 10 percent during rush hours. How do you think these changes would affect the queuing patterns of taxis and passengers? Do you think the proposal is a good one from the pas-

sengers' point of view? From the cabbies' point of view? From the standpoint of efficiency? Discuss.

6. **Rent control.** Turn to part b of Exhibit 3.11 (page 73), which shows the long-run effects of rent control. If the controls are enforced and there are no disguised rent charges, landlords move down the supply curve to E_2. Buildings are abandoned or converted because of the low rent they bring in. Now consider some alternative possibilities:

   a. Suppose the controls are poorly enforced so that landlords, through key deposits, furniture sales, or some other means, are able to charge as much as the market will bear. What will be the resulting equilibrium price and quantity taking both open and disguised rental charges into account?

   b. Now suppose the controls are enforced against landlords so that they really cannot collect more than $250 per month. However, the controls are not enforced against tenants who sublet. What will be the equilibrium quantity and the equilibrium price, including both the rent paid to landlords and the disguised rental payments made by subtenants to their sublessors?

Case for Discussion
Good News and Bad News for the Coal Industry

There is good news and bad news for the coal industry. The bad news is that the drop in oil prices has sent coal prices into a tailspin. The good news is that given time, new technology is on the way that could make coal more competitive with oil than ever in the electric utility market.

First the bad news. After 1970, the U.S. coal industry rode high. It can thank OPEC for that. For a quarter of a century after World War II, coal prices hovered around $5 per ton. After 1970, when OPEC came to power, coal prices rose in tandem with oil prices, peaking at $28. But now oil prices are dropping. Switching back to oil has already begun. In April 1986, when electric power production rose more than 1 percent, the quantity of coal burned went down more than 5 percent.

Coal miners checking in after a shift.

Now the good news. A big barrier to selling more coal to electric utilities is the pollution that results when coal is burned. Adding stack scrubbers to remove the pollution is so expensive that many utilities use oil instead. Now a new technology is on the horizon: fluidized bed combustion of coal. This improvement in the technology of burning coal to generate electricity could make the cost of burning coal less than that of burning oil for many utilities, even if oil prices stay low.

Source: James Cook, "Coal Comfort," *Forbes*, August 11, 1986, 62–63. Excerpted by permission of *Forbes* magazine. © Forbes Inc., 1986. Photo Source: Russell Lee, 1946. Records of the Solid Fuels Administration for War.

Questions

1. Are coal and oil complements or substitutes? How can you tell from this article?

2. Draw a supply and demand diagram showing the effect on the coal market of the increase in oil prices caused by OPEC in the 1970s.

3. Draw a pair of supply and demand diagrams, one representing the market for coal and the other the market for electric power. How will the development of fluidized bed combustion affect the market for electric power? Will the supply curve shift? Will the demand curve shift? Will both shift? Explain why. How will the new technology affect the market for coal in terms of shifts in the supply and/or demand curves? Show equilibrium in each market before and after the introduction of the new technology. (Assume that oil prices are constant in this part of the problem.)

Suggestions for Further Reading

Baird, Charles W. *Rent Control: The Perennial Folly.* Washington, D.C.: The Cato Institute, 1980.

This book describes the history and recent practice of rent control in the United States and elsewhere.

Breit, William, and Roger L. Ransom. *The Academic Scribblers,* 2d ed. New York: Holt, Rinehart and Winston, 1982.

Chapter 3 is an essay on Alfred Marshall, the founder of modern supply and demand analysis. Chapters 1 and 2 provide useful background.

Campbell, Colin D., ed. *Wage and Price Controls in World War II: United States and Germany.* Washington, D.C.: American Enterprise Institute, 1971.

This book provides vivid descriptions and insightful analyses of what happens when governments overrule the law of supply and demand.

Marshall, Alfred. *Principles of Economics,* various editions.

First published in 1891, this book remains remarkably amenable to browsing even by beginning students.

4 The Role of Business: The Firm, Financial Markets, and Corporate Control

After reading this chapter, you will understand . . .

- Why business firms exist in so many different sizes and organizational forms.
- Why all the business in an economy cannot be handled by one big firm.
- What can be learned by looking at a firm's balance sheet.
- The role that financial markets play in the economy.
- What lies behind headlines dealing with corporate control, takeovers, and insider trading.

Before reading this chapter, make sure you know the meaning of . . .

- Markets and their functions (Chapters 1 and 2)
- Entrepreneurship (Chapter 2)
- Supply and demand (Chapter 3)

Chrysler to Buy American Motors

Lee A. Iacocca

MARCH 10, 1987. Chrysler Corporation yesterday announced plans to buy American Motors Corporation for a total of more than $1.5 billion in a deal that would reduce to three the number of homegrown U.S. car manufacturers.

The buyout proposal is contained in a letter of intent signed by Chrysler and French auto maker Regie Nationale des Usines Renault, which owns 46.1 percent of AMC.

The agreement is contingent upon approval by the boards of directors of the two companies and by AMC stockholders. Because Renault is government-owned and because of American antitrust laws, the French and U.S. governments must also approve the deal.

"This is an agreement in principle. Much work remains to be done before the deal is complete," said Chrysler Chairman Lee A. Iacocca, who steered his own company away from the brink of bankruptcy eight years ago.

"But we believe our decision to acquire American Motors is right for both companies, for the immediate future and the long haul. It'll strengthen both of us in what's already become a tough market," Iacocca said.

AMC, which has lost a total of $856.6 million since 1980, was too short of cash and product lines to survive much longer, according to auto industry analysts and officials. The firm's strength has been in its Jeep products—four-wheel drive sports-utility vehicles such as the Jeep Wrangler and Wagoneer, and pickups like the Comanche. But the Japanese are zeroing in on those models also, leaving AMC desperate for new ammunition and the kind of undisputed marketing savvy exhibited by Iacocca's Chrysler.

"It's a reasonable deal all around," said David Healy, an analyst with Drexel Burnham Lambert Inc. in New York. "Chrysler needs the additional capacity that AMC has to offer, and Chrysler certainly could use AMC's Jeep products."

Source: Warren Brown, "Chrysler to Buy American Motors," *The Washington Post*, March 10, 1987, p. 1. Reprinted with permission. Photo Source: Courtesy of Chrysler Corporation.

CLOSE reading of this news item raises a number of questions about the role of business firms in the U.S. economy. What exactly is a corporation? Who owns and controls giant corporations such as Chrysler? Where do these firms get the billions of dollars they need to do business? Why do some firms grow to be giants, while others prosper on the small scale of a corner store? These and other questions will be addressed in this chapter.

At the same time, the item raises questions about the role of government. Why is it that the vast bulk of goods and services in the United States are produced by private firms rather than by government-owned firms such as France's Renault? What is the government's role in regulating business transactions? If the government plays only a minor role in the production of goods and services, what does it do with all the billions that it collects in taxes? We will look at these questions in Chapter 5. Together this chapter and Chapter 5 will establish themes that will be developed in detail throughout the macro- and microeconomics courses.

Forms of Business Organization

Business firms vary widely in terms of their size and scope of operations. They also differ in terms of their form of organization. In this section we discuss the three most common types of firms—sole proprietorships, partnerships, and corporations—and briefly examine a few less common ones.

The Sole Proprietorship

Sole proprietorship
A firm that is owned and usually operated by one person, who receives all the profits and is responsible for all of the firm's liabilities.

A **sole proprietorship** is a firm that is owned and operated by a single person who receives all of its profits and is personally responsible for all of its liabilities. Sole proprietorships are very common. As Exhibit 4.1 shows, more than three-quarters of U.S. firms take this form. However, they are usually small. Together proprietorships account for less than 10 percent of total business receipts. Proprietorships are common in farming, construction, and wholesale and retail trade but far less so in other sectors of the economy.

Advantages of Proprietorships

Proprietorships have a number of advantages that make them well suited to small firms. Perhaps the biggest one is that they are easy to form. Starting a proprietorship requires little more than registering the firm's name. Proprietorships are also easy to dissolve: The owner simply stops doing business, and the firm ceases to exist.

A second advantage of the proprietorship is the fact that its owner receives all the profits (if any) directly. Income from a proprietorship is subject only to the personal income tax.

Finally, proprietors have the advantage of working for themselves without being accountable to employers or other owners. Many people value this independence so highly that they are willing to run their own businesses in return for lower incomes than they could earn working for someone else.

Disadvantages of Proprietorships

Proprietorships have certain drawbacks that limit their usefulness for large ventures. One is the owner's unlimited liability. Just as the owner receives all the

Exhibit 4.1   Forms of Business Organization

These charts show the distribution of firms in the United States according to form of ownership. Proprietorships are by far the most numerous. They are the main form of ownership in agriculture and are also common in retail trade and construction. However, most proprietorships are small; in terms of total receipts, they are overshadowed by corporations. The corporate sector, in turn, is dominated by the small number of firms (some 418,000 in 1980) that have reported receipts of $1 million or more.

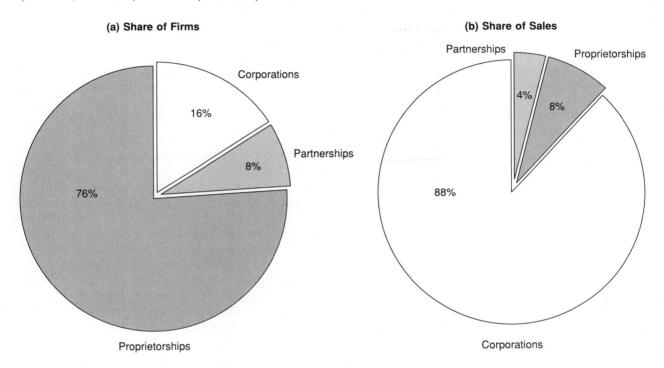

Source: U.S. Department of Commerce, *Statistical Abstract of the United States: 1984*, 104th ed. (Washington, D.C.: Government Printing Office, 1984), Tables 887, 888.

profits, he or she must bear any losses. Any liabilities that the firm incurs, such as business debts, lawsuits, or damages for breach of contract, are borne by the proprietor. Thus, a bankrupt proprietorship means a bankrupt owner.

The fact that a proprietorship cannot be separated from its owner is another drawback. The firm's growth may require more capital than the owner can purchase with his or her own funds, and it is difficult for a proprietorship to tap outside sources of funds. Also, the legal life of a proprietorship comes to an end upon the proprietor's death.

The Partnership

A **partnership** is an association of two or more people who operate a business as co-owners. Partnerships are the least common of the three major forms of business organization. They account for only about 7 percent of all U.S. firms and less than 4 percent of all business receipts. Partnerships are most often found in professions, such as law, medicine, and accounting. In these fields, state laws

Partnership
An association of two or more people who operate a business as co-owners by voluntary legal agreement.

restrict the use of the corporation by groups of professionals. Some of these laws have been relaxed in recent years, however, and professional corporations are becoming more common.

Advantages of Partnerships

Forming a partnership is one way for a proprietorship to grow. Two or more partners can pool their skills and financial resources to create a firm that is larger and stronger than either could support alone. Also, in certain situations partnerships have tax advantages over corporations.

Disadvantages of Partnerships

Offsetting these advantages are some serious drawbacks. One is the partners' unlimited liability. In terms of liability, a partner is worse off than a proprietor because he or she bears the liabilities of the entire firm. If the firm fails, a partner can lose far more than was put into it. A partner in a professional partnership may even be held liable for damages awarded in suits against other firm members.

Continuity is another serious problem for partnerships, since the death of any partner ends the firm's legal life. A partner's withdrawal can also create problems. If a partner wants to leave the firm, someone—either a new partner or the existing ones—must be willing to buy his or her interest in the firm. Until a buyer is found, the partner's investment may be "frozen," that is, unable to be withdrawn as cash or invested in another business.

Limited Partnerships

For some purposes, such as real estate ventures, a special kind of partnership called a *limited partnership* is used in order to avoid the problem of unlimited liability. A limited partnership includes one or more general partners who are in charge of running the firm and have much the same status as the co-owners of an ordinary partnership. It also includes one or more limited partners who put in funds and share profits but whose liability can never exceed the amount they have invested. A limited partnership has many of the advantages of a corporation in terms of raising funds with which to acquire capital. At the same time, it retains the tax advantages of a partnership.

The Corporation

Corporation
A firm that takes the form of an independent legal entity with ownership divided into equal shares and each owner's liability limited to his or her investment in the firm.

The corporation is the third major form of business organization. A corporation is a business that is organized as an independent legal entity, with ownership divided into shares. The corporation is the dominant form of organization for large firms. Only about 14 percent of all U.S. firms are corporations, but they account for more than 85 percent of all business receipts. Exhibit 4.2, which lists the 25 largest industrial corporations in the United States, contains many familiar names. Small corporations are also common, however; one-quarter of all corporations report receipts of less than $25,000 a year.

Advantages of Corporations

The usefulness of the corporate form for large businesses stems from two facts: (1) The corporation is a legal entity apart from its owners, and (2) the owners have limited liability.

The legal independence of the corporation makes it stable and long-lived.

Exhibit 4.2   The 25 Largest U.S. Industrial Corporations

Each year *Fortune* magazine publishes a list of the 500 largest industrial corporations in the United States, ranked by sales. This list of the top 25 contains many familiar names.

Rank	Company	Sales ($ thousands)	Net Income ($ thousands)
1	General Motors	102,813,700	2,944,700
2	Exxon	69,888,000	5,360,000
3	Ford Motor	62,715,800	3,285,100
4	International Business Machines	51,250,000	4,789,000
5	Mobil	44,866,000	1,407,000
6	General Electric	35,211,000	2,492,000
7	American Telephone and Telegraph	34,087,000	139,000
8	Texaco	31,613,000	725,000
9	E.I. du Pont de Nemours	27,148,000	1,538,000
10	Chevron	24,351,000	715,000
11	Chrysler	22,513,500	1,403,600
12	Philip Morris	20,681,000	1,478,000
13	Amoco	18,281,000	747,000
14	RJR Nabisco	16,998,000	1,064,000
15	Shell Oil	16,833,000	883,000
16	Boeing	16,341,000	665,000
17	United Technologies	15,669,157	72,727
18	Procter & Gamble	15,439,000	709,000
19	Occidental Petroleum	15,344,100	181,100
20	Atlantic Richfield	14,585,802	615,116
21	Tenneco	14,558,000	−39,000
22	USX	14,000,000	−1,833,000
23	McDonnell Douglas	12,660,600	277,500
24	Rockwell International	12,295,700	611,200
25	Allied-Signal	11,794,000	605,000

Source: *FORTUNE* 500; © 1987 Time Inc. All rights reserved. Reprinted by permission.

Stockholders can enter or leave the firm at will. Creditors and customers have only one legal entity to deal with rather than a number of partners. Further, the firm can own property and enter into contracts in its own name rather than just in its owners'.

Limited liability means that stockholders cannot suffer a loss greater than the sum they have invested in the business. This is the stockholder's most important protection. A person can own shares in dozens of corporations without ever facing the risks that a partner or proprietor does.

Together these two features make the corporation ideal for raising large sums from many small investors. We will discuss some of the ways in which this is done later in the chapter.

Disadvantages of Corporations

Corporations also have some disadvantages. (If they didn't, every firm would be a corporation.)

One disadvantage is the relative cost and difficulty of forming or dissolving a corporation. Although each state has its own laws in this area, forming a corporation usually requires the services of a lawyer and the payment of fees. These costs make the corporation poorly suited to many small or temporary business ventures.

Corporations also have a major tax disadvantage in that corporate income is taxed twice. When earned, it is subject to corporate income taxes; when paid out to stockholders as dividends, it is subject to the personal income tax. This double taxation can be very costly. If state and federal taxes take 40 percent of a firm's profit when earned and personal income taxes take 40 percent of the remainder when paid out as dividends, the firm's owners receive only $.36 of each dollar earned.

Not-for-Profit Firms

In addition to profit-seeking proprietorships, partnerships, and corporations, the private sector contains many not-for-profit firms. These include churches, colleges, charities, labor unions, country clubs, and the like. Like profit-seeking firms, these organizations participate in markets, produce goods and services, and provide jobs.

Most not-for-profit firms are corporations. Unlike profit-seeking corporations, however, they have no stockholders. They are run by independent boards of trustees whose members are chosen under rules set forth in the organization's bylaws. In a typical private college, for example, the trustees are elected by alumni, faculty, and sometimes students.

Some not-for-profit firms depend on donations for their income. Many also receive income from fees and sales of goods and services, as is the case with not-for-profit hospitals, publishers, and theater groups. If a not-for-profit firm takes in more donations and sales revenues than it spends, it is required by law to plow the surplus back into the business.

Cooperatives are closely related to not-for-profit firms. They are formed by consumers, farmers, and sometimes factory workers to run a business for their mutual benefit. Unlike not-for-profit firms, however, cooperatives may distribute any surplus they earn to their members. For example, the surplus of a co-op supermarket might be distributed to members at the end of the year on the basis of each member's total purchases during that period.

Unlike ordinary corporations, however, cooperatives do not always have profits as their main goal. Other benefits of forming a cooperative include consumers' chance to pool their purchasing power and buy at wholesale prices and farmers' opportunities to control the marketing of their crops.

The Firm as Coordinator

Whatever their form of organization, all business firms have one thing in common: They coordinate economic activity. They are responsible, in large part, for deciding what goods are made, who makes them, and how they are made. They do this by means of two types of coordination, which we will call *market coordination* and *managerial coordination*.

Coordinating the work of many people requires a system of incentives. It also requires a means by which people can communicate with one another. **Market coordination** uses the price system both as a means of communication

Market coordination
A means of coordinating economic activity that uses the price system to transmit information and provide incentives.

and as a source of incentives. As prices change in response to supply and demand, buyers are led to substitute lower-priced goods and services for higher-priced ones. At the same time, changing prices create new profit opportunities for entrepreneurs who expand their output of goods whose prices have been bid up by strong consumer demand. All this is done in a decentralized fashion; no central authority makes decisions or issues commands.

However, there are large areas of economic activity in which market coordination is not used. Take, for example, the coordination of work in a television factory. Workers do not decide on their own, in response to price changes, that they will spend the day making portables rather than cabinet models. Instead, they make portables because their boss tells them to. This is an example of **managerial coordination,** which is based on directives from managers to subordinates. The subordinates follow the directives because they have agreed to do so as a condition of employment.

Managerial coordination
A means of coordinating economic activity that uses directives from managers to subordinates.

Coordination within the Firm

In a well-known essay on the nature of the firm, Ronald Coase posed a question about these two ways of coordinating economic activity[1] (see "Who Said It? Who Did It? 4.1"). If the market works as well as economists say it does, Coase asked, why is managerial coordination used at all? Why must workers in a television factory take orders from a boss? If market coordination were used everywhere, all TV cabinets and picture tubes would be built by independent firms working on contract. Changes in the relative prices of various components would keep the right number of workers on each job and the right amounts of goods flowing to consumers.

Coase found an answer to his question. He said that market coordination is not used in every case where coordination is needed because it entails transaction costs. **Transaction costs** are incidental costs incurred by buyers and sellers in the process of making a transaction. They include the costs of gathering information about market conditions; the costs of negotiating contracts, writing invoices, and making payments; and the costs of straightening things out when contracts are not carried through.

Transaction costs
Incidental costs to buyers and sellers of making a transaction, including the costs of gathering information, making decisions, carrying out trades, writing contracts, and making payments.

Transaction costs limit the use of the market as a means of coordination. Imagine that you had to negotiate with each person who helped build a TV set that you wanted—the one who built the cabinet, the one who put the finish on, the one who installed the picture tube, and so on. The transaction costs of all these dealings would make buying a TV set a very expensive proposition. To avoid these costs, you might have a local shop build a set from scratch. But then the benefits of large-scale production would be lost, and the set would still cost a lot. When a firm like Magnavox acts as an intermediary between you and all the people who build the set, thousands of transactions are avoided. You can buy your TV set in a store, and the job of building it is coordinated within the firm through the issuing of directives that workers carry out.

Coase realized, though, that in answering one question he had raised another, namely, if managerial coordination works so well, why use the market at all? Why not run the entire economy as one big firm, with all people acting as employees and a single, central manager running the whole show? Then coordination would be a matter not only of giving TV or autoworkers instructions for

---

[1]Ronald H. Coase, "The Nature of the Firm," *Economica* (November 1937): 386–405.

WHO SAID IT? WHO DID IT?   4.1

Ronald Coase: Interpreter of Economic Institutions

Economists are sometimes charged with expressing their models in such abstract mathematical or graphical form that they lose all touch with real-world economic institutions. But not Ronald Coase. Through his own writings and work as editor of the *Journal of Law and Economics*, Coase has fostered a cross-fertilization between analytic and institutional economics. In the approach Coase favors, one selects an economic institution and poses two related questions:

Photo Source: Courtesy of the University of Chicago Law School Publications; Photographer: David Joel.

1. What are the effects of this particular institution on the allocation of resources?

2. How can one account for the evolution and continued existence of the institution in terms of an analysis of its effects on resource allocation?

Coase, who was born and educated in London, began his studies of economic institutions early in his career. His paper on the nature of the firm was published in 1937 and brought him international recognition. He came to the United States in 1951 to teach first at the University of Buffalo, then at the University of Virginia, and finally at the University of Chicago. In 1961, his most famous paper, "The Problem of Social Cost," appeared in the *Journal of Law and Economics*. At that time, the journal was new and the study of law and economics hardly existed as an independent specialty within either profession. Coase's probing analysis of the nature of the law as an economic institution sparked so much interest among both economists and lawyers that economic analysis of law soon became one of the most exciting fields of study available. Within a little over a decade, all leading law schools had economists on their staffs and were offering courses in the new approach.

---

the day but also of giving high school graduates orders concerning whether to become technicians or welders. Not only would the question of how many portables and how many cabinet-model TVs be answered by managerial coordination, such questions as how many factories should be in each industry and where they should be located would be answered as well.

However, managerial coordination has its own costs. Under managerial coordination, the person who actually does a job need not know all the reasons for doing it—and that is a saving. But offsetting this is managers' need to learn a great deal about all the jobs they coordinate. Sometimes the costs of giving information to a central decision maker are greater than those of giving information to people close to the job. Once central managers get the information they need to make decisions, they must transmit clear instructions back to middle managers and then to workers. The further central managers are from the workers doing the job, the more costly is the coordination process, the longer are the delays, and the greater is the chance of error. At some point, the costs of managerial coordination become so great that it loses its advantage over market coordination.

Limits of the Firm

Coase saw that the two coordinating mechanisms we have discussed are the key to understanding the nature of the firm and its role in the economy. A firm, he said, uses managerial coordination for its internal activities. It uses the market to coordinate its activities with those of people on the outside. Each firm finds it worthwhile to expand its operations only to the point at which the managerial costs of organizing one more task within the firm equal the transaction costs of organizing the same task outside the firm through the market.

In some cases, this principle leads to very large firms. Magnavox, for example, is a large firm in itself. It is also part of the Philips organization, one of the 50 or so largest firms in the world. Such a firm coordinates a vast number of activities. It builds hundreds of different products, makes parts in one plant for products that will be assembled in another halfway around the world, and so on. But even a firm like Philips does not do everything for itself. If it wants to ship goods by rail, it does not build a railroad. Some jobs are so big that even the largest firms find it more efficient to use outside specialists.

In other cases, Coase's principle leads to firms that are very small. Bullard's Welding of Chelsea, Vermont, is an example from the millions of small business firms in the U.S. economy. Bullard does a few things for himself that most firms of that size would not do. For example, he built his own furnace to heat his shop. But he does not make the parts for the diesel engines he repairs or set up a rolling mill to make the sheet steel he needs or hire a lawyer as an employee. Instead, he finds it cheaper to buy those goods and services on the market.

In Bullard's case, as in Philips', allowing each firm to expand to its optimal size while leaving coordination among firms to the market keeps total coordination costs down when both the transaction costs of market coordination and the managerial costs of coordination within firms are taken into account. The concept of the firm as a means of making economic coordination more efficient should be kept in mind throughout the study of economics.

Financing Private Business

The Balance Sheet

Regardless of their size or legal form, all private firms need financial resources in order to purchase capital and carry on their operations. One way to understand how a firm obtains and uses financial resources is to look at its **balance sheet**—a financial statement that shows what the firm owns and what it owes. Exhibit 4.3 shows a balance sheet for an imaginary firm, Great Falls Manufacturing Inc. (GFMI).

The left-hand column of the balance sheet lists the firm's **assets,** which are all the things to which it holds a legal claim. GFMI's assets include $10 million in cash and accounts receivable; $15 million in inventory; and $100 million in property, plant, and equipment. Its assets thus total $125 million.

The right-hand column of the balance sheet lists the firm's liabilities and net worth. A firm's **liabilities** are all the legal claims that outsiders hold against it. For GFMI, these include $5 million in accounts payable; $15 million in short-term loans from banks; and $55 million in long-term debts, such as mortgages on its property. The final item on the right-hand side of the balance sheet is the firm's **net worth,** also known as **owners' equity,** which is the difference between total assets and total liabilities. The firm's net worth represents its owners' claims against its assets. The fact that GFMI's net worth is $50 million means that if its owners closed it down, sold all its assets at the values listed on the balance sheet, and paid off all its liabilities, they would have $50 million left over.

Balance sheet
A financial statement showing a firm's or household's assets, liabilities, and net worth.

Assets
All the things to which a firm or household holds legal claim.

Liabilities
All the legal claims against a firm by nonowners or against a household by nonmembers.

Net worth (owners' equity)
A firm's or household's assets minus its liabilities.

Exhibit 4.3   Balance Sheet of Great Falls Manufacturing Inc.

A firm's balance sheet gives a snapshot of its financial position. The left-hand side lists the firm's assets—all the things to which it holds legal claim. The right-hand side lists the firm's liabilities—claims against it by nonowners—and its net worth, or owners' equity. According to the accounting equation, assets always equal liabilities plus net worth.

Assets (Millions)		Liabilities and Net Worth (Millions)	
Cash and accounts receivable	$ 10	Accounts payable	$ 5
Inventory	15	Short-term debt	15
Property, plant, and equipment	100	Long-term debt	55
		Total liabilities	$ 75
		Net worth	50
Total assets	$125	Total liabilities plus net worth	$125

The balance sheet gets its name from the fact that the totals of the two columns always balance. This follows from the definition of net worth. Because net worth is defined as assets minus liabilities, liabilities plus net worth must equal assets. In equation form, this basic rule of accounting reads as follows:

$$\text{Assets} = \text{Liabilities} + \text{Net worth.}$$

As a firm grows, so do the entries on its balance sheet. A growing firm will need more plant and equipment and a larger inventory. It will also need more cash, and its accounts receivable will increase as it does business with more workers, customers, and suppliers.

According to the accounting equation, the firm's liabilities, net worth, or both must grow along with its assets. If the firm is profitable, it can obtain funds for growth by plowing profits back into the business. If it does this, its assets will grow without a corresponding increase in its liabilities; therefore, by definition, its net worth will grow. Thus, by plowing profits back into the business, owners increase their stake in the firm. If the firm does not make enough profits to finance its own growth, it must turn to outside sources of funds.

Broadly speaking, there are two outside sources of funds to which the firm can turn. One is to bring in more owners—new partners for a partnership, new stockholders for a corporation, or new members for a cooperative. The funds raised from these new owners are entered on the firm's balance sheet as additions to its net worth. The alternative is to borrow funds from individuals, banks, or other lenders. If the firm does this, its liabilities will increase.

Financial Markets

Financial markets
Markets through which borrowers obtain funds from savers.

The markets in which a firm obtains funds are known as **financial markets**. A basic understanding of these markets is useful, since they play key roles in both macro- and microeconomics.

Exhibit 4.4 gives an overview of financial markets. Such markets serve as a link between economic units that are *net savers* (those that spend less than they earn) and units that are *net borrowers* (those that spend more than they earn). Some households are net borrowers, but the total saving of all households exceeds their total borrowing. Therefore, the household sector is shown in Exhibit

Exhibit 4.4   Financial Markets

This chart shows how financial markets channel investment funds from households (net savers) to nonfinancial businesses (net borrowers). Two types of financing are shown. Direct financing is the sale of claims against firms (such as stocks or bonds) directly to households. Indirect financing channels the funds through financial intermediaries—firms that gather funds from households and use them as a basis for making loans to other firms. The chart shows flows of funds as solid arrows and flows of financial claims issued in exchange for funds as dotted arrows.

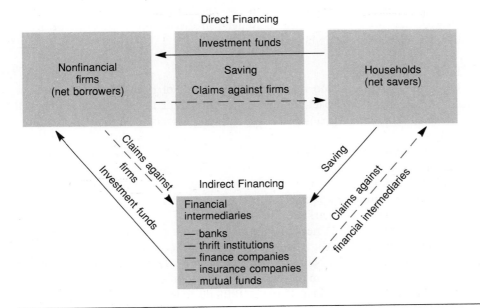

4.4 as a source of funds for financial markets. Some nonfinancial firms take in more funds than they use and thus are net savers, but the total borrowing of nonfinancial business firms exceeds their total saving. Thus, the nonfinancial business sector is shown as a user of funds provided through financial markets.

Direct Financing
One way for a firm to raise funds is to approach net savers—households or other nonfinancial firms—directly. This process is called **direct financing.** In exchange for the funds they provide, these net savers receive claims against the firm. These claims take several forms, the most common of which are bonds and stocks.

A **bond** is a promise, given in return for borrowed funds, to make interest payments at an agreed-upon rate over a set period, plus a final payment equal to the amount borrowed. Most bonds are issued in denominations of $1,000 for periods of 10 to 30 years. Suppose that GFMI wanted to raise $1 million to buy some new injection-molding equipment. It could sell 1,000 bonds with a face value of $1,000 each, promising to pay the lenders, say, $150 a year for 30 years and to repay the $1,000 at the end of that period.

Instead of borrowing funds by selling bonds, GFMI could raise the $1 million by selling stock. A share of **common stock** is a certificate of part ownership in the firm. In return for their funds, the new stockholders become co-owners

Direct financing
The process of raising investment funds directly from savers.

Bond
A promise, given in return for borrowed funds, to make a fixed annual or semiannual payment over a set number of years plus a larger final payment equal to the amount borrowed.

Common stock
A certificate of part ownership in a corporation that gives the owner a vote in the selection of the firm's directors and the right to a share of dividends, if any.

with all other stockholders. Unlike bondholders, though, common stockholders are not promised a fixed return on their investment. Instead, they expect to be rewarded for their investment through dividends or capital gains. *Dividends* are payments to stockholders that are made out of profits. *Capital gains* are sums that are realized when and if stockholders are able to sell their shares at a higher price than they paid for them. Firms also sometimes issue *preferred stock*, which is stock that has guaranteed dividends but no voting rights.

Stocks and bonds are only two of a great many types of financial instruments that firms issue. Others include *commercial paper* (similar to bonds but scheduled for repayment in a year or less) and *convertible bonds* (bonds that can be exchanged for stock at a set price). A detailed discussion of these securities is beyond the scope of this book.

Indirect Financing

Direct financing is by no means the only source of funds for a firm such as GFMI. Instead of approaching households directly, a firm can turn to financial intermediaries such as banks, savings and loan associations, insurance companies, mutual funds, and pension funds. **Financial intermediaries** gather funds from net savers and pass them along to net borrowers by either making loans or buying stocks, bonds, or other securities from them. The process of raising funds through financial intermediaries is known as **indirect financing.** Indirect financing accounts for about two-thirds of all funds raised by nonfinancial sectors in U.S. financial markets.

Suppose that GFMI needs $100,000 to build a new warehouse. Instead of seeking the funds directly from households or other nonfinancial firms, it applies to the Great Falls National Bank for a mortgage loan. In return for the funds, GFMI gives the bank a mortgage note promising to repay the $100,000, with interest, over a period of 15 years. If it fails to make the payments, the bank can take possession of the warehouse.

Where does the bank get the funds it needs to make the loans? It gets them by accepting checking and savings deposits from the citizens of Great Falls. As Exhibit 4.4 shows, indirect financing involves a double exchange of funds and claims. Households give their funds to the bank in return for claims against it, and the bank passes the funds along to GFMI in return for a claim against the new warehouse.

Indirect financing has a number of advantages over direct financing. First, it is more flexible. A bank could, for example, lend a retail store a few thousand dollars for 90 days to finance an inventory buildup for the Christmas season. Selling securities for this purpose would be impractical for a small firm. Second, indirect financing can be used by small firms, including proprietorships and partnerships. Because these firms are not widely known and do not always have high credit ratings, they may find it difficult to sell stocks or bonds. Finally, financial intermediaries perform a useful service by matching the needs of borrowers and lenders. For example, the Great Falls National Bank would be able to give GFMI a 15-year mortgage loan for $100,000 even though none of its depositors may have that much in savings or want the savings tied up for such a long period.

Not all indirect financing takes the form of loans. Sales of stocks, bonds, or other financial instruments to financial intermediaries also count as indirect financing. Pension funds, mutual funds, and insurance companies have large holdings of corporate financial instruments.

Financial intermediaries
Financial firms, including banks, savings and loan associations, insurance companies, pension funds, and mutual funds, that gather funds from net savers and provide funds to net borrowers.

Indirect financing
The process of raising investment funds via financial intermediaries.

Secondary Financial Markets

The financial markets shown in Exhibit 4.4 are called **primary financial markets** because they are markets in which newly issued claims against firms are exchanged for new investment funds. There are also many **secondary financial markets,** in which firms and households buy and sell previously issued bonds, stocks, and other securities. The best known of these secondary markets is the New York Stock Exchange. Stocks and bonds are also traded in so-called over-the-counter markets, which are networks of dealers who do business by telephone or computer hookup.

The prices of stocks and other securities traded in secondary markets vary hour by hour and day by day as buyers and sellers revise their expectations regarding general economic conditions and profits of individual firms. Each day financial newspapers publish multipage reports on the latest prices of stocks, bonds, and other securities. Averages of the prices of selected stocks, such as the Dow Jones Industrial Average, are widely reported on radio and television as well as in newspapers.

Secondary markets allow shareholders who become disillusioned with their firms' management to sell out and invest elsewhere. As we will see in the next section, these markets play a key role in determining who controls corporate policy.

Primary financial markets
Markets in which newly issued stocks, bonds, and other securities are sold.

Secondary financial markets
Markets in which previously issued bonds, stocks, and other securities are traded among investors.

Corporate Control, Takeovers, and Insider Trading

Because corporations contribute such a large share of the total output of the U.S. economy, the question of who controls these firms is important. For example, the news article that opens this chapter refers to "Lee Iacocca's Chrysler Corporation." In what sense is it "his" company? Who makes decisions such as Chrysler's takeover bid for American Motors? Who decides whether such bids succeed? This section looks briefly at these important issues.

Stockholders' Rights

One of the advantages of the corporation is that it can raise funds from many thousands of people, none of whom need invest much in any one firm. In most corporations, the stockholders have the legal power to control the firm by electing its board of directors, who in turn appoint its top managers. In such a corporation, the stockholders are the *principals* in whose interest the firm is supposed to be run. Directors and managers—the Lee Iacoccas—are the stockholders' *agents.* It is their legal duty to serve the stockholders' interests, particularly their interest in earning a return on the funds they have invested.

In practice, however, many corporations' stockholders exercise little day-to-day power over the firm's policies. This is especially true when ownership is divided among many stockholders, none of whom holds a significant percentage of the total stock. Typically, stockholders own shares in many different corporations; this is true of both individual stockholders and institutional stockholders such as pension funds and insurance companies. If they disapprove of the policies of one firm's managers, they can simply sell that stock and buy stock of another company rather than voicing their concerns via shareholder meetings and election of directors.

However, many observers have asked, if stockholders take this attitude, what guarantee exists that directors and managers will act in stockholders' interests? What will keep them from turning corporations into private fiefdoms in which they rule from lavish penthouse suites, gad about in corporate jets, and pay themselves extravagant bonuses while the business goes to pot?

Incentives and Bonuses

One way to keep manager-agents working in the interests of their stockholder-principals is to set incentives and bonuses that are tied to the firm's profitability. A common type of profit-sharing plan is the stock option, which gives a manager the right to buy a certain number of shares of the firm's stock at a set price before a specified date. Suppose that in July 1987 a manager is given the option to buy 1,000 shares of the firm's stock at any time until 1992 at the 1987 price of $25. If the manager does a good job of running the firm, the price of the stock is likely to rise. If it rises to, say, $45 by 1992, the option to buy 1,000 shares at $25 is worth $20,000. This is a nice reward for a job well done. But if the company is poorly managed and the stock's price falls below $25, the option will be worthless.

Takeovers

An even more powerful incentive for managers to heed stockholders' interests is the threat of a takeover. We have noted that when stockholders do not like a firm's policies, they are likely to sell their shares and buy shares in another firm. If many stockholders decide to sell at the same time, the price of the stock is driven way down. The firm then may be subject to a *takeover* bid, that is, a bid by a new owner to buy a block of shares large enough to control election of the firm's directors.

Sometimes takeovers are friendly, such as the one between Chrysler and American Motors discussed in the article that opens this chapter. In such cases, managers see mutual interests in a merger. But other takeovers are not friendly. If the price of its stock sags, the firm may face the prospect of a hostile takeover, in which the buyer—if successful—will throw out the present management team and install its own.

A hostile takeover bid may be made by an individual, a group, or, most often, another corporation. One tactic is to make a *tender offer,* meaning an offer to buy a controlling interest in the firm's stock at a stated price, usually well above the stock's current market price. Another tactic is to ask stockholders for *proxies,* that is, promises to vote for a new board of directors at the next stockholder meeting. In either case, if the takeover succeeds, the new management will do its best to raise profits. When investors realize this, the price of the firm's stock will be bid up and the takeover group will reap handsome gains.

Some economists have argued that it is the right to sell out to a raider staging a takeover, rather than attendance at stockholder meetings, that is the true basis of stockholders' power to discipline management. Together with stock options and other profit-sharing devices, takeovers act as carrots and sticks to keep managers from straying too far from their duty of earning profits for their stockholders. However, not all observers share this view. The debate as to whether takeovers are good for the economy revolves around three principal sets of issues: debt, defensive strategies, and short-run bias.

Debt versus Equity

In order to persuade stockholders to sell out, raiders offer to buy a company's shares at a price substantially higher than its current market value. They finance the purchases with borrowed money. As a result, after the takeover the company has more debt in relation to its net worth than before. Economists critical of takeover practices say that all that debt makes the firm financially weak. The reason debt makes a company financially weak is that a firm has a legal obligation to make payments to its bondholders or to banks from which it has borrowed whether or not it is earning a profit. These fixed-payment obligations can force a firm into bankruptcy in a period when its sales and profits have slipped. In contrast, equity funding gives the corporation more flexibility. The firm has no legal obligation to make dividend payments to its stockholders each year. Omitting dividends during hard times can give the firm the breathing space it needs to work its way back to profitability in the long run.

Critics worry that the tendency to replace owners' equity with debt will weaken the corporate sector as a whole and reduce its ability to survive an economic downturn. In the period 1984 to 1986 alone, more than $300 billion of owners' equity was exchanged for debt through a variety of financial restructuring methods. However, raiders—and those economists who side with them—say not to worry: The debt can be repaid with higher earnings once the old management is replaced by a stronger one. Also, some of the debt can be paid off by selling real estate, subsidiaries, and other assets that the corporation has been using inefficiently.

Defensive Strategies

Critics claim that fear of takeover prompts managers to adopt defensive strategies that hurt the company. They may sell off the firm's "crown jewels"—its most profitable assets or divisions. They may load up the firm with debt to make it less attractive. They may design "poison pills"—complex financial traps that they hope would-be raiders will choke on. They may pay "greenmail"—huge ransoms to raiders who agree to go away—that leaves the firm impoverished.

Defenders of the takeover mechanism agree that these tactics can be harmful. They see them as an expression of contempt for shareholders on management's part. If raiders can oust such managers, the sooner the better.

Short-Run Bias

The threat of takeover, say economists who are critical of certain widely used tactics, forces managers to stress the short run over the long run. Managers do everything they can to keep short-term profits up, hoping that this will boost their firms' stock prices and keep them from becoming takeover targets. In so doing, they allegedly slight research and development and pass over risky but potentially profitable long-term projects.

However, many economists tend to be skeptical of this argument. It assumes that stockholders systematically overvalue the stocks of firms that pursue short-sighted goals and undervalue those of companies that invest in long-term profitability. In fact, the very things that managers must do to resist a takeover—restructure, sell assets they cannot manage well, and so on—are more likely to strengthen than weaken the firm in the long run.

Takeovers and Insider Trading

Although many economists defend takeovers on the grounds that they improve efficiency by replacing bad managers with good ones, the people who actually play the takeover game are not in it to make the world a better place. They are in it to make money. Because the sums of money involved in a major corporate merger such as Chrysler/AMC are enormous, the issue of takeovers has become entangled with another controversy: *insider trading*. The explosive mixture of takeovers and insider trading has led to some of the most spectacular headlines to come out of Wall Street; "Economics in the News 4.1" provides a case in point.

The Mechanics of Insider Trading

First we must understand why insider trading is so profitable. Let Ace Corporation be a poorly run, plodding dog of a company with much greater potential than its current managers have been able to extract. On the basis of current management performance, its stock is trading at $15 per share. Now comes Zeus Corporation, a go-go outfit that employs teams of researchers to identify firms like Ace. Zeus's management figures that by selling off some of Ace's timber holdings, revamping its line of women's shoes, and doing some heavy-duty cost cutting, it can so boost profitability that Ace's stock will rise to a market value of $25. Having planned how to turn Ace around, Zeus will go into the stock market on June 1 with a public tender offer, bidding $20 per share for any or all of Ace's

---

ECONOMICS IN THE NEWS   4.1

Another Wall Street Insider Pleads Guilty

FEBRUARY 14, 1987. Martin A. Siegel, one of Wall Street's premier investment bankers, pleaded guilty yesterday to criminal charges that he participated in an illegal information swapping and stock trading scheme with high-ranking executives of Goldman, Sachs & Co. and Kidder, Peabody & Co.

Siegel agreed to pay the government more than $9 million to settle charges that he violated federal securities laws. He also pleaded guilty to income-tax evasion charges.

The 38-year-old investment banker also was charged yesterday by the Securities and Exchange Commission with selling secret information about corporate takeovers to stock speculator Ivan F. Boesky, who used the tips to make more than $33 million in the stock market.

For the illegal stock tips, Boesky paid Siegel $700,000, which was delivered by aides who handed over briefcases containing cash after exchanging secret passwords with Siegel in public places, the SEC said.

Siegel resigned yesterday from his multimillion-dollar-a-year job as cohead of the merger department at Drexel Burnham Lambert Inc. An executive at Kidder for 15 years before he joined Drexel last year, Siegel helped arrange more than 500 corporate takeovers and helped develop novel takeover defense strategies for corporations, including Martin Marietta Corp. Drexel said that all of the charges against Siegel involve activities that took place before he joined the firm.

"I swapped material, nonpublic information with Robert Freeman of Goldman, Sachs, for the mutual benefit of Goldman, Sachs and Kidder, Peabody," Siegel replied when U.S. District Judge Robert J. Ward asked what he had done. Ward then asked Siegel if he knew what he had done was wrong. "Yes, your honor," Siegel replied, after he wiped tears from his cheeks.

Siegel, dressed in a dark suit, light blue shirt and red tie, stood alongside other defendants who were pleading guilty to crimes ranging from drug-pushing to assault. He faces up to 10 years in prison on information swapping and tax evasion charges. He was released on his own recognizance after the hearing.

Source: David A. Vise and Michael Schrage, "Another Wall Street Guilty Plea." *The Washington Post*, February 14, 1986, p. A1. Reprinted with permission.

10 million outstanding shares. Zeus hopes that Ace's present stockholders will be happy with a $5 capital gain. If its hunch that better management will boost the stock price to $25 is right, the additional $5 a share will give Zeus a fat profit from the takeover. All this is honorable, ethical, and legal—exactly how the system is supposed to work.

Now comes Dwight the Insider. Dwight is a lawyer who works for the law firm that represents Zeus. When asked to draw up a set of legal papers in conjunction with the coming tender offer, he sees an opportunity. Borrowing $1.75 million from a friendly banker (with whom he perhaps shares his tip), Dwight buys 100,000 shares of Ace during the month of May. His trading boosts demand for the stock enough to push up its price, making him pay an average of $17.50 a share. Even so, when Zeus makes its tender offer, Dwight sells out at $20 and clears a cool quarter-million, less brokerage commissions and interest on the loan.

The Case against Insider Trading

Dwight's actions are illegal. If detected by the Securities and Exchange Commission, he can be forced to forfeit his profits and possibly serve a jail term as well. What has he done to deserve such harsh treatment?

The case against insider trading rests on the view that every player in the stock market should have an equal chance of profiting from an upward or downward move in a stock's price. The insider who trades on information not yet available to the public is seen in the same light as a blackjack dealer who plays with marked cards. In our example Dwight, by buying Ace's stock at $17.50, can be seen as robbing the sellers of a chance to profit from Zeus's coming tender offer.

In Support of Insider Trading

Not everyone, however, is persuaded that insider trading is reprehensible. If the stock market is viewed as a mechanism for using information in the service of efficient resource allocation, it is not so clear that Dwight's actions are damaging.

For one thing, there are winners as well as losers among the people with whom the insider trades. The case against insider trading assumes that someone— let's say Ellen—who owns Ace stock would have held it until June 1 had Dwight not come along. But stock in every company is bought and sold every day. What about Margaret, who needed to sell her Ace holdings by May 31 in order to meet her daughter's college tuition bill? Thanks to Dwight, she sells at $17.50 instead of $15.

The important thing, say defenders of insider trading, is that such trading moves stock prices in the right direction—right from an efficiency point of view, that is. In a well-functioning stock market, the price of each share should reflect each firm's true long-term earning potential. In this case, Zeus has discovered a defect in the constellation of prices. Ace stock is underpriced, due to the clumsy practices of its present managers. From the standpoint of efficiency, the sooner the price goes up, the better.

. . . But Not All Insider Trading

The above arguments suggest that Dwight the Insider may have helped as many people as he hurt and probably improved the efficiency of stock prices. Does this mean he did nothing wrong? Even among those who see insider trading as beneficial, there is one disturbing element in the story. Dwight is an attorney employed by Zeus to help with its takeover attempt. But by running up the stock price prematurely, Dwight is potentially damaging his client. With the stock's price already on the rise, Zeus's $20 tender offer may not look so good after all; it may have to bid $21, or $22, or $24.75. Thus, it appears that in the end Dwight has acted unethically. However, the real victim is not Ellen, the innocent bystander, but Zeus, his client.

It is easy to see that our fictional case of Dwight the Insider has elements in common with the case of Martin A. Siegel reported in "Economics in the News 4.1." Whether or not the deals Siegel cut with Ivan Boesky and others moved stock prices in the "right" direction, critics charge that Siegel stole from his employer and the clients that hired the firm to conduct their merger business. Trading on information obtained through abuse of a position of trust, the critics say, is little different, ethically speaking, from pocketing $5 bills from the cash register at the corner gas station.

Looking Ahead

As you continue your study of economics, you will draw on the material in this chapter at many points. Both macroeconomics and microeconomics deal frequently with financial markets. Firms' ability to attract funds with which to invest in new capital is crucial to their own performance and to the growth of the economy as a whole. The balance sheet concepts of assets, liabilities, and net worth are necessary for understanding the operation of the banking system (a part of macroeconomics) and of individual firms (a part of microeconomics). Sometimes economists deal with simplified models in which firms are treated as identical, interchangeable units. However, you should keep in mind that behind those models lies a real world in which business firms come in all sizes, shapes, and legal forms.

Summary

1. **Why do business firms exist in so many different sizes and organizational forms?** Different forms of business organization suit different firms depending on their size and scope of operations. The most common type of firm is the *sole proprietorship*. Small firms often choose this form because of its flexibility and the complete control it gives the owner. However, limited liability and continuity make the *corporation* a more suitable form of organization for large firms. In between, some firms, especially those in the professions, assume the *partnership* form of organization.

2. **Why cannot all business in the economy be handled by one large firm?** Business firms play a major role in solving the economic problems of what, how, and for whom. They do so by means of both market and managerial coordination. *Market coordination* uses the price system as a means of communication and a source of incentives. *Managerial coordination* relies on directives from managers to subordinates. Each form

of coordination entails certain costs that limit its usefulness. Firms tend to expand their operations to the point at which the managerial costs of organizing one more task within the firm equal the *transaction costs* of organizing the same task through the market. This is what sets an upper limit on the efficient size of firms.

3. **What can be learned by looking at a firm's balance sheet?** A firm's *balance sheet* is a financial statement that shows what it owns and what it owes. The firm's *assets*—all the things to which it holds a legal claim—are listed on the left-hand side of the balance sheet. Its *liabilities*—all the claims that outsiders hold against it—are listed on the right-hand side. The right-hand side of the balance sheet also lists *net worth (owners' equity)*, which is the difference between total assets and total liabilities. Owners' equity represents owners' claims against the firm according to a relationship known as the accounting equation: Assets = Liabilities + Net worth.

4. **What role do financial markets play in the economy?** *Financial markets* are the markets in which firms obtain funds for operations and investment. They serve as a link between savers and borrowers. With *direct financing*, firms borrow directly from or sell securities directly to households or other nonfinancial firms. With *indirect financing*, they deal with households or other nonfinancial firms via *financial intermediaries* such as banks, insurance companies, and pension funds. Markets in which newly issued securities are sold are called *primary financial markets;* those in which previously issued securities are traded are called *secondary financial markets.*

5. **What lies behind headlines dealing with corporate control, takeovers, and insider trading?** Stockholders have the legal power to control the corporations they own. Their main channel of control is the right to elect the firm's board of directors. However, in practice managers have a good deal of day-to-day independence from stockholders. Stockholders get into the corporate control act in a major way only when the firm is faced with a takeover bid. Takeovers are controversial because of their questionable effects on the economy and their links to insider trading scandals.

Terms for Review

- sole proprietorship
- partnership
- corporation
- market coordination
- managerial coordination
- transaction costs
- balance sheet
- assets
- liabilities
- net worth
- owners' equity
- financial markets
- direct financing
- bond
- common stock
- financial intermediaries
- indirect financing
- primary financial markets
- secondary financial markets

Questions for Review

1. List the main advantages and disadvantages of the sole proprietorship, the partnership, and the corporation.

2. What are the advantages of market coordination? Give an example of a situation in which transaction costs

limit its use. In what way do the costs of managerial coordination limit the firm's size?

3. What kinds of items would be listed as assets of a typical manufacturing firm? As its liabilities? What is the relationship among the firm's assets, liabilities, and net worth?

4. Distinguish between direct and indirect financing. List some common types of financial intermediary, and explain their role in financial markets.

5. What are the main mechanisms through which stockholders exercise control of corporations? Why is their control often less than complete?

Problems and Topics for Discussion

1. **Examining the lead-off case.** What benefits does each corporation hope to realize from the proposed merger of AMC and Chrysler? How does the secondary market in AMC stock make it possible for AMC's stockholders to share in these benefits? How might Chrysler president Lee Iacocca personally benefit from bringing about the merger?

2. **Types of business organization.** Look around your community for businesses organized as proprietorships, partnerships, corporations, and not-for-profit firms. Do you think each firm has chosen the most appropriate form of organization? Why or why not?

3. **Examining a corporate balance sheet.** Obtain a copy of a corporation's annual report. (You may find one in your library. If not, you can get one by writing or telephoning the corporation, or you can borrow one from a friend or relative who is a corporate stockholder.) At the back of the report, you will find the firm's balance sheet. Compare this balance sheet with the one given in Exhibit 4.3. What similarities do you see? What differences?

4. **A personal balance sheet.** Howard Winters is a graduate student in economics at Catatonic State University. He owns a 1974 Chevrolet worth about $800; a $1,000 stereo system; and about $500 worth of other personal possessions. He has $420 in his checking account and no other financial resources. Over the past seven years he has borrowed $8,700 under a student loan program, which he plans to pay back after he has received his degree and landed a job. He also owes $125 on a credit card account.

   Draw up a personal balance sheet for Winters. Which items go on the right-hand side? On the left-hand side? What is his net worth? Which of his "assets" (not listed on his balance sheet) have made it possible for him to borrow so much money?

5. **Secondary financial markets in the news.** Each day for one week, look at the stock and bond market re-

ports in a newspaper with a good financial section. (*The Wall Street Journal* has the most complete reports, but any big-city paper will do.) Also, look for stories that discuss increases or decreases in the prices of stocks and bonds traded in secondary financial markets. What reasons for the price changes are given?

6. **Mergers and acquisitions in the news.** Scan recent issues of business magazines like *Business Week*, *Fortune*, or *Forbes* for a story about a merger that has recently taken place or is being considered. What reasons for the merger are given? Do you think the merger makes sense in terms of Coase's theory of the firm? Is this a "friendly" merger, in which the acquired company's management is cooperating or a hostile takeover that management is trying to resist? What controlling role, if any, are the acquired firm's stockholders expected to play in the merger?

Harrison J. Goldin

Case for Discussion
A Bill of Rights for Corporate Shareholders

Kings of corporate management beware: Your once loyal and passive subjects have declared their independence by adopting the Shareholder Bill of Rights.

No longer will your biggest stockholders stand idly by as you take away their right to vote on questions as crucial as who will rule the corporate kingdom. Gone are the days when shareholders will watch silently as top executives adopt antitakeover devices that entrench management and depress stock prices.

Instead, with the Shareholder Bill of Rights as its guide and more than $160 billion in assets as its economic weapon, the Council of Institutional Investors is preparing to launch a campaign in support of shareholder democracy.

"We have done something very important, even revolutionary," said Harrison J. Goldin, comptroller of New York City and cochairman of the council.

The first demand in the Bill of Rights is that each share of common stock have an equal vote. "The right to vote is inviolate and may not be abridged," the Bill of Rights says.

The bill's "one-share, one-vote" rule is violated by some public companies, which have different classes of common stock with unequal voting rights. Unequal voting rights is the most effective antitakeover device in existence, because it typically is used to give control of a company to friends of management, who own stock that may have 10 votes per share, while stock owned by the public has only one vote per share.

"A share of stock without a vote is truly a crippled instrument," said Roland Machold, who directs $16 billion in pension assets for 380,000 state and municipal policemen, teachers, firemen, judges and public employees in New Jersey. He said the fundamental problem in many public companies is that the interests of shareholders and top management differ. If top management owns relatively little stock in the company, it usually will favor two classes of voting stock and any other device that deters takeovers and preserves its jobs. But shareholders, including pension funds, are interested in getting the highest price for their stock. Thus, shareholders typically favor the generous takeover bids that managements oppose.

The Bill of Rights also charges that corporate managements are making too many critical decisions without consulting shareholders. The bill calls on corporations to allow shareholders to vote on greenmail payments, the sale of significant corporate assets, the lucrative compensation arrangements for executives known as golden parachutes, and poison-pill provisions—corporate devices that can be activated to make a company less attractive—which many managements have adopted recently to deter takeovers.

Source: David A. Vise, "'Bill of Rights' Seeks to Boost Power of Shareholders," *The Washington Post*, April 13, 1986, p. F-1. Reprinted with permission. Photo Source: Courtesy of Office of the Comptroller, New York City.

Questions

1. According to this news item, why do the interests of shareholders and managers diverge? What does each party want?

2. You have your choice between buying two kinds of stock in XXX corporation: Class A stock, with 1 vote, and Class B stock, with 10 votes. Each share will pay equal dividends and represents an equal fraction of ownership in every other respect. For which will you pay more? Why?

3. Do you think there should be a law to enforce one-share, one-vote and other provisions of the Shareholder Bill of Rights? Or do you think that because no one is forced to buy stock in a company with policies that violate the bill the matter can safely be left to the parties involved?

4. Some critics of takeovers say that raiders do not really improve the management of the firms they acquire—they just make a quick buck at the expense of the firms' long-term profit prospects. If this is true, would you expect the price of a firm's stock to rise or to fall after implementing antitakeover measures like unequal voting rights?

5. Why would incompetent managers be able to persuade their "friends" to buy and hold large blocks of stock in the firms they are mismanaging? Wouldn't this be asking a lot of their friends? Discuss.

Suggestions for Further Reading

Galbraith, John Kenneth. *The New Industrial State.* Boston: Houghton Mifflin, 1967.

In this unorthodox book, Galbraith suggests that the market plays little or no role in coordinating the U.S. economy and that corporations are run not by their stockholders but by something called the technostructure.

Gordon, Scott. "The Close of the Galbraithian System," *Journal of Political Economy* 76 (July/August 1968): 635–644.

A critique of Galbraith's view of the economy and the corporation.

Keating, Barry P., and Maryann O. Keating. *Not for Profit.* Glen Ridge, N.J.: Thomas Horton and Daughters, 1980.

An analysis of the not-for-profit sector of the U.S. economy. Covers government as well as private not-for-profit firms.

Malkiel, Burton G. *A Random Walk Down Wall Street.* New York: Norton, 1975.

A readable and informative introduction to the stock market.

5 The Role of Government: Market Failures, Rent Seeking, and Privatization

After reading this chapter, you will understand . . .

- How large the government sector of the U.S. economy is.
- Why government action is needed to control pollution.
- Why the Army, Navy, and Air Force are not private firms.
- Why the government does not leave the questions of what, how, and for whom entirely to the market.
- Why some government programs seem designed to enrich private firms and individuals rather than promote the goals of efficiency and fairness.
- Which government roles might be better turned over to the private sector.

Before reading this chapter, make sure you know the meaning of . . .

- Opportunity costs (Chapter 1)
- Entrepreneurship (Chapter 2)
- Supply and demand (Chapter 3)
- Price ceilings and supports (Chapter 3)

Jails—Public or Private?

Bay County Jail in Panama City, Florida

PANAMA CITY, FLORIDA. The nation's fledgling private corrections companies have a lot riding on the county jail here.

In October, 1985, the Bay County jail, then faced with two state corrections department lawsuits that included charges of overcrowding, fire safety violations and inadequate medical care and staffing, became the first large maximum-security jail to be turned over to a private company, Corrections Corp. of America. The Nashville, Tennessee, company's managers, most of whom learned the corrections business in the state systems whose bureaucratic clumsiness they now disparage, say they can do a better job when they aren't manacled by government red tape.

In Florida, as in some other states, the county sheriff normally operates the county jail and hires and fires its staff. So when the Bay County Commission decided to take control of the jail away from the sheriff, it immediately became a volatile political issue. County Commissioner Helen Ingram says that for her the issue wasn't politics, but saving money. Construction of a new jail work camp and other renovations blur comparisons, but the bottom line is this: The county was able to budget $700,000 less for the jail under CCA than it estimates it would have if the sheriff were still in control.

CCA is making major renovations to the existing jail building. Extra staff has been added and there is better medical care. The inmates are seeing lots of little amenities, such as new mattresses and sheets and new color television sets in cell pods.

Most of the sheriff's jail staff stayed on to work for CCA and they are taking home bigger paychecks. They have learned to call their charges "residents," and they have traded in their traditional deputy uniforms for brown blazers that sport the CCA logo. Stephen Toth, the jail's former administrator who stayed on to become the jail's security chief under CCA, has adopted the company's businesslike perspective on treatment of inmates. "You want to do the right thing. Lawsuits cost a lot of money."

103

Some prisoner-rights advocates fear companies like CCA will become a forceful lobby for more prisons and harsher sentences to keep the cells full. But so far, the most vocal opposition to privately run prisons has come from public employee unions concerned about losing turf. Bay County employees weren't unionized, but Florida sheriffs almost succeeded in persuading the legislature to completely ban private jails. The legislature did make it harder for counties to turn over their jails to private companies by requiring a four-fifths majority vote of county commissioners to do so. But that may have only helped slow the push. Already, several other Florida counties are talking to private companies.

Source: Ed Bean, "Private Jail in Bay County, Fla., Makes Inroads for Corrections Firms, but the Jury Is Still Out," *The Wall Street Journal*, August 29, 1986, p. 38. Reprinted by permission of *The Wall Street Journal*, © Dow Jones & Company, Inc. 1986. All Rights Reserved. Photo Source: Courtesy of Corrections Corporation of America.

W E are used to the idea of a division of labor between private business and government. It seems natural that cars be made by private firms and jails run by government. But a closer look at things shows that the division of labor is by no means as clear-cut as we might expect. The article that opened Chapter 4 noted that American Motors, before Chrysler's takeover bid, was largely owned by the French government. The story did not note that Lee Iacocca, a vociferous advocate of free enterprise, rescued his own Chrysler Corporation from bankruptcy only with the help of a massive infusion of funds from the U.S. government. Having noted the government's involvement in the automobile industry, we now find that private firms are involved in the running of jails. The division of labor between business and government, it turns out, is not so clear-cut after all.

This chapter gives an overview of the role of government in the U.S. economy. We begin with a general description of government in terms of its size and finances. Next, we look at two theories that have been advanced to explain the scope of government activity. Finally, we examine the issue of *privatization*—the process of moving government functions to the private sector—as exemplified in the case of the Bay County jail.

Government in the U.S. Economy

The government sector of the U.S. economy consists of federal, state, and local units. Of the nearly $1.5 trillion spent by all government levels in 1986, the federal government accounted for just under 70 percent, with state and local governments making up the rest. For purposes of economic analysis, the three levels of government are often combined. Therefore, unless specific reference to government level is being made, we will assume that "government" includes the federal, state, and local levels.

The Growth of Government

Exhibit 5.1 shows how government in the United States has grown since 1955. Two different measures are used to show the size of federal, state, and local governments in relation to the economy as a whole.

Exhibit 5.1   Growth of Government in the United States, 1955–1986

This chart shows the growth of the federal, state, and local governments combined using two measures. In terms of government purchases of goods and services, the government sector stayed roughly steady at 20 percent of GNP over the period. When transfer payments are taken into account, however, the government sector grew from about one-quarter to over one-third of GNP.

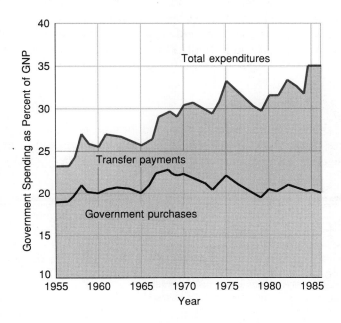

Source: *Economic Report of the President* (Washington, D.C.: Government Printing Office, 1987), Table B-77.

The first measure is **government purchases of goods and services,** or simply **government purchases.** It includes all the goods bought by governments—from submarines to typewriter ribbons—plus the cost of hiring the services of government employees and contractors—from the President to the courthouse janitor. As Exhibit 5.1 shows, purchases by federal, state, and local governments have remained roughly constant at about 20 percent of GNP for over 30 years. **Transfer payments,** on the other hand, have grown a great deal. These include all payments by governments to individuals that are not made in return for current services, for example, social security benefits, unemployment compensation, and welfare. Until 1967, transfer payments by all government levels were about 5 percent of GNP; since then, they have grown to almost 15 percent.

Which is a better measure of government growth—government purchases or total expenditures, including transfers? The answer depends on what we are trying to measure. Government purchases measure the percentage of GNP that is "used up" by government; they represent real resources that are shifted from satisfying private wants to satisfying public wants. According to this measure, government has grown little—if at all—since the mid-1950s. Transfer payments, in contrast, are funds that flow through the government without being used up. Even after they have been collected (through taxation) and paid back out, they are available for the satisfaction of private wants.

Government purchases of goods and services (government purchases)
Purchases of finished goods by government plus the cost of hiring the services of government employees and contractors.

Transfer payments
Payments by government to individuals that are not made in return for goods and services currently supplied.

Nevertheless, total expenditures, including transfers, are in some ways a better measure of government growth than are government purchases alone. The reason is that although transfer payments do not use up resources, the transfer process determines who uses them and how they are used. Total government spending thus measures the share of the economy for which government decision making replaces market decision making. In terms of this measure, government has continued to grow.

However, even though the economic role of government in the United States is expanding, it is still modest by world standards. In Sweden, government expenditures exceed 60 percent of GNP; in Norway and the Netherlands, they are over 50 percent; and in West Germany and the United Kingdom, they exceed 40 percent.

Patterns of Expenditure

Exhibit 5.2 shows what the federal, state, and local governments buy with their expenditures. Part a shows the pattern of federal government expenditures. The biggest category is income security; this includes social security, unemployment

Exhibit 5.2   Government Expenditures by Program

These charts compare federal government expenditures with those of state and local governments by program. Income security, which includes social security, unemployment benefits, public welfare, and so on, is the largest federal item, followed by national defense. Because of high interest rates and extensive federal borrowing, interest on the national debt has grown rapidly. Education is the largest item for state and local governments, followed by public welfare, highways, health and hospitals, and police and fire protection.

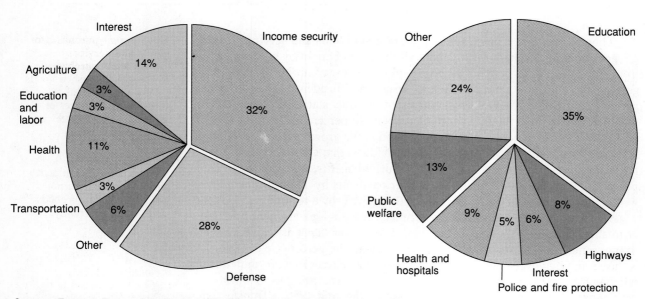

(a) Federal

Interest 14%
Agriculture 3%
Education and labor 3%
Health 11%
Transportation 3%
Other 6%
Defense 28%
Income security 32%

(b) State and Local

Other 24%
Education 35%
Public welfare 13%
Health and hospitals 9%
Police and fire protection 5%
Interest 6%
Highways 8%

Sources: *Economic Report of the President* (Washington, D.C.: Government Printing Office, 1987), Table B-74; U.S. Department of Commerce, *Statistical Abstract of the United States: 1987*, 107th ed. (Washington, D.C.: Government Printing Office, 1987), Table 446.

compensation, public assistance (welfare), and federal employee retirement and disability benefits. Income security has been the largest category of federal expenditures only since 1974. Before then, national defense, now in second place, took a larger share of the budget. As recently as 1968, national defense accounted for 40 percent of federal spending. By 1980, its share had fallen to 20 percent. Under the Reagan administration, it has grown again, to 28 percent.

Although defense outlays have commanded an increasing share of the federal budget under the Reagan administration, they have not been the most rapidly growing category. Because of large federal deficits, interest payments on the national debt grew from 9 to 14 percent of the budget during the 1980 to 1986 period. Still faster-growing categories during this period were health, including medicare (from 6 to 11 percent), and agricultural subsidies (from about 1.5 to more than 3 percent).

Part b of Exhibit 5.2 shows the pattern of state and local government spending. State governments have accounted for about two-fifths of this. By far, the largest item in state and local government budgets has been education, followed by highways, welfare, police and fire protection, and hospitals and health programs.

Financing the Public Sector

The other side of government budgets concerns sources of funds. These are shown in Exhibit 5.3. Part a shows the sources of funds for the federal government for the 1986 budget year. Personal income taxes were the largest source of revenue, closely followed by social security taxes paid by employers and employees. Corporate income taxes, excise taxes, and items such as customs receipts accounted for another 14 percent. The remaining 22 percent was raised by borrowing.

Part b of Exhibit 5.3 gives similar information for state and local governments. For state governments, sales taxes were the largest source of revenue, and property taxes were the largest source for local governments. Personal and corporate income taxes and other sources, such as fees and charges for services, were also significant. The federal government contributed substantially to state and local funds through a variety of programs, including highway and sewage treatment grants, medicaid, income security programs, and general revenue sharing. The data on which the exhibit is based do not reflect the operations of liquor stores, utilities, and pension trust funds of state and local governments. Some state and local units relied on borrowed funds during the period for which data are given, but the state and local government sector as a whole showed a small budget surplus for that period.

The Economic Role of Government: Externalities and Other Market Failures

The preceding section gives some idea of government size and the kinds of programs government undertakes. We now turn to the question of why the government does certain things and not others, that is, to the economic justification of government functions. This section is devoted to a theory according to which the role of government is to compensate for market failures. **Market failures** are instances in which markets fail to meet accepted standards of effi-

Market failure
An instance in which a market fails to meet accepted standards of efficiency or fairness in performing its functions of transmitting information, providing incentives, and distributing income.

Exhibit 5.3   Sources of Government Funds

These charts show the sources of funds for federal, state, and local governments. The personal income tax is the largest federal item, followed by employer and employee social security contributions. In 1986, 22 percent of federal spending was financed by borrowing. Individual and corporate income taxes are less important at the state and local levels. Sales taxes are the largest source of revenue for state governments and property taxes the largest source for local governments. The federal government has provided a large share of state and local funds through revenue sharing and other programs. State and local governments have had a modest budget surplus; thus, borrowing does not appear as a source of funds.

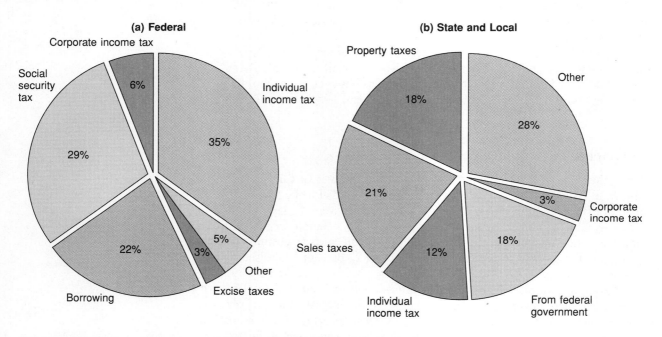

Sources: *Economic Report of the President* (Washington, D.C.: Government Printing Office, 1987), Table B-74; U.S. Department of Commerce, *Statistical Abstract of the United States: 1987*, 107th ed. (Washington, D.C.: Government Printing Office, 1987), Table 446. The data for state and local governments do not reflect the activities of state utilities and liquor stores or those of state and local trust funds and pension funds.

ciency or fairness in performing their functions of transmitting information, providing incentives, and distributing income. The next section looks at a different theory of government known as the theory of *rent seeking*. The final section looks at private-sector alternatives to government action.

Externalities

The first instance of market failure we will examine concerns a failure of the market to perform its function of transmitting information about scarcity in the form of prices. In order for markets to perform their job efficiently, the prices they transmit should reflect the opportunity costs of producing the goods or services in question.

Ordinarily, market prices do reflect at least a reasonable approximation of opportunity costs. As we saw in the discussion of the supply curve in Chapter 3, producers of a good or service normally must receive a price at least equal to opportunity costs or they will employ their factors of production elsewhere. However, situations arise in which producers' actions (and consumers') have effects on *third parties*, that is, people other than the buyer and seller who carry out a transaction. These third-party effects, which are not reflected in prices, are known as **externalities.** When externalities are present, the price system fails to transmit accurate information. Let us consider some examples.

Externality
An effect of producing or consuming a good whose impact on third parties other than buyers and sellers of the good is not reflected in prices.

Pollution

The classic example of an externality is pollution. Suppose that a steel mill burns coal in its blast furnaces. The costs of fuel, capital, and labor come to $100 per ton of steel produced. These are called *internal costs* because they are borne by the steel mill itself. These costs are reflected in market transactions—payments to coal producers, workers, stock- and bondholders, and so on. Internal costs are part of the opportunity cost of making steel because they represent the forgone opportunities of using the same natural resources, capital, and labor in some other industry. In order to stay in business, the mill must receive a price of at least $100 per ton, that is, a price at least equal to the internal opportunity costs.

But the internal costs are not the only costs of making steel. In the process of burning coal, the mill spews out clouds of sulphur dioxide, soot, and other pollutants. The pollution damages health, kills trees, and ruins paint in areas downwind of the plant. These effects are *external* costs of generating electricity because they are borne by third parties—people who are neither buyers nor sellers of steel or any of the inputs used in making it. External costs are also part of the opportunity cost of making steel in that they represent the value of the factors destroyed by the pollution (dead trees, workers in firms other than the steel producer taking sick leave) or required in order to repair its effects (repainting houses, treating pollution-related diseases).

Suppose that pollution damage of all kinds comes to $20 per ton of steel produced. Added to the $100 in internal costs, the $20 of external costs makes the overall opportunity cost of steel $120 per ton. This figure reflects the value of the factors of production used directly by the mill plus those destroyed or diverted from other uses by the pollution.

If the price of steel is set by supply and demand in a competitive market, it will tend toward the level of $100 per ton that just covers internal costs. But this sends a false signal to steel users: It tells them that producing a ton of steel puts a smaller drain on the economy's scarce factors of production than is really the case. Thus, steel users will use more steel than they should. They will be less inclined to find substitutes for steel, recycle steel, design products so as to use less steel, and so on. In short, the market will fail to achieve efficient resource allocation because prices will have sent users the wrong information.

Crowding

Another common type of externality results from crowding of common property. By **common property** economists mean property that is open to use by all members of a community. Ocean fishing grounds, parks, and city streets are examples of common property.

Common property
Property to which all members of a community have open access.

Consider the case of ocean fishing grounds. In order to enter the fishing business, an operator must bear a number of internal costs, including the capital costs of a boat, crew members' pay, the cost of fuel, and so on. These costs are fully reflected in transactions between boat owners and their suppliers. When many boats compete, fish prices are set by supply and demand at a level that reflects these internal costs.

However, when the fishing ground reaches a certain level of crowding, there begin to be external costs as well. When fishing strains the ability of the fish population to reproduce, the total catch of all boats will fall as more boats enter the fleet. With more boats going after fewer fish, the costs per ton of fish and the market price of fish rise.

The effects of crowding are a type of externality in which the third parties on whom the external costs fall are other participants in the activities—in this case, other fishing boats. The measure of the external costs is the amount by which the entry of an additional boat reduces the daily catch of the boats already there and hence raises the cost per ton of fish they catch. Thus, the true opportunity cost of adding one boat to the fleet is greater than the internal costs of capital, wages, fuel, and so on that the new entrant bears. As the fishing grounds become increasingly crowded, consumers must pay an ever higher price for fish in order to insure that each boat will continue to earn enough to cover internal costs.

External Benefits

Pollution and crowding generate external costs, that is, effects that harm third parties. However, some externalities are beneficial. For example, a person who raises bees to produce honey benefits the owners of neighboring orchards by improving pollination. If the price of honey does not reflect the value of the pollination services, the price overstates the opportunity cost of producing honey, resulting in too little honey produced and consumed. This too can be considered a market failure.

The examples of steel, fish, and honey all relate to externalities of production. There are also externalities of consumption, both harmful and beneficial. Exhaust pollution from cars is an example of a harmful externality of consumption; so is a noisy party in a quiet neighborhood. A commuter using a crowded highway generates an externality of consumption in the form of crowding. Raising flowers in one's yard, on the other hand, produces an external benefit for neighbors and passersby.

The Role of Government

Market failures resulting from externalities are widely believed to require corrective action by government. There are many possible kinds of corrective action. Take the case of steel mill pollution. One option is to require the mill to use stack scrubbers and other pollution abatement equipment. Another is to place a tax (in this case, of $20 per ton) on steel so that users will bear the full opportunity cost. Still another is to allow those injured by pollution to seek redress from the mill through federal or state courts. The objective in each case is the same: By imposing the cost of buying pollution control equipment, a tax, or the cost of lawsuits, the external costs will be "internalized," that is, brought to bear on the parties involved in the transaction that is the source of the externality. A closer study of pollution and its remedies is part of the microeconomics course.

In addition to taking action against external harms such as pollution, some see a role for government in cases of external benefits. Beekeepers might be paid a subsidy; property owners might be subject to laws requiring them to keep their property presentable; and so on.

Private Action to Internalize Externalities

Although externalities are often seen as calling for government action, sometimes private alternatives exist. Problems of externalities are closely linked to the nature of property rights (Ronald Coase pointed this out in his article on social costs; see "Who Said It? Who Did It? 4.1," page 88). Contracts among private property owners can sometimes internalize externalities that would otherwise require government action. For example, in many residential developments, private covenants among property owners control both beneficial and harmful externalities associated with property upkeep, subdivision of lots, type of construction, and so on. Beekeepers often contract with fruit growers to bring their hives to the orchard at blossom time. The owners of private amusement parks, private fishing lakes, and so on are able to control crowding through fees that they can raise during periods of peak demand.

Public Goods

A second category of market failure that is widely held to call for government action occurs in the case of *public goods*. In the terminology of economics, **public goods** are goods and services that cannot be provided for one person without being provided for that person's neighbors and that, once provided for one person, can be provided for others at no extra cost.

Perhaps the closest thing to a pure public good is national defense. One person cannot be protected against nuclear attack without the protection being extended to everyone. Also, it costs no more to protect a single resident of an area than to safeguard an entire city or region. Police and fire protection are public goods in part (police and fire departments also provide many individual services). Some people think the space program and even the national parks are public goods too. The idea is that people everywhere get satisfaction from reading or hearing about them even if they themselves do not take a ride in orbit or a hike in the mountains.

It is difficult for private firms to make a profit selling products that, once provided to one customer, become available to others at no additional cost. The reason is that people who do not pay their share of the cost of the good cannot be excluded from enjoying its benefits. To see why the market may fail in such cases, imagine that someone tries to set up a private missile defense system, Star Wars Inc., to be paid for by selling subscriptions to people who want protection from a nuclear attack. If my neighbors subscribed and got their houses protected, I would not need to subscribe myself; instead, knowing that their homes' protection would be my home's as well, I would be tempted to become a "free rider."

However, my neighbors would probably reason the same way. They would not subscribe, hoping that I would; then they could be the free riders. If some of them were willing to pay their fair share, that would not be enough to cover the whole cost. Those few public-spirited people would have to pay far more than

Public good
A good or service that (1) cannot be provided for one person without also being provided for others and (2) once provided for one person can be provided for others at zero added cost.

their fair share to keep the service from going bankrupt. In short, it is unlikely that a private missile defense firm would ever get off the ground.

The free-rider problem, which is always present in the case of public goods, means that government may have to provide those goods if they are to be provided at all (we say "may" because, as "Applying Economic Ideas 5.1" illustrates, some things that have the characteristics of public goods are provided by private firms). However, it should be noted that many goods and services provided at public expense are not public goods in the sense that the term is used in economics. Take education, for example. The primary beneficiaries of public education are students. It is not impossible to exclude students from the schools. Only a few schools, public or private, operate on an "open admission" basis. Others select their students according to neighborhood, or ability to pay, or scholastic achievement. Nor can students be added to the schools at no expense. The more students a school has, the more teachers, classrooms, laboratories, and so on it needs. Thus, education does not fit the definition of a public good. It may, however, have certain external benefits in the form of promoting good citizenship. As we saw in the preceding section, such external benefits would—in some people's eyes, at least—justify a government role in education whether or not it is a true public good.

Insufficient Competition

Still another source of market failure that many economists think justifies government action is insufficient competition. As we have seen, market prices should reflect opportunity costs if they are to guide resource allocation efficiently. In the case of harmful externalities, market failure occurs because prices fall below opportunity costs. Where competition is insufficient, however, market failure can occur because prices are too *high*.

As an extreme case, consider a market in which there is only a single seller of a good or service—that is, a *monopoly*. Public utilities such as residential electric and telephone service are a frequently cited example. Suppose, for instance, that Metropolitan Electric can generate power at an opportunity cost of $.10 per kilowatt hour. Selling power to customers at that price would guide them in making efficient choices between electricity and other energy sources, such as oil or coal, and in undertaking energy-saving investments, such as home insulation and high-efficiency lighting.

If homeowners could buy electricity from anyone they wanted, as they can eggs or gasoline, the forces of competition, acting through supply and demand, would push the market price toward the level of opportunity costs. The utility would not sell power for less than the opportunity costs because doing so would put it out of business (we assume that appropriate government policies would internalize any externalities of pollution). Further, in a competitive market, any one seller that tried to raise prices much above the opportunity costs would be undercut by others seeking to take its customers away.

However, utilities do not compete in sales to residential customers. Every home, after all, is connected to only one set of power lines. In this case a utility, left to its own devices, could substantially increase its profits by charging a price higher than the opportunity costs. Of course, raising the price would mean that less power would be sold as customers moved up and to the left along their demand curves. But up to a point, the greater profit per kilowatt hour sold

APPLYING ECONOMIC IDEAS 5.1

Private Marketing and the Public Goods Problem: The Case of Computer Software

To a substantial degree, computer software has the properties of a public good. Once a game program, word processing system, or spreadsheet system has been provided for one user, others are likely to make copies for their own use. Further, the cost of copying many kinds of software is near zero. Yet despite these traits, the writing and selling of computer software is a multi-million-dollar private business. How do firms do it?

One technique is to "copy protect" software before it is sold. A program that cannot be copied no longer resembles a public good. Lotus Development Corporation, creator of the popular *1-2-3* spreadsheet program for personal computers, uses this strategy. However, copy protection has its drawbacks. For one thing, the codes used to protect the software can be broken and the means for doing so spread quickly along the computer user grapevine. Also, copy-protected software is somewhat less convenient to use, a fact that gives competitors an advantage.

For these reasons, other major software suppliers sell their programs in a form that can be easily copied. Buyers are required as part of their purchase contract to pledge that they will not copy the program except to make extra copies for their own convenience. However, there is no barrier to copying by dishonest users. Ashton-Tate, which sells the *MultiMate* word processing program, is an example of a firm that permits copying only by contract. The fact that thousands of users pay several hundred dollars for the firm's programs rather than using pirated copies attests to the fact that most are honest.

A third approach to the free-rider problem relies even more directly on user honesty: the Freeware™ approach developed by Headlands Press of Tiburon, California. This firm does not sell its popular program *PC-Talk* through computer stores or other retail channels. Instead, a message encoded in the program invites new users to make copies of the program and distribute them to their friends in return for a modest contribution to Headlands Press. This unusual business strategy has earned tens of thousands of dollars (he won't say exactly how much) for computer author Andrew Fluegelman, Freeware's inventor. This example shows that despite the marketing challenges it creates, the free-rider problem is not an absolute barrier to the private marketing of products with the properties of a public good.

would more than outweigh the effect on overall profit of the reduction in quantity demanded. (The microeconomics course explores the profit-maximizing calculus of the monopolist in detail.)

If too high a price is charged, homeowners will get a false message regarding the opportunity cost of electricity. They may make substitutions that are not economically justified. For example, they may switch from electricity to oil for heat even in regions where cheap hydroelectric power is available or from electric air conditioning to gas air conditioning even in areas where the opportunity cost of electricity is below that of gas.

Many economists think that market failures due to insufficient competition are not limited to the extreme case of monopoly. As the microeconomics course explains, they think that competition among a small number of firms may also lead to higher prices, especially if the firms collude with one another to keep prices high.

Several kinds of government actions aim to prevent market failures due to insufficient competition. In some cases, the government may assume ownership of monopoly public utilities, as does the Tennessee Valley Authority. In others, the utilities remain in private hands but are subject to price regulation. In other markets, *antitrust policy* is used to insure a reasonable number of competing firms in each market. For example, although the government normally permits mergers between nondominant firms such as Chrysler and American Motors, it would oppose a merger of Ford and General Motors. Even given competition from imports, it would be feared that there would be insufficient competition in the auto industry following a merger of two such dominant firms. Antitrust laws and monopoly regulation are covered in greater detail in the microeconomics course.

Income Distribution

In the cases of externalities, public goods, and insufficient competition, the market fails in that it does not achieve an efficient resource allocation. In terms of the economic questions of Chapter 2, mistakes are made with respect to *which* outputs are produced and *how* they are produced. In addition, many observers feel, the market may fail to achieve a fair distribution of income; in other words, its answer to the question of *for whom* goods are to be produced is unacceptable.

As pointed out in Chapter 1, opinions differ as to what constitutes a fair distribution of income. Some ideally would like to do away with almost all inequality of income. Others would be satisfied with a system that guaranteed an adequate minimum income. Still others think that there are certain **merit goods,** such as education and health care, that should be distributed more or less equally, whereas other goods and services, such as cosmetics or airline travel, matter less. These are all variations of the egalitarian view of fairness. As Chapter 1 also pointed out, some people take a libertarian point of view, under which they see fairness as applying mainly to freedom and equality of opportunity rather than to a particular income distribution.

Those who believe the market fails to achieve a fair distribution of income favor a variety of government remedies. Transfer payments, from social security to food stamps, are one type of cure. Free or below-cost provision of merit goods, such as education, is another. Programs intended to raise the earnings of low-income workers, including the federal minimum wage, are still another possibility. These programs also are given more detailed treatment in the microeconomics course.

Merit good
A good to which all citizens are entitled regardless of ability to pay.

The Macroeconomic Role of Government

All of the market failures mentioned so far are microeconomic in nature. However, many economists see yet another role for government in correcting macroeconomic failures of the market economy. In their view, a capitalist economy is inherently unstable, subject to cycles of inflation alternating with periods of high unemployment and slow or negative economic growth.

The macroeconomics course looks at the policy tools that the government has available for promoting macroeconomic stability. These include federal tax and expenditure policies and policies related to control of money, interest rates, and financial markets. The macroeconomics course also examines the views of economists who think that the private economy is not so unstable after all. In their eyes, much of the inflation and unemployment experienced in the past was caused by policy mistakes on the part of officials who might better have taken a hands-off approach.

The Rent-Seeking Theory of the Government's Economic Role

The market failure theory of the role of government is largely a *normative* theory. As such, it attempts to define the role that government ought to play in the economy: The government should promote efficient allocation of resources; insure a fair distribution of income; and do all it can to stabilize the macroeconomy.

But when we look at what government actually does rather than what it ought to do, we find many programs that poorly fit the categories of market failure. In fact, some programs seem designed to promote inefficiency and inequality in markets that would function reasonably well without government intervention. Consider, for example, price supports for farm products. As we saw in Chapter 3, these hold farm prices above equilibrium levels, thus causing huge surpluses. This is hardly efficient. Further, although some benefits go to farmers in financial difficulty, thus serving the goal of fairness, most of the subsidies, as "Economics in the News 5.1" points out, go to farmers who are financially well off.

It appears, then, that at least some government programs cannot be adequately explained in terms of the market failure theory of government. Gordon Tullock of George Mason University and others have advanced a theory of *rent seeking* as an alternative.[1]

The Nature of Economic Rents

In everyday language, a *rent* simply means a payment made for the use of something, say, an apartment or a car. Economists use the term in a more specialized sense, however. An **economic rent** is any payment to a factor of production in excess of its opportunity costs. The opportunity cost of supplying a factor of production, in this case, means its value in its best alternative use. The concept is broad and can apply to any factor of production. For example:

Economic rent
Any payment to a factor of production in excess of its opportunity costs.

- Ralph Singer owns two fields, one flat and one hilly, on which he grows hay worth $50 a year net of growing costs. The opportunity cost of the fields (that is, the payment needed to bid them away from hay growing) is $50 a year. A youth club agrees to pay $100 per year to rent the flat field for playing baseball. Of the $100 received for the flat field, $50 covers its opportunity cost and the remaining $50 is economic rent.

- Billingham Pharmaceuticals Inc. holds a patent on a lotion claimed to cure baldness. The lotion costs only $1 a jar to produce, but since it has no competition, it can be sold for $8 per jar. Of the $8, $7 can be considered economic rent.

- Joe Zmud is an autoworker with 20 years' seniority. Ford Motor Company pays him $20 an hour. Given his age and specialized skills, the best alternative job he could get would probably pay only half his cur-

---

[1]For a representative collection of papers on the theory of rent seeking, see James M. Buchanan, Robert D. Tollison, and Gordon Tullock, eds., *Toward a Theory of the Rent-Seeking Society* (College Station, Tex.: Texas A&M Press, 1980).

ECONOMICS IN THE NEWS   5.1

Farm Subsidies Often Benefit the Strong

In Hollywood and Washington, there is a sharp image of the American farm problem: a family enterprise, passed down from one hard-working generation to the next, now threatened by low prices but ready to rise strong and healthy once more if only given a helping hand. However, the reality is more complex. Certainly there are many farms that fit the classic family-farm description. But of the $26 billion a year that the federal government spends on farm subsidies (as of 1986), much of it misses farmers in need and ends up in other pockets. Items from the news:

- To evade a $50,000-per-farmer cap on government payments, a California rice farm was leased to 56 tenants, each of whom qualified for the top payment and then split the $1.5 million income with the landlord. At least eight of the tenants were related to the owner.

- To benefit corn growers by increasing the demand for their crop, the government subsidizes the production of gasohol, a blend of ethanol distilled from corn and gasoline. In 1986, $29,230,000 was paid to Archer Daniels Midland, a huge, Illinois-based agribusiness that reported record profits that year. This sum represented 54 percent of total government payments under the program, which critics have christened "corporate food stamps."

- Mohammed Aslam Khan grows rice in Butte City, California. He is a U.S. citizen, but four relatives, passive investors in the farm, are not—they live in Faisalabad, Pakistan. Uncle Sam paid the four $152,010 for Khan's 1984 crop.

- In Vincennes, Indiana, Dennis Carnahan's family has pushed corn production costs so low that they could probably turn a profit if the farm program were abolished. But the 33-year-old farmer figures that the program is "the best ball game in town." The Carnahans expect to collect $81,180 from the government for the corn grown on their 3,800-acre farm this year.

The *Des Moines Register* is considered the most influential newspaper in the farm belt. What does it think of the government's programs? "American farm policy is a colossal hoax. It is a hoax on the countryside as well as on urban taxpayers," says the *Register*. Noting that less than one dollar in three spent on farm subsidies goes to a farmer in need, it suggests limiting payments to a safety net for small and medium-size farms. Under current policy, "Never before have Americans spent so many tax dollars on agriculture, and never have the results been more destructive to the kind of rural life that Americans profess to want."

Sources: Ward Sinclair, "Loophole Allows Extra Farm Subsidies," *Washington Post*, January 20, 1987, A3; Michael Isikoff, "Ethanol Producer Reaps 54 Percent of U.S. Subsidy," *Washington Post*, January 29, 1987, A14; Wendy L. Wall and Charles F. McCoy, "New Farm Law Raises Federal Costs and Fails to Solve Big Problems," *The Wall Street Journal*, June 17, 1986, 1; "Sacred Farmers," *The Wall Street Journal*, March 5, 1987, 28. The quotations from the *Des Moines Register* are as given in "Sacred Farmers."

rent wage. Thus, he can be considered as earning $10 per hour in economic rent.

As the above examples show, rents are very nice for those who receive them. However, they are not always easy to come by. Ralph Singer was just lucky to have inherited one of the few flat fields in his hilly county. Billingham had to spend millions on research and thousands more on patent lawyers to secure its position as the sole maker of baldness lotion. Zmud and his predecessors at Ford staged many bitter strikes before attaining the current wage scale.

Moreover, rents not only are hard to come by but are under constant threat in the form of competition. Someone else might lease a baseball field more cheaply. A competitor might come up with a different baldness formula and undercut Billingham's price. Buyer preference for Toyotas and Yugos might force Zmud to seek work selling shoes.

In short, a rent is something that must be first won and then defended. The process of obtaining and defending rents is known as **rent seeking.**

Rent seeking
The activity of obtaining and defending rents.

The Process of Rent Seeking

One way to seek and defend rents is through entrepreneurship. As competition forces prices toward opportunity costs, rents are eroded. They can be reestablished by exploring new opportunities, finding new ways of doing things, and inventing means of satisfying consumer wants. Rents earned by entrepreneurs as the reward for creating new value are commonly called *profits.* But business firms are not the only ones who earn rents as a reward for entrepreneurship. In labor markets, the first workers to move into a fast-growing region or a new specialty often earn rents in the form of higher wages than they could obtain in older, more crowded labor markets. These entrepreneurial types of profit seeking and rent seeking are an essential part of the market process in a capitalist economy.

However, instead of taking the entrepreneurial route, firms, workers, and resource owners may turn to government in their search for rents. A rent earned through a government program that raises prices or cuts costs is just as good, dollar for dollar, as a rent that is won in the marketplace. In some cases it may even be better, because government can not only create rents but shield them from erosion by competition.

Agricultural price supports are an example of rents obtained through government action. As "Economics in the News 5.1" points out, the bulk of farm subsidies go to farmers who are not in trouble. This reflects the fact that whether the price is set by the market or by the government, most farmers will receive enough to cover their opportunity costs. Those with better than average land or managerial skills will receive rents even at the market price, although the rent will be even higher if the government sets a price above the market price. In a period when production costs are rising or demand for the product is falling, some farmers with average or below-average land and skills will be unable to cover their costs and will be in financial difficulty, but this will not happen to all farmers at once.

According to the rent-seeking model of government, the reason farm programs are not more narrowly targeted is that broad-ranging programs that generate rents for all farmers will draw much wider political support. Without the political support of the relatively prosperous farmers who draw the bulk of the subsidies, say the rent-seeking theorists, programs for troubled farmers would not get the votes they need in Congress. This line of reasoning is discussed in detail in the microeconomics course under the heading of *public choice theory.*

Subsidies are one important tactic of rent seeking, but not the only one. Restrictions on competition are another way of generating rents. We have seen that competition from other producers—especially from those who can produce at lower costs—tends to erode rents in a free market. Such rents can be protected by laws that restrict competition.

Restrictions on imports are a leading example. Tariffs and import quotas on clothing, cars, sugar, steel, and other products shield domestic firms and their employees from competition. The firms are thus able to earn rents in the form of higher profits and the employees to earn rents in the form of higher wages.

From the standpoint of the rent-seeking theory of government, a policy such as import quotas on automobiles is perfectly understandable in view of the political power of the firms and their unions. However, it is more difficult to reconcile with the market failure theory. It clearly does not promote efficiency, since it interferes with specialization according to comparative advantage. Also, it is questionable whether it promotes equity in view of the fact that automakers' stockholders and unionized employees have higher average incomes than the typical auto buyer.

Examples of government restrictions on competition can be found within the domestic economy as well. Banking regulations prohibit commercial banks from competing with investment banks in the securities business. Licensing fees and examinations restrict the number of competitors who can enter such professions as law and medicine and often even such occupations as manicuring and hair styling. The article that leads off this chapter notes that public employee unions in Florida tried, with partial success, to get the state legislature to block competition from private prisons. Also, recently tightened immigration control has generated rents for some U.S. citizens by reducing the supply of competing immigrant workers.

Ironically, even successful rent seekers do not always come out ahead. A major reason is that the activity of seeking rents is itself costly. Firms sometimes spend millions on lawyers, lobbyists, and public relations firms in the hope of winning an arms contract, television license, or offshore drilling site. Expenditures on rent seeking are sometimes seen as a major waste of resources.

Rent Seeking and the Concept of Government Failure

Much work on the theory of market failure aims to identify cases in which government action could, if properly carried out, enhance efficiency or fairness. However, it is important to realize that government programs themselves may fail to work efficiently. Rent seeking is one major reason.

For examples, we can run right down the list of programs designed to correct market failures. Let's start with national defense. Defense is a public good and might well be inadequately supplied by private firms. But the defense budget is also a major source of rents for defense contractors, communities hosting military bases, and so on. Each year the U.S. defense department itself publishes a "Pentagon pork" list of billions of dollars' worth of unwanted bases that it is forced to keep open and ineffective weapons that it is made to buy because they generate rents in the home district of some powerful member of Congress.

Next, consider pollution control. Government regulations often frustrate private firms' efforts to reduce pollution at the lowest cost. For example, regulators have forced some utilities to use "stack scubbers" to clean the sulphur dioxide from coal smoke rather than the cheaper method of burning low-sulphur Western coal to begin with. The reason: rent seeking by politically powerful producers of high-sulphur Eastern coal.

Regulation of monopolies may also fall victim to rent seeking. In some cases, regulated firms manage to "capture" regulatory agencies. The agencies then end up protecting the rents of producers rather than insuring low prices and efficient service for consumers. The relationship between the Interstate Commerce Commission and the trucking industry prior to the regulatory reforms of the early 1980s is a case in point.

Even programs designed to redistribute income to the poor are distorted by rent-seeking behavior. For instance, in the 1970s and early 1980s a program designed to encourage construction of low-cost housing became a multi-billion-dollar tax shelter for wealthy doctors, lawyers, and stockbrokers.

The point of these examples is not that government always makes a mess of things or that the market always functions perfectly; rather, they demonstrate that both the market and government are imperfect institutions. In deciding whether to transfer a function to government from the market, the possibilities of government failure must be weighed against those of market failure. As the next section reveals, these types of comparisons often lead to the conclusion that some functions of government should be moved to the private sector.

Privatization

Privatization means the turning over of government functions to the private sector. In part, privatization is the opposite of nationalization. *Nationalization,* once popular in many countries, means the transfer of private firms in communications, transportation, heavy industry, and finance to government ownership. Under privatization, such firms are now being returned to private ownership in many countries. Privatization can also mean contracting with private firms to provide services for which the government continues to pay. The private jail in Bay County, Florida, described at the beginning of this chapter is an example of this alternative form of privatization.

Privatization
The turning over of government functions to the private sector.

Privatization in Action

Privatization is a worldwide phenomenon. As the following examples indicate, privatization is underway in advanced industrial nations, the Third World, and even the Soviet Union and other socialist countries. In the United States, steps toward privatization have been taken at all government levels.

The United Kingdom under Prime Minister Margaret Thatcher is, in many respects, the world leader in privatization. Major state-owned industries sold to the public include British Telecom (the telephone company), British Airways, and, biggest of all, the $7.9 billion British Gas. France is not far behind, having recently sold the large glassmaker Saint-Gobain and Paribas, a major bank. In the British and French styles of privatization, shares are sold to individual investors; for example, 1.5 million French investors bought shares in Saint-Gobain and 4.5 million Britons bought shares in British Gas. By widely distributing shares, the governments hope to maximize political support for the programs. Industrial countries outside Europe are also privatizing. Japan, like the United Kingdom, has sold its national telephone company and is planning to sell its railway system and airline. Israel and Canada have also taken privatization steps.

Privatization is not limited to the advanced industrial countries. State-owned telephone and telegraph companies are being sold in Bangladesh, Mexico, Thailand, South Korea, Malaysia, and Sri Lanka; state-owned airlines in Thailand, Singapore, Bangladesh, Malaysia, and South Korea; state-owned banks in Chile, South Korea, Bangladesh, the Philippines, and Taiwan; and sugar refineries in Jamaica and Uganda.[2]

---

[2]Peter Young, "Privatization around the Globe: Lessons for the Reagan Administration," *Policy Report No. 120* (Dallas: National Center for Policy Analysis, January 1986).

Privatization is even underway in some socialist countries, with farming and service industries the main focus. China under Deng Xiaoping has privatized much of its vast farm sector. Private restaurants and retail shops are now common. State-owned housing has been sold to tenants in China, as is also being done in Cuba. In Eastern Europe, Hungary sports the only private hotel in the Soviet Bloc. The Soviet Union under Gorbachev has been cautious, but some small-scale private service businesses, such as automobile and shoe repair, have been permitted.

In the United States, state and local governments have moved ahead of the federal government. In Farmington, New Mexico, a private firm runs the airport control tower. Chandler, Arizona, buys sewage treatment services from a private firm. In Virginia, a private firm wants to build a 10-mile toll road through rapidly growing Louden County, and another wants to build a rapid transit system to link Dulles Airport to the Washington, D.C., subway system. And, of course, there is that private jail in Florida.

At the federal level—despite some pro-privatization claims by the Reagan administration—there have been few major actions. This is partly because the U.S. government has never become as involved in ownership of transportation, communications, and heavy industry as have the governments of European countries. The one major privatization step taken was the sale of Conrail, the dominant railroad in the Northeast. After an aborted plan to sell Conrail to Norfolk Southern, the government sold shares to the public following the British and French models.

Perceived Benefits of Privatization

The perceived benefits of privatization vary among countries and industries. However, there are some common elements.

Political and Ideological Motives

In some cases, political and ideological motives are behind privatization. For example, the conservative governments of Britain and France hope that the millions of shareholders in newly privatized industries will feel they have a stake in the capitalist system and thus vote conservative in future elections. One of the most effective moves reportedly has been the sale of hundreds of thousands of British public housing units to current tenants.

Improved Administration

A more widespread motivation for privatization is the hope of improved administration. Government bureaucracies are not designed for the creativity and quick reactions needed for managing a modern business. The hallmarks of bureaucracy are caution, job security, and decisions by the book. There is no "bottom line" to spur government managers to better performance.

Cost Savings through Competition

With large-scale European-type privatization, it is hoped that cost savings will be realized once subsidies are cut off and firms are exposed to competition in the international marketplace. In the kind of privatization practiced by state and local governments in the United States, the savings come through competitive bidding for contracts to collect garbage, repair transit equipment, and so on. As the article that opens this chapter notes, Bay County, Florida, turned to a private prison operator largely because this would save $700,000 a year.

Suppression of Rent Seeking

As we have seen, one of the reasons many government undertakings are inefficient is that they become the focus of rent seeking. For example, in cities whose sanitation and transit workers are public employees, wage scales have been pushed far above private-sector levels and restrictive work rules have sharply cut productivity in contrast to private contractors. Both employees and managers of government programs may practice a form of rent seeking in which power, prestige, and salary are enhanced by maximizing the number of people who work in an agency rather than by minimizing costs.

Improved Service Quality

Private firms often are able not only to supply services at lower costs than government agencies but to improve service quality as well. Anyone who has compared the process of getting a driver's license with that of getting a haircut knows the difference. In the Soviet Union and Eastern Europe, better service quality is seen as the most important benefit of privatization.

Potential Limitations of Privatization

Despite privatization's current popularity, it is unlikely that government participation will disappear. Privatization has inherent limitations. Some of these stem from the notion of market failure discussed earlier in the chapter. There is no practical way to supply some public goods at a profit. In these cases, the government may contract with private operators to provide services but continue to foot the bill.

Even where public goods are not involved, there is the problem that some government enterprises are too unprofitable to attract private buyers. The French automaker Renault is an example, at least for the time being. In the United States, the government rail passenger system Amtrak provides a case in point. Conrail could be sold because as an all-freight operation, it can be run at a profit. Amtrak, on the other hand, shows little promise of doing the same.

Finally, rent seeking can become a problem even when government is involved as a buyer of privately supplied services. The opening article to this chapter mentions the fear that private jailers will campaign for harsh prison sentences in order to keep their cells full. This is a small-scale variant of the notorious rent-seeking activities of the private arms makers who comprise the so-called military industrial complex in the United States.

In the final analysis, then, drawing the line between government and private sectors of the economy will always be a matter of balancing the imperfections of one set of institutions against those of the other.

Summary

1. **How large is the government sector of the U.S. economy?** The government sector of the U.S. economy consists of federal, state, and local units. The federal government accounts for about 70 percent of total government expenditures and state and local governments for the remainder. *Government purchases*

of goods and services at federal, state, and local levels combined equal about 20 percent of GNP. When *transfer payments* are added, total government expenditures rise to over one-third of GNP.

2. **Why is government action needed for controlling pollution?** According to one theory, the role of government is to compensate for *market failures. Externalities*—the effects of an economic activity on third parties—are one important source of market failure. Pollution is a case in point. If producers do not have to limit pollution or pay for the damages it causes, the price system will transmit distorted information about opportunity costs and efficiency will suffer. Crowding of *common property* is another example of an externality.

3. **Why are the Army, Navy, and Air Force not private firms?** National defense is an example of a *public good*— a good or service that cannot be provided to one person without being provided to that person's neighbors and that once provided to one person can be provided to others at no extra cost. Public goods often cannot be sold at a profit by private firms because "free riders" who use the goods but do not help pay for them cannot be excluded from enjoying their benefits. Providing public goods is thus seen as a government role.

4. **Why does the government not leave the questions of what, how, and for whom entirely to the market?** Market failures associated with externalities, public goods, and insufficient competition result in inefficient allocation of resources. These market failures represent defects in the market's method of handling the questions of what and how. Many government programs are designed to compensate for such market failures and, in so doing, improve efficiency. In addition, many people think that the market distributes income unfairly, that is, offers an unacceptable answer to the question of for whom goods and services will be produced. Transfer payments are designed to address this problem. Finally, the government also attempts to control inflation, unemployment, and economic growth, although not always successfully.

5. **Why do some government programs seem designed to enrich private firms and individuals rather than to promote the goals of efficiency and fairness?** Some government policies, such as farm price supports and import restrictions, rate poorly in terms of efficiency and fairness. Some economists think that such programs can be explained as the result of *rent seeking* by private firms and individuals. An *economic rent* is any payment to a factor of production in excess of its opportunity costs.

6. **Which of the roles of government might be better turned over to the private sector?** In the 1980s, there has been a global movement toward *privatization*, meaning the turning over of government functions to the private sector. One type of privatization is the sale of government-owned business firms to private owners; examples are the sale of British Gas, the Japanese telephone system, and the U.S. railroad Conrail. Another form of privatization involves contracts with private firms to provide services for which the government continues to pay; examples include the operations of jails, airports, garbage collection, and transit services.

Terms for Review

-   government purchases of goods and services (government purchases)
-   transfer payments
-   market failure
-   externality
-   common property
-   public good
-   merit good
-   economic rent
-   rent seeking
-   privatization

Questions for Review

1. As a measure of the size of government, what is revealed by the share of government purchases in GNP? By the share of government expenditures, including transfer payments?

2. What is an externality? Give five examples of externalities other than those mentioned in the chapter, including at least one beneficial externality.

3. Is police protection a public good? If so, in whole or in part? Consider police actions aimed at (a) reducing the level of street crime and (b) releasing the kidnapped child of a rich industrialist.

4. Why may the prices charged by a monopolist fail to reflect the opportunity costs of the good or service produced?

5. Give three examples, other than those mentioned in the chapter, of government programs that you think reflect rent seeking.

Problems and Topics for Discussion

1. **Examining the lead-off case.** Why do you think jails are usually run by the government? Is this govern-

ment activity better explained by the market failure approach or the rent-seeking approach—or do both theories fit the case of jails to some degree?

2. **Growth of government.** Using the latest *Economic Report of the President* or other source, update the information given in Exhibit 5.1. Has government grown more rapidly or more slowly than GNP over the past year?

3. **Externalities of traffic congestion.** Some cities are testing a new technology to reduce traffic congestion in downtown areas. A special device called a "transponder" is attached to the license plate of every car registered in the area. When a transponder-equipped car drives over wires embedded in the pavement along certain busy streets and highways, a computer records the license number. At the end of the month, the car's owner receives a bill reflecting how often he or she used the busy streets. The charge is higher if the car passed the detector during rush hour. How would this technology "internalize" externalities of traffic congestion? Do you think it would improve efficiency? Would it be a fair way to pay for street repair, police patrol, and so on? If the technology proved successful, would it become possible to privatize city streets by selling or leasing them to private firms that would regulate traffic, make repairs, and collect fees? Discuss.

4. **Economics of education.** A variety of arguments have been advanced in support of public funding for primary and secondary education. Some claim that education is a public good. Others say that education has beneficial externalities. Still others say that education is a merit good. What do you think? Do you believe that the same arguments apply to college education?

5. **Superstar rents.** Luciano Pavarotti reputedly is a very accomplished chef as well as one of the world's greatest opera tenors. Suppose that by running a restaurant he earns, say, $100,000 per year as opposed to $1 mil-

lion during a season of singing operas and recitals. What part of his earnings as a singer is economic rent? Do you think Pavarotti's rent is threatened by competition? Can the high earnings of superstars in other areas be explained in terms of the concept of rent? Discuss.

6. **Rent controls as a form of rent seeking.** Review the discussion of rent controls in Chapter 3. Of the monthly rental payments received by landlords for apartments, which portion represents economic rent? Is the answer the same in a long-run context as in a short-run context? We saw that some tenants benefit from rent control, especially those who live in rent-controlled apartments for an extended period. In what sense, if any, are the gains of such tenants analogous to economic rents? Should political support of rent control by tenant groups be considered a form of rent seeking?

7. **Private versus public universities.** In the field of higher education, private colleges and universities compete with government-run institutions. Write a short essay either in favor of or in opposition to privatization of public universities. First, consider the possibility that private firms are hired to run the schools but ownership remains in government hands and tuition is kept at the current level. Second, consider the possibility that universities will be sold outright to private operators who will cover all costs through tuition or alumni contributions. Would you feel differently about privatization of state universities if the private organizations that took them over from government were not-for-profit firms rather than profit-seeking corporations? If you attend a public college or university, are any university services privatized or are all the service providers employees of the school? What about cafeteria services? Custodial services? Security services? If none of these are privatized at your school, do you think they should be?

Case for Discussion

Backdoor Spending

You might think that, with huge federal budget deficits, Congress would be stymied. The deficits clearly make big new spending programs or tax cuts more difficult. How, then, can members of Congress do something for their constituents? Don't worry. The solution is to create new government benefits and make someone else pay for them.

Politically, the logic is powerful. A shrewdly designed program focuses benefits on a selected constituency while spreading costs across a large population

Since 1986, the Democrats do most of the "backdoor spending."

that won't realize it's paying. The economic logic is less compelling. At best, these programs simply redistribute society's wealth from A to B. At worst, they create pressures that make noninflationary economic growth more difficult. Everyone loses.

Although the political charms of backdoor spending appeal to both Republicans and Democrats, the Democrats—having regained control of Congress in 1986—are mainly responsible for its new-found importance. It allows them to create a legislative agenda without busting the budget. Consider:

- Sen. Edward Kennedy (D-Massachusetts) wants to raise the minimum wage $1 an hour or more over the current $3.35, with the increase spread over three or four years. Automatic annual changes would then keep the minimum at 50 percent of average hourly earnings.

- Sen. Tom Harkin (D-Iowa) and Rep. Richard A. Gephart (D-Missouri) would improve farmers' incomes by having the government restrict the size of crop plantings. Higher food prices would then raise farmers' profits.

- Many southern members of Congress—Republicans as well as Democrats—propose tighter import restrictions on textiles and apparel. Other industries will also probably seek relief.

- Rep. Patricia Shroeder (D-Colorado) and Sen. Christopher Dodd (D-Connecticut) would require most businesses to give parents four and a half months of unpaid leave on the birth of a child. The bill also requires unpaid leave for workers to care for sick children or family members.

Source: Robert J. Samuelson, "Backdoor Spending," *The Washington Post*, February 25, 1987, F1. Reprinted with permission.

Questions

1. Discuss each of the programs mentioned. Is the program justified as a government action for correcting market failure? If so, what kind of a failure? Or is the program better understood as an example of rent seeking? Could a program possibly fit both theories of the role of government?

2. Compare the Harkin-Gephart plan of crop restrictions with the support price program for milk discussed in Chapter 3. What are the similarities? What are the differences? Who would benefit from the crop restriction program—just farmers in need or all farmers? If plantings were to be restricted, would you favor an equal cutback in production by all farmers or giving proportionately larger allotments to the most efficient farmers or those farmers in greatest financial need? Discuss the pros and cons of each choice.

Suggestions for Further Reading

Buchanan, James M., Robert D. Tollison, and Gordon Tullock, eds. *Toward a Theory of the Rent-Seeking Society*. College Station, Tex.: Texas A&M Press, 1980.

A collection of papers by several authors applying the theory of rent seeking in various areas.

Coase, Ronald. "The Problem of Social Cost," *Journal of Law and Economics* 3 (1960).

A classic discussion of the problem of externalities and their relationship to property rights.

Goodman, John C. *Privatization*. Dallas: National Center for Policy Analysis, 1985.

A collection of papers on privatization, including several on the British experience. Includes an appendix on privatization at the state and local levels in the United States.

Hyman, David N. *Public Finance*, 2d ed. Hinsdale, Ill.: The Dryden Press, 1987.

Public finance is the name of the economics field devoted to the role of government. This is a comprehensive textbook on the subject.

Introduction to Microeconomics

Part Two

6 Applying Supply and Demand

After reading this chapter, you will understand . . .

- How the responsiveness of quantity demanded to a price change can be expressed in terms of the notion of *elasticity*.

- How the notion of elasticity can be applied to situations other than the responsiveness of quantity demanded to a price change.

- What determines the distribution of the economic burden of a tax.

- In what way the notion of elasticity is useful for understanding the problems of the farm sector.

Before reading this chapter, make sure you know the meaning of . . .

- Supply and demand (Chapter 3)
- Substitutes and complements (Chapter 3)
- Normal and inferior goods (Chapter 3)

A Novel Sales Ploy: Cut Prices

General Motors Corp. has come up with a plan that might keep its 10-year-old Chevrolet Chevette alive a bit longer.

The plan is simple: cut the price.

To producers of things other than cars, that might seem a fairly obvious tack. But in the auto industry, it is novel, even outlandish.

Chrysler Corp. tried it last spring with its Omni/Horizon models, eight-year-old subcompacts that compete with Chevette. And it worked.

Chevette price cuts increase the quantity demanded.

Chrysler knocked $710 off the base price of the Omni/Horizon, added some equipment and the "America" name to the car line, and offered the package for $5,499. The result has been a 26.2 percent increase in sales of cars that were on Chrysler's scrap list. The company sold 165,300 Omni/Horizon models in the first nine months of this year, compared with 130,968 in the same period last year.

GM seems to be taking the same approach with the pricing of its Chevettes for the coming year, auto industry analysts say. GM has trimmed nearly $800 from the price of these rear-wheel-drive, four-cylinder autos, and has made standard some formerly optional equipment. The base price is $4,995.

Still, the days of the oft-maligned, oft-praised Chevette are numbered, GM officials say.

"The car is continuing to sell fairly well, particularly in fleet sales," said Ralph Kramer, Chevrolet's director of public relations. Fleet buyers accounted for about 65 percent of the 75,761 Chevettes sold last year, industry analysts say.

If Chevette sales miss the 100,000-mark in the coming year, it is likely that GM will proceed with plans to discontinue production of that model next spring, he said.

"We tend to think in modules of 100,000 units to justify gearing up a plant for production," Kramer said. "We obviously are well below that capacity with the Chevette."

Source: Warren Brown, "Chevette Sales Ploy: Cut Prices," *The Washington Post*, October 15, 1986, F1. © 1986 *The Washington Post*, reprinted with permission. Photo Source: Courtesy of Chevrolet Motor Division.

IN this chapter, we build on the basic supply and demand model developed in Chapter 3. In doing so, we shift our focus somewhat. Instead of looking only at the *direction* of changes that result from changing supply and demand conditions, we stress the *size* of the changes.

As the case of the General Motors price cuts shows, the size of the response to a change in price is crucial. The law of demand tells us that except in rare cases, a price cut will increase the quantity demanded. But when the loss of revenue per unit and the producer's costs are taken into account, will the greater quantity be enough to make the price cut profitable? This chapter begins the task of providing a framework for answering this question.

Elasticity

Elasticity
A measure of the responsiveness of quantity demanded or supplied to changes in the price of a good or in other economic conditions.

Supply and demand analysis stresses that buyers' and sellers' plans change as prices change. It is often useful to know how responsive such plans are to changes in economic conditions. In such situations, economists commonly use the concept of **elasticity**, which is based on percentage changes in prices, quantities, and other variables. We begin with the most common application of the elasticity concept, namely the measurement of the responsiveness of quantity demanded to changes in price.

Price Elasticity of Demand

Price elasticity of demand
The ratio of the percentage change in the quantity demanded of a good to a given percentage change in its price, other things being equal.

Revenue
Price times quantity sold.

The measure of the responsiveness of quantity demanded to a change in price is the **price elasticity of demand**; it is the ratio of the percentage change in the quantity of a good demanded to a given percentage change in its price.

Exhibit 6.1 presents three demand curves showing different degrees of price elasticity of demand. In part a, the quantity demanded is highly responsive to a change in price. In this case, a decrease in price from $5 to $3 causes the quantity demanded to increase from three to six units. Because the percentage change in quantity is greater than that in price, the drop in price causes total revenue from sales of the good to increase. **Revenue** means the price times the quantity sold. On a supply and demand diagram, revenue can be shown as the area of a rectangle drawn under the demand curve, with a height equal to price and a width equal to quantity demanded. In this case, comparison of the shaded

Exhibit 6.1   Elastic, Inelastic, and Unit Elastic Demand

These graphs show the relationship between changes in price and changes in revenue for three demand curves. As the price of good A decreases from $5 to $3, revenue increases from $15 to $18; the demand for good A is elastic. As the price of good B decreases over the same range, revenue falls from $15 to $12; the demand for good B is inelastic. As the price of good C decreases, revenue remains unchanged; the demand for good C is unit elastic.

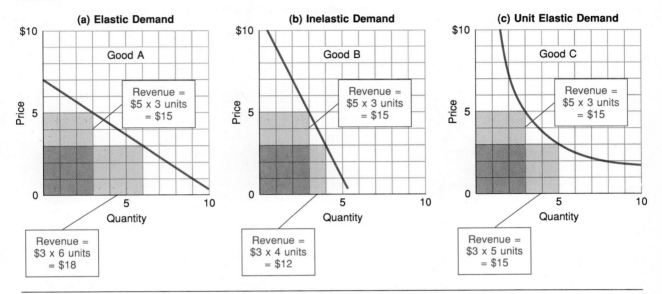

rectangles representing revenue before ($5 per unit × 3 units = $15) and after ($3 per unit × 6 units = $18) shows that revenue is greater after the price has been reduced. When the quantity changes by a greater percentage than price so that a price decrease causes total revenue to increase, demand is said to be elastic.

Part b of Exhibit 6.1 shows a case in which the quantity demanded is much less responsive to a change in price. Here a $2 decrease in price, from $5 to $3 per unit, causes the quantity demanded to increase by just one unit—from three to four. This time the percentage change in quantity is less than that in price. As a result, the decrease in price causes total revenue to fall (again note the shaded rectangles). In such a case, demand is said to be inelastic.

Part c shows a case in which a change in price causes an exactly proportional change in quantity demanded so that total revenue does not change. When the percentage change in quantity demanded equals the percentage change in price, demand is said to be unit elastic.

Besides the cases of elastic, inelastic, and unit elastic demand shown in Exhibit 6.1, there are two limiting cases, which are shown in Exhibit 6.2. Part a shows a demand curve that is perfectly vertical. Regardless of the price, the quantity demanded is five units—no more, no less. Such a demand curve is said to be **perfectly inelastic.** Part b shows a demand curve that is perfectly horizontal. Above a price of $5, no units of the good can be sold; but as soon as the price drops to $5, producers can sell as much of the good as they care to produce

Elastic demand
A situation in which quantity demanded changes by a larger percentage than price and total revenue therefore increases as price decreases.

Inelastic demand
A situation in which quantity demanded changes by a smaller percentage than price and total revenue therefore decreases as price decreases.

Unit elastic demand
A situation in which price and quantity demanded change by the same percentage and total revenue therefore remains unchanged as price changes.

Perfectly inelastic demand
A situation in which the demand curve is a vertical line.

Exhibit 6.2   Perfectly Elastic and Perfectly Inelastic Demand

Part a of this exhibit shows a demand curve that is a vertical line. No matter what the price, the quantity demanded is five units. Such a demand curve is described as perfectly inelastic. Part b shows a perfectly elastic demand curve, which is a horizontal line. Above the price of $5, no units of the good can be sold. At that price, suppliers can sell as much of the good as they want without further price reductions.

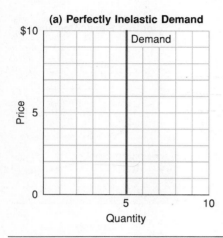
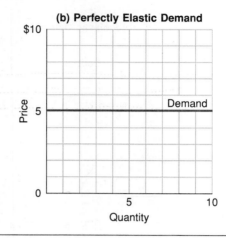

without further cutting the price. A horizontal demand curve such as this is described as **perfectly elastic.**

Measuring Elasticity of Demand

It is often useful to attach numerical values to elasticity of demand. The basis for such values is the definition of elasticity of demand as the ratio of the percentage change in quantity demanded to the percentage change in price.

Percentage Changes

In order to apply this definition to the measurement of elasticity, we need a way to measure percentage changes. Everyday methods for doing this are not very useful. Suppose, for example, that we are dealing with a $.25 increase in the price of strawberries, from $.75 to $1 a pint. Ordinarily we would use the initial price as the denominator in calculating a percentage change; thus, we would call this a 33 percent increase (.25/.75 = .33). However, suppose the initial price is $1 a pint and we are considering a $.25 decrease in price to $.75 a pint. In that case, we use $1 in the denominator and call it a 25 percent decrease (.25/1 = .25).

In measuring elasticity, it is awkward to have to state whether we are dealing with a price increase or a price decrease before we can calculate the percentage change. We can get around this problem by using the *midpoint* of the price range as the denominator in calculating the percentage change for both increases and decreases in price. To find the midpoint, we take the sum of the initial price and the final price and divide by 2. In this case, the midpoint is (.75 + 1)/2 = .875.

Perfectly elastic demand
A situation in which the demand curve is a horizontal line.

Using the midpoint value of .875 as the denominator, the percentage change in price becomes (approximately) .25/.875 = .285—a 28.5 percent change for both an increase and a decrease over the specified price range.

With P_1 representing the price before the change and P_2 the price after, the midpoint formula for calculating the percentage change in price can be written as

$$\text{Percentage change in price} = \frac{P_2 - P_1}{(P_1 + P_2)/2}.$$

The same approach can be used to define the percentage change in the quantity demanded that results from a given price change. Suppose that when the price of strawberries falls from $1 to $.75, the quantity demanded rises from 100 to 150 pints a day. We use the midpoint of the quantity range as the denominator in calculating the percentage change in quantity. If Q_1 and Q_2 are the quantities before and after a price change, the midpoint formula for the percentage change can be written as

$$\text{Percentage change in quantity} = \frac{Q_2 - Q_1}{(Q_1 + Q_2)/2}.$$

Applying this formula to the above example, we say that either an increase in quantity from 100 to 150 or a decrease from 150 to 100 represents a 40 percent change in quantity:

$$\text{Percentage change in quantity} = \frac{150 - 100}{(150 + 100)/2} = .40.$$

An Elasticity Formula

Defining percentage changes in this way allows us to write a useful formula for calculating elasticities. The formula can be applied to the elasticity of either supply or demand. With P_1 and Q_1 representing price and quantity before a change and P_2 and Q_2 representing price and quantity after, the midpoint formula for elasticity is

$$\begin{matrix}\text{Price} \\ \text{elasticity} \\ \text{of demand}\end{matrix} = \frac{(Q_2 - Q_1)/(Q_1 + Q_2)}{(P_2 - P_1)/(P_1 + P_2)} = \frac{\text{Percentage change}}{\text{Percentage change}} \begin{matrix}\text{in quantity} \\ \text{in price}\end{matrix}.$$

The following problem illustrates the use of this formula.

Problem: A change in the price of strawberries from $1 to $.75 a pint causes the quantity demanded to increase from 100 to 150 pints per day. What is the price elasticity of demand for strawberries over the given range of price and quantity?

Solution:

- P_1 = price before change = $1
- P_2 = price after change = $.75
- Q_1 = quantity before change = 100
- Q_2 = quantity after change = 150

$$\text{Elasticity} = \frac{(150 - 100)/(100 + 150)}{(\$.75 - \$1)/(\$1 + \$.75)}$$

$$= \frac{50/250}{-\$.25/\$1.75}$$

$$= \frac{.2}{-\$.1428} = -1.4.$$

Because demand curves have negative slopes, this formula yields a negative value for elasticity. The reason is that the quantity changes in the direction opposite to that of the price change. When the price decreases, $(P_2 - P_1)$, which appears in the denominator of the formula, is negative whereas $(Q_2 - Q_1)$, which appears in the numerator, is positive. When the price increases, the numerator is negative and the denominator is positive. However, in this book we follow the widely used practice of dropping the minus sign when discussing price elasticity of demand. Thus, the elasticity of demand for a good will be given as, say, 2 or .5 rather than as −2 or −.5. Applying this convention to the above problem, the elasticity of demand for strawberries would be stated as 1.4 over the range of price and quantity shown.

A numerical elasticity value such as 1.4 can be related to the basic definition of elasticity in a simple way. That definition stated that price elasticity of demand is the ratio of the percentage change in quantity to a given percentage change in price. Thus, an elasticity of demand of 1.4 means that the quantity demanded will increase by 1.4 percent for each 1 percent change in price; an elasticity of .5 means that quantity demanded would change by .5 percent for each 1 percent change in price; and so on.

Elasticity Values and Changes in Revenue

Earlier in the chapter, we defined *elastic, inelastic, unit elastic, perfectly elastic,* and *perfectly inelastic demand* in terms of the relationship between change in price and change in total revenue. Each of these terms corresponds to a numerical value or range of values of elasticity as calculated using the elasticity formula. A perfectly inelastic demand curve has a numerical value of 0, since any change in price produces no change in quantity demanded. The term *inelastic* (but not *perfectly inelastic*) *demand* applies to numerical values from 0 up to, but not including, 1. *Unit elasticity,* as the name implies, means a numerical value of exactly 1. *Elastic demand* means any value for elasticity that is greater than 1. *Perfectly elastic demand,* represented by a horizontal demand curve, is not defined numerically; as the demand curve becomes horizontal, the denominator of the elasticity formula approaches 0 and the numerical value of elasticity approaches infinity.

Varying- and Constant-Elasticity Demand Curves

The midpoint formula for calculating the elasticity of demand shows the elasticity of demand over a certain range of prices and quantities. Measured over some other range, the elasticity of demand for the same good may or may not differ. Whether the elasticity of demand for a good changes along the demand curve depends on the curve's exact shape. This can be seen in Exhibits 6.3 and 6.4.

Exhibit 6.3   Variation in Elasticity along a Straight-Line Demand Curve

These graphs show how elasticity varies along a straight-line demand curve. At low quantities, demand is elastic; for example, in the range of 10 to 20 units, the elasticity of demand is 5.66. At 50 units of output (halfway down the curve), a point of unit elasticity is reached. From there to 100 units of output, demand is inelastic; in the 70-to-80-unit range, for example, elasticity is .33. Part b shows that total revenue increases as the quantity rises over the elastic portion of the demand curve and decreases as the quantity increases over the inelastic portion. Total revenue reaches a maximum at the point of unit elasticity.

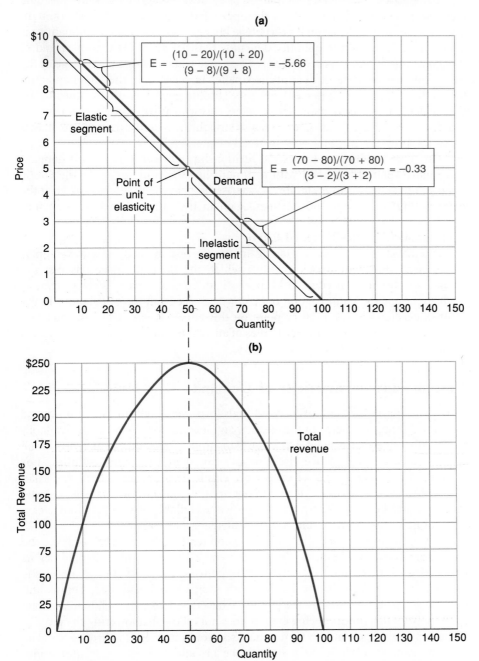

(a)

$$E = \frac{(10 - 20)/(10 + 20)}{(9 - 8)/(9 + 8)} = -5.66$$

$$E = \frac{(70 - 80)/(70 + 80)}{(3 - 2)/(3 + 2)} = -0.33$$

(b)

A Linear Demand Curve

First look at Exhibit 6.3, which shows a demand curve that, like most of those in this book, is a straight line. The elasticity of demand is not constant for all ranges of price and quantity along this curve. For example, measured over the price range $8 to $9, the elasticity of demand is 5.66; measured over the range $2 to $3, it is .33. (The calculations are shown in the exhibit.)

This illustrates the general rule that elasticity declines as one moves downward along a straight-line demand curve. It is easy to see why. With a straight-line demand curve, a $1 reduction in price always causes the same absolute increase in quantity demanded. At the upper end of the demand curve, though, a $1 change in price is a small percentage change, but the change in quantity is a large percentage of the quantity demanded at that price. At the lower end of the curve, the situation is reversed: A $1 change is now a large percentage of the price, but the increase in quantity is smaller in relation to the larger quantity demanded. Because it is percentages, not absolute amounts, that count in elasticity calculations, the demand curve is less elastic near the bottom than near the top. Because elasticity changes along a straight-line demand curve, it makes sense to apply the formula only to small changes.

Part b of Exhibit 6.3 shows the relationship between elasticity of demand and total revenue for a good with a straight-line demand curve. In the elastic range of the demand curve, total revenue rises as price falls, reaches a peak at the point of unit elasticity, and declines again in the range of inelastic demand.

A Constant-Elasticity Demand Curve

If the demand curve is not a straight line, these results need not always apply. There is an important special case in which the demand curve has just the amount of curvature needed to keep elasticity constant over its entire length. Such a curve is shown in Exhibit 6.4. As we can see from the calculations in the exhibit, elasticity is 1.0 at every point on this curve. It is possible to construct demand curves with constant elasticities of any value. Such curves are often used in statistical studies of demand elasticity.

Determinants of Elasticity of Demand

Why is the price elasticity of demand high for some goods and low for others? The most important factor in the elasticity of demand for a good is the availability of substitutes. If a good has close substitutes, demand for it tends to be elastic, since when its price rises, people can switch to the substitutes. For example, the demand for olive oil is more elastic than it would be if other salad oils could not be substituted for it. Likewise, the demand for cars is less elastic than it would be if public transportation were available everywhere, since cars and public transportation can be substituted for each other.

It also follows that the demand for a good tends to be more price elastic the more narrowly it is defined. The news item with which this chapter begins provides an illustration. GM expects the demand for Chevettes to be elastic because they compete in the market with their close substitutes, Omnis and Horizons. Thus, by lowering the price of Chevettes, GM may well increase total revenue from this product. However, it does not follow that lowering the price of all makes and models of cars simultaneously would increase total revenue of the auto industry as a whole. Demand for the broadly defined good automobiles could well be inelastic even though the demand for any given model is elastic.

Exhibit 6.4   A Demand Curve with Constant Elasticity

It is possible for a demand curve to have constant elasticity throughout its length. This demand curve, for example, has an elasticity of 1.0 wherever it is measured. Constant-elasticity demand curves are often used in estimating demand elasticity.

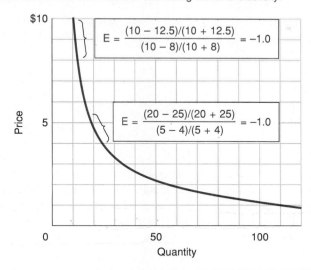

$$E = \frac{(10 - 12.5)/(10 + 12.5)}{(10 - 8)/(10 + 8)} = -1.0$$

$$E = \frac{(20 - 25)/(20 + 25)}{(5 - 4)/(5 + 4)} = -1.0$$

The existence of complements can also play a role in determining elasticity. If something is a minor complement to an important good, its demand tends to be inelastic. For example, the demand for motor oil tends to be inelastic because it is a complement to a more important good—gasoline. The price of gasoline has more of an effect on the amount of driving a person does than the price of motor oil.

Elasticity is also influenced by the portion of a person's budget spent on a good. There are substitutes for matches, for example; yet the demand for matches is somewhat inelastic because people spend so little on them that they hardly notice a price change. In contrast, goods such as housing and transportation are hard to do without, but demand for them is not perfectly inelastic partly because they account for a large part of people's budgets; thus, changes in their prices cannot be ignored.

Finally, elasticity of demand is influenced by time. Demand often is less elastic in the short run than in the long run. Consider the demand for home heating fuel. In the short run, people find it hard to cut back the amount they use when the price goes up. They are used to keeping their homes at a certain temperature and dressing a particular way. Given time, however, they may find ways to cut back—they can put better insulation in their homes, dress more warmly, or even move to a warmer climate.

Other Elasticities

So far we have applied the concept of elasticity only to the price elasticity of demand for a good. However, this concept has other applications. All of them are based on the ratio of the percentage change in one variable to the percentage change in another.

Income elasticity of demand
The ratio of the percentage change in the demand for a good to a given percentage change in consumer income, other things being equal.

Income Elasticity of Demand

As shown in Chapter 3 and again earlier in this chapter, changes in income can cause changes in the demand for a good. The **income elasticity of demand** for a good is defined as the ratio of the percentage change in demand for that good to the percentage change in income. In measuring the income elasticity of demand for a good, it is assumed that the good's price does not change. Using Q_1 and Q_2 to represent quantities before and after the income change and y_1 and y_2 to represent income before and after it, the formula for income elasticity of demand can be written as

$$\text{Income elasticity of demand} = \frac{(Q_2 - Q_1)/(Q_1 + Q_2)}{(y_2 - y_1)/(y_1 + y_2)} = \frac{\text{Percentage change in quantity}}{\text{Percentage change in income}}.$$

The income elasticity of demand for a good is closely linked to the concepts of *normal* and *inferior* goods. For a normal good, an increase in income causes demand to rise. Because income and demand change in the same direction, the income elasticity of demand for a normal good is positive. For an inferior good, an increase in income causes demand to decrease. Because income and demand change in opposite directions, the income elasticity of demand for an inferior good is negative.

Cross-Elasticity of Demand

Cross-elasticity of demand
The ratio of the percentage change in the demand for a good to a given percentage change in the price of some other good, other things being equal.

Another factor that can cause a change in the demand for a good is a change in the price of some other good. The demand for lettuce is affected by changes in the price of cabbage, the demand for motor oil by changes in the price of gasoline, and so on. The concept of elasticity can be applied here also: The **cross-elasticity of demand** for a good is defined as the ratio of the percentage change in demand for the good to a given percentage change in the price of another good. The formula for cross-elasticity of demand is the same as that for price elasticity of demand, except that the numerator shows the percentage change in the quantity of one good while the denominator shows the percentage change in the price of some other good.

Cross-elasticity of demand is related to the concepts of *substitutes* and *complements*. Because lettuce and cabbage are substitutes, an increase in the price of cabbage causes a rise in the quantity of lettuce demanded; the cross-elasticity of demand is positive. Because motor oil and gasoline are complements, an increase in the price of gasoline causes a decrease in the quantity of motor oil demanded; the cross-elasticity of demand is negative.

"Applying Economic Ideas 6.1" shows how the concepts of price elasticity, cross-elasticity, and income elasticity of demand can be applied in a real-life situation—that of the demand for intercity rail passenger service.

Price Elasticity of Supply

Price elasticity of supply
The ratio of the percentage change in quantity supplied to a given percentage change in the price of a good, other things being equal.

The definition of the **price elasticity of supply** for a good closely resembles that of the price elasticity of demand: the percentage change in the quantity of the good supplied divided by the percentage change in the good's price. The formula for calculating price elasticity of supply is the same as that for determining price elasticity of demand. Because price and quantity change in the same direction along a positively sloped supply curve, the formula gives a positive value for

Demand for Amtrak Passenger Service

The National Railroad Passenger Corporation (Amtrak) was formed by Congress in 1970 to take over the rapidly disappearing passenger services of private railroads. At the time Amtrak came into being, total passenger miles traveled by train had been declining for half a century and railroads had been losing money on passenger services for more than 30 years. Like every other passenger railroad, Amtrak has found it hard to make a profit on passenger service. Recently, its revenues have covered approximately two-thirds of its costs.

Much of Amtrak's difficulty in turning a profit has been caused by the demand conditions it faces. The price elasticity, cross-elasticity, and income elasticity of demand for rail passenger service have all been studied in the hope of finding a segment of the intercity passenger market that Amtrak can serve successfully.

In most markets, the price elasticity of demand is quite high—about 2.2 on the average, according to a study by Amtrak. This means that Amtrak cannot automatically raise fares without losing large amounts of revenue. A fare cut would bring in many more passengers, but unless the cost of serving the added passengers is less than the gain in revenue, more passengers just mean greater losses. The Northeast corridor—Washington, D.C., to Boston—is an exception. The price elasticity of demand there is estimated at .67. This low elasticity is believed to be linked with the high percentage of business-related trips in the Northeast. In the rest of the nation, most intercity trips are taken for pleasure.

High price elasticity of demand is typical of goods and services that have close substitutes. Estimates of cross-elasticity give an idea of what the substitutes are. A 1977

study found a cross-elasticity of .6 with air travel and 1.29 with bus travel, indicating that intercity bus service was Amtrak's closest competitor. Since then, lower average air fares have forced buses to keep their fares low as well. This has not improved Amtrak's situation.

In the past, intercity rail service was viewed as an inferior good. Estimates of income elasticities of demand made in the 1950s found a value of −.6 for rail compared to values of +1.2 for automobile and +2.5 for air. Because incomes have grown steadily and will continue to do so, these numbers would make Amtrak's job almost hopeless if it tried to compete head-on with automobile and airline travel. However, Amtrak believes that the demand for recreational and vacation travel by rail has a positive income elasticity. In effect, there may be a market for the unique comfort and ambiance of train travel even when it is not the cheapest mode, for somewhat the same reason that cruise ships have prospered, while transatlantic ocean travel has all but disappeared.

Source: George W. Hilton, *Amtrak: The National Railroad Passenger Corporation* (Washington, D.C.: American Enterprise Institute, 1980). Photo Source: Courtesy of Amtrak.

the elasticity of supply. Exhibit 6.5 applies the elasticity formula to two supply curves, one with constant elasticity and the other with variable elasticity.

Applications of Elasticity

The concept of elasticity has many applications in both macro- and microeconomics. In macroeconomics, it can be applied to money markets, to the aggregate supply and demand for all goods and services, and to foreign exchange

Exhibit 6.5   Calculating Price Elasticity of Supply

This exhibit uses four examples to show how price elasticity of supply is calculated. Price elasticity of supply is shown for two ranges on each of the two supply curves. Supply curve S_1, which is a straight line passing through the origin, has a constant elasticity of 1.0. Supply curve S_2, which is curved, is elastic for small quantities and inelastic for larger ones.

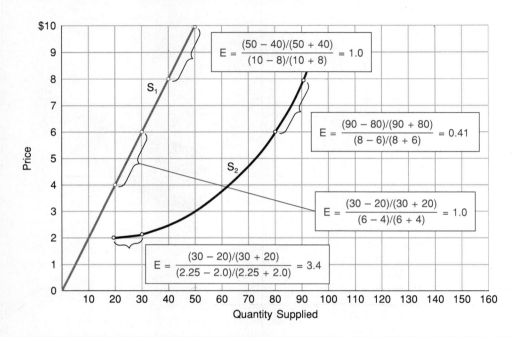

$$E = \frac{(50-40)/(50+40)}{(10-8)/(10+8)} = 1.0$$

$$E = \frac{(90-80)/(90+80)}{(8-6)/(8+6)} = 0.41$$

$$E = \frac{(30-20)/(30+20)}{(6-4)/(6+4)} = 1.0$$

$$E = \frac{(30-20)/(30+20)}{(2.25-2.0)/(2.25+2.0)} = 3.4$$

markets, to name just a few. We will see that in microeconomics elasticity plays a role in discussions of consumer behavior, firms' profit-maximizing behavior, regulatory policy, labor market policy, and many other areas. For further familiarization, we conclude this chapter with two specific applications of the notion of elasticity—tax incidence and the farm problem.

Elasticity and Tax Incidence

Who pays taxes? One way to answer this question would be to look at government records to find who wrote the checks received in payment of taxes. That would show that property owners pay property taxes, gasoline companies pay gasoline taxes, and so on. However, looking at who writes the checks does not always answer the question of who bears the economic burden of a tax—or, to use the economist's term, the issue of **tax incidence.**

> **Tax incidence**
> The issue of who bears the economic burden of a tax.

     The economic incidence of a tax may not fall entirely on the party who hands over tax payments to the government, because it is often possible to pass along the tax burden, in whole or in part, to someone else. The degree to which the burden of a tax may be passed along turns out to depend on the elasticities of supply and demand. Let's consider some examples.

Incidence of a Gasoline Tax

As a first illustration, consider the familiar example of a gasoline tax. Specifically, suppose that the state of Virginia decides to impose a tax of $.50 a gallon on gasoline beginning from a situation in which there is no tax.

Exhibit 6.6   Incidence of a Tax on Gasoline

S_1 and D are the supply and demand curves before imposition of the tax. The initial equilibrium price is $1 per gallon. A tax of $.50 per gallon shifts the supply curve to S_2. In order to induce sellers to supply the same quantity as before, the price would have to rise to $1.50. However, as the price rises, buyers reduce the quantity demanded, moving up and to the left along the demand curve. In the new equilibrium at E_2, the price rises only to $1.40. After the tax is paid, sellers receive only $.90 per gallon. Thus, buyers bear $.40 of the tax on each gallon and sellers the remaining $.10. Buyers bear the larger share of the tax because demand, in this case, is less elastic than supply.

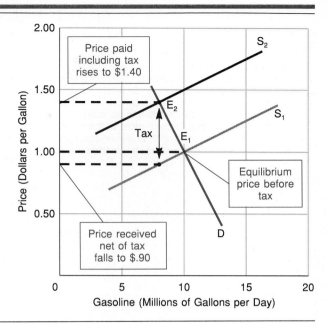

Exhibit 6.6 uses the supply and demand model to show the effects of the tax. Initially the demand curve intersects supply curve S_1 at E_1, resulting in a price of $1 per gallon. The supply curve is elastic in the region of the initial equilibrium. The elasticity of supply reflects the fact that we are dealing with the gasoline market in just one state; only a slight rise in the price of gasoline in Virginia is needed to divert additional quantities from elsewhere in the nation. The demand for gasoline is less elastic than the supply in the region of the initial equilibrium. Motorists—except, perhaps, those who live near the state line—cannot go elsewhere to buy gasoline when the price rises in Virginia. However, they are not entirely unresponsive to a rise in prices, since they can decide to drive less or switch to more fuel-efficient cars.

The effect of the tax is to shift the supply curve upward by $.50. Because sellers must now turn over $.50 to the state government for each gallon of gas sold, they would have to get $1.50 per gallon in order to be willing to sell the same quantity (10 million gallons per day) as initially. However, when sellers attempt to pass the tax on to motorists, motorists respond by cutting back the quantity of gasoline they buy. As the quantity sold falls, sellers are moved down and to the left along supply curve S_2 to a new equilibrium at E_2.

In the new equilibrium, the price is $1.40 per gallon—just $.40 higher than the original price. After paying the $.50 tax, sellers net $.90 per gallon—$.10 less than formerly. The amount of the tax—$.50 per gallon—is shown by the vertical gap between the supply and demand curves. The economic burden of the tax is divided between buyers and sellers, but in this case it falls more heavily on the buyers.

Incidence of a Tax on Apartment Rents

In the previous example, the incidence of the gasoline tax falls more heavily on buyers than on sellers because demand is less elastic than supply. If the elasticities are reversed, the results will also be reversed, as can be seen in the case of a tax on apartment rents.

Exhibit 6.7   Incidence of a
Tax on Apartment Rents

This exhibit shows the incidence of a tax imposed in a
market in which supply is less elastic than demand. Initially
the equilibrium rent is $500 per month. A $250-per-month
tax on apartment rents shifts the supply curve to S_2. The
new equilibrium is at E_2. Landlords end up absorbing all but
$50 of the tax. If they tried to pass more of the tax on to
renters, more renters would switch to owner-occupied
housing and the vacancy rate on rental apartments would
rise.

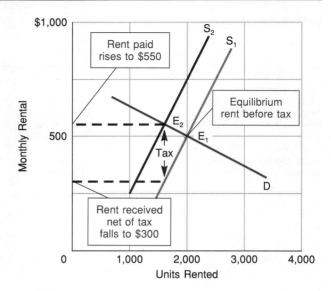

In Exhibit 6.7, the market for rental apartments in a certain small city is
initially in equilibrium at $500 per month. The supply of rental apartments is
inelastic. An increase in rents will cause a few new apartments to be built, and a
reduction will cause a few to be torn down, but the response will moderate. On
the other hand, demand is fairly elastic, because potential renters consider
houses or condominiums a fairly close substitute for rental apartments.

Given this situation, the local government now decides to impose a tax of
$250 per month on all apartments rented in the town. As in the previous exam-
ple, the supply curve shifts upward by the amount of the tax. After the shift, the
market reaches a new equilibrium at E_2. Here the price rises to only $550 per
month—just $50 per month higher than initially. After the $250-per-month tax
is paid, landlords net only $300 a month—$200 less than before. Thus, in this
case, because supply is inelastic and demand is elastic, suppliers bear most of the
incidence of the tax and buyers only a little.

It is not always as easy to measure the incidence of taxes as it is in these
examples. One reason is that it may be hard to get good estimates of elasticities of
supply and demand. Another is that more than two parties may be involved; for
example, the burden of a corporate income tax may be shared among the firms'
customers, stockholders, and employees. Finally, taxes interact with one another in complex ways. Thus, the incidence of an income tax may depend on the
sales and property taxes that are already being paid. However, in these more
complex cases, as in the simple ones we have examined, it remains true that
elasticities are a key determinant of tax incidence.

Elasticities and the Farm Problem

The history of agriculture in the United States has been one of steady technological advances and rising productivity. Yet these breakthroughs have not brought
uniform prosperity to the farm economy. Instead, the record has been one of

volatile prices and periodic downward pressure on farm incomes. Many aspects of the farm problem can be explained in terms of elasticities.

Implications of Inelastic Demand

As part a of Exhibit 6.8 shows, demand for many important farm products is inelastic. The more inelastic the demand for a product, the more the price will vary in response to changes in output. Also, with inelastic demand good weather and a large crop will mean a drop in farm revenue; poor weather and a bad crop will mean an increase in revenue.

The historical instability of farm prices is shown in part b of Exhibit 6.8 in terms of the **parity-price ratio.** This is the ratio of an index of prices that farmers receive to an index of prices that they pay. The ratio uses the years 1910 to 1914 as a base period, which was one of relative farm prosperity.

As Exhibit 6.8 shows, the parity-price ratio has experienced wide swings, indicating volatility of prices of farm output relative to those of farm inputs. In the worst period, from 1929 to 1932, the ratio fell from 92 to 64 in just over three years. The collapse of demand in those early years of the Great Depression pushed all prices down; but because agricultural demand is so inelastic, farmers were hit worse than anyone else. The index of prices paid by farmers dropped a great deal over this period—from 160 to 112. The index of prices received fell even more sharply—from 149 to a mere 65.

Farm prices recovered along with the rest of the economy during World War II. Then, during the 1950s and 1960s, farm prices, as measured by the parity-price ratio, declined steadily but without the sharp fluctuations of earlier periods. Any hope that agricultural markets had become more stable, however, was not borne out by what happened in the 1970s and early 1980s.

In 1973 a combination of factors, ranging from bad weather in the Soviet Union to the failure of the Peruvian anchovy catch, created a worldwide food shortage. Farm prices skyrocketed. The parity-price ratio rose to an average of 91 for 1973 and in August of that year briefly touched the 100 mark for the first time in 20 years. Many farmers saw this as the beginning of a trend in which U.S. agriculture would increasingly be relied on to feed a hungry and populous world. They responded by borrowing heavily to invest in new equipment and to buy land. The price of farmland rose sharply, and farm indebtedness climbed with it.

However, the high prices of the early 1970s proved transitory. The parity-price ratio fell again as quickly as it had risen. By the mid-1980s, it had hit new lows. The "green revolution" boosted farm output throughout the world, and even such one-time agricultural basket cases as India and China became self-sufficient in grain. As prices fell, many farmers found themselves unable to pay off debt incurred in the 1970s. Thousands of operators were forced out of business, often taking equipment dealers, bankers, and small-town merchants with them. These troubles occurred despite billions of dollars spent by the federal government on price support programs.

Long-Term Adjustment and Income Elasticity

The parity-price ratio tells the story of one part of the farm problem—short-term instability. The second part of the story concerns the problem of long-term adjustment to rising productivity.

The long-term problem can be seen as the result of demand for farm products being not only price inelastic but income inelastic as well. As per capita

Parity-price ratio
The ratio of an index of prices that farmers receive to an index of prices that they pay.

Exhibit 6.8 Elasticity of Demand for Farm Goods

As part a of this exhibit shows, the demand for many major farm goods is inelastic. When demand is inelastic, a small shift in either the supply curve or the demand curve can cause a relatively large change in price. The volatility of farm prices over time is shown in part b in terms of the parity-price ratio, the ratio of an index of prices that farmers receive to an index of prices that they pay.

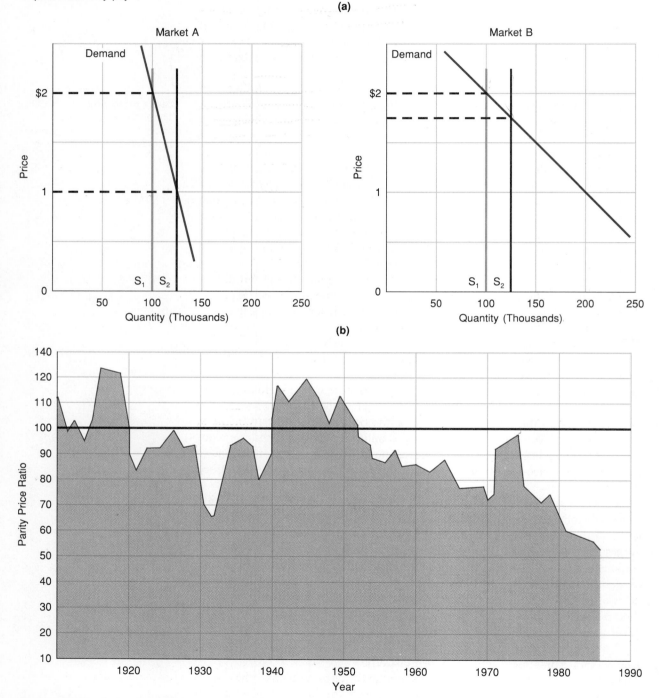

Sources: President's Council of Economic Advisers, *Economic Report of the President* (Washington, D.C.: Government Printing Office, 1977); Bureau of the Census, *Statistical Abstract of the United States, 1984*, 107th ed. (Washington, D.C.: Government Printing Office, 1987), 634; U.S. Department of Commerce, *Survey of Current Business*, various issues.

income grows, the demand for agricultural output increases, but not as rapidly as income does. The result of slowly growing demand and rapidly improving farm productivity has been a steady decline in the number of farmers needed to meet the demand for agricultural goods. Fifty years ago, 25 percent of the U.S. population was engaged in farming. Today the figure is less than 5 percent.

The marketplace has a way of telling people to leave an overcrowded sector: It offers them a lower income than is available elsewhere. Thus, throughout the period of declining farm population, per capita income in farming has been below that of the rest of the economy. In the 1970s, the gap narrowed so that by some measures farm families caught up with the nonfarm population. However, renewed difficulties in the 1980s have pushed relative farm incomes down again.

As the farm population has fallen, the role of the family farm—the farm with sales in the $40,000 to $100,000 range that is the main source of income for the family that owns and operates it—has changed. Farms of this type have shaped most nonfarmers' image of rural life and also have strongly influenced farm policy. Today, however, they are becoming increasingly overshadowed by two other kinds of farms. On the one hand, there are the 70 percent of farms with sales under $40,000 per year whose operators depend on other jobs for most of their incomes. On the other, there are professionally managed farms with sales of $100,000 or more per year. The 12 percent of farms in this size class—which tend to be the most productive and technologically advanced—account for about two-thirds of gross farm income.

Looking Ahead

By enriching the supply and demand model with the notion of elasticity, this chapter has set the stage for a discussion of a number of questions.

First, what really lies behind the supply and demand curves? We have seen some broad explanations of the shapes of these curves, but now we must consider their meaning in terms of people's efforts to deal with the problems of scarcity and choice. This explanation will take up several chapters.

Next, do the principles of supply and demand apply to all markets or to only certain types? This chapter limited its examples to markets, such as those for chicken and strawberries, in which there are many buyers and sellers who are all relatively small. But we also need to know how to apply these principles to markets that are dominated by one or a few large sellers.

Finally, how can we use the principles of supply and demand to help us understand the role of government in the economy? In many markets, government regulations have a strong impact on the prices and quantities of goods that consumers can buy and producers can sell.

The following chapters will answer these questions by building on the basics covered here.

Summary

1. **How can the responsiveness of quantity demanded to a change in price be expressed in terms of the notion of elasticity?** *Elasticity* is the responsiveness of quantity demanded or supplied to changes in the price of a good or in other factors. The *price elasticity of demand* between two points on a demand curve is

computed as the percentage change in quantity divided by the percentage change in price. If the demand for a good is *elastic*, a decrease in price will increase total *revenue*. If it is *inelastic*, an increase in price will increase total revenue.

2. **How can the notion of elasticity be applied to situations other than the responsiveness of quantity demanded to a price change?** The concept of elasticity can be applied to many situations besides movements along demand curves. The *income elasticity of demand* for a good is the ratio of the percentage change in quantity demanded to a given percentage change in income. The *cross-elasticity of demand* between two goods is the ratio of the percentage change in the quantity of the first good demanded to a given percentage change in the price of the second good. The *price elasticity of supply* is the ratio of the percentage change in the quantity of a good supplied to a given change in its price.

3. **What determines the distribution of the economic burdens of a tax?** The way in which the economic burdens of a tax are distributed is known as the *incidence* of the tax. The incidence depends on the relative elasticities of supply and demand. If supply is more elastic than demand, buyers will bear the larger share of the tax burden. If demand is more elastic than supply, the larger share of the burden will fall on sellers.

4. **How is the notion of elasticity useful for understanding the problems of the farm sector?** For a given shift in demand, the more inelastic demand is, the more the market price will fluctuate. Also, when demand is inelastic, an increase in quantity will cause a reduction in total revenue. The instability of farm prices and incomes can be attributed, at least in part, to the inelasticity of demand for many farm products. Also, demand for many farm products is income inelastic as well as price inelastic. This means that as U.S. per capita income has risen, the demand for farm goods has increased only moderately—not enough to keep up with the rate of increase in farm productivity. Thus, a much smaller proportion of the population is engaged in farming today than formerly. The exit of farm operators continues in the 1980s.

Terms for Review

- elasticity
- price elasticity of demand
- revenue
- elastic demand
- inelastic demand
- unit elastic demand
- perfectly inelastic demand
- perfectly elastic demand
- income elasticity of demand
- cross-elasticity of demand
- price elasticity of supply
- tax incidence
- parity-price ratio

Questions for Review

1. Sketch examples of demand curves that are elastic, inelastic, unit elastic, perfectly inelastic, and perfectly elastic. Can a demand curve have different elasticities at various points? If so, give an example.

2. Write the formula for price elasticity of demand. Sketch two or three demand curves on a piece of graph paper. Calculate the price elasticity of demand at two or three points on each demand curve.

3. How does revenue change in response to changes in price under conditions of elastic, inelastic, and unit elastic demand? Sketch a straight-line demand curve and a second curve showing total revenue for each point along the demand curve.

4. What factors affect the elasticity of demand? What role do substitutes and complements play? What is the effect of the amount of time consumers are given to adjust to a change in the price of a good?

5. Show how the concept of elasticity can be extended to income elasticity of demand, cross-elasticity of demand, and price elasticity of supply.

6. Under what conditions will the economic burden of a tax be divided evenly between buyers and sellers? Under what conditions will it fall more heavily on buyers? On sellers?

7. How have price inelasticity and income inelasticity affected the farm sector of the U.S. economy?

Problems and Topics for Discussion

1. **Examining the lead-off case.** Using the data provided in the lead-off article, estimate the price elasticity of demand for Chrysler's Omni/Horizon. If Chevette sales were to increase to 100,000 in the year following the price cut, what would be the price elasticity of demand for that car? *Bonus question:* Suppose that demand for the Chevette is elastic so that the firm's revenues will increase if the price is cut. Does that automatically mean that its profits will increase? Think about this question now, and return to it after Chapter 10.

2. **Elasticity and shifts in demand curves.** Measurements of elasticity such as those you made in problem 1 carry an "other-things-being-equal" condition. Spe-

cifically, they are accurate only if it is assumed that the demand curve did not shift between the two periods. How would the measurement for elasticity of demand for the Omni/Horizon be distorted if, between the two years for which data are given, consumer incomes increased and you know that cars are normal goods? Use a diagram to show the nature of the distortion.

3. **Elasticity of demand and revenue.** Assume you are an officer of your campus film club. You are at a meeting at which ticket prices are being discussed. One member says, "What I hate to see most of all is empty seats in the theater. We sell out every weekend showing, but there are always empty seats on Wednesdays. If we cut our Wednesday night prices by enough to fill up the theater, we'd bring in more money." Would this tactic really bring in more revenue? What would you need to know in order to be sure? Draw diagrams to illustrate some of the possibilities.

4. **Cross-elasticity of demand.** Between 1979 and 1981, the price of heating oil rose by 104 percent while the price of LP gas, also used for home heating, rose by just 56 percent. Over the period, use of fuel oil fell slightly while use of LP gas rose. What does this suggest about the cross-elasticity of demand for LP gas with respect to the price of fuel oil? Draw a pair of diagrams to illustrate these events. (Suggestion: Draw upward-sloping supply curves for both fuels. Then assume that the heating oil supply curve shifts upward while the LP gas supply curve stays the same.)

Airlines fight for passengers through selective price cuts.

Case for Discussion
The Changing Face of Airline Fare Wars

The early 1980s saw repeated fare wars in the airline industry. Low-cost newcomers such as People Express and New York Air slashed fares across the board. They offered no-frills service—no hot meals, sometimes less convenient terminals—but they filled their planes. The established carriers often matched their fares, or nearly so, in order to avoid losing passengers. At one point in 1983, 88 percent of all passengers flew on discount fares. The industry as a whole lost money.

By the mid-1980s, competition was still vigorous but the nature of the fare wars had changed. In 1983 United, American, and other major airlines cut fares across the board. After 1984, they were more selective: They cut fares on routes for which they competed with the discount airlines, but they raised fares on other routes. They sold few discount tickets on midweek flights favored by business travelers but many on weekend flights popular with vacationers. Also, they added restrictions on discount tickets: Travelers were forced to buy their tickets up to a few weeks in advance if they wanted to qualify for the lower fares, and they were not always offered their money back if they changed their plans. With this selective price cutting, the major carriers hoped to fight the competition without the painful loss of revenue they had suffered in 1983.

Source: UPI/Bettmann Newsphotos.

Questions

1. What assumptions do the major airlines seem to be making about the elasticity of demand for their services on routes for which they face competition compared with routes for which they do not?

2. What assumptions do the major airlines appear to be making about the cross-elasticity of demand between their own flights and those of the low-cost airlines? Are they making different assumptions for business and vacation travelers? Discuss.

Suggestions for Further Reading

Browning, Edgar K., and Jacquelene M. Browning. *Public Finance and the Price System*. New York: Macmillan, 1979, Chapter 10.

Public finance is the name of the branch of economics that studies taxation and government expenditures from both a micro- and macroeconomic point of view. This or any other public finance text will provide additional details on the topic of tax incidence.

Gardner, Bruce. *The Governing of Agriculture*. Lawrence, Kan.: Regents Press of Kansas, 1981.

An excellent overview of farm policy.

Nicholson, Walter. *Intermediate Microeconomics and Its Applications*, 4th ed. Hinsdale, Ill.: Dryden Press, 1987, Chapter 5.

This or any other intermediate microeconomics text will give further details on the definition of elasticity and practical problems in measuring elasticity of demand.

7 Rational Choice and Consumer Behavior

After reading this chapter, you will understand . . .

- What elements are involved in consumers' rational choices.
- How consumers balance their selection of goods and services to achieve an equilibrium.
- What lies behind the effect of a price change on the quantity of a good demanded.
- Why demand curves have negative slopes.
- Why consumers and producers both gain from exchange in free markets.
- Why the burden of a tax exceeds the revenue raised by government.

Before reading this chapter, make sure you know the meaning of . . .

- Real and nominal quantities (Chapter 1)
- Substitutes and complements (Chapter 3)
- Normal and inferior goods (Chapter 3)
- Incidence of a tax (Chapter 6)

Danger: Children and Pedestrians!

Can government regulations requiring the use of seat belts or airbags in cars endanger bicyclists and pedestrians? Can government regulations requiring safety caps on aspirin bottles endanger children? Strange as it may seem, some economists think they can.

Economist Sam Peltzman started the controversy over seat belts with a study that found that when people felt their cars to be safer, they reacted by driving faster and less cautiously. The number of pedestrians and bicyclists they mowed down rose as much as the number of drivers and passengers who were killed fell. Other studies have challenged the finding of no net gain in safety from seat belts and airbags, but many of these also found that safer cars result in at least a little more danger to people on the street.

A similar effect may apply to safety caps on aspirin bottles. A study by W. Kip Viscusi found that the safety-cap regulation did not reduce the rate of aspirin poisoning among children. In fact, safety-capped aspirin bottles have accounted for a greater proportion of poisonings than of aspirin sales. The reason may be that the caps are hard for even adults to use—especially those with fingers stiffened from arthritis who take aspirin for relief. To save themselves trouble, these people leave the caps off the bottles altogether. Children then find the open bottles and poison themselves.

Are these findings evidence of human stupidity? Of irrationality? Of evil intent? Economists think not; rather, they are simply an outcome of the logic of consumer choice—a logic that government regulators do not always take into account.

Please buckle up.
You may never get another chance.

"My children, Matt and Jaime, and I were not safety belt users. But minutes before this crash, we put them on. Experts tell us we'd have been killed without safety belts. I share this with you out of love. So please buckle up. You may never get another chance."

Barbara Mandrell

Do drivers wearing seat belts drive less *cautiously than those who don't?*

Sources: Sam Peltzman, "The Effects of Automobile Safety Regulation," *Journal of Political Economy* 83 (August 1975): 677–725; Robert W. Crandall and John D. Graham, "Automobile Safety Regulation and Offsetting Behavior: Some New Empirical Estimates," *American Economic Review* 74 (May 1984): 328–331; W. Kip Viscusi, "The Lulling Effect: The Impact of Child-Resistant Packaging on Aspirin and Analgesic Ingestions," *American Economic Review* 74 (May 1984): 324–327. Photo Source: Courtesy of National Safety Council.

A chapter title like "Rational Choice and Consumer Behavior" may evoke an image of people filling their shopping carts in a supermarket. To be sure, the economic theory of consumer behavior does apply to the supermarket—but its uses extend much further, as the cases of seat belts and aspirin bottle safety caps suggest. In fact, it applies to any scenario in which people are faced with the need to get the most satisfaction they can in a situation of scarcity given the alternatives and opportunity costs that they face. But let's not get ahead of the story. As usual, we must begin with the basics.

Utility and the Rational Consumer

When it comes to consumer behavior, the most basic question we can ask is why people consume goods and services at all. The answer that people usually give when they think about their own motivations is that consumption of goods and services is a source of pleasure and satisfaction. A loaf of bread to eat, a warm bed to sleep in, or a book to read each serves some want. Economists have their own term for this: The use or consumption of goods and services gives people **utility.**

Utility
The pleasure, satisfaction, or need fulfillment that people get from the consumption of goods and services.

Objectives, Alternatives, and Constraints

Utility is your *objective* as a consumer. There are many ways in which you can achieve utility—eating pie, listening to music, driving a nice car. Economists refer to these as your *alternatives*. However, scarcity limits your ability to take advantage of the alternatives available to you. In many situations, scarcity expresses itself in the form of a limited budget: You have only $5 to spend for lunch, so you must pass up the filet mignon and champagne and settle for a cheeseburger and a soft drink. Also, you may be faced with a scarcity of time: You can't both go to the concert and study economics. Whatever its form, scarcity imposes *constraints* on your choice of alternatives.

Objectives, alternatives, and constraints set the scene for **rational choice.** *Rational*, in this sense, simply means "purposeful"—you are acting rationally if you set goals and make a systematic effort to achieve them given the alternatives available to you and the constraints you face. Acting rationally does not have to mean using a computer to calculate everything to the last decimal point before making a move. Trial and error, experimentation, and the use of short-cut rules of thumb are consistent with rationality provided you keep your goals in mind and learn from your mistakes.

Rational choice
Purposeful choice directed systematically toward the achievement of objectives given the alternatives and constraints of the situation.

Economists do not claim that people behave rationally, even in this broad sense, at all times. People are subject to periods of aimlessness when it seems too much effort to make a choice. They may experience fits of frustration or even rage. And they sometimes make choices that are inconsistent with their expressed objectives, for example, wolfing down pie when they claim to be on a diet. Psychologists find these behaviors interesting. They may try to construct models in which, say, episodes of rage are related to chemical or electrical activity in certain parts of the brain. But economists, for the most part, have been content to limit their models to rational choice.

William Stanley Jevons and Marginal Utility Theory

The English economist William Stanley Jevons is credited with the first systematic statement of the theory of marginal utility. Jevons was trained in mathematics and chemistry. With this background, it is not surprising that when his interest turned to economics he tried to restate economic theories in mathematical terms. It was this effort that led him to the theory of marginal utility.

In his *Theory of Political Economy*, published in 1871, Jevons set forth the principle of diminishing marginal utility as follows:

Photo Source: Historical Pictures Service, Chicago.

Let us imagine the whole quantity of food which a person consumes on an average during twenty-four hours to be divided into ten equal parts. If his food be reduced by the last part, he will suffer but little; if a second tenth part be deficient, he will feel the want distinctly; the subtraction of the third part will be decidedly injurious; with every subsequent subtraction of a tenth part his sufferings will be more and more serious until at length he will be upon the verge of starvation. Now, if we call each of the tenth parts an *increment*, the meaning of these facts is, that each increment of food is less necessary, or possesses less utility, than the previous one.

Jevons was the first economist to put the new theory into print, but he shares credit for the "marginal revolution" with at least three others who were working along the same lines simultaneously. The Austrian economist Karl Menger published his version of marginal utility theory in 1871. Three years later, the Swiss economist Leon Walras, who knew neither Jevons' nor Menger's work, came out with still another version. Finally, Alfred Marshall worked out the basics of marginal utility theory at about the same time in his lectures at Cambridge, although he did not publish them until 1890.

The Principle of Diminishing Marginal Utility

In the late nineteenth century, William Stanley Jevons and other economists working independently took a major step forward in their understanding of rational choice when they unearthed the principle of diminishing marginal utility (see "Who Said It? Who Did It? 7.1"). To a consumer, the **marginal utility** of a good is the amount of added utility that he or she gains from consuming one additional unit of that good, other things being equal. The **principle of diminishing marginal utility** says that the greater the quantity of any good consumed, the less the marginal utility from consuming one more unit.

This principle was arrived at less through observation than through introspection. Chances are you have experienced diminishing marginal utility yourself. Suppose you arrive at a party. You are thirsty. Your host has thoughtfully provided a cooler filled with ice and cans of cold soda. You grab a can. Ah—satisfaction! Your mental utility meter hits a 10. A few minutes later, you grab another can. It's still good even though there is no matching the satisfaction of that first can. Give this one a 7. Still later, you reach for your third can. You take a few swallows, but it tastes overly sweet. You set it down unfinished. Your utility meter has hit zero: Those last remaining swallows would give you no satisfaction at all.

Of course, utility is a subjective concept. No one has yet invented a "utility meter" that can be hooked up to a person to read utility the way it is possible to read blood pressure. But suppose there is such a meter. If you allowed yourself

Marginal utility
The amount of added utility gained from a one-unit increase in consumption of a good, other things being equal.

Principle of diminishing marginal utility
The principle that the greater the consumption of some good, the smaller the increase in utility from a one-unit increase in consumption of that good.

to be hooked up to it during the above party and recorded the results, they would look something like Exhibit 7.1.

Diminishing Marginal Utility and Consumer Choice

The party situation represented in Exhibit 7.1 is not a typical example of consumer choice because it lacks the elements of alternatives (choice between two or more goods) and constraints (a limited budget). We now look at how the principle of diminishing marginal utility can be applied to a slightly more complex situation.

Assume you are at a lunch counter where pizza is being sold at a price of $2 for a rather skimpy slice and soda is being sold at a price of $1 for a small glass. You have $10 to spend on lunch. What will you order?

Your objective is to choose a lunch that will give you the greatest possible utility. Will you spend all your money to buy five pieces of pizza? Probably not. However much you like pizza, you won't get as much satisfaction out of the fifth piece as the first—at least according to the principle of diminishing marginal utility. Probably you will be willing to pass up the fifth piece of pizza to have a couple of glasses of soda with which to wash the first four down. Doing so will increase your total utility, because the first two sodas will give you a lot of satisfaction and the last piece of pizza only a little. How about the fourth piece of pizza? Maybe you will be willing to give up half of it for one more glass of soda. As you cut back on pizza and increase your consumption of soda, the marginal utility of pizza rises and that of soda falls. Finally, you get to the point where you cannot further increase your utility by spending less on one good and more on the other within a given budget. You have reached a point of **consumer equilibrium.**

Consumer equilibrium
A state of affairs in which a consumer cannot increase the total utility gained from a given budget by spending less on one good and more on another.

You reach consumer equilibrium when the marginal utility you get from a dollar's worth of one good equals the marginal utility you get from a dollar's worth of the other. Another way to state this is that the ratio of the marginal utility of a good to its price must be the same for all goods:

$$\frac{\text{Marginal utility of good A}}{\text{Price of good A}} = \frac{\text{Marginal utility of good B}}{\text{Price of good B}}.$$

Suppose, for example, that you have adjusted the quantities of pizza and soda you buy so that you get 10 "utils" from another slice of pizza at a price of $2 per slice and 5 utils from another glass of soda with a price of $1 per glass. At these ratios, you get no more added satisfaction from an extra dollar's worth (one half-slice) of pizza than from an extra dollar's worth (one glass) of soda. It is not worthwhile to trade off some of either good for some of the other. You are in equilibrium.

On the other hand, suppose you get 18 utils from another slice of pizza (9 utils per half-slice) and 4 from another glass of soda, still given the same prices. Now you are not in consumer equilibrium. Cutting back by one soda would lose you just four utils. You could then use the dollar you saved to buy another half-slice of pizza, gaining nine utils. By making this adjustment in your consumption pattern, you would not only gain total utility—you would also move closer to consumer equilibrium, because the marginal utility you would get from pizza would fall slightly as you consumed more and the marginal utility you would get from soda would rise a little as you consumed less.

Exhibit 7.1   Diminishing Marginal Utility

As the rate at which a person consumes a good increases, the utility gained from one additional unit decreases. This graph shows hypothetical utility data for the consumption of soda by a certain consumer. The numbers are only illustrative; in practice, utility cannot be measured.

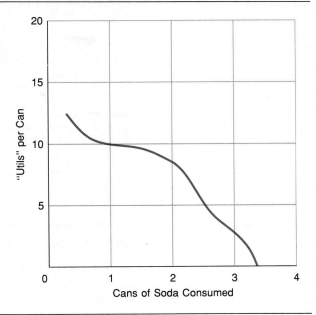

Putting numbers on things in this way helps explain the principle involved. Remember, however, that in practice consumer choice is a much more subjective process. Some people count calories when they sit down to lunch; some count the pennies in their pockets; but no one counts "utils"—they cannot really be counted. Utility is something we feel, not something we think about. Because some people feel differently about what they eat than others, they make different choices. Perhaps you would rather have a cold squid salad and a glass of iced coffee than either pizza or soda. But although the outcome of your choice might differ from that of someone else's, the logic of the decision—the calculus of utility, the concept of equilibrium—is the same.

From Consumer Equilibrium to the Law of Demand

The concepts of consumer equilibrium and diminishing marginal utility can be combined to give an explanation of the law of demand that is useful even though not entirely precise. The explanation goes as follows. Suppose you have adjusted your pattern of consumption until you have reached an equilibrium in which, among other things,

$$\frac{\text{MU of pizza}}{\$2} = \frac{\text{MU of soda}}{\$1}.$$

As long as this equality holds, it will not benefit you to increase your consumption of pizza; doing so would, according to the principle of diminishing marginal utility, soon push down the marginal utility of pizza. The marginal utility per dollar's worth of pizza would drop below the marginal utility per dollar's worth of soda, making you better off if you switched back toward more soda.

But what if the price of pizza were to drop to, say, $1.50 per slice, upsetting the equality just given? To make the two ratios equal again given the new price of pizza, either the marginal utility of soda would have to rise or that of pizza would have to fall. According to the principle of diminishing marginal utility, one way to get the marginal utility of pizza to fall is to consume more pizza, and one way to get the marginal utility of soda to rise is to consume less soda. Perhaps you would do a little of both—that is, cut back a little on soda and consume a little more pizza. In so doing, you would be acting just as the law of demand would predict: A fall in the price of pizza would have caused you to buy more pizza.

This line of reasoning connects the law of demand with the principle of diminishing marginal utility in a way that appeals to common sense. However, that is not good enough for all economists. In the next section, we look at an alternative line of reasoning.

Substitution and Income Effects

In the view of some economists, the whole concept of utility is suspect because of its subjective, unmeasurable nature. Is there a way to explain the law of demand without relying on utility? There is—an approach based on the concepts of substitution and income effects of a change in price.

Substitution Effect

Substitution effect
The part of the increase in quantity demanded of a good whose price has fallen that is caused by substitution of the good that is now relatively cheaper for others that are now relatively more costly.

One reason people buy more of a good whose price falls is that they tend to substitute that good for others that are now relatively more expensive. In our earlier example, we looked at the effects of a drop in the price of pizza. This change in price will cause people to substitute pizza for other foods that they might otherwise have eaten—hamburgers, nachos, whatever. Broader substitutions are also possible. With the price of pizza lower than before, people may substitute eating out for eating at home or a pizza party for an evening at the movies. The part of the increase in the quantity demanded of a good whose price has fallen that is caused by the substitution of the now relatively cheaper good for others that are now relatively more costly is known as the **substitution effect** of a change in price.

Income Effect

There is a reason other than the substitution effect why the change in a good's price will cause a change in quantity demanded. This reason has to do with the effect of price changes on real income.

In Chapter 1, we introduced the term *nominal* to refer to quantities measured in the ordinary way—in current dollars—and the term *real* to indicate quantities adjusted for the effects of price changes. The distinction between real and nominal income is a typical application. If your monthly paycheck is $1,000, that is your nominal income—the number of dollars you earn. If your nominal income stays at $1,000 while inflation doubles the average prices of all goods and services, however, your *real* income—your ability to buy things taking price changes into account—will fall by half. With less real income, you will buy less of things that are normal goods and more of things that are inferior goods. If your nominal income stays at $1,000 while the average prices of goods and services drop by half, your real income will double. Because of the increase in real income, you will buy more of normal goods and less of inferior goods.

In macroeconomics, we tend to focus on the effects of inflation or deflation that take the form of changes in the prices of many goods at once. Microeconomics, on the other hand, tends to emphasize the effects of price changes of one good at a time. Nonetheless, if the price of even one good changes while the prices of others remain constant, there will be some effect on the average price level and, hence, on real income.

With this in mind, let us return to our example. Again suppose that the price of pizza falls while your nominal income and the prices of all other goods and services remain the same. While pizza occupies only a small place in your budget, a fall in its price means a slight fall in the average level of all prices and, hence, a slight increase in real income. If you continue to buy the same quantity of pizza and all other goods and services as before, you will have a little money left over. For example, if the price of pizza goes down by $.50 a slice and you usually buy 10 slices a month, you will have $5 left over after your usual purchases. This is as much of an increase in your real income as you would get were your paycheck increased by $5 while all prices remained constant.

The question now is: On what will you spend the $5? You will use it to buy more of things that are normal goods. If pizza is a normal good, one of the things you will buy with your increased real income is more pizza. The part of the change in quantity demanded of a good whose price has fallen that is caused by the increase in real income resulting from the price change is known as the income effect of the price change.

Income effect
The part of the change in quantity demanded of a good whose price has fallen that is caused by the increase in real income resulting from the price change.

Income and Substitution Effects and the Demand Curve

In the case of a normal good, the income effect is an additional reason, logically distinct from the substitution effect, for buying more of a good when its price falls. With two effects causing the quantity demanded to increase when the price falls, we can be certain that the demand curve for a normal good will have a negative slope. Note that we can reach this conclusion with no reference to the messy concept of "utility." So far, so good.

If we are dealing with an inferior good, however, the situation is a little different. Let's say that hot dogs are an inferior good for you. You eat them if you are hungry and they are all you can afford, but if your income goes up enough to buy pizza, you phase out hot dogs. Now what will happen if the price of hot dogs goes down while the prices of all other goods and services remain constant?

First, there will be a substitution effect. Hot dogs are relatively cheaper than before compared to soda, pizza, pretzels, haircuts, or whatever. Taken by itself, the substitution effect will cause you to buy more hot dogs. Other things being equal—other things including real income, that is—the rational consumer will always buy more rather than less of something when its opportunity cost (in this case, its price relative to other goods) goes down. But here other things are not equal. At the same time that the fall in the price of hot dogs tempts you to substitute hot dogs for other things, it also slightly raises your real income. Taken in isolation, that increase in real income will cause you to buy fewer hot dogs, because hot dogs are an inferior good for you. Thus, we see that in the case of an inferior good, the substitution and income effects work at cross-purposes when the price changes.

What, then, is the net effect of a decrease in the price of hot dogs? Will you buy more or less of them than before? In the case of a good that makes up only a small part of your budget, such as hot dogs, it is safe to assume that a fall in price will cause you to buy more and a rise in price to buy less. The reason is that a change in the price of something of which you buy only a little anyway will cause only a minuscule income effect, which will be outweighed by the substitution effect. Thus, when the substitution effect is larger than the income effect, the demand curve for even an inferior good will still have a negative slope.

However, there exists the remote possibility that the demand curve for an inferior good might have a positive slope if it makes up a large part of a person's budget so that the income effect is significant. Imagine, for example, a family that is so poor that they spend almost all of their income on food. They eat bread as a special treat on Sunday, but the rest of the week they must make do with inferior-tasting but cheaper oatmeal. One day the price of oatmeal goes up, although not by enough to make it more expensive than bread. The rise in the price of oatmeal is devastating to the family's budget. They are forced to cut out their one remaining luxury: The Sunday loaf of bread disappears and is replaced by oatmeal. The paradoxical conclusion, then, is that a rise in the price of oatmeal causes this family to buy more oatmeal, not less. The family's demand curve for oatmeal has a positive slope.

Now one more question: So what? If you are in the pizza business—or even in the oatmeal business—you can be essentially certain that, taking the world as it really is, raising the price of any good or service will cause people to buy less of it and cutting the price will cause them to buy more. Experience tells us that demand curves have negative slopes. However, the pure logic of rational choice by itself cannot prove that there will never be a situation in which the demand curve (for an inferior good) might be an exception to general experience.

Applications of Income and Substitution Effects

The law of demand and the concepts of income and substitution effects can be applied to many situations besides the ones discussed so far—in fact, to every situation of consumer choice. This is true even when the choices are not between goods for sale in a store and the opportunity costs of the choices are not stated in terms of money.

Substitution and Safety

The studies of safety regulations cited at the beginning of this chapter illustrate this point. First, take the case of automobile safety equipment. When you get in a car to go somewhere, you face a trade-off between travel time and safety. A quick trip is good, but so is a safe one. Making the trip safer by driving more slowly, stopping for yellow lights, and so on has an opportunity cost in terms of time. Cutting travel time by driving faster and going through yellow lights has an opportunity cost in terms of safety.

If the opportunity costs change, the choices drivers make also tend to change. For example, suppose there is snow on the road; that makes the road less safe and raises the opportunity cost of speed. When it snows, then, drivers shift their choices away from speed and toward safety, just as the substitution effect would predict.

A change in the design of cars to make them safer also changes the opportunity cost of speed relative to that of safety. Cutting travel time by speeding up and running yellow lights entails giving up less safety in a car with airbags than in one without them. Logically, the substitution effect would cause people to drive faster and less carefully in safer cars. A side effect of this choice would be more pedestrian and bicyclist deaths. This is the result found by the studies cited earlier. The studies disagree on the size of the effect, but not on its direction.

Some of the studies have found an income effect as well as a substitution effect on driving behavior. The studies by Crandall and Graham indicate that safety is an inferior good. It seems that as people's incomes go up, they begin to feel that their time is too valuable to spend in a car. Perhaps they speed up so they can get to their high-paying jobs or fancy parties more quickly. If they decide to run a greater risk of killing themselves and others along the way—well, that's part of the logic of consumer choice. Maybe people with less exciting destinations have less reason to be in a hurry.

The aspirin bottle case described in the opening case of this chapter can also be explained in terms of the logic of consumer choice. Putting the cap back on the aspirin bottle has a benefit: It decreases the chance that young children will poison themselves. If the cap is a safety cap, the benefit is greater still, since it is even less likely that a young child will open the bottle. However, putting the cap back on the bottle also has an opportunity cost: It will be harder to grab an aspirin the next time you have a headache. If the cap is a safety cap, the opportunity cost will be greater, since safety caps are often hard for even adults to remove. Thus, fitting aspirin bottles with safety caps raises both the benefit in terms of safety and the cost in terms of convenience. If the increase in cost outweighs the increase in benefit, putting a safety cap on the bottle raises the opportunity cost of safety. Following the logic of the substitution effect, people shift their behavior away from safety and toward convenience. The result, Viscusi found, is that 73 percent of all aspirin poisonings involve bottles with safety caps, even though only half of all aspirin bottles sold have such caps. Further, half of all the poisonings involve bottles that were left open.

Are Animals Rational Consumers Too?

Studies such as those described can be interpreted as illustrations of income and substitution effects and the law of demand. There are problems with these interpretations, however. In the real world, it is never possible to observe how people's behavior changes, "other things being equal," because other things are changing too. Thus, studies of responses to changes in automobile safety have been clouded by changes in speed limits, the average age of drivers, the quality of roads, and other factors. Similarly, studies of aspirin bottle safety caps have been clouded by changes in total aspirin use, marketing of new painkillers, and so on.

Because the real world is such a messy place, economists have often envied the controlled laboratory environments of their scientist colleagues. Now some economic researchers have begun to do laboratory experiments too. "Applying Economic Ideas 7.1" reports the results of an experiment on the consumer behavior of white rats. The rats, it seems, are subject to the substitution effect just as people are. Think about that the next time you are threading your way through the maze of aisles in your local supermarket.

APPLYING ECONOMIC IDEAS   7.1

Testing Consumer Demand Theory with White Rats

Two white male rats were placed in standard laboratory cages, with food and water freely available. At one end of each cage were two levers that activated dipper cups. One dipper cup provided a measured quantity of root beer when its lever was depressed; the other provided a measured quantity of nonalcoholic Collins mix. Previous experimentation had shown that rats prefer these beverages to water.

Within this setup, each rat could be given a fixed "income" of so many pushes on the levers per day. The pushes could be distributed in any way between the two levers. Experimenters could also control the "price" of root beer and Collins mix by determining the number of pushes the rat had to "spend" to obtain one milliliter of liquid.

In an initial experimental run lasting 2 weeks, the rats were given an income of 300 pushes per day, and both beverages were priced at 20 pushes per milliliter. Under these conditions, rat 1 settled down to a pattern of drinking about 11 milliliters of root beer per day and about 4 millili-

ters of Collins mix. Rat 2 preferred a diet of almost all root beer, averaging less than one milliliter of Collins mix per day.

Next came the crucial test. By manipulating incomes and prices, could the rats be induced to shift their consumption patterns in the way economic theory predicts? To see if they could, the experimenters proceeded as follows. First, the price of root beer was doubled and the price of Collins mix was cut in half. At the same time, each subject's total income of pushes was adjusted to make it possible for each to afford to continue the previous consumption pattern were it chosen. (This adjustment in total income was made in order to eliminate any possible income effect of the price change and to concentrate solely on the substitution effect.) Economic theory predicts that under the new conditions the rats would choose to consume more Collins mix and less root beer than before, even though they would have the opportunity to keep their behavior the same as before.

The rats' behavior exactly fitted these predictions. In 2 weeks of living under the new conditions, rat 1 settled down to a new consumption pattern of about 8 milliliters of root beer and 17 milliliters of Collins mix per day. Rat 2, which had chosen root beer almost exclusively before, switched over to about 9 milliliters of root beer and 25 milliliters of Collins mix.

Source: Adapted by permission from John H. Kagel and Raymond C. Battalio, "Experimental Studies of Consumer Demand Behavior," *Economic Inquiry* 8 (March 1975): 22–38, Journal of the Western Economic Association.

Consumer Surplus

This chapter has related consumer choice to the demand curve from two perspectives—that of utility theory and that of the income and substitution effects. In both cases, the demand curve was viewed as answering the question: How much of a good will consumers wish to purchase at any given price? In this section, we turn to a different question to which the demand curve can also provide an answer: How much will consumers be willing to pay for an additional unit of a good given the quantity they already have?

Demand Curve as Willingness to Pay

Exhibit 7.2 shows a demand curve for apples for Elizabeth Carellas, a student at George Mason University. Carellas eats lunch each day in the student union cafeteria and often includes an apple in her menu. The demand curve given in

Exhibit 7.2   Consumer Surplus

The height of a demand curve shows the maximum that this consumer would be willing to pay for an additional unit of a good. For example, she would be willing to pay up to $.38 for a first apple each month but only $.26 for a seventh. The maximum she would willingly pay for each unit is shown by a vertical bar. In this case, the market price is $.20; thus, she buys 10 apples a month, paying a total of $2. The difference between what she actually pays at the market price and the maximum she would have been willing to pay, shown by the shaded area, is called *consumer surplus.*

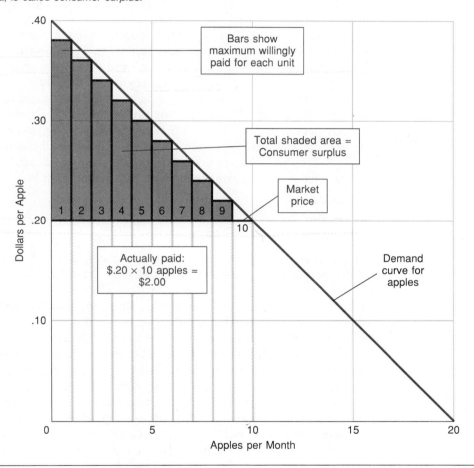

the exhibit shows that the number of apples she eats each month depends on their price. Currently the price of an apple is $.20. At this price, she buys 10 per month. On other days she substitutes an orange or a banana.

The demand curve indicates that $.20 is the maximum that Carellas would be willing to pay for the tenth apple. If the price rose to $.22, she would substitute some other fruit for the tenth apple. However, she would not cut out apples altogether. Although $.20 is the maximum she is willing to pay for the tenth apple, she would not give up the ninth apple unless the price rose above $.22. Similarly, she would be willing to pay up to $.24 before giving up the eighth apple, up to $.26 before giving up the seventh, and so on. The height of the demand curve at each point, then, emphasized here by a vertical bar, shows the maximum she would willingly pay for each unit consumed. This maximum decreases as the quantity consumed increases in accordance with the principle of diminishing marginal utility.

Measuring the Surplus

Exhibit 7.2 shows us the maximum that Carellas is willing to pay for various quantities of apples, but it also shows that she need not actually pay this amount. At the going price of $.20, she pays only a total of $2 for the 10 apples she buys each month. Except in the case of the last unit purchased, she gets each unit for less than what she would willingly have paid for it. The difference between what she would willingly have paid for each unit and the amount actually paid at the market price is called the **consumer surplus** for that unit. The consumer surplus on each unit is shown by the shaded portion of the corresponding vertical bar. For example, the surplus on the first apple, for which Carellas would have willingly paid $.38 if necessary, is $.18, since she actually paid only $.20. The total consumer surplus on all units purchased is shown by the sum of the shaded portions of the bars. The area of the triangle between the demand curve and the market price is an approximate measure of consumer surplus.[1]

Consumer Surplus, Producer Surplus, and Gains from Exchange

The reasoning behind the notion of consumer surplus can be extended to the producers' side of the market as well. Consider Exhibit 7.3, which shows supply and demand curves for a typical market. The equilibrium market price is established where the two curves cross. The demand curve, as we have seen, measures consumers' maximum willingness to pay for each unit sold; for example, they will pay no more than $1.50 for the 1,000th unit. Consumer surplus is a measure of the difference between the maximum that consumers would have been willing to pay and what they actually pay at the market price.

Now turn to the supply curve. The height of the supply curve at any point represents the minimum that producers would willingly accept for the unit. For example, producers would be unwilling to accept less than $.75 for the 1,000th unit sold. If they could not get at least that much, the producers would put their resources to an alternative use rather than produce the 1,000th unit of this product.

However, as the exhibit is drawn, producers receive the market price of $1 per unit for all units sold, including the 1,000th. On that unit, they earn a producer surplus of $.25. The **producer surplus** earned on each unit is the difference between the market price of $1 and the minimum that the producers would have been willing to accept in exchange for that unit—$.75 in the case of the 1,000th unit in our example. The total producer surplus earned on all units is shown by the area between the supply curve and the market price.

Thus, there is a symmetry to the market. Consumers buy the goods, except

Consumer surplus
The difference between the maximum that a consumer would be willing to pay for a unit of a good and the amount that he or she actually pays.

Producer surplus
The difference between what producers receive for a unit of a good and the minimum they would be willing to accept.

---

[1] The intermediate-level microeconomics course will explain that for reasons associated with the income effect, this triangle does not provide a precise measure of consumer surplus. However, the approximation is close for goods that make up only a small part of consumers' total expenditures.

Exhibit 7.3   Gains from Trade

This exhibit shows that both consumers and producers gain from trade in free markets. Here the equilibrium market price is $1 per unit. The demand curve shows the maximum that consumers would willingly pay for each unit. Consumers' gain from trade takes the form of consumer surplus, shown by the area between the demand curve and the market price. The supply curve shows the minimum that producers would willingly accept rather than put their resources to work elsewhere. Producers earn a surplus equal to the difference between what they actually receive at the market price and the minimum they would have been willing to accept. This producer surplus is shown by the area between the supply curve and the market price. Total gains from trade are thus the entire area between the supply curve and the demand curve up to the equilibrium point.

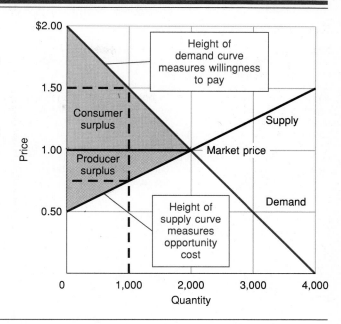

for the very last unit, for less than they would have been willing to pay, and producers sell the goods, except for the very last unit, for more than the minimum they would have been willing to accept. In other words, *both buyers and sellers gain from exchange*. That is why markets exist. As long as participation is voluntary, they make everyone who buys and sells in them better off than they would be if they did not participate. The total gains from trade—consumer surplus plus producer surplus—equal the entire triangle between the supply and demand curves in Exhibit 7.3.

Application: The Excess Burden of a Tax

Exhibit 7.4 provides an application of the concepts of consumer and producer surplus. The example is based on Exhibit 6.6 (page 141), which analyzes the incidence of a tax on gasoline. There we showed that a $.50-per-gallon tax on gasoline raised the equilibrium price, including tax, from $1 to $1.40 per gallon. The price received by sellers, after tax, fell from $1 to $.90 per gallon. We concluded that the economic burden of this particular tax fell more heavily on consumers than on suppliers, although both bore a share.

The concepts of consumer and producer surplus offer additional insight into the issue of tax incidence. Exhibit 7.4 shows that the tax brings in $4 million per day in revenue to the government. This equals the after-tax quantity Q_2, which is 8 million gallons, times the amount of the tax, which is $.50 per gallon. Part of this revenue is paid by consumers at the expense of the consumer surplus they otherwise would have earned by being able to buy 8 million gallons at $1 rather than at $1.40. Part is paid by suppliers at the expense of the producer surplus they would have earned by being able to sell 8 million gallons at $1

Exhibit 7.4   Excess Burden of a Tax

Imposition of a tax of $.50 per gallon on gasoline raises the equilibrium price from $1 to $1.40 per gallon. The price that sellers receive after the tax is paid falls to $.90. Revenue collected by the government equals the tax times Q_2, the equilibrium quantity after tax. The economic burden of the revenue is divided between consumers and sellers. There is also an *excess burden,* which takes the form of the consumer and producer surpluses that would be realized from sale of the additional quantity that would be sold without the tax. This is shown by the area of the triangle between the supply and demand curves and between the pretax quantity, Q_1, and the after-tax quantity, Q_2.

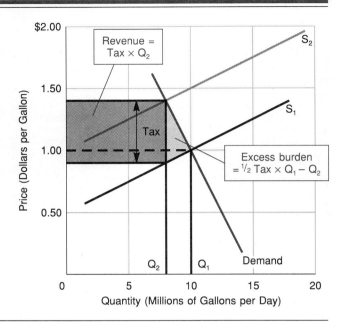

Excess burden of a tax
The part of the economic burden of a tax that takes the form of consumer surplus and producer that is lost because the tax reduces the equilibrium quantity sold.

rather than at $.90. The sum of this part of the consumers' burden and this part of the producers' burden is equal to the tax revenue collected by the government.

However, there is an additional burden on consumers and producers that is not reflected in the government's revenue from the tax. This burden is associated with the reduction in quantity from 10 million to 8 million gallons per day because of the tax. Consumers would have enjoyed a surplus on this extra 2 million gallons equal to the triangle above the pretax price of $1 between Q_1 and Q_2; producers would have enjoyed a surplus equal to the triangle below the pretax price between Q_1 and Q_2. This lost consumer-plus-producer-surplus is called the **excess burden of the tax.**

The common sense behind this is that the tax imposes a burden on consumers and producers that is larger than the amount the government takes in as revenue. It does so because the tax discourages buyers and sellers from doing as much business as they would have done without the tax. The potential mutual gains from pushing exchange in the gasoline market all the way out to 10 million gallons per day are lost. In geometric terms, the size of the excess burden can be calculated by applying the rule that the area of a triangle equals one-half of its height times its base. The height is the tax ($.50), and the base is $Q_1 - Q_2$ (2 million gallons). Thus, the excess burden is $500,000 per day. The total burden on consumers plus producers equals the $4 million collected by the government plus this $500,000 excess burden, or $4.5 million.

This example can be generalized in that virtually any tax causes firms or individuals to change their behavior by doing less of the taxed activity. For instance, income taxes have an excess burden related to their reduction of incentives to work and save. Similarly, taxes on imports (tariffs) have an excess burden related to the fact that they discourage international trade following the principle of comparative advantage. The excess burden of taxes is part of the opportunity cost of government services.

Looking Ahead

In this chapter, we have taken a behind-the-scenes look at the demand curve. Although the basic idea that people buy more of a good when its price goes down can be understood without formal training in economics, an understanding of the logic of rational choice permits extensions and applications of demand theory to less familiar areas. Examples in this chapter have included consumer safety policy, animal experiments, and the excess burden of a tax.

In the next two chapters, we will leave the demand curve for a time in order to take a similar behind-the-scenes look at the supply curve. After that, we will apply the concepts underlying the supply and demand curves together to a wide range of theoretical problems and policy issues.

Summary

1. **What elements are involved in rational choice by consumers?** Objectives, alternatives, and constraints provide the setting for rational choice by consumers. Consumers choose rationally when they set goals and make systematic efforts to achieve them. The objective of consumer choice is *utility*—the pleasure and satisfaction that people get from goods and services. The added utility obtained from a one-unit increase in consumption of a good or service is its *marginal utility*. The greater the rate of consumption of a good, the smaller the increase in utility from an additional unit consumed.

2. **How do consumers balance their selection of goods and services to achieve an equilibrium?** Typically, a consumer must choose among many alternative goods given the constraint of a fixed budget. *Consumer equilibrium* is said to occur when the total utility obtained from a given budget cannot be increased by shifting spending from one good to another. In equilibrium, the marginal utility of a dollar's worth of one good must equal the marginal utility of a dollar's worth of any other good.

3. **What lies behind the effect of a price change on the quantity of a good demanded?** The change in quantity demanded that results from a change in a good's price, other things being equal, can be separated into two parts. The part that comes from the tendency to substitute cheaper goods for more costly ones is the *substitution effect*. The part that comes from the increase in real income that results when the price of a good falls, other things being equal, is the *income effect*.

4. **Why do demand curves have negative slopes?** For a normal good, the substitution and income effects work in the same direction. The demand curves for normal goods therefore slope downward. For inferior goods, the income effect of a price change works in the opposite direction from that of the substitution effect. For inferior goods, therefore, the demand curve will slope downward only if the substitution effect outweighs the income effect. In practice, this seems to always be the case.

5. **Why do both consumers and producers gain from exchange in free markets?** When consumers buy a product at a given market price, they pay the same amount for each unit purchased. However, because of the *principle of diminishing marginal utility*, the first units purchased are worth more to them than the last. The difference between what consumers actually pay for a unit of a good and the maximum they would be willing to pay is the *consumer surplus* gained on that unit of the good. Similarly, the difference between what sellers actually receive for a good and the minimum they would have accepted is known as *producer surplus*.

6. **Why does the burden of a tax exceed the revenue raised by government?** When a tax is imposed on a good or service, the equilibrium price including tax rises while the equilibrium price net of the tax falls. As

a result, the equilibrium quantity falls, making both consumers and producers forgo some surplus. This forgone surplus not captured in the form of tax revenue is called the *excess burden of the tax*. It is a burden on consumers and producers over and above the sum that the government collects as tax revenue.

Terms for Review

- utility
- rational choice
- marginal utility
- principle of diminishing marginal utility
- consumer equilibrium
- substitution effect
- income effect
- consumer surplus
- producer surplus
- excess burden of a tax

Questions for Review

1. Do all goods give consumers utility? What form does the utility gained from a hamburger take? From a house? From a novel? Do you think these different kinds of utility have enough in common that we can speak of trade-offs between them?

2. Assume that soft drinks cost $.50 a cup and popcorn $.75 a box. Under what conditions would a consumer be in equilibrium in the consumption of soft drinks and popcorn assuming that he or she buys at least some of each?

3. Suppose that packaged chocolate chip cookies are a normal good and flour for baking cookies is an inferior good. Explain how the quantity of each good demanded is affected by an increase in its price, taking into account both the substitution and income effects.

4. What role do income and substitution effects play in determining the slope of the demand curve for a normal good? For an inferior good?

5. Why does the maximum amount that a consumer is willing to pay for a good decline as the quantity of the good purchased increases?

6. Why does a tax on a good or service reduce the total gains from trade between producers and consumers by more than the amount of revenue raised by government?

Problems and Topics for Discussion

1. **Examining the lead-off case.** The increase in pedestrian and bicyclist deaths resulting from drivers' use of seat belts or airbags is an example of an externality (see Chapter 5). What could the government do to prevent this externality while still achieving the policy goal of increased driver safety? *Bonus question:* If you complete the appendix to this chapter, analyze the trade-off between speed and safety using an indifference curve diagram. How does the installation of seat belts in a car change the budget line?

2. **Can there be increasing marginal utility?** Can there be increasing marginal utility in some cases? For example, suppose it would take eight rolls of wallpaper to decorate your kitchen. If someone gave you seven rolls of wallpaper, you would get only limited utility from them. An eighth roll, however, would bring great utility. Do you think this is a valid exception to the principle of diminishing marginal utility?

3. **Consumer equilibrium, marginal utility, and prices.** Martha Smith consumes two pounds of pork and five pounds of beef per month. She pays $1.50 a pound for the pork and $2 per pound for the beef. What can you say about the ratio of the marginal utility of pork to the marginal utility of beef assuming that this pattern represents a state of consumer equilibrium for Smith? Is the ratio 3/4, 4/3, 5/2, 2/5, or none of these?

4. **An exception to the law of demand?** A family living in Minnesota spends each January in Florida. One year the price of home heating fuel goes up sharply. The family turns the thermostat down a little, but even so the heating bills go up so much that the family cannot afford to go to Florida that year. Staying home in January means that the house must be kept heated during that month. The extra fuel burned during January is more than what the family has been able to save with a lower thermostat setting in other months. Thus, the total quantity of fuel burned in the winter rises as a result of the increase in the price of heating fuel. Analyze this case in terms of the income and substitution effects, and compare it to the oatmeal example given in the chapter. (Hint: Winter vacations spent in Minnesota are an inferior good for this family. Heating fuel is a complement to winter vacations in Minnesota and thus is also an inferior good.)

5. **Excess burden of a tax.** Exhibit 6.7 (page 142) demonstrates the incidence of a tax on apartment rents. Using the approach outlined in this chapter, calculate the revenue raised by and the excess burden of this tax. How much of the excess burden is borne by landlords? How much by tenants?

Case for Discussion
Homes Get Dirtier as Women Seek Jobs

CHICAGO. This stately old Victorian house would make a stately old Victorian squirm.

Household cleanliness declines as women join the job force.

Dust coats the classics on the living room bookcase and combines with dog hair to form soft curls that ride the drafts in the hardwood hallway upstairs. Light switches are mottled with fingerprints. In the dining room, the silver tea set has turned golden.

The lady of this particular house is a lawyer. "She raised five kids and got burned out on housework and now has better things to do," says Brenda Bell, digging away with a mop at some stubborn wax buildup in a kitchen corner. Bell, a cleaning lady, now tries to do weekly in five hours what used to take most ladies all week. "Mostly I just try to maintain and keep it from getting worse," she says.

This house, in Chicago's fashionable Hyde Park neighborhood, could be anywhere, for cleanliness is no longer next to godliness. Gone are the days when housekeepers dusted even their lightbulbs to perfection and waxed their floors to reflection. "There's a whole new generation of women out there who wouldn't be caught dead on their hands and knees scrubbing a floor," says Mary Powers, associate director of the Good Housekeeping Institute.

Sales of scouring powder, mildew removers, floor wax and dishwashing liquid slipped again last year, continuing a 10-year trend, according to Selling Areas Marketing Inc., a New York research company. In contrast, sales of paper plates and aluminum baking pans (the kind you can throw away) boomed. So did a new type of toilet-bowl cleaner that purports to eliminate the need for scrubbing. For much of the year, air fresheners also did a sweet business—the better to cover up bad odors.

Even Heloise, the archetypal homemaker whose nationally syndicated column has been advising women for 26 years on how to get gum out of the carpet and scum off the shower tile, admits that she has relaxed her standards. "Oh my goodness yes, I believe in neat and tidy but definitely not in spic and span," says the 33-year-old Texan who inherited the column from her mother. She recently caught herself dusting her word processor with the corner of her bathrobe. "That's how bad things get around here," she says.

Questions

1. In times past, women had little access to high-paying careers outside the home in such fields as law, finance, and medicine. How has the emergence of such career possibilities changed the opportunity cost of household cleanliness? How does the change in opportunity cost explain the decline in cleanliness? Do you conclude simply that people today are slobs, or are the trends discussed an example of rational choice?

2. On the basis of this article, would you conclude that cleansers, mildew removers, and so on are inferior goods? Why or why not?

3. Is the decline in household cleanliness in upper-income, dual-earner homes

attributable to an income effect? A substitution effect? Some of each? Explain.

4. *Bonus question:* If you complete the appendix to this chapter, analyze the cleanliness issue in terms of indifference curves. (Hint: Use a diagram with "time spent on housework" on the horizontal axis and "consumer goods" on the vertical axis. The consumer goods are purchased with money earned in a job outside the home.) Assume a time budget of 10 hours a day total to be divided between housework and work at an outside job. Draw a budget line for a person whose best job outside the home pays $3.25 an hour as a supermarket clerk and another for a person whose best outside job pays $25 an hour as an accountant.

Suggestions for Further Reading

Blaug, Mark. *Economic Theory in Retrospect*, 3d ed. Cambridge, England: Cambridge University Press, 1978.

Chapter 8 discusses the origins of utility theory and the work of William Stanley Jevons. Chapter 9 discusses Alfred Marshall's refinements of utility theory and its modern restatement in terms of preference and indifference.

Nicholson, Walter. *Intermediate Microeconomics and Its Applications*, 4th ed. Hinsdale, Ill.: Dryden Press, 1987.

Chapters 3 through 6 of this book (or comparable chapters in any other intermediate microeconomics text) discuss the logic of consumer choice in detail.

Appendix to Chapter 7 — Indifference Curves

Chapter 7 described two versions of the theory of consumer choice—one based on marginal utility and the other on income and substitution effects. This appendix gives a third version that uses what are known as *indifference curves*. Indifference curves are not featured in this book, but they are often used in intermediate- and advanced-level economic writings. Many students and instructors find it worthwhile to study them, albeit briefly, as part of an introductory course. This appendix will serve their needs.

Constructing an Indifference Curve

Begin by supposing that I am an experimenter and you are my subject. I want to find out how you feel about consuming various quantities of meat and cheese. It would be convenient if I had a utility meter, but I do not. Therefore, to find out your attitudes toward the consumption of these goods, I offer you a number of baskets (two at a time) containing varying amounts of meat and cheese.

As I offer each pair of baskets, I ask: "Would you prefer the one on the left to the one on the right? The one on the right to the one on the left? Or are you indifferent between the two?" In this way, I hope to get a meaningful answer from you. I know I have a better chance of getting such an answer this way than I would if I asked you how many utils you would get from each basket.

At some point in the experiment, I offer you a basket A, which contains eight pounds of meat and three pounds of cheese, and basket B, which contains six pounds of meat and four pounds of cheese. I ask you the usual questions, and you answer that you are indifferent between the two baskets. You feel that the extra pound of cheese in basket B just makes up for the fact that it has two pounds less meat than basket A. This gives me a useful bit of information: It tells me that for you baskets A and B belong to an **indifference set**—a set of consumption choices each of which yields the same amount of satisfaction such that no member of the set is preferred to any other. Exploring the matter further, I find that two other baskets, C and D, also belong to the same indifference set, which now has the following four members:

Indifference set
A set of consumption choices of which each yields the same utility so that no member of the set is preferred to any other.

Basket	Meat (Pounds)	Cheese (Pounds)
A	8	3
B	6	4
C	5	5
D	4	7

I thank you for taking part in my experiment and get out a piece of graph paper. First I draw a pair of axes, as in Exhibit 7A.1. Pounds of meat are

Exhibit 7A.1   An Indifference Curve

Each point in this diagram stands for a basket of meat and cheese. A, B, C, and D are baskets among which a certain consumer is indifferent. All give equal utility. Those points and all the others on a smooth curve connecting them form an indifference set. An indifference curve is a graphic representation of an indifference set.

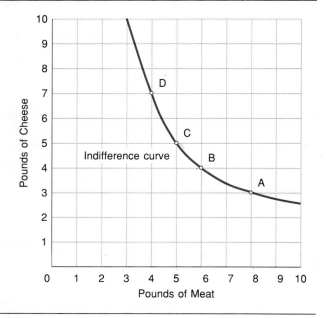

measured on the horizontal axis and pounds of cheese on the vertical axis. Each basket of goods can be shown as a point in the area between the two axes. The points representing baskets A through D are shown in their proper places on the graph. These points and all those between them that lie on the smooth curve joining them are members of the same indifference set. The curve itself is an **indifference curve**—a curve composed of points that are all members of the same indifference set.

Indifference curve
A graphic representation of an indifference set.

Some Characteristics of Indifference Curves

Indifference curves have characteristics that reflect certain regularities in patterns of consumer preferences. Five of these are of interest to us:

1. *Indifference curves normally have negative slopes.* For example, the curve in Exhibit 7A.2 is not possible if both meat and cheese are desired goods— that is, if the consumer prefers more to less, other things being equal. The basket shown by point A contains more of both goods than that shown by point B. This implies that if greater amounts of meat and cheese give greater satisfaction, A must be *preferred* to B; it cannot be a member of the same indifference set as B.

2. *The absolute value of the slope of an indifference curve at any point is the ratio of the marginal utility of the good on the horizontal axis to the marginal utility of the good on the vertical axis.* For example, look at Exhibit 7A.1. Between D and C, the slope of the curve is approximately −2 (or simply 2 when the minus sign is removed to give the absolute value). This shows that the marginal utility of meat is approximately twice that of cheese when the amounts consumed are in the region of baskets C and D. Because the marginal utility of

Exhibit 7A.2   Indifference
Curves Have Negative Slopes

Indifference curves normally have negative slopes. The
positively sloped portion of the indifference curve shown
here is impossible if both goods give increased satisfaction
with increased quantity. A has more of both goods than B.
Therefore, point A should be preferred to point B and,
hence, could not lie on the same indifference curve.

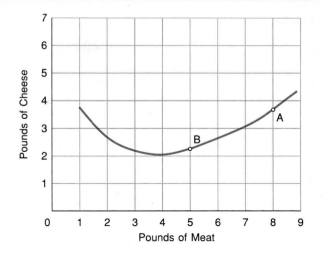

meat is twice that of cheese in this region, the consumer will feel neither a
gain nor a loss in total utility in trading basket D for basket C, that is, in
giving up two pounds of cheese for one extra pound of meat. Because it
shows the rate at which meat can be substituted for cheese without a gain or
loss in satisfaction, the slope of the indifference curve is called the **marginal
rate of substitution** of meat for cheese.

3. *Indifference curves are convex; their slopes decrease as one moves downward and
   to the right along them.* This implies that the ratio of the marginal utility of
   meat to the marginal utility of cheese (or the marginal rate of substitution of
   meat for cheese) decreases as one moves downward and to the right along
   the curve. Look once more at Exhibit 7A.1. In the region between D and C
   the curve's slope is approximately −2, indicating that the ratio of the marginal utility of meat to that of cheese is approximately 2 to 1. By comparison,
   in the region between B and A the slope is only about −1/2. The ratio of the
   marginal utility of meat to the marginal utility of cheese is now approximately 1 to 2.

4. *An indifference curve can be drawn through the point that represents any basket
   of goods.* Exhibit 7A.3 shows the same indifference curve as in Exhibit
   7A.1, but here the curve is labeled I_1. Point E, which represents a basket
   containing seven pounds of meat and five pounds of cheese, is not a member
   of the indifference set represented by this curve. Because it lies above and to
   the right of point B and has more of both products than B, it must be
   preferred to B. Other points, such as F and G, have more cheese and less
   meat than E and, on balance, give the same satisfaction as E. The consumer
   is indifferent among E, F, G, and all other points on curve I_2 and prefers all
   of these points to any of those on I_1.
       Any point taken at random, along with the other points that happen to
   give the same amount of satisfaction, can form an indifference curve. Several other (unlabeled) curves are sketched in Exhibit 7A.3. Were all possible curves drawn in, they would be so close together that the lines would run
   into a solid sheet, completely filling the space between the axes. A selection

**Marginal rate of
substitution**
The rate at which one good
can be substituted for
another with no gain or loss
in satisfaction.

Exhibit 7A.3   Multiple Indifference Curves

An indifference curve can be drawn through any point. Here curve I_1 represents an indifference set containing points A, B, C, and D and I_2 a set composed of points E, F, and G. All points on I_2 are preferred to all points on I_1. A representative set of indifference curves like the one shown here can be called an *indifference map*.

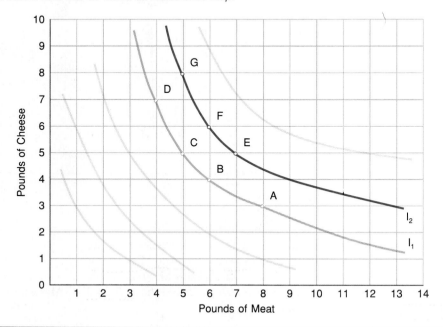

Indifference map
A selection of indifference curves for a single consumer and pair of goods.

Transitivity
The principle that if A is preferred to B and B is preferred to C, A must be preferred to C.

of indifference curves showing their general pattern but leaving enough space to make the graph easy to read is called an **indifference map.**

5. *Indifference curves do not cross.* Consumer preferences are **transitive,** meaning that if you prefer A to B and B to C, you will prefer A to C. Looking at Exhibit 7A.4, you can see that crossed indifference curves are not possible. Consider points A, B, and C. A and B lie on the same indifference curve, I_1; hence, the consumer is indifferent between them. A and C both lie on I_2; thus, the consumer is indifferent between them, too. Since consumer preferences are transitive, if B is as good as A and A is as good as C, C is as good as B. But C lies above and to the right of B. It represents a mix of goods that contains more of both meat and cheese. If more is better, the consumer must prefer C to B. Since crossed indifference curves imply a contradictory set of preferences, we must conclude that they cannot cross.

The Budget Line

The range of choices open to a consumer with a given budget and with given prices can be shown on the same kind of graph we have used for indifference curves. Exhibit 7A.5 shows how this can be done. Suppose you have a food

Exhibit 7A.4   Indifference Curves Cannot Cross

Because consumer preferences are transitive, indifference curves cannot cross. The impossible curves shown here represent contradictory preferences. A and B are both on I_1; thus, the consumer must be indifferent between them. A and C are both on I_2; hence, the consumer must be indifferent between them as well. Transitivity implies that the consumer is indifferent between B and C, but this is impossible because C contains more of both goods than B does.

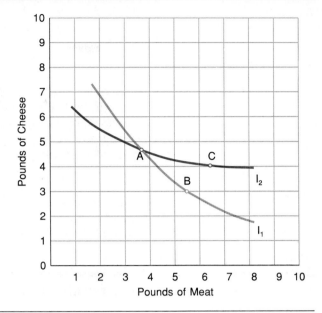

budget of $10 per week, the price of meat is $2 a pound, and the price of cheese is $1 a pound. If you spend all your money on meat, you can have up to 5 pounds of meat; if you spend all your money on cheese, you can have up to 10 pounds of cheese. Combinations such as two pounds of meat and six of cheese or four pounds of meat and two of cheese are also possible. Taking into account the possibility of buying a fraction of a pound of meat or cheese, these choices can be

Exhibit 7A.5   The Budget Line

Suppose you have a food budget of $10 per week. You can spend your money on meat at $2 a pound, on cheese at $1 a pound, or on some mix of the two. The consumption opportunity line (budget line) shows all the possible combinations given these prices and your budget.

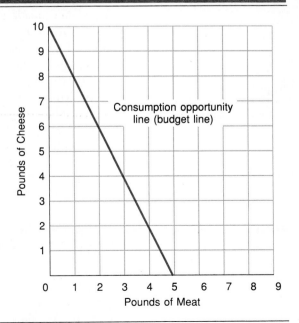

Consumption opportunity line (budget line)

Budget line
A line showing the various combinations of goods and services that can be purchased at given prices within a given budget.

shown on the graph as a diagonal line running from 10 on the cheese axis to 5 on the meat axis. This line is called the **budget line.**

Using m to stand for amount of meat and c for amount of cheese, the equation for the budget line can be written as

$$2m + 1c = 10.$$

This equation simply says that the number of pounds of meat bought times the price of meat plus the number of pounds of cheese bought times the price of cheese must add up to the total budget if no money is left unspent. In more general terms, the equation for a budget line for goods x and y—with P_x the price of x, P_y the price of y, and B the consumer's total budget—is

$$P_x x + P_y y = B.$$

The slope of such a budget line is $-P_x/P_y$. In the case shown in Exhibit 22A.5, where the price of meat is \$2 a pound and the price of cheese is \$1 a pound, the slope of the budget line is -2.

A Graphic Representation of Consumer Equilibrium

Indifference curves and the budget line can be used to give a graphic representation of consumer equilibrium. Exhibit 7A.6 shows the budget line from Exhibit 7A.5 superimposed on an indifference map like the one shown in Exhibit 7A.3. In this way, we can easily compare consumer preferences and consumption choices. For example, point B is preferred to point A because it lies on a "higher" indifference curve (one that at some point, such as C, passes above and to the right of A). By similar reasoning, point B is preferred to point D. Of all the points on or below the budget line, it is clear that point E, which represents 2.5 pounds of meat and 5 pounds of cheese, is the most preferred, since all the other points on it lie on lower indifference curves. Every point that, like F, is better lies outside the range of consumption choices.

Because E is the point that gives the greatest possible satisfaction, it is the point of consumer equilibrium. At E, the relevant indifference curve is just tangent to the budget line; this means that the slopes of the curve and the budget line are the same at this point. The slope of the indifference curve, as shown earlier, equals the ratio of the marginal utility of meat to the marginal utility of cheese. The slope of the budget line equals the ratio of the price of meat to the price of cheese. Thus, it follows that in consumer equilibrium,

$$\frac{\text{Marginal utility of meat}}{\text{Marginal utility of cheese}} = \frac{\text{Price of meat}}{\text{Price of cheese}}.$$

This is the condition for consumer equilibrium given in Chapter 7.

Derivation of the Demand Curve

This appendix concludes with Exhibit 7A.7, which shows how a demand curve for meat can be derived from a set of indifference curves. Along with the curves, Exhibit 7A.7 shows a set of budget lines. Each line is based on the assumption

Exhibit 7A.6   Consumer Equilibrium

E is the point of consumer equilibrium given the indifference curves and budget line shown. All points that are better than E (such as F) lie outside the budget line. All other points for goods that the consumer can afford to buy (such as A and D) lie on lower indifference curves than E and thus are less preferred.

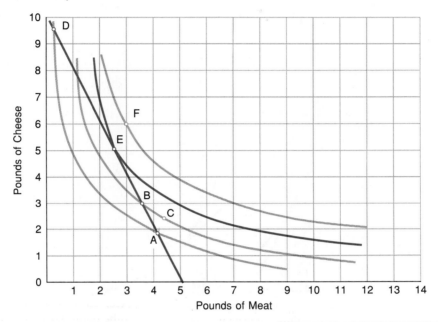

that the price of cheese is $1 a pound and the consumer's budget is $10, as before. Now, however, each budget line assumes a different price, P, of meat. The budget line running from 10 on the vertical axis to 2.5 on the horizontal axis assumes that P = $4. The budget line running from 10 on the vertical axis to 5 on the horizontal axis assumes that P = $2. (This is the same budget line as the one in Exhibits 7A.5 and 7A.6.) The other two budget lines assume that P = $1.50 and P = $1, respectively.

The equilibrium pattern of consumption differs for each price of meat, other things being equal. When P = $4, point A, which represents six pounds of cheese and one pound of meat, is the best the consumer can do; when P = 2, B is the most preferred point.

Given this information, it is a simple matter to draw the consumer's demand curve for meat. Part b of Exhibit 7A.7 shows a new set of axes, with the quantity of meat on the horizontal axis as before but the price of meat on the vertical axis. From part a of Exhibit 7A.7, when P = $4 the consumer chooses combination A, which includes one pound of meat. In part b, therefore, point a is marked as the quantity of meat demanded at a price of $4; then point b (which corresponds to point B in part a) is added; and so on. Drawing a smooth line through points a, b, c, and d gives the consumer's demand curve for meat. As expected, it has the downward slope predicted by the law of demand.

Exhibit 7A.7   Derivation of a Demand Curve

Part a of this exhibit shows a consumer's indifference map for meat and cheese and a set of budget lines. Each budget line corresponds to a different price, P, of meat. All four budget lines assume the price of cheese to be $1 and the total budget to be $10. Points A, B, C, and D in part a show the choices the consumer makes at meat prices of $4, $2, $1.50, and $1. In part b, the data on meat consumption at the various prices is plotted on a new set of axes. The smooth line connecting points a, b, c, and d is the consumer's demand curve for meat.

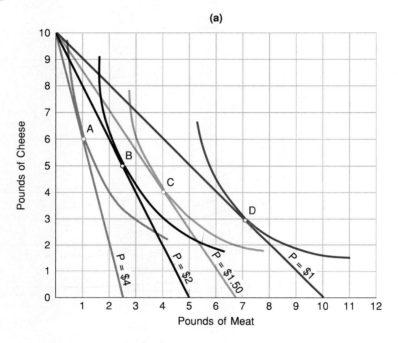

(a)

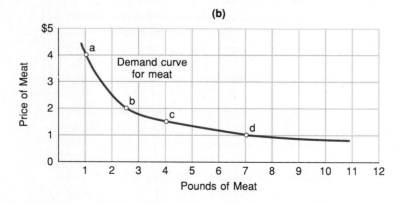

(b)

Terms for Review

- indifference set
- indifference curve
- marginal rate of substitution

- indifference map
- transitivity
- budget line

Theory of the Firm

Part Three

8 Cost and Production

After reading this chapter, you will understand . . .

- How economists view the concepts of cost and profit.
- How short-run and long-run time horizons are distinguished.
- How costs vary in response to changes in the quantity of a variable input.
- How a firm's cost structure can be represented geometrically.
- What choices a firm faces in the course of long-run expansion.

Before reading this chapter, make sure you know the meaning of . . .

- Opportunity cost (Chapter 1)
- Entrepreneurship (Chapter 2)
- Rent (Chapter 5)
- Nature of the firm (Chapter 4)

Sharing a Dream

Andrea and Ralph Martin shared a dream with millions of Americans: having a business of their own. For some that dream means a hamburger franchise, a dry cleaning shop, or a few hundred acres of soybeans. The Martins were more ambitious: They dreamed of having their own computer company.

The Martins had no illusions about the entrepreneurial life. They knew that starting their own firm would take hard work and sacrifice. Both were engineers with high-paying jobs at large corporations. On their combined income of $80,000 a year, they could have lived the good life—a house in the suburbs, a Mercedes in the driveway, and a condominium in the Virgin Islands. Instead, they lived in a small apartment and saved every dollar they could to build a nest egg with which to start their firm.

The Martins knew they couldn't take on IBM in hand-to-hand combat. They needed to find a corner of the computer market where they could start small and offer customers something new. Ralph's job with an oil company gave him an idea. On his visits to refineries and drilling sites, he often carried a notebook-size computer with which to record data and make on-the-spot computations. But all the small computers available were designed for use in offices. Out in the heat and dust of the field, they often broke down. Ralph was sure there would be a market for a more ruggedly built computer for use under field conditions. Andrea was sure she could design one.

The design for the new machine took shape on paper. The company, Fieldcom Inc., took shape on paper too. Then one day it was time to take the plunge. The Martins quit their jobs, hired two technicians and an office manager, and went into production. Their factory was an abandoned service station available at a rock-bottom rent. Within a month the first of their new products, the Fieldcom I, rolled off the assembly line.

Fieldcom Inc. needed to find a niche in a competitive market.

179

IN this and the next chapter, we will use Fieldcom Inc. as a case study around which to build a theory of supply in competitive markets. Along with the theory of consumer choice that underlies the demand curve, this theory will give us a better understanding of the factors that affect equilibrium prices and quantities in a market economy. The first step, which we will take in this chapter, will be to develop a theory of production and cost. In Chapter 9, we will show how costs interact with demand conditions to determine the amount of output that the firm supplies.

The Nature of Costs

One of the most basic ideas in economics is that all costs arise from the need to choose among possible uses of scarce resources; in other words, all costs are opportunity costs. The true measure of the cost of doing something is the value of the best alternative use of the same resources.

Implicit and Explicit Costs

The opportunity costs that a firm such as Fieldcom faces include the payments it must make to suppliers of parts, materials, and services plus the incomes it must provide to workers, investors, and owners of resources in order to attract factors of production away from alternative uses. These costs are of two kinds—explicit and implicit.

Explicit costs
Opportunity costs that take the form of payments to outside suppliers, workers, and others who do not share in the firm's ownership.

   Explicit costs are opportunity costs that take the form of payments to outside suppliers, workers, and others who do not share in the firm's ownership. These include payments for the labor and raw materials used in production, the services of hired managers and salespeople, insurance, legal advice, transportation, and many other things.

Implicit costs
Opportunity costs of using resources owned by the firm or contributed by its owners.

   Implicit costs are the opportunity costs of using resources owned by the firm or contributed by its owners that are not obtained under contracts calling for explicit payments. Like explicit costs, they represent real sacrifices by the firm. Unlike explicit costs, however, they do not take the form of explicit payments to outsiders. When a firm uses a building that it owns, it need not make a payment to anyone, but it gives up the opportunity to receive payments from someone else to whom it could rent the building. As another example, if the proprietor of a small firm works along with the firm's hired employees, he or she gives up the opportunity to earn a salary by working for someone else. Firms normally do not record implicit costs in their accounts, but that does not make these costs any less real.

Costs and Profits

Pure economic profit
The sum that remains when both explicit and implicit costs are subtracted from total revenue.

Accounting profit
Total revenue minus explicit costs.

The distinction between explicit and implicit costs is important for understanding the concept of profit. As economists use the term, profit means the difference between a firm's total revenues and its total costs, including both explicit and implicit costs. This concept is called **pure economic profit.** Special care must be taken to distinguish the concept of economic profit from two other uses of the term *profit.*

   First, in the world of business the term *profit* is often used to mean revenue minus explicit costs only. Economists call this concept **accounting profit** to distinguish it from pure economic profit as defined above. The relationship between these two concepts is as follows:

Pure economic profit = Accounting profit − Implicit costs.

Second, the term **normal profit** is sometimes used to refer to the opportunity cost of capital. Let's say, for example, that the Martins use $200,000 of their own savings as capital for their new business. They could instead have placed these funds in a certificate of deposit in a bank, where they would have earned a 10 percent rate of return, or $20,000 per year. That $20,000 would be the opportunity cost of capital—the return the funds would have earned in their best alternative use. However, the $20,000 they "normally" would earn on the capital if invested elsewhere is really a part of implicit costs; thus, it is somewhat misleading to call it "normal profit." *Normal return on capital* or *opportunity cost of capital* are more accurate terms.

Exhibit 8.1 uses Fieldcom Inc. to illustrate the concepts of pure economic profit, accounting profit, and "normal profit." The exhibit shows Fieldcom as having earned total revenues of $500,000. Explicit costs—materials purchased and salaries paid to employees—came to $350,000. This left an accounting profit of $150,000.

These explicit costs do not include all of the firm's opportunity costs, however. Both Andrea and Ralph Martin gave up high-paying jobs to start the firm. Their combined former income of $80,000 is listed in Exhibit 8.1 as an implicit cost of production. Also listed as an implicit cost is $20,000 of forgone income that the Martins could have earned on their $200,000 had they invested it elsewhere. This is the firm's opportunity cost of capital—the "normal profit" required to attract capital to this use rather than the best alternative one. When both explicit and implicit costs (including "normal profit") are subtracted from revenue, the firm is left with a pure economic profit of $50,000.

Normal profit
A term sometimes used to describe the opportunity cost of capital.

Profit, Rents, and Entrepreneurship

Pure economic profit, as we have defined it, is the difference between what a firm receives for the products it sells and the opportunity cost of producing them. We encountered the notion of payments in excess of opportunity costs in Chapter 5, where we called them *economic rents*. Profit, then, is a type of economic rent. Nonetheless, the two terms are not fully interchangeable.

For one thing, rent is a broader notion than profit. "Profit" is usually used in connection with the activities of a business firm, whereas "rents" can be said

---

Exhibit 8.1   Accounts of Fieldcom Inc.

This exhibit shows the implicit and explicit costs of the Martins' firm, Fieldcom Inc. Total revenue minus explicit costs equals accounting profit. Subtracting implicit costs from this quantity yields pure economic profit.

Total revenue	$500,000
Less explicit costs:	
Wages and salaries	300,000
Materials and other	50,000
Equals accounting profit	$150,000
Less implicit costs:	
Forgone salary, Andrea Martin	40,000
Forgone salary, Ralph Martin	40,000
Opportunity cost of capital ("normal profit")	20,000
Equals pure economic profit	$ 50,000

to be earned by any factor of production. For example, rock stars, top sports professionals, and other people with exceptional talents often earn more than the minimum they would accept rather than leave their chosen line of work. Their extraordinary earnings can thus properly be called economic rents, but they normally would not be considered profits.

A distinction is also sometimes made between *profit seeking* and *rent seeking*. Profit seeking is commonly associated with the activity of entrepreneurship. Entrepreneurs seek profits by finding ways to use readily available factors of production, purchased at market prices, to create goods and services of greater value or at lower costs than others have been able to do in the past. The Martins of our opening case are an example of entrepreneurs seeking profits by finding a new way to satisfy customer needs. Thus, *profit seeking* means finding ways to create new value.

However, as we pointed out in Chapter 5, some firms seek to increase their revenues not through innovation and cost reduction but by seeking restrictions on competition. For example, the Martins might try to boost their firm's earnings by persuading Congress to ban imports of similar computers made in Japan and Korea. This is an example not of entrepreneurship but of rent seeking.[1]

The distinction between profits earned by entrepreneurs and rents earned by rent seekers is certainly not watertight. In both cases, we are dealing with revenues that exceed opportunity costs. Data such as those in Exhibit 8.1 do not tell us all we might want to know about the origin of the $50,000 of "pure economic profit." Was that $50,000 earned by entrepreneurial creation of a new product superior to those of competitors, or was it earned by rent seeking—say, by import restrictions that drove the superior products of foreign competitors from the market? The issues raised by this kind of question go beyond the cost and revenue data with which we deal in this and the next chapter, but we will return to them in later chapters.

Production and Costs in the Short Run

Having pinned down the economic meaning of cost, our next step is to build a theory of cost. The job of this theory is to explain how costs vary with the amount of output a firm produces and, in the process, provide a basis for the firm's supply curve. Our discussion of the theory of cost will be divided into two parts corresponding to two time horizons—the short run and the long run. We will first examine the distinction between them.

Long Run versus Short Run

A firm uses many kinds of inputs to produce its output. The amounts of inputs it uses vary as the amounts of output change. The amount of some inputs used can be adjusted quickly, but others are more difficult to modify. The latter inputs can be thought of as those that define the size of the firm's plant, such as the physical size of structures and the production capacity of machinery. These are

---

[1] See James M. Buchanan, "Rent Seeking and Profit Seeking," in James M. Buchanan, Robert D. Tollison, and Gordon Tullock, eds., *Toward a Theory of the Rent-Seeking Society* (College Station, Tex.: Texas A&M University Press, 1980), 3–15.

ECONOMICS IN THE NEWS 8.1

Labor Costs: Fixed or Variable?

Hourly labor is usually considered a variable cost of production. When demand for a firm's product declines, layoffs of hourly workers are often one of the first steps taken to adjust to a lower output rate. However, some firms' contracts with their unions make hourly labor a fixed rather than variable cost, at least in part.

The big steel firms' contract with the United Steel Workers is a case in point. It calls for pensions, health and life insurance, unemployment benefits, and severance pay when a plant is closed. The benefits can cost up to $70,000 per employee.

Source: Thomas F. O'Boyle, "High Cost of Liquidation Keeping Some Money-Losing Plants Open," *The Wall Street Journal*, November 29, 1982, 29.

If labor costs remain fixed even when a plant is closed, it may make sense to keep a plant running even if it is losing money. For example, in 1980 Kaiser Steel's directors voted to keep 11,000 workers on the job because shutting down would have cost the company more than $350 million in benefits. In another case, the need to treat labor costs as fixed prompted a firm to adopt an unusual strategy to get rid of a money-losing operation. In 1981, National Steel decided that it could no longer afford to invest in its Weirton, West Virginia, steel division. Closing the plant would have cost the firm about $320 million in benefits for former employees. To escape this burden, National sold the Weirton operation to its 10,000 employees. They have kept the plant open and are hoping that wage cuts and increases in productivity will make it profitable again.

---

known as **fixed inputs.** In some cases, the services of hard-to-replace employees can also be viewed as fixed inputs.

In addition to fixed inputs, the firm uses **variable inputs** that can be adjusted quickly and easily within a plant of a given size as output changes. Raw materials, energy, and hourly labor are variable inputs for most firms. It should be kept in mind that which inputs are fixed and which are variable depends on the situation. As "Economics in the News 8.1" shows, inputs that are variable for some firms may be fixed for others.

The distinction between fixed and variable inputs is the basis for that between the short run and the long run in cost theory. The **short run** is a time horizon that is too short to permit changing the size of a firm's plant, allowing variations in output to come only from changes in the amounts of variable inputs used. The **long run** is a time horizon that is long enough to permit changes in the amounts of fixed inputs and the size of the firm's plant.

Production with One Variable Input

Most firms have many inputs that can be varied. A change in any one of them will have some effect on output, other things being equal. Let's turn once again to Fieldcom for an example.

A key variable input for Fieldcom, as for most other firms, is labor. Exhibit 8.2 shows what happens to the daily production rate measured in physical terms, or **total physical product,** as the number of workers is varied from zero to eight.

If no workers are employed, no production can take place. One worker alone cannot produce anything either—some parts of the job require a minimum of two people working together. Two workers can get production moving, but because they waste a lot of time setting up work and changing from job to job,

Fixed inputs
Inputs that cannot be easily increased or decreased in a short time.

Variable inputs
Inputs that can be easily varied within a short time in order to increase or decrease output.

Short run
A time horizon within which output can be adjusted only by changing the amounts of variable inputs used while fixed inputs remain unchanged.

Long run
A time horizon that is long enough to permit changes in both fixed and variable inputs.

Total physical product
Total output of a firm measured in physical units.

Exhibit 8.2   Response of Output to
Changes in One Variable Input

This exhibit shows how the output of computers at Fieldcom Inc. responds to changes in one variable input—labor. All other inputs remain constant while the number of workers is varied. One worker can produce nothing, since some equipment takes a minimum of two employees to operate. Output increases—at first rapidly, then more slowly—as more workers are used. After seven workers are on the job, all equipment is in use; thus, additional workers add nothing more to output. Column 3 of part a and the chart in part b show the amount of added output that results from each added worker. This is known as the *marginal physical product* of the variable input.

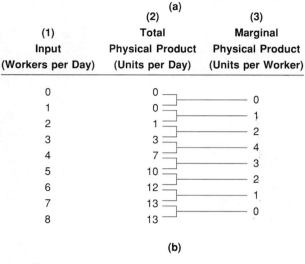

(a)

(1) Input (Workers per Day)	(2) Total Physical Product (Units per Day)	(3) Marginal Physical Product (Units per Worker)
0	0	
		0
1	0	
		1
2	1	
		2
3	3	
		4
4	7	
		3
5	10	
		2
6	12	
		1
7	13	
		0
8	13	

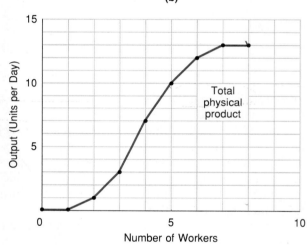

(b)

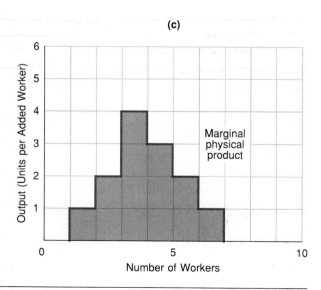

(c)

they are able to produce at a rate of only one computer per day. When the third worker is added, some degree of specialization is made possible, and production picks up to three units per day. A fourth worker gets things moving really smoothly, and production rises to seven units per day. Adding workers 5, 6, and 7 boosts the plant's output to its maximum of 13 computers per day. At that point, it does no good to add more workers; all the tools and equipment are in use, and the extra workers would have to stand around waiting for a turn to use them.

Of course, output could be increased by adding *other* inputs in addition to workers—more assembly tables, more test equipment, and so on. But for the moment, we are looking at the effects of increasing just one variable input, other things being equal.

Marginal Physical Product

The chart in part b and columns 1 and 2 in part a of Exhibit 8.2 show the relationship between labor inputs and the total daily output rate. In the range of one to seven workers, output rises as labor input increases, but not at a constant rate. Column 3 of the table and the chart in part c of the exhibit show how much output is added by each additional worker. This is called the **marginal physical product** of the variable input. As labor input is increased from one to two workers, the marginal physical product is one unit of output; as it is stepped up from two to three workers, marginal physical product rises to two units; and so on. The step from three workers to four gives the greatest boost to output. After that, output increases at a diminishing rate with each added worker. Finally, once staffing reaches seven workers, the marginal physical product drops to zero.

Marginal physical product
The increase in output, expressed in physical units, produced by each added unit of one variable input, other things being equal.

Law of Diminishing Returns

The example just given illustrates a long-established principle known as the **law of diminishing returns**. According to this principle, as the amount of one variable input is increased with the amounts of all other inputs remaining fixed, a point will be reached beyond which the marginal physical product of the input will decrease.

The law of diminishing returns applies to all known production processes and to all variable inputs. It applies in manufacturing, as illustrated in the Fieldcom case. But the law could be demonstrated just as well by an example from farming with, say, fertilizer as the variable input: As more fertilizer is added to a field output increases, but beyond some point the gain in output brought about by an additional ton of fertilizer tapers off. (In fact, too much fertilizer could poison the plants, in which case marginal physical product would become negative.) Oil refineries, power plants, barber shops, government bureaus—indeed, *any* production process—could be used to illustrate the law of diminishing returns.

Law of diminishing returns
The principle that as one variable input is increased with all others remaining fixed, a point will be reached beyond which the marginal physical product of the variable input will begin to decrease.

From Marginal Physical Product to Marginal Costs

Our next step is to move from the marginal physical product of an input to the marginal cost of output. **Marginal cost** means the increase in cost required to raise the output of a good or service by one unit. As before, we will use Fieldcom as an example.

Marginal cost
The increase in cost required to raise the output of some good or service by one unit.

Exhibit 8.2 shows how output increases as labor input increases. Exhibit 8.3 continues the story. The first step is to rearrange the data so that column 1 shows output rather than input and to flip the charts over so that output rather than labor input occupies the horizontal axis. Next, we convert physical units of input to costs stated in dollars by multiplying the number of workers by the daily wage rate—$100 per day. The chart in part b of the exhibit, which shows total variable costs, can then be plotted from columns 1 and 3 of the table. Taking the rearrangement of the axes and the change in units into account, this curve can be recognized as the mirror image of the total physical product curve shown in Exhibit 8.2.

Next, column 4 of the table is filled in to show marginal cost, that is, added cost in dollars per added unit of output. Increasing output from zero to one requires adding two workers, so the added cost per unit in that range is $200; increasing output by two more units (from one to three) requires one more worker at $100 per day, so the cost per added unit of output in that range is $50; and so on. The marginal cost curve shown in part c of the exhibit is plotted from columns 1 and 4 of the table in part a. Again considering the change in units and rearrangement of the axes, this chart is the mirror image of the marginal physical product curve shown in part c of Exhibit 8.2.

More Than One Variable Input

The Fieldcom example assumes that only one input is varied. In practice, short-run increases or decreases in Fieldcom's output would require changes in many—though not all—inputs. For example, if the firm wanted to raise its output, it might burn more fuel to keep the shop heated longer each day and double the rate at which it orders parts as well as hiring additional workers. At the same time, its costs for certain fixed inputs—office staff, test equipment, and rent—might remain fixed.

The appendix to this chapter outlines a way of analyzing changes in two or more variable inputs. Without going into details, we can say that taking more variable inputs into account and allowing them to be varied in smaller steps tend to smooth out the steps in the crude cost curve shown in Exhibit 8.3. The result is a total variable cost curve with a smooth reverse-S shape and a smooth U-shaped marginal cost curve.

A Set of Short-Run Cost Curves

A set of smoothed-out total variable cost and marginal cost curves as described above are shown in Exhibit 8.4. These curves are only two of a set of short-run cost curves that can be constructed for Fieldcom. The exhibit also contains some often-used formulas and abbreviations that pertain to cost curves.

Total variable cost is shown graphically in part a of Exhibit 8.4 and numerically in column 2 of part c. In addition to these variable costs, there are fixed costs (office staff, test equipment, rent, and so on) that are assumed to be $2,000, as shown in column 3 of part c. Adding fixed cost to variable cost gives short-run total cost, which is shown in column 4. Total fixed cost and total cost curves are plotted together with the total variable cost curve in part a. Because fixed cost by definition does not vary as output changes, the total fixed cost curve is a horizontal line $2,000 above the horizontal axis. Adding fixed cost to variable cost gives

Exhibit 8.3   Cost and Output
with One Variable Input

This exhibit shows how the cost of production at Fieldcom Inc. changes as output varies. The table and graph are based on the same data used in Exhibit 8.2, but here they are recast to stress cost assuming a daily wage of $100 per worker. Column 3 of the table and the chart in part b show total labor cost for various output levels. Column 4 and the chart in part c show marginal cost—the amount by which cost increases per added unit of output. For example, increasing the number of workers from three to four raises output from three to seven computers per day. Over this range, then, the cost of each added computer is one-quarter of a day's wage, or $25.

(a)

(1) Output (Units per Day)	(2) Labor Input	(3) Total Labor Cost	(4) Marginal Cost
0	0	$ 0	
1	2	200	$200
3	3	300	50
7	4	400	25
10	5	500	33
12	6	600	50
13	7	700	100

(b)

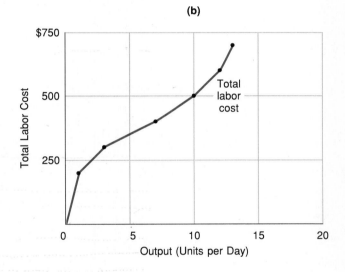

(c)

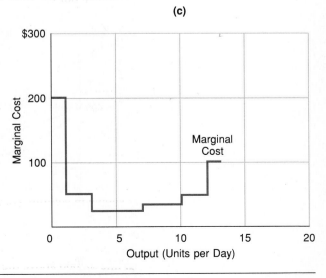

Exhibit 8.4   A Set of Short-Run Cost Curves

A whole set of short-run cost curves can be derived from data on fixed and variable costs, as this exhibit shows. The data are presented in the form of a table and a pair of graphs. The exhibit also lists a number of useful abbreviations and formulas.

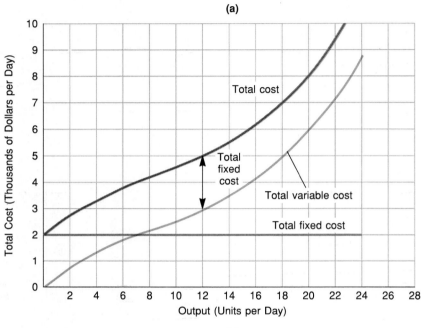

(a)

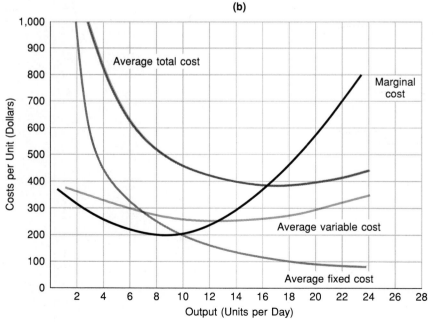

(b)

(c)

Quantity of Output (Units) (1)	Total Variable Cost (2)	Total Fixed Cost (3)	Total Cost (4)	Marginal Cost (Dollars per Unit) (5)	Average Variable Cost (Dollars per Unit) (6)	Average Fixed Cost (Dollars per Unit) (7)	Average Total Cost (Dollars per Unit) (8)
0	$ 0	$2,000	$ 2,000		—	—	—
				$380			
1	380	2,000	2,380		$380	$2,000	$2,380
				340			
2	720	2,000	2,720		360	1,000	1,360
				305			
3	1,025	2,000	3,025		342	667	1,009
				275			
4	1,300	2,000	3,300		325	500	825
				250			
5	1,550	2,000	3,550		310	400	710
				230			
6	1,780	2,000	3,780		296	333	629
				215			
7	1,995	2,000	3,995		285	286	571
				205			
8	2,200	2,000	4,200		275	250	525
				200			
9	2,400	2,000	4,400		266	222	488
				205			
10	2,605	2,000	4,605		260	200	460
				215			
11	2,820	2,000	4,820		256	181	437
				230			
12	3,050	2,000	5,050		254	169	421
				250			
13	3,300	2,000	5,300		254	154	408
				275			
14	3,575	2,000	5,575		255	143	398
				305			
15	3,880	2,000	5,880		259	133	392
				340			
16	4,220	2,000	6,220		264	125	389
				380			
17	4,600	2,000	6,600		271	118	389
				425			
18	5,025	2,000	7,025		279	111	390
				475			
19	5,500	2,000	7,500		289	105	394
				530			
20	6,030	2,000	8,030		302	100	402
				590			
21	6,620	2,000	8,620		315	95	410
				655			
22	7,275	2,000	9,275		331	91	422
				725			
23	8,000	2,000	10,000		348	87	435
				800			
24	8,800	2,000	10,800		367	83	450

(d)

Common abbreviations:

Q	Quantity of output
TC	Total cost
TFC	Total fixed cost
TVC	Total variable cost
MC	Marginal cost
AVC	Average variable cost
AFC	Average fixed cost
ATC	Average total cost

Useful formulas:

$$TC = TFC + TVC$$

$$MC = \frac{\text{Change in TC}}{\text{Change in Q}} = \frac{\text{Change in TVC}}{\text{Change in Q}}$$

$$AVC = \frac{TVC}{Q}$$

$$AFC = \frac{TFC}{Q}$$

$$ATC = \frac{TC}{Q}$$

total cost. The total cost curve parallels the total variable cost curve at a higher level. The distance between the total cost and total variable cost curves equals total fixed cost.

The next column in part c of Exhibit 8.4 is marginal cost. These data appear on lines between the total cost entries in order to stress the fact that marginal cost shows how total cost changes as the level of output varies. The marginal cost curve is plotted in part b of the exhibit.

The last three columns in the table are average cost concepts: average variable cost, average fixed cost, and average total cost. Average variable cost equals total variable cost divided by quantity of output; average fixed cost equals total fixed cost divided by output; and average total cost equals total cost divided by output. The three average cost curves are drawn together with the marginal cost curve in part b of the exhibit.

Some Geometric Relationships

Parts a and b of Exhibit 8.4 demonstrate some important geometric relationships among the cost curves. First, let us compare the marginal cost curve with the total variable cost curve drawn above it. The bottom of the U-shaped marginal cost curve lies at exactly the level of output at which the slope of the reverse-S-shaped total variable cost curve stops flattening out and starts getting steeper. This occurs because the slope of the total variable cost curve is the rate at which that curve is rising, just as marginal cost measures the rate at which total variable cost is rising. In *graphic* terms, then, the *height* of the marginal cost curve always equals the *slope* of the total variable cost curve.

A second feature of the cost curves in Exhibit 8.4 deserves comment. The marginal cost curve intersects both the average variable cost and average total cost curves at their lowest points. This is not a coincidence; it is a result of a relationship that can be called the **marginal-average rule.** This rule can be explained as follows. Beginning at any given point, ask what the cost of making one more unit will be. The answer is given by marginal cost. Then ask whether this cost is more or less than the average cost of all units produced up to that point. If the added cost of the next unit made is less than the average cost of previous units, making that unit will have the effect of pulling down the average. If the next unit costs more, its production will pull the average up. It follows that whenever marginal cost is below average variable cost, the average variable cost curve must be falling (that is, negatively sloped), and whenever marginal cost is above average variable cost, the average variable cost curve must be rising (positively sloped). This, in turn, implies that the marginal cost curve cuts the average variable cost curve at its lowest point. All this is equally true of the relationship between marginal cost and average total cost.

The marginal-average rule is not unique to economics; it can be seen in many everyday situations. Consider, for example, the effect of your grade in this course on your grade point average. You could call this grade your "marginal grade," because it represents the grade points earned by taking one more course. If your grade in this course (that is, your marginal grade) is higher than your average grade in other courses, the effect of taking this course will be to pull up your average. Your grade point average must be rising if your marginal grade exceeds your average grade. If you do worse than average in this course, your grade point average will fall. When your marginal grade falls short of your average grade, your grade point average must be falling. This is the same as the

Marginal-average rule
The rule that marginal cost must equal average cost when average cost is at its minimum.

relationship between marginal cost and average cost. If the cost of making one more unit is less than the average cost of making previous units, the average will be pulled down; if it is more, the average will be pulled up.

Some people find it easier to remember the relationships among the various cost concepts if they are presented as formulas. If you are one of these, you may find the formulas in part d of Exhibit 8.4 useful. The exhibit also gives some common abbreviations. These are not used in this text, but you may want to use them in your note taking, and your instructor will probably use them on the blackboard.

Long-Run Costs and Economies of Scale

It is sometimes said that firms "operate in the short run and plan in the long run." This slogan reflects the distinction between variable and fixed costs: In the short run, a firm varies its output within a plant of fixed size; in the long run, it plans (and carries out) expansions or contractions of the plant itself.

The previous section, then, can be thought of as an analysis of the cost factors that affect operating decisions. Many key aspects of economics turn on the operating decisions that firms make within plants of given sizes. How will farmers change the quantities of the crops they grow? During a recession, how much will a firm reduce its output and how many workers will it lay off? Should a moving and storage company charge higher rates during its peak moving season? Any change in prices or quantities supplied that does not involve a change in plant size will be affected by the shape and position of the short-run cost curves of the firms involved.

In many other cases, however, we need to know something about the factors that affect firms' plans for expansion or contraction of their plants. We might want to know, for example, how the price of milk would be affected by a reduction in federal dairy subsidies once farmers had eliminated their surplus production capacity. We might wonder how coal output would respond to increases in oil prices once time had been allowed for new mines to be opened and new equipment installed. Such questions would require an analysis of long-run costs, to which we now turn.

Planning for Expansion

Put yourself in the position of an entrepreneur about to set up a small firm like Fieldcom. You think it will be wise to start with a small plant, but you want to do some long-range planning, too. After consulting with specialists in the field, you sketch some average cost curves for various plant sizes. Five such curves are drawn in Exhibit 8.5. The first one shows short-run average costs for the range of output that is possible with a very small plant; the second one corresponds to a slightly larger plant; and so on.

The size of plant you actually choose will depend on the level of output you plan to produce in the long run. Moving from one plant size to another involves a major commitment to fixed costs. The curves in Exhibit 8.5 are drawn to show average total costs assuming that these fixed costs can be spread over a long operation period at the output level for which a plant is designed. A small firm cannot afford to take on the costs of a permanently larger plant just to fill a single

Exhibit 8.5   Short- and Long-Run Average-Cost Curves

The position of the short-run average total cost curve for a firm depends on the size of the plant. In the long run, the firm has a choice of operating with any size of plant it chooses. Each plant size can be represented by a U-shaped short-run average total cost curve. Five such curves are shown in this graph. A new firm might begin with a plant that can be represented by a curve such as the first one shown here. Then, as demand for its product expands, it might move to one of those further to the right. The firm's long-run average cost curve is the "envelope" of these and other possible short-run average total cost curves; that is, it is a smooth curve drawn so that it just touches the short-run curves without intersecting any of them.

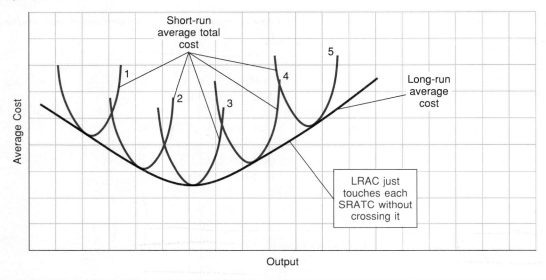

order. (This point is illustrated in "Applying Economic Ideas 8.1" with an episode from the early days of Sony Corporation as recounted by the firm's founder and chairman, Akio Morita.) Assuming, however, that the firm expects its output rate to increase permanently, it can move with confidence from one of the short-run curves shown in Exhibit 8.5 to the next.

Of course, the five short-run cost curves in the exhibit represent only a sampling of plant sizes; other positions are possible. Taking into account the short-run curves that correspond to intermediate-size plants as well as those shown, we can draw a *long-run average-cost curve* such as the one shown in the exhibit. This curve is the "envelope" of all the possible short-run average cost curves, meaning that it just touches each of the possible short-run curves without crossing them. The size of plant chosen for each output in the long run will be the one that corresponds to a short-run average total cost curve that is just tangent to the long-run average total cost curve at that point.

Exhibit 8.5 makes it clear that there is one best plant size for any given level of output that the firm plans to produce in the long run. Typically, a plant designed for one level of output can be run at a higher or lower output level only at a penalty in terms of cost. As a young firm expands, it must build more or larger plants as it moves along the downward-sloping portion of the long-run average total cost curve. Likewise, a firm that is planning to reduce its output

A Young Sony Corporation Faces Costs and Opportunities

Akio Morita is chairman of the Japanese electronics giant, Sony Corporation. His firm, like most others, started small. Here he recalls an episode from Sony's early days.

Our first transistor radio of 1955 was small and practical—not as small as some of our later efforts, but we were very proud of it. I saw the U.S. as a natural market. I took my little $29.95 radio to New York and made the rounds of possible retailers.

While making the rounds, I came across an American buyer who looked at the radio and said he liked it very much. He said his chain, which had about 150 stores, would need large quantities. He asked me to give him a price quotation only on quantities of 5,000, 10,000, 30,000, 50,000 and 100,000 radios. What an invitation!

But back in my hotel room, I began pondering the possible impact of such grand orders on our small facilities in Tokyo. We had expanded our plant a lot since we outgrew the unpainted, leaky shack on Gotenyama [a hill on the southern edge of Tokyo]. We had moved into bigger, sturdier buildings adjacent to the original site and had our eye on some more property. But we did not have the capacity to produce 100,000 transistor radios a year and also make the other things in our small product line. Our capacity was less than 10,000 radios a month. If we got an order for 100,000, we would have to hire and train new employees and expand our facilities even more. This would mean a major investment, a major expansion and a gamble.

Source: Adapted from *Made in Japan: Akio Morita and Sony* by Akio Morita with Edwin M. Reingold and Mitsuko Shimomura. Copyright © 1986 by E. P. Dutton, a division of NAL Penguin Inc. Reprinted by permission of the publisher, E. P. Dutton, a division of NAL Penguin Inc.

I was inexperienced and still a little naive, but I had my wits about me. I considered all the consequences I could think of, and then I sat down and drew a curve that looked something like a lopsided letter U. The price for 5,000 would be our regular price. That would be the beginning of the curve. For 10,000 there would be a discount, and that was at the bottom of the curve. For 30,000 the price would begin to climb. For 50,000 the price per unit would be higher than for 5,000, and for 100,000 units the price would have to be much more per unit than for the first 5,000.

My reasoning was this: If we had to double our production capacity to complete an order for 100,000, and if we could not get a repeat order the following year, we would be in big trouble, perhaps bankrupt, because how, in that case, could we employ all the added staff and pay for the new and unused facilities? . . . In Japan, we cannot just hire people and fire them whenever our orders go up or down. We have a long-term commitment to our employees and they have a commitment to us.

I returned the next day with my quotation. The buyer looked at it and blinked as though he couldn't believe his eyes. He put down the paper and said, patiently, "Mr. Morita, I have been working as a purchasing agent for nearly 30 years, and you are the first person who has ever come in here and told me that the more I buy the higher the unit price will be. It's illogical!" I explained my reasoning to him, and he listened carefully to what I had to say. When he got over his shock, he paused for a moment, smiled, and then placed an order for 10,000 radios—at the 10,000 unit price—which was just right for him and for us.

---

will eliminate some plant rather than keep production facilities operating at lower levels of output than those for which they were designed.

Economies of Scale

Economists have developed some special terms to describe what happens to long-run average costs as output increases. In any output range in which long-run average cost *decreases* as output increases, the firm is said to experience **economies of scale.** In any output range in which long-run average cost *increases*, the firm is said to experience **diseconomies of scale.** Finally, if there is

Economies of scale
A situation in which long-run average cost decreases as output increases.

Diseconomies of scale
A situation in which long-run average cost increases as output increases.

Constant returns to scale
A situation in which there are neither economies nor diseconomies of scale.

any range of output for which long-run average cost does not change as output varies, the firm is said to experience **constant returns to scale** in that range.

The long-run average cost curve in Exhibit 8.5 is smoothly U shaped, but that is not the only possible shape for such a curve. In fact, statistical studies suggest that L-shaped long-run average cost curves are the rule, at least in many manufacturing industries. Such a curve appears in Exhibit 8.6, which shows a range of economies of scale followed by a range of roughly constant returns to scale. The curve could turn out to be a flat-bottomed U if it were followed out far enough (as the broken extension of the curve in Exhibit 8.6 shows). In a given industry, however, there may be no firms that are large enough to show diseconomies of scale. In that case, the upward-sloping portion of the curve will not be represented in the statistical sample.

Minimum efficient scale
The output level at which economies of scale cease.

Statistical studies of long-run average cost often try to measure the level of output at which economies of scale end and constant returns to scale begin. This level is called the firm's **minimum efficient scale.** As shown in Exhibit 8.6, it corresponds to the point at which the L-shaped long-run average cost curve stops falling and begins to level out. If the cost curve does not have a sharp kink at this point—and there is no reason to think it does—the minimum efficient scale can only be approximated. This is not a major problem, however, since statistical studies of cost must deal in approximations in any case.

Sources of Economies of Scale

Where do economies of scale come from? Why is it ever true that a large firm can produce at a lower unit cost than a smaller firm? Economists who have studied these questions have found that there is no single source of economies of scale for all firms; rather, there are a number of sources, whose degree of importance depends on the industry involved.

When most people think of economies of scale, they probably have in mind an automobile assembly plant or a steel mill. Costs per unit tend to fall with the output rate per plant in industries such as autos and steel for a number of reasons. One is that a metal-forming machine or steel furnace designed to produce twice as much as another is likely to cost less than twice as much to build. Another is that larger plants can take advantage of more specialized divisions of

---

Exhibit 8.6   An L-Shaped Average Cost Curve

Statistical studies have found that long-run average cost curves are often L shaped, as shown here. The point at which economies of scale end and the curve begins to flatten out is called the firm's *minimum efficient scale.* If a firm continued to expand without limit, long-run average costs probably would begin to rise. However, in many industries there are no firms operating in the range of diseconomies of scale.

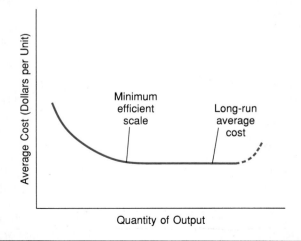

labor. The automobile assembly line, on which each worker performs a single operation on each car as it moves by, is the classic example of this.

However, not all economies of scale are linked with increases in the output rate of a single plant. Sometimes they originate in the total amount of a product or model that is produced rather than in the rate at which it is produced. With a long production run, the costs of product design, equipment setup, and training can be spread over a large number of units.

In addition to the rate and volume of production at a single plant, multiplant operation can yield economies of scale. The McDonald's hamburger chain provides a good example. The minimum efficient scale for a single plant (restaurant) is very small in the fast-food industry. Yet McDonald's gains some important economies by running a large number of restaurants as a system. Some of these are production economies: Individual food items and ingredients can be made in central kitchens; workers can be trained at "Hamburger University"; and so on. A multiplant firm like McDonald's also realizes economies of scale in such areas as finance, advertising, and marketing.

Looking Ahead

This chapter has only scratched the surface of the theory of cost. The appendix to this chapter and the books listed in the end-of-chapter bibliography extend the theory in many ways. Nevertheless, the treatment of cost theory given here is sufficient to serve as a basis for analyzing supply decisions in the next few chapters.

Chapter 9 shows how short- and long-run cost curves can be used to derive supply curves for an industry in which there are a large number of competing firms. Chapter 10 uses cost curves to analyze markets in which a single firm has a monopoly. Chapters 11 and 12 look at intermediate cases, and later chapters apply cost theory to problems of public policy.

Summary

1. **How do economists view the concepts of cost and profit?** *Explicit costs* of production take the form of payments to workers, suppliers, and other nonowners of the firm. *Implicit costs* are opportunity costs of using resources owned by the firm or contributed by its owners. Implicit costs include the *normal profit*, or opportunity cost of capital, needed to attract owners' capital to the firm. If only explicit costs are subtracted from revenue, the result is *accounting profit*. Revenue minus all costs, both implicit and explicit, results in *pure economic profit*.

2. **How are short-run and long-run time horizons distinguished?** *Fixed inputs* are those that cannot be easily increased or decreased in a short time; they are linked with the size of the firm's plant. *Variable inputs* can be quickly and easily varied in order to increase or decrease output; these include hourly labor, energy, and raw materials. The *short run* is a period within which only variable outputs can be adjusted. In the *long run*, changes can be made in fixed inputs, including plant size.

3. **How do costs vary in response to changes in the quantity of a variable input?** As the amount of one input to a production process increases while the amounts of all other inputs remain fixed, output will increase, at least over some range. The amount of output added by each one-unit increase in the variable input is known as the *marginal physical product* of that input. According to the *law of diminishing returns*, as the amount of one variable input used in a production process increases (with the amounts of all other inputs remaining fixed), a point will be reached beyond which the amount of output added per unit of added variable input (that is, the marginal physical product of the variable input) will begin to decrease. This principle applies to all production processes.

4. **How can a firm's cost structure be represented geometrically?** A whole set of cost curves can be constructed for a firm given data on its fixed and variable costs. The most commonly used cost curves are total cost, total fixed cost, total variable cost, average fixed cost, average variable cost, average total cost, and *marginal cost*. According to the *marginal-average rule*, the marginal cost curve cuts the average variable cost and average total cost curves at their lowest points.

5. **What choices does a firm face in the course of long-run expansion?** In the long run, a firm can adjust the amounts of fixed inputs that it uses by expanding or reducing its plant. Each possible plant size has a U-shaped short-run average total cost curve. The firm's long-run average cost curve is a shallower U-shaped curve based on a set of short-run curves. When long-run average cost decreases as output increases, the firm is said to experience *economies of scale*. When long-run average cost increases as output increases, the firm is said to experience *diseconomies of scale*. If there are neither economies nor diseconomies of scale, the firm is said to experience *constant returns to scale*.

Terms for Review

- explicit costs
- implicit costs
- pure economic profit
- accounting profit
- normal profit
- fixed inputs
- variable inputs
- short run
- long run
- total physical product
- marginal physical product
- law of diminishing returns
- marginal cost
- marginal-average rule
- economies of scale
- diseconomies of scale
- constant returns to scale
- minimum efficient scale

Questions for Review

1. Why are implicit and explicit costs both opportunity costs? Give examples of some implicit and explicit costs for a typical firm.

2. How are the concepts of short run and long run related to the concepts of fixed and variable inputs?

3. What happens to a typical firm's output as one variable input is increased while all other inputs are kept fixed?

4. Illustrate the law of diminishing returns for a vegetable garden in which the area of soil and the amounts of seeds and fertilizer are fixed while the amount of labor used varies.

5. Write a formula for each of the following:
   a. The relationship between total cost on the one hand and total fixed and total variable costs on the other
   b. The relationship between marginal cost and changes in total cost or total variable cost
   c. The relationship between average variable cost and total variable cost and the similar relationships for average fixed cost and average total cost

6. How do average costs vary in the long run as the size of a firm's plant is increased? Draw a sketch to show the relationship between short-run and long-run average cost curves.

7. What is the difference between diminishing returns and diseconomies of scale? Draw sketches to illustrate the concepts of economies of scale, diseconomies of scale, and constant returns to scale.

Problems and Topics for Discussion

1. **Examining the lead-off case.** One of the opportunity costs borne by the Martins is that of exchanging the secure life of employees of large firms for the risky life of entrepreneurs. Do you think they would be willing to do this if they expected to earn no more than their previous salaries plus a "normal profit" on the capital they invested in the firm? Do you think that pure economic profit can be viewed as compensation to entrepreneurs for the risk they bear? Discuss.

2. **Implicit and explicit costs.** List the basic costs of owning and operating an automobile. Which are explicit costs? Which are implicit costs? Does driving an automobile impose any opportunity costs on the economy as a whole that do not show up on your list as either implicit or explicit costs? If so, what are they?

3. **Fixed and variable costs.** Divide the costs of owning and operating an automobile into fixed and variable costs. Suppose you were deciding whether to drive to a nearby college's football game or to take the bus instead. Would you take both fixed and variable costs into account? Suppose you were deciding whether to buy a house in a neighborhood in which you could walk to work or a house in one in which you would have to buy a second car to drive to work every day. Would you then take both fixed and variable costs into account? Explain the difference between the two situations.

4. **Economies and diseconomies of scale.** Do you think the business of running a college is subject to economies or diseconomies of scale? Which parts of the col-

lege's operation (such as library, dormitories, faculty salaries, moving students between classes, and so on) are subject to economies of scale, diseconomies of scale, or constant returns to scale?

5. **Total cost curves.** On a piece of graph paper, draw a set of coordinate axes. Label the x axis "quantity of output" (0 to 20 units) and the y axis "cost" (0 to 20 units). Plot the following (x, y) points on your graph: (0, 4); (2, 6); (4, 7); (7, 8); (9, 9); (11, 11); and (13, 14). Connect these points with a smooth curve, and label it "total cost." Working from this curve, construct a total fixed cost curve and a total variable cost curve for the same firm.

6. **Marginal and average cost curves.** On another piece of graph paper, draw a second set of coordinate axes. Label the horizontal axis "quantity" (0 to 20 units) and the vertical axis "cost per unit" (0 to 2 units, in tenths of a unit). Using as a basis the total cost, total variable cost, and total fixed cost curves you drew for problem 4, construct the following curves on your new graph: marginal cost, average total cost, average variable cost, and average fixed cost.

7. **Relating the long-run and short-run cost curves.** Turn to Exhibit 8.5. Copy the diagram onto a sheet of graph paper, drawing the long-run average total cost curve and one of the short-run average total cost curves. Use these curves to construct the corresponding long-run and short-run total cost curves. Both total cost curves should be reverse-S shaped and tangent to each other at the same output level for which the average total cost curves are tangent.

8. **Diminishing returns.** Suppose you examine the relationship between the amount of coal burned per week in a certain power plant and the amount of electricity generated per week. You find that for minute amounts of coal—too small to even bring the boiler up to the temperature needed to make steam—no electricity can be produced. After a certain minimum amount of coal is burned, the plant begins to operate. From that point on, the added amount of electricity generated per added ton of coal burned is constant over a wide range. Then a ceiling is reached beyond which burning more coal produces no more electricity. Sketch the total physical product curve for this plant, and draw a graph showing how marginal physical product varies as output changes. Does this production process obey the law of diminishing returns?

9. **More on diminishing returns.** It has been said that were it not for the law of diminishing returns, all the food that the world needs could be grown in a flowerpot. Discuss this statement. (Suggestion: Think of land as the only fixed factor and fertilizer as the only variable factor. How much food could be grown in the flowerpot if the marginal physical product of fertilizer were constant regardless of the amount used per unit of land?)

Case for Discussion
Cruel Days in Tractorville

In the 1970s, farmers flourished as grain exports boomed. Lured by interest rates that seemed low when adjusted for inflation and by tax incentives—investment credits and accelerated depreciation—farmers went on an equipment-buying spree. High prices in the used-equipment market helped spur them on. After using a tractor for four years or so, a farmer could trade it in for nearly as much as its initial cost. It hardly mattered that inflation was steep and a new tractor cost 50 to 60 percent more; much of the increase was recovered in tax savings.

The tractor slump forced firms to cut back their level of operations.

Then, in 1981, the bottom fell out. A lethal combination of high interest rates, falling commodity prices, a strong dollar, and a decline in grain and soybean exports clobbered farm income. Deflation in land values was another villain. Notoriously big users of credit, farmers had borrowed heavily, using land as collateral, to expand their operations in the 1960s and 1970s. As inflation spiraled upward, so did farmland values. When inflation slowed during the Reagan administration, land values in the midwestern farm belt fell—by an average of 25 percent between 1981 and 1984. Farmers were left with less borrowing power with which to buy new equipment, and many found themselves trapped in debt at continuing high interest rates.

All this made for hard times in the tractor industry. Tractor sales had peaked at over 180,000 units in 1979. By 1984, output had fallen to under 120,000 units.

Towering above the industry's problems was overcapacity, which at most companies dictated a strategy of downsizing. "We thought the boom would last forever, or at least for the foreseeable future," said Emmett Barker, president of the Farm and Industrial Equipment Institute. The tractor market was expected to improve somewhat in the late 1980s, but most observers thought the 1979 sales peak would not recur in the near future.

Working on the basis of this forecast, the leading tractor makers scrambled to cut their losses. Plant closings were a major factor in most firms' strategies. Massey-Ferguson had built $700 million worth of new plant; after 1980, half of its total plant was scrapped or sold. Ford closed its European headquarters and began assembling tractors at fewer locations. Even John Deere, the strongest firm in the market, was forced to close a combine plant. J. I. Case, the fifth largest tractor maker, ceased business as an independent maker, joining with the tractor division of International Harvester to produce the Case-International line.

Source: Faye Rice, "Cruel Days in Tractorville," *Fortune*, October 29, 1984, 30–36. Photo Source: © 1987 Phyllis Woloshin.

Questions

1. Faced with the prospect of a permanent drop in sales, why would a tractor firm shut down some plants rather than keep all of its plants running at reduced output levels? Would the firm react the same way to a temporary drop in sales? Why or why not?

2. The tractor slump forced all firms to cut back their level of operations. Why might this situation force Case, the smallest of the major tractor makers, out of the business entirely? State your explanation in terms of cost theory.

3. In retrospect, were firms wise to respond to the boom of the 1970s by expanding their plants? Use a diagram similar to Exhibit 8.5 to show the choices actually made by the tractor industry, and compare them with the alternative approach it would have taken had it known that the boom in equipment sales was going to be only temporary.

Suggestions for Further Reading

Alchian, Armen A. "Costs and Outputs." In *The Allocation of Economic Resources*, edited by Moses Abramovitz et al. Stanford, Cal.: Stanford University Press, 1959. Reprinted in William Breit and Harold M. Hochman, eds. *Readings in Microeconomics*, 2d ed. New York: Holt, Rinehart and Winston, 1968.

An attempt to clarify certain aspects of the theory of costs. Alchian emphasizes that cost varies in response to variations in total expected volume of output as well as variations in the output rate.

Blaug, Mark. *Economic Theory in Retrospect*, rev. ed. Homewood, Ill.: Irwin, 1968.

Chapter 10 discusses Alfred Marshall's contributions to cost theory.

Peters, Thomas J., and Robert H. Waterman. *In Search of Excellence*, Chapter 8. New York: Harper & Row, 1982.

The authors of this best-selling book on management point out that there is more to keeping average costs low than building the biggest plant possible—in fact, bigness may be the enemy of productivity.

Cost and Output with Two Variable Inputs

Appendix to
Chapter 8

In Chapter 8, we looked at the relationship between cost and output when just one input is varied and all other inputs are kept constant. In this appendix, we extend the theory of cost to the case in which more than one input is varied.

Substitution of Inputs

The main new feature of situations in which more than one input is varied is the possibility of substituting one input for another. Consider the case of Henry Hathaway, a farmer who makes his living growing corn. Hathaway spends all his time working on his farm and does not hire anyone to help him. For him, the amount of labor used in growing corn is a fixed input. In addition to fixed amounts of labor and machinery, he uses two variable inputs: land and fertilizer.

Hathaway can grow any given quantity of corn—say, 200 bushels—in many different ways. Some of the possibilities are shown in Exhibit 8A.1. One way to grow 200 bushels of corn is to use 2.5 tons of fertilizer and 10 acres of land. This is represented by point P on the graph. If Hathaway wants to grow the same amount of corn on less land, he can substitute fertilizer for land. For example, at point Q he can grow 200 bushels of corn on 5 acres by using 5 tons of fertilizer. By substituting still more fertilizer for land, he can move to point R, where the 200 bushels are grown on just 2.5 acres using 10 tons of fertilizer.

Diminishing Returns in Substitution

In Chapter 8, we defined the law of diminishing returns as it applies to a situation in which one input is varied while all others remain constant. In that situation, after a certain point the amount of the variable input needed to make an extra unit of output increases. (This is another way of saying that the marginal physical product of the variable input decreases.) A similar principle applies when one input is substituted for another in such a way as to keep output at a constant level: As the amount of input x is increased, the amount of x needed to replace one unit of y increases.

Exhibit 8A.1   An Isoquantity Line

This graph shows an isoquantity line, or isoquant, for the production of 200 bushels of corn. The variable inputs are land and fertilizer; the other inputs, labor and machinery, are assumed to be fixed. Points P, Q, and R represent various ways of growing the given quantity of corn. A movement downward along the isoquant represents the substitution of fertilizer for land while output is maintained at 200 bushels per year. As more and more fertilizer is substituted for land, the isoquant becomes flatter because of diminishing returns.

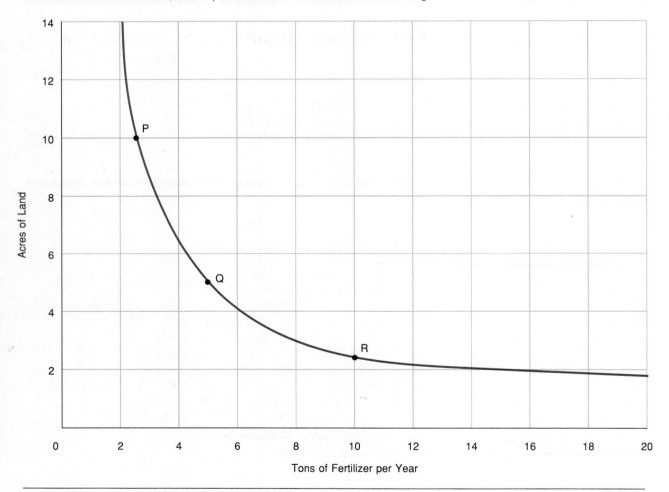

The example in Exhibit 8A.1 illustrates this principle. In moving from point P to point Q, 2.5 tons of fertilizer replace 5 acres of land while output stays constant at 200 bushels. But in moving from point Q to point R, 5 more tons of fertilizer are needed to replace just 2.5 acres of land.

As a result of the law of diminishing returns in substituting one input for another, a curve connecting points P, Q, and R becomes flatter as one moves downward and to the right along it. This reflects the decreasing ratio of the marginal physical product of fertilizer to the marginal physical product of land as more fertilizer is substituted for land.

Choosing the Least-Cost Production Method

The line connecting points P, Q, and R in Exhibit 8A.1 is called an **isoquantity line or isoquant,** because it shows the combinations of inputs that can be used to produce a given amount of output. (The prefix *iso* comes from a Greek word meaning "equal.") But while all the points on the isoquant are equal in terms of output, they are not equal in terms of cost. To see how a producer can choose the least-cost method of producing a given level of output, we need to know the prices of the inputs.

In the appendix to Chapter 7, we used budget lines as a graphical device to represent the prices of consumer goods. As Exhibit 8A.2 shows, the same technique can be used to represent the prices of inputs. The graph assumes a cost of $50 a ton for fertilizer and a rental price of $50 per year for land. The sum of $400 can buy 8 tons of fertilizer and no land, 8 acres of land with no fertilizer, or any of the other points on line A; the sum of $500 will buy 10 tons of fertilizer, 10 acres of land, or any of the other points on line B; and so on.

When the isoquant for 200 bushels of corn is drawn on top of a set of budget lines for the inputs, it is easy to see the least-cost method of producing that output level: It is the method that uses 5 tons of fertilizer and 5 acres of land. This corresponds to point Q on the graph, where the isoquant just touches budget line B. Points P and R are possible ways of growing 200 bushels of corn, but they lie on budget line C, which corresponds to a cost of $625—and a budget of less than $500 (say, $400, as shown by budget line A) is not enough to reach the 200-bushel isoquant no matter how it is split between fertilizer and land.

Isoquantity line (isoquant)
A line showing the different combinations of variable inputs that can be used to produce a given amount of output.

Response to Changes in Input Prices

If input prices change, the least-cost combination of inputs is likely to change as well. Suppose that the suburbs begin to expand in the direction of our friend Hathaway's farm, driving up the price of land. Now land that used to rent for $50 per acre per year rents for $200 per acre. The price of fertilizer remains unchanged at $50 a ton.

The results of the increase in the price of land are shown in Exhibit 8A.3. Now $500 will not be enough to buy the combinations of inputs that fall along budget line B. Even if all the money were spent on land, only 2.5 acres could be rented. The new $500 budget line is C, which does not reach the 200-bushel isoquant at any point.

To grow 200 bushels, Hathaway must now spend more than $500. As he increases his budget for land and fertilizer, the budget line shifts upward but stays parallel to C. When the budget line reaches D, which corresponds to spending $1,000 on inputs, it just touches the isoquant at R. We see, then, that now $1,000 is the lowest cost at which 200 bushels of corn can be grown, given a price of $50 a ton for fertilizer and $200 an acre for land. With those prices, R is the least-cost combination of inputs.

In this case, the effect of an increase in the price of an input is typical. Less of the input whose price has gone up is used, and the other input, which has become relatively less costly, is substituted for it. We will return to this topic in later chapters, where we discuss the markets for the factors of production.

Exhibit 8A.2   Finding the Least-Cost Production Method

This graph shows how the least-cost method of production can be found from among the points on an isoquant given the prices of the variable inputs. Here the price of fertilizer is assumed to be $50 a ton and the rental price of land $50 per year. A set of budget lines is drawn to represent various levels of spending on inputs. Line A, which corresponds to a total variable cost of $400, does not provide enough inputs to produce 200 bushels of corn. Line C, which corresponds to a total variable cost of $625, provides enough inputs to grow 200 bushels of corn using methods P or R. Line B, which corresponds to a total variable cost of $500, permits the 200 bushels to be grown using method Q, which is the least-cost method given these input prices.

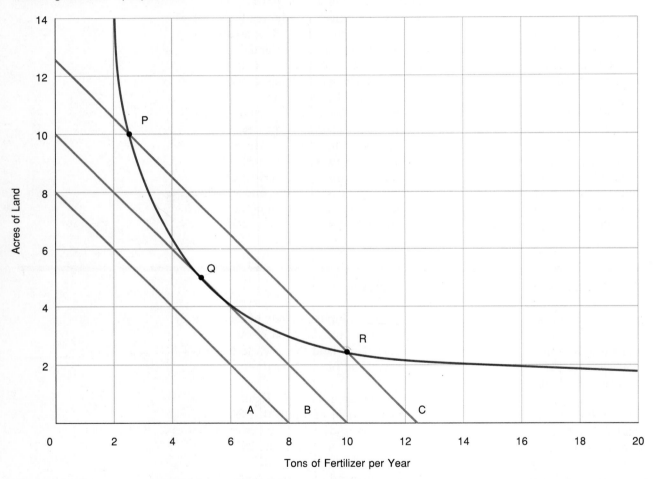

Varying Output

The isoquant technique can also be used to analyze variations in output with two variable inputs. Part a of Exhibit 8A.4 shows an isoquant "map" with three sets of points that correspond to three output levels. As before, P, Q, and R represent three ways of growing 200 bushels of corn. Points S, T, and U represent

Exhibit 8A.3   Effects of a Change in Input Prices

If the rental price of land increases from $50 to $200 per year while the price of fertilizer remains fixed at $50 a ton, 200 bushels of corn can no longer be produced for $500. The $500 budget line shifts from position B to position C and now falls short of the 200-bushel isoquant. Increasing the amount spent on variable inputs to $1,000 shifts the budget line up to position D, where it just touches the isoquant at point R. The increase in the price of land thus not only raises the total variable cost of growing 200 bushels of corn but causes fertilizer to be substituted for land, which is now relatively more costly.

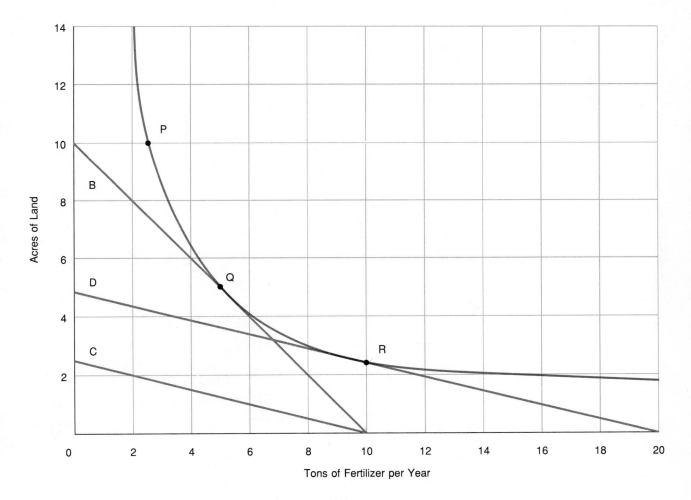

three ways of growing 100 bushels, and points V, W, and X are three ways of growing 300 bushels. An isoquant has been drawn through each set of points.

In this exhibit, we return to the assumption that land costs $50 an acre and fertilizer $50 a ton. Using these prices, a set of budget lines has been drawn, each corresponding to a different total variable cost. Budget line A corresponds to a total variable cost of $300, B to a cost of $500, and C to a cost of $1,000.

As the graph clearly shows, there is a least-cost method for producing each output level given these prices. Point T is the best way to produce 100 bushels;

Exhibit 8A.4   Expansion of Output and Total Variable Costs

Part a of this exhibit shows three isoquants for the production of corn corresponding to outputs of 100, 200, and 300 bushels. Assuming input prices of $50 an acre for land and $50 a ton for fertilizer, budget lines can be drawn to show the minimum total variable cost for each output level. As output expands, the firm will move from T to Q and then to W along the expansion path. Part b of the exhibit plots the amount of output and the total variable cost for each of these points. The result is a reverse-S-shaped total variable cost curve that shows the effects of diminishing returns for output levels above 200 bushels per year.

(a)

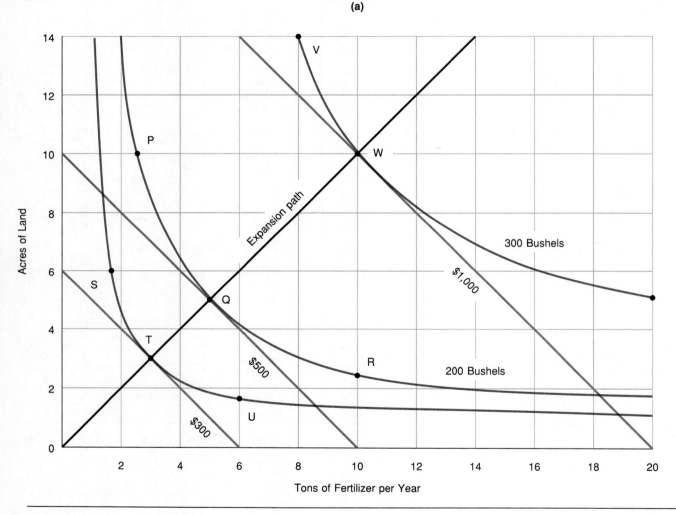

Q is best for 200 bushels; and W is best for 300 bushels. Other output levels would be possible as well; these would lie along the line drawn from the origin through points T, Q, and W. This is called the firm's *expansion path.* As the firm moves along its expansion path, more of both the variable inputs, land and fertilizer, is used. Meanwhile, the fixed inputs—labor and machinery, in Hathaway's case—remain constant.

(b)

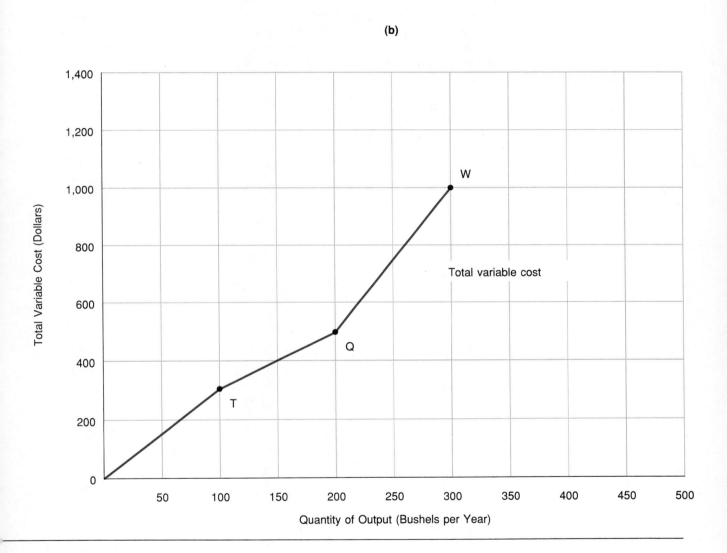

Deriving a Cost Curve from the Isoquant Map

Once the expansion path has been identified, it is easy to construct a total variable cost curve. All we need do is construct a graph that links each point on the expansion path with the variable cost level of the corresponding budget line.

This is done in part b of Exhibit 8A.4. At the origin, both output and total variable cost are zero. At point T, output is 100 bushels and total variable cost is $300; at Q, we have 200 bushels and $500; and at W, 300 bushels and $1,000. Plotting these points and connecting them give the firm's total variable cost curve.

Note that this curve has the same reverse-S shape as the cost curve of Fieldcom Inc. discussed in Chapter 8. This shape results from the law of diminishing returns, applied to the case in which two inputs vary while all others remain fixed. Beyond point Q, the amounts of inputs needed to produce each added unit of output begin to rise, just as they did when only one input was allowed to vary. Only if all inputs are allowed to vary and none to remain fixed can a firm escape the effects of the law of diminishing returns.

Term for Review

- isoquantity line (isoquant)

9 Supply under Perfect Competition

After reading this chapter, you will understand . . .

- What characteristics define the structure of a market.
- What determines the profit-maximizing output level in the short run for a perfectly competitive firm.
- Under what conditions a firm will continue to operate even if it sustains a loss.
- How a firm's short-run supply curve is related to its cost curves.
- What are the conditions for long-run equilibrium in a perfectly competitive industry.
- What determines the shape of the long-run supply curve for a perfectly competitive industry.

Before reading this chapter, make sure you know the meaning of . . .

- Entrepreneurship (Chapter 2)
- Supply and demand (Chapters 3 and 6)
- Perfectly elastic demand (Chapter 6)
- Marginal and average costs (Chapter 8)
- Long run and short run (Chapter 8)

The World
by the Tail

When Ralph and Andrea Martin
started Fieldcom Inc., they thought
they had the world by the tail. Their
rugged portable computer, the first
one designed for use under hot and
dusty field conditions, would be a sure
source of profits. With only a small
investment, they quickly got their
firm off the ground and their computer into production. No one had a
product that would come close to what
theirs would do.

Then the structure of the market
began to change. What the Martins
didn't realize was that the very factors
that made the portable-computer market easy for them to enter would make

Fieldcom's success in the market created a new obstacle: competition.

it easy for everyone else to enter too. As soon as their machine proved there was
a market for rugged portable computers, copies sprang up on all sides. Makers
of office-type portable computers beefed up their carrying cases and shock-
mounted their components. Other start-up firms brought out machines that,
from the user's point of view, were just as good as Fieldcom's. Equipment
supply dealers contracted with little-known electronics firms in the Far East to
produce rugged portable computers for sale under the dealers' own brand
names. In the office computer market, "clones" of the famous IBM PC had
made desktop personal computers a "commodity"—a good that consumers saw
as very much the same from one brand to another and bought only if the price
was the lowest available. Now clones of Fieldcom's rugged portable computer
were doing the same to this market.

Within a year there were many similar products available, none of which
was able to capture a dominant share of the growing market. The pressure to
trim prices was relentless. At the end of their second year in business, the
Martins were working hard just to break even when the full opportunity costs of
their firm were taken into account.

IN Chapter 8, we looked at Fieldcom by itself. However, firms like the Martins' do not operate alone in the real world; they face competition. Competition may take the form of giants such as General Motors and Toyota struggling to dominate a market or of advertising campaigns by rivals trying to woo fickle consumers. Sometimes it takes the form of rapid increases in the number of brands and styles, as often happens in the markets for breakfast cereal and clothing. Sometimes, as in Fieldcom's case, it takes the form of many small firms selling essentially identical products in a market in which entry and exit are easy.

The Concept of Market Structure

Market structure
The key traits of a market, including the number and size of firms, the extent to which the products of various firms are different or similar, and the ease of entry and exit.

Economists refer to the conditions under which competition occurs in a market as **market structure.** Market structure is defined in terms of the number and size of firms, the nature of the product, and the ease of entry and exit. The concept of market structure is useful in organizing the theory of supply and profit maximization.

Varieties of Market Structure

Perfect competition
A market structure that is characterized by a large number of small firms, a homogeneous product, and freedom of entry and exit.

In this course, we will look at four market structures. The first, to which this chapter is devoted, is **perfect competition.** This is defined as a market in which there are many firms, none with a significant share of the market; in which the product is homogeneous; and in which firms can enter or exit from the industry with ease. By a "significant" share of the market, we mean a share sufficiently large that the actions of a single firm are enough to noticeably affect the market price. By a "homogeneous product," we mean that the various firms' products are alike in all important respects. By "ease of entry," we mean that firms just starting to produce this product can do so on an equal footing with existing firms in terms of such matters as the prices they pay for inputs, their knowledge of production techniques, access to government permits or licenses, and so on. Finally, by "ease of exit," we mean that firms face no legal barriers to leaving the market and are able to find buyers or other uses for their fixed inputs.

Monopoly
A market structure in which there is only one firm selling a unique product and protected from the entry of rivals.

Oligopoly
A market structure in which there are a few firms, at least some of which are large in relation to the size of the market.

Monopolistic competition
A market structure in which there are many small firms, a differentiated product, and easy entry and exit.

At the opposite extreme is the case to be examined in the next chapter, namely **monopoly.** This is a market in which there is a single firm selling a unique product and adequately protected from the entry of new competitors. The third market structure, known as **oligopoly,** is defined as a market with a few firms, at least some of which have a significant share. The product may be either homogeneous or differentiated, and there may or may not be significant barriers to entry. The fourth and final market structure is **monopolistic competition.** This structure resembles perfect competition in that there are many small firms and easy entry and exit. However, under monopolistic competition the various firms' products are differentiated. Oligopoly and monopolistic competition will be discussed in Chapter 11.

The characteristics of the four market structures are summarized in Exhibit 9.1.

Exhibit 9.1   Market Structures

The structure of a market refers to the conditions under which firms compete in it—the number and size of firms, the nature of the product, and the ease of entry and exit. Perfect competition and monopoly are "ideal" types of structures. Few—if any—markets fit their definitions perfectly. Monopolistic competition and oligopoly are descriptive of most markets in the U.S. economy.

	Number and Size of Firms	Nature of Product	Entry and Exit Conditions
Perfect Competition	Many firms, all small	Homogeneous	Easy
Monopolistic Competition	Many firms, all small	Differentiated	Easy
Oligopoly	Few firms, at least some of them large	Differentiated or homogeneous	May be some barriers to entry
Monopoly	One firm	Unique product	Complete protection from entry of rivals

Descriptive versus Ideal Structures

The four market structures listed in Exhibit 9.1 fall into two classes. Oligopoly and monopolistic competition are *descriptive* of a great many real-world markets. Examples of oligopoly include such manufacturing industries as automobiles, aluminum, cigarettes, and breakfast cereals and such service industries as long-distance telephone service and network TV broadcasting. The characteristics of monopolistic competition accurately describe a large number of service industries, such as restaurants, service stations, and consumer banking services, as well as some manufacturing industries, such as clothing. There is no hard-and-fast line between the two structures with respect to how large the biggest firm must be in order to make the industry an oligopoly rather than one of monopolistic competition. How a market is classified may depend on how the product is defined. For example, the broad category "magazine publishing" would probably be best described as monopolistically competitive, whereas the narrower category "weekly news magazines" is an oligopoly dominated by Time Inc.

Perfect competition and monopoly, on the other hand, are not descriptive of real-world markets; rather, they are "ideal types" that certain real-world markets can only approximate. For example, it is hard to find markets that exactly fit perfect competition, because the various firms' products are rarely identical in every respect, entry and exit are seldom totally free, and individual firms are rarely microscopic in size. Some markets approximate these requirements fairly closely; the markets for some farm products, such as wheat and corn, and certain financial markets are often cited as examples. On the other hand, it is difficult to find markets that are perfect monopolies, because no product is ever so unique that it has no substitute and no market is ever perfectly insulated from the entry of new rivals. Consider long-distance phone service, cited in textbooks of a generation ago as a nearly perfect example of monopoly. The entry of MCI, Sprint, and other firms has turned this into an oligopoly, while express mail and satellite computer links provide close substitutes.

The ideal and descriptive classes of market structures play different roles in economics. The power of the ideal types—perfect competition and monopoly—comes from the fact that we can construct precise models of their workings. There may be few markets to which these models exactly apply, but the models nonetheless provide insight into the operation of markets that only approximately fit them. For example, the market for rental apartments is not perfectly competitive, because not all apartments are alike; yet an understanding of the abstract model of perfect competition can help us see how the market for apartments works. The descriptive market structures—oligopoly and monopolistic competition—have the advantage of fitting many real-world markets, but, as we will see, it is much more difficult to construct formal models that accurately reflect how they work. Nevertheless, study of these markets can also produce useful insights.

Competition and Entrepreneurship

A major reason that it is hard to construct precise models of oligopoly and monopolistic competition is the importance of entrepreneurship in these markets. In Chapter 2, we defined *entrepreneurship* as the process of looking for new possibilities: utilizing new ways of doing things, being alert to new opportunities, and overcoming old limits. Everyday life in oligopolistic and monopolistically competitive markets is dominated by rivalry among entrepreneurs—head-to-head contests of product design, advertising, personal selling, service quality, and pricing strategy. There is no way to capture entrepreneurs' behavior precisely in terms of equations or graphs, because the notion of entrepreneurship is itself one of change, uncertainty, and innovation. Even the basic concept of equilibrium becomes a moving target in such markets rather than a fixed point at which lines cross on a graph.

On the other hand, it is possible to construct accurate models of perfect competition and monopoly precisely because most aspects of entrepreneurial rivalry are assumed away in the definition of these market structures. Perfectly competitive firms do not innovate or advertise; their products are by definition identical, both in substance and in the eyes of consumers. They do not have complex pricing strategies; each small firm simply takes the market price as a given. Entrepreneurship is absent from pure monopoly for various reasons. The monopoly has no rivals; buyers do business with it, or else. Nor does it have to worry about pricing strategies of other firms in its market, because it is the only firm in that market.

Entrepreneurship therefore will receive little attention in this and the next chapter while the ideal types of models are being constructed. It will reappear in Chapters 11 and 12.

Perfect Competition and Supply in the Short Run

Having defined perfect competition, we now turn to the main topic of this chapter: building a model to fit this market structure. The model-building process has the following objectives: (1) to show how the profit-maximizing decisions of individual firms determine the quantity they will supply at various prices and (2) to show how individual firms' decisions generate market supply curves. We will look first at the short run and then at the long run.

The Perfectly Competitive Firm as a Price Taker

Because all firms in a perfectly competitive industry are small and have homogeneous products, they are **price takers.** This means that the price at which each firm sells its output is determined by forces beyond the firm's control; the price is set by supply and demand conditions in the market as a whole. From the individual firm's point of view, the market price is a given.

Price taker
A firm that sells its outputs at prices that are determined by forces beyond its control.

Market Demand and Demand for the Firm
This situation is illustrated in Exhibit 9.2. Part a shows the supply and demand curves for the market for chicken as given in earlier chapters. The equilibrium price is $.40 per pound and the equilibrium quantity 2 billion pounds per year.

Part b of Exhibit 9.2 shows how the market looks from the viewpoint of an individual chicken farm. This firm thinks in terms of thousands rather than billions of pounds. As far as it is concerned, the demand is *perfectly elastic* (horizontal) at the market price. The reason is that the market price will not be perceptibly affected by this one farm's decision to produce 10,000, 20,000, or 40,000 pounds of chicken a year. A 10,000-pound movement is too small even to see on the scale of the market supply and demand curves.

Exhibit 9.2 Market Demand and Demand
for the Perfectly Competitive Firm

The perfectly competitive firm is a price taker. It is so small relative to the market as a whole that its decisions do not significantly affect the market price. In this example, the market equilibrium price is $.40 per pound. This price will not be much affected if the individual firm shown in part b produces 20,000 rather than 40,000 pounds out of the billions of pounds produced in the market as a whole. Because the individual competitive firm is a price taker, the demand curve it faces is perfectly elastic. Among other things, that means that marginal revenue equals price for a perfectly competitive firm.

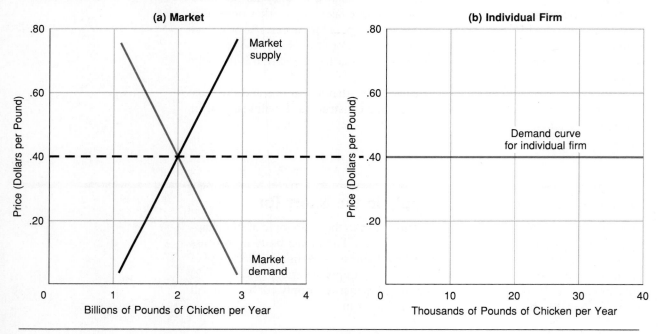

Perfectly Elastic Demand and Marginal Revenue

In Chapter 8, we introduced the term *marginal cost* to refer to the amount by which total cost changes when output changes by one unit. Now we can introduce a similar term, **marginal revenue,** to refer to the amount by which total revenue changes as the result of a one-unit change in output. Recall that *revenue* means price times quantity sold. For a firm with a perfectly elastic demand curve, then, marginal revenue simply equals price. For example, if the price of chicken is $.40 per pound, the firm will receive a revenue of $40.00 from the sale of 100 pounds and a revenue of $40.40 from the sale of 101 pounds. A one-pound increase in output gives a $.40 increase in revenue, that is, an increase in revenue equal to the product's price. Therefore, throughout this chapter we can treat marginal revenue and price as equal from the individual firm's viewpoint.

Marginal revenue
The amount by which total revenue increases as a result of a one-unit increase in quantity sold.

Short-Run Profit Maximization for the Firm

Let's turn from the market for chicken to the market for portable computers in which Fieldcom operates. For purposes of this chapter, we will treat this market as perfectly competitive, bearing in mind that no real-world market exactly fits the ideal type. The next step in our model building will be to see how a typical perfectly competitive firm such as Fieldcom chooses the output level that earns it the maximum profit in the short run.

A Total Cost–Total Revenue Approach

Part a of Exhibit 9.3 shows short-run cost data for Fieldcom as first given in Chapter 8. It also shows the revenue Fieldcom earns from the sale of each quantity of output assuming a constant price of $500 per unit.

Subtracting total cost in column 3 from total revenue in column 2 gives the total profit the firm earns at each output level. The maximum is reached at 19 units per day, where a profit of $2,000 per day is earned. This profit-maximizing output level is shown graphically in part b of Exhibit 9.3. There the firm's total profit is indicated by the distance between the total revenue and total cost curves. That distance is greatest at 19 units of output.

A Marginal Approach

Instead of comparing total cost and total revenue, we can use a marginal approach to find the profit-maximizing output level. Look first at columns 5 and 6 of part a of Exhibit 9.3. Column 5 gives data on marginal cost. (As before, these data are printed on lines between the entries in the first four columns to show that marginal cost is the change in cost as output moves from one level to another.) Column 6 shows marginal revenue, which, as explained, is equal to the product's price. Each computer that Fieldcom sells adds $500 to its total revenue.

As the table shows, both total cost and total revenue rise as output increases. If the increase in revenue exceeds the increase in cost (that is, if marginal revenue is greater than marginal cost), boosting output by one unit increases total profit. If the increase in cost exceeds that in revenue (that is, if marginal cost is greater than marginal revenue), raising output by one unit reduces total profit. It follows that in order to maximize profit, a firm should expand its output as long as marginal revenue exceeds marginal cost and stop as soon as marginal cost begins to exceed marginal revenue. A comparison of columns 5 and 6 of Exhibit 9.3 shows that for Fieldcom this means producing 19 units of output per day—the same number at which we arrive when we compare total cost and total revenue.

The marginal approach to short-run profit maximization is shown graphically in part c of Exhibit 9.3. At up to 19 units of output, the marginal cost curve lies below the marginal revenue curve so that each added unit of output increases profit. Beyond 19 units, the marginal cost curve is above the marginal revenue curve so that each added unit of output reduces profit. The point of profit maximization—at which the marginal cost and marginal revenue curves intersect—matches the point in part b at which the spread between total revenue and total cost is greatest.

In part c, the vertical distance between the demand curve, which shows price and marginal revenue, and the average total cost curve shows the average profit per unit. This is multiplied by the number of units to give total profit. Thus, from the standpoint of part c, total profit equals the area of the shaded rectangle.

Minimizing Short-Run Losses

In the example just given, Fieldcom was able to make a profit at a price of $500. However, market conditions are not always so favorable. Suppose, for example, that the market price drops to $300. A lower market price means a downward

Exhibit 9.3 Short-Run Profit Maximization

This exhibit shows the profit-maximizing level of output chosen by a perfectly competitive firm, Fieldcom Inc., given a market price of $500 per unit. The output can be found by comparing total cost and total revenue, as shown in parts a and b. It can also be found by comparing marginal cost and marginal revenue. (Because the firm is a price taker, marginal revenue is equal to price.) Profit increases up to the point at which marginal cost begins to exceed marginal revenue; after that point, it declines. Regardless of the approach used, the profit-maximizing output is 19 units per day and the maximum profit per day is $2,000.

(a)

Quantity of Output (1)	Total Revenue (2)	Total Cost (3)	Total Profit (2) − (3) (4)	Marginal Cost (5)	Marginal Revenue (6)
0	$ 0	$ 2,000	−$2,000		
1	500	2,380	−1,880	$380	$500
2	1,000	2,720	−1,720	340	500
3	1,500	3,025	−1,525	305	500
4	2,000	3,300	−1,300	275	500
5	2,500	3,550	−1,000	250	500
6	3,000	3,780	−780	230	500
7	3,500	3,995	−495	215	500
8	4,000	4,200	−200	205	500
9	4,500	4,400	100	200	500
10	5,000	4,605	395	205	500
11	5,500	4,820	680	215	500
12	6,000	5,050	950	230	500
13	6,500	5,300	1,200	250	500
14	7,000	5,575	1,425	275	500
15	7,500	5,880	1,620	305	500
16	8,000	6,220	1,780	340	500
17	8,500	6,600	1,900	380	500
18	9,000	7,025	1,975	425	500
19	9,500	7,500	2,000	475	500
20	10,000	8,030	1,970	530	500
21	10,500	8,620	1,880	590	500
22	11,000	9,275	1,725	655	500
23	11,500	10,000	1,500	725	500
24	12,000	10,800	1,200	800	500

shift in the firm's perfectly elastic demand curve. Being a price taker, the firm can do nothing about the price and will have to adjust its output as best it can to meet the new situation. The required adjustments are shown in Exhibit 9.4.

  There is no output level at which the firm can earn a profit. Unable to earn a profit, the firm must focus on keeping its losses to a minimum. With a price of $300 per unit, the minimum loss occurs at 14 units of output. As in the previous

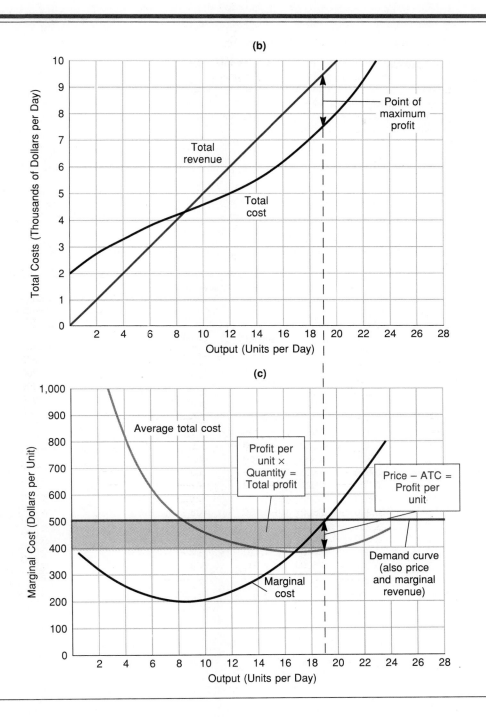

(b)

(c)

case, this is the output level beyond which marginal cost begins to exceed the product's price.

The two graphs in Exhibit 9.4 give two views of Fieldcom's situation. Part b presents the total cost–total revenue approach. Because the total cost curve is higher than the total revenue curve at all points, the firm cannot make a profit. Total revenues come closest to total costs at 14 units of output.

Exhibit 9.4   Minimizing Short-Run Losses under Perfect Competition

If the product's market price is too low to permit earning a profit, the firm must try to keep its losses to a minimum. For this firm, given a price of $300 per unit, the point of minimum loss is 14 units of output per day. Note that the marginal cost curve intersects the marginal revenue curve at a point higher than average variable cost but lower than average total cost. Each unit of output sold earns more than its share of variable cost but not enough to pay for its share of total cost when its share of fixed cost is included.

(a)

Quantity of Output (1)	Total Revenue (2)	Total Cost (3)	Total Profit or Loss (4)	Average Total Cost (5)	Average Variable Cost (6)	Marginal Cost (7)	Marginal Revenue (8)
0	$ 0	$2,000	−$2,000	—	—		
1	300	2,380	−2,080	$2,380	$380	$380	$300
2	600	2,720	−2,120	1,360	360	340	300
3	900	3,025	−2,125	1,009	342	305	300
4	1,200	3,300	−2,100	825	325	275	300
5	1,500	3,550	−2,050	710	310	250	300
6	1,800	3,780	−1,980	629	296	230	300
7	2,100	3,995	−1,895	571	285	215	300
8	2,400	4,200	−1,800	525	275	205	300
9	2,700	4,400	−1,700	488	266	200	300
10	3,000	4,605	−1,605	460	260	205	300
11	3,300	4,820	−1,520	437	256	215	300
12	3,600	5,050	−1,450	421	254	230	300
13	3,900	5,300	−1,400	408	254	250	300
14	4,200	5,575	−1,375	398	255	275	300
15	4,500	5,880	−1,380	392	259	305	300
16	4,800	6,220	−1,420	389	264	340	300
17	5,100	6,600	−1,500	389	271	380	300

Part c shows how this looks from the marginal point of view. This graph shows both the average total cost and average variable cost curves. The point at which marginal cost equals price lies between the two average cost curves. Because the demand curve is below the average total cost curve, there is a loss on each unit sold. The total loss is equal to the shaded rectangle (loss per unit times

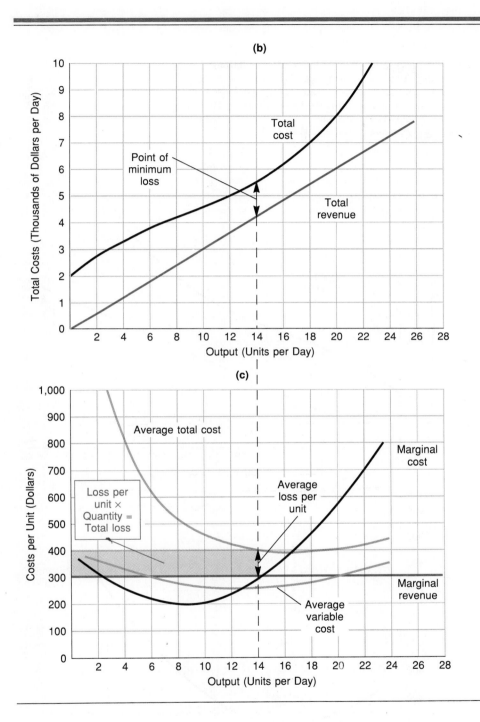

(b)

(c)

quantity). However, the demand curve lies above the average variable cost curve. This means that revenue per unit is more than enough to cover variable cost and, hence, each unit sold makes at least some contribution to fixed cost. Thus, losses are smaller than they would be if no output were produced, but fixed costs still must be paid.

Exhibit 9.5   Shutting Down to Minimize Short-Run Loss

Sometimes the price of a firm's output may drop so low that the firm must shut down in order to keep short-run losses to a minimum. This is illustrated here at a price of $225 per unit. Marginal cost rises above marginal revenue at 11 units of output. This output yields a smaller loss ($2,345) than those slightly greater or lower. However, the loss can be reduced to just $2,000 a day if the firm shuts down. Note that the marginal cost curve in this case intersects the marginal revenue curve at a point below average variable cost. That is the signal to shut down.

(a)

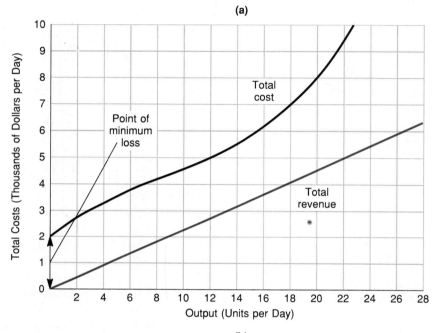

(b)

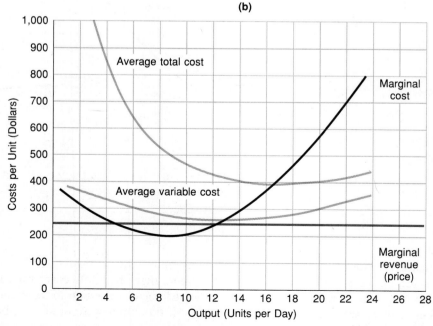

(c)

Quantity of Output (1)	Total Revenue (2)	Total Cost (3)	Total Profit or Loss (4)	Average Total Cost (5)	Average Variable Cost (6)	Marginal Cost (7)	Marginal Revenue (8)
0	$ 0	$2,000	−$2,000	—	—		
1	225	2,380	−2,155	$2,380	$380	$380	$225
2	450	2,720	−2,270	1,360	360	340	225
3	675	3,025	−2,305	1,009	342	305	225
4	900	3,300	−2,400	825	325	275	225
5	1,125	3,550	−2,425	710	310	250	225
6	1,350	3,780	−2,430	629	296	230	225
7	1,575	3,995	−2,420	571	285	215	225
8	1,800	4,200	−2,400	525	275	205	225
9	2,025	4,400	−2,375	488	266	200	225
10	2,250	4,605	−2,355	460	260	205	225
11	2,475	4,820	−2,345	437	256	215	225
12	2,700	5,050	−2,350	421	254	230	225
13	2,925	5,300	−2,375	408	254	250	225
14	3,150	5,575	−2,425	398	255	275	225
15	3,375	5,880	−2,505	392	259	305	225
16	3,600	6,220	−2,620	389	264	340	225
17	3,825	6,600	−2,775	389	271	380	225

As an aid to understanding the logic of this loss-minimizing decision, suppose for a moment that wages are the firm's only variable cost and that rent on its building is its only fixed cost. At the point shown, the firm is bringing in more than enough revenue to pay its wage bill (variable costs); the remainder will help pay the rent. If the firm shuts down temporarily, it will have to pay the rent with no help at all from current revenue. That would mean even more of a loss than at 14 units of output per day.

Shutting Down to Cut Short-Run Losses

What would happen if the price of portable computers dropped even lower than $300? Would it always be worthwhile for the firm to keep making computers even though it was losing money? The answer, as shown in Exhibit 9.5, is no.

This exhibit assumes a price of $225 per unit. It is clear that with such a low price the firm again cannot make a profit at any output level. But this time, the best thing for the firm to do in the short run is to shut down. A short-run shutdown is not the same as going out of business. While it is shut down, the firm keeps its plant intact, pays its rent, and so on and thus does not escape its fixed costs. If things get better and the price rises again, the firm can resume making computers. If things never improve, the firm will have to wind up its affairs and go out of business. When it goes out of business, it sells its equipment, gives up the lease on its building, and so on. Only at that point are its fixed costs finally eliminated.

In the shutdown case, it can be misleading to follow the rule of expanding output until marginal cost begins to exceed marginal revenue. With the price at $225, such a point is reached at about 11 units of output. That output level does give the firm a lower loss than does one slightly higher or slightly lower. But in this case, the firm takes an even smaller loss by not producing at all.

The reason 11 units of output does not minimize loss is that the demand curve lies below the average variable cost curve at that point. Suppose again that wages are the firm's only variable cost and rent its only fixed cost. At 11 units of output, revenue is not enough even to meet the firm's payroll. The firm will do better to send its workers home and save the cost of wages, even though when it does this the owners will have to pay the entire rent out of their own pockets.

The Firm's Short-Run Supply Curve

The examples just given provide the information needed to draw a short-run supply curve for a perfectly competitive firm. Let's turn to Exhibit 9.6 and work through it, starting with a price of $500. As we saw earlier, Fieldcom will turn out 19 computers a day at this price. Point E_1 of the firm's short-run marginal cost curve is thus a point on its supply curve.

Now suppose that the demand for portable computers slackens and the market price begins to fall. As it does, the point at which marginal revenue equals marginal cost moves downward along the firm's marginal cost curve. Soon point E_2 is reached—the point at which marginal cost and average total cost are equal. This occurs at an output of about 17 units and a price of about $385. At that price, the best the firm can do is break even; either a greater or a smaller output will result in a loss.

If the price falls still lower, the firm's problem becomes one of keeping its loss to a minimum rather than making the maximum profit. At a price of $300, for example, the firm minimizes its loss by making 14 units (point E_3). In the range of prices between minimum average total cost and minimum average variable cost, the supply curve continues to follow the marginal cost curve.

At about $250, the price reaches the lowest point on the average variable cost curve. Here the firm is just on the edge of shutting down—it is covering its variable costs with nothing to spare. Loss is equal to fixed cost. At any lower price, the firm minimizes its losses by shutting down. This point—E_4—is the lowest point on the marginal cost curve that can be considered part of the firm's supply curve.

All that we have learned so far about the firm's short-run supply decision can be summed up in the following statement: *The short-run supply curve of a profit-maximizing firm operating in a perfectly competitive market coincides with the upward-sloping part of the marginal cost curve lying above its intersection with the average variable cost curve.*

The Industry's Short-Run Supply Curve

We can now construct the supply curve for a whole industry on the basis of the supply curves for the firms in that industry. Exhibit 9.7 shows the supply curves for three firms. To get the total supply of this three-firm industry at each price, the quantities supplied by each firm are added together. In the graph, this means adding the supply curves horizontally. For an industry with many firms, it would be necessary to simply add the supply curves of increasing numbers of firms in the same way.

It should be noted that in adding the firms' supply curves together we assumed that input prices did not change as output expanded. For a small firm in a perfectly competitive industry, this is a realistic assumption. However, if all firms in an industry try to grow at the same time, the assumption may not hold; in fact, input prices will rise unless the supply curve for the input is perfectly

Exhibit 9.6   Derivation of the Short-Run Supply Curve

This graph shows how a short-run supply curve for Fieldcom Inc. can be derived from its cost curves. When the price is $500, the firm will produce at point E_1. As the price falls, the firm will move downward along its short-run marginal cost curve, as shown by points E_2 and E_3. The firm will continue to produce at the point at which price equals marginal cost until marginal cost falls below average variable cost. E_4 is thus the lowest point on the firm's supply curve. Below that price, the firm will shut down.

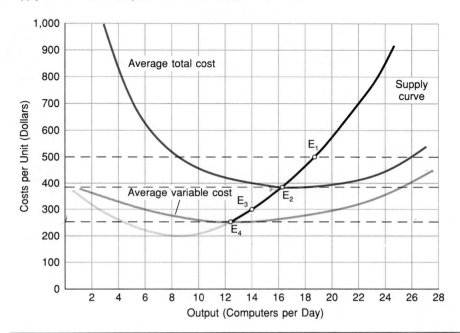

elastic. If input prices rise as the industry's total output grows, each firm's cost curves will shift upward as the output of all firms increases. This will make the short-run industry supply curve somewhat steeper than the sum of the individual supply curves.

Long-Run Equilibrium under Perfect Competition

Up to this point, we have considered changes in industry output that result from firms' decisions to produce more or less as the market price changes. In doing so, however, we have neglected an important part of a competitive industry's response to changes in demand: the process of entry and exit.

Consideration of entry and exit moves us from the realm of the short run to that of the long run. In Chapter 8, we made the distinction that all inputs can be varied in the long run but some are fixed in the short run. It is the ability to vary all inputs in the long run—even durable ones such as land, structures, and major pieces of equipment—that allows firms to enter a market for the first time, starting with a new plant and work force. It also means they can leave a market for good, releasing all their employees and selling their plant and equipment. (Sometimes firms leave peacefully, with the owners selling the firms' assets and dividing up the proceeds. Other times they leave the market only when forced to

Exhibit 9.7   Derivation of a Short-Run Industry Supply Curve

A short-run industry supply curve can be obtained by summing the supply curves of individual firms. Here this method is shown for an industry with only three firms. If the prices of inputs change as industry output varies, it will be necessary to adjust the industry supply curve.

(a)

Price	Firm X	Firm Y	Firm Z	Total
		Quantity Supplied		
$ .40	1,500			1,500
.80	5,500	3,000	3,333	11,833
1.20	9,500	7,000	10,000	26,500
1.50	12,500	10,000	15,000	37,500

(b)

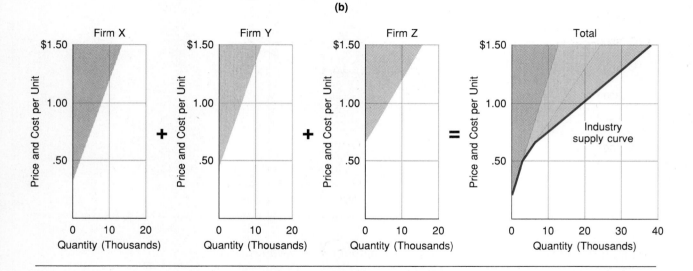

do so, such as when creditors resort to a bankruptcy court to force a sale of the firm's assets in order to pay the debts that it owes.) Typically, as an industry expands and contracts, many firms enter and leave it. The case of the chocolate chip cookie store industry, discussed in "Economics in the News 9.1," is a typical example.

Free entry and exit of firms is one of the basic traits of a perfectly competitive market. Free entry in this case does not mean that firms can enter at no cost. They may have to pay a great deal to set up shop, hire employees, gain useful contacts, and so on. Free entry simply means that if they are willing to invest the needed capital, new firms are free to compete with existing ones on a level playing field. They are not kept out by patents or licensing requirements, trade secrets, collusion by firms already in the industry, or lack of location or raw materials. Likewise, free exit means that firms face no legal barriers to shutting down or moving out of town if they find they cannot make a profit and that they can find buyers for the fixed assets for which they no longer have a use.

Free entry and exit did not play a direct role in our discussion of a firm's short-run supply decision. However, as we will now see, it is crucial to understanding how a competitive market works in the long run.

Cookie Stores Feel the Bite as Market Shifts

Ever since Wally Amos opened the first Famous Amos cookie store on Hollywood's Sunset Boulevard in 1975, the fresh-baked chocolate chip cookie business has appealed to entrepreneurs.

"The cookie business looked like such an easy business that every doctor or dentist with a brother-in-law out of work opened a cookie store," says Don Sawyer, president of Famous Amos Chocolate Chip Cookie Co. "There was an explosion of amateur cookie store owners." Today, he estimates, there are at least 1,200 cookie stores in the United States.

But the number of independent companies is shrinking as smaller cookie retailers close stores or sell to larger competitors. Even some of the bigger companies are feeling the squeeze. David's Cookies Inc., a market leader with about 170 stores, has lost at least 21 company-owned and franchised outlets, including seven in its New York City home market.

The main reason: The market for munchies on the run is moving on; new confectionary concoctions and other snack foods are competing for consumers' attention. Says Sawyer, "The competition for the snack dollar is way up."

No one is suggesting that the fresh-baked chocolate

chip cookie will go the way of the Hula Hoop. But many mom-and-pop operations are dropping out. Mrs. Fields Inc. alone has gobbled up some two dozen smaller companies that decided to call it quits.

Other entrepreneurs are determined to stay in the market, but they are finding it tough going. Jackie Kamin, who has launched seven Jackie's Cookie Connection stores on the East Coast since 1979, now is down to only two shops. Though she intends to stay in the business (she has two more stores in the works), Kamin concedes that the industry "isn't anything like it was. The competition is pretty stiff."

Source: Steven P. Galante, "Fresh-Cookie Stores Feel the Bite as Snack Food Market Shifts," *The Wall Street Journal,* February 24, 1986, 37. Photo Source: Copyright © 1987 B. E. White. All rights reserved.

Long-Run Equilibrium for a Competitive Firm

At a number of points, we have used the term *equilibrium* to refer to a state of affairs in which buyers and sellers are satisfied with the outcome of their economic plans. For a perfectly competitive firm, short-run equilibrium means being satisfied with the current output level. As we have seen, this is the case when marginal cost is equal to marginal revenue, that is, to the product's price. In the long run, equilibrium under perfect competition has two other requirements: (1) Each firm must be content with the size of its current plant (that is, with the amount of fixed inputs it uses), and (2) firms not already in the market must be willing to stay out and existing firms to stay in.

Exhibit 9.8 shows how these three requirements are met in the long-run equilibrium for a perfectly competitive firm. First, marginal cost equals price at the chosen output level. In the short run, there is no reason for the firm to either increase or decrease its output. Second, the firm has a plant that is just the right size to make short-run average total cost equal to the lowest possible long-run average cost at the chosen output level. No change in the amount of fixed inputs

Exhibit 9.8   A Perfectly Competitive Firm in Long-Run Equilibrium

Long-run equilibrium in a perfectly competitive industry requires that the typical firm (1) have
no short-run incentive to change the level of its output; (2) have no long-run incentive to
change the size of the plant used to produce its output; and (3) have no long-run incentive
to enter or leave the industry. This requires that price, short-run marginal cost, short-run
average total cost, and long-run average cost all have the same value in equilibrium as
shown here.

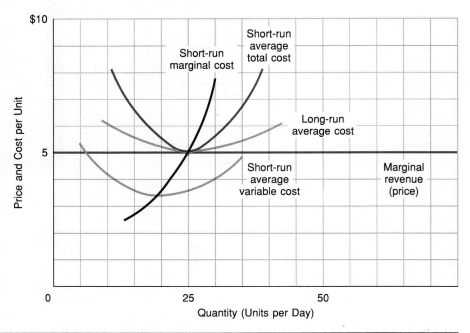

can cut average cost. Third, both long-run and short-run total average cost are
equal to price at the equilibrium level of output.

As always, average total cost comprises both explicit and implicit costs,
including the opportunity cost of capital, or "normal profit." When price equals
average total cost, then, capital employed in the industry is earning exactly
normal profit—no more and no less. (Another way of saying this is that firms are
earning zero *economic profit*.) Earnings above normal profit (a positive economic
profit) will attract new capital into the industry. Earnings below normal profit
(economic loss) will cause capital to leave the industry.

These three conditions for long-run equilibrium can be expressed in the
following equation:

$$\text{Price} = \frac{\text{Marginal}}{\text{cost}} = \begin{array}{c}\text{Short-run}\\\text{average}\\\text{total cost}\end{array} = \begin{array}{c}\text{Long-run}\\\text{average}\\\text{cost}\end{array}$$

If any part of this equation does not hold, firms will have a reason to change their
plans. If price does not equal marginal cost, they will want to change the output
level given the size of their plants. If short-run average total cost does not equal
long-run average total cost, they will want to change the size of the plants they
are using to produce their current output. If price is lower than long-run average

cost, firms in the industry will want to leave it; if price is above long-run average total cost, firms outside the industry will want to enter it. Unless all parts of the equation hold, then, the market cannot be in long-run equilibrium.

Industry Adjustment to Falling Demand

A state of long-run equilibrium such as that shown in Exhibit 9.8 exists only so long as outside conditions do not change. Suppose, though, that those conditions do change—for example, there is a long-run decrease in the demand for the firm's product. Exhibit 9.9 shows what will happen.

Part a of Exhibit 9.9 shows a set of cost curves for a typical firm. Part b is a supply and demand diagram for the market as a whole. The short-run industry supply curves shown are built up from those of the individual firms in the market (see Exhibit 9.7). The demand curves are market demand curves.

Suppose that initially the short-run market supply and demand curves are in the positions S_1 and D_1. The equilibrium price is $5. Each firm takes this price as given and adjusts its output on that basis, producing 25 units. At that price

Exhibit 9.9   Long-Run Adjustment to Declining Demand

Part a represents a typical firm in a perfectly competitive industry; part b represents the industry as a whole. At first, both the firm and the industry are in long-run equilibrium at a price of $5. Then something happens to shift the market demand curve leftward from D_1 to D_2. In the short run, the price falls to $4 at the intersection of D_2 and S_1. The firm's short-run response is to move downward along its marginal cost curve. After a while, some firms (not the one shown) get tired of taking losses and leave the industry. This causes the market supply curve to shift toward S_2 and the market price to recover. The typical firm returns to the breakeven point. The market has traced out part of its long-run supply curve as shown by the large arrow.

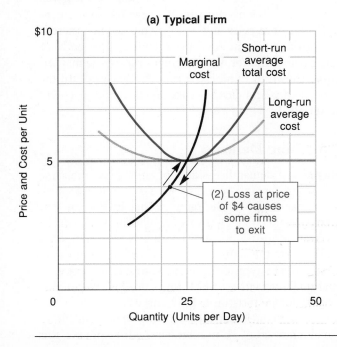

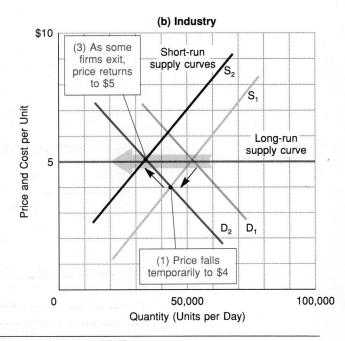

and output, a typical firm would just break even. (Remember, though, that "breaking even" in the economic sense means earning enough to cover all costs, including the opportunity cost of capital.)

Now something happens—say, a change in consumer tastes or incomes—that shifts the demand curve to a new position, D_2. The short-run result is a drop in the market price to $4. Each firm, being a price taker, will view the decline in price as beyond its control and will adjust to it as best it can. As shown in part a of Exhibit 9.9, this means cutting back output slightly in order to keep losses to a minimum but not shutting down completely. Each firm's movement back along its marginal cost curve is what causes the movement of the market as a whole downward and to the left along short-run supply curve S_1.

However, this new situation cannot be a long-run equilibrium, because each firm is operating at a loss. Owners are not earning enough to cover the opportunity costs of keeping their capital invested in the industry. (We could also say they are not earning a "normal profit.") If the market demand curve shows no hope of shifting back to the right, some owners will pull their capital out of the industry. Some may go bankrupt. Others will sell their plant and equipment and get out while they can. Still others will keep their firms running but change over to making goods for other, more profitable markets.

There is no way to tell which firms will be the first to go, but let us assume that the typical firm shown in Exhibit 9.9 is not one of the first. Look what happens to it as some of the others leave. As some firms withdraw, the market loses their output. The market supply curve, which is now made up of fewer individual supply curves, shifts to the left toward S_2. As it does, the market price begins to move upward along demand curve D_2. When the price gets all the way back to $5, the firms remaining in the industry will no longer be losing money. Firms will stop leaving the industry, and the market will have reached a new long-run equilibrium. In the new equilibrium price, marginal cost, short-run average total cost, and long-run average cost will once again be equal.

This sequence of events has traced out a portion of the industry's *long-run supply curve*, as shown by the arrow. A long-run supply curve for an industry shows the path along which equilibrium price and quantity move when there is a lasting change in demand. Movement along this curve requires time both for firms to adjust the sizes of their plants and for firms to enter or leave the market.

The long-run supply curve shown in Exhibit 9.9 is perfectly elastic. In the long run, the leftward shift of the demand curve causes no change in price but only a decrease in quantity supplied.

Industry Adjustment to Rising Demand

When there is a long-run increase in demand, freedom of entry plays the same role that freedom of exit plays when demand falls. This case is shown in Exhibit 9.10. The starting position in this exhibit is the same as that in Exhibit 9.9. Short-run supply curve S_1 and demand curve D_1 give an equilibrium price of $5. The individual firm breaks even at an output of 25 units. Now watch what happens as the demand curve shifts to the right to D_2. The short-run result is an increase in the market price to $6. The typical firm adjusts to the new price by moving upward along its marginal cost curve. As all firms do this, the market moves upward and to the right along short-run supply curve S_1.

But again this short-run adjustment is not the new long-run equilibrium, because now all firms are making a profit. Entrepreneurs will soon spot this healthy, growing market as a good one in which to invest. Some of them may

Exhibit 9.10   Long-Run Adjustment to an Increase in Demand

In this exhibit, both the firm and the industry start out in equilibrium at a price of $5. Then
something happens to shift the market demand curve rightward to D_2. In the short run, the
price rises to $6 at the intersection of D_2 and S_1. The firm's short-run response is to move
upward along its marginal cost curve, earning better-than-normal profits. After a while, these
high profits attract new firms into the industry. As these firms enter, the market supply curve
shifts toward S_2. Profits for the typical firm return to normal, and new firms stop entering the
industry. Again the market has traced out part of its long-run supply curve as shown by the
large arrow.

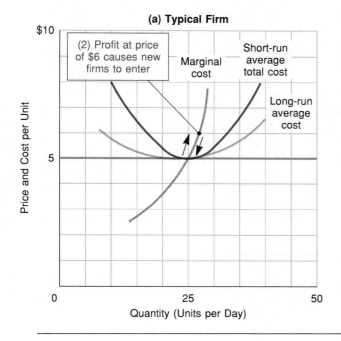

(a) Typical Firm

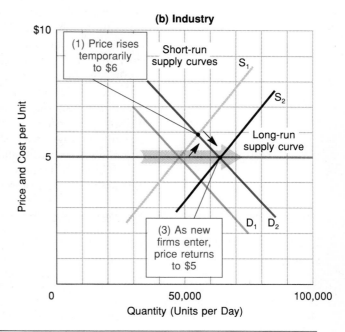

(b) Industry

start new firms in this market; others may shift plant and equipment from making something else to making goods for this industry. It does not matter whether
the entry is by new firms or by existing ones that are producing for this market
for the first time. In either case, new entries will cause the supply curve to shift
to the right toward S_2.

As the supply curve shifts, the price falls. It does not fall far enough to drive
the new entrants out, but it does fall sufficiently to drive everyone's profits back
to the normal level. Entry of firms into the industry will stop, and the market
will be in a new long-run equilibrium at the intersection of S_2 and D_2.

Once again a portion of the long-run supply curve for the industry has been
traced out, as shown by the large arrow in Exhibit 9.10. Also, this long-run
supply curve again is perfectly elastic. A rightward shift in the demand curve
has, in the long run, produced an increase in quantity supplied but no rise in
price.

Other Long-Run Supply Curves

The long-run industry supply curve need not always be perfectly elastic as in the
examples just given. Supply curves that are upward sloping, downward sloping,
and U shaped are also possible.

Which shape the long-run industry supply curve takes depends mainly on what happens to the industry's input prices in the long run as output expands. If the long-run supply curve for all inputs is perfectly elastic, the prices of those inputs will not change as the quantity of them demanded by the industry increases. It may also be that the industry uses such a small part of the total supply of each input that any change in input prices that does occur will be slight. For example, the cookie store business uses such a small part of the total supply of flour and eggs produced in the economy that expansion or contraction of such stores will have no effect on the price of those inputs. Industry output can therefore expand without affecting the costs of the individual firms, and the supply curve will be perfectly elastic. This was the case in Exhibits 9.9 and 9.10.

Suppose, however, that the industry is a heavy user of relatively specialized inputs whose outputs can be boosted only at increasing cost. For example, consider the home construction business. This uses a substantial portion of all the lumber produced in the country. An expansion of the construction industry will cause lumber suppliers to exhaust the lowest-cost stands of trees and move to harvesting higher-cost timber. The home construction industry also uses a significant proportion of all carpenters in the country. If the industry expands, carpenters' wages may have to rise relative to those of, say, auto mechanics in order to attract additional workers into this occupation.

Exhibit 9.11 shows what happens in such an industry as a permanent increase in demand causes output to expand. As in the previous case, the shift in

Exhibit 9.11   A Positively Sloped Long-Run Industry Supply Curve

In Exhibits 9.9 and 9.10, it was assumed that input prices do not change as industry output expands. This pair of diagrams shows what happens if industry expansion causes input prices to rise. As output expands, rising input prices push up the firm's marginal cost curve from MC_1 to MC_2 and its average total cost from ATC_1 to ATC_2. The result is a new long-run equilibrium price that is higher than the initial price. The long-run industry supply curve thus has a positive slope.

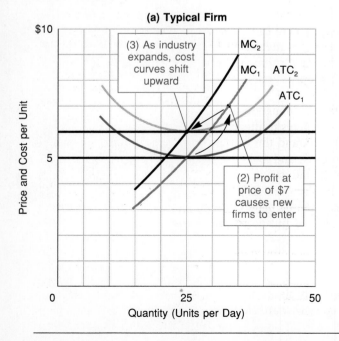

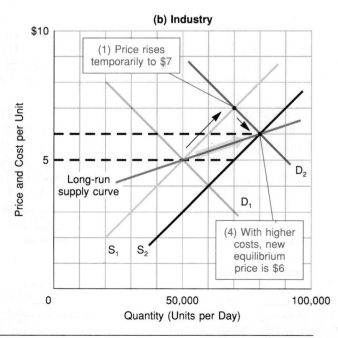

demand first pushes up price along the short-run supply curve. New firms enter the market. However, expansion of the industry now raises input prices. Each firm's marginal cost and average total cost curves are shifted upward from MC_1 to MC_2 and from ATC_1 to ATC_2 as shown. As a result, the new long-run equilibrium is at a higher price than the initial equilibrium. The long-run industry supply curve, drawn through the two points of short-run equilibrium, thus has a positive slope.

It is also possible for the price of an input to decrease as the industry's total output increases. For example, as sales of electronic equipment expand, the firms that make the components that go into it may be able to use cheaper production methods. If this occurs, the cost curves for all firms will drift downward as new firms enter the industry. The long-run supply curve will then be downward sloping.

Finally, it is possible for a combination of forces to be at work. Long-run supply is at first influenced by the falling price of one special input; but beyond a certain point, some other special input becomes a limiting factor that causes the long-run supply curve to bend upward. The long-run industry supply curve then becomes U shaped.

As we have seen, many variants are possible. Only through direct observation of the industry in question can we tell which possibility applies.

Summary

1. **What characteristics define the structure of a market?** A *market structure* is defined in terms of the number and size of firms, the nature of the product, and the ease of entry and exit. A *perfectly competitive* market has the following traits: (1) There are many buyers and sellers, each small compared with the market as a whole; (2) the product is homogeneous; and (3) entry into and exit from the market are easy. Other market structures to be studied in this course include *monopoly, oligopoly,* and *monopolistic competition.*

2. **What determines the profit-maximizing output level in the short run for a perfectly competitive firm?** In the short run, the relationship between marginal cost and *marginal revenue* (price) determines the profit-maximizing output level for a perfectly competitive firm. The firm should expand output to the point at which marginal cost rises to the level of marginal revenue provided that marginal revenue is at least equal to average variable cost at that point.

3. **Under what conditions will a firm continue to operate even if it sustains a loss?** If marginal revenue is below average total cost at the point at which marginal cost and marginal revenue are equal, the firm cannot earn a profit. It will minimize loss in the short run by staying open if marginal revenue is above average variable cost. If marginal revenue is below average variable cost at the same point, the firm will minimize loss by shutting down.

4. **How is a firm's short-run supply curve related to its cost curves?** The short-run supply curve for a perfectly competitive firm is the upward-sloping part of the marginal cost curve lying above its intersection with the average variable cost curve.

5. **What are the conditions for long-run equilibrium in a perfectly competitive industry?** Long-run equilibrium in a perfectly competitive industry requires that (1) price be equal to marginal cost so that each firm is content with the level of output it is producing; (2) short-run average total cost be equal to long-run average cost so that firms are satisfied with the size of their plant given their output rate; and (3) price be equal to long-run average cost so that there is no incentive for new firms to enter the industry or for existing firms to leave it.

6. **What determines the shape of the long-run supply curve for a perfectly competitive industry?** A perfectly competitive industry adjusts to long-run changes in demand through exit of firms (in the case of a drop in market demand) or entry of new firms (in the case of a rise in market demand). If input prices do not change as the industry's output changes, the industry's long-run supply curve will be flat. If input prices rise, the long-run supply curve will have a positive slope; if they fall, it will have a negative slope.

Terms for Review

- market structure
- perfect competition
- monopoly
- oligopoly
- monopolistic competition
- price taker
- marginal revenue

Questions for Review

1. What characteristics define the structure of a market?

2. Name three traits that define the market structure of perfect competition.

3. What is the relationship between the total cost and total revenue curves at the point of short-run profit maximization for a perfectly competitive firm? What is the relationship between the marginal cost and marginal revenue curves at the same point?

4. Under what conditions will a perfectly competitive firm find it worthwhile to operate even if it operates at a loss in the short run?

5. What part of the perfectly competitive firm's supply curve coincides with its marginal cost curve in the short run? What part does not?

6. List four quantities that must be equal in order for a perfectly competitive firm to be in long-run equilibrium.

7. Under what conditions will the long-run supply curve for a perfectly competitive industry be perfectly elastic?

Problems and Topics for Discussion

1. **Examining the lead-off case.** What assumptions are made about the market in which Fieldcom operates that permit that market to be treated as perfectly competitive? In what respects does the market for computers in the real world meet these conditions? Does it matter what kind of computers you consider—pocket calculators, personal computers, large "mainframe" computers? Discuss.

2. **Market structures.** Give examples other than those presented in the text of industries that fit, or approximate, the four market structures of perfect competition, monopolistic competition, oligopoly, and monopoly.

3. **Buyers as price takers.** The concept of being a price taker can apply to buyers as well as sellers. A price-taking buyer is one who cannot influence prices by changing the amount purchased. Are you a price taker for the goods you buy? Can you give an example of a firm that might not be a price taker in the market in which it buys one or more of its inputs?

4. **Changes in fixed cost and the supply curve.** Fieldcom buys some automated equipment in order to speed up production of its computers. The equipment adds $500 per day to the firm's fixed costs, but it saves $50 per unit in variable costs. Rework the graph in Exhibit 9.6 to show how the new equipment affects Fieldcom's supply curve. (You may want to rework part a of Exhibit 9.3 as a basis for the new supply curve.) What is the minimum price the firm must now charge in order to continue operating in the short run? What is the lowest price at which it can break even?

5. **Long-run supply with falling input prices.** Exhibit 9.11 shows the long-run adjustment of a competitive industry to an increase in demand in the case in which input prices rise as output increases. Assume instead that input prices fall as output rises. Draw a new set of diagrams to show how a typical firm and the industry as a whole respond to an increase in demand.

Case for Discussion

Independent Truckers as a Perfectly Competitive Industry

The next time you are out on the highway, take a look at the trucks that are passing you. You will see many that belong to large firms, such as Yellow Freight, that haul large numbers of small shipments all over the country on regular schedules. You will also see trucks that bear the names of companies such as Sears or Sun Oil, for which transportation is a sideline.

If you look closely, though, you will see that about one truck in four looks a little different. The tractors, many of which are brightly painted and highly chromed, often have sleepers attached. The trailers, often refrigerated, are likely to be filled with farm produce moving to market. These are the trucks of independent owner-operators, who move much of the nation's output of farm goods and some manufactured goods.

Each firm in this market consists of a person who owns and drives just one truck. There are many such firms—as many as 35,000, by some estimates.

From the shipper's point of view, one refrigerated truck is about as good as another, as long as it is headed in the right direction. And most independent truckers will go wherever their loads take them.

Entry is easy. Some people go into business with a used truck and as little as $5,000. Most operators buy their trucks on credit. Exit is also easy—too easy, some say. Many independent truckers go broke every year, and the number of firms rises and falls with the state of the economy.

People who run the giant trucking companies that haul manufactured goods often look down their noses at the independent truckers with their loads of apples and potatoes. They call them "gypsies" or worse. But this system succeeds in putting fresh produce on the dinner table in every town every day.

As many as 35,000 independent truckers operate in the United States.

Questions

1. In what ways does the independent trucking industry meet the requirements of perfect competition? Are there any ways in which it does not?

2. On average, the firms in a perfectly competitive industry earn no pure economic profits. However, average conditions do not always apply. What would you expect to happen to the profits of independent truckers when the economy enters a recession? When it enters a period of prosperity? What do you think would happen to the number of firms in the industry at such times?

3. Diesel fuel is a major input for independent truckers. What would you expect to happen to the profits of independent truckers and the number of firms in the industry as the price of fuel rises and falls? Outline the sequence of events in each case (drawing a graph may help).

Suggestions for Further Reading

Nicholson, Walter. *Intermediate Microeconomics and Its Application*, 4th ed. Hinsdale, Ill.: Dryden Press, 1987.

Chapter 11 of this text parallels this chapter. Chapter 9 contains a useful discussion of the profit maximization assumption and some alternatives.

Robinson, Joan. "What Is Perfect Competition?" *Quarterly Journal of Economics* 49 (November 1934): 104–120.

This classic paper attempts to pin down some of the fine points of the concept of perfect competition. Not all of the issues it raises have as yet been laid to rest.

10 The Theory of Monopoly

After reading this chapter, you will understand . . .

- How price and revenue are related for a monopoly.
- How the profit-maximizing price and output are determined for a monopoly.
- Why monopolies and other firms sometimes engage in price discrimination.
- Why monopoly is a source of market failure.
- Why "natural monopolies" such as electric utilities are regulated and what problems regulation poses.

Before reading this chapter, make sure you know the meaning of . . .

- Market failure (Chapter 5)
- Consumer and producer surplus (Chapter 7)
- Normal profit (Chapter 8)
- Market structure (Chapter 9)

Cracking the Beryllium Monopoly

Lighter than aluminum, yet stronger than steel, beryllium is one of the world's magic metals. Prized by Pentagon planners and electronics makers, it is used in computers, satellites, missiles and nuclear reactors. Beryllium's mystique is heightened because it's so hard to find. For nearly 20 years there has been only one beryllium-bearing mine in the Free World (the Soviet Union and China have their own supply), a hole in the ground in Utah owned by Cleveland-based Brush Wellman. Now Hecla Mining Co., in Coeur d'Alene, Idaho, the biggest U.S. silver miner, has its hands on a huge deposit in Canada. "We are very excited," says Hecla President Arthur Brown.

Until recently, there was only one beryllium-bearing mine in the Free World.

With the price of silver having bobbed as low as $4.90 recently, and still $6 or so an ounce, it's hard to blame Brown for his enthusiasm. After all, beryllium is a can't-miss metal, right? Maybe not. "Hecla is never going to be able to market all of that [beryllium]. Sometimes it's hard to explain to miners that first you worry about where you can sell it before you spend millions doing mine plans," says Al Kuestermeyer, a mining and beryllium consultant in Tucson.

The catch is that while beryllium may be a wonder metal, its uses, so far, are limited. A mere 1.1 million pounds of the stuff was purchased last year, compared with, say, 26 million pounds of silver. Hecla's mine, if company projections are realized, would dump the equivalent of another 20 percent a year into the world market. If worrying about a glut isn't problem enough, Hecla must try to break Brush Wellman's near monopoly. Brush Wellman refines beryllium into various alloys, ceramics, and beryllium metal itself—average price $400 per pound—which means 24 percent operating margins and a price-earnings ratio of 24 for its stock.

Hecla, nonetheless, wants in, but its plan has several holes. It wants to produce beryllium only in an intermediate form, such as beryllium oxide, and sell it to customers who would then convert it into final beryllium products such as alloys. But only a handful of companies can convert it. Hecla's only realistic way to make a beryllium investment pay may be to manufacture beryllium alloys and the like and go head to head with Brush Wellman. That would put Hecla in the highest-profit end of the business, but it could cost another $30 million to get there. It would also put the company into a manufacturing business it knows nothing about.

Source: Excerpted by permission of *Forbes* Magazine, from Barry Stavro, "Long Shot," October 20, 1986, 127–128. © Forbes Inc., 1986. Photo Source: UPI/Bettmann Newsphotos.

IN Chapter 9, we defined a monopoly as a market in which there is a single firm selling a unique product, protected from the entry of competitors. As a market structure, monopoly is an ideal type, a theoretical construct that exists in its pure form only as an economic model. In the real world, the conditions of monopoly can only be approximated. Brush Wellman's 20-year near monopoly of beryllium is about as good an approximation as can be found. But in illustrating the model, it also reveals the model's limitations:

- It is rare to find a market that is truly served by only a single firm. Brush Wellman is the sole firm producing beryllium in the West, but it accounts for only two-thirds of the world total, counting China and the Soviet Union.

- The concept of a "unique" product implies one with no substitutes. In practice, however, every product faces competition from substitutes. As an element beryllium certainly has a unique atomic weight, distinct chemical properties, and so on, but in economic terms it faces competition from other strong, light materials—titanium, magnesium, carbon-fiber composites, and even plain old aluminum.

- Most important, no firm faces absolute protection from competition. Ownership of a rare mineral deposit is pretty good protection—but, as this case shows, another deposit may be discovered. Even monopolies that are protected by law, such as the U.S. Postal Service, must face the possibility that the law can be changed.

If there are no true monopolies, why develop the model? The answer is that the study of monopoly provides a benchmark with which to compare the behavior of firms that lie in the vast territory between monopoly and its opposite ideal type, perfect competition. In a sense, there is an element of monopoly in every firm that has some degree of control over the price of its product—every firm, that is, that operates in a market that is not perfectly competitive—and that takes in a great many firms indeed.

Profit Maximization for the Pure Monopolist

If for the sake of discussion we set aside the question of how closely firms like Brush Wellman fit the ideal type, we can concentrate on the key difference between monopoly and perfect competition: A monopolist is not a price taker.

The fact that a monopolist's choice of output level directly affects the product's price is the starting point of the theory of monopoly.

Output, Price, and Marginal Revenue under Monopoly

Exhibit 10.1 illustrates the relationships among output, price, and revenue under monopoly. Columns 1 and 2 of the table in part a give data on the demand for the product of a pure monopolist. Part b presents the data as a demand curve. As the table and the graph make clear, the greater the output, the lower the price at which buyers will be willing to purchase the entire amount produced.

As the monopolist raises or lowers output, changes in both price and quantity affect the firm's total revenue (part c). For any output, total revenue equals price times quantity. Starting from zero, as output increases, total revenue first rises, then reaches a maximum at about 17 units of output, and then falls.

Exhibit 10.1 Demand, Total Revenue, and Marginal Revenue for a Monopolist

This exhibit shows how demand, total revenue, and marginal revenue are related for a typical monopolist. Total revenue is found by multiplying price by quantity at each point on the demand curve. Marginal revenue is the increase in total revenue that results from a one-unit increase in output. When demand is elastic, marginal revenue is more than zero and total revenue is increasing. When demand is inelastic, marginal revenue is less than zero and total revenue is decreasing. Marginal revenue is less than price at all output levels.

(a)

Quantity (1)	Price (2)	Total Revenue (3)	Marginal Revenue (4)
1	$10.00	$10.00	
2	9.70	19.40	$9.40
3	9.40	28.20	8.80
4	9.10	36.40	8.20
16	5.50	88.00	
17	5.20	88.40	.40
18	4.90	88.20	−.20
33	.40	13.20	
34	.10	3.40	−9.80
35	.00	.00	−3.40

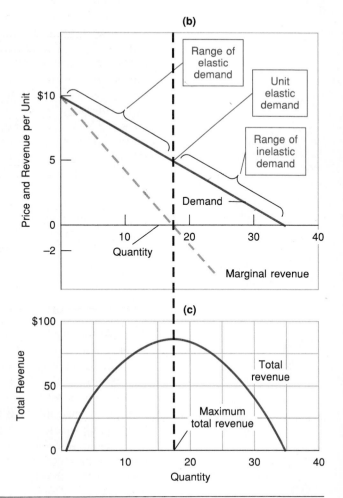

We first noted this relationship between price and total revenue along the demand curve when the concept of elasticity was introduced. At that time, we showed that when demand is *elastic* a drop in price causes total revenue to rise. (The reason is that in percentage terms, the quantity sold rises by more than the price falls; thus, the product of the two increases.) In contrast, when demand is *inelastic* revenue falls when the price drops. (This is because with inelastic demand, the percentage increase in quantity is less than the percentage decrease in price.) With a straight-line demand curve such as the one in part b of Exhibit 10.1, the upper half is elastic and the lower half inelastic. That accounts for the shape of the "revenue hill" drawn as a separate graph in part c.

The relationship between output and revenue for a pure monopolist can also be viewed in marginal terms. In Chapter 9, we defined *marginal revenue* as the change in total revenue that results from a one-unit increase in a firm's output. Column 4 of part a of Exhibit 10.1 gives data on marginal revenue for the firm in this example. The figures in the column are the differences between the entries in column 3. Part b shows the firm's marginal revenue curve. The marginal revenue curve is above the horizontal axis when total revenue is increasing (elastic demand) and below it when total revenue is decreasing (inelastic demand). It intersects the horizontal axis at the point of maximum total revenue (part c).

There is an easy rule that will help in sketching the marginal revenue curve that corresponds to any straight-line demand curve: *The marginal revenue curve for a straight-line demand curve always cuts the horizontal distance from the demand curve to the vertical axis exactly in half.* Following this rule, the horizontal intercept of the marginal revenue curve can be placed halfway between the origin and the horizontal intercept of the demand curve. (In Exhibit 10.1, the marginal revenue curve cuts the horizontal axis at 17.5, half of 35.) The vertical intercept of the marginal revenue curve is the same as that of the straight-line demand curve. (The vertical intercept is at $10 in Exhibit 10.1.) This rule does not work for curved demand curves, but the examples in this book are being kept simple.

Note that the marginal revenue curve is always below the demand curve. This means that the increase in total revenue that the monopolist gets from the sale of one additional unit is less than the price at which that unit is sold. The reason is that the monopolist must cut the price on all units sold, not just on the last one sold, in order to increase total sales volume. The price cut on earlier units thus partly or wholly offsets the revenue gain from increasing the amount sold.

Profit Maximization

The relationship between output and revenue for a pure monopolist is one key set of data needed to determine the profit-maximizing output level for a monopolist. The model is completed by adding data on cost, as is done in Exhibit 10.2.

As in the case of perfect competition, we can proceed by either comparing total cost with total revenue or taking a marginal approach. Total cost for the firm at various output levels is given in column 6 of part c of Exhibit 10.2. Subtracting this from total revenue (column 3) gives total profit (column 7). A glance at column 7 shows the profit-maximizing output level to be 13 units. The total revenue–total cost approach to profit maximization is shown graphically in part a of the exhibit. Total profit equals the vertical gap between the total cost

Exhibit 10.2   Profit Maximization for a
Monopolist

A monopolist maximizes profits by producing the amount of output for which marginal cost equals marginal revenue. The price it charges for the product is determined by the height of the demand curve (rather than of the marginal revenue curve) at the profit-maximizing quantity. Note that maximizing profit is not the same as maximizing revenue. Beyond 13 units of output (the profit-maximizing level in this case), total revenue continues to rise for a while, but profit falls because total cost rises even more rapidly.

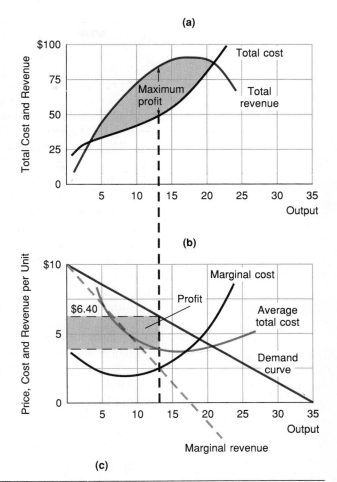

(a)

(b)

(c)

Output (1)	Price (2)	Total Revenue (3)	Marginal Revenue (4)	Marginal Cost (5)	Total Cost (6)	Total Profit (7)
1	$10.00	$10.00			$23.80	−$13.80
			$9.40	$3.40		
2	9.70	19.40			27.20	−7.80
			8.80	3.05		
3	9.40	28.20			30.25	2.05
			8.20	2.75		
4	9.10	36.40			33.00	3.40
			7.60	2.50		
5	8.80	44.00			35.50	8.50
			7.00	2.30		
6	8.50	51.00			37.80	13.20
			6.40	2.15		
7	8.20	57.40			39.95	17.45
			5.80	2.05		
8	7.90	63.20			42.00	21.20
			5.20	2.00		
9	7.60	68.40			44.00	24.40
			4.60	2.05		
10	7.30	73.00			46.05	26.95
			4.00	2.15		
11	7.00	77.00			48.20	28.80
			3.40	2.30		
12	6.70	80.40			50.50	29.90
			2.80	2.50		
13	6.40	83.20			53.00	30.20
			2.20	2.75		
14	6.10	85.40			55.75	29.65
			1.60	3.05		
15	5.80	87.00			58.80	28.20
			1.00	3.40		
16	5.50	88.00			62.20	25.80
			.40	3.80		
17	5.20	88.40			66.00	22.40

and total revenue curves. It reaches a maximum at 13 units of output, where the two curves are furthest apart.

Note that maximizing profit is not the same as maximizing revenue. Between 13 and 17 units of output, total revenue continues to rise. But total cost rises even more rapidly; hence, profit falls.

The alternative marginal approach is based on the data given in columns 4 and 5 of part c. Marginal revenue is the amount by which total revenue increases when output is increased by one unit; marginal cost is the amount by which total cost increases. It follows that as long as marginal revenue exceeds marginal cost, adding one more unit of output adds more to total revenue than to total cost and hence adds to total profit. Beyond 13 units of output, marginal revenue falls below marginal cost; thus, any further expansion of output reduces total profit.

Part b of Exhibit 10.2 compares marginal revenue and marginal cost in graphic terms. The profit-maximizing quantity is found where the marginal cost and marginal revenue curves intersect. It matches the point of maximum profit, which is shown in part a of Exhibit 10.2 as the point at which the gap between the total revenue and total cost curves is greatest. Profit per unit is equal to the vertical gap between the demand curve (which shows the price at which the product is sold) and the average total cost curve. Profit per unit times quantity of output equals total profit, as shown by the shaded rectangle in part b of Exhibit 10.2.

It is important to remember that the intersection of the marginal cost and marginal revenue curves in Exhibit 10.2 gives the profit-maximizing output level for the firm, but the profit-maximizing price is given by the height of the demand curve for that level. For a pure monopolist, this price is always above marginal cost when profit is being maximized. For the firm in our example, marginal cost at 13 units of output is $2.60 per unit but, according to the demand curve, consumers are willing to buy 13 units for as much as $6.40. Therefore, $6.40 is what the monopolist will charge for the 13 units of output in order to earn the maximum profit.

Profit Maximization or Loss Minimization?

If market conditions are unfavorable, a monopolist, like a perfectly competitive firm, may be unable to earn a profit in the short run. If that is the case, it will try to keep losses to a minimum. Whether a profit is possible depends on the position of the demand curve relative to the monopolist's average total cost curve.

The possibility of a loss is shown in Exhibit 10.3. The demand curve lies below the average total cost curve at all points. This might be the case, for example, during a recession, when incomes fall. Following the usual rule, the profit-maximizing (here loss-minimizing) level of output is found where the marginal cost and marginal revenue curves intersect—at about 10 units. According to the demand curve, that much output cannot be sold for more than $4 per unit, but average total cost at 10 units of output is $4.60. At a price of $4 per unit, then, the monopolist will lose $.60 on each unit sold. This total loss is shown by the shaded rectangle.

Exhibit 10.3   A Monopolist
Suffering a Short-Run Loss

Sometimes demand may not be high enough to allow a
monopolist to earn a profit. In this graph, for example, the
demand curve lies below the average total cost curve at all
points. The best the monopolist can do in the short run is
cut losses by producing at the point at which marginal cost
equals marginal revenue. If the demand curve were to shift
downward even further, preventing the firm from obtaining a
price that would cover average variable cost, the short-run
loss-minimizing strategy would be to shut down.

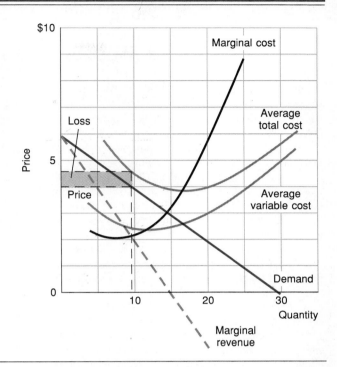

Although the monopolist suffers a loss at 10 units of output, no other output
level will yield a smaller loss. As Exhibit 10.3 is drawn, $4 per unit is more than
enough to cover average variable costs. The monopolist, like the perfectly competitive firm, is better off staying in business in the short run, even at a loss, as
long as the price at which it can sell its output is greater than the average variable
cost. But if the demand curve shifts so far to the left that it falls below the average
variable cost curve at all points, a pure monopolist, like a perfectly competitive
firm, will minimize short-run losses by shutting down.

In the long run, if demand conditions do not improve, the firm shown in
Exhibit 10.3 will be in trouble despite its monopolistic position. If it must depend entirely on private sources of capital, it will go out of business because it
will be unable to offer potential investors a return sufficient to cover their opportunity costs; they will put their capital elsewhere. However, as "Applying Economic Ideas 10.1" shows, if the monopoly provides an essential public service, it
may be kept in business by means of a government subsidy.

Long-Run Profit Maximization

One of the basic conclusions reached in Chapter 9 was that in the long run,
pure economic profits are impossible under perfect competition. The reason is
that when an increase in demand for the product raises the market price above
average total cost, new firms are drawn into the industry. As they enter, the total

Subsidized Monopoly: The Case of Mass Transit

If demand conditions turn against a private monopoly to the point where it cannot expect to charge a price at least equal to average total cost in the long run, it will have to go out of business. However, if the monopoly provides a service that is essential to the public, it may continue to operate under a government subsidy. The mass transit systems of many cities are in this position. They used to be able to make a profit as private monopolies. Over time, however, rising costs and falling demand cut into their earnings. At that point, many transit systems were taken over by local governments.

Public mass transit systems face a dilemma in their pricing decisions. From the viewpoint of taxpayers who are not regular users of mass transit, the proper pricing policy would be to equate marginal cost and marginal revenue in order to keep the subsidy to a minimum. However, several considerations suggest a lower fare and a larger subsidy.

One factor is efficiency. A market works most efficiently when the price (in this case, the fare) equals the opportunity cost of providing an additional unit of the good or service, that is, the marginal cost. A subsidy-minimizing price would, like the profit-maximizing price of a private monopolist, be higher than marginal cost and thus higher than the efficient level.

A second consideration is the desire to relieve traffic congestion. Traffic congestion is a type of negative externality that in itself results in inefficient use of transportation resources. A low transit fare that draws riders from crowded highways is thus often advocated as a means of offsetting the adverse effects of traffic congestion.

Finally, low transit fares are often proposed as a means of benefiting low-income households. These tend to be heavy users of public transportation. Without affordable public transportation as a means of getting to work, it is argued, some of these households would have to rely on public welfare payments for support.

In practice, most mass transit systems do not set fares so as to minimize the subsidies. To do so would require raising the price until the system was operating on the elastic part of its demand curve—the part of the demand curve on which further fare increases would reduce total revenue. However, fare increases on most systems result in higher revenues, showing that they are on the inelastic portion of the demand curve. The rule seems to be to keep the price low and the subsidy high until the taxpayers scream and then raise fares a little—but not all the way to the point at which the subsidy could be kept to a minimum.

quantity supplied to the market increases, driving the price back to the level of average total cost.

For an ideal-type monopoly, in contrast, pure economic profits can continue as long as demand conditions are favorable. The reason is that a monopolist is protected against competition. Even if short-run demand conditions permit a rate of return higher than the opportunity cost of capital, no other firm can enter the market. If nothing happens to disturb the favorable position of its cost and demand curves, a monopolist can earn pure economic profits above and beyond the opportunity cost of capital even in the long run.

Entrepreneurial Competition, Rent Seeking, and Limit Pricing

As we have repeatedly seen, no real-world firm is ever fully protected from competition in the long run. The reason is that a pure economic profit earned by a monopolist acts as a beacon to entrepreneurs, who will focus their ingenuity on finding a way to break into the market. Brush Wellman's beryllium monopoly is a case in point. Although this firm reigned for 20 years as the West's only supplier of beryllium, it had to contend with rapid innovation by producers of other strong, lightweight materials such as titanium and carbon-fiber composites. In addition, other entrepreneurs were on the lookout for new beryllium deposits, and such a deposit was finally found.

What can a monopolist do to protect itself from such entrepreneurial competition? One possibility is to persuade the government to bar entry into the industry. This is an example of *rent seeking*, as discussed in Chapter 5. A well-known illustration is the long battle that AT&T waged in court and in Congress to protect its one-time monopoly on long-distance telephone service from competition by new entrants such as MCI and Sprint. Another example is the U.S. Postal Service. The USPS retains a legally protected monopoly on first-class mail service even though it now faces competition in parcel delivery and express mail. (See the case for discussion at the end of this chapter for additional details.) However, rent-seeking activities such as lobbying and lawsuits are themselves costly. They raise the level of a monopolist's average total cost curve, thereby cutting into its long-run monopoly profit.

An alternative way to limit competitive attack from substitutes and new entrants is to dim the beacon that attracts other entrepreneurs by charging less than the price that would maximize short-run profit. This strategy is known as **limit pricing.** In the case of beryllium, for example, a limit-pricing strategy for Brush Wellman would mean charging a price just low enough to make it less than worthwhile for Hecla to enter the market. In fact, as the lead-off case for this chapter suggests, Hecla's entry is not guaranteed to be successful. Without information on costs and demand that is accessible only to the firm, we cannot know whether the $400-per-pound price quoted by Brush Wellman is calculated strictly on the basis of short-run marginal costs and revenues or is influenced by the desire to limit entry and the development of substitutes.

Limit pricing
The practice by the dominant firm in a market of charging less than the short-run profit-maximizing price in order to limit the likelihood of new competitors' entry.

Price Discrimination

Up to this point in our discussion, we have assumed that the monopolist sells all units of output at the same price. Such a policy is forced on the monopolist whenever resale by buyers is possible. For example, it is unlikely that your campus bookstore (a monopoly on many campuses) could get away with selling economics texts at list price to seniors and at a 25 percent discount to everyone else. If it tried to do so, some clever sophomore would soon go into business buying books for resale to seniors at a split-the-difference price. The bookstore's list price sales would soon fall to zero.

Some firms, however, do not sell their product to all customers at the same price. Such sellers are said to practice **price discrimination.** Two things are required for price discrimination to be possible. First, resale of the product by consumers must be impossible or at least inconvenient. Second, the seller must be able to classify consumers into groups based on the elasticity of their demand for the good. Those with highly inelastic demand can then be charged high prices and those with more elastic demand lower prices.

The conditions for price discrimination are not found in every market, but they are not rare. "Economics in the News 10.1" discusses the method of price discrimination used by colleges and universities. The system works as follows. First, the business office sets tuition at some high level. Then the admissions office gives its approval to a certain number of qualified applicants. Next, the

Price discrimination
The practice of charging different prices for various units of a single product when the price differences are not justified by differences in cost.

ECONOMICS IN THE NEWS 10.1

How Colleges Make Financial Aid Decisions

Roughly half the college applicants awarded financial aid are puzzled enough about the process to ask for clarifications, administrators say.

The information used to make college-aid decisions is pretty straightforward, consisting of data provided by the family on salaries, savings, taxes, and so forth. But how the numbers are evaluated is apparently anything but clear to many college-bound students and their parents.

"The biggest surprise is that their assets are included in the calculations," says Haskell Rhett, a vice-president of the New York–based College Board, one of three organizations that make the preliminary decisions for colleges and other groups that give scholarships.

A key factor in the decision is the equity of the family home or homes. "If you've got two families, one sitting in a $300,000 home and one in a more modest situation, with a mortgage, the first family has greater financial strength,

Source: Alexandra Peers, "Here's the Way Colleges Decide Financial Aid," *The Wall Street Journal*, April 30, 1987, 33. Reprinted by permission of *The Wall Street Journal*, © Dow Jones & Company, Inc. 1987. All Rights Reserved.

and we have to take that into account," says Karl Furstenberg, director of admissions and financial aid for Wesleyan University in Middletown, Connecticut.

Mom and Dad's retirement nest egg also isn't sacrosanct. But aid officials do give older parents a break. The amount of savings that's considered available is prorated on the basis of the age of the older parent. The thinking, says Margaret Dean-Colman, director of financial-aid services for American College Testing, is that younger parents will have more years to save for retirement.

After the family's resources are added up, subtractions are made for expenses, including a living allowance. In the case of a family of four with one child in college, for instance, this allowance figures $12,890 for most outlays other than those for housing, medical expenses, and taxes.

What's left of the family resources after allowable expenses are deducted is called "adjusted available income." A percentage of this amount—ranging from 22 percent for families with adjusted available incomes of $7,500 or less to 47 percent for those with adjusted available incomes of more than $15,101—is the amount the family is expected to contribute toward its child's college education. If the family contribution exceeds college costs, no aid is given.

financial aid office gives selective price rebates, called *scholarships*, to students who it thinks will be unwilling or unable to attend if they are charged full tuition.

A college or university is in an ideal position to practice price discrimination. For one thing, the product cannot be transferred. If you are admitted to both Harvard and Dartmouth, you cannot sell your Dartmouth admission to someone who got into neither place. As "Economics in the News 10.1" explains, the college also has access to a great deal of information on families' willingness and ability to pay. Finally, an applicant's high school grades help a college estimate his or her elasticity of demand. A student with relatively high grades probably has many alternatives and, hence, relatively elastic demand. A student with lower grades may be lucky to get into one decent college. It is partly for this reason that colleges offer some aid to superior students regardless of financial need.

It is not necessary for a firm to be a monopolist in order to practice price discrimination, provided other conditions are satisfied. Examples of price discrimination are found at theaters that offer lower prices for children than for adults; stores that give senior-citizen discounts; airlines that find ways to charge business travelers more than vacation travelers; and in many other markets.

Price discrimination is often viewed as unfair, especially by those who pay the higher prices. Attempts have been made to outlaw price discrimination in some markets. However, the example of price discrimination in the form of college scholarships suggests that this practice may have benefits as well as draw-backs. When price discrimination allows some people who otherwise would be excluded from the market to buy the good but still insures that everyone pays a price at least as high as marginal cost, it is likely to have some value. After all, price discrimination makes it possible for some students to attend colleges that they otherwise could not afford. It allows parents to take young children to the movies. It makes it possible for standby passengers who cannot afford the full fares that business travelers pay to fill airplane seats that otherwise would be empty.

Monopoly and Market Failure

From the beginning of this course, we have repeated the point that a key function of market prices is to transmit information on opportunity costs. Buyers and sellers of goods and services rely on this information in choosing how best to use scarce resources to meet their wants. If all goes well, the economy operates efficiently. By this we mean that markets point the way to opportunities to satisfy some people's wants more fully with no harm to others and provide the incentives needed to take advantage of those opportunities. However, as pointed out in Chapter 5, markets sometimes fail to do their job as well as might be desired. One of the categories of market failure is monopoly. Comparing the model of monopoly presented in this chapter with that of perfect competition presented in Chapter 9 will show why monopoly is considered a source of market failure.

Prices and Opportunity Costs

Under perfect competition, market prices reflect opportunity costs in both a short-run and a long-run sense. In the short run, prices in a competitive market are equal to marginal costs. When both explicit and implicit costs are taken into account, marginal cost measures the opportunity cost of producing an additional unit of the good or service in question. In the long run, prices reflect opportunity costs in another sense. When a perfectly competitive industry is in long-run equilibrium, the market price equals not only marginal cost but also average total cost; that is to say, the long-run equilibrium price in a perfectly competitive market equals the full opportunity cost of the good or service, including those elements that are fixed and those that are variable in the short run.

The situation is different under monopoly. As we have seen, the monopolist's profit-maximizing price is always higher than marginal cost. Also, under favorable demand conditions and given protection from competition, the monopolist can hold the price above the level of average total cost indefinitely.

Because the price the monopolist charges is greater than the opportunity cost of producing a unit of the good or service in question, buyers get a false signal of the item's scarcity. For example, if beryllium users see a market price of $400 per pound when the opportunity cost of producing this metal is, say, $300, they will waste resources by overinvesting in a search for substitutes or they will cut back on their use of beryllium even when it is the most efficient material for a given job.

Consumer and Producer Surplus under Monopoly

An alternative to looking at monopoly market failure in terms of prices and opportunity costs is to apply the concepts of consumer and producer surplus introduced in Chapter 7.

Part a of Exhibit 10.4 reviews consumer and producer surplus for a competitive market. Here the demand curve measures the maximum amount that consumers would willingly pay for a given quantity. The supply curve, based on the marginal cost curves of individual firms, measures the opportunity cost of producing each additional unit. The equilibrium price is $20 and the equilibrium quantity 200 units. Consumers, who would be willing to pay more than $20 for all but the 200th unit, earn a consumer surplus equal to the area beneath the demand curve but above the market price. Producers, who produce all but the 200th unit at an opportunity cost of less than $20, earn a producer surplus equal to the area above the supply curve but beneath the market price. These surpluses represent consumers' and producers' mutual gains from trade.

Under competitive conditions, production is carried to the point at which all potential gains from trade are exhausted. Nothing would be gained from producing beyond the 200-unit mark. From the 201st unit on, the opportunity cost of

Exhibit 10.4   Consumer and Producer Surplus under Monopoly and Competition

Under perfect competition, shown in part a, production is carried out to the point where the price consumers are willing to pay for the last unit produced just equals the opportunity cost of producing it. All possible gains from trade are realized in the form of producer and consumer surplus. Under monopoly, production stops short of that point. Consumer surplus is smaller and producer surplus larger than under competition, but the total of the two is smaller. Some potential gains from trade go unrealized. This deadweight loss is the reason monopoly is considered a form of market failure.

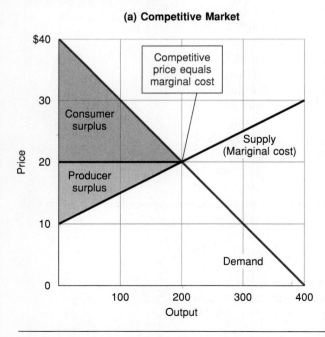

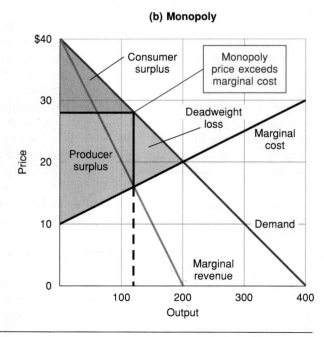

the unit to producers as measured by the supply curve would exceed its value to producers as measured by the demand curve.

Now consider the situation under monopoly, as shown in part b of Exhibit 10.4. For ease of comparison, the demand and marginal cost curves for the monopolist in question are assumed to be the same as the market demand and supply curves for the competitive industry.

Maximizing profits, the monopolist limits production to 120 units and charges a price of $28 per unit. Even at this price, consumers are better off than they would be were the good entirely unavailable. They realize a surplus equal to the area beneath the demand curve but above the $28 price. The monopolist, on the other hand, realizes a very substantial producer surplus. The 120th unit, which is sold for $28, costs only $16 to produce, for a producer surplus of $12 on that unit alone. Surpluses on earlier units, which are produced at lower opportunity cost, are correspondingly greater. The total producer surplus equals the shaded area above the marginal cost curve but below the $28 price, bordered on the left by the vertical axis and on the right by the profit-maximizing quantity.

Comparing the competitive case with the monopoly case shows three differences:

1. Consumer surplus is smaller under monopoly.
2. Producer surplus is larger under monopoly.
3. The total of producer and consumer surplus is smaller under monopoly.

The third difference reveals the inefficiency of monopoly. It indicates that some potential gains from trade are unrealized. Other things being equal, production of units 121 through 200 would provide benefits to consumers that exceed their costs. This would make both producers and consumers better off. The potential gains from trade that are "wasted" are shown by the triangle lying between the supply and demand curves and bordered on the left by the monopolist's profit-maximizing quantity. This is labeled a **deadweight loss**—a term often used to refer to any benefit lost to one party but not gained by another. The excess burden of a tax, illustrated in Chapter 6, is another example of a deadweight loss.

Deadweight loss
A loss of consumer or producer surplus that is not balanced by a gain to someone else.

If producing another 80 units of output would make both producers and consumers better off, one might ask why this isn't done. The answer lies in the fact that in this case, "holding other things equal" must include holding the price of the first 120 units at $28 while selling units 121 through 200 at a price of, say, $20. Because this is not possible for a nondiscriminating monopolist, as we have seen, the point at which the marginal cost and marginal revenue curves meet marks the limit of such a monopolist's willingness to produce. In a sense, then, the deadweight loss of monopoly can be attributed to the monopolist's inability to price discriminate.

Natural Monopoly and Its Regulation

Concern over market failures resulting from monopoly has led many economists to favor policies that would prevent one firm, or a few firms acting in concert, from gaining control over a market. We will discuss policies of this type in later chapters. However, there may be cases in which there is no practical way to avoid monopoly. In this section, we examine policies intended to improve the performance of these markets.

Characteristics of Natural Monopoly

Natural monopoly
An industry in which average total costs are kept to a minimum by having just one producer serve the entire market.

A natural monopoly is an industry in which total costs are kept to a minimum by having just one producer serve the whole market. Local telephone service often is cited as a natural monopoly; gas, electric, cable TV, and water services are other examples. It is easy for one such utility to hook up more customers once it has run its lines into their neighborhood, but it is wasteful and costly for different companies to run lines down the same street.

Although the term *natural monopoly* is well established in economics, it should be interpreted with care. It is not nature so much as human regulations and technology that determine the conditions for natural monopoly. For example, long-distance telephone service was once considered as much of a natural monopoly as local telephone service. Today, with optical fiber systems, satellite communications, and microwave relays, it is possible for many long-distance services to compete efficiently with one another. The breakup of AT&T into a long-distance service that faces many rivals on the one hand and a number of regional telephone monopolies for local service on the other was largely spurred by these technological changes.

The Policy Problem

The policy problem raised by a natural monopoly is how to keep the firm from taking advantage of its position to raise prices and restrict output. Consider the example shown in Exhibit 10.5. That firm, an electric utility, has constant marginal costs and an L-shaped long-run average cost curve. The demand curve intersects the long-run average cost curve at quantity Q_1, not far from the minimum efficient scale of production. If this output were divided between even two firms, each of which produced half of quantity Q_1, the cost per unit would be a lot higher—and still more so if there were more than two firms.

If one unregulated firm operates in a market, it can be expected to act like a pure monopolist. Instead of producing Q_1 it will produce Q_2, which corresponds to the intersection of the firm's marginal revenue and marginal cost curves. The price that corresponds to this output is P_2, which is far above marginal cost. This is too small an output and too high a price to permit efficient production.

The Regulatory Solution

It appears, then, that in a natural monopoly competition by two or more firms is inefficient, as is monopoly pricing by a single firm. The traditional solution is to allow just one firm to operate but to regulate the price at which it can sell its output. For example, the firm may be limited to a price of no more than P_1, the price at which the demand curve intersects the long-run average cost curve in Exhibit 10.5. With this price ceiling in force, the firm becomes a price taker for output levels up to Q_1, because keeping output below that level would prevent it from further raising the price. The maximum profit is earned under the regulated price by producing Q_1 units of output. This is a larger price and greater quantity than would result from either an unregulated pure monopoly or dividing production between two or more competing firms.

In order for the market to be perfectly efficient, the price would have to be reduced to the level of marginal cost, which is slightly lower than P_1. At any price lower than P_1, however, the firm would suffer a loss. It could survive in the

Exhibit 10.5   Regulation of a Natural Monopoly

This graph shows the cost and demand curves for a natural monopoly such as an electric utility. As an unregulated monopolist, the firm would make the maximum profit by charging price P_2 and selling quantity Q_2. If regulators impose a maximum price of P_1, the firm will find it worthwhile to produce quantity Q_1.

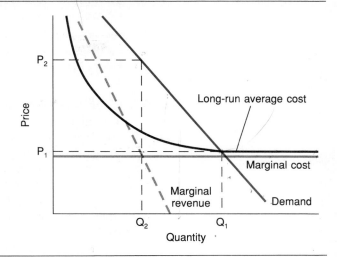

long run only if it were subsidized. By allowing the firm to charge price P_1, which is high enough to cover all costs, the regulators would avoid the need for a subsidy while giving up only a small degree of efficiency.

Rate of Return as a Focus of Regulation

It is not difficult to identify the correct regulated price in Exhibit 10.5 because the shapes and positions of the demand and cost curves are right there on the page. In the real world, however, regulators do not have complete information about demand and cost. Lacking this information, they set the regulated price indirectly by focusing on the rate of return that the firm earns. The rate of return is the firm's accounting profit expressed as a percentage of its net worth.

To see why the rate of return is a useful focus of regulatory policy, consider the implications of setting various prices. If the price is set equal to average total cost, the firm will earn exactly a "normal profit," that is, a rate of return equal to the opportunity cost of capital. If the price is higher than average total cost, the firm will earn more than a normal profit, that is, enough to cover the opportunity cost of capital with some left over as economic profit. If the price is set below average total cost, the firm will earn less than a normal profit. Because revenue is insufficient to meet all opportunity costs, including that of capital, the firm will then suffer an economic loss.

Armed with this reasoning, the regulators proceed in five steps:

1. They measure the value of the firm's capital, which for the firm in our example is, say, $1.2 million. This is called the *rate base.*

2. They measure the average rate of return for the economy, that is, the normal rate of profit. Suppose this turns out to be 15 percent per year. (In practice, steps 1 and 2 are more difficult than they sound, but for our purposes the regulators can be given the benefit of the doubt.)

3. They multiply the rate base by the permitted rate of return to calculate a total cost of capital for the firm—in this case, $180,000 per year. This sum should be enough to both make interest payments on the portion of the firm's capital that was acquired by borrowing and give an accounting profit high enough to compensate the owners for their investment in the firm.

Rate of return
A firm's accounting profit expressed as a percentage of its net worth.

4. They ask the firm to propose a price or set of prices that it thinks will allow it to meet its capital costs.

5. As time goes by, they keep track of the firm's actual rate of return, cutting the price if it rises above the normal level and allowing it to rise if returns fall below the target.

Limits on Rate-of-Return Regulation

For a number of reasons, rate-of-return regulation may not always achieve its goals of lower prices and greater output. One possible reason is that regulators may be guided by goals other than economic efficiency. This may occur, for example, if regulated firms "capture" the regulatory agency by gaining control over the appointment of regulators or if regulators follow lax policies in the hope of finding well-paying jobs in the industry after their terms as regulators end. On the other hand, regulatory agencies in some areas have been "captured" by groups that represent consumers. They seek the short-run political gains that come from keeping rates low without regard for the regulated firms' long-run capital needs.

Another possible problem is that regulators may not know enough about the industry to control its rate of return. It is by no means easy to measure such factors as the regulated firm's stock of capital, its actual rate of return, and the opportunity cost of capital. The more regulators must rely on guesswork, the less likely they are to be effective.

Finally, there is the fact that regulation, by putting the firm on a cost-plus basis, distorts incentives. If a firm is allowed to earn revenues that exceed its cost by a certain maximum amount, why should it try to minimize its costs at all? Minimizing costs is hard work for managers. Why not relax and take things easy? Why not take Wednesday mornings off for golf? Install new carpeting in the boardroom? Give the president's nephew a job? There is no incentive to put effort into keeping costs down.

Distortions Caused by the Wrong Rate of Return

For several reasons, then, regulators may set rates of return that are either higher or lower than the opportunity cost of capital. In either case, there will be problems. A study by Harvey Averch and Leland Johnson, for example, suggested that in the 1960s regulated rates for electricity tended to be too high.[1] They allowed utilities to achieve a rate of return that was higher than the opportunity cost of capital. This gave the utilities' stockholders an indirect way of taking advantage of their monopoly position. They could raise new capital to build new plants, whether or not they were needed, and add these into their rate base. The regulators then would allow them to raise their rates enough to not only pass along the costs of the new plants but earn a pure economic profit as well. The outcome—now known as the *A-J effect*—was that too high a rate of return led to wasteful overinvestment in the regulated industry.

In the 1980s, the situation changed. Some economists are now afraid that rates of return are too low. If so, this will cause the A-J effect to operate in reverse. Utilities will avoid investing in new plants even when they would be justified from the consumer's point of view. Such a policy of "rate suppression" might keep rates low for consumers for many years before problems become

[1] Harvey A. Averch and L. L. Johnson, "Behavior of the Firm under Regulatory Constraint," *American Economic Review* (December 1962): 1052–1069.

apparent. But as old plants wear out, the quality of service falls. Some writers predict serious shortages of electric power by the end of the century if rate suppression continues.

Not all economists agree that rate suppression is widespread. It is no easier for outside observers to know whether a utility is charging just the right rates than it is for the regulators. It is widely agreed, however, that the A-J effect cuts both ways: Either too high or too low an allowed rate of return is harmful. Thus, in their search for efficiency regulators must walk a narrow line between two kinds of errors.

Distortions Caused by Average Cost Pricing

Even if regulators are able to adjust utilities' rates of return to exactly the right level, regulation can still lead to inefficiency. One source of inefficiency arises from the use of average rather than marginal cost pricing. Exhibit 10.5 glosses over this problem by assuming that the marginal cost of producing electric power is constant and that it is not very different from average total cost at the output level at which the utility operates.

In practice, many utilities have plants of different ages that operate at various levels of marginal cost. Regulatory agencies tend to look at the historical costs of these plants in setting prices. Plants built many years ago are listed at the cost that was paid for them at the time they were built, even though this may be far below the cost of replacing them or adding to their capacity. Average cost as measured in historical terms falls far short of marginal cost, since the cost of generating an added kilowatt-hour means the cost of generating it in new facilities. Setting prices below marginal cost can lead to wasteful use. It provides insufficient incentive for conservation measures such as insulation and thermostat timers. It also fails to provide enough motivation for shifting electricity use from peak periods, when the least efficient generators must be brought on line, to periods of lower generating costs.

Cross-subsidization is another problem created by average cost pricing. This is a form of price discrimination—the practice of setting prices that cover total costs on the average but charging some customers more than the cost of their services while charging other customers less. The case of telephone service is an example. When AT&T was a regulated monopoly, it charged prices to long-distance customers that were higher than the cost of the service and charged less than the cost of service to local customers. On the average, telephone costs covered total costs.

Cross-subsidization is highly favored by people who receive the low-cost services. People liked free directory assistance service, which saved them the trouble of reaching for the telephone directory; they liked house calls by telephone installers and servicepeople, which spared them the effort of shopping for phones as they would for hair dryers. But business users did not like having to pay high rates for long-distance and other business services. They began turning to upstart competitors. Eventually, the competition won. Long-distance phone service was extensively deregulated, and newly independent local phone companies lost the source of their subsidies.

Can Competition Be Brought to Natural Monopolies?

Problems of regulation have created interest in the possibility of bringing some degree of competition to natural monopolies, especially the electric utilities. This has led to efforts to distinguish between areas in which a natural monopoly will

Cross-subsidization
The practice of setting prices that cover total costs on the average by charging some customers more than the cost of their services while charging other customers less than that cost.

continue to require regulation and areas in which technological change has made competition more feasible.

In the electrical power industry, local service to homes and business firms has many of the features of a natural monopoly. On the other hand, the actual generation of electrical power may no longer be a natural monopoly. Rising energy costs and technological advances have combined to make certain types of small-scale generating plants more competitive with large, centralized power stations. One example is industrial cogeneration, in which a firm that needs steam for a certain process, such as brewing, may simply install a turbine to extract electrical power from the steam before it is used to heat the vats. When the boiler is already in place, it costs relatively little to add the turbine and generator. To make the generator worthwhile, however, the brewery must have a market for any power it produces beyond its own needs.

In addition to competition in the form of small-scale generation, it is also possible for utilities to compete by transmitting power to one another's territories. This practice traditionally has been limited by regulation even where technologically feasible. Future technological change, perhaps even including superconducting transmission lines, will make this type of competition increasingly possible if regulators permit it.

Ultimately, a market might develop in which local electric service would remain a regulated utility but local "distribution" utilities would be free to buy power in a competitive market from suppliers ranging from backyard windmills to distant coal or nuclear plants.

Looking Ahead

It would be tempting to wrap up this chapter with a sweeping comparison of monopoly and competition: Competition is good; monopoly is flawed. But not so fast! The conclusions we can safely draw from the models presented so far are more limited than they appear. Also, a lot more groundwork must be laid before we can draw even those limited conclusions.

The problem is that our models of both perfect competition and pure monopoly have taken such factors as technology, product quality, and consumer tastes as given, which is to say they have largely ignored the element of entrepreneurship in business decision making. Before reaching any conclusions on the merits of various market structures, we need a more complete picture of these entrepreneurial aspects of competition. We must recognize that comparing two models, one competitive and the other monopolistic, is not the same as figuring out how any one market would perform under two different market structures.

In practice, it is rarely—if ever—possible to change the structure of a market without affecting the incentives faced by entrepreneurs in that market. Thus, any change in market structure (number of firms, conditions of entry, nature of the product) is likely to affect costs, product quality, and the pace of innovation as well. If competition reduces costs, improves the product, and speeds innovation, its advantage over monopoly may be much greater than the deadweight-loss triangle in Exhibit 10.4 shows. On the other hand, if dividing production among many firms raises costs, reduces quality, or slows innovation, those effects may more than outweigh the benefits of competition. It would be premature to make any comparisons between perfect competition and monopoly until we have studied the other market structures that lie between and before we have taken a closer look at the role played by entrepreneurship on market performance. We turn to these issues in the next two chapters.

Summary

1. **How are price and revenue related for a monopoly?** A monopolist is not a price taker. As output is increased or decreased, both price and quantity change, causing changes in total revenue. For a firm with a straight-line, downward-sloping demand curve, marginal revenue is always below price. In such a case, the marginal revenue curve cuts the horizontal distance from the demand curve to the vertical axis in half.

2. **How are the profit-maximizing price and output determined for a monopoly?** A monopoly makes the maximum profit by producing the output level that makes marginal cost equal to marginal revenue. The price is determined by the height of the demand curve at the profit-maximizing level. If a monopoly cannot earn a profit in the short run, it will try to keep its loss to a minimum. If the loss-minimizing price is above average variable cost, the firm will continue to operate in the short run. If the loss-minimizing price is below average variable cost, it will shut down.

3. **Why do monopolies and other firms sometimes engage in price discrimination?** A monopolist or other firm that is not a price taker can practice *price discrimination* if its product cannot be resold by buyers and if it has some way of classifying buyers by elasticity of demand. Although price discrimination is resented by buyers who must pay higher prices, it may increase efficiency by allowing some customers who value the product more than its marginal cost to buy the product rather than being shut out of the market.

4. **Why is monopoly a source of market failure?** A monopoly is a source of market failure because the amount of output it produces is less than the amount that would make marginal cost equal to the price charged. This means that some consumers who would be willing to pay a price higher than marginal cost are unable to buy from a monopolist. Because some gains from trade (consumer and producer surplus) are not realized under monopoly, there is a *deadweight loss* to the economy.

5. **Why are natural monopolies regulated, and what are the problems of regulation?** A *natural monopoly* is an industry in which total costs are kept to a minimum by having just one producer serve the entire market. This happens when the minimum efficient scale of operation in the industry is as large as or larger than demand when output is sold at a price equal to average total cost.

Terms for Review

- limit pricing
- price discrimination
- deadweight loss
- natural monopoly
- rate of return
- cross-subsidization

Questions for Review

1. Why is it difficult, if not impossible, to find pure examples of monopoly in the real world?

2. Why is marginal revenue always less than price for a monopolist? Under what elasticity conditions will marginal revenue be positive, negative, and zero?

3. Given data on cost and demand, how is the profit-maximizing output level for a monopolist determined? Given the profit-maximizing output, how is the price determined?

4. Under what conditions can a monopolist practice price discrimination? Who gains and who loses from price discrimination? Is price discrimination always inefficient?

5. What is meant by the *deadweight loss* of a monopoly?

6. Why are natural monopolies subject to regulation? Is the regulation always successful in achieving efficient market functioning?

Problems and Topics for Discussion

1. **Examining the lead-off case.** "A monopolist can always make a profit because with no competition it can charge any price it likes." Do you think this statement is true? What, if anything, restrains the price that Brush-Wellman has been charging for beryllium?

2. **Short-run shutdown for a monopolist.** Redraw the graph in Exhibit 10.3, shifting the demand and marginal revenue curves to illustrate the case in which a monopolist will shut down in the short run rather than continue to produce at a loss.

3. **Price discrimination.** The form of price discrimination discussed in the text involves charging different prices to various customers when the price difference is not justified by variations in cost. Can you think of any examples in which different prices are justified by differences in cost? Discuss.

4. **Public ownership of utilities.** In some cities, utilities such as electric companies and gas pipelines are owned by the city government. What do you think are the advantages and disadvantages of public ownership of a natural monopoly compared with both regulated and unregulated private ownership?

5. **Mass transit pricing and market failure.** Reread the sections of Chapter 5 dealing with market failure and rent seeking. Can it be argued that the market failure

theory of government justifies public ownership and subsidy of mass transit systems? What particular types of failure are involved here? What pricing policy would be called for under the market failure theory?

Do you think there are any elements of mass transit policy that can be explained under the theory of rent seeking?

The U.S. Postal Service has a monopoly on the delivery of first-class mail.

Case for Discussion
The Postal Monopoly

The U.S. Post Office was organized in 1789 and immediately began losing money. One of the reasons it lost money was competition. The Post Office charged the same price to deliver a letter anywhere in the country, but its costs were not the same in every case. For letters mailed between points in the East, the Post Office charged more than cost; for letters mailed to points in the West, it charged less than cost.

Competitors flocked to the routes on which costs were low. For example, in the 1840s Henry Wells, who later founded the famous Wells-Fargo Company, set up a mail service between Philadelphia and New York. He charged $.06 for a first-class letter compared to the Post Office's rate of $.25. By the early 1840s, private firms were carrying at least a third of all mail in the United States.

To fight off the competition, the Post Office turned to Congress. In 1845, Congress strengthened the restrictions on private first-class mail service. This saved the Post Office from extinction and allowed it to continue its policy of uniform rates regardless of cost of service. This policy remains in force for first-class mail to this day. The cost of mailing a letter to any address in the United States is the same whatever the distance. However, the cost of delivering the letter clearly is not the same for all addresses. Deliveries to post office boxes are least expensive; deliveries to homes in suburban neighborhoods are a bit more costly; and rural free delivery service is more expensive still.

Source: Reprinted by permission from *Economics of Public Policy*, 2d ed. (Chapter 11) by John C. Goodman and Edwin G. Dolan. Copyright © 1982 by West Publishing Company. All rights reserved. Photo Source: © 1987 Phyllis Woloshin.

Questions

1. Do you think the practice of charging the same price when costs differ from one customer to another should be viewed as price discrimination? Do you think it has any benefits? Why or why not?

2. Although the U.S. Postal Service (as it is now called) has retained its monopoly of ordinary first-class mail, it allows competition from firms such as United Parcel Service and Federal Express in carrying overnight and third-class mail (parcels). In these cases, both the USPS and its private competitors charge different prices according to weight and distance and to whether pickup and delivery services are provided. Why does a policy of one price regardless of cost not work in a market in which competition exists?

Suggestions for Further Reading

Bork, Robert H. *The Antitrust Paradox: A Policy at War With Itself.* New York: Basic Books, 1978.

Chapter 4 presents an excellent summary of the economic theory of monopoly, stressing its implications for efficiency.

Kahn, Alfred E. *The Economics of Regulation.* 2 vols. New York: Wiley, 1971.

A detailed work on the theory of regulation. The author has served as chairman of the New York State Public Service Commission, the Civil Aeronautics Board, and President Carter's Council on Wage and Price Stability.

Nicholson, Walter. *Intermediate Microeconomics and Its Applications,* 4th ed. Hinsdale, Ill.: Dryden Press, 1987.

Chapter 12 discusses monopoly and includes a graphic treatment of price discrimination.

11 Industrial Organization, Monopolistic Competition, and Oligopoly

After reading this chapter, you will understand . . .

- The extent to which markets are dominated by a few large firms.
- How in an oligopoly each firm's decisions depend on those of other firms.
- How collusion among rival firms may bring increased profits at the expense of consumers.
- What conditions affect the performance of concentrated markets.
- What attempts to measure market performance have revealed.
- How profits are maximized under monopolistic competition.

Before reading this chapter, make sure you know the meaning of . . .

- Consumer and producer surplus (Chapter 7)
- Economies of scale (Chapter 8)
- Market structure (Chapter 9)
- Limit pricing (Chapter 10)

Battle of the Corn Kernel

There are dark accusations of double-dealing, conspiracy, collusion, jockeying for position, and inferior ingredients.

This is serious stuff.

This is the popcorn war.

About the only thing the combatants agree on that is obvious: Where just a few months ago a single pushcart was selling popcorn for $1 a box, now four carts are doing battle at prices as low as 25 cents.

"It's competition," said Noul Moheyeldin, who operates one of the 25-cent carts in the combat zone at the corner of 15th and L streets NW in Washington, D.C.

In the context of "the popcorn war," competition refers to business rivalry.

"This is full-fledged war, man," said a vendor at the 50-cent competitor, who would not give his name. "Nowhere in Washington can you find [such] cheap popcorn." He said he was helping his niece, Alem Eyob, who owns the cart, but he indicated that he knew a lot about the business.

It's hard to tell which side has the advantage. Yesterday afternoon, the two 25-cent carts were doing a brisk business, with customers walking away with armfuls of boxes.

But the 50-cent carts also were doing well, relying, their proprietors said, on a steady stream of loyal customers willing to pay a premium for what the vendors claim is superior corn.

The battle began last summer, when Mohamed Moawad, who had operated a cart at 15th and L for another owner ($1 a box), got his own cart and cut his price to 50 cents.

The spurned owner set Eyob up in competition. Business boomed.

Roman Seyoum, who operates that cart, said she thought the location was a prime one, despite the existing competition, because of its heavy foot traffic.

Moawad, however, charges collusion. He claims Seyoum is in cahoots with the Eyob cart, a charge the other side denies.

"They're trying to run me out of this spot," Moawad said. So he escalated the hostilities. A few days ago, he had his cousin, Moheyeldin, bring his cart to the corner from elsewhere in the city. Then they cut the price to 25 cents a box, and the battle was joined.

Moawad says he'll keep his price at 25 cents even if the competition is driven off, while the 50-cent vendors say they'll maintain their price, relying on loyal customers to keep business going.

Whatever the outcome of the hostilities, the big winners will doubtless be the customers. "It's a giveaway," one man said as he forked over his quarter to Moawad.

Source: Mark Potts, "The Battle of the Corn Kernel Pops On," *The Washington Post*, February 19, 1987, E1. © 1987 *The Washington Post*, reprinted with permission. Photo Source: © 1987 Phyllis Woloshin.

"IT'S competition," says Noul Moheyeldin, speaking of the popcorn war. But the popcorn war highlights the fact that the term *competition* has more than one meaning. In the phrase "perfect competition," it refers to *market structure*. A market is perfectly competitive if it has large numbers of small firms, a homogeneous product, and easy entry and exit of firms. In contrast, in the context of the popcorn war, competition refers to *business rivalry*. In this sense, "rivalry" refers to the activities of entrepreneurs, not just those of business managers who are responding to conditions that they accept as given for their markets.

There is no rivalry and no entrepreneurship in ideal-type perfectly competitive markets of the kind described in Chapter 9. In such markets, each firm sees every other firm as too small to have a significant impact on market conditions. Rivalry and entrepreneurship are also absent from the ideal-type pure monopoly, because there is only one firm in the market. An ideal-type monopolist can make a profit forever just by doing the same thing day after day. In most markets, however, rivalry plays too big a role to be pushed into the background. Most markets have more than a single firm and, hence, are not pure monopolies. However, most markets also fall short of perfect competition in that they either have too few firms or lack a homogeneous product. These "in-between" markets have the market structures of *oligopoly* or *monopolistic competition*. This chapter deals with these two market structures.

The chapter focuses on the following question: *Is perfect competition required for satisfactory market performance, or is competition in the sense of rivalry among entrepreneurs enough even when there are only a few firms?* Some economists say yes, and some say no. While this chapter does not offer a definitive answer to this controversial question, it can at least provide a map of the territory.

Market Concentration

Market concentration
The degree to which a market is dominated by a few large firms.

We begin this chapter by examining some of the factors that determine market concentration. **Market concentration** is the degree to which a market is dominated by a few large firms, ranging from total concentration in the case of monopoly to no significant concentration in the case of perfect competition.

Measuring Market Concentration

Concentration ratios give a rough-and-ready measure of the extent to which markets are dominated by a few firms. The most common of these ratios is the four-firm concentration ratio, which measures the percentage of sales accounted for by the top four firms in a given market, and the eight-firm concentration ratio, which measures the share of the top eight firms.

Exhibit 11.1 gives data on concentration ratios for selected U.S. industries. At the top of the chart are "tight" oligopolies; here a handful of firms control almost the whole market. In other industries, shown in the middle of the chart, are "loose" oligopolies, in which the top four firms account for less than half of total sales. At the bottom of the chart, the category of oligopoly shades into monopolistic competition, in which there are "many" firms, each of which is "small" relative to the market's size.

Concentration ratio
The percentage of all sales that is accounted for by the four or eight largest firms in a market.

Exhibit 11.1   Concentration Ratios for Selected Industries

Concentration ratios measure the percentage of an industry's output that is accounted for by the largest firms. This list of 31 U.S. industries shows a wide range of ratios. The figures given here do not take into account foreign competition or the fact that some industries produce mainly for local markets.

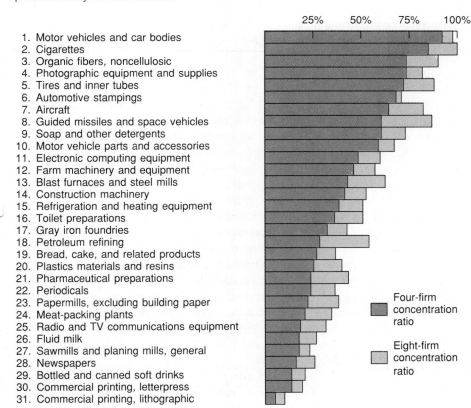

1. Motor vehicles and car bodies
2. Cigarettes
3. Organic fibers, noncellulosic
4. Photographic equipment and supplies
5. Tires and inner tubes
6. Automotive stampings
7. Aircraft
8. Guided missiles and space vehicles
9. Soap and other detergents
10. Motor vehicle parts and accessories
11. Electronic computing equipment
12. Farm machinery and equipment
13. Blast furnaces and steel mills
14. Construction machinery
15. Refrigeration and heating equipment
16. Toilet preparations
17. Gray iron foundries
18. Petroleum refining
19. Bread, cake, and related products
20. Plastics materials and resins
21. Pharmaceutical preparations
22. Periodicals
23. Papermills, excluding building paper
24. Meat-packing plants
25. Radio and TV communications equipment
26. Fluid milk
27. Sawmills and planing mills, general
28. Newspapers
29. Bottled and canned soft drinks
30. Commercial printing, letterpress
31. Commercial printing, lithographic

Four-firm concentration ratio

Eight-firm concentration ratio

Source: U.S. Department of Commerce, Bureau of the Census, *Statistical Abstract of the United States*, 98th ed. (Washington, D.C.: Government Printing Office, 1977), 808–809.

Unfortunately, the data given in Exhibit 11.1 are misleading in one crucial respect: They ignore import competition. A few markets—cigarettes, for example—are almost entirely dominated by domestic firms, but one could hardly say the same for motor vehicles or photographic equipment. Most of the industries listed in Exhibit 11.1, in fact, operate in world markets characterized not only by imports and exports of finished goods but by integrated multinational manufacturing. Thus, the degree of concentration of world markets is much less than Exhibit 11.1 suggests.

Increased international competition has eroded the effective concentration of U.S. markets. However, even when the effects of international competition are ignored, there is evidence that U.S. markets are becoming less concentrated over time. A study by William G. Shepherd, for example, found that industries that were virtual monopolies, with one firm supplying nearly 100 percent of output, accounted for 3.1 percent of U.S. output in 1958 but just 2.5 percent in 1980. Markets in which the single largest firm had 50 percent or more of the market declined from 5 to 2.8 percent over the same period. Tight oligopolies in which no one firm had half the market but the four-firm concentration ratio exceeded 60 percent declined from 35.6 percent of output in 1958 to 18 percent in 1980.[1]

Causes of Market Concentration

Why are some markets more concentrated than others? There is no single theory that explains concentration, but a variety of hypotheses have been advanced. We will discuss these under the headings of *economies of scale* and *barriers to entry*.

Economies of Scale

Chapter 8 introduced the concept of economies of scale. A firm is said to experience economies of scale if its long-run average cost declines as its output increases. At one extreme is the case of natural monopoly, discussed in Chapter 9, in which economies of scale are so strong that minimum-cost production requires that the entire market supply be produced by a single firm. In less extreme cases, it is possible that the *minimum efficient scale* for a firm—the point at which the average total cost curve stops falling and begins to flatten out—is so large that only a few firms can efficiently coexist in a market.

Exhibit 11.2 gives estimates of the minimum efficient scale for a single plant in several industries, stated as a percentage of U.S. consumption of the product. The third column shows the theoretical minimum four-firm concentration ratio implied by the minimum efficient plant size. The industry could not be any less concentrated than this without forcing some firms to use plants that are too small to produce at minimum long-run average cost. The fourth column shows the actual four-firm concentration ratio for each industry. In every case, this ratio is much larger than the theoretical minimum. It is clear that, with the possible exception of refrigerators, economies of scale *at the plant level* are insufficient to explain the observed degree of market concentration.

Some caution should be used in interpreting the data in Exhibit 11.2. The study from which they are taken defined *economies of scale* quite narrowly. Thus, the numbers given should be viewed as lower bounds for the minimum efficient

[1] William G. Shepherd, "Causes of Increased Competition in the U.S. Economy, 1939–1980," *Review of Economics and Statistics* (November 1982): 613–626.

Exhibit 11.2   Plant-Level Economies of Scale and Market Concentration

Column 2 of this exhibit gives estimates of the minimum efficient scale for a single plant in 12 industries. Multiplying these estimates by 4 gives column 3, the theoretical minimum four-firm concentration ratio for each industry. Comparing columns 3 and 4 tells us that all the industries shown are much more concentrated than plant-level economies of scale alone can explain.

(1) Industry	(2) Minimum Efficient Plant Size as Percent of U.S. Consumption	(3) Theoretical Minimum Four-Firm Concentration Ratio	(4) Actual 1967 Four-Firm Concentration Ratio
Ball and roller bearings	1.4	5.6	54
Beer brewing	3.4	13.6	40
Cement	1.7	6.8	29
Cigarettes	6.6	26.4	81
Cotton and synthetic fabrics	0.2	0.8	36
Glass containers	1.5	6.0	60
Paints	1.4	5.6	22
Petroleum refining	1.9	7.6	33
Refrigerators	14.1	56.4	73
Shoes	0.2	0.8	26
Storage batteries	1.9	7.6	61
Wide strip steel works	2.6	10.4	48

Source: F. M. Scherer, Alan Beckenstein, Erich Kaufer, and R. D. Murphey, *The Economics of Multi-Plant Operation: An International Comparisons Study* (Cambridge, Mass.: Harvard University Press, 1975), Table 3.11, p. 80. All Rights Reserved. Reprinted by permission.

[handwritten margin note:] Note: firms are bigger than they need to be. Bigger seems to give them advantages in marketing, pricing than smaller firms.

[handwritten margin note:] Price Leadership — can't be proven as illegal therefore it gives firms an advantage.

scale even at the plant level. Also, as stressed in Chapter 8, there are many sources of economies of scale above the plant level. Operating more than one plant may result in savings in scheduling, transportation, research and development, finance, marketing, and administration costs. To the extent that cost savings in producing a given product or model depend on "learning by doing," a plant with a large market share builds up experience more quickly than one with a small market share. These kinds of economies of scale may lie beyond the ability of economists and accountants to measure accurately.[2]

Even after all such qualifications are taken into account and the minimum efficient scales shown in Exhibit 11.2 are increased several times, it appears that economies of scale alone do not fully account for the degree of concentration found in U.S. industry. Let's turn, then, to the role of barriers to entry.

Barriers to Entry

Barriers to entry by new firms are one reason that an industry may be more concentrated than economies of scale alone would indicate. For our purposes, a barrier to entry may be defined as any factor that prevents a new firm from

Barrier to entry
Any factor that prevents a new firm in a market from competing on an equal footing with existing ones.

[2] See John S. McGee, "Efficiency and Economies of Size," in Harvey J. Goldschmid, H. Michael Mann, and J. Fred Weston, eds., *Industrial Concentration: The New Learning* (Boston: Little, Brown, 1974), 55–96.

competing on an equal footing with existing firms. In a market with neither large economies of scale nor high barriers to entry, growth will tend to occur mainly through the entry of new firms, leading to a decrease in concentration over time. With the presence of barriers to entry, the first firms in the industry may be able to maintain their market shares as the industry grows, even without the help of economies of scale.

Sometimes barriers to entry into oligopolistic industries are deliberately created by federal, state, or local governments. In such cases, the government stops short of creating a pure monopoly but still limits the number of firms to a figure below that which would exist under conditions of free entry. For example, the Federal Communications Commission controls the number of radio and TV stations allowed in each community. In most places, the number of stations permitted is smaller than the number that would be technically possible. At the state level, entry into many professions—law, medicine, plumbing, and hairdressing, to name only a few—is limited by licensing boards. In many areas, entry into rental housing or retailing is limited by local zoning regulations. The list of such barriers continues indefinitely.

A second kind of barrier to entry is ownership of a nonreproducible resource. A classic example is the market for beryllium, which was discussed in the lead-off case in Chapter 10. In other markets, the nonreproducible resources are human; for example, entry into the movie industry may be difficult if all the top stars are under contract to existing firms. Whatever the reason, ownership of a nonreproducible resource gives existing firms an advantage over new ones and in this way acts as a barrier to entry.

Patents and copyrights, another class of barriers to entry, are important in both oligopoly and monopoly. A patent or copyright can be treated as a restrictive regulation. Alternatively, it can be considered just like ownership of any other nonreproducible resource. In either case, patents and copyrights clearly can make entry difficult and contribute to market concentration.

As the term is used here, a *barrier to entry* is something that keeps new firms from duplicating the performance of existing ones in terms of cost or product quality. It does not mean that every effort or expense that a firm must undertake to enter a market should be thought of as a barrier. In order to start a new firm, an entrepreneur must take risks, find investors, recruit workers, attract customers, and so on. All these activities are hard work—hard enough to discourage some people from making the effort. But the need for hard work is not a barrier to entry in the economic sense. When entrepreneurs are free to buy the building blocks for their new firms on the same terms as existing ones, even huge markets can be cracked by new entrants. Examples include Honda's entry into the automobile market, starting from the base of its motorcycle business; the entry of Texas Air, New York Air, and People Express (all now combined with Continental) into the national airline market; and the entry of Kuwait's Q8 brand into a European retail gasoline market formerly dominated by such giants as Shell and British Petroleum.

Random Influences

Finally, even in a market with no great economies of scale and no barriers to entry, random influences may lead to concentration over time. Suppose a large number of firms start out with equal opportunities in an industry that grows at an average rate of 6 percent per year. By chance, in any given year some firms will grow more quickly and others more slowly than average. A few firms can be expected to be lucky and grow more rapidly than average several years in a row. Once they lead the pack, it will be hard for the others to catch up. The leaders will maintain a large market share even if their performance eventually becomes average. Computerized studies suggest that random factors alone can explain a large part of the concentration of U.S. industry.[3]

The Theory of Oligopoly: Interdependence and Collusion

Chapters 9 and 10 presented simple models of profit maximization for the market structures of perfect competition and monopoly. However, there is no widely accepted and generally applicable model of profit maximization under oligopoly. The reason lies in what is called **oligopolistic interdependence.** This refers to the need for each firm to take its rivals' likely reactions into account when making decisions related to price, output, and other elements of business strategy.

Oligopolistic interdependence
In an oligopolistic market, the need to pay close attention to the actions of rival firms when making price or production decisions.

The popcorn price war described at the beginning of this chapter illustrates the problem of oligopolistic interdependence in miniature. If there were just one firm in the market, the profit-maximizing strategy would be based on the ideas of marginal cost and marginal revenues—or at least on the vendor's seat-of-the-pants estimates of these variables. The price of $1 a box that prevailed when there was only one vendor may have approached this profit-maximizing price. If, on the other hand, there were enough firms in the market for perfect competition to exist, each firm would care only about an impersonal market price, not individual rivals' reactions. The price would be treated as a given and output would be adjusted by each firm until the price equaled marginal cost.

With four vendors on the corner of 15th and L, however, the pricing decision depends not only on each vendor's estimates of marginal cost and marginal revenue but also on each one's estimates of rivals' actions. The $.50 strategy is based on the hunch that the 25-centers will get tired of working so hard for so little profit before all the customers loyal to the $.50 carts shift to the cheaper popcorn. The $.25 strategy is based on the guess that the 50-centers' customers are not so loyal after all so that increased sales volume will allow them to earn a profit even at the low price. Thus, the price charged and quantity produced in an oligopoly can change as a result not only of changes in "objective" conditions such as cost and demand but also as a result of purely subjective estimates of such human traits as stubbornness, loyalty, patience, and anger.

The Theory of Cartels

Oligopolistic interdependence may lead to intense rivalry, as in the case of the popcorn war, but it can also result in collusion. *Collusion* occurs when the firms in an oligopoly realize that they can jointly increase their profit by raising the

---

[3] Such an experiment is described in F. M. Scherer, *Industrial Market Structure and Economic Performance*, 2d ed. (Chicago: Rand McNally, 1980), 145–150.

Cartel
A group of producers that jointly maximize profits by fixing prices and limiting output.

product's price and working out an agreement for dividing the market. When collusion is open and formal and involves all or most producers in the market, the result is called a **cartel.**

A simple example will show how cartels work. Imagine an industry made up of 100 small firms. Assume that the marginal cost of production for all firms in the industry is $1 per unit regardless of the amount produced. Because marginal cost is the same for all units of output, the marginal cost curve also serves as the long-run average cost curve and the long-run supply curve for the industry. This perfectly elastic long-run supply curve is shown, along with a demand curve for the industry, in Exhibit 11.3.

The industry's equilibrium price and output level depend on how the market is organized. Initially, suppose that all firms act like perfect competitors. Under the theory set forth in Chapter 9, this will result in an equilibrium in which the market price is $1 per unit (equal to long-run average cost and long-run marginal cost) and 400,000 units of output are produced each month. In this equilibrium, firms earn no economic profit.

Forming a Cartel

Now suppose that one day the heads of the 100 firms meet to form a cartel. They hope that by replacing competition with cooperation they can all benefit. They elect a cartel manager, who is asked to work out a production and marketing plan that will result in the maximum total profits for the industry and to divide them fairly among its members.

The profit-maximizing problem the cartel manager faces is exactly the same as that faced by a monopolist. Industry profits are highest at the output level at

---

Exhibit 11.3   Profit Maximization for a Cartel

This graph shows an industry made up of 100 firms, each producing at a constant long-run average and marginal cost. If the firms act like perfect competitors, the industry will be in equilibrium at the point at which the demand and marginal cost curves intersect. If the firms form a cartel, however, they can jointly earn profits by restricting output to the point at which marginal cost equals marginal revenue and raising the price from $1 to $2.

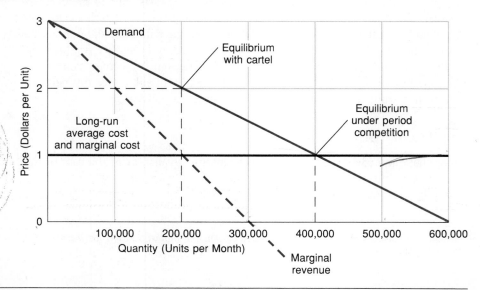

which marginal revenue equals marginal cost—200,000 units per month. If output is restricted to that quantity, the price can be raised to $2 per unit, which will yield $200,000 per month of pure economic profit.

To divide this profit among all the cartel members, the manager will give each firm an output quota of 2,000 units a month, half as much as each was producing before the cartel was formed. In this way, the member firms will reap the benefits of pure monopoly despite their small size and large number.

The Stability Problem

Although cartels are good for their members, they are not so good for consumers. For them, cartels mean a smaller supply of goods and higher prices. Fortunately for consumers, cartels have some built-in problems that make them hard to form and unstable.

The first problem from which cartels suffer is control over entry. As we saw in Chapter 9, any industry that has prices above the level of long-run average cost tends to attract new firms. Since the whole point of a cartel is to raise prices above the competitive level, a cartel acts as a magnet for entrepreneurs. But the entry of new firms does not increase the total amount the cartel can sell at the profit-maximizing price. More firms only mean that the profits must be divided into smaller shares. Any cartel, then, needs to find a way to control entry into its market if it is to serve the interests of its founding members.

The second—and even more serious—inherent problem of cartels is enforcing output quotas. In a cartel, each member has an incentive to cheat by producing output beyond its quota. Take the cartel in Exhibit 11.3. The quota for each of the 100 members is 2,000 units per month—just half of what each would produce under perfect competition.

What would happen if one firm cheated on its quota by stepping up its output while the others went on playing by the rules? The answer is simple: An extra 2,000 units per month would have only a small effect on the market price, since it would represent only a 1 percent increase in industry output. By producing 4,000 units a month, the cheater would double its monthly profit—as long as others did not cheat too.

But what if the other 99 firms did cheat and stepped up their output to 4,000 units while the remaining firm stuck to its quota? With industry output at 398,000 units, the price would be forced down to the competitive level of $1. The firm that played fair would gain nothing for having done so.

The conclusion to which this leads is that every member of a cartel will have an incentive to cheat if it expects other members to play fair—and to cheat if it expects others to cheat as well.

Cartels in Practice

The problems of entry and cheating affect all cartels. The cartel known as the Organization of Petroleum Exporting Countries (OPEC) is a well-known case. In 1973, OPEC controlled about 60 percent of the oil output of the industrialized countries. Taking advantage of its market power, it proceeded to increase crude oil prices some tenfold in the next eight years to a level approaching $40 per barrel. Output was divided among members in proportion to formulas agreed upon at meetings of the oil ministers of the various OPEC countries. Saudi Arabia, the largest producer, had the greatest influence and the largest quota.

The price increase brought the OPEC countries fabulous wealth in the short run. However, it also spurred output in non-OPEC areas such as the North Sea, Alaska, and Mexico. Also, the demand for oil proved more elastic in the long run than in the short run as factories installed energy conservation equipment and consumers bought more efficient cars. As a result of these changes, OPEC lost half of its former market share. As it did, Saudi Arabia cut back its own output to less than 25 percent of capacity and tried to persuade smaller members to accept lower quotas as well. But cheating in terms of both price and quantity became widespread. By 1986, the OPEC cartel was in disarray. The world oil price plunged to near $10 a barrel before stabilizing, at least temporarily, at a little under $20. OPEC still has vast reserves. If new discoveries outside its territory are not made as fields in Alaska, the North Sea, and elsewhere are depleted, its ability to control the world oil market may return. But for the time being, its market power is but a shadow of what it once was.

Other cartels have met similar fates. In 1986, about the same time OPEC's problems were reaching a head, the 30-year-old international tin cartel collapsed. A few years earlier, the century-old diamond cartel headed by the South African company De Beers was shaken by the development of a giant new mine in Australia and by cheating on the part of Zaire. Cooperation by the Soviet Union allowed De Beers to stave off collapse, but only at the cost of concessions to the Australians and a reduction in the firm's own quota.

In short, cartels that depend on voluntary cooperation among members sooner or later run into problems. However, not all cartels depend on voluntary cooperation. Some have succeeded by enlisting the government to enforce quotas and restrict entry. In the United States, agricultural cartels known as *marketing orders* are a case in point (see "Economics in the News 11.1"). Other cartels have succeeded by using criminal action to discourage cheating; garbage collection service in some parts of the United States fits this pattern. As the operator of one such service put it, "Anybody takes my customers, I'll burn his house and kill his kids."[4]

Coordination without Collusion

Formal cartels are not unknown, but they are rare. They are uncommon partly because of their inherent instability, as explained in the previous section. Also— in the United States, at least—most cartels are illegal under the antitrust laws. (These laws will be described in Chapter 17.) But that leaves the question of whether the firms in an oligopoly can, even without open collusion, tacitly coordinate their price and output decisions in a way that will jointly maximize their profit. Put another way, will an industry in which there are only a few firms but no formal cartel perform more nearly like the model of perfect competition or that of monopoly?

There have been a number of attempts to answer this question with formal models similar to those of perfect competition and monopoly. These attempts have not been particularly successful, however, because there is no simple way to handle the problem of oligopolistic interdependence—the dependence of each firm's behavior on its rivals' decisions.

To construct a formal model, one must make a specific assumption about how each firm reacts to what its rivals do and how it expects them to react to what it does. One model, for example, assumes that each firm reacts to its rivals' changes in prices or output but expects them not to respond to changes in its own prices and output. Another model assumes that rivals will always match

---

[4]See James Cook, "The Garbage Game," *Forbes*, October 21, 1985, 121–130.

Independent Farmers Fight the Orange Cartel

SANGER, CALIFORNIA. Inside a big metal building on the Riverbend International Corp. farm here, shiny oranges bounce jauntily along conveyor belts and down chutes, automatically joining like-sized fruit in boxes bound for Pacific Rim markets.

But outside, in orchards that stretch across the San Joaquin Valley, oranges just as fine plop off trees and rot in the scorching heat. Perry Walker, Riverbend's vice president, says that the fruit wouldn't be going to waste if it weren't for restrictions imposed by a government-backed cartel.

Rotting fruit and lost profits have become a cause. Walker has joined a growing group of independent fruit and nut farmers and packers who are fighting what they see as 1930s-bred socialism. Fifty-year-old federal regulations allow farmers to form cartels to control supplies, share marketing efforts and allocate production rights through "marketing orders" approved and enforced by the U.S.

Agriculture Department. Says one grower, "Even the Communists don't do what we're doing—destroying good food."

Using petitions, lawsuits and other legal maneuvers, the farmers and packers are winning some battles. In California, Florida and the Upper Midwest, they have gotten rid of some of the nation's 47 marketing orders and begun to weaken others.

At stake is the enormous power of huge produce-marketing cooperatives. Because of their big market shares, co-ops like Sunkist, Sun-Diamond and the California Almond Growers Exchange have most of the votes on the committees that administer the marketing orders. Without the protection from competition that the production limits provide, the co-ops might lose farmer members and valuable markets to the independents.

Consumers and many farmers stand to gain if the independents' campaign succeeds. More fruit and nuts on the market would lower retail prices, the U.S. Small Business Administration advocacy office has concluded.

"The system's a house of cards," says James Moody, a Washington, D.C. lawyer who has worked for the growers for the past eight years. "If you keep banging away at it, it will fall."

Source: Marj Charlier, "Independent Farmers Oppose Rules Letting Cartels Decide Output," *The Wall Street Journal*, June 17, 1987, 1. Reprinted by permission of *The Wall Street Journal*, © Dow Jones & Company, Inc. 1987. All Rights Reserved.

price cuts but never price decreases. Still another assumes that each firm expects its rivals to do the worst thing possible and plans accordingly.

These formal models are described in the appendix to this chapter. None of them, however, has been accepted as a valid and general solution to the question of how price and output decisions are made under oligopoly. Instead, much of the writing on oligopoly deals with informal theories that, while less elegant than formal ones, are more realistic. These theories consist of conjectures about the conditions that tend to make cooperation by oligopolists easier or more difficult. Under conditions that facilitate formal, tacit coordination, price and output may tend to more closely resemble the result of a cartel. Under conditions that make coordination more difficult, price and output may tend to more nearly approximate the result of perfect competition. Some of the most common themes struck by the informal theories are described next.

Number and Size of Firms

There is little doubt that the number and size of the firms in a market make a big difference. Tacit coordination is easier in a market with only two or three large firms of roughly equal size than in one in which a dozen equal-size firms have half the market and the rest consists of smaller firms. If the number of firms is large enough and the size of the largest firms sufficiently small, the market ceases to be an oligopoly altogether. With a homogeneous product it becomes perfectly competitive, as discussed in Chapter 9. With a differentiated product it becomes monopolistically competitive, a case that we will analyze later in this chapter.

The relative size and number of the various firms in the market are considered important on the grounds that cooperation is easier in an industry in which there is one dominant firm. That firm may be able to act as a price leader. Under the strongest form of **price leadership,** firms are no longer uncertain about how their rivals will react to price changes. The leader knows that the others will follow it both up and down. The others know that if they follow the leader others will too, but not if they raise or lower prices on their own. When it works, this arrangement is tantamount to a cartel in that the dominant firm's efforts to maximize its own profit will also maximize the entire industry's.

Nature of the Product

The nature of the product also affects the ease or difficulty of coordination. A homogeneous product with a smooth flow of orders tends to make coordination easier. A variable product with an irregular flow of orders tends to make it more difficult. In the latter case, there are simply too many things to coordinate. It is not enough that all firms tacitly agree to sell at the same price; they must also agree on a set of price variations for changes in quality, speed of delivery, size of order, and so on. Under these conditions, an agreement to raise the price above the competitive level, even if it can be sustained, is unlikely to lead to higher profits. It is more apt to lead to an outbreak of competition in terms of quality, scheduling, volume discounts, and so on. These factors will add to the cost of doing business until excess profits disappear.

Growth and Innovation

The rates of growth and innovation in a market are another factor that is likely to affect the ease or difficulty of coordination among rival oligopolists. In a market in which product features, production techniques, and buyers' and sellers' personalities do not change from year to year, an agreement among firms, whether tacit or overt, will never have to be revised. In a market with rapidly changing elements, any agreement will soon be made obsolete by changing conditions or disrupted by the entrance of new buyers or sellers. Given the uncertainties of tacit agreements and the fact that overt ones are illegal, one would expect that the faster the pace of growth and change, the less successful rival firms will be at coordinating their activities.

Ease of Entry and Exit

Barriers to entry play an important role in the price and output decisions of an oligopoly. Even if there are only a few firms in the market, the threat of entry by new firms may force existing ones to practice limit pricing to avoid attracting new rivals. Under limit pricing, as explained in Chapter 10, the price is set below the profit-maximizing level implied by short-run demand, marginal revenue, and marginal cost curves.

Barriers to entry are also important in considering the effect of mergers on price and output decisions in an oligopoly. A merger within an oligopoly reduces the number of firms in the industry and, if the larger members are involved, increases the concentration ratio. Taken in isolation, a reduction in the number and an increase in the size of firms would tend to make coordination easier,

Price leadership
In an oligopoly, a situation in which increases or decreases in price by one dominant firm, known as the *price leader,* are matched by all or most of the other firms in the market.

ECONOMICS IN THE NEWS 11.2

Start-up Book Publishers Fill Gap Left by Big-Firm Mergers

The literary world is jittery about a wave of mergers among book publishers. News America Holdings Inc.'s purchase of Harper and Row this month and last September's acquisition of Doubleday & Co. by West Germany's Bertlesman AG were only the latest in a string of big mergers. The resulting giants, some authors fear, will publish only blockbuster books, dooming unknown writers to remain so.

Those worries, however, don't take into account a number of start-ups in the book-publishing world. And though the new publishing houses are small now, they don't intend to stay that way. "We are small because you have to start somewhere," says Hy Steirman, chairman of Richardson & Steirman Inc., a two-year-old publishing house in New York. The company expects revenue of "around $2 million" this year, Steirman says, adding: "Right now, we are looking for venture capital because we think we can be a $10 million to $15 million company in a few years."

Source: Steven P. Galante, "Start-Up Book Publishers Fill Gap Left by Big-Firm Mergers," *The Wall Street Journal*, April 27, 1987, 27. Reprinted by permission of *The Wall Street Journal*, © Dow Jones & Company, Inc. 1987. All Rights Reserved.

Barney Rosset, a veteran New York publisher who founded a new company, Rosset & Co., last fall, adds: "There is a booming small-publishing business in this country." Rosset, best known as the founder of maverick publisher Grove Press Inc., which he sold in 1985, says small houses are flourishing partly because these days they can subcontract for more services, such as printing, jacket design, distribution and marketing. "It's gotten cheaper" to enter publishing, Rosset says.

The new publishers are getting into fiction and general-interest nonfiction—a market dominated by the large "trade" publishers, such as Random House Inc., Simon & Schuster Inc., and Macmillan Inc. "We're trying to avoid the small-press mentality, which is unnecessarily defensive," says Juris Jurjevics, who established Soho Press Inc. in New York last year.

However, ventures like Soho aren't going head to head with the publishing giants. Rather, they are publishing "midlist" authors big houses can't afford to put in print. "If we sell 5,000 copies of a book, we can make a profit," says Steirman, "whereas a big publisher has to sell 20,000 to make a profit."

---

perhaps leading to a more cartel-like result. In some industries, however, new firms quickly enter to fill any gaps left by mergers. The book publishing industry, in which several mergers have taken place in recent years, is a case in point (see "Economics in the News 11.2").

Finally, it has been pointed out that ease of exit from the industry can be just as important as ease of entry in determining an oligopoly's performance. The reasoning is that entrepreneurs will be more willing to risk entering a market if entry does not involve large *sunk costs*—costs that cannot be recovered later.

For example, compare the airline and hotel industries. Both airliners and hotels are very expensive pieces of capital. However, the decision to enter the market for airline travel between Denver and Houston has far lower sunk costs than the decision to enter the Denver hotel market. If the airline puts several planes in service between Denver and Houston and then fails to attract enough passengers to make a profit, it can simply cut back its Denver-Houston schedule and move the planes to another route. But if an entrepreneur builds a hotel in Denver and fails to attract enough patrons to make a profit, there is no way to move the hotel. Because exit is easier from the airline market, then, it takes a smaller magnet, in the form of potential profit, to draw new entrants.

Contestable market
A market in which barriers
to entry and exit are low.

A market in which the costs of both entry and exit are low is called a **contestable market.**[5] In such markets, the prevailing price and quantity can be expected to approximate the outcome of perfect competition even if there are few firms actually in the market at a given time. The market for air travel to and from a given city is contestable because of the ease of moving planes around, despite the fact that an airliner costs many millions of dollars. In the book publishing industry (discussed in "Economics in the News 11.2"), the possibility of subcontracting services from specialists makes the market more contestable than it otherwise would be. Both entry and exit in this industry are facilitated by the fact that specialist firms can be hired for printing, jacket design, and so on. If each firm had to have its own printing plant, employ its own staff of designers, and provide all the other needed special services on its own, existing firms would have to make higher profits before start-up publishers would be attracted.

Measuring Market Performance under Oligopoly

Neither the formal theories discussed in the appendix to this chapter nor the informal rules of thumb just presented give conclusive answers to the question asked at the beginning of the chapter—whether rivalry among a few firms in a concentrated market is enough to insure good market performance. In this context, good market performance means performance like that of a perfectly competitive market, with prices equal or close to marginal cost, so that the sum of producer and consumer surplus is maximized. Poor performance means performance like that of a monopoly or cartel, in which prices remain higher than marginal cost, making potential gains from trade go unrealized.

Unable to answer questions about market performance by means of pure theory, economists turn to statistical methods. Because there is no direct way to measure whether a gap exists between a firm's output prices and its marginal costs, the common approach is an indirect one. If firms in concentrated industries can be shown, on average, to earn returns that exceed the opportunity cost of capital, one can infer that they are behaving more like monopolists than like perfect competitors. If, on the other hand, firms in concentrated industries earn only "normal profits"—that is, rates of return on capital no higher, on average, than those of firms in less concentrated industries—one can conclude that oligopolies perform about as well as more competitive industries.

Early Empirical Studies
The first person to try this approach in a systematic way was University of California professor Joe Bain. In 1951, he published the results of a study of 42 selected industries for the years 1936 to 1940. According to Bain's analysis of the data, industries with concentration ratios of over 70 earned higher profits than less concentrated ones. The link between profits and concentration was neither perfect nor strong, but it did exist.

During the 1950s and 1960s, many of Bain's students and followers repeated his studies for other industries and years. Most of them got the same results—a weak but persistent link between profits and concentration. It became one of economists' general beliefs that the more highly concentrated an industry, the

---

[5] See William J. Baumol, "Contestable Markets: An Uprising in the Theory of Industry Structure," *American Economic Review* 72 (March 1982): 1–15.

more it will tend to perform like a cartel or a monopoly. This would be true even if there were no agreement among rivals to raise prices and divide markets.

More Recent Results

As faith in this idea grew, economists tried as hard as they could to prove it, using the more advanced statistical techniques and better data that became available each year. But the harder they tried, the more elusive the connection became. Some studies showed that if the data were adjusted for the size of firms in different markets, the link between concentration and profits tended to disappear. Others indicated that if the data were adjusted for differences in advertising expenditures, the connection would evaporate. Still others suggested that results like Bain's held only in periods of recession and disappeared with the return of prosperity.

Moreover, as the link between concentration and profits was becoming more ambiguous, economists were growing less certain about how such a link should be interpreted even if it could be confirmed. New reasons were found to explain why firms in more concentrated industries might appear to earn higher profits than firms in less concentrated ones. These suppositions had nothing to do with monopoly pricing or tacit coordination. For example, a concentrated industry that was growing rapidly might need to earn high profits to attract more capital. Perhaps the high profits of the largest firms in each concentrated industry might simply reflect those firms' superior efficiency relative to smaller firms in the same industry. Finally, the higher profits that some concentrated industries appeared to earn might not be profits at all in the economic sense; they might merely reflect the fact that the categories accountants use to record business transactions differ from those used by economic theorists.

One major problem that prevented a final resolution of the dispute lay in the nature of the available data. Until quite recently, most data on profits and concentration were gathered at the company level, whereas the theories being tested were stated in terms of markets. In one market after another, the firms with big market shares were highly diversified with respect to either the product markets or the geographic markets in which they participated. Thus, relationships that might have been present at the market level simply failed to show up clearly enough in data collected at the company level. Recent information on market-by-market concentration ratios and market shares indicates that larger firms are indeed more profitable. However, the source of profits seems to be lower costs rather than higher prices.[6]

The Theory of Monopolistic Competition

Up to this point, we have looked at industries in which many small firms produce a homogeneous product and at others in which a few large firms make products that need not be alike. These cases leave out a very large class of markets in which there are many small firms, each of which makes a product that differs slightly from those of its competitors. This is the market structure known as *monopolistic competition*. Examples include restaurants, service stations, bakeries, some types of book publishing companies, and countless others.

---

[6] See Bradley T. Gale and Ben Branch, "Concentration and Market Share: Which Determines Performance and Why Does It Matter?" *Antitrust Bulletin* 27 (Spring 1982).

Profit Maximization under Monopolistic Competition

While there is no general agreement on a formal model for oligopoly, there is a widely accepted model of monopolistic competition. As its name implies, this model, which dates from work done in the 1930s by Edward H. Chamberlin and independently by Joan Robinson, blends monopolistic and competitive aspects. Like a monopolist, the monopolistically competitive firm is assumed to face a negatively sloped demand curve; changes in the price it charges will affect the quantity it can sell. However, like the perfectly competitive firm, the monopolistic competitor is assumed to share the market with many other similar firms of small size. For this reason, the model of monopolistic competition ignores oligopolistic interdependence. It assumes that each firm is so small that none are significantly affected by—or pay much attention to—what other firms in the market do.

The theory can be understood with the help of Exhibit 11.4, which shows short- and long-run equilibrium positions for a typical firm under monopolistic competition. The demand curve has a negative slope because each firm's product is a little different from its competitors'. Each firm therefore can raise its price at least slightly without losing all its customers, because some customers attach more importance than others to the special style, location, or other marketing advantage the firm offers. Given this negatively sloped demand curve, the short-run profit-maximizing position shown in panel a of the exhibit is found in the same way as that for a pure monopolist: The output level is determined by the intersection of the marginal cost and marginal revenue curves and the price charged by the height of the demand curve at that point.

However, this short-run equilibrium cannot also be a long-run equilibrium under monopolistic competition. The reason is that monopolistically competitive markets are highly contestable, with easy entry and exit. In the short-run position shown in part a of Exhibit 11.4, the firm is earning a pure economic profit; this is shown by the fact that price exceeds average total cost.

But profits attract new firms. As new firms enter the market, two things happen. First, the demand curves of existing firms shift downward. This happens because the new firms' products, although not identical to those of the original firms, are substitutes for them. Second, in reaction to the new competition, firms already in the market may step up advertising, improve their product in some way, or take other steps to win back customers. These efforts cause the firms' average total cost curves to shift upward. The downward shift in the demand curves of the original firms, the upward shift in their cost curves, or both continues until there are no more profits to attract new firms. The result is the long-run equilibrium position shown in part b of the exhibit.

Performance of Monopolistically Competitive Industries

At one time, the long-run equilibrium position shown in Exhibit 11.4 was thought to indicate poor performance by monopolistically competitive industries. For one thing, as under pure monopoly, each firm stops short of the output level that would maximize the sum of producer and consumer surplus. Likewise, the gap between price and marginal cost indicates potential added production that would benefit both the firm and its customers. In addition, under monopolistic competition a firm does not operate at the lowest point on its long-run average cost curve. If there were fewer firms, each producing a greater

Exhibit 11.4   Short-Run and Long-Run Equilibrium
under Monopolistic Competition

Under monopolistic competition, each firm has a downward-sloping demand curve but there are no barriers to entry by new firms. In the short run, a firm that produces at the point at which marginal cost equals marginal revenue can earn pure economic profits, as shown in part a. In the long run, however, new firms are attracted to the market. This diverts part of the demand from firms that are already in the market, thus lowering each one's demand curve. Also, those firms may fight to keep their share of the market, using means that will increase their costs. Entry by new firms will continue until a long-run equilibrium is reached in which profits are eliminated, as shown in part b.

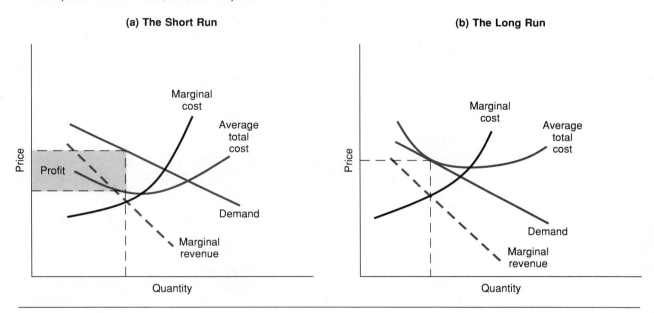

amount of output, the same quantity of goods could be provided at a lower total cost. Following this reasoning, it was said that the hallmark of monopolistic competition is too many gas stations, supermarkets, and restaurants, each operating at a fraction of capacity and each charging inefficiently high prices. Yet despite the high prices, each earns only the minimum return it needs to stay in business.

Today these criticisms of monopolistic competition are less widely accepted. Many articles have been written on the subject, and several variations on the theory have been suggested. Setting aside differences in detail, most of the arguments for the efficiency of monopolistic competition come down to the idea that monopolistic competition and perfect competition are not really very different.

One argument is that the belief in a difference comes from a mistaken idea about the nature of the product being sold. For example, the restaurants in any town sell meals that are highly varied in terms of location, cuisine, atmosphere, service, and many other features. But perhaps meals are not really the product; instead, all of the restaurants can be thought of as selling a homogeneous good called "dining pleasure." The differences among restaurants should be considered not variations in product but differences in the methods used to produce dining pleasure as well as in the "packages" of dining pleasure being sold. This is somewhat similar to potato farming: Different farmers grow potatoes in assorted sizes and use a variety of farming methods, but the potato market is still thought to be perfectly competitive, or close to it. By this line of reasoning, the dining pleasure market is just like the potato market.

A variation on this argument acknowledges differences among products but points out that such differences are themselves valuable. Suppose it were true, as the theory of monopolistic competition suggests, that prices would be a little lower if there were fewer barbershops, each somewhat less conveniently located; or fewer supermarkets, each a little more crowded; or fewer ice cream flavors, even if that meant leaving out some people's favorites. Would a move in that direction benefit consumers? Not if consumers were willing to pay something for variety. Imagine that there was some way to split the market for, say, ice cream into two markets—one for the good called "ice cream" and the other for the good called "variety." In that case, each good could have its own price and each market could be perfectly competitive. But such a scenario is impossible. In the real world, a single market for both goods with the structure known as monopolistic competition is as close as one can come to the ideal.

Looking Ahead

We began this chapter with the question of whether business rivalry will produce satisfactory market performance even when the conditions for perfect competition are not met. After reviewing various formal and informal theories, the answer seems to be maybe yes, maybe no.

However, we have not yet said all there is to say on the subject of competition and market performance. All the models we have looked at are limited in that they focus narrowly on one aspect of business decision making—the search for maximum profits under given conditions of demand, technology, and resource availability. Except when discussing entry of new firms, we have said little about the entrepreneurial elements of business decision making. Entrepreneurship involves more than entry into new markets and exit from old ones. It also concerns changes made by firms operating within markets whose structure remains constant—changes that focus on such aspects of nonprice competition as product enhancement, improvements in customer service, advertising, and so on. In the next chapter, we examine some of these factors.

Summary

1. **To what extent are markets dominated by a few large firms?** *Concentration ratios* are a common measure of the degree to which a market is dominated by a few firms. The most often used ratios measure the share of total sales in the market accounted for by the top four or eight firms in it. There appears to be a trend toward less concentration in many U.S. markets, especially when international competition is taken into account.

2. **In an oligopoly, how do each firm's decisions depend on those of other firms?** *Oligopolistic interdependence* refers to the need for each firm in an oligop-

oly to pay close attention to its rivals' actions. For example, in the airline industry, some fares are changed each day. Whenever one airline changes a fare, its rivals must decide whether to stand pat, match the new fare, undercut it, or take some other action.

3. **How may collusion among rival firms bring increased profits at the expense of consumers?** A group of producers that jointly maximize profits by fixing prices and limiting output is known as a *cartel*. Profits are maximized for a cartel by setting output at a level corresponding to the intersection of industry

marginal cost and marginal revenue curves. Cartels tend to be unstable because of the difficulty of controlling entry and preventing cheating.

4. **What conditions affect the performance of concentrated markets?** A major question in oligopoly theory is how well concentrated markets perform—that is, how closely they approach the outcome of perfect competition, in which equilibrium prices equal market cost. Among the factors thought to affect market performance are the number and size of firms, the presence or absence of *price leadership*, the nature of the product (homogeneous or varied), the pace of growth and innovation, and the ease of entry and exit. If barriers to entry and exit are low, a market is said to be *contestable*. Contestable markets are thought to perform well even if highly concentrated.

5. **What has been revealed by attempts to measure market performance?** Early studies suggested that firms in industries with high concentration ratios earn higher profits than those in less concentrated industries. This was taken as a sign that firms in concentrated industries engage in tacit coordination and earn joint monopoly profits. More recent research suggests that the connection is not so simple and that at least part of the higher profits in more concentrated industries is accounted for by the fact that firms with dominant market shares tend to have lower production costs than smaller firms.

6. **How are profits maximized under monopolistic competition?** A monopolistic competitor maximizes profit at the output level at which marginal cost equals marginal revenue. In the long run, competition in such an industry results in an equilibrium in which price equals average total cost. In this equilibrium, price does not equal marginal cost and production does not take place at the point of minimum average total cost; nevertheless, consumers enjoy the benefit of product variety.

Terms for Review

- market concentration
- concentration ratio
- barrier to entry
- oligopolistic interdependence
- cartel
- price leadership
- contestable market

Questions for Review

1. What are the key traits of oligopoly? Of monopolistic competition?

2. What is the most common method of measuring the degree of a market's concentration in the hands of a few firms? What has been the concentration trend in the United States?

3. List some examples of oligopolistic interdependence.

4. What problems affect the long-run stability of cartels?

5. How is an oligopoly's performance affected by the number and size of firms in the industry? By the nature of the product? By the pace of growth and innovation?

6. Give examples of markets that are contestable even though they are not perfectly competitive.

7. What evidence suggests that concentrated industries do not perform as efficiently as perfectly competitive ones? How has this idea been challenged?

8. Give some examples of monopolistically competitive markets. How well do these markets perform?

Problems and Topics for Discussion

1. **Examining the lead-off case.** Would you classify the market for popcorn sold by street vendors as monopolistically competitive or oligopolistic? Does it make a difference whether you consider "the market" to be the whole city or a single street corner? Is the popcorn market contestable? Do you think that on the whole this market serves consumers well or poorly?

2. **Oligopolistic interdependence in action.** Look around your community for a case in which a firm is conducting a special sale or product promotion. To what extent, if at all, is the firm's action a response to something its rivals have done? To what extent, if at all, have its rivals reacted with their own sales or promotions?

3. **Concentration outside of manufacturing.** The data on market concentration in Exhibit 11.1 relate only to manufacturing, the sector of the economy that has received the most attention in oligopoly studies. To what extent do you think the agriculture, transportation, services, retail trade, and communications sectors of the economy are concentrated? What do you think accounts for the degree of concentration (or lack of it) in each sector?

4. **Barriers to entry.** "Barriers to entry are lower in the restaurant industry than in the airline industry because a restaurant requires only a few workers and a few thousand dollars in capital, whereas even a small airline requires many workers and millions of dollars in capital." Do you agree? Why or why not?

5. **The market for college education.** What market structure do you think best fits the market for college education? What factors do you believe affect the

structure of the college education industry? How important are economies of scale? Barriers to entry and exit? Chance factors?

6. **Labor unions as cartels.** In what ways do labor unions resemble cartels? In what ways do they differ? Do you think labor unions ever suffer from the stability problems that plague cartels? (We will return to the subject of labor unions in Chapter 14.)

7. **Moscow versus New York restaurants.** In downtown Moscow, there are far fewer restaurants than in New York. The Moscow restaurants are, on the average, much larger and busier than those in New York. The quality of the food served is high in some cases, though the service leaves something to be desired by U.S. standards. Do these facts suggest to you that the central planners who control Moscow's restaurants have designed their system to perform better than the restaurant market in New York? Using what you have learned about monopolistic competition, argue both sides of this question.

Case for Discussion

Bonus Coupon Wars Hit Supermarket Profits

Bonus couponing plays havoc with retailers' profits.

Star Supermarkets' profits fell 10 percent last year and were flat in the first quarter of this year, victims of the practice of "bonus" couponing—paying consumers double or even triple the face value of coupons that appear in newspapers and magazines and sometimes in the mailbox. But Theodore Levinson, president of the upstate New York chain, isn't about to halt the self-defeating promotions.

"I'm not ready to give them up until my competitors do," he says. "I will protect my market share." Levinson isn't alone. In Cleveland, it took 34 Stop-N-Shop supermarkets six months to recoup profits lost during four days of triple couponing in 1980. During the first two months of this year, the chain was at it again with double coupons.

And in Connecticut, store managers for Mott's Super Markets keep "double coupon" signs in their offices to post as soon as competitors announce similar deals. Bonus couponing has reached record proportions: It can be found in about three dozen major cities and, says Zal Venet, president of a New York ad agency with several supermarket clients, "has become a basic, though expensive, marketing tool."

The supermarket manager's dilemma: Bonus couponing usually is started by one of a region's smaller chains to steal market share. If the leaders ignore the challenger, they stand to lose sales. If they reciprocate, they stimulate a coupon war.

Source: Excerpted from Jeffrey H. Birnbaum, "Bonus Coupon Wars Produce Only Victims, Analysts Warn," *The Wall Street Journal*, June 4, 1981, 29. Reprinted by permission of *The Wall Street Journal*, © Dow Jones & Company, Inc., 1981. All Rights Reserved. Photo Source: © 1987 Phyllis Woloshin.

Questions

1. Is bonus couponing an example of oligopolistic interdependence? Why or why not?

2. How do incentives for small and large chains differ in deciding whether to start bonus coupon campaigns? Whether to follow campaigns begun by others?

3. The title of the article suggests that coupon wars produce "only victims." Do consumers too suffer from coupon wars?

Suggestions for Further Reading

Brozen, Yale, ed. *The Competitive Economy*. Morristown, N.J.: General Learning Press, 1975.

Many of the articles reprinted in this book are relevant to this chapter. Brozen is skeptical of the view that concentration implies poor market performance, and many of the readings reflect this point of view.

Goldschmid, Harvey J., Michael H. Mann, and Fred J. Weston, eds. *Industrial Concentration: The New Learning*. Boston: Little, Brown, 1974.

This book takes the form of a series of debates among representatives of contrasting views on many of the problems discussed in this chapter. Especially relevant are Chapter 2 (a debate between F. M. Scherer and John S. McGee on economies of scale as a cause of concentration) and Chapter 4 (which matches Harold Demsetz against Leonard Weiss on the concentration-profits issue).

McGee, John S. "Ocean Freight Rate Conferences and the American Merchant Marine," *University of Chicago Law Review* 27 (Winter 1960): 191–314.

This book-length article discusses cartels and their problems (with many useful references) and applies the general analysis to ocean-shipping cartels.

Scherer, F. M. *Industrial Market Structure and Economic Performance*, 2d ed. Chicago: Rand McNally, 1980.

This is the definitive text on all facets of industrial organization theory.

Formal Theories of Oligopoly

Over the years, many economists have tried to state a formal theory of oligopoly. The goal of such a theory would be to determine the equilibrium price and output level for an oligopolistic firm and its industry given such aspects of market structure as number of firms, concentration ratio, cost and technology, and demand curve. No general theory has been developed, but some useful partial theories and interesting analyses of special cases exist. These provide some insight into the broader problem of oligopoly. The three theories discussed in this appendix are a sample from the literature on formal theories of oligopoly.

The Cournot Theory and Its Variations

The oldest attempt at a theory of oligopoly began with a work published by Augustin Cournot in 1838. Cournot recognized the problem of oligopolistic interdependence—the need for each firm to take its rivals' behavior into account when deciding on its own market strategy. The way to understand the behavior of rival firms, Cournot thought, was to make a simple assumption about the way each firm would react to its rivals' moves.

In his initial statement of the problem, Cournot assumed that each firm would act as if it did not expect its rivals to change their output levels even if it changed its own. Later theorists who expanded Cournot's theory, however, usually made price rather than quantity the crucial variable. In the price-based version of the Cournot theory, each firm is assumed to set its price as though it expects other firms in the industry to leave their prices unchanged.

Exhibit 11A.1 shows how the price-based Cournot theory might work for an industry with just two firms. Each firm has a definite price that will yield maximum profits for each price that its rival may charge. These prices are shown in the form of the firms' *reaction curves*. For example, firm 1's reaction curve indicates that it will charge $60 if its rival charges $50 (point S). If firm 2 charges $150, firm 1 will charge $130 (point T). In the limiting case, firm 2 may charge so much that it will price itself out of the market, leaving firm 1 with a pure monopoly. In that event, firm 1 will maximize its profits by charging $150, as shown by the broken line labeled "Firm 1's monopoly price." Firm 2's monopoly price is shown in the same way. The two reaction curves can be derived from the two firms' cost and demand curves. The derivation is not given here, but it can be found in many advanced texts.

Exhibit 11A.1   The Cournot Theory of Oligopoly

The Cournot theory assumes that each firm will set its price as though it expects its rivals' prices to remain fixed. The reaction curves show the best price for each of two firms given the other's price. For example, point S on firm 1's reaction curve indicates that firm 1 should charge $60 if firm 2 charges $50. If firm 1 has a monopoly, it will set a price of $150. If firm 2 then enters the market, it will touch off a price war, moving the industry step by step to points A, B, C, D, and finally E. Point E is a stable equilibrium.

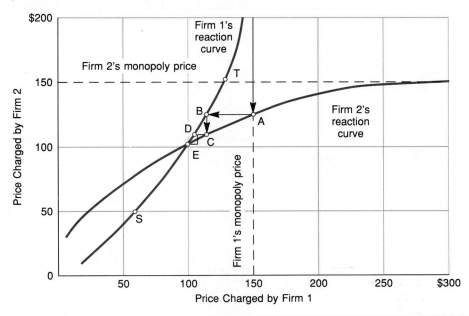

Given these reaction curves, the oligopoly story, according to Cournot, can be told somewhat as follows. Imagine that at first firm 1 is the only producer of the good in question. Since it has a pure monopoly, it maximizes profits by setting a price of $150. Then firm 2 enters the market. Under the Cournot theory, firm 2 will set its price as though it expected firm 1 to go on charging $150 indefinitely. Given this assumption, firm 2 sets its price at $125, as shown by point A on firm 2's reaction curve.

At this point, firm 1 begins to notice its rival. Seeing that firm 2 has taken away many of its customers with its much lower price, it moves to point B on its reaction curve, cutting its own price to $115.

Firm 2, which entered the market on the assumption that firm 1 would maintain its price at $150, must react next. Given firm 1's $115 price, firm 2 cuts its price to $108 (point C). That sparks a price cut by firm 1, which goes to $107 (point D). After a series of increasingly smaller moves and countermoves, the two firms' prices converge at an equilibrium of $100 at point E.

Two things are appealing about the Cournot theory. First, it gives a stable equilibrium. At prices above the intersection of the two reaction curves, each firm has an incentive to undercut its rival's price. At prices below the intersection, each firm has an incentive to charge more than its rival. Thus, given the assumptions, there is only one price that the market can reach. Second, as the theory is expanded beyond two firms to allow for multifirm oligopolies, it can be shown that the equilibrium price moves steadily away from the monopoly price and toward a price equal to marginal cost. Thus, the Cournot equilibrium for an industry with one firm equals the monopoly price; that for an industry with an infinite number of firms equals the competitive price; and those for oligopolies of various sizes occur along a continuum between these extremes.

Still, there is one feature of the Cournot story that has always troubled economists. The structure of the theory depends on each firm's assuming that its rivals will not react to its price changes. Yet daily life in the Cournot world proves that assumption to be wrong. In the example in Exhibit 11A.1, firm 2 enters on the assumption that firm 1 will pay no attention to its entry and capture of a large chunk of firm 1's sales. But firm 1 does react, as does firm 2. Instead of this mindless price war, wouldn't each firm have second thoughts about its price cutting, fearing its rival's reaction? The Cournot theory fails to acknowledge this possibility.

The Kinked Demand Curve Theory

A century after Cournot, in 1939, another major theory of oligopoly came along. This was the so-called *kinked demand curve theory*, which was proposed at about the same time by British economists R. L. Hall and C. J. Hitch and the American economist Paul M. Sweezy. Like the Cournot theory, the kinked demand curve theory begins from a simple assumption about oligopolists' reaction to price changes made by their rivals. Each firm is supposed to assume that if it cuts its price, its rivals will match the cuts, but if it raises its price, no other firms will follow.

Exhibit 11A.2 shows how the market looks to an oligopolist who makes these two assumptions. Let P be the price ($1.70, in this case) that happens to prevail in the market. If the firm cuts its price below P, other firms will lower their prices in turn. Sales in the industry as a whole will expand. The firm in question will keep about the same share of the market and will move down the lower slope of the demand curve. In contrast, if the firm raises its price, the others will not follow suit. Instead of keeping its share of the market, our firm will lose customers to its rivals. As a result, the part of the firm's demand curve above price P is much more elastic than the part below it.

Now bring marginal cost and marginal revenue into the picture. Give the firm a short-run marginal cost curve with the usual upward slope. The marginal revenue curve contains a step that corresponds to the kink in the demand curve. To the left of the step, marginal revenue is very high, showing that revenue will be lost quickly if the firm moves up the very elastic part of the demand curve. To the right of the step, marginal revenue is much lower, indicating that little extra revenue can be obtained by moving down the less elastic part of the demand curve. As drawn, the marginal cost curve cuts the marginal revenue curve right at the step. The prevailing price is an equilibrium price for the firm, since it will be unprofitable to move in either direction.

The kinked demand curve equilibrium for an oligopolist is a very stable kind of equilibrium. Unlike a pure monopolist, the oligopolist with a kinked demand curve will not change its price or output in response to small or medium-size changes in cost. The level of marginal cost shown in Exhibit 11A.2

Exhibit 11A.2   The Kinked Demand
Curve Theory of Oligopoly

An oligopolist will have a kinked demand curve if its rivals
will follow any price decrease it makes but no increase.
There is a sharp step in the marginal revenue curve that
corresponds to the kink in the demand curve. Here the
marginal cost curve crosses the marginal revenue curve just
at the step. This makes the equilibrium very stable.

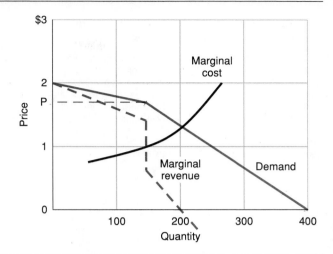

can move by as much as $.30 in either direction, and the firm will not change its
price or output. The marginal cost curve will still cross the marginal revenue
curve at the step. Only if marginal cost changes by more than $.30 will the firm
break with the prevailing price.

Like the Cournot theory, the kinked demand curve theory is simple and
elegant. Its assumptions about the way each oligopolist views its rivals' actions
are clearly more plausible than Cournot's. But the kinked demand curve theory
has a major flaw of its own. Although it explains why an oligopolist might be
reluctant to change its price once set, it fails to show how the price comes to be
set at any particular level in the first place. The theory thus provides an answer
to a question that is not central to the analysis of oligopoly.

Game Theory and Oligopoly Behavior

It has often been remarked that oligopoly is really a game of sorts—one in
which, as in chess or poker, each player must try to guess the opponent's moves,
bluffs, countermoves, and counterbluffs as many moves ahead as possible.
Hence, economists who specialize in oligopoly theory were excited by the appearance in 1944 of a thick, highly mathematical book entitled *The Theory of
Games and Economic Behavior*.[1] Could it be that the authors, John von Neumann
and Oskar Morgenstern, had at last solved the oligopoly puzzle?

Clearly, Neumann and Morgenstern had taken a major step. Instead of
using as their starting point an assumption about how one firm would react to
others' moves, they decided to ask, in effect, what *optimal assumption* each firm
should make about its rivals' behavior.

A simple example of an oligopoly game will convey the spirit of the Neu-

---

[1] John von Neumann and Oskar Morgenstern, *The Theory of Games and Economic Behavior*
(Princeton, N.J.: Princeton University Press, 1944).

Exhibit 11A.3　Profits for Alpha Company
under Various Pricing Strategies

This exhibit shows the profits Alpha Company would earn
under various pricing strategies for itself and its rival, Zed
Enterprises. If both firms set their prices at $5, each will
earn $400. If both cut their prices to $4, they will continue to
split the market and each will earn $360. If Alpha cuts its
price while Zed does not, Alpha will steal many of Zed's
customers and earn $450. If Zed cuts its price while Alpha's
remains at $5, Zed will steal many of Alpha's customers,
leaving Alpha with only $240 in profits.

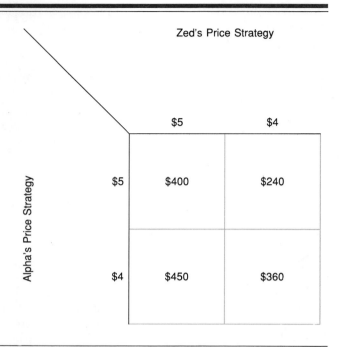

Zed's Price Strategy

	$5	$4
$5	$400	$240
$4	$450	$360

Alpha's Price Strategy

mann-Morgenstern approach. Imagine a market in which there are only two
firms—Alpha Company and Zed Enterprises. Their product costs $1 a unit to
make. If each firm sets its price at $5 a unit, each will sell 100 units per month at
a profit of $4 a unit, for a total monthly profit of $400. If each sets its price at $4
a unit, each will sell 120 units at a profit of $3 a unit, for a total profit of $360.
Which price will the firms actually set? Clearly, $5 is the price that will maxi-
mize their joint profits, but under oligopoly this price may not be a stable equilibrium.

Exhibit 11A.3 shows why. It presents the pricing strategies available to
Alpha Company. Besides the two already mentioned, Alpha must consider two
more. One is to cut its price to $4 while Zed holds at $5. That will allow Alpha to
take away a lot of Zed's customers and sell 150 units, for a profit of $450. The
other is for Alpha to hold its price at $5 while Zed cuts its price to $4. Then Zed
will take away many of Alpha's customers and leave Alpha selling only 60 units,
for a total profit of $240.

So what will happen? One way to seek an answer is to look at the effects of
different assumptions that each firm might make about the other's behavior. If
Alpha assumes that Zed will charge $5, Alpha will be best off charging $4. If
Alpha assumes that Zed will charge $4, it will again be best off charging $4. It
looks as though Alpha will be best off charging $4 regardless of what Zed does.
Alpha will also be aware that Zed's view of the game is the mirror image of its
own. After considering the likely effects of the different assumptions, each firm
will see that it is rational to assume the worst. Unless the two firms can agree to
keep the price at $5 (and such agreements are assumed to be against the rules of
the game as it is played here), $4 seems to be the equilibrium price.

Despite the high hopes of oligopoly theorists, however, it turned out that game theory could not be used to solve the general problem of oligopoly. Some games had a structure that made it impossible to come up with the kind of determinate solution in our example. Further, efforts to expand the game to three or more players quickly became bogged down in a swamp of mathematical complications. Thus, game theory has remained little more than a brilliant solution to an extremely small set of special cases.

12 Entrepreneurship and the Market Process

After reading this chapter, you will understand . . .

- The role that entrepreneurship plays in the market process even when markets are not in equilibrium.
- How economists view the area of business activity known as *marketing*.
- How advertising affects market performance.
- How market structure affects efficiency in both a static and a dynamic sense.

Before reading this chapter, make sure you know the meaning of . . .

- Entrepreneurship (Chapter 2)
- Market structure (Chapter 9)
- Monopoly (Chapter 10)
- Oligopoly and monopolistic competition (Chapter 11)

Darwinism in the Bathroom Cabinet

The 1980s will long be remembered as a time of innovation and entrepreneurship. Just think of the triumphs of technology—the personal computer, the space shuttle, genetic engineering, the toothpaste pump. . . .

Yes, the toothpaste pump. What will future archaeologists think when they dig these little gizmos out of late-twentieth-century landfills? In a stratum that will be shown by carbon-14 dating techniques to belong to the mid-1980s, they will note the appearance of Colgate-Palmolive's Colgate brand, Procter & Gamble's Crest brand, and Lever Brothers' Aim brand. They will find that the pumps have two kinds of innards—one works by vacuum and the other by direct mechanical pressure.

The toothpaste pump is an example of entrepreneurship.

Dates, brands, mechanics—these are facts for the archaeologists to note in their journals. But what will they make of the subjective aspects of the toothpaste pump? What Darwinian forces could have caused the toothpaste pump, at this moment in history, to begin to displace the toothpaste tube—the dominant life form in the bathroom cabinet for over 100 years? Why indeed, when the tube is so much simpler, so much cheaper, and (if squeezed from the bottom) so much less wasteful?

If future linguists are still able to translate the ancient language of *The Wall Street Journal*, they will find a simple explanation: The pump introduces an element of gadgetry, and fun, to the humdrum process of brushing one's teeth. And who could resist the chance to pay 20 percent more for toothpaste if by doing so one could brighten one of the dullest moments of the day?

Source: Based on Stephen MacDonald, "Competing Designs of Toothpaste Pumps Are Vying for Supremacy in Marketplace," *The Wall Street Journal*, November 13, 1984, 35. Photo Source: © 1987 Phyllis Woloshin.

THE example of the toothpaste pump reminds us that something is missing from our account of the workings of the market economy. In three chapters, we looked in depth at models of four market structures—perfect competition, monopoly, oligopoly, and monopolistic competition. In each case, we focused on just two aspects of business decision making—price and quantity. In focusing on price and quantity as variables, we treated such matters as cost curves, demand curves, and product characteristics as known and unchanging features of the environment in which business decisions are made. In this chapter, we take a broader view of the way markets operate—one in which there are many more variables than price and quantity, in which market conditions are uncertain and constantly changing, and in which business decision makers do not merely react passively to change but work actively to shape it. In short, we take a view in which entrepreneurship becomes a central feature of markets.

In earlier chapters, we treated entrepreneurship as the activity of looking for new possibilities, making use of new ways of doing things, being alert to new opportunities, and overcoming old limits. In the first section of this chapter, we explore alertness to opportunities and innovation as key aspects of entrepreneurship. In the remaining sections, we examine entrepreneurship at work.

Entrepreneurship and the Market Process

The models of various market structures covered in Chapters 9 through 11 are products of the neoclassical school of economics whose origins trace back to the work of Alfred Marshall at the close of the nineteenth century. (See "Who Said It? Who Did It? 3.1," page 75.) A key trait of neoclassical economics is the focus on *equilibrium*—a state of affairs in which the plans of buyers and sellers match. In equilibrium, both buyers and sellers are able to carry out their plans; no one is forced to change his or her plans for the coming period.

The neoclassical notion of equilibrium is one of the most powerful metaphors of economics. It conveys the idea that buyers and sellers will stop seeking gains from trade only when those gains have been exhausted. It shows how two separate sets of considerations—those that govern consumers' choices and those that govern producers'—interact to determine market prices. In addition, the neoclassical approach allows the application of the tools of graphical and mathematical modeling to economic questions.

However, as mentioned several times in earlier chapters, the neoclassical models have their limitations. They are like lenses that focus sharply on some features of the market economy but at the cost of narrowing the field of vision. Their chief limitation is their tendency to treat the conditions that determine cost and demand as givens. Neoclassical models are not adept at dealing with those aspects of entrepreneurship that, through innovations in organization and technology, seek to shift cost curves. Nor are they well suited to aspects of entrepreneurship that seek to shift demand curves or to create new products for which demand curves previously did not exist at all. In short, although the neoclassical models can help us understand the factors that determine the equilibrium price of toothpaste, they are of little use in explaining the sudden appearance of toothpaste pumps as a replacement for tubes.

While neoclassical economics has treated entrepreneurship as a side issue, another school of thought—the Austrian school—has made it a focal point. The Austrian school traces its origins to the work of Carl Menger, Friedrich von Wieser, and Eugen von Böhm-Bawerk, who worked in Vienna in the latter part of the nineteenth century. In the twentieth century, the Austrian tradition was brought to the United States by Ludwig von Mises and Friedrich von Hayek, among others. Today the modern Austrian school continues to have a strong following in the United States. In this section, we look at the contributions of the Austrian school to our understanding of entrepreneurship.

Spontaneous Order and the Market Process

Like the neoclassicists, economists of the Austrian school treat the market economy as a system of *spontaneous order*. By this they mean that it is an orderly structure that has been established not through the explicit plan of any person or group but as the unintended outcome of individual choices made with narrower ends in mind. As Adam Smith put it, "It is not from the benevolence of the butcher, the brewer, or the baker that we expect our dinner but from their regard to their own interest. . . . [Each] intends only his own gain, and is in this, as in many other cases, led by an invisible hand to promote an end which was no part of his intention."

In the Austrian view, the spontaneous order of the marketplace is best viewed not in terms of an equilibrium that exists at a given moment in time but in terms of a *process* that takes place continuously through time. The central player in the market process is the entrepreneur. It is the entrepreneur's efforts to move resources from less valued to more valued uses (making a profit in doing so) that make the process an orderly one. Success in these efforts requires (1) being aware of opportunities presented by the marketplace and (2) creating new opportunities. Let's look at each of these in turn.

Entrepreneurship and Arbitrage

As an example of the way in which entrepreneurs take advantage of opportunities that markets present, consider arbitrage. **Arbitrage** is the activity of buying something at a low price in one market and reselling it at a higher price in another. By its nature, arbitrage cannot exist when markets are in equilibrium, for equilibrium is a state of affairs in which buyers' and sellers' plans mesh on the basis of one price at which trades are expected to be carried out. Opportunities for arbitrage, then, arise when circumstances change, throwing plans out of alignment and throwing markets out of equilibrium.

Arbitrage is important in organized markets for agricultural commodities, precious metals, and securities. In these markets, a trader peering at a computer screen might learn that tin is trading at a slightly higher price in the London market than in the Chicago market. An order to buy tin in Chicago and sell it in London will earn the trader a quick profit. Although not part of their intention, the profit-seeking activities of arbitrageurs, together with those of other buyers and sellers of tin, contribute to the efficiency of the world economy by sending signals, in the form of prices, about changes in the opportunity cost of using tin. "Who Said It? Who Did It? 12.1" gives an example used by Hayek to make this point.

Arbitrage appears in its purest form in organized commodity exchanges, but it is not limited to markets of that kind. To take a broader example, any type of

Arbitrage
The activity of earning a profit by buying something at a low price in one market and reselling it at a higher price in another.

WHO SAID IT? WHO DID IT?   12.1

Friedrich von Hayek on Markets and Information

Friedrich von Hayek, a recipient of the Nobel Memorial Prize for economics, was a pioneer in monetary theory and, early in the century, helped develop the field we now know as macroeconomics. Born and educated in Vienna, he is considered a key contributor to the approach to economics known as the *Austrian school*. With such books as *The Road to Serfdom* and *The Constitution of Liberty*, he also gained a reputation as a leader in political philosophy.

A distinguishing feature of the Austrian school is its focus on the process through which markets adjust to changing circumstances. In Hayek's view, the role of markets as transmitters of information is a key to understanding the market process. In 1945, Hayek presented his views on this matter in a classic article, "The Use of Knowledge in Society."

Suppose, says Hayek, that a major new use for tin arises. It may be in manufacturing, electronics, medicine—it doesn't matter. Also, it is important for understanding the role of markets that the exact nature of the new use does not matter. All that tin users really need to know is

that the opportunity cost of using tin has gone up—that is, that some of the tin they previously used can now be more profitably used elsewhere—and, as a consequence, they must economize on tin. The great majority of them need not know what the new use is but only that there is some new, more urgent use. If only some of them know the nature of the new use and switch resources over to it, and if the people who are aware of the resulting gap in turn fill it from still other sources, the effect will spread rapidly. It will influence the uses not only of tin but of its substitutes, substitutes for the substitutes, the supply of all things made of tin, the supply of all things made of its substitutes, and so on. All of this will happen with the great majority of those involved unaware of the exact cause of the original disturbance.

How will people be notified of the change in the tin market? The means of communication that Hayek has in mind is not television, newspapers, or government directives but the market price of tin. It is a rise in the price of tin that will notify each user that a more urgent use has arisen elsewhere.

Prices are an efficient means of communicating this information because they allow each tin user to concentrate on the details of the work at hand while giving just enough information about opportunity costs to guide decisions in the right direction. As Hayek puts it, "The whole acts as one market not because any of its members survey the whole field, but because their limited individual fields of vision sufficiently overlap so that through many intermediaries the relevant information is communicated to all."

In recent years, there has been a resurgence of interest in the Austrian school among U.S. economists. A common theme in the new Austrian literature is the need to understand that markets are more than curves crossing on a graph. They are the nerve fibers along which messages pass from one part of the economic organism to another, thus allowing the whole to adapt to a constantly changing environment.

Source: F. A. von Hayek, "The Use of Knowledge in Society," *American Economic Review* 35 (September 1945): 519–530.

international trade that follows the principle of comparative advantage can be considered an example of arbitrage. In this case, entrepreneurs—who may be selling agents for a manufacturer, purchasing agents for a retailer, or independent brokers—compare the prices at which some good can be bought and sold in various countries. The prices indicate the opportunity costs of production in one place or another. By buying each good in the country in which its domestic opportunity cost is low and selling it where its domestic opportunity cost is higher, international arbitrageurs make a profit. They also—albeit unintentionally—contribute to the efficiency of resource allocation in the world economy.

In securities markets, buying and selling of stocks, bonds, and other financial instruments by arbitrageurs tends to move these instruments into the hands of those who place the highest estimates on their values. This kind of arbitrage is especially important in the case of common stock because, as we saw in Chapter 4, ownership of common stock carries the right to vote on corporate control. Thus, one aspect of financial arbitrage in the stock market is the takeover process, through which more effective management replaces less effective management.

As mentioned, arbitrage can take place only when markets are in a state of disequilibrium. However, disequilibrium in a market does not mean disorder. The reason is that arbitrage does not cause prices to move at random; it causes them to move in the direction of equilibrium. To take a simple case, suppose a boom in construction in the Northeast has raised the wages of construction workers there, while a slump in the Southwest has lowered construction workers' wages. Building contractors, playing the role of arbitrageur, will place ads in southwestern newspapers and send agents to that area to hire workers, perhaps offering to pay moving expenses. As workers flow from one part of the country to the other, wages will be bid up in the Southwest and fall in the Northeast. The market will move toward a new equilibrium in which differences in wages reflect only differences in cost of living, climate preferences, and so on.

In practice, circumstances often change before the new equilibrium is reached. Murray Rothbard compares this aspect of the market process to what goes on at a racetrack at which a mechanical rabbit is used to urge the dogs to run. In Rothbard's view, equilibrium is "like the mechanical rabbit being chased by the dog. It is never reached in practice, and it is always changing, but it explains the direction in which the dog is moving."[1]

Entrepreneurship and Innovation

Arbitrage is an example of alertness to changes stemming from forces beyond the entrepreneur's own control. The change might come from outside the market system entirely, as in the case of a flood or a drought. It might simply come from outside the entrepreneur's own local market, as in Hayek's example, in which a change in the supply of tin causes reactions in distant markets. Whatever the case, change is the rabbit and the entrepreneur the pursuer.

However, entrepreneurs do not always wait for things to happen and then react. They also make things happen—that is, they innovate. They seek to improve products, thus shifting demand curves. They seek new production techniques and organization methods, thus shifting cost curves. And they develop entirely new products, thus creating new markets with entirely new cost and demand curves.

The goal of innovation, like that of arbitrage, is profit. The first firm to come out with a new product or to introduce a new cost-saving production method is able, at least for a time, to sell its product at a price higher than its opportunity cost. Before long, competitors will react. As other suppliers pick up

[1] Murray Rothbard, *Man, Economy, and State* (Los Angeles: Nash, 1962), 250. As quoted by Jack High, "Equilibration and Disequilibration in the Market Process," in *Subjectivism, Intelligibility and Economic Understanding*, ed. Israel M. Kirzner (New York: New York University Press, 1986), 112.

the innovation, the forces of supply and demand will once again drive the price toward the level of opportunity cost. But by that time, with a little hard work, another innovation will be ready to be brought to market.

The Market Process as a Process of Selection

Arbitrage and innovation complement each other as parts of the market process. An innovation is introduced—the compact disk player, fluidized-bed combustion for electric power plants, the limited partnership for real estate ventures, or whatever. This innovation disrupts the old equilibrium, creating a profit opportunity for the first firm to introduce it and very likely threatening competitors with a loss. Because of the innovation, buyers' and sellers' plans no longer mesh at the old set of prices, not only in the market in which output is sold but also in input markets, markets for substitutes and complements, and so on. Arbitrageurs set to work to exploit the profit opportunities that the innovation has created, and the effects ripple throughout the economy.

We have already seen that this process tends to move the market toward a new equilibrium, one that may move before it is reached in the manner of a dog chasing a rabbit. To complete the picture, however, we must also take into account the fact that entrepreneurs often make mistakes. An arbitrageur may buy wheat at $2.50 a bushel, hoping to sell at $2.75, but good weather at harvest time causes the price to fall to $2.25 instead. A corporate marketing staff may bring out a product like New Coke that seemed to be a good idea but is not accepted by the marketplace. In these cases, the entrepreneurs that made the initial move suffer a loss.

Losses and profits are the selection mechanism of the market economy. When a firm makes a profit, its capital grows and its power to influence market events increases. When a firm suffers a loss, its capital shrinks and its power to influence market events wanes. Nineteenth-century economists recognized a similarity between the selection process of the market and the process of natural selection that Charles Darwin saw as the driving force in the evolution of plant and animal species: Innovation spurs many variations; profit and loss determine those that survive.

Three forces, then, are at work to drive the market process:

- Arbitrage and related forms of alertness to new opportunities, which use information in the form of prices to steer the economy toward an equilibrium.

- Innovation, which disrupts the old equilibrium and creates new opportunities for arbitrage.

- Selection through loss and profit, which enhances the likelihood of survival for innovations that move resources from lower- to higher-valued uses and weeds out those that move resources in the wrong direction.

As economists of the Austrian school are fond of pointing out, these forces taken together mean that the market is not chaotic even though it is rarely in equilibrium. The forces of entrepreneurship make the market process an orderly one, steering markets toward improved resource allocation, even during—in fact, especially during—episodes of disequilibrium.

Marketing as a Form of Entrepreneurship

The preceding discussion of entrepreneurship was very general. For a better understanding, it will be worthwhile to look at some examples of entrepreneurship in action in the world of business. One of the most fruitful places to look for examples of entrepreneurship is in the activity that businesspeople refer to as *marketing*.

Marketing means the process of finding out what customers want and channeling a flow of goods and services to meet those wants. Marketing is a topic often neglected by economists. For example, the models examined in Chapters 7 through 11 assume, for the most part, that the problem of marketing has been solved before the analysis begins. They are set in a world in which both firms and consumers are assumed already to know what kinds of goods and services will meet their wants and how they will be made available. The only function performed by the market in these models is that of providing a forum in which buyers and sellers can agree on the price of each good and the quantity to be sold. In this section, we go beyond the limits of the neoclassical models in order to take a look at the economics of marketing that maintains an emphasis on entrepreneurship.

Marketing
The process of finding out what customers want and channeling a flow of goods and services to meet those wants.

To organize the discussion, we will follow the traditional division of marketing into four activities. The first is creating a *product* that will meet consumer needs. The second is getting the product to a *place* where consumers can conveniently buy it—an activity that includes not only physical transportation but the whole process of wholesale and retail trade. The third is *promoting* the product through advertising, personal selling, and other means. The fourth—the one economists have not neglected—is putting the right *price* on the product. These four activities are often called the "four Ps" of marketing. As Exhibit 12.1 shows, the costs of the four Ps account for about half of all consumer spending in the United States. Let's look at the role that each activity plays in a competitive economy.

Competition and the Product

In a perfectly competitive market, the product—wheat, trucking services, or whatever—is thought of as given. Some oligopolies also have products that change little from year to year—the aluminum and cement industries come to mind (although someone with closer knowledge would probably be aware of changes in those products, too). But there are a great many markets in which shaping the product to fit consumer needs is a key element of competition.

Innovation, Diversity, and Quality

Innovation is one major aspect of product competition. Consider the case of stereo equipment. Here it is clear what customers want—music in their living rooms that sounds like a live performance. That is an ideal that is never quite reached, but long-playing records, metal-oxide cassette tapes, Dolby noise suppression systems, and compact disks each represent a step closer to it. The first competitor to take each step has at least a temporary advantage.

Diversity is another aspect of product competition. Consumers have different needs and tastes. Economists talk about "the market" for cars, but this

Exhibit 12.1   Marketing Costs and Consumer Spending

As this chart shows, marketing costs account for about half of all consumer spending. The costs and profits of wholesale and retail trade are the largest single item, followed by freight transportation. Advertising, although the most visible of marketing activities, accounts for only about 3 percent of the cost of consumer goods and services. All aspects of marketing are important to the process of competition.

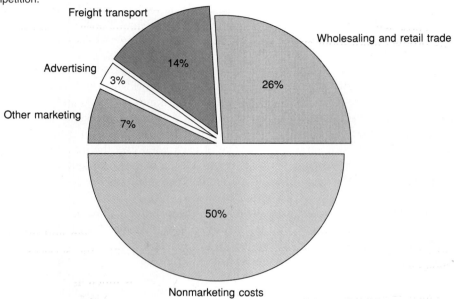

market is really composed of many segments: the markets for economy cars, vans, sports cars, and so on. Competition insures that products will be made that will meet the needs of consumers in each segment; a neglected segment will soon attract a firm in search of profits.

Quality is yet another dimension of product competition—one that has been getting more attention in recent years. The quality of many U.S.-made goods has been improving for years. Tires last longer; fabrics wash more easily; contact lenses give better vision. However, the demand for quality seems to have risen even more rapidly than the supply. Foreign firms—especially Japanese ones—have gained a competitive advantage in many markets by being the first to respond to this demand for quality. As U.S. firms scramble to catch up, consumers come out the winners.

Product Innovation and Market Performance

From time to time, however, economists have challenged the notion that product diversity is beneficial to consumers. One line of reasoning is that actions taken by a firm to distinguish its product more clearly from those of its rivals have the effect of making the firm's demand curve less elastic. The less elastic the demand curve, it is argued, the greater the gap between price and marginal cost in equilibrium and, hence, the less efficient the market.

As we saw in Chapter 11, this argument has been used in comparing monopolistic competition unfavorably with perfect competition. The defense of monopolistic competition turned, in part, on the notion that diversity itself is a good that benefits consumers even if they must pay more to get it. But that notion has its detractors, too.

The alleged problem is that some kinds of diversity add no objective value to the product. To be sure, it is good that consumers are offered a choice between snow tires and smooth-tread tires, since each serves a distinct purpose. But what about something like the toothpaste pump described in the article that leads off this chapter? Is it not blatant exploitation of consumers to make them pay more than before for the same product just because it is packaged differently?

Those who see product diversity as beneficial commonly answer that even silly product innovations such as toothpaste pumps should be judged in light of the principle of consumer sovereignty. So long as plain, boring old tubes share drugstore shelves with fun, fancy new pumps, consumers are not being exploited. Never mind that toothpaste pumps add nothing to the objective value of the product—in this case, its tooth-cleaning power. In a free market, the prices at which goods change hands reflect the subjective values that consumers place on them. Thus, toothpaste pumps must be adding subjective value for at least some consumers, or they would not sell given their higher prices.

Competition in Distribution

The second of the four Ps of marketing—place—refers to all the activities necessary for getting a product to consumers. It includes transportation and other aspects of physical distribution and—even more important—the services of wholesale and retail firms.

Innovation and diversity affect distribution systems as much as they affect products themselves. Tried-and-true methods of retailing such as supermarkets and department stores, which were radical innovations by entrepreneurs of the past, have now come under pressure from a new generation of entrepreneurs. On the one hand, specialized, boutique-type retailers and direct-mail companies are winning a bigger share of the wealthiest consumers. On the other, discount stores, off-price retailers, and warehouse-type food stores are making inroads among budget-conscious consumers. Often the prize in competition among manufacturing firms goes to those with the best distribution networks.

However, the patterns of distribution that arise in a competitive economy also have their critics. As Exhibit 12.1 shows, wholesale and retail trade—even when the transportation aspect of distribution is excluded—account for some $.26 out of every dollar consumers spend. What do people get in return for all they spend to support the vast wholesale and retail trade establishment? Why don't rational consumers bypass these "middlemen," as they used to be called?

The answer most commonly given by economists is that consumers are buying services with that $.26. Provision of information is one such service; visiting a car dealer or a department store is often the most efficient way for a consumer to learn about product availability and characteristics. Convenience is the service provided by many branches of retailing. It is the reason that a 7-Eleven store can charge more for a gallon of milk than the supermarket across the street. It is the reason that many people buy motor oil a quart at a time at the gas station instead of buying it by the case and servicing their cars in their driveways.

Consumers are not forced to buy the services that retailers offer. In an economy characterized by consumer sovereignty, there are low-cost, low-service options for buying almost any good. Clothing, toys, and groceries can be bought at off-price stores, where there are few clerks and incomplete selections but very low prices. Computers, tools, and veterinary supplies can be bought from discount mail-order houses; while this entails some waiting and the goods cannot be examined in advance, prices are much lower than in local stores. In some communities, consumer cooperatives have been formed for buying goods in bulk and reselling them to members at reduced prices. Even with all these available low-price alternatives, however, many people prefer to pay the extra $.26 on the dollar for the additional services they get at department stores and convenience markets, just as people often choose to eat in restaurants rather than preparing meals more cheaply at home.

Competition in Promotion

Advertising is the most visible aspect of competition in many markets—so visible, in fact, that many people are surprised to find that it accounts for only $.03 out of the consumer dollar, as shown in Exhibit 12.1. Advertising, together with other promotional activities such as personal selling, store displays, and public relations, is the communication link between producers and their customers.

A major part of promotion is spreading information. The models of consumer choice and perfect competition that we examined in earlier chapters begin from the assumption that consumers are well informed about the choices available to them, but in the real world information is a scarce resource and, as such, cannot be obtained without incurring an opportunity cost. One way in which consumers can get information is by reading publications such as *Consumer Reports* or *Car and Driver* that test and compare the products sold by many firms. This entails an opportunity cost to the consumer in the form of the publications' cost and the time taken to read them. Advertising, personal selling, and other promotional activities are another channel through which consumers can learn about prices, product features, and where to buy desired goods and services. These too have an opportunity cost, which consumers pay in the form of higher prices for advertised brands.

The marketplace allows for competition among these sources of information. It offers consumers a choice between nationally advertised brands and lower-priced local brands or unbranded "generic" products. It offers a choice between stores with many sales clerks and those with few. The fact that some firms find heavy spending on promotion profitable can be taken as an indication that advertising, personal selling, and the rest are, at least in some cases, an efficient means of providing information.

Advertising and Its Critics

However, it is well known that advertising does more than just inform consumers; it also shapes their tastes and, as shown in "Perspective 12.1," even their perceptions. The power of advertising to shape tastes and perceptions has made this aspect of marketing a subject of controversy.

One line of argument, used by economist John Kenneth Galbraith, among others, is that a distinction should be made between true wants and those created by advertising. In the critics' view, advertising that goes beyond a simple statement of the facts about a product is at best a waste and at worst harmful to consumer welfare. Others, however, doubt that there exist such things as true or natural wants other than the very basic needs for food, security, affection, self-esteem, and so on. Advertising may affect which goods people choose to satisfy

PERSPECTIVE   12.1

The Effect of Advertising on Consumer Perceptions

In an experiment to determine the effect of a well-known brand name on consumer preferences, 150 subjects from Detroit were presented with two plates, on each of which was a slice of turkey meat. Although the two slices were actually from the same turkey, they had different labels. One bore a brand name that was heavily advertised and well known in Detroit, and the other bore a name that was much less familiar. Of the 150 subjects, only 10 percent thought the two samples tasted alike; 56 percent expressed a strong preference for the known brand, and 34 percent preferred the unknown brand.

In another part of the experiment, 61 subjects were

presented with two plates. On one was a slice of tender turkey meat and on the other a slice of tough turkey meat. When no brand names were used, 49 of the subjects preferred the tender meat, 4 preferred the tough meat, and 8 could not tell the difference. After they had said which slice they preferred, they were asked to say which brand they thought the slices belonged to—the advertised brand or the unknown brand. Thirty-four of the subjects said that the turkey they preferred must have been the known brand; 18 thought the slice they liked was probably the unknown brand.

The experimenter concluded that advertising affected the consumers' perceptions even when the samples were identical and that when the samples were not identical, advertising created an expectation that the better sample would be the advertised one.

Source: James C. Makens, "Effect of Brand Preferences upon Consumers' Perceived Taste of Turkey Meat," *Journal of Applied Psychology* 49 (November 4, 1965): 261–263.

these needs. It may cause them to choose round-toed rather than square-toed boots to keep their feet dry, but that does no harm. Economists who take this point of view believe that efforts to limit consumer choice in the name of giving people what they "truly" want are a greater threat to consumer sovereignty than is advertising.

Advertising, Product Differentiation, and Barriers to Entry

In addition to creating false wants in consumers' minds, advertising and other promotional activities, according to critics, lead to reduced market performance. Advertising appears chiefly under oligopoly and monopolistic competition, market structures that have been criticized for poor performance for reasons examined in Chapter 11. Like product differentiation, advertising is said to make things worse because it overstates the differences among the products of various firms (or even creates differences where none exist). This, in turn, makes each firm's demand curve less elastic than it otherwise would be and increases the gap, in equilibrium, between price and marginal cost. Further, in the case of oligopoly advertising is seen as a barrier to entry by new firms and, as such, a force that leads to high levels of market concentration—and concentration, as we have seen, is linked with poor market performance in some economists' views.

The way in which advertising is said to act as a barrier to entry is by creating brand loyalties. Supposedly consumers who might otherwise treat all cola drinks as close substitutes are divided into opposing camps, some fiercely loyal to one brand, others to its rival. If brand loyalty were strong enough, each firm could raise its price with little fear that doing so would cause its customers to go elsewhere. Further, no firm would have to worry about the resulting high profits attracting new firms to the market, since the new firms not only would have to spend money to build plants and hire workers but would also have to mount expensive advertising campaigns.

In 1967, this view of the effects of advertising got a major boost from economists W. S. Comanor and T. A. Wilson. They looked at the statistical link between advertising spending and profits in 41 industries and reached the following conclusion:

> It is evident that . . . advertising is a highly profitable activity. Industries with high advertising outlays earn, on the average, at a profit rate which exceeds that of other industries by nearly four percentage points. This differential represents a 50 percent increase in profit rates. It is likely, moreover, that much of this profit rate differential is accounted for by the entry barriers created by advertising expenditures and by the resulting achievement of market power.[2]

However, other economists reject the idea that advertising is a barrier to entry. Instead, they see it as a key tool used by entrepreneurs to penetrate new markets and break down old barriers to entry. Yale Brozen is one who takes this view.[3] According to Brozen, existing firms have no advantage over new ones in buying advertising. Advertising agencies will sell their services to anyone who will pay their fees. In practice, he says, firms aim their advertising less at building up loyalty in their own customers than at getting their rivals' customers to try their products. The real way to create a barrier to entry and protect existing firms, in this view, would be to ban advertising. Then it would be far harder for a new firm to enter a market.

Brozen thinks that the Comanor and Wilson study is flawed by a confusion between categories of accounting and those of economic theory. Partly because of the way tax laws are written, accountants treat advertising as a current expense, like wages or supply purchases. However, advertising is in fact an investment that has long-term effects. A brand image takes years to develop, and after that it is a long-lasting asset for the company that created it. If advertising is viewed as an investment and its accumulated result as an asset, profits expressed as a percentage of assets will no longer be higher for firms that advertise heavily than for those that do not.

Advertising and Market Performance

The debate over the benefits of advertising and other marketing techniques seems to turn on two opposing views of the world. Would a world without advertising be one in which consumers treat all sources of supply as alike and move freely among them in response to small changes in price? Or would it be one in which lack of incentive and information causes consumers to cling to familiar sources of supply, giving each firm a monopoly with regard to its own customers? Further, does advertising set up barriers among firms, thereby adding to their monopoly power, or does it break down barriers, thus destroying that power? Several kinds of evidence might help answer these questions.

One form of evidence comes from studies of consumer behavior such as that described in "Perspective 12.1." There it is shown that advertising affected the

---

[2] W. S. Comanor and T. A. Wilson, "Advertising, Market Structure, and Performance," *Review of Economics and Statistics* 49 (November 1967): 437.

[3] For a representative exposition of Brozen's views, see Yale Brozen, "Entry Barriers: Advertising and Product Differentiation," in *Industrial Concentration: The New Learning*, ed. Harvey J. Goldschmid, H. Michael Mann, and J. Fred Weston (Boston: Little, Brown, 1974), 115–137.

perceived tastes of different samples of meat that all came from the same turkey. This study implies that advertising can increase brand loyalty. But other studies, such as that in the "Case for Discussion" in this chapter, suggest that brand loyalty can arise even in the absence of advertising.

Another kind of evidence comes from studies of how firms use advertising. For example, it has been shown that new products are advertised more heavily than old ones. This may indicate that makers of old products tend to depend on consumer loyalty and that advertising is a way of breaking down that loyalty. It has also been shown that consumers in markets in which advertising is heavy are less loyal to one brand than those in markets with light advertising. This too might indicate that advertising helps make consumers more willing to try substitute products.[4]

Perhaps most interesting of all, real-life experiments have been done in which advertising was introduced into a market in which it had been prohibited before. The market for legal services, discussed in "Perspective 12.2," is one such case. There the introduction of advertising seems to have spurred a wave of entrepreneurial activity by lawyers and, ultimately, to have improved market performance. Another study compared the prices of eyeglasses in states in which advertising was restricted with prices in states that permitted unlimited advertising for that product. It found the prices in states without advertising to be more than twice as high.[5] And so the debate goes on.

Price as a Marketing Tool

This brings us to price, the central tool of competition in economic models. How is this last of the four Ps viewed by marketing theorists? Does it fade to insignificance compared with product, place, and promotion, or does it still have a key role to play?

Writers on marketing agree with economists that good pricing decisions are vital to a firm's success. But in the real world, they say, the right price cannot be found by picking a point on a graph. Pricing decisions are entrepreneurial in nature too and must be coordinated with other marketing decisions in order to serve consumer wants as effectively as possible.

Take quality and variety, for example. Some consumers are willing to pay top price for top quality, while others would prefer less than top quality at a lower price. That is why premium-quality brands can be found next to standard-quality "house" labels on any supermarket shelf. Some consumers are willing to pay high prices to satisfy unusual tastes; others prefer to save by following the crowd in their tastes. Thus, for example, the few people who buy books of poetry pay more for them than those who prefer mass-market crime or romance novels.

Pricing is a key factor in distribution, too. Often the same goods are available at different prices in swanky boutiques and barnlike off-price outlets. Some consumers prefer one, some the other.

Finally, price and promotion interact. While some consumers will pay extra

---

[4]The article by Brozen cited in footnote 3 discusses and provides the references to these and similar studies.

[5]Lee Benham, "The Effect of Advertising on the Price of Eyeglasses," *Journal of Law and Economics* 15 (October 1972): 337–352.

PERSPECTIVE   12.2

Practicing Law in the Advertising Age

By today's standards, the ad seems staid, even timid. "Do you need a lawyer?" inquired Phoenix lawyers John Bates and Van O'Steen, promising "legal services at very reasonable rates."

The young lawyers' advertisement in the *Arizona Republic* for their legal clinic trumpeted no celebrity endorsements, no holiday-special discounts, but it drew the wrath of Arizona bar authorities. They accused the pair of violating a disciplinary rule, similar to that in force in almost every state, prohibiting lawyers from publicizing themselves through newspaper ads, radio or television announcements, or even display advertisements in the *Yellow Pages*.

That local disciplinary action ended up before the Supreme Court, in *Bates* v. *State Bar of Arizona*. In the view of many legal scholars, the decision handed down on June 27, 1977, revolutionized the practice of law in this country more than any other Supreme Court decision in history.

Rejecting the warnings of the organized bar that freeing lawyers to compete in the "hustle of the marketplace" would "tarnish the dignified public image of the profession," the high court ruled 5 to 4 that lawyers have a constitutional right to advertise their services.

Today advertising has become a way of life for many American lawyers. The practice of law has evolved into a more cutthroat, dollar-oriented business, a change due in large measure to the loosening of restrictions. And the debate outlined in the *Bates* case rages on.

Many lawyers are appalled at what they regard as the shameful spectacle of lawyers hawking their wares on billboards and matchbook covers. Retired chief justice Warren E. Burger has said he would "dig ditches" before resorting to advertising and bemoaned the marketing of legal services like "other commodities from mustard, cosmetics and laxatives to used cars."

Indeed, some ads have been tasteless. "Holiday special—give that spouse of yours something he or she has been wanting for a long time—a divorce," a Florida lawyer's ad urged.

But others—even some officials of the legal establishment, which battled vigorously against the *Bates* result—view advertising as a healthy unleashing of market forces that has cut the cost of basic legal services for many consumers, once befuddled about where to turn for legal help.

In a 1983 study of the effect of advertising on the cost of legal services, the Federal Trade Commission concluded that fees for legal services such as wills, bankruptcies, uncontested divorces, and uncomplicated accident cases were 5 to 13 percent lower in the cities that had the fewest restrictions on advertising.

"As advertising increases in the legal service market, prices will decline," said the FTC, which surveyed 3,200 lawyers in 17 states.

Advertising "forced lawyers to become more efficient," said Gail Meyers, a founding partner of Jacoby & Meyers, a 150-office legal chain that is one of the country's heaviest advertisers. "In midtown Manhattan an uncontested divorce cost $1,500 thirteen years ago," she said. "Our fee now is about $500."

A 1979 American Bar Foundation survey of 74 Los Angeles residents found that the 22 who went to Jacoby & Meyers were more satisfied with their lawyers' services than the 52 who went to traditional firms.

Source: Ruth Marcus, "Practicing Law in the Advertising Age," *The Washington Post*, June 30, 1987, A6. © 1987 *The Washington Post*, reprinted with permission.

for advertised brands, others prefer low-priced generic goods that don't even have brand names.

In sum, when all aspects of marketing are taken into account, competition begins to look like a much more complex process than it appears to be on a graph, where price and quantity are the only variables. It is much less a matter of calculating a maximum on the basis of given conditions and much more an issue of entrepreneurship—of looking for new possibilities, utilizing new ways of doing things, being alert to new opportunities, and overcoming old limits.

Entrepreneurship and Market Dynamics

In marketing, entrepreneurial energies are largely focused on creating new products or shifting demand curves for existing ones. Now we turn our attention to entrepreneurship from the standpoint of efficiency in production. Up to this point, our discussions of economic performance have concentrated on static efficiency—the ability of an economy to get the greatest possible amount of consumer satisfaction with given resources and technology. Static efficiency is a measure of how close an economy comes to its production possibility frontier. Now we turn to the issue of the economy's dynamic efficiency—its success in increasing the rate of output per unit of resources. Dynamic efficiency is a measure of the rate at which the production possibility frontier shifts outward over time.

Of the two kinds of efficiency, dynamic efficiency is much more important in the long run. In the past, the most important single factor in U.S. economic growth was gains in knowledge, that is, innovation and technological change. Economic growth from this source alone has been estimated at 1.5 percent per year out of an average growth rate of about 2.5 to 3 percent for the post–World War II period.[6] The remaining economic growth is due to capital accumulation, population growth, increased education, and other factors. The contribution of innovation and technological change is very large compared to the loss in static efficiency caused by monopolistic and oligopolistic market structures. The very highest serious estimates of loss from monopoly and oligopoly have been about 2.5 percent of gross national product. Innovation and technological change add more than that to GNP every two years.

The Schumpeter Hypothesis

If every policy that promotes static efficiency also contributed to dynamic efficiency, the distinction would hardly matter. However, there are reasons to think that this may not necessarily be the case. One key issue is the relationship between market structure and market performance. In earlier chapters, we saw that neoclassical models imply that perfectly competitive markets are the most efficient in the static sense. According to these models, monopoly is the least efficient in the static sense, with oligopoly and monopolistic competition lying somewhere in between. However, when efficiency is viewed in dynamic terms, the superiority of perfect competition is not so clear. It has been argued that the traditional categories of market structure are largely irrelevant to market performance measured in dynamic terms. This view is often referred to as the *Schumpeter hypothesis*, named after the Austrian economist Joseph Schumpeter, who first brought it to widespread attention (see "Who Said It? Who Did It? 12.2"). Schumpeter and others suggested that in some cases large, oligopolistic firms may very well outperform small, perfectly competitive firms in dynamic terms.

According to Schumpeter, the source of innovation and growth is competition—but competition among entrepreneurs, not the kind found in perfectly

Static efficiency
The ability of an economy to get the greatest degree of consumer satisfaction from given resources and technology.

Dynamic efficiency
The ability of an economy to increase consumer satisfaction through growth and innovation.

[6] See Edward F. Denison, *Accounting for U.S. Economic Growth, 1929–1969* (Washington, D.C.: The Brookings Institution, 1974), 124–150.

Joseph Schumpeter on Competition and Entrepreneurship

Joseph Schumpeter was born in Austria in 1883. He studied law at the University of Vienna and attended lectures by the leading economists of the day, including some of the founders of the Austrian school. He served briefly as minister of finance after World War I. In 1932 he left Austria for Harvard University, where he wrote most of the works for which he is known today.

Schumpeter had little use for the kind of economics that reduces everything to graphs and equations. He

Source: Joseph Schumpeter, *Capitalism, Socialism, and Democracy* (New York: Harper & Row, 1942), 84–85, 106.

thought economic theories paid too little attention to the role of the entrepreneur. He saw competition among entrepreneurs rather than the abstract notion of perfect competition as the source of economic progress. As he wrote in *Capitalism, Socialism, and Democracy,*

> The competition that counts is the competition from the new commodity, the new technology, the new source of supply, the new type of organization (the largest scale unit of control, for instance)—competition which commands a decisive cost or quality advantage and which strikes not at the margins of the profits and the outputs of the existing firms, but at their foundations and their very lives. This kind of competition is as much more effective than the other as a bombardment is in comparison with forcing a door, and so much more important that it becomes a matter of comparative indifference whether competition in the ordinary sense functions more or less promptly; the powerful lever that in the long run expands output and brings down prices is in any case made of other stuff. . . .

"In this respect," Schumpeter added elsewhere, "perfect competition is not only impossible but inferior, and has no title to being set up as a model of ideal efficiency."

competitive markets. He saw two ways in which entrepreneurial competition promotes dynamic efficiency even when it leads, at least temporarily, to some degree of monopoly power.

First, Schumpeter points out, the hope of achieving monopoly power is often the entrepreneur's chief incentive for competition. The first firm to obtain new knowledge and put it to use is able to make pure economic profits because its new discovery gives it a temporary monopoly. If each new product had to be brought out at a price that just covered cost, or if each cost-reducing innovation had to be followed by a matching reduction in price, there would be little reason to innovate at all. If the first firm to adjust to changing conditions were unable to increase the gap between costs and revenues by doing so, there would be no incentive to be first. Competition among entrepreneurs is competition for monopoly power, at least in the short run. In this sense, monopoly is not the opposite of competition but a normal result of it.

Second, monopoly power acts to spur competition. This is true in the sense that an industry in which monopoly profits are being made tends to attract entrepreneurs from the outside. This applies both to the entry of new firms and to indirect competition by substitutes. For example, OPEC's attempts to exploit its monopoly power in the 1970s led to a speedup in the rate of oil exploration and also to innovations in alternative energy sources and conservation techniques. In this sense, monopoly is an impetus to competition.

Can the Schumpeter Hypothesis Be Tested?

The Schumpeter hypothesis poses a sweeping challenge to economic theory and policy. Not surprisingly, many attempts have been made to verify or refute it by studying the data on economic growth, market concentration, and innovation. The results to date, however, have been inconclusive.[7]

The main problem in testing the Schumpeter hypothesis lies in measuring innovation. Schumpeter had in mind a fairly broad view of innovation. Inventing new products or techniques, figuring out how to apply new inventions, working out new forms of business organization, finding new ways of financing investment, and creating new methods of marketing and distribution were, to Schumpeter, all major sources of dynamic efficiency. But most of them clearly can be measured only indirectly, and some not at all. As a result, attempts to test the Schumpeter hypothesis have had to make do with rather crude substitutes for some of its central concepts.

One indirect test has used research and development (R&D) spending to indicate firms' innovative efforts. The answer to the simple question "Do large firms in concentrated industries account for more than their share of all R&D spending?" seems to be yes. The 400 to 500 largest firms, each with 5,000 or more employees, account for 80 to 90 percent of all R&D spending and only 25 to 30 percent of all output. This alone is enough to suggest that the Schumpeter hypothesis cannot be dismissed out of hand.

However, a number of qualifications must be added. For example, using patented investments rather than R&D spending as a measure of innovative activity appears to weaken the link between concentration and innovation. Also, such factors as the nature of the industry's product or the scientific environment in which the industry operates seem to have a major effect on innovative activity. Finally, some studies have suggested that size of firms and degree of market concentration affect innovation only up to a certain threshold, with giant firms having no advantage over firms that are merely large.

Perhaps the safest conclusion is that innovation—in Schumpeter's sense—is simply too complex to be subjected to quantitative analysis. Looking at all the studies in perspective, we find that under favorable conditions firms of all sizes in markets with all degrees of concentration are able to contribute to the dynamic efficiency of the economy as a whole. This implies that neither a policy of breaking up large firms into smaller ones nor one of welding small firms into larger ones can be counted on to speed the pace of innovation. The ability of large corporations to assign R&D teams to solve tough technical problems is important, but so is the flash of insight that may come to a lone inventor. In short, for all we know, the present mix of large and small firms may be just about right from the viewpoint of dynamic efficiency.

Looking Ahead

In this chapter, we have tried to expand our understanding of how markets work by adding an entrepreneurial dimension to the static neoclassical models intro-

---

[7]For a survey of these efforts, see Jesse W. Markham, "Concentration: A Stimulus or Retardant to Innovation?" in *Industrial Concentration: The New Learning*, ed. Harvey J. Goldschmid, H. Michael Mann, and J. Fred Weston (Boston: Little, Brown, 1974), 247–272.

duced earlier. The resulting view of the economy cannot be captured so neatly in graphic form, but it is in important ways more realistic.

As we continue our discussion of microeconomics, we will make use both of formal, neoclassical models and of the insights regarding entrepreneurship contributed by economists of the Austrian school and others. Especially when we encounter issues of economic policy, as we will in many of the following chapters, it will be important to keep both perspectives in mind.

Summary

1. **What role does entrepreneurship play in bringing order to the market process even when markets are not in equilibrium?** Economists of the Austrian school view the market as a place in which spontaneous order is maintained even when the market is not in equilibrium. The activities of entrepreneurs are crucial to the market process through which this order is maintained. *Arbitrage* uses information in the form of prices to steer the economy toward an equilibrium, although conditions may change again before equilibrium is reached. Innovation disrupts the old equilibrium and creates new opportunities for arbitrage. Selection through loss and profit enhances the likelihood that beneficial innovations will survive.

2. **How do economists view the area of business activity known as *marketing*?** Many examples of entrepreneurship at work can be found in marketing. *Marketing* means finding out what customers want and channeling a flow of goods and services to meet those wants. It consists of four activities: making a product that will meet consumer needs; getting it to a place where consumers can buy it conveniently; promoting it through advertising, personal selling, and other means; and putting the right price on it.

3. **How does advertising affect market performance?** Some economists view advertising as a barrier to entry of a market by new firms and a source of monopoly profits. Others dispute these claims, contending that advertising is used more by entrepreneurs entering a market than by existing firms. They also suggest that if more realistic accounting concepts are used, firms that advertise heavily are not more profitable, on the average, than other firms.

4. **How does market structure affect efficiency in both a static and a dynamic sense?** *Static efficiency* means the ability of an economy to get the greatest amount of consumer satisfaction from given resources and technology. *Dynamic efficiency* means achieving growth in the rate of output per unit of resources. Joseph Schumpeter suggested that market structure, as conventionally understood, may have little to do with dynamic efficiency and that at least in some cases, rel-

atively concentrated markets may actually be more dynamically efficient than perfectly competitive ones. In his view, the hope of achieving at least a temporary monopoly is a spur to innovation. Modern research suggests that this is probably true in at least some markets, though not necessarily in all.

Terms for Review

- arbitrage
- marketing
- static efficiency
- dynamic efficiency

Questions for Review

1. What three aspects of entrepreneurship interact to insure that the market process will be orderly even when the market is not in equilibrium?

2. What are the "four Ps" of marketing?

3. How is arbitrage important in establishing an efficient pattern of international trade?

4. Use a production possibility frontier to show the difference between static and dynamic efficiency.

5. How did Schumpeter think market structure was related to dynamic efficiency? What have tests of his hypothesis shown?

Problems and Topics for Discussion

1. **Examining the lead-off case.** How does the example of toothpaste pumps illustrate entrepreneurship and what Austrian economists call the *market process?* How does the case illustrate marketing? Do you think toothpaste pumps cater to "true" or "false" consumer needs, or is this an invalid distinction?

2. **The "four Ps" of marketing.** Look through recent issues of such business magazines as *Fortune*, *Forbes*, and *Business Week* for examples of each of the four Ps of marketing. Do the examples bear out the notion that advertising is an entrepreneurial activity?

3. **Advertising and its critics.** Critics of advertising often claim that it causes consumers to buy things they don't "really" want or need. Can you think of an example of something that you yourself buy because of advertising but don't really want or need? If so, why do you buy it? If not, do you think you are an exception—that advertising has no adverse effect on you but does on other people? Discuss.

4. **Entrepreneurship.** Review "Economics in the News 3.1" (page 58) and "Economics in the News 3.2" (page 68). How does each case illustrate what economists of the Austrian school call the *market process?* What aspects of entrepreneurship are shown in each case?

Case for Discussion

Brand Loyalty without Brands

The brewing industry is an oligopoly dominated by a few major brewers.

In a study of brand loyalty, a random sample of 60 beer drinkers was drawn from Stanford University students living in married-student housing. The subjects were told that they were taking part in a marketing test of three types of beer produced by a local brewer.

Once a week the subjects were presented, in their homes, with a chance to choose from among three bottles labeled "M," "L," and "P." They were told that brand M was a high-priced beer, brand L a medium-priced beer, and brand P a bargain-priced beer. The subjects did not have to pay for their beer; but to make the price difference more realistic, the medium-priced beer had a $.02 "refund" taped to the bottle while the low-priced beer had a $.05 "refund." The subjects could keep the refunds.

In point of fact, the three brands of beer were all drawn from the same production run at the brewery; only the labels differed. However, this did not prevent the development of fierce brand loyalty by many of the subjects. (Subjects were considered to be brand loyal if they chose the same brand four times in a row.) Although at first the subjects experimented with the three brands, by the end of 24 trials 57 of the 60 had developed brand loyalty. Of those 57, 26 chose brand M, 12 brand L, and 19 brand P.

Since the beer was all the same, it is surprising how firmly set in their opinions some of the subjects became. One subject reported, "M is a good, strong, malty beer, but I like L because it is lighter. Mmm!!! P would poison me—make me ill." Another subject, who developed a strong taste for P, once tried a bottle of M and reported, "Worst I've ever had; you couldn't give it away."

Source: J. Douglass McConnell, "The Development of Brand Loyalty: An Experimental Study," *Journal of Marketing Research* 5 (February 1968): 13–19. Photo Source: Copyright © B. E. White, 1987. All Rights Reserved.

Questions

1. Critics of advertising blame it for creating brand loyalty. This, in turn, is said to create barriers to entry in oligopolistic industries and to make the demand curves of firms in monopolistically competitive industries less elastic than they otherwise would be. In both cases, advertising is thought to contribute to poor market performance. What does this case suggest about the connection between advertising and brand loyalty? Does it support a policy of setting limits on advertising as a means of improving market performance in the beer industry?

2. Economies of scale have led to a high degree of concentration in the brewing

industry. That industry is now an oligopoly dominated by a few major brewers. Yet those brewers still produce a great many brands of beer. If one looked only at the number of brand names displayed in a typical store, one would think brewing was an example of monopolistic competition. What does brand loyalty have to do with this type of market structure? Do you think market performance would be improved by limiting each large firm to just one brand? By returning to a situation in which each brand was made by a different firm? Discuss.

Suggestions for Further Reading

Galbraith, John Kenneth. *The Affluent Society*. Boston: Houghton Mifflin, 1958.

Contains an attack on advertising as a violation of consumer sovereignty.

Goldschmid, Harvey J., Michael H. Mann, and Fred J. Weston, eds. *Industrial Concentration: The New Learning*. Boston: Little, Brown, 1974.

Chapter 3 is a debate between Yale Brozen and H. Michael Mann on advertising as a barrier to competition. In Chapter 5, Jesse W. Markham discusses market concentration and innovation, citing several attempts to test the Schumpeter hypothesis.

Kirzner, Israel M., ed. *Subjectivism, Intelligibility and Economic Understanding*. New York: New York University Press, 1986.

A collection of essays by members of the modern Austrian school. The papers by Jack High and Urlich Fehl are particularly useful in providing an overview of the theory of the market process.

Schumpeter, Joseph. *Capitalism, Socialism, and Democracy*. New York: Harper & Row, 1942.

Part 2 of this book contains Schumpeter's discussion of the link between market concentration and dynamic efficiency.

von Hayek, Friedrich A. "The Non Sequitur of the Dependence Effect." *Southern Economic Journal* 27 (April 1961).

A critique of Galbraith's attack on consumer sovereignty.

Factor Markets

Part Four

13 Pricing in Factor Markets

After reading this chapter, you will understand . . .

- The role that factor markets play in determining how and for whom goods are produced.

- What determines demand for a factor of production.

- What determines the supply curve for labor.

- What are the characteristics of equilibrium in a competitive labor market.

- What are the characteristics of labor market equilibrium with only one or a few employers.

- Why wages are not the same for all labor markets and all individuals within a labor market.

Before reading this chapter, make sure you know the meaning of . . .

- Income and substitution effects (Chapter 7)

- Marginal physical product and diminishing returns (Chapter 8)

- Perfect competition (Chapter 9)

- Theory of monopoly (Chapter 10)

Helping Workers Work Smarter

Before the line began to roll at General Motors' new truck plant in Fort Wayne, Indiana, each assembly line worker received 400 to 500 hours of paid training. Electricians and other skilled maintenance workers got 1,000 hours apiece—the equivalent of almost 6 months—with full pay and benefits. All told, training for the Fort Wayne work force came to more than 1 million hours. The cost: an estimated $32 million in wages and benefits alone and millions more for instructors and facilities. The factory itself cost $500 million.

Though the amount of training the Fort Wayne workers got is extraordinary by the standards of most industries, it represents a powerful new trend. Many companies are coming to regard training expenses as no less a part of their capital costs than plant and equipment. Anthony Patrick Carnevale, chief economist for the Washington-based American Society for Training and Development, a professional group, estimates that corporate expenditures on formal training and education, away from the office or shop floor, now total roughly $30 billion a year, or almost a third of what the United States spends on all college-level education. That's a conservative estimate, Carnevale says. When you add wage and benefit costs, the total may well match the $238 billion annual bill for all public education.

Less than 1 percent of that goes for remedial teaching to make up for the failures of the American educational system. Most reflects the demands of the second industrial revolution spreading through the United States. The factory Henry Ford created is scrap, even if some backward managements haven't realized it yet. At the turn of the century, industrial engineer Frederich W. Taylor's hated inspectors, stopwatches in hand, tried to turn jobs and workers into irreducible, brainless minimums of time and motion. But today's workplace is filled with sophisticated machinery, and it is increasingly organized to make workers responsible for what they do. The workers at Fort Wayne, for example, learned how to handle the plant's new equipment and master new quality-control tech-

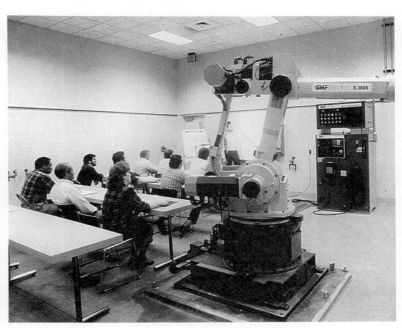

Corporate expenditures on formal training and education total roughly $30 billion a year.

niques. But they were also schooled in such subjects as team production systems, group problem-solving methods, and the tough competition their products would face.

The results at many companies have been dramatic. For example, Motorola spends an amount equal to 2.6 percent of its wage bill on training each year. Bill Wiggenhorn, training head at Motorola, says, "We've documented the savings from the statistical process control methods and problem-solving methods we've trained our people in. We're running at a rate of return of about 30 times the dollars invested—which is why we've gotten pretty good support from senior management."

Source: Michael Brody, "Helping Workers Work Smarter," *FORTUNE*, June 8, 1987, 86–88. © 1987 Time Inc. All rights reserved. Reprinted with permission. Photo Source: Courtesy of General Motors Corporation.

Factor markets

The markets in which the factors of production—labor, capital, and natural resources—are bought and sold.

THE issue of worker training draws attention to an important set of markets to which we have referred only indirectly up to this point: **factor markets,** which are the markets in which labor, capital, and natural resources are bought and sold. Factor markets perform two major functions in a market economy: They help determine (1) how goods and services are produced and (2) for whom they are produced. In this and the next two chapters, we will look at both functions.

Factor markets are important in determining how goods and services are produced because most goods and services can be produced in more than one way. Wheat, for example, can be grown by means of extensive cultivation of large areas of land with a lot of machinery and little labor or with intensive cultivation of small areas with little machinery and much labor. Cars can be made using a large work force of relatively unskilled workers or a smaller work force of more highly trained workers. The choice of production methods depends on the relative prices of the factors. As those prices change, production methods can change too. Factors that are relatively cheap are used intensively; those that are relatively expensive are used sparingly.

At the same time, factor markets help determine for whom output is produced, because most people earn their incomes by selling whatever factors of production they own. The majority sell their labor services. Later in the chapter, we will see some of the considerations—including training and education—that determine how much they receive for these services. Many people also sell or rent capital or natural resources that they own. Because markets determine factor prices, they also determine how much of the total product will go to the owners of labor services, capital, and natural resources.

In the first part of this chapter, we will outline marginal productivity theory—the foundation of the economics of factor markets. Here we will treat factors of production, including labor, as though they consisted of identical, interchangeable units. Later in the chapter, we will apply the theory of marginal productivity to the more complex reality of factor markets—especially labor markets—in which each unit of the factor is a unique individual. In Chapter 14, we will take up the topic of labor unions and collective bargaining. Finally, in Chapter 18 we will examine the problem of poverty. There we will see how the operation of factor markets helps determine the incidence of poverty and discuss government policies aimed at reducing or eliminating poverty.

The Demand for Factors of Production

In many ways, factor markets are much like the product markets we have already studied. The theories of supply and demand and the tools of marginal analysis apply to factor markets just as they do to product markets. However, factor markets differ from product markets in one major respect: In factor markets, firms are the buyers and households are the sellers, rather than the other way around. A theory of the demand for factors of production must be based on the same considerations of price, revenue, and profit that determine the supply of products. A theory of factor supply must be an extension of the theory of consumer choice.

In taking the first steps toward a theory of factor demand, we will assume, as always, that firms aim to maximize their profits. Each profit-maximizing firm must take three things into account when it buys factors of production: (1) the amount of output produced by a unit of the factor in question; (2) the revenue derived from the sale of the output that will be produced; and (3) the cost of obtaining the factor.

Marginal Physical Product

In Chapter 6, we defined the *marginal physical product of a factor* as the increase in output that results from a one-unit increase in the input of that factor when the amount of all other factors used stays the same. For example, if using one additional worker-hour of labor in a light bulb factory yields an additional output of five light bulbs when no other input to the production process is increased, the marginal physical product of labor in that factory is five bulbs per hour.

The Law of Diminishing Returns

As Chapter 6 showed, the marginal physical product of a factor varies as the amount of it used changes, other things being equal. In particular, as the quantity of a single factor increases with the quantities of all other factor inputs remaining fixed, a point will be reached beyond which the marginal physical product of the variable factor will decline. This principle is known as the *law of diminishing returns*.

Exhibit 13.1 shows total and marginal physical product curves for a firm that is subject to the law of diminishing returns over the range from 0 to 20 units of factor input. (At this point, it does not matter whether the factor in question is labor, capital, or natural resources; the principle is the same for all.) As the amount of this factor is increased with the amount of all other factors used held constant, output increases—but at a diminishing rate. The first unit of the factor yields a marginal physical product of 20 units of output, the second a marginal physical product of 19 units of output, and so on. After the twentieth unit of output, marginal physical product drops to zero. This implies that some ceiling has been reached such that adding more of the variable factor cannot produce more output unless the inputs of some of the fixed factors are also increased. For example, if the variable factor is labor, it may be that adding more than 20 workers will do nothing to increase output unless the amount of, say, machinery available for the workers' use is increased as well. Beyond 20 units of output,

Exhibit 13.1 Total and Marginal Physical
Product of a Factor of Production

As the quantity of one factor increases with the quantity of
other factors remaining unchanged, total physical product
increases, but at a decreasing rate. As parts a and c of this
exhibit show, marginal physical product decreases as the
quantity of the employed factor increases. This decrease is a
direct result of the law of diminishing returns.

(a)

Quantity of Factor (1)	Total Physical Product (2)	Marginal Physical Product (3)
0	0	
1	20	20
2	39	19
3	57	18
4	74	17
5	90	16
6	105	15
7	119	14
8	132	13
9	144	12
10	155	11
11	165	10
12	174	9
13	182	8
14	189	7
15	195	6
16	200	5
17	204	4
18	207	3
19	209	2
20	210	1

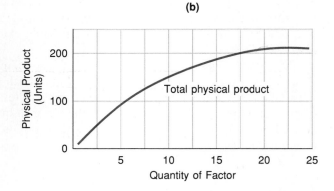

(b)

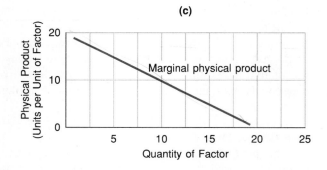

(c)

where the marginal physical product of the variable factor drops to zero, the total
physical product curve becomes horizontal.

Marginal Revenue Product

To determine what quantity of each factor of production it should buy to maximize its profit, a firm must take into account the revenue it will earn from the
sale of the output of an added unit of factor input as well as the size of the
marginal physical product. Here a new term will be useful. The change in revenue that results from the sale of the output produced by one additional unit of
factor input is called the **marginal revenue product** of that factor.

The Perfectly Competitive Firm

We begin with the case of a perfectly competitive firm. As Chapter 9 showed,
such a firm is a price taker. It faces a perfectly elastic demand curve so that the
quantity of output it produces has no effect on the price at which its output is
sold. Marginal revenue for the competitive firm thus equals the price of the

Marginal revenue product
The change in revenue that
results from the sale of the
output produced by one
additional unit of a factor of
production.

firm's output, which is constant for all quantities of output. For such a firm, then, marginal revenue product equals the **value of marginal product,** that is, marginal physical product times the output's price.

Value of marginal product
Marginal physical product times the product's per-unit price.

Exhibit 13.2 gives an example. The marginal physical product schedule is the same as that given in Exhibit 13.1, and a constant price of $1 per unit of output is assumed.

The Imperfectly Competitive Firm

If the firm is not perfectly competitive, the price at which it sells its output will tend to vary as the amount of output changes. Any firm facing a negatively sloped demand curve must decrease the price at which it sells its product each time it wants to increase the quantity sold. Because the price per unit decreases as output increases, marginal revenue per unit of output is always less than price per unit for a monopolist. It follows, then, that the marginal revenue product for such a firm is less than the value of marginal product.

Exhibit 13.3 shows how marginal revenue product is calculated for a firm with a negatively sloped demand curve. The exhibit uses the same total physical product schedule as in Exhibits 13.1 and 13.2. Column 3 gives the firm's product demand curve, showing that the price at which output can be sold drops from $1.40 per unit at 20 units of output to $.45 at 210 units. Multiplying price

---

Exhibit 13.2   Marginal Revenue Product for a Typical Price-Taking Firm

For a price-taking firm, the marginal revenue product of a factor equals the value of marginal product, that is, the factor's marginal physical product times the product's price. This exhibit assumes that the product price is $1 per unit and that marginal physical product is the same as in Exhibit 13.1.

Quantity of Factor (1)	Total Physical Product (2)	Marginal Physical Product (3)	Revenue per Unit (Price) (4)	Marginal Revenue Product (5)
0	0			
1	20	20	$1	$20
2	39	19	1	19
3	57	18	1	18
4	74	17	1	17
5	90	16	1	16
6	105	15	1	15
7	119	14	1	14
8	132	13	1	13
9	144	12	1	12
10	155	11	1	11
11	165	10	1	10
12	174	9	1	9
13	182	8	1	8
14	189	7	1	7
15	198	6	1	6
16	200	5	1	5
17	204	4	1	4
18	207	3	1	3
19	209	2	1	2
20	210	1	1	1

by total physical product gives the total revenue that corresponds to each quantity of factor input, shown in column 4.

The differences among successive entries in the total revenue column give the marginal revenue product data, shown in column 5. For example, as the amount of factor input increases from 4 to 5 units, total output increases from 74 to 90 units, while the price falls from $1.13 per unit to $1.05. As column 4 shows, total revenue increases from $83.62 when 4 units of factor input are used to $94.50 when 5 units of factor input are used. This gives a marginal revenue product of $10.88 in the range from 4 to 5 units of factor input.

It can be verified that this marginal revenue product is less than the value of marginal product (not shown in the exhibit). The product price is $1.13 when 4 units of the factor are used and $1.05 when 5 units of the factor are used, thus averaging $1.09 over the corresponding output range. Multiplying this by the marginal physical product of 16 (column 6 of the exhibit) gives a value of marginal product of $17.44 at the midpoint of the output range in question, compared to a marginal revenue product of $10.88.

Exhibit 13.3   Marginal Revenue Product for a Monopolist

This exhibit shows how marginal revenue product varies as the quantity of factor input changes for a firm that faces a negatively sloped demand curve for its product. As column 3 shows, price falls as outputs increase in accordance with the demand for the firm's product. Total revenue begins to decrease after 10 units of output, as marginal revenue per unit of output becomes negative, even though marginal physical product remains positive. Marginal revenue product can be calculated either as the difference between each entry in the total revenue column or as the product of marginal physical product and marginal revenue per unit of output.

Quantity of Factor (1)	Total Physical Product (2)	Price of Output (3)	Total Revenue (4)	Marginal Revenue Product (5)	Marginal Physical Product (6)	Marginal Revenue per Unit of Output (7)
0	0	—	0			
1	20	$1.40	$ 28.00	$28.00	20	$1.40
2	39	1.31	50.90	22.90	19	1.21
3	57	1.22	69.26	18.36	18	1.02
4	74	1.13	83.62	14.36	17	.84
5	90	1.05	94.50	10.88	16	.68
6	105	.98	102.38	7.88	15	.52
7	119	.91	107.70	5.32	14	.38
8	132	.84	110.88	3.18	13	.24
9	144	.78	112.32	1.44	12	.12
10	155	.73	112.38	.06	11	.01
11	165	.68	111.38	−1.00	10	−.10
12	174	.63	109.62	−1.76	9	−.20
13	182	.59	107.38	−2.24	8	−.28
14	189	.56	104.90	−2.48	7	−.35
15	195	.53	102.38	−2.52	6	−.42
16	200	.50	100.00	−2.38	5	−.47
17	204	.48	97.92	−2.08	4	−.52
18	207	.47	96.26	−1.66	3	−.55
19	209	.46	95.10	−1.16	2	−.58
20	210	.45	94.50	−.60	1	−.60

Note: Figures in columns 3, 4, 5, and 7 are rounded to the nearest cent.

As the price continues to fall, marginal revenue eventually becomes negative. Beyond that point, additional units of factor input, even though they increase total physical product, reduce total revenue. The turning point comes at 10 units of factor input. Beyond that amount, marginal revenue product is negative even though marginal physical product remains positive.

At every level of factor input, the marginal revenue product of the factor equals the marginal physical product times the marginal revenue per unit of output. This relationship is shown in columns 5 through 7 of Exhibit 13.3. The marginal revenue figures in column 7 are expressed in terms of dollars per unit of output, whereas those in column 5 are expressed in terms of dollars per unit of factor input.

Marginal Factor Cost

The third thing a firm must consider in determining the profit-maximizing quantity of a factor is the cost of obtaining each additional unit of that factor—its **marginal factor cost.**

To keep things simple for the moment, let us consider only the case in which a firm is a price taker in the market where it buys its factors of production. This will happen if the firm is only one of a large number of firms that are competing to hire that particular factor and if the amount of the factor it uses is only a small fraction of the total used by all firms. For a firm that buys as a price taker, marginal factor cost equals the factor's market price. For example, if the market wage rate for typists is $7 an hour, the marginal factor cost for this particular type of labor is $7 an hour for any firm that is a price taker in the market for typists.

Marginal factor cost
The amount by which a firm's total factor cost must increase in order for the firm to obtain an additional unit of that factor of production.

Profit Maximization

In order to maximize profits, a firm must hire just enough of each factor of production to equalize marginal revenue product and marginal factor cost. If marginal revenue product exceeds marginal factor cost, hiring one more unit of the factor will add more to the revenue than to the cost and, hence, will increase profit. If marginal factor cost exceeds marginal revenue product, *reducing* input of that factor by one unit will reduce cost by more than revenue and thus increase profit. Only when marginal revenue product and marginal factor cost are equal will it be impossible for any change in factor input to raise profit. In equation form, this rule can be stated as

$$\text{mfc} = \text{mrp},$$

where mfc stands for marginal factor cost and mrp for marginal revenue product. The rule applies both to a firm that is a perfect competitor in its output market and to a monopolist.

Exhibit 13.4 illustrates this profit maximization rule. Both the table and the corresponding graph assume that the firm is a perfect competitor in the output market and sells its product at $1 per unit, as in Exhibit 13.2. The firm is also assumed to be a price taker in the factor market, buying inputs of the factor at $5 per unit. Note that profit rises as more of the factor is purchased—up to the fifteenth unit of input. The firm just breaks even on the purchase of the sixteenth unit of input, and thereafter profit declines. It is between the fifteenth and sixteenth units of factor input that marginal revenue product becomes exactly equal to marginal factor cost.

Exhibit 13.4   Profit Maximization for a Price-Taking Firm

Maximizing profits requires that a firm buy just enough of each factor of production to
equalize marginal revenue product and marginal factor cost. Here it is assumed that the firm
is a price taker, as in Exhibit 13.2. The point of profit maximization falls between 15 and 16
units of input.

(a)

Quantity of Factor (1)	Marginal Revenue Product (2)	Marginal Factor Cost (3)	Total Variable Cost (4)	Fixed Costs (5)	Total Revenue (6)	Total Profit (7)
1			$ 5	$100	$ 20	−$85
2	$19	$5	10	100	39	−71
3	18	5	15	100	57	−58
4	17	5	20	100	74	−46
5	16	5	25	100	90	−35
6	15	5	30	100	105	−25
7	14	5	35	100	119	−16
8	13	5	40	100	132	−8
9	12	5	45	100	144	−1
10	11	5	50	100	155	5
11	10	5	55	100	165	10
12	9	5	60	100	174	14
13	8	5	65	100	182	17
14	7	5	70	100	189	19
15	6	5	75	100	195	20
16	5	5	80	100	200	20
17	4	5	85	100	204	19
18	3	5	90	100	207	17
19	2	5	95	100	209	14
20	1	5	100	100	210	10

(b)

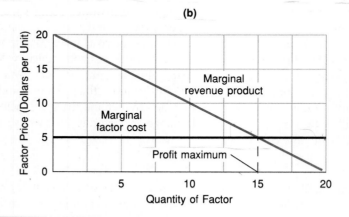

Factor Demand Curves

It follows from this analysis that when a firm is a price taker in the factor market,
its marginal revenue product curve for a factor is also its demand curve. A
demand curve must indicate the quantity demanded at each price, and it has
been shown that the quantity of the factor demanded by such a firm will be
whatever quantity makes the factor's price (and, hence, its marginal factor cost)
equal to marginal revenue product.

The same profit-maximizing concept that underlies the demand curves of individual firms can be extended to all firms hiring a given factor to get a market demand curve for that factor. Such a market demand curve is said to be a *derived demand curve*, because the demand for a factor of production does not arise from the usefulness of the factor services themselves; instead, it is indirectly derived from the usefulness of the products the factor can produce. The market demand for farmland is derived from the market demand for food, the market demand for printers from the market demand for books, and so on.

Changes in Factor Demand

Like the demand for products, the demand for factors changes in response to changes in economic conditions. Look at Exhibit 13.5. Suppose that demand curve D_0 is the market demand curve for some factor of production. A change in the market price of that factor will cause the quantity of the factor demanded to change. This is represented by a movement along the demand curve, as shown by the arrow parallel to D_0. Changes in economic conditions other than a change in the factor's price can cause a change in demand for a factor—for example, a shift in the demand curve from D_0 to D_1 or D_2.

Three kinds of changes are capable of causing shifts in the demand curve for a factor of production. First, an increase in demand for the output that the factor produces will shift the factor demand curve to the right and a decrease will shift it to the left. Second, a change in the price of another factor of production that is used in combination with the given factor can also cause the demand for the given factor to shift. An increase in the price of a factor that is a substitute for the given factor will cause the demand curve for the given factor to shift to the right; an increase in the price of a factor that is a complement to the given factor will cause the demand curve of that factor to shift to the left. Third, any change in technology that increases the marginal physical productivity of a factor will cause its demand curve to shift to the right, other things being equal; any de-

Exhibit 13.5   Movements along a Factor Demand Curve and Shifts in the Curve

Changes in the price of a factor, other things being equal, will produce movements along a factor demand curve, as shown by the arrow. Other kinds of changes can shift the curve. An increase in demand for the product produced by the factor might shift the curve from D_0 to D_1. An increase in the price of another factor that is a complement to the given factor might shift the curve from D_0 to D_2.

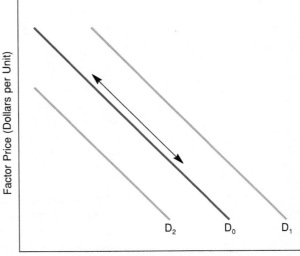

Factor Price (Dollars per Unit)

D_2 D_0 D_1

Quantity of Factor Demanded

crease in the marginal physical product of the factor will shift the curve to the left.

Supply and Demand in the Labor Market

Up to this point, we have discussed marginal productivity and factor demand only in general terms. Now we will turn to the specifics of markets for particular factors. In this section, we will begin the analysis of such markets by looking at the supply and demand for labor. Our discussion will be limited at first to the case in which individual workers compete with one another for jobs. In Chapter 14, we will take up the case of organized labor markets, in which workers form unions to bargain with employers rather than competing with one another for jobs. Finally, in Chapter 15, we will look at markets for capital and natural resources.

The Labor Supply Curve

We can apply our general analysis of factor demand from the previous section to the labor market with no major changes. However, we need a labor supply curve to go with the labor demand curve. We will begin the analysis with a look at the labor supply decision for an individual worker.

Labor Supply for an Individual

Individuals' decisions regarding how much labor to supply to the market are part of the general problem of consumer choice and can be analyzed in terms of the theory developed in Chapter 7. The best way to approach the problem is to think in terms of a trade-off between two sources of utility—leisure and the consumption of purchased goods and services. Leisure is valued for relaxation, recreation, and the completion of certain household tasks. Time spent at leisure is time taken away from work, however, and thus is time diverted from earning income that could be used to buy goods and services. Within the limits of a 24-hour day, people balance the advantages of work and leisure to achieve an equilibrium in which, ideally, the marginal utility per hour of leisure exactly equals the marginal utility of the goods that can be bought with an hour's earnings.

The hourly wage rate can be thought of as the price—or, more precisely, the opportunity cost—of leisure to the worker in that it represents the dollar equivalent of the goods and services that must be sacrificed in order to enjoy an added hour of leisure. As the wage rate increases, it affects work-versus-leisure decisions in two ways. First, there is a substitution effect; the increased wage rate provides an incentive to work more, because each hour of work now produces more income to be spent on goods and services. In effect, purchased goods and services are substituted for leisure. Second, however, the increase in the wage rate has an income effect that tends to reduce the number of hours worked. The higher wage rate—assuming that the prices of goods and services remain unchanged—increases workers' real incomes. With higher real incomes, workers tend to consume more of goods that are normal goods and less of those that are inferior goods. Leisure is a normal good. Other things being equal, people generally seek more leisure, in the form of shorter working hours and longer vacations, as their incomes rise. Taken by itself, then, the income effect of a wage increase is a reduction in the amount of labor supplied by workers.

It can be seen, therefore, that the net effect of an increase in the wage rate on the amount of labor supplied by an individual worker depends on the relative strengths of the substitution and income effects. It is generally believed that for very low wage rates the substitution effect predominates, and therefore the quantity of labor supplied increases as the wage rate rises. As the wage rate increases, however, the income effect becomes stronger. People tend to treat leisure as a luxury good; after they have assured themselves of a certain material standard of living, they begin to consider "spending" any further wage increases on more time off from work. The labor supply curve for such a person has a backward-bending shape like the one shown in Exhibit 13.6. Over the positively sloped low-wage section, the substitution effect of wage changes predominates; over the negatively sloped high-wage section, the income effect prevails.

Market Labor Supply Curves

Although the labor supply curves for individual workers may bend backward, at least over some range of wages, the supply curve for any given type of labor as a whole is likely to be positively sloped throughout. Consider, for example, the supply of electrical engineers in New York, of typists in Chicago, or of farm laborers in Texas. Beyond some point, each individual engineer, typist, or laborer might respond to a wage increase by cutting back on the number of hours worked. For the market as a whole, however, this tendency would be more than offset by new workers drawn into that labor market from other occupations or areas. Thus, other things being equal, if the wage rate for electrical engineers in New York rose, more engineering students would take up that specialty; if the wage rate for typists in Chicago rose, more people would become typists than, say, filing clerks; and if the wage rate for farm laborers in Texas rose, workers would be drawn in from Arizona, Florida, and Mexico. As a result, for any discussion of the market for a particular category of labor at a specific time and place, it is reasonable to draw the labor supply curve with the usual positive

Exhibit 13.6   An Individual's Labor Supply Curve

On the one hand, a higher wage tends to increase the amount of work that a person is willing to do, since the extra income compensates for time taken away from leisure pursuits. On the other hand, a higher wage allows a person to take more time off from work and still enjoy a high standard of living. Taken together, the two effects tend to give the individual labor supply curve the backward-bending shape shown here.

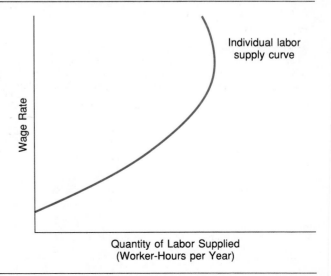

Individual labor supply curve

Wage Rate

Quantity of Labor Supplied
(Worker-Hours per Year)

Exhibit 13.7 A Hypothetical
Supply Curve for Typists

Although each individual typist may have a backward-
bending supply curve, the supply curve for typists in any
local market will have the usual upward-sloping shape. As
the wage rises, people will be drawn into this occupation
from other kinds of work or other localities.

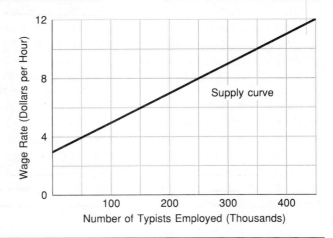

slope, as in Exhibit 13.7, regardless of the shape of the individual labor supply
curves underlying it.

Competitive Equilibrium

Determining the wage rate in a labor market that is fully competitive on both
sides is a simple matter of supply and demand analysis. Exhibit 13.8, for example, shows supply and demand curves for the labor market for typists in Chicago. It assumes that a large number of typists compete for jobs and a large
number of employers compete for typists so that both are price takers. The
demand curve for typists is derived from the demand curves for individual
firms. The supply curve is the same as that in Exhibit 13.7.

Equilibrium in this market requires a wage rate of $7 an hour, with 200,000

Exhibit 13.8 Determination of the Equilibrium
Wage in a Competitive Labor Market

When both employers and workers are price takers in the
labor market, the point of equilibrium is found where the
supply and demand curves intersect. Here the equilibrium
wage rate is $7 an hour and the equilibrium quantity of labor
is 200,000 typists.

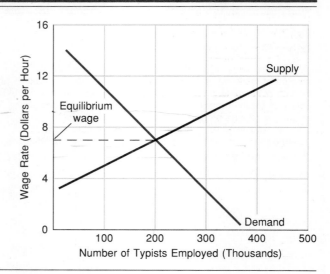

typists employed. If the wage rate were lower, there would be a shortage of typists. Some firms, unable to fill all their job openings, would offer premium wages to workers from other jobs or regions. The wage rate would thus be driven up to the equilibrium level. If, on the other hand, the wage rate were above $7 an hour, there would be a surplus of typists. Many people would be looking for typing jobs and not finding them. After a sufficiently long search, some would be willing to accept work at lower-than-expected wages, thereby pushing the wage rate down toward equilibrium; others would drift into other occupations or regions.

In a labor market such as this—where both employers and employees are price takers—the equilibrium wage rate equals the marginal revenue product of labor. In the special case in which all employers are price takers (perfect competitors) in the market where they sell their output as well as in the market where they purchase inputs, the equilibrium wage rate also equals the value of marginal product.

Shifts in Demand and Movement among Labor Markets

The supply of any given occupational group of workers is more elastic in the long run than in the short run, because differences in wages among labor markets will affect people's decisions regarding choice of occupation. This principle is illustrated in Exhibit 13.9. Two closely related labor markets are pictured— the market for typists and the market for word processor operators. As word processors replace typewriters in many offices, the demand for word processor operators shifts to the right and that for typists shifts to the left. The wage rate for word processor operators rises from W_1 to W_2 as this market moves up along the short-run supply curve to a new equilibrium at E_2. At the same time, the wage rate of typists falls.

This situation cannot prevail in the long run, however. It is no more difficult to learn how to use a word processor than it is to use a typewriter. Not all experienced typists will learn how to use the new machines, but most of those entering secretarial occupations will. In the long run, then, we expect the supply curve for both typists and word processor operators to be more elastic than in the short run. Here we assume the long-run supply curves in both markets to be perfectly elastic. In this case, we can expect the wage differential between word processor operators and typists to disappear in the long run. As that happens, the markets will move to long-run equilibriums at E_3 and e_3, respectively.

Earlier in the chapter, we discussed various sources of shifts in labor demand curves. In the case of typists and word processor operators, the shifts were caused by a fall in the price of word processors. Because word processors are a complement to the labor of word processor operators, their falling price shifts the demand curve for those workers to the right. At the same time, word processors are a substitute for the labor of typists; thus, a decline in their price shifts the demand curve for typists to the left.

Because the demand for factors of production is a derived demand, shifts in labor demand curves can also be caused by shifts in demand for the product. For example, in recent years the demand for restaurant meals has increased more rapidly than the average demand for other goods and services. This has shifted the demand curve for restaurant workers to the right.

Exhibit 13.9   Demand Shifts and Relative Wages

Shifts in demand have a larger effect on relative wages in the short run than in the long run. This pair of graphs compares the market for word processor operators with that for typists. In the short run, increasing demand for word processor operators shifts that demand curve to the right and pushes wages up. Meanwhile, the demand for typists decreases, leading to a fall in wages. In the long run, the supply curves for both types of workers will be more elastic than in the short run. If the demand curves remain in their new positions, then, the difference in pay will disappear.

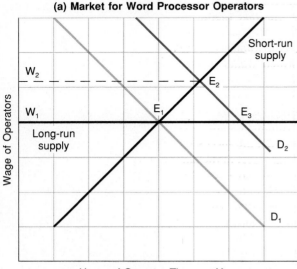

(a) Market for Word Processor Operators

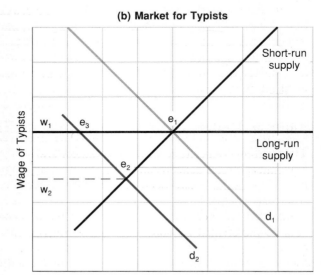

(b) Market for Typists

The Marginal Productivity Theory of Distribution

Supply and demand determine how much each worker earns as well as how much labor will be used in making each product. When employers are price takers in the markets in which they buy inputs, profit maximization requires that each factor be used up to the point at which its marginal revenue product will equal its price. This suggests that each unit of each factor receives a reward that equals the contribution it makes to the firm's revenue. The idea that factors are rewarded according to their marginal productivity is known as the **marginal productivity theory of distribution.**

Marginal productivity theory of distribution
A theory of the distribution of income according to which each factor of production receives a payment equal to its marginal revenue product.

In an economy in which all markets—output as well as input—are perfectly competitive, the marginal productivity theory applies even more directly. In this case, marginal revenue product equals output price times marginal physical product. In such an economy, the reward that each unit of each factor receives equals the value of marginal product. If an extra hour spent pulling weeds in a cabbage patch increases production by 20 pounds and cabbage sells for $.50 per pound, the wage rate must be $10 an hour—no more, no less.

The principle of distribution, in which every factor receives a reward equal to the value of its marginal product, appeals to some people as being both efficient and fair. The reward of every worker is exactly equal to that worker's contribution to the productive process. If a worker or a factor owner withholds a unit of productive services from the market, that person will suffer a loss of earnings exactly equal to the value of production that is lost to the economy as a whole.

Monopsony

Not every factor market meets the conditions required for the marginal productivity theory of distribution to apply. The extreme situation in which there is only one buyer in a market is called **monopsony**. Unlike a firm that is a perfect competitor in the market in which it buys its inputs, a monopsonist is not a price taker. For such a firm, the wage rate is not a given; instead, the wage that must be paid rises as the number of workers hired increases.

Compare the situation of a retail store in Albuquerque that wants to hire a few security guards with that of the U.S. government, which wants to hire soldiers for its volunteer army. The retail store is a price taker in the market for security guards. If the going wage for such guards is, say, $11,000 a year, it can call an agency or put an ad in the paper and get as many guards as it wants at that price. The situation of the government as the employer of volunteer soldiers is very different. Experience with the volunteer army has shown that the success of recruitment efforts depends on the level of military pay. For example, in the late 1970s real military pay decreased somewhat because nominal pay increases failed to keep up with inflation. This left some military specialties understaffed. In the early 1980s, a combination of military pay raises and slack demand for labor in the civilian economy made it possible to fill many of those positions again.

In practice, the theory of monopsony can be extended from the ideal-type case in which there is only one employer in a labor market to the more common case of employers that are not alone in their markets but are still large enough that the quantity of labor they hire affects the wage rate. Normally, if a monopsonist decides to raise its wage offer in order to attract new workers, it must also raise the wages of the workers who are already on its payroll by a comparable amount. To do otherwise—that is, to pay newly hired workers more than those who have been on the job for some time—would be harmful to worker morale. But the need to pay a higher wage to all workers—not just those newly hired— means that the monopsonist's marginal factor cost is actually higher than the wage rate paid to the new workers themselves. Exhibit 13.10 shows why, using as an example the supply of typists in a small town in which one big employer— say, an insurance company—employs a large percentage of the town's typists.

The supply schedule for typists shows that no one will work as a typist at a wage rate of $3 an hour or less. Above the $3 wage, each extra $.02 per hour will attract one more worker. Suppose that the monopsonistic employer has hired 150 typists at a rate of $6 an hour, making the total labor cost for this size of labor force $900 an hour. What will happen to the firm's total labor cost per hour if it expands its labor force by one worker?

According to the supply curve, hiring 151 typists requires a wage of $6.02 an hour. That wage must be paid not just to the 151st worker but to all workers. The total cost of a labor force of 151 typists, then, is $6.02 times 151, or $909.02 per hour. The addition of one more worker has raised the total labor cost per hour from $900 to $909.02—a marginal factor cost of $9.02. The result is much the same regardless of the chosen starting point. In every case, the monopsonist's marginal factor cost exceeds the factor price (in this case, the wage rate).

Monopsony
A situation in which there is only a single buyer in a market.

Exhibit 13.10   Marginal Factor Cost under Monopsony

Under monopsony, marginal factor cost exceeds factor price. Consider an increase in
quantity from 150 to 151 units of labor. The wage rate must be raised from $6 to $6.02 not
just for the 151st employee but for all the previous 150 as well. Marginal labor cost in this
range is thus $9.02 rather than $6.02 an hour.

(a)

Quantity of Labor Supplied (1)	Wage Rate (2)	Total Factor Cost (3)	Marginal Factor Cost (4)
1	$3.02	$ 3.02	$ 3.06
2	3.04	6.08	3.10
3	3.06	9.18	
150	6.00	900.00	9.02
151	6.02	909.02	9.06
152	6.04	918.08	
200	7.00	1,400.00	11.02
201	7.02	1,411.02	11.06
202	7.04	1,422.08	

(b)

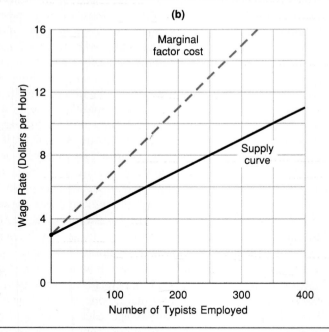

Part b of Exhibit 13.10 shows a marginal factor cost curve based on the
marginal factor cost column of the table in part a. This curve lies above the
supply curve at every point. The graph shows that the relationship between the
supply curve and the marginal cost curve for the monopsonist is similar to that
between a monopolist's demand and marginal revenue curves.

Monopsony Equilibrium

Given the monopsonist's marginal factor cost curve—derived from the factor's
market supply curve—determining the equilibrium level of employment for the
firm is a routine matter. Exhibit 13.11 shows the monopsonistic employer's

Exhibit 13.11   Determination of
Wages under Monopsony

Here are a monopsonist's marginal revenue product of labor
curve, labor supply curve, and marginal factor cost curve.
The quantity of labor required for maximizing profits is found
at the point at which the marginal revenue product and
marginal factor cost curves intersect. The equilibrium wage
rate is not shown by the intersection of the marginal factor
cost and marginal revenue product curves. Instead, the rate
is equal to the height of the supply curve directly below that
intersection.

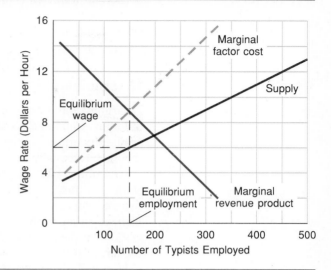

marginal revenue product curve along with the labor supply and marginal factor
cost curves from Exhibit 13.10. Following the general rule that profit is maximized when marginal factor cost equals marginal revenue product, the monopsonist will hire 150 typists at a wage rate of $6 an hour.

When a labor market is in monopsony equilibrium, the wage rate is lower
than both the marginal factor cost and the marginal revenue product of labor. In
the example just given, the equilibrium wage rate is $6 an hour (which is equal
to the height of the labor supply curve), although the marginal revenue product
is $9 an hour at the point at which the marginal revenue product and marginal
factor cost curves intersect. Despite the gap between the wage rate and the
marginal revenue product, adding to the amount of labor hired would not raise
revenue by enough to offset higher labor costs. The reason is that the cost of
hiring another worker is not just the $6.02 an hour that must be paid to the 151st
worker but that sum plus the extra $.02 per hour by which the wages of all 150
previously hired workers must be raised. The complete marginal factor cost for
the 151st worker is thus $6.02 + $3.00, or $9.02 an hour.

We see, then, that the marginal productivity theory of distribution does not
apply in a monopsonistic labor market. In such a market, workers are paid
a wage that is less than their contribution, at the margin, to the employer's
revenue.

Why Wage Rates Differ

All people are created equal, according to a widely shared concept of justice. But
if that is so, why do people's earnings in labor markets differ so substantially?
Why do different people receive different wages within a given labor market,
and why do the wage structures of some markets differ markedly from others'?
In this section, we turn to the question of what causes wages to differ. Why are
typists in New York City paid more than people doing the same job in Goshen,
Indiana? Why are people with engineering degrees paid more to work in industry than to teach engineering at a university? Why are the average wages of

blacks and women less than those of white men? Without treating these subjects exhaustively, we will look at some considerations that help explain wage differences. The topic of labor unions, which also contribute to wage differences, is covered in Chapter 14.

Discrimination

Discrimination is one demand-related factor that can affect the relative wages of different groups and occupations. Employers can be said to *discriminate* against a group of workers if they are unwilling to hire them at the same wage rate that they pay to equally productive members of a more favored group.

Exhibit 13.12 shows the effects of discrimination by employers. Part a shows the supply and demand curves for workers in the favored group. The demand curve in this market is the marginal revenue product curve, as explained earlier in the chapter. Part b shows the supply and demand curves for workers in the disfavored group. In this market, the demand curve is shifted to the left relative to the marginal revenue product curve. This indicates that employers will hire members of the disfavored group only if they are more productive than members of the favored group or if they are equally productive but will work for less.

Exhibit 13.12   Effects of Discrimination on Wage Rates and Hours Worked

This exhibit shows the effect of discrimination in a labor market that can be divided into a group of workers who are favored by employers and a group who is disfavored. The two groups are assumed to be equal in terms of productivity, but the demand curve for the disfavored group is shifted to the left of the corresponding marginal revenue product curve. If there are no equal-pay laws, the disfavored group's pay will fall to W_2, below the level of W_1 received by members of the favored group. If the law requires equal pay, both groups will receive wage W_1 but fewer members of the disfavored group will be employed. Many disfavored-group members who would be willing to work in this occupation at wage W_1 will be forced into other, less attractive sectors of the job market or into unemployment. With or without the equal-pay law, then, discrimination is harmful to the disfavored group.

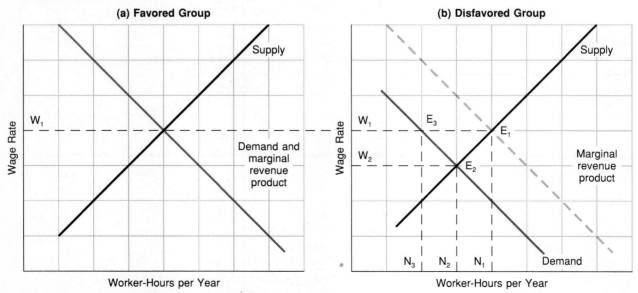

Equilibrium under Discrimination

Two types of equilibrium are possible under discrimination.

First, let us assume that there are no legal restrictions on discrimination. In this case, the wage rate for the disfavored group in Exhibit 13.12 will fall to W_2 compared to a wage of W_1 for the favored group. Workers from the two groups will then work side by side, doing the same job, but will receive different pay. All members of the disfavored group who want to work at wage W_2 will be able to find jobs in this market.

In the second case, we assume that the law prohibits paying different wages to members of different groups for doing the same work. This is the situation in the United States since passage of the Equal Pay Act of 1963. In this case, employers must pay wage W_1 to members of both the favored and disfavored group. As a result, they will employ only N_3 worker-hours per year from the disfavored group.

The effect of the equal-pay law on members of the disfavored group is mixed. On the one hand, members of that group who are employed in this market get paid more than they would without the law. On the other hand, fewer workers from the disfavored group get jobs at wage W_1. Those who do not get jobs in this market either remain unemployed or are crowded into some other sector of the labor market, possibly one in which employers do not discriminate. However, whether or not employers in those other markets discriminate, wages there will be pushed down by the increased supply of workers who are unable to find jobs in the market shown in Exhibit 13.12.

In the end, then, discrimination lowers the average wage of members of the disfavored group even when the law requires equal pay for all workers doing a given job and there are some markets in which employers do not discriminate. Many women's-rights activists see this as a major factor in the pay gap between men and women. They think that discrimination holds down the number of women employed in high-paying executive and skilled-labor positions. As a result, wages are forced down in such occupations as nursing, teaching, and secretarial work, in which employers are as willing to hire women as they are men.

Competition and Discrimination

Now that we have examined the effects of discrimination on workers, we turn to the effect on employers. At first it might seem that employers gain from discrimination in that it pushes down the wages of members of disfavored groups. However, this is true only to the extent that employers are united in their desire to discriminate. Looking at the matter from the viewpoint of a single employer, there is a strong incentive not to discriminate.

Consider the case in which there is no equal-pay law. In that situation, the wage rate for workers from the disfavored group is lower than that of workers from the favored group. Employers who set aside their prejudices and hire only workers from the disfavored group will have a distinct cost advantage over those who discriminate. This cost advantage will allow them to undercut their competitors' prices, perhaps driving them out of the market or at least forcing them to change their hiring practices. In the long run, competition will tend to erode both the practice of discrimination and the pay gap.

Even if there is an equal-pay law, an employer can gain a competitive advantage by not discriminating. In this case, although all employers pay the same wage, the nondiscriminating employer can skim off the most productive mem-

Discrimination and the Law
in the Jim Crow South

In the southern United States in the Jim Crow era (the 1890s through the early 1950s), there was no lack of discrimination against black workers. Especially in the early part of the period, the economy was dominated by white planters who employed large numbers of blacks. As a group, they had an interest in holding down the wages of black farm workers, both to boost their own profits and to maintain the dominant position of the white race.

There was one problem, however. The greed of many white employers overcame racial solidarity. Despite warnings in newspapers that "white men must stick together," the employers competed for black labor. Black workers often left their jobs for higher-paying ones, especially at harvest time, when labor was in short supply. In addition, labor recruiters from the North would appear in the South to entice black workers to come to work in the North's growing industries at wages that, while low by today's standards, were still better than those paid by the southern planters. Something had to be done to protect the traditional system of exploitation against erosion by market forces. The solution was the following set of labor laws, which were passed in most southern states between 1890 and 1910:

- *Enticement laws* made it a crime for white employers to "entice" a worker who had a contract with another employer. The aim was to prevent competition for workers that might bid up wages.

- *Contract enforcement laws* made it a crime for a

black worker to break a labor contract with a white employer in order to seek work elsewhere. The standard contract period was one year. The aim was to prevent competition at harvest time, when the demand for labor was strongest.

- *Vagrancy laws* made it a crime for any person who was able to work to "wander or stroll in idleness." The aim was to keep black workers in the labor force and to prevent them from spending time between jobs shopping around for the best wage offer.

- *Emigrant-agent laws* curbed the activities of labor recruiters from other states or even other counties. For example, a law passed by the city of Montgomery, Alabama, imposed a $100 fine or six months in jail on anyone who printed, published, wrote, delivered, posted, or distributed any advertisement that tried to persuade people to leave the city to seek work elsewhere.

- The *convict lease system* allowed black prisoners, including those who had been imprisoned for violating contract or vagrancy laws, to be leased to private employers. Being on the chain gang was worse than being a slave: Since the lease was short term, the employer, unlike a slave owner, did not even have an interest in preserving the worker's health.

Economist Jennifer Roback, in a study of the Jim Crow labor laws, finds that they were effective in keeping wages down and limiting migration. She concludes that without the laws, competition would have undermined the system of exploitation.

Source: Jennifer Roback, "Exploitation in the Jim Crow South: The Market or the Law?" *Regulation* (September-December 1984): 37–44. A longer version of the article appears in *University of Chicago Law Review* (Fall 1984).

bers of the disfavored group. The advantage gained by doing so can be seen in Exhibit 13.12 as the vertical gap between wage rate W_1 and the marginal revenue product curve at employment level N_1. Once again this competitive advantage would tend to bring an end to discrimination.

All in all, the situation of discrimination in the labor market is much like that of a cartel, which was discussed in Chapter 11. Discriminating employers or cartel members can gain as long as they are united. But in practice, each has an incentive to cheat on the system. Just as cartel members are pulled by the profit motive to undercut their fellow members, so are employers pulled by the profit motive to abandon established patterns of discrimination. "Perspective 13.1" looks at these forces in the case of the southern states of the United States in the Jim Crow era. There competition and the profit motive so undermined discrimination that states had to pass laws that, in effect, forced employers to discriminate.

Most economists see competition as a force that tends to break down discrimination, but this does not mean that competition alone will eliminate discrimination. Pockets of discrimination can survive for a number of reasons. In some cases, discrimination might originate with the customer rather than the employer. If, say, car owners didn't trust women mechanics to fix their cars, there would be an incentive for employers of mechanics not to hire women even if they knew them to be competent. In other cases, discrimination can arise with fellow workers. For instance, until the 1880s, professional baseball teams hired some black players, but white players eventually insisted that the practice be discontinued.

In still other cases, employers might be shielded from market forces. Government employers are one example. It is no accident that some of the major targets of the drive for equal pay for women have been city and state governments. Further, in Chapter 4 we mentioned the belief of some economists that managers of large corporations do not always share their stockholders' interest in maximum profits. If the male head of such a corporation liked to hire only white males even when more highly qualified women or minority candidates were available, he might be able to get away with doing so, at least for a time. Finally, it is possible that some employers simply are unaware of the costs of discrimination.

Nonwage Job Characteristics

Discrimination is hardly the only thing that causes wages to differ. Another reason that one company may pay its typists or truck drivers less than another concerns the nonwage characteristics of jobs—their interest, safety, prestige, challenge, and so on. Other things being equal, workers are willing to supply their services at lower wages to employers who offer jobs with attractive nonwage characteristics. Many employers know this and try to make the jobs they offer safe, attractive, and challenging.

Of course, not everyone's idea of a good job is the same. Some economists see differences in nonwage job characteristics as one of the reasons for the pay gap between jobs that are held mainly by men and those held chiefly by women. For example, women, on the average, have entered and left the labor force much more often than men—at least in the past. The desire to do so may lead many women to choose occupations, such as clerical and secretarial work, in which it is relatively easy to enter and leave employment even though these jobs do not pay as well as some others. Some studies have found that the pay gap between women who have never married and men is smaller than that between men and married women. This may be partly because never-married women tend to spend more of their working-age years in the labor force and, hence, are more likely to choose careers in which steady labor force membership is important.[1]

---

[1] See Walter Williams, "Explaining the Economic Gender Gap" (National Center for Policy Analysis, Dallas, November 1983). Among other studies, Williams cites one by Solomon Polachek that found that married female college graduates spend 36 percent of their working-age years in the labor force compared with 89 percent for never-married female college graduates.

Human Capital

Ability is another factor that affects the supply of labor for certain occupations. Some people are born with special abilities, or at least with unusual potential for developing them. The enormous salaries of professional ballplayers, first-rate opera singers, and so on are a direct result of the scarcity of those abilities.

But abilities with which people are born are only part of the story. Training is a more important factor in the supply of workers for most occupations. The salaries of lawyers, accountants, glassblowers, and hairdressers depend to a large extent on the cost of training. The natural abilities required for these occupations are not very rare. Many more people could acquire the training needed to practice them than actually do so.

Economists view the costs of training as a form of investment. Taking courses to become an accountant, in this view, is much like buying a dump truck in order to go into the gravel-hauling business. In both cases, one makes an expenditure now to acquire something that will increase one's future earning power. The main difference lies in the fact that the dump truck operator acquires capital in the form of a machine, whereas the accountant acquires **human capital**—capital in the form of learned abilities.

According to human-capital theory, the earnings of each occupation that requires special training must be high enough to make up for the opportunity cost of getting the training. In the case of a person going to college to acquire a degree in accounting, the opportunity cost includes both the costs of tuition, books, and so on and the income that he or she could have earned if the college years had been spent working in an occupation that required no college degree. Other things being equal, we would expect occupations that require longer or more expensive training to pay more than those that demand less. Thus, we would expect doctors to earn more than lawyers, lawyers to earn more than hairdressers, and so on—and this is in fact the case.

Of course, allowance must be made for factors other than human capital that also affect the supply of workers for various occupations. If certain occupations are more exciting or prestigious than others, people may be willing to enter them even if the pay alone is not enough to justify the investment in training. For example, college graduates earn more than nongraduates, but not sufficiently more, in many cases, to offset the full opportunity costs of spending four years in college. However, people do not go to college solely for the monetary rewards of doing so. In part, they are motivated by the nonwage characteristics of the jobs for which they are preparing; they may also be partly motivated by a perception that the college experience itself is enjoyable.

Formal education is by no means the only way to invest in human capital. As the case study that opens this chapter shows, on-the-job training is also important. On-the-job training may be specific, such as learning how to run certain kinds of machinery, or general, such as learning good work habits, how to work with other people, or how to supervise others.

Differences in human capital are believed to be another factor in explaining the pay gap between men and women. For one thing, the large numbers of women who entered the labor force for the first time during the 1970s had less education and experience, on the average, than male workers. Also, the fact that in the past women have spent a smaller percentage of their working-age years in the labor force has affected their human capital. This is partly because they have acquired less human capital on the job and partly because such women, knowing

Human capital
Capital in the form of learned abilities that have been acquired through formal training or education or through on-the-job experience.

that they would not work full-time for all of their working-age years, have had less incentive to invest in formal education and training.

It is likely that the human-capital gap between men and women will narrow in coming years and that the wage gap will shrink with it. This will happen partly because the large numbers of women who have entered the labor force in the past 15 years will gain in experience and seniority. In addition, young women today appear to expect to be in the labor force throughout their working-age years and therefore are more willing to invest in training and education.

Efficiency Wage Theory

Human capital theory suggests that the ability to perform a job better causes an increase in the wage rate of a worker or group of workers. However, another theory suggests that the opposite may be true—that higher pay may itself lead to better on-the-job performance. This line of reasoning is referred to as **efficiency wage theory**.

Efficiency wage theory
The theory that wages higher than the minimum necessary to attract qualified workers can raise productivity and hence increase profit.

Efficiency wage theory poses the following question: Why do many firms pay a wage that is higher than necessary to attract workers of the desired minimum qualifications? Anyone who has ever looked for a job has probably had the experience of hearing about an employer who offered a high wage for given skills and working conditions, only to learn that the employer had hundreds of applications on file and a low turnover rate. According to the simple supply and demand model, the profit-maximizing strategy for such a firm would be to lower the wage rate, allowing the backlog of job applications to shrink to just the level necessary to cover turnover. Yet this is not always done.

The explanation offered by efficiency wage theory is that the high wage stimulates increased productivity. Several mechanisms have been suggested, including improved morale, lower absenteeism, and lower labor turnover. Also, workers at a high-wage firm are likely to be less willing to take a chance of losing their jobs because of poor performance and thus may work to the best of their abilities with less supervision and monitoring.

"Perspective 13.2" discusses an example sometimes cited in support of efficiency wage theory: the introduction of the $5 day at Ford Motor Company in 1914.

Looking Ahead

In this chapter, we looked at a number of things that affect the pay of one job versus that of another. Some result from choices made by workers themselves—choices based on nonwage characteristics of jobs, choices involving investment in human capital, and choices concerning whether to remain in the labor force full-time or only part-time. Other factors that affect wage rates are beyond the control of individual workers—shifts in demand, discrimination, and natural abilities. Two other factors that affect wages remain to be discussed: labor unions, which will be covered in the next chapter, and minimum wage laws, which will be covered in Chapter 16. What, if anything, can we conclude about the system by which wages are determined? Is it a good one? A fair one?

Economists generally praise wages determined by supply and demand as an efficient solution to the problem of how to produce goods and services. Market-based wages encourage employers to balance the marginal productivity of labor against that of other factors of production in such a way as to choose more

PERSPECTIVE 13.2

Henry Ford's $5 Day

The Ford Motor Company was founded in 1903, but it remained small for its first five years. By 1908, it had just 450 employees, most of them skilled craftsmen and machinists. Cars were assembled from parts that were not made to high tolerances, so that much custom machining and fitting was required. The work was complex, and workmen had broad discretion and control over their jobs. In 1908, the firm produced just 10,607 cars.

Over the next five years, the company underwent a radical transformation. The model T was introduced and became the only car that Ford made. Ford wanted his cars to be all alike—"just like one pin is like another pin when it comes from the pin factory."

The new car required a new approach to manufacturing. The world's first moving assembly line was introduced. Specialized, single-purpose machine tools replaced conventional multipurpose tools. Parts supplied from outside had to be made to tolerances that allowed them to be interchangeable without special fitting.

These changes in production methods were accompanied by a major change in Ford's work force. By 1913 the work force had reached nearly 14,000, almost all of it unskilled. Three-quarters of the work force was foreign born, and many did not speak English. These unskilled workers did simple, very finely subdivided jobs, such as attaching a single nut or bolt. The training required for these jobs was a matter of five or ten minutes in many cases. Output of cars rose to 5,000 per week.

Source: Daniel M. G. Raff and Lawrence H. Summers, "Did Henry Ford Pay Efficiency Wages?" (Working Paper No. 2101, National Bureau of Economic Research, December 1986).

There were problems, though. One of them was high labor turnover and absenteeism. In 1913, turnover was almost 400 percent, and Ford had to hire 50,000 men to maintain its average work force of just under 14,000. On any given day, 10 percent of the work force failed to show up for work. The turnover and absenteeism cut productivity and were symptoms of other problems, such as arbitrary practices by supervisors.

To cope with these labor problems, a new policy was announced in January 1914. Wages for most male workers aged 22 or older were raised from roughly $2.32 per day to a minimum of $5 per day, and at the same time the workday was cut from nine to eight hours. This was done despite the fact that there had never been a shortage of applicants for available jobs even at the old wage.

The results of this program fit the pattern predicted by efficiency wage theory. Productivity rose: from 1913 to 1914, output went up by 15 percent while the work force shrank by 15 percent and the workday was shortened. Turnover fell from 400 percent to 28 percent, and absenteeism also plummeted. Ford's profit in the first year of the $5 day rose by 15 percent to $30 million and then rose another 20 percent the following year.

Work at the Ford plant was very hard. As one employee put it, "You've got to work like hell at Ford's. From the time you become a number in the morning until the bell rings for quitting time, you have to keep at it. You can't let up. You've got to get out the production and if you can't get it out, you get out." Nonetheless, after the $5 day was introduced, thousands of men lined up outside the plant, waiting all night in blizzard conditions, to apply for jobs. As for those already inside the plant, "it would almost have required the use of a rifle to separate the average Ford employee from the payroll."

---

efficient production methods. Market wages give people an incentive to invest in human capital—a major source of growth for the economy. Finally, markets tend—though not always perfectly—to punish employers who waste human resources through discriminatory hiring practices.

There is less agreement on the fairness of a system in which women, on the average, earn only 64 percent as much as men, blacks only 77 percent as much as whites, Hispanics only 78 percent as much as the average for all workers, and so on. Many economists emphasize that a substantial part of these discrepancies results from differences in education, age, experience, career choices, and so forth. The important thing, these people say, is to insure that everyone has an opportunity to compete for jobs on equal terms. As long as that is the case, there is no reason to insist on equality of results.

Others, however, do not see formal equality of opportunity as enough. They see women and minority group members as victims of discrimination, often in forms that are too subtle to be dealt with by existing laws. These views have given rise to demands for stronger laws governing the pay practices of both private and public employers. The debate is sure to remain a lively one for years to come.

Summary

1. **What role do factor markets play in determining how and for whom goods are produced?** *Factor markets* play an important role in determining how goods and services are produced. When factor prices change, firms tend to modify their production methods, using less of factors that have become more expensive and more of those that have become cheaper. At the same time, factor markets help determine for whom goods and services are produced, since payments for the services of labor, capital, and natural resources are the main source of income for most households.

2. **What determines the demand for a factor of production?** For a perfectly competitive firm, the *marginal revenue product* of a factor is equal to the factor's *value of marginal product*, that is, to marginal physical product times the product's price. For a monopolistic firm, it is equal to marginal physical product times marginal revenue and is thus less than the value of marginal product. In both cases, the firm makes the maximum profit by buying each factor up to the point at which marginal revenue product equals *marginal factor cost*. Hence, the marginal revenue product curve is the factor demand curve for the firm. The demand for a factor of production is said to be a *derived demand* because it depends on the demand for the goods or services that the factor produces.

3. **What determines the supply curve for labor?** Labor supply curves depend on the trade-off that people make between leisure and the goods and services they can buy with income earned in the labor market. The labor supply curve for an individual worker, and perhaps for the economy as a whole, may bend backward above a certain wage rate. However, the supply curve for a single labor market (say, the supply of typists in Chicago) is positively sloped throughout its length.

4. **What are the characteristics of equilibrium in a competitive labor market?** In a labor market in which employers compete for workers and workers compete for jobs, the equilibrium wage rate will be equal to the marginal revenue product of labor. This is known as the *marginal productivity theory of distribution*. If employers are also perfect competitors in the market in which they sell their output, the equilibrium wage rate will be equal to the value of the marginal product. Shifts in the demand for a factor of production can cause wages in one labor market to differ from those in another. Over time, the differences are reduced as workers move from one market to the other.

5. **What are the characteristics of labor market equilibrium with only one or a few employers?** *Monopsony* means a situation in which there is only one buyer of factor services in a given market. The marginal factor cost curve for such a firm lies above the supply curve for labor. Equilibrium is established at the intersection of the marginal factor cost curve and the marginal revenue product curve. In such a market, the equilibrium wage does not equal marginal revenue product. The same principle applies to markets with more than one employer provided each firm faces an upward-sloping labor supply curve.

6. **Why are wages not the same for all labor markets and all individuals within a labor market?** Wages differ among markets and among individuals for a variety of reasons. Some wage differences can be explained in terms of discrimination, although market forces tend to erode discriminatory differences over time. Other wage differences stem from differences in *human capital* among individuals or from differences in nonwage characteristics of jobs. According to *efficiency wage theory*, some employers pay more than the going wage because doing so results in higher productivity.

Terms for Review

- factor markets
- marginal revenue product
- value of marginal product
- marginal factor cost
- marginal productivity theory of distribution
- monopsony
- human capital
- efficiency wage theory

Questions for Review

1. What role do factor markets play in determining how goods and services are produced? In determining for whom they are produced?

2. What is the relationship between the marginal revenue product of a factor of production and the price of the product when the firm is a perfect competitor in the market in which it sells its output? When it is a monopolist in that market?

3. What is the factor market equilibrium condition for a profit-maximizing firm?

4. Why is it possible for one person's labor supply curve to have a negatively sloped section above a certain wage rate? Why do the labor supply curves for individual labor markets lack such negatively sloped sections?

5. According to the marginal productivity theory of distribution, what is the relationship between the wage rate and the value of the product in equilibrium?

6. In what way is the factor market equilibrium condition for a monopsonistic firm similar to that for a competitive firm? In what way is it different?

7. List three changes in economic conditions that can cause the demand curve for a factor of production to shift to the left or right. How do such shifts affect the relative wages of different jobs in the short run? In the long run?

8. In what sense do market forces tend to erode wage differences based on discrimination? Why does the market not always eliminate discrimination completely?

Problems and Topics for Discussion

1. **Examining the lead-off case.** Compare the case of GM's Fort Wayne plant with that of the early Ford Motor Company ("Perspective 13.2"). How do the two cases compare in terms of investment in human capital? Why would both firms have an incentive to pay higher wages than the average of all manufacturing firms of their times?

2. **Households as buyers in factor markets.** This chapter discusses only factor markets in which the buyers are firms. Are households ever direct buyers of factors of production? For example, are you the direct buyer of a factor of production when you hire someone to type a term paper for you? How would the theory of factor markets have to be modified to take into account cases in which the buyers of factor services are households rather than firms?

3. **Isoquants and factor demand.** This question is for readers who have completed the appendix to Chapter 8 on isoquants or wish to read that appendix now. Use an isoquant diagram to derive the demand curve for a factor of production. You may need to refer to the derivation of a product demand curve in Exhibit 7A.7 (page 176).

4. **A case of backward-bending labor demand?** In his historical novel *Chesapeake*, James Michener describes the unsuccessful efforts of early European colonists to run their plantations with hired Native American labor. Among the many factors that led to the breakdown of relationships between the planters and local tribes were some economic problems. For example, Michener reports the frustration of a planter who finds that an offer of higher wages does not discourage his native workers from quitting their jobs in the fields after a few weeks of work; in fact, the workers seem to quit sooner when their pay is raised. Does what you have learned in this chapter shed any light on this situation? Discuss.

5. **Monopsony and monopoly.** Is a monopsonist always a monopolist, and vice versa? Try to imagine a firm that is a monopsonist in its factor market but a perfect competitor in its product market. Then try to visualize a firm that is a monopolist but not a monopsonist.

6. **The relationship of "how" and "for whom."** Discuss the following statement: "It is a good idea to let factor markets determine how things are produced, but the matter of for whom things are produced should be handled according to need, not according to supply and demand." Is it possible to separate the "how" and "for whom" functions of factor markets?

7. **Supply of and demand for dentists.** Turn to "Economics in the News 3.2" (page 68), which discusses the market for dentists' services. In this case, how have demand shifts affected the earnings of dentists relative to those of other workers? How long is the "long run" in the case of dentists? What evidence do you find in the discussion that a long-run adjustment is taking place? How will the short-run and long-run equilibria in this market be affected by investment in human capital?

8. **Trends in the pay of men and women.** In the last 10 years, the male-female wage gap has narrowed somewhat, and it is expected to narrow further later in this century with or without new legislation to combat wage discrimination. Do you think the narrowing of the wage gap has anything to do with the facts that (1) women are more than proportionately represented in service occupations and (2) demand for services is growing more rapidly than demand for goods? Discuss.

9. **Affirmative action.** "Equal pay for equal work is not enough. Employers must also be required to follow affirmative-action guidelines or hiring quotas for members of disfavored groups." Comment on this statement in light of what you have learned in this chapter.

Case for Discussion

Government: Friend or Foe of Women in the Labor Market?

Any reliance on government to increase women's position in the labor force is ironic, writes economist Deborah Walker, in that analysis shows that government legislation, even when well intentioned, has not always been helpful to women. Historically, legislation has restricted women from entering certain occupations for several reasons. During the early 1900s, women were banned from working in establishments that sold liquor so that immoral and disorderly situations would not develop. Women were also prohibited from working in mines and at night jobs in order to prevent "unregulated mingling of men and women" in dark places. "Specific evil effects of long hours on childbirth and female functions" was the basis for restricting the number of hours women could work.

Job-related regulations are usually not *helpful to women.*

Job-related regulations initially were seen as helpful to women. Most of them, however, proved to be just the opposite. One female economist realized this very early. In 1906, Sophonisha P. Breckenridge wrote:

> Such legislation is usually called "protective legislation" and women workers are characterized as a "protected class." But it is obviously not the women who are protected. For them, some of this legislation may be a distinct limitation. For example, the prohibition against work in mines or against night work may very well so limit the opportunities of women to find employment as to result in increased congestion and decreased wages in such other occupations as are open to them. . . . But no one should lose sight of the fact that such legislation is not enacted exclusively, or even primarily, for the benefit of women themselves.

Walker notes other examples of laws that adversely affect women in the labor market. Laws that fix wage rates at certain levels for the purpose of benefiting workers create side effects, including discrimination. When a minimum-wage law is imposed, many new job applicants enter the market hoping to get paid this wage rate. This activity creates a surplus of people searching for jobs and allows employers to be discriminatory at a very low cost. Further, many of the job applicants whose skills are not worth the minimum wage to employers will not be hired at all. For [various] reasons, many of these applicants will be women.

Source: Deborah Walker, "Value and Opportunity: The Issue of Comparable Pay for Comparable Work," Cato Policy Analysis No. 38, May 31, 1984. Photo Source: Baker Library, Harvard Business School.

Questions

1. Use supply and demand analysis to show how a law excluding women from certain occupations will tend to depress the wages of women workers.

2. According to Sophonisha Breckenridge, restrictive legislation is not enacted exclusively, or even primarily, for the benefit of women themselves. Who would be the real beneficiaries? Explain, using supply and demand analysis.

3. Review the discussion of rent control in Chapter 3 beginning on page 72. There it was explained that rent control makes it easier and less costly for landlords to discriminate. In what way are the labor market effects of a minimum-wage law similar to the effects of a rent control law?

4. A contemporary labor market issue concerns exposure in the workplace to chemicals or radiation that may be harmful to pregnant women but harm-

less—or at least less harmful—to men and nonpregnant women. What course should policy take in such cases? Should there be a law prohibiting pregnant women from working under conditions that expose them to these hazards? Should there be a law prohibiting employers from discriminating against pregnant women in job assignments even when possible hazards are involved? Or should the matter be left to the discretion of the employers and employees concerned? Discuss the pros and cons of each approach.

Suggestions for Further Reading

Aaron, Henry J., and Cameran M. Lougy. *The Comparable Worth Controversy.* Washington, D.C.: The Brookings Institution, 1986.

A brief survey of the problem of differences in pay for work of "comparable worth" by men and women, including some recommended solutions.

Kaufman, Bruce E. *The Economics of Labor Markets and Labor Relations.* Hinsdale, Ill.: Dryden Press, 1986.

This text provides in-depth coverage of the material in this and the following chapter.

Wallace, Mark J., and Charles H. Fay. *Compensation Theory and Practice.* Boston: Kent, 1983.

Discusses issues of pay from a business manager's point of view.

14 Labor Unions and Collective Bargaining

After reading this chapter, you will understand . . .

- How labor unions have developed over time in the United States.
- The main provisions of U.S. labor law.
- How wage rates are determined in unionized markets.
- What unions do in addition to bargaining over wages and benefits.

Before reading this chapter, make sure you know the meaning of . . .

- Economic rent (Chapter 5)
- Producer surplus (Chapter 7)
- Monopsony (Chapter 13)
- Efficiency wage theory (Chapter 13)

"If I'd Had Anything I'm Really Sold on, It's the UAW"

"Everybody has to have something they're really sold on. Some people go to church. If I'd had anything I'm really sold on, it's the UAW [United Auto Workers].

"I started working at Fisher Body in 1917 and retired in '62, with 45 and $\frac{8}{10}$ years service. Until 1933, no unions, no rules: you were at the mercy of your foreman. I could go to work at seven o'clock in the morning, and at seven fifteen the boss'd come around and say: you could come back at three o'clock. If he preferred somebody else over you, that person would be called back earlier, though you were there longer.

"I left the plants so many nights hostile. If I were a fella big and strong, I think I'd a picked a fight with the first fella I met on the corner. It was lousy. Degraded. You might call yourself a man if you was on the street, but as soon as you went through the door and punched your card, you was nothing more or less than a robot. Do this, go there, do that. You'd do it.

"We got involved in a strike in Detroit, and we lost the strike. Went back on our knees. That's the way you learn things. I got laid off in the fall of '31. I wasn't told I was blackballed, but I was told there was no more jobs at Fisher Body for me."

Source: From an interview with Bob Stinson, former autoworker, in Studs Terkel, *Hard Times: An Oral History of the Great Depression*, © 1970 Pantheon Books, A Division of Random House, Inc., p. 129. Reprinted with permission. Photo Source: UPI/Bettmann Newsphotos.

IN the labor markets discussed in Chapter 13, workers competed with one another for jobs as individuals. However, many autoworkers, steelworkers, truck drivers, garment workers, and others do not enter the labor market as individuals; rather, they do so as members of unions. When Bob Stinson was fired from General Motors' Fisher Body division in 1931, unions were poised for a period of growth that brought their membership to 35 percent of the nonfarm labor force by 1945 (see Exhibit 14.1). Union membership has fallen since then, but even though fewer than one-fifth of all workers belong to unions today, they still deserve a separate chapter. This is partly because they are strongest in such key industries as automobiles, steel, and transportation. It is also because wage settlements and labor-management relations in unionized firms strongly influence those in nonunionized firms.

In this chapter, we examine what labor unions are and what they do. We begin with a brief history of unions in the United States. Next, we look at the effects of unions on wages. Finally, we discuss some of the effects of unions on nonwage aspects of work life.

Exhibit 14.1   Labor Union Membership in the United States, 1935–1984

After the passage of the Wagner Act in 1935, unions began a period of rapid growth. Membership peaked at a little over a third of the nonfarm labor force 10 years later. Since then, union membership as a percentage of the nonfarm labor force has declined steadily.

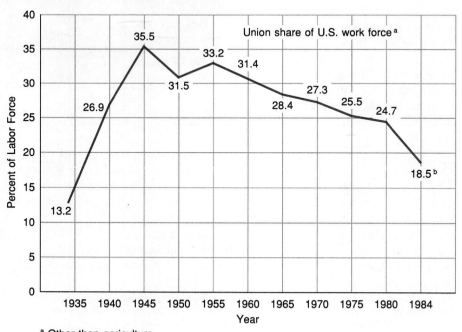

[a] Other than agriculture.
[b] Troy and Shefflin.

Source: For 1935–1980, Bureau of Labor Statistics. The official series was discontinued in 1980. Later data are estimates by Leo Troy and Neil Sheflin of Rutgers University.

History of Unionism in the United States

Earliest Beginnings

Unions had their start in the United States toward the end of the eighteenth century. In the 1790s craft workers, including printers, shoemakers, and carpenters, formed local associations to further their economic interests. These earliest labor groups, called **craft unions,** were organizations of skilled workers who were in the same trade. Their skills and shared interests made it relatively easy for them to work together in union activities and gave their organizations some degree of monopoly power in employer dealings.

Craft union
A union of skilled workers who all practice the same trade.

However, most of the early local craft unions were short-lived and problem ridden. It was not until 1842, for example, that the courts recognized unions as legal. But even after that date, the courts were often unfriendly. Further, few of the early local unions were strong enough to survive the frequent business downturns of that period. As soon as business activity declined, they lost most of their bargaining power. They then faded away, to be organized again in the next period of prosperity.

The Knights of Labor

Unionism did not take root on a wide scale until after the Civil War. Before then, there had been some attempts to form national unions, but these did not prove lasting. After the war, new national organizations appeared. The most prominent of the national labor organizations in the post–Civil War period had the colorful name of Noble Order of the Knights of Labor. This organization was founded as a secret society in 1869, but its growth began only after it abandoned secrecy in 1878. Membership reached a peak of more than 700,000 workers in 1886.

Many local unions of skilled craft workers were affiliated with the Knights of Labor, but the Knights were much more than an association of craft unions. They welcomed anyone who worked for a living, including farmers, farm workers, and unskilled laborers, excluding only such "undesirables" as bankers, liquor dealers, Pinkerton detectives, and lawyers. The Knights' program was not limited to issues of wages and working conditions; it also stressed worker education and producer cooperatives as ways of combating the "evil of wealth."

The broad scope of the Knights of Labor permitted rapid growth, but it also led to the group's eventual decline. After 1886, conflicts between the Knights and its member unions increased, and some of the more discontented unions left the organization. Moreover, public hostility was aroused by the killing of a policeman during Chicago's Haymarket Riot of 1886, although no connection of the Knights with that event was ever proved. From that year on, however, the Knights of Labor lost ground to the American Federation of Labor.

The AFL

The American Federation of Labor, or AFL (first called the Federation of Organized Trades and Labor Unions), was founded in 1881. Its founders included some independent craft unions and some local craft affiliates of the Knights of

Labor that felt that the bargaining power of skilled craft workers would be wasted in efforts to win benefits for unskilled workers. Since 1886, the AFL has played a dominant role in union history.

The AFL found strong leadership under Samuel Gompers, its president for all but one year from 1886 until his death in 1924 (see "Who Said It? Who Did It? 14.1"). Gompers sought to avoid the mistakes that had led to the downfall of the Knights of Labor. The AFL owes its success largely to three features of its organization and philosophy:

1. The AFL was based solidly on the principle of craft unionism. Its leaders thought that the dangers of economic depressions and employer opposition could be overcome only by relying on skilled workers who could not easily be replaced during strikes. The AFL itself was, in effect, an umbrella organization of national craft unions.

2. The AFL emphasized business unionism; that is, it devoted most of its energies to bread-and-butter issues of pay and working conditions. Unlike many European labor unions, it was content to work within the capitalist system. It did not seek the overthrow of private property or the establishment of socialism.

3. The AFL limited its political role. Again in contrast to European labor movements, it did not found a labor party. Gompers thought that excessive political involvement would lead to internal conflict within the labor movement and hence weaken its ability to achieve concrete economic goals.

The AFL grew slowly at first and then more rapidly. By 1904, it had 2 million members. Membership peaked at about 5 million in 1920 but declined to around 3 million in 1930.

Early Industrial Unions

Industrial union
A union of all the workers in an industry, including both skilled and unskilled workers in all trades.

Although the AFL dominated the union scene in the decades around the turn of the century, the principle of craft unionism was not accepted everywhere. In some places, there were notable early successes in organizing industrial unions—unions that included workers of all crafts and skill levels within a given industry. Brewery workers organized in 1886, soon followed by the organization of the United Mine Workers in 1890. After 1900, three successful industrial unions emerged in the clothing industry, the strongest one being the International Ladies' Garment Workers' Union. During the same years, however, industrial unionism suffered some major failures. Strike efforts by steel and railway workers were defeated after clashes involving Pinkerton detectives, state troopers, and strikebreakers and the jailing of labor leaders.

On another front, the AFL was challenged by unionists who were unwilling to work within the capitalist system. The most notable of their organizations was the International Workers of the World (IWW), whose members were known as "Wobblies." The IWW campaigned for "one big union" that would embrace all workers of all skills and crafts; it also called for worker management of industry. It was successful in organizing lumberjacks and agricultural workers. However, during World War I the IWW opposed the U.S. war effort—a stand that brought it under intense political attack. Many of its leaders and members were jailed, and the organization faded rapidly.

Samuel Gompers and the AFL

Samuel Gompers was born in a London tenement; he was the son of a skilled cigar maker. When he was 13, he and his family moved to the United States and settled on the East Side of New York. Gompers followed his father into the cigar trade.

Although his formal education ended at age 10, Gompers was very active in the workers' self-education movement. In the cigar-making shops, jobs were organized on a piecework basis. Groups of workers would have one of their members read to them while they worked. They paid the reader by making his cigars for him. In this way, Gompers became acquainted with the works of Marx, Engels, and other European socialists. Often he was chosen as the reader.

The cigar makers' union to which Gompers belonged

Photo Source: AFL–CIO.

fell apart during the depression of 1873. Gompers rebuilt it as a craft union like those he was later to unite in the American Federation of Labor. Key features of this union were high membership dues, central control of funds, national officers with control over local unions, and union-organized accident and unemployment benefits for members.

Gompers became disillusioned with radical socialism. The main role of unions, in his view, was to look after their members' economic interests. He wrote:

> Unions, pure and simple, are the natural organization of wage workers to secure their present material and practical improvement and to achieve their final emancipation. . . . The working people are in too great need of immediate improvements in their condition to allow them to forego them in the endeavor to devote their entire energies to an end however beautiful to contemplate. . . . The way out of the wage system is through higher wages.

During the 1890s, a socialist faction emerged within the AFL. It adopted a program that called for collective ownership of all means of production and other radical measures. Gompers opposed the group, and in the 1895 election for the AFL presidency, he was defeated. He fought back, however, and succeeded in regaining the presidency the following year. He remained president until his death in 1924.

Gompers was an ardent patriot throughout his career. During World War I, he opposed pacifism and supported the war effort. In 1918 he said, "America is a symbol; it is an ideal; the hopes of the world can be expressed in the ideal—America."

The 1930s and the CIO

Unionism waned in the 1920s, but during the Great Depression the decline was reversed. The revival of organized labor was brought about largely by favorable legislation passed during this period. That legislation (to be discussed in some detail later in the chapter) removed the main legal barriers to union organization and crippled employers' antiunion efforts.

In the improved legal climate, there was increased pressure to organize workers in the mass production industries—steel, rubber, automobiles, and others—in which earlier attempts had failed. This led to serious conflicts within the AFL, whose old-line craft unionists did not believe that stable unions could be formed in those industries. These unionists also resented the efforts of industrial unions to recruit skilled workers in their industries, believing that such workers ought to join existing craft unions. As a result of this dispute, an opposition group formed within the AFL, led by John L. Lewis of the United Mine Workers. In 1938, the group was expelled from the AFL and formed the rival

Congress of Industrial Organizations, or CIO (originally known as the Committee for Industrial Organization).

The CIO scored some major successes during the 1930s, most notably the unionization of the steel industry. (The industry leader, U.S. Steel, agreed to collective bargaining in 1937.) Successful unionization campaigns were carried out around the same time in the rubber, automobile, electrical, meat-packing, and textile industries, to name just a few. By the end of 1938, the CIO's membership of 4 million exceeded the AFL's membership of 2.9 million.

The CIO's successes made it clear that craft unionism was not the only workable recipe for labor organization. They also contributed to a rapid growth in union membership—although the AFL also grew quickly during that period. By 1939, union membership had risen to 29 percent of nonagricultural employees—more than double the figure of just four years earlier. By 1945, over a third of nonagricultural workers had been organized.

The AFL-CIO Merger

After World War II, unions faced more difficulties. The political and legislative climate began to turn against them. Unionization drives in the South, which had been expected to yield millions of new members, were relatively unsuccessful. At the same time, leadership of both the AFL and the CIO passed into the hands of men who had not been directly involved in the bitter disputes that had led to the split between the two unions. The distinction between craft and industrial unions seemed less important now that it was clear that each type had its place. The outcome was an agreement to merge the two labor federations, which was signed in December 1955.

The Present and Future

The formation of the AFL-CIO did not reverse the fall in union membership or prevent further decline. Many factors have contributed to the problems of union organizers in recent decades. For one thing, blue-collar workers, traditionally the easiest to organize, now make up a much smaller percentage of the labor force than in the past. Women, who comprise an increasing fraction of the labor force, have never belonged to unions in proportion to their numbers. Moreover, unions have not successfully followed the shift of jobs from the industrial Northeast and Midwest to the Sunbelt states. Finally, some observers believe that younger workers do not consider unions important to their well-being. In sum, despite some success in the organization of state and local government and agricultural workers, the prognosis for unionization is continued gradual decline.

Public Policy toward Unions

Labor unions do not operate in a vacuum. They function in an environment of law and public policy that has been a topic of heated debate since unions began. Some have argued that all unions should be suppressed as illegal restraints on trade. Others have advocated government support for unions to promote industrial stability and high living standards for all. Still others have favored a laissez-faire policy that would let workers and management bargain without government interference. The debate has been clouded by disagreements about the true effect of unions on relative and absolute wages and on industrial efficiency. Without taking a position, in the next section we will survey the changing course of government policy over time, seeing how first one and then another opinion has become dominant.

Early Court Hostility

Unions have had trouble with the courts from their earliest days. Under precedents from English common law, they were often treated as illegal conspiracies in restraint of trade. In *Commonwealth* v. *Hunt*, a landmark case decided in Massachusetts in 1842, the court declared that unions were not necessarily illegal in themselves but restricted the aims unions could pursue and the means they could use in achieving them.

In the early twentieth century, the legal climate for unions grew even more hostile. In a series of cases from 1908 through the 1920s, the Sherman Antitrust Act was applied to unions despite considerable doubt as to whether Congress had intended the act to be interpreted in this way.

During this period, the main legal weapon used against unions was the *injunction* (court order). If a firm believed that union activities threatened it in any way, it could get an injunction barring the union from striking, picketing, publicizing labor disputes, assembling to promote its interests, and virtually anything else. Often the courts issued such injunctions without even hearing the union's side of the case.

Norris–La Guardia Act

As union membership sank to a low point in 1932, the legal climate was changed dramatically by the passage of the Norris–La Guardia Act. This act deprived antiunion employers of the injunction, formerly their biggest weapon. The law declared, in effect, that the government should remain neutral in labor disputes. The courts could still intervene to protect tangible property and prevent the use of violence. However, as long as unions remained nonviolent, they had the right to strike, picket, boycott, assemble, and persuade others to do these and other things.

Wagner Act

The growing prolabor climate of the 1930s led to the passage of further labor legislation. The Wagner Act of 1935 took government policy out of the neutral position in which the Norris–La Guardia Act had left it and put the government squarely on the side of the unions.

The Wagner Act declared that "employees shall have the right to self-organization, to form, join, or assist labor organizations, to bargain collectively through representatives of their own choosing, and to engage in concerted activities, for the purpose of collective bargaining or other mutual aid or protection." The law created its own enforcement agency in the form of a three-member National Labor Relations Board (NLRB). This board was to oversee enforcement of the act, arrange for representative elections, and serve as judge and jury whenever the act was violated.

The Wagner Act also outlawed a specific list of "unfair employer labor practices." Employers could no longer use lockouts, intimidation, blacklists, or spying. They could no longer force employees to sign contracts that made non-membership in a union a condition of employment. In some cases, employers were even barred from speaking against unions.

Taft-Hartley Act

The Wagner Act gave such a boost to labor unions that people began to worry about whether it was working too well. Unions became strong and powerful. They could call strikes that could paralyze a region and even threaten national welfare. After a series of damaging strikes in 1946, a Republican Congress passed legislation that amended the Wagner Act.

The Taft-Hartley Act of 1947 tried to move public policy back toward a neutral position on labor issues. It modified the structure of the NLRB and removed its prosecutorial powers. It retained the list of unfair employer labor practices but added one of unfair union labor practices. The new list included restraint or coercion of employees by unions, strikes and boycotts aimed at forcing self-employed people to join unions, and secondary boycotts (strikes or boycotts intended to force an employer to cease dealings in the product of an-other firm involved in a labor dispute). The act limited the closed shop, under which union membership is a condition of employment. It also provided for federal intervention in strikes that threaten to create a national emergency.

Landrum-Griffin Act

The last major piece of legislation defining government policy toward unions was the Landrum-Griffin Act of 1959. It put government in the business of policing the internal affairs of unions. A series of scandals and congressional hearings had brought several cases of corrupt or criminal practices on the part of union officials to public attention. This legislation was an attempt to "clean up" unions.

A major provision of the act was a bill of rights for rank-and-file union members. It guaranteed their right of free speech, their right to vote in union elections, and so on. The act also mandated union reports on finances, regulated the term of office of union officials, specified election procedures, and strength-ened the Taft-Hartley Act's provisions against secondary boycotts.

Collective Bargaining and Wage Rates

From its earliest days through the turmoil of the 1930s and continuing today, unionism has had two faces. On the one hand, unions can be seen as organiza-tions that attempt to exercise monopoly power in order to raise their members' wages. On the other, they can be regarded as the collective voice of workers, bargaining for safety, democracy, and dignity in the workplace as well as wages and benefits and striving to serve the diverse interests of more and less skilled members, older and younger workers, and union leadership as well as rank and file. In this section, we will look at both faces of unions as they affect the wage bargain. In the final section, we will examine some issues that go beyond wages.

The Union as a Maximizer

One approach to understanding labor unions is to treat them as maximizing organizations in much the same way as firms and households. Consider, for example, the case of a union that was formed in a competitive market and now seeks higher wages through the threat of a strike. Exhibit 14.2 sets the stage. It shows a labor market in which the competitive equilibrium wage rate is $8 an hour and the equilibrium level of employment is 300,000 worker-hours per year (point E_1).

Now suppose that the newly organized workers tell employers that they want $10 an hour or else they will go on strike. The strike threat is shown in the graph by a change in the shape of the supply curve. Initially the supply curve had the usual upward-sloping shape. After the strike threat, employers face a supply curve that contains a kink. The horizontal left-hand branch of the kinked supply curve shows that if the employers do not pay at least $10 an hour, no

Exhibit 14.2   Effect of Unionization in a Competitive Labor Market

A union formed in a competitive labor market can use a strike threat to bargain for higher wages. Here the union threatens to strike unless the wage is raised from its competitive level of $8 an hour ($E_1$) to $10 an hour. At that point, the supply curve for labor becomes horizontal at $10 an hour up to 400,000 worker-hours per year. A new equilibrium is reached at E_2, where the new supply curve intersects the demand curve. The wage is higher than before, but the quantity of labor employed is smaller.

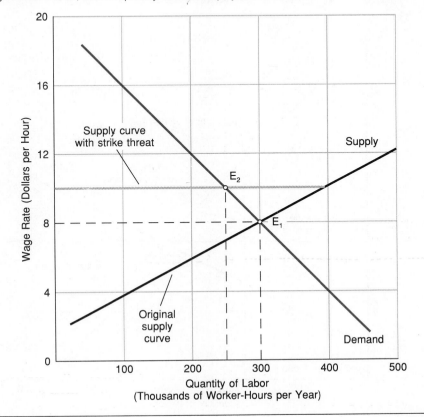

workers will be available. Up to 400,000 worker-hours will be supplied at $10 an hour. To hire more labor than that, the wage will have to be raised above what the union is demanding.

If the employers decide that they have no choice but to accept the union's demand, they will react by shifting to a new equilibrium at point E_2, where the demand curve and the horizontal part of the new supply curve intersect. There they will hire 250,000 worker-hours per year at $10 an hour. The union will have succeeded in raising its members' wage, but only at the cost of reducing the amount of work available from 300,000 to 250,000 worker-hours per year.

In this example, we see that the union can win a higher wage rate only at the expense of jobs for its members. This trade-off raises two questions: What do unions maximize? How far up the demand curve should they try to move, if at all, in attempting to serve their members' interests? These questions have puzzled economists for many years. A number of answers have been proposed, but

Exhibit 14.3   The Wage-Job Trade-off

Unions in industries in which employers are price takers may choose various ways of dealing with the wage-job trade-off. If the union's goal is to maximize employment, it will not bargain for a wage higher than the competitive equilibrium. If the labor demand curve is inelastic at the competitive equilibrium point, total income of union members can be increased by raising the wage to the point at which the demand curve becomes unit elastic. If unions take workers' opportunity costs into account, they may want to raise wages higher to the level that will maximize worker rents.

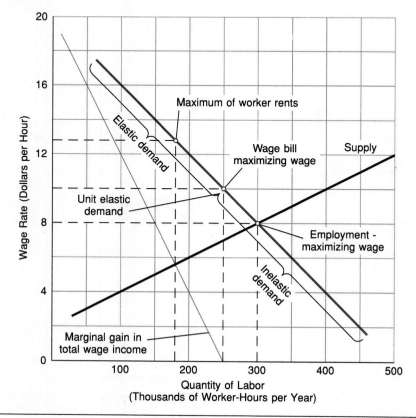

none have ever been found to apply to all cases. Several of those answers are illustrated in Exhibit 14.3.

Maximize Employment

One possibility is for a union to maximize employment for its members. In Exhibit 14.3, this will require a wage of $8 an hour, as shown by the intersection of the supply and demand curves. At that wage, 300,000 worker-hours per year will be employed. At any higher wage, employers will be unwilling to use so much labor. At any lower wage, workers will not be available. However, $8 an hour is the same as the competitive wage that would prevail in a competitive market without a union. An employment-maximizing union thus might represent workers politically or might provide social benefits, but it would be unable to do anything to raise the wage. (An exception is the case in which the union faces a monopsonist, which we will discuss shortly.)

Maximize Wage Bill

A more widely accepted suggestion is that unions seek to maximize the *total wage bill*—that is, the product of the wage rate and the number of hours worked per year. As Exhibit 14.3 shows, the wage bill is maximized at $10 an hour—the point at which the elasticity of labor demand is 1. Keeping the wage at this level, however, creates an excess supply of labor. Workers will be willing to supply 400,000 hours per year, but only 250,000 will be required. The union can simply allow workers to compete for jobs on a first-come, first-served basis and not worry about who can get a job. Alternatively, it can try to divide up the available work among all the workers who want jobs in the industry. Each worker will be able to put in only a limited number of hours. Whatever the route taken, the union must be organized well enough to prevent nonunion workers from undercutting it—something that is not easy to do.

Maximize Worker Rents

The wage-bill maximization approach has been criticized by some economists for neglecting the opportunity costs that workers face. To any individual worker, the opportunity cost of taking a job is the value of the best alternative use of the workday—usually another job. The height of the labor supply curve at any point can be taken as a measure of this opportunity cost. In Exhibit 14.3, for example, no more than 100,000 worker-hours will be supplied at $4, because the remaining workers have other ways of using their time that are worth more than $4 an hour. However, if the wage is raised to $6 an hour, another 100,000 worker-hours will be supplied, representing workers whose opportunity costs are more than $4 an hour but less than or equal to $6 an hour.

Using the labor supply curve as a measure of opportunity costs makes it possible to calculate the *economic rent* that each worker receives from employment, that is, the difference between the wage received and the opportunity cost of taking a given job rather than the best available alternative. Graphically, the total rent workers receive equals the area above the labor supply curve and below a line drawn at the height of the wage rate. (The geometry is the same as that for producer surplus as shown in Chapter 7.)

Some economists have reasoned that rather than trying to maximize the wage bill, it would be more logical for unions to try to maximize worker rents. To do this, they should permit employment to expand only to the point at which the marginal gain in total wage income for their members will begin to fall below the opportunity cost of supplying the marginal unit of labor. The marginal gain in total wage income for members can be represented by a line that is related to the labor demand curve in the same way that, in the product market, a firm's marginal revenue curve is related to the demand curve for its product. Such a line is drawn in Exhibit 14.3. The point at which this line intersects the labor supply curve (which represents the opportunity cost of supplying labor) is the point at which worker rents are maximized.

Union versus Monopsonist

The question of what it is that unions maximize stems largely from the trade-off between wages and jobs that most unions face. However, there is one case in which unions do not face that trade-off—the case in which a union faces an employer that is a monopsonist. This situation is illustrated in Exhibit 14.4.

Initially workers are assumed to be unorganized. The equilibrium quantity of labor hired, shown by the intersection of the employer's demand curve and the marginal labor cost curve, is 220,000 worker-hours per year. The wage rate,

Exhibit 14.4   Effects of Unions in a Monopsony Labor Market

When a union faces a monopsonistic employer, it can sometimes raise both wages and employment. Here the initial equilibrium wage is $6.50 an hour, with 220,000 worker-hours per year employed (point E₁). A strike threat changes the shape of the monopsonist's marginal labor cost curve. The monopsonist is now a price taker up to 400,000 worker-hours per year. The new equilibrium occurs at E₂, where both the wage rate and the number of worker-hours employed is greater than at E₁.

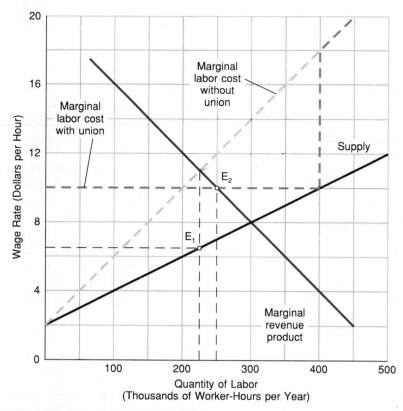

shown by the height of the supply curve for that quantity of labor, is $6.50 an hour. This equilibrium point is labeled E_1.

Now consider what happens if the workers unionize and threaten to go on strike if they are not paid $10 an hour. As in Exhibit 14.2, the union's action puts a kink in the labor supply curve. What is more important, along the horizontal part of the new labor supply curve the monopsonist's marginal labor cost equals the wage rate. The union says, in effect, that the firm can hire as many workers as it wants at no more and no less than $10 an hour—which means that changes in the quantity of labor hired no longer require changes in the wage rate. One more worker-hour raises total labor costs by no more and no less than $10.

Suppose that the union is strong enough to make the monopsonist accept its wage demand on a take-it-or-leave-it basis. The new equilibrium will then be found where the new marginal labor cost curve intersects the marginal revenue product curve—at E_2. There the wage rate is $10 an hour and 250,000 worker-hours per year are employed. Both the wage rate and employment are higher than in the previous monopsonistic equilibrium.

However, there is a limit on the power of a union facing a monopsonist to raise wages without losing jobs. This limit is set by the extent to which the original monopsony wage fell short of the competitive wage. Once the wage rate begins to exceed the level at which the supply and marginal revenue product curves intersect, further raises will reduce employment; in fact, in Exhibit 14.4 the wage of $10 an hour is already in the trade-off region. Maximum employment is reached at $8 an hour, which is equal to the competitive wage.

Bilateral Monopoly

The example just given assumes that the monopsonistic employer will accept the union's demand on a take-it-or-leave-it basis. However, this is not the typical case. Normally the collective bargaining process proceeds through an exchange of demands and offers in which neither party acts as a price taker. This situation is often called **bilateral monopoly.**

The outcome of collective bargaining under bilateral monopoly cannot be predicted by economic analysis alone. Economic analysis can only state a range of outcomes within which a settlement can take place. The actual outcome depends on the relative bargaining strengths and skills of the two sides. The headline-making disputes in which "big labor" clashes with "big business" are usually examples of bilateral monopoly.

Bilateral monopoly
A market situation in which both the buyer and the seller have some monopoly or monopsony power and neither behaves as a price taker.

Union Politics and Wage Bargaining

Models of unions as maximizers treat labor organizations as though they were firms. In these models, unions are seen as single-mindedly pursuing some goal just as a firm pursues the goal of profits. However, the maximizing models have been criticized for glossing over one crucial difference between a labor union and a business firm, namely that union members have no common interest that unites them in the way that profits unite a firm's owners.

Consider the case of a corporation that is trying to decide whether to raise the price of its product, knowing that a higher price will mean fewer units sold. It compares marginal cost with marginal revenue. If product demand is elastic, less output will mean less revenue. However, if the marginal revenue forgone is less than the marginal cost of producing the units in question, a higher price and lower output will mean more profit. This profit will be shared among all the owners—the partners in a partnership or the stockholders in a corporation. Thus, if the marginal cost–marginal revenue calculations are favorable, all owners can be expected to agree to the increase in product price.

The situation of a union bargaining for an increase in the wage rate is fundamentally different. If the wage is increased, jobs will be lost as the employer is forced up and to the left along the labor demand curve. Depending on circumstances, the increase in the wage rate may, as was shown earlier, increase the total wage bill, total worker rents, or both, but the gain will not be shared equally among union members. Instead, some will lose their jobs altogether, while those who remain on the job will reap all the gains.

Following this reasoning, it would appear that each worker's "maximizing" wage would be different from every other's. Whether or not a given worker will favor a given wage increase will depend on whether he or she will lose the job as a result. If, as is often the case, layoffs are made in reverse order of seniority, the more senior the worker, the higher will be the wage he or she favors.

Bruce E. Kaufman has suggested that under some circumstances, the equilibrium wage rate for a labor market will not be the wage that maximizes anything; rather, it will be determined by the interests of the *median worker*—the one in the middle of the seniority scale. This reasoning assumes that union leadership is responsive to the wishes of a majority of the membership, either through a formal voting process or through less formal channels of influence. The idea is that the median worker plus all more senior workers compose a majority voting bloc within the union. This bloc can, in principle, override the interests of less senior workers, who are the most threatened by layoffs.[1]

Of course, Kaufman and everyone else who has studied internal union politics recognize that the median-worker model is in its own way as much of an oversimplification as the maximizing models examined earlier. Taken at face value, the median-worker model suggests that 50 percent of the union plus one member would force through a wage increase that would get the rest of the membership sacked; the next year, half of those left might force through another such wage increase; and so on until only one worker remained on the payroll. Obviously there is more to union politics than this. Union leaders in the bargaining process and workers voting on contract ratification must take many more variables into account than wage rates and seniority. There is the risk that driving too hard a bargain will drive the employer out of the market altogether. There are trade-offs between wages and working conditions. Union leaders may have an interest in keeping the union membership large to enhance their own prestige, and workers may have feelings of solidarity with their fellows who are lower on the seniority scale.

Nonetheless, the point remains that once unions are viewed as political entities, no simple maximizing model analogous to the profit-maximizing model of the firm can do justice to the process of collective bargaining.

Evidence on Wage Effects

Despite their different points of departure, both the maximizing models and political models of unions imply that unions will tend to raise wages above levels

---

[1] Bruce E. Kaufman, *The Economics of Labor Markets and Labor Relations* (Hinsdale, Ill.: Dryden Press, 1986), 461–463.

that would otherwise prevail. But by how much will they raise wages? Theory alone cannot answer this question.

The answer depends partly on conditions in the product market. Recall that the demand for labor is a derived demand. The greater the elasticity of demand for the employer's product, the less possible it will be for the employer to pass wage increases along to customers. In the case of an employer that sells its product in a perfectly competitive market, a union would be able to win no wage increase at all.

A union's power to raise its members' wages is enhanced if the entire industry is unionized and the union bargains with employers as a group. This has long been true in such industries as steel, automobiles, and trucking. In such cases it is the elasticity of the industry demand curve that counts, not that of each employer. However, although industry demand tends to be less elastic than the demand of any one firm within the industry, employers' ability to pass along wage increases is not unlimited. Unions in the steel and automobile industries have learned that high costs, based in part on high union wages, have caused customers to turn to foreign producers. In the trucking industry, the powerful Teamsters Union was humbled by competition from nonunion truckers after the industry was deregulated in the early 1980s.

In short, the ability of unions to raise wages varies from one industry to another. In a recent study, economists Richard B. Freeman and James L. Medoff concluded that unions raised the wages of their members by somewhat more than 20 percent and, in some cases, by more than 30 percent (see "Perspective 14.1").[2] It should be noted that Freeman and Medoff's data come from the 1970s. Many observers think that the union/nonunion wage differential has decreased in the 1980s under the impact of international competition, deregulation, and other forces.

What Else Do Unions Do?

To focus entirely on unions' effects on wages would be misleading; unions do many other things besides bargain over wages. This has been true from the earliest days of unionism, when the Knights of Labor campaigned for worker education and self-improvement, to the present, when unions provide social activities, help members with personal and family problems, and serve as a channel for participation in national politics. Some of the things that unions do reach beyond the scope of economics. But even on the economic level, unions affect more than wages.

For one thing, unions give workers a voice in how the workplace is run. In an economy based on free labor markets, a worker can always seek another job if he or she does not like the way the workplace is run. But unions offer an alternative. They can bargain with employers over health and safety conditions in the workplace. They can help settle workers' grievances in matters ranging from job assignments to company policy to conflicts with supervisors. They can bargain over issues of fairness, such as the role of seniority in layoffs and recalls.

Freeman and Medoff point out that these union activities can improve labor-management relations, reduce employee turnover and absenteeism, and raise

---

[2] Richard B. Freeman and James L. Medoff, *What Do Unions Do?* (New York: Basic Books, 1984).

PERSPECTIVE   14.1

Estimates of the Impact of Unions on Wages

How much do unions raise the wages of their members? Crude data suggest that on the average, union members have earned about 15 percent more than nonmembers as of 1980. However, these overall data mean little, because they fail to consider such factors as the type of work done, age, gender, and so on. A study by Richard B. Freeman and James L. Medoff attempted to estimate the impact of unions on wages in a way that would take such differences into account. They used several data sources and examined several groups of workers. Their results are given in the accompanying table.

Freeman and Medoff also looked into the impact of unions on fringe benefits. They found these to be more strongly affected than wages. The level of fringe benefits of unionized workers averaged 68 percent higher than those of nonunionized workers. Pensions, life and accident insurance, and vacation pay showed the most significant effects.

Finally, Freeman and Medoff looked at the impact of unions on the distribution of wages. The traditional view has been that unions increase income inequality among wage earners. As we have seen, union wage gains tend to come at the cost of fewer jobs in unionized industries. The reduction in employment in unionized industries increases the supply of workers for nonunionized ones, driving wages down in those industries. If the industries that were most likely to be unionized tended to be low-wage industries in the first place, this effect might make the distribution of wages more equal. However, the opposite is the case. Unions tend to be strongest among relatively skilled workers, including airline pilots, skilled construction workers, and semiskilled workers such as autoworkers. They tend to be weak among the lowest-paid worker categories, such as farm workers and retail clerks. In this regard, then, collective bargaining increases the inequality of income between unionized and nonunionized workers.

Freeman and Medoff note, however, that this does not mean that unions make earnings more unequal for the labor force as a whole. For one thing, wages tend to be more equal within unionized firms than within nonunionized ones. In addition, because blue-collar workers are more highly unionized than better-paid white-collar workers, unionization reduces the pay inequality between the two groups. Freeman and Medoff go so far as to claim that these equalizing effects more than offset the tendency of unions to widen the pay gap between their members and nonunionized blue-collar workers.

Source: From *What Do Unions Do?* by Richard B. Freeman and James L. Medoff. The table is based on their Table 3-1, p. 46. Copyright © 1984 by Basic Books, Inc. Reprinted by permission of the publisher.

Source of Estimates	Year	Number of Observations	Approximate Percentage Gain in Wages Due to Collective Bargaining
Data on individuals:			
May Current Population Survey, Bureau of Labor Statistics	1979	16,728	21
Panel Study of Income Dynamics, University of Michigan	1970–1979	11,445	26
Older men, National Longitudinal Survey, Ohio State University	1976	1,922	25
Younger men, National Longitudinal Survey	1976	2,335	32
Mature women, National Longitudinal Survey	1977	1,724	25
Younger women, National Longitudinal Survey	1978	2,068	21
Data on establishments:			
Expenditures for Employee Compensation Survey, Bureau of Labor Statistics	1972–1976	15,574	27

How Top Nonunion Companies Manage Employees

What do managers of top nonunion companies, such as Black & Decker, Eli Lilly, Gillette, Grumman, IBM, and Polaroid, see as the chief benefit of managing in a nonunion environment? According to a study by Fred K. Foulkes, they see not a lower level of wages but a higher level of productivity. The higher productivity comes partly from lower employee turnover and less absenteeism, partly from greater worker loyalty, and partly from wider acceptance of new technology.

Foulkes found that managers of these top nonunion companies made special efforts to give workers a voice in company affairs and to improve the quality of work life. For example:

- Managers work hard to create a sense of equality. Executive status symbols such as exclusive dining rooms and country clubs are avoided. In many firms, managers and workers park in the same parking lots and eat in the same cafeterias.

- Many firms do everything they can to avoid layoffs. Instead, they handle slack periods by reducing hours or producing for inventory. They respond to peak demand with part-time or recently retired workers rather than with newly hired workers who would have to be laid off when the peak had passed.

- The firms tend to promote from within. They post notices of job openings in their plants and offer training to workers who want to upgrade their skills.

- Many firms offer wages and fringe benefits that are competitive with those in unionized firms. (Exceptions can be found in such industries as steel, airlines, and trucking, where union wage scales are unusually high.) They also tend to pay blue-collar workers monthly salaries rather than hourly wages.

- Managers are good listeners, and they keep their office doors open. They are very careful about the handling of grievances. They pay attention to workers' suggestions as well as complaints.

Should these practices be viewed as evidence that unions are not really necessary in a well-managed firm? Or should they be considered evidence that the threat of unionization causes nonunion firms to treat their workers better? You be the judge.

Source: Fred K. Foulkes, "How Top Nonunion Companies Manage Employees," *Harvard Business Review* (September-October 1981): 90–96.

productivity. The fact that unions do these same things while also raising wages is consistent with the notion of *efficiency wage theory* discussed in Chapter 13. It is also consistent with the fact that many top nonunion firms strive to give workers a voice in company affairs. (See "Perspective 14.2.") This chapter began began with the comments of a long-time General Motors worker who saw the United Auto Workers as the union that brought an end to an era of hostility, degradation, and "do this, go there, do that." Side by side with this worker's views, it is interesting to quote those of former General Motors chairman Thomas Murphy, who once said of the UAW, "What comes to my mind is the progress we have made, by working together, in such directions as providing greater safety and health protection, in decreasing alcoholism and drug addiction, in improving the quality of work life."[3]

However, there is a darker side to unions' voice in company affairs. Cooperation in improving productivity and quality of work life is not always the rule. Sometimes unions fight new technology that they fear will eliminate jobs; they

---

[3] Quoted in Freeman and Medoff, p. 4.

battle inroads by women, minority groups, and immigrants into what tradition-ally have been jobs for white males; they stir up worker hostility to make them-selves seem more needed; and they oppose nonunion competition with threats and violence.

Because unions have this negative as well as positive side, managers of non-unionized firms tend to be less than enthusiastic about inviting unions in. Some firms take a negative stance: They fight the unions tooth and nail, sometimes staying within the law and sometimes overstepping it. But today many managers are aware that "do this, go there, do that" is the wrong approach to labor relations, union or nonunion. They see high productivity and better labor rela-tions, rather than lower wages, as the main benefit of not having a union. How-ever, low turnover, high loyalty, and acceptance of new technology by workers do not come by accident, as was shown in "Perspective 14.2."

It may well be, then, that one of the most useful functions unions perform is that of pressuring managers to manage better. Labor-management relations will always be a delicate balance of conflict and cooperation. To some extent, unions have been a means for workers to defend themselves against bad management. Today the power of unions in the United States seems to be on the decline. But if at the same time the quality of management is increasing, the decline of union power need not mean a return of hard times for workers.

Summary

1. **How have labor unions developed over time in the United States?** The earliest labor unions appeared in the United States almost 200 years ago. They were *craft unions*—unions of skilled workers who practiced the same trade. The modern labor movement dates from 1881, when the American Federation of Labor, an association of craft unions, was founded. *Industrial unions*—which include all the workers in an industry regardless of trade—were a later development. Most of the big industrial unions, such as the United Auto Workers and the United Steel Workers, date from the 1930s, although brewery workers, mine workers, and garment workers were organized earlier. Union mem-bership reached its peak in 1945 at about a third of the labor force.

2. **What are the main provisions of U.S. labor law?** U.S. labor law has evolved over time. Until 1930, the courts were generally hostile to unions, limiting the goals they could pursue and the means they could employ. The Norris–La Guardia Act of 1932 was in-tended to place the government in a neutral position with respect to unions. Three years later, the Wagner Act swung the power of government to the union side. This act created the National Labor Relations Board, set procedures under which workers could form unions, and limited the antiunion tactics that employ-ers could use. The Taft-Hartley Act of 1947 limited union powers somewhat and gave the government the power to intervene in strikes that threatened the na-tional interest. Finally, the Landrum-Griffin Act of 1959 gave the government the power to intervene in unions' internal affairs in order to fight corruption and insure union democracy.

3. **How are wage rates determined in unionized mar-kets?** A union wage demand, backed by a strike threat, changes the shape of the labor supply curve an employer faces. The supply curve becomes horizontal at the wage demanded. In a competitive labor market, any increase in the wage brought about by unioniza-tion tends to reduce employment. In the case of mo-nopsony, unionization can increase both the wage rate and employment up to the point at which the wage rate reaches the competitive level. Attempts have been made to analyze the equilibrium wage level in terms both of maximizing models and of unions' internal political processes. Evidence indicates that unions indeed raise members' wages above levels that would otherwise prevail, but by how much is difficult to de-termine.

4. **What do unions do in addition to bargaining over wages and benefits?** Besides affecting wages, unions give workers a voice in how the workplace is run. Often this voice is used in a constructive way—to improve health and safety conditions, increase fair-ness in hiring and layoffs, and so on. Sometimes it is used in a negative way—to fight new technology and

limit competition. Managers of top nonunion firms recognize that productivity is enhanced when workers are allowed a voice in company affairs.

Terms for Review

- craft unionism
- industrial unionism
- bilateral monopoly

Questions for Review

1. When were the earliest unions in the United States founded? The earliest national union organizations? When did union membership as a percentage of the labor force reach its peak?

2. List four major U.S. labor laws and the main provisions of each.

3. Use supply and demand curves to show how a union affects wages and employment in a competitive industry and a monopsonistic industry.

4. What key difference between unions and firms limits the applicability of maximizing models to labor unions?

5. By how much, on the average, do unions raise their members' wages? How do unions affect the level of fringe benefits? How do they influence equality of wages among workers?

6. What do unions do besides bargain over wages?

Problems and Topics for Discussion

1. **Examining the lead-off case.** Discuss the wage and nonwage functions of unions from the standpoint of the former autoworker whose views are expressed in this case. Why do many employers today, both union and nonunion, want to create a different work environment than the one that prevailed in the auto industry half a century ago?

2. **Regional differences in unionization.** Only 18 percent of blue-collar workers in the South belong to unions compared to 38 percent in the Northeast. In what way, if any, would union workers in the Northeast gain if unionization became more widespread in the South? Which southern workers, if any, would gain? Which southern workers, if any, would lose?

3. **Unionization on campus.** Is the nonteaching staff of your college unionized? Is the teaching faculty unionized? Are there any efforts under way to unionize either of these groups? Interview one member of the nonteaching staff and one member of the faculty to learn their attitudes toward unionization.

4. **Labor unions and cartels.** Review the section on cartels in Chapter 11 beginning on page 263. In what ways do unions resemble cartels? How do they differ from cartels? Do you think that public policy should treat unions and producer cartels differently? Discuss.

5. **Labor unions in the news.** Examine recent copies of *The Wall Street Journal, Fortune, Forbes, Business Week,* and other business publications for news of labor unions and collective bargaining. Have recent rounds of bargaining centered on issues of wages and benefits or on matters such as job security and productivity? Give examples.

6. **Labor practices of nonunion firms.** Review "Perspective 14.2." Comment on the labor practices of nonunion firms in terms of the theory of efficiency wages outlined in Chapter 13.

Case for Discussion
Productivity and Job Security Often Overshadow Wages in Collective Bargaining

The ritual takes place every three years in Detroit.

With cameras clicking and reporters scribbling, United Auto Workers representatives extend the traditional handshakes across the table to officials of General Motors Corp. Across town, Ford Motor Co. holds a similar ceremony, and another round of national talks begins.

In contrast, virtually no one was on hand in Columbus, Ohio, on February 2, 1987. That's when UAW Local 969 signed an agreement with a GM plant that changed certain seniority and wage provisions, cutting production costs by $17 million a year and saving about 770 jobs in the aluminum moldings department. Or the following week in Flint, Michigan, when 750 workers at another GM plant combined various job classifications and slashed the price of producing an oil filter by 22 percent.

Yet such little-noticed local negotiations are going on in more and more factories in a wide range of industries, and their cumulative effect may be greater—on companies, unions, and the overall economy—than anything occurring at national bargaining tables.

Wages, the main focus of national negotiations, are becoming less important than work rules, which are usually handled in local contracts. That's where U.S. companies are furthest behind their major international competitors and can make the most progress. Thus, when General Electric Co. announced that it would resume production of color-television sets in the United States, it said its decision hinged not on wage reductions but on the willingness of the International Brotherhood of Electrical Workers local in Bloomington, Indiana, to help improve plant efficiency.

When Chrysler negotiated "modern operating agreements" at 5 of its 31 factories, it figured that the changes increased net income some $28 to $35 million. But not only the companies are benefiting from the changes. For industrial workers, job security has become the top issue. While union leaders are struggling to make some headway in that area at the national table, the companies are making it clear that a "competitive" local contract is the best thing a union can do to keep a plant open or to retain work in-house.

GM was scheduled to close its Fairfax, Kansas, plant by the end of 1987, but in 1985, it said it would replace it with a new plant that it might put near the antiquated facility. Two months after the union local signed a letter of intent saying it would consider drastic changes, the company agreed to build the new plant there. Local 31 believes that its cooperation was "damn important" to preserving 4,900 hourly jobs, says Charles Knott, the local's president. "Had we taken a hard line and said we weren't willing to look at anything, chances are we wouldn't have a $1.05 billion plant along the Missouri River."

Source: Jacob M. Schlesing, "Plant-Level Talks Rise Quickly in Importance; Big Issue: Work Rules," *The Wall Street Journal*, March 16, 1987, 1. Reprinted by permission of *The Wall Street Journal*, © Dow Jones & Company, Inc. 1987. All Rights Reserved.

Questions

1. Many union work rules, such as those that prevent one worker moving from one job to another within a plant or specify minimum crew sizes larger than the number actually needed to operate equipment, initially were established in an attempt to preserve jobs. Why are these restrictive work rules now being eliminated in the name of job security?

2. What factors do you think explain whether a given union local will be willing to accept a certain work rule change? Do you think such decisions could be better characterized in terms of a maximizing model or in terms of a model that emphasizes internal union political processes?

3. What do you think is the relationship between the downward trend in union membership and the current trend toward granting work rule concessions? Could the loss of union membership be related to restrictive work rules at unionized plants?

Suggestions for Further Reading

Freeman, Richard B., and James L. Medoff. *What Do Unions Do?* New York: Basic Books, 1984.

A comprehensive look at labor unions and their functions.

Kaufman, Bruce E. *The Economics of Labor Markets and Labor Relations.* Hinsdale, Ill.: Dryden Press, 1986.

Chapters 10 through 12 of this text discuss the economics of labor unions.

Reynolds, Morgan O. *Power and Privilege: Labor Unions in America.* New York: Universe Books, 1984.

A critique of the role of labor unions that addresses some of the points made by Freeman and Medoff.

15 Rent, Interest, and Profit

After reading this chapter, you will understand . . .

- What role interest plays in credit markets and markets for capital.
- How payments made at different points in time can be properly compared.
- How the theory of rent can be applied to land as a factor of production.
- Where profits come from in the views of various economists.

Before reading this chapter, make sure you know the meaning of . . .

- Economic rent (Chapter 5)
- Tax incidence (Chapter 6)
- Arbitrage (Chapter 12)
- Marginal revenue product (Chapter 13)

Pittsburgh, Henry George, and the Land Tax

In passing out credit for the remarkable urban comeback of Pittsburgh, Pennsylvania, consider the contribution of the nineteenth-century American economist Henry George. Pittsburgh is the only large city anywhere to embrace the Henry George theory of real estate taxation, a theory that says land should be taxed heavily and buildings and improvements on the land not at all.

Pittsburgh has had a modified "land tax" since 1913. Some say the tax was crucial in helping the city grow at the same time that local steel mills were shutting down. Others say Henry George's ideas haven't made a dime's worth of difference in Pittsburgh's renaissance.

Pittsburgh's land tax promotes development and discourages slums.

The land tax (often called the "two-rate tax" or the "split tax") is widely used in Australia and New Zealand. Pennsylvania, however, is the only state in the United States that has given its municipalities the option of substituting a land tax for the more conventional property tax. And this raises questions. If Henry George's theory is a dud, why have six other Pennsylvania municipalities, including Scranton and Harrisburg, opted for a land tax in recent years? But if it works—and George's ideas were acclaimed worldwide when they were published in 1897—why hasn't it caught on elsewhere in the United States?

The genius of the land tax, in the eyes of George's present-day disciples, is that it promotes development and discourages slums and land speculation. Property taxes commonly give great weight to the value of the home or building on a piece of land. Fix up your home, or build a skyscraper on a lot downtown, and what happens? Your tax bill goes up.

But there are skeptics as well as fans. A driver who spends an hour looking for a parking place in downtown Pittsburgh wonders if gridlock is the inevitable byproduct of a tax with a high-rise bias.

Source: Eugene Carlson, "It's the Land Tax, by George, That Sets Pennsylvania Apart," *The Wall Street Journal*, March 12, 1985, 33. Reprinted by permission of *The Wall Street Journal*, © Dow Jones & Company, Inc. 1985. All Rights Reserved. Photo Source: AP/Wide World Photos.

THE Pittsburgh land tax draws attention to land and other natural resources—factors of production to which we have given little attention in the last two chapters. In this chapter, we complete the story of factor markets by examining the markets for capital and natural resources. We also extend the discussion of profit and entrepreneurship and show how these concepts relate to factor markets.

Interest and Capital

The term *interest* is used to express both the price paid by borrowers to lenders for the use of loanable funds and the market return earned by capital as a factor of production. A person who loans $1,000 to another in return for a payment of $100 a year (plus repayment of the principal on a set date) is said to earn 10 percent interest per year on the money. At the same time, a person who buys a machine for $1,000 and earns $100 a year by using the productive services of that machine is said to earn 10 percent interest on the capital.

Consumption Loans

We begin our discussion of interest and capital by considering how credit markets work in a simple economy in which households are the only suppliers of credit—that is, of loanable funds. Savers are households that earn income now but consume less than they earn in order to put something aside for future needs. However, not all households in the economy are savers; some want to consume more than their current incomes permit. The latter may be households that are faced with a temporary decrease in income or households with steady incomes that are unwilling to wait to buy a car or take a vacation. These and other households that borrow are one source of demand for loanable funds. The loans they take out are called *consumption loans*.

Exhibit 15.1 shows how credit markets look in an economy in which consumption loans are the only source of demand for loanable funds and personal saving is the only source of supply. Under these conditions, savers' willingness to save at various interest rates determines the shape and position of the supply curve. Borrowers' eagerness to borrow at various interest rates determines the shape and position of the demand curve. The intersection of the two curves determines the market rate of interest.

The Productivity of Capital

So far we have said nothing about production or capital. Opportunities to use capital as a factor of production are a second source of demand for loanable funds. In order to understand the demand for loans of this kind, we need to understand why capital is productive.

Using capital means using a roundabout rather than direct method of production. Consider a person whose business is making bricks. There are two ways to make bricks. The direct way is to form them by hand out of raw clay scooped up from the ground and to bake them over an open fire. Suppose that by using this method a worker can make 100 bricks a month. The other way of making bricks is a roundabout one. The brickmaker first spends a month forming bricks

Exhibit 15.1   Determination of the Interest
Rate for Consumption Loans

If consumption loans were the only kind made, the interest
rate would be determined as shown here. The supply curve
for loanable funds is determined by the willingness of savers
to lend their money. The demand curve is determined by the
eagerness of borrowers to consume now and pay later. The
intersection of the two curves determines the interest rate.

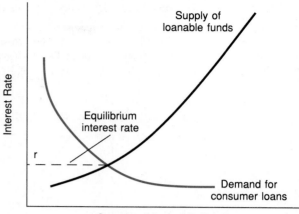

by hand and putting them together to make a kiln. When the kiln is completed,
its hotter fire and lower fuel consumption make it possible to produce 110 bricks
a month from then on. This method, which uses capital (the kiln), lengthens the
period between the time work starts and the time finished bricks begin to appear. In return, it increases the rate of output. That is the sense in which capital
is productive.

The brickmaker's experience is repeated whenever a firm makes a capital
investment. Making cars on an assembly line is a roundabout method of production compared to making them one by one using hand tools. Constructing a
building in which to hold economics classes is a roundabout method of education compared with holding classes outside under a tree. In both cases, time is
taken to construct aids to production in order to produce more effectively later
on.

The same reasoning applies to decisions to invest in human capital. A person who takes four years to complete college is taking a roundabout route to
establishing a career compared with someone who begins working straight out of
high school. A person who takes several more years to complete medical school
or law school is taking an even more roundabout route. However, in each case it
is hoped that a greater investment in human capital will result in higher earnings
later on.

Investment Loans

The brickmaker in the above example invested directly by actually building the
needed capital equipment. However, in a market economy firms need not build
their own capital equipment. Anyone who sees an opportunity to increase output
by using a more capital-intensive (that is, more roundabout) production process
can borrow money and buy capital. The productivity of capital thus creates a
source of demand for loanable funds in addition to the demand for consumption
loans. Loans that are used to buy capital can be called *investment loans*.

Exhibit 15.2 shows how the interest rate is determined when the demand for
investment loans is added to the demand for consumption loans. The diagram
reveals that the interest rate is higher when both types of loan demand are taken

Exhibit 15.2   The Interest Rate with Consumption and Investment Loans

This exhibit shows how the interest rate is determined in an economy in which there are both consumption and investment loans. In this case, the demand for investment loans is added to the demand for consumption loans to get the combined demand for loanable funds. The equilibrium interest rate, r, is higher than it would be if only consumption loans were taken into account.

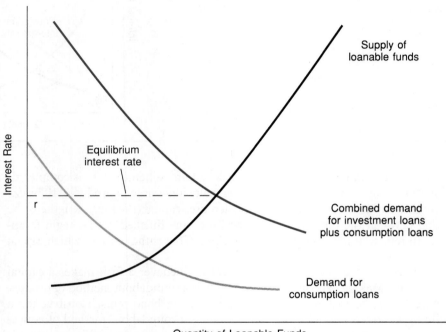

into account than it is when only consumption loans are considered. In practice, the investment demand for loanable funds is much greater than the consumption demand, which means that the investment demand is the more important factor in determining the interest rate.

Capital and Interest

We now turn from the determination of the interest rate in the credit market to the link between the demand for loanable funds and the demand for capital as a means of production. We will begin with the case in which capital is leased for a monthly or yearly payment, which we will call the *lease price*. Much capital equipment is leased this way rather than owned by the firm that uses it. We will start with the lease market for capital equipment because it more closely resembles the labor market, which we examined in the last two chapters.

Exhibit 15.3 shows the short-run lease market for capital equipment—machines, buildings, and the like. As we saw in Chapter 8, in the short run capital can be treated as a fixed input. With a fixed existing stock of capital equipment, the supply curve is perfectly inelastic. As in other factor markets, the demand curve is the marginal revenue product curve for the services of capital equipment. The two determine the lease value of capital equipment.

Exhibit 15.3   The Lease Price
of Capital Equipment

In the short run, the lease price of capital equipment is
determined by the existing stock of capital and the demand
(marginal revenue product) curve for the services of capital.
In the long run, new investment causes the supply curve to
shift to the right. This drives down the rental price, other
things being equal. In practice, however, innovations
constantly shift the demand curve for capital to the right;
hence, the lease price does not fall as much as shown here.

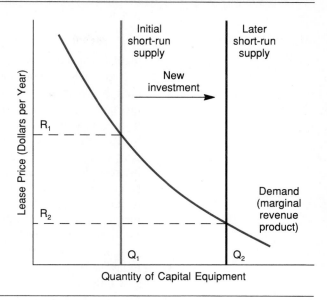

If the short-run lease price of capital equipment is high enough and the
expected real interest rate sufficiently low, it will be worthwhile to build more
such equipment. (We will see exactly how one determines whether an item of
capital equipment will pay for itself in the next section.) Over time, as investment proceeds and capital builds up, the short-run supply curve for capital shifts
to the right. In the long run, this tends to drive down the lease price of capital
equipment and reduce the incentive to invest. The investment demand for loanable funds decreases, and the interest rate falls.

In theory, the economy can end up in a steady-state equilibrium in which all
worthwhile investment projects are completed and consumption loans constitute
the only remaining demand for loanable funds. In practice, the steady state
never arrives. Technological change is constantly pushing up the demand curve
(marginal revenue product curve) for capital services. The short-run lease value
of capital equipment thus is kept high enough to justify investing in new capital
equipment year after year.

Discounting and Investment Decisions

The preceding analysis of the lease market for capital equipment raises the question of how a firm decides whether it is worth acquiring an item of capital given
its lease value and the prevailing interest rate. Making this decision requires
comparing payments made at different points in time—the cost of the equipment, which must be borne now, and the income from it, which will be received
only in the future. In this section, we will set out some of the basic principles
involved in this type of decision.

Discounting

If a firm puts funds to work earning interest by placing them in a bank account,
making a loan, or buying a security, the original sum it invests will grow year by
year. At 10 percent interest per year, $100 invested today will be worth $110 a

year from now; after two years, it will be worth $121; after three years, it will be worth $133.10; and so on. The $11 gain in the second year reflects interest of $10 on the original principal and $1 interest on the $10 interest earned in the first year. The payment of interest on previously earned interest gives this process the name *compound interest.*

In a world in which funds can be loaned out at compound interest, it is always advantageous to receive a payment earlier rather than later. The opportunity cost of receiving a sum later rather than sooner is the interest that could have been earned otherwise. Consider, for example, the cost of receiving a sum of $100 a year from now rather than today assuming the same interest rate of 10 percent per year. Delaying receipt of the sum would mean forgoing a year's interest. Rather than give up that interest, a firm would be just as well off receiving a smaller sum now than the $100 a year from now. To be precise, it would be just as good to get $91 now as $100 a year from now, because the $91 placed for a year at 10 percent would grow to $100 (give or take the odd dime). Similarly, $100 payable two years from now is equivalent to about $83 today assuming 10 percent interest; $100 three years from now is worth about $75 today; and so on.

This kind of example can be generalized to any time period and any interest rate. Let V_p be the sum of money that if invested today at r percent interest will grow to the sum V_t after t years. V_p is known as the **present value** of the sum V_t, payable t years from now, discounted at r percent per year. **Discounting** is the term for the procedure by which the present value is calculated. The formula for calculating the present value of any future sum is:

$$V_p = \frac{V_t}{(1 + r)^t}.$$

Present value
The present value of a sum, V_t, payable t years in the future, discounted at r percent interest, is the sum V_p that if invested today at r percent interest would grow to the value V_t in t years; the present value formula is $V_p = V_t/(1 + r)^t$.

Discounting
The procedure by which the present value of a sum payable in the future is calculated.

Applying the Discounting Formula

The discounting formula can be used to determine whether a given item of capital equipment is worth purchasing given a certain interest rate and the equipment's purchase price, lease value, and scrap value at the end of its useful life. An example is presented in Exhibit 15.4. This concerns the purchase of a subcompact automobile by an auto rental company. The purchase price is $8,000. The car can be rented at a lease price of $2,000, net of maintenance expenses, for four years. At the end of that time, it will be worth $4,000 in the used-car market. For simplicity, each year's cash flow is treated as though it took place on the last day of the year.

Is it worth buying the car? An unsophisticated approach to the matter would be to simply add up the income from the car and compare it to the price. Four years' lease income at $2,000 plus the $4,000 resale value comes to $12,000, compared with the $8,000 purchase price. But before deciding whether the car is worth buying, the firm must discount the various sums to determine their present values.

These calculations are performed in Exhibit 15.4 assuming first a 10 percent interest rate and then an 18 percent rate. Discounted at 10 percent, the value of the first year's lease income is $1,820 ($2,000 × .91), the value of the second year's lease income is $1,660, and so on. The $4,000 resale value, which is assumed to be realized at the end of the fourth year, has a present value of $2,720 ($4,000 × .68). Thus, the sum of the present value of all payments that the firm will receive from the car comes to $9,060 when the calculation is made assuming

Exhibit 15.4   Discounting and Investment Decision Making

These tables illustrate how a car rental agency might evaluate the advisability of purchasing a new car for its fleet. The car is assumed to cost $8,000 initially and to bring in $2,000 a year in lease income for four years. (For simplicity, all the income is assumed to arrive on the last day of each year.) At the end of the fourth year, the car can be sold for $4,000. It will be profitable to buy the car so long as the discounted value of the lease income plus the discounted used-car value exceed the purchase price. As the numbers show, this is the case when the prevailing interest rate is 10 percent but not when it is 18 percent.

(a)
10% Interest Rate

Year	Outlay (−) or Income	Discount Factor	Discounted Outlay (−) or Income
0	−8,000	1.00	−8,000
1	2,000	.91	1,820
2	2,000	.83	1,660
3	2,000	.75	1,500
4	6,000	.68	4,080
		Sum of discounted net cash flows	$1,060

(b)
18% Interest Rate

Year	Outlay (−) or Income	Discount Factor	Discounted Outlay (−) or Income
0	−8,000	1.00	−8,000
1	2,000	.85	1,700
2	2,000	.72	1,440
3	2,000	.61	1,220
4	6,000	.52	3,120
		Sum of discounted net cash flows	−$520

a 10 percent interest rate. This is considerably less than the $12,000 undiscounted sum, but $9,060 still compares favorably with the $8,000 purchase price. If funds for buying the car can be raised at an interest cost of 10 percent, the firm should add the car to its rental fleet.

Turning to part b of Exhibit 15.4, we see the importance of the interest rate. There the calculations have been reworked using an 18 percent rate. Given the higher interest rate, the present value of each future payment is less than when discounted at the lower interest rate. This time the sum of the discounted future payments comes to only $7,480, which is less than the purchase price of the car. Thus, at an 18 percent interest rate it will not be worthwhile for the firm to add the car to its fleet.

The Markets for Land and Natural Resources

We now turn from markets for capital to markets for natural resources. We will begin with the example of land and the rent that is earned from its ownership.

Pure Economic Rent

In Chapter 5, we defined *rent* as any income to a factor of production in excess of its opportunity cost. Land, which in this context means the natural productive powers of the earth and the locational advantages of particular sites, is a special case in that its supply is perfectly inelastic. No matter how high its rental price, the amount of land is fixed, and no matter how low the price, the land is always there. We will not consider artificial improvements to land or reclamation of land—say, by drainage—because such improvements count as capital. To the extent that they raise the lease price of a parcel of land, the added income counts as interest on the capital invested, not as rent.

Pure economic rent
The income earned by any factor of production whose supply is perfectly inelastic.

The income earned by a factor of production whose supply is perfectly inelastic in the long run is called a **pure economic rent.** It is "pure" because such a factor has no opportunity cost from the standpoint of the economy as a whole, and thus all the income it earns is economic rent.

Exhibit 15.5 shows how pure economic rent is determined by supply and demand in a competitive market. It considers a specific type of land—Kansas wheatland. The supply curve for Kansas wheatland is a vertical line because the amount of land supplied does not vary with changes in the rent that it earns. The demand curve is the marginal revenue product curve for that land as seen by Kansas wheat farmers. The marginal product of land falls as more land is used in combination with fixed quantities of labor and capital because of diminishing returns. The demand curve thus slopes downward and to the right.

The rent the land earns is determined by the intersection of the supply curve, which represents the scarcity of land, and the demand curve, which represents its productivity. If the rent is higher than the equilibrium shown, not all of the land will be put to use. The rent will then fall as landowners compete to find tenants. If the rent is lower than the equilibrium rate, farmers will be unable to find all the land they want. They will bid against one another for the limited supply and drive rents up.

Capitalization of Pure Economic Rents

The price paid per year for the use of land is called *rent*, but much land is used by the person who owns it and therefore is not rented by a tenant from an owner. That fact does not change the way supply and demand determine the value of land. It does imply, however, that it is sometimes useful to speak of the price of land in terms of a lump sum sales price rather than as a rent per month or year.

Exhibit 15.5   Determination of Rent by Supply and Demand

Pure economic rent is earned by a factor whose supply is perfectly inelastic. This exhibit shows hypothetical supply and demand curves for Kansas wheatland. No account is taken of the possibility that such land could be created or destroyed; thus, the supply curve is vertical. As in the case of other factors of production, the demand curve is based on the land's marginal revenue product.

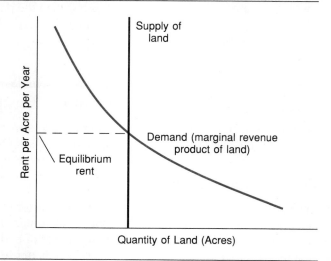

There is a simple relationship between the value of a piece of land expressed as a rent and the price at which that parcel can be sold in the market. The market price of a piece of land is said to be the **capitalized value of its rent**—the sum that would earn an annual return equal to the annual rent if it were invested at the market rate of interest.

The relationship among the market price of a piece of land, its annual rental income, and the market rate of interest is determined according to the discounting formula given in the previous section. However, in the case of land, the stream of rental income continues into the indefinite future, since the land (as distinct from improvements to it) does not have a finite life. When the discounting formula is applied over an infinite time horizon to a piece of land with an expected rental income of R dollars per year and assuming an interest rate r, the result can be given by the formula R/r. Thus, a piece of land that is expected to produce, say, $5,000 a year rental income for the indefinite future has a capitalized value of $50,000 assuming a 10 percent interest rate, of $100,000 assuming a 5 percent rate, and so on.

The formula also makes it clear that either a change in the expected income from a piece of land or a change in the interest rate will affect its price, other things being equal. Recent years have seen some dramatic examples of these effects in the case of farmland, especially in the midwestern United States. A combination of factors put a squeeze on farm income in the early 1980s. For a farmer, the economic rent of land means the income it yields after allowing for the costs of other inputs, including labor, capital, fuel, and fertilizer. As this rental income fell, and at the same time interest rates rose, the price of farmland dropped. Many farmers had used their land as collateral on bank loans. When the market price of the land fell below the value of the loans, some banks foreclosed on the loans, putting the farmers out of business. After about 1985, however, the prices of farmland began to recover somewhat, at least in some areas. This recovery reflected, in part, an improvement of expected farm income, and also a general decline in interest rates from the high levels of the early 1980s.

The Theory of Rent and the Land Tax

The theory of rent can be applied to the case of the Pittsburgh land tax discussed in the opening case of this chapter. The nineteenth-century economist Henry George, who inspired the land tax, saw the connection between rent and perfectly inelastic supply. He reasoned that if a tax were placed on land, whose supply is perfectly inelastic, the owners would be unable to pass the tax along to their tenants. The entire tax would be borne by the landowners. Further, if no land were withdrawn from the market, the tax would have no excess burden.

Exhibit 15.6 contrasts the effects of a land tax with those of a tax on buildings or other improvements to land. The supply of buildings is not perfectly inelastic. A tax on these properties means an increase in costs for their owners. The increase shifts the supply curve upward. As the market price rises, a portion of the tax is passed along to tenants in the form of higher rental payments. (Recall that the rental payments on a store or apartment are not pure economic rents.) At the same time, the quantity of buildings supplied decreases. Some new buildings are not constructed and some existing buildings deteriorate because improvements are not made and the buildings are inadequately maintained.

Capitalized value of a rent
The sum that would earn annual interest equal to the annual rent if it were invested at the current market rate of interest.

Exhibit 15.6   Economics of the Land Tax

This exhibit explains the logic of a land tax such as that used in Pittsburgh, Pennsylvania.
Part a shows the market for land. The equilibrium rental value is $2 per square foot per
year. When a tax of $1 per square foot is imposed on this market, the quantity supplied
does not change. Competition among landowners prevents them from passing along the tax
to tenants who occupy their lots; thus, the rent tenants pay remains at $2 per square foot.
Part b shows the market for buildings constructed on the same land. At first, the rental price
of buildings is also $2 per square foot. A tax of $1 per square foot is a cost to building
owners and shifts the supply curve upward from S_1 to S_2. Part of the tax is passed on to
tenants in the form of an increase in the rental price to $2.50 per square foot. The quantity
of floor space provided falls by half a million square feet. The shaded area shows the
excess burden of the tax.

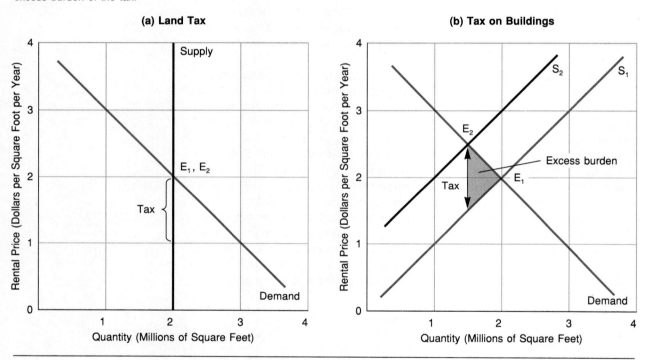

Profit and Entrepreneurship

The term *pure economic profit* was introduced in Chapter 8 to refer to the income, if any, remaining for the owners of a firm after they have deducted all
implicit and explicit costs of production. Explicit costs include factor payments
to workers, owners of resources, and suppliers of capital together with the costs
of any semifinished inputs that are purchased from other firms. Implicit costs
include the opportunity cost of capital supplied by owners of the firm plus the
opportunity costs of using natural resources or labor supplied by the firm's
owners or owned by the firm itself. What is left over is pure economic profit.

This definition of profit does not answer two important questions: Why does
a firm ever earn any pure economic profit, and why is the entire value of the
product of all firms not divided up among the owners of the labor, natural
resources, and capital used in the production process?

Theories of Profit

The question of the origin of profits has occupied the minds of many economists over the years. No answer to the question has won universal acceptance. In this section, we look at several explanations that have been offered.

Risk and Profit

According to one theory, profits are a reward that the owners of businesses receive for bearing risk. Every business venture is subject to the risk of failure; that is the nature of economic life in a world in which the future is not known with certainty. People who merely hire out their factor services largely avoid risk. A new business usually is expected to guarantee its employees that the payroll will be met even if the firm loses money. It is also expected to offer security against default to banks or bondholders who supply it with credit. The firm's owner(s) (stockholders if the firm is a corporation) bear most of the risk of loss if the firm fails. In return they get the right to keep the profits if revenues turn out to be more than enough to pay off the firm's obligations to hired factors.

Why is it, though, that the profits earned by successful risk takers are not exactly offset by the losses of those who do not succeed? One proposed answer concerns people's attitudes toward risk. It is possible that some people are indifferent to risk. A person who is indifferent to risk will be indifferent between the opportunity to earn $10,000 a year with absolute certainty and the opportunity to try for $20,000 subject to a 50-50 chance of earning nothing. A person who is indifferent to risk will be willing to launch new businesses even when the profit expected if the business succeeds is exactly offset by the loss expected if the business fails.

In practice, however, most people dislike risk. If they know they can earn a sure $10,000 a year, they will not launch a business with a 50-50 chance of failure unless it will pay more than $20,000 if successful. Because most people dislike risk, somewhat fewer business ventures are launched than would otherwise be the case. That makes opportunities slightly more favorable, on the average, for those who are willing to bear some risk. When successes and failures are averaged out over the whole economy, profits more than offset losses. The excess of profits over losses is thus seen as the reward earned by the people who bear business risks. Factor owners are willing to accept less than the whole value of the firm's product to the extent that they are shielded from those risks.

Profits as Factor Income

Many economists of the neoclassical school have interpreted profits as the reward to a fourth factor of production—entrepreneurship. The case for considering entrepreneurship as a factor of production begins with the observation that entrepreneurs, like workers, resource owners, and suppliers of capital, earn a reward for their contribution to production. Like the other factors, entrepreneurship is scarce. Not everyone is able to organize business ventures and recognize new opportunities to make a profit. Also, as is true for labor, natural resources, and capital, production cannot take place without entrepreneurship. Thus, entrepreneurs are able to earn an income in the form of the profit that remains after all the costs of their firms have been covered.

There is a limit, however, to how far the parallel between entrepreneurship and other factors can be pushed. One problem is that entrepreneurship cannot be measured; there is no numerical unit of entrepreneurship and, hence, no way to determine a price per unit. Applying supply and demand analysis to this fourth factor of production just does not work. In addition, there is the fact that profit, the return to entrepreneurship, disappears when the economy is in equilibrium. In equilibrium, the entire value of each firm's product must be paid out to the owners of labor, capital, and natural resources. Profit and entrepreneurship are found only in a state of disequilibrium—a fact that sets entrepreneurship apart from the three other factors of production in a very basic way.

Austrian Theories of Profit

As discussed in Chapter 12, economists of the Austrian school also have linked profit to entrepreneurship. In the Austrian literature, however, profit is interpreted not as a type of factor income but as the reward for the activities of arbitrage and innovation.

Recall that arbitrage is the activity of buying a good at a low price in one market and selling it at a higher price in another. Examples of pure arbitrage can be found in markets for agricultural commodities, precious metals, foreign currencies, and the like, in which standardized goods are traded at different locations.

Consider the gold markets in London and Hong Kong. Economic policies, news events, and so forth may affect supply and demand in these two markets differently. A political crisis in the British government, for example, may prompt an increase in demand in the London market, sending up the price of gold there relative to its price in Hong Kong. Before the two prices grow very far apart, however, arbitrageurs in Hong Kong will start buying gold at the low Hong Kong price for resale at the higher London price. This activity will raise the demand in Hong Kong and the supply in London until the price in the two markets is equalized. (In practice, because of various transaction costs the prices will be only roughly equal on any given day.) In the process of forming a crucial link in the transmission of information through the price system, the arbitrageurs will make a handy profit.

Arbitrage cannot always be seen in as pure a form as in the international gold market. However, Israel Kirzner points out that there is an element of arbitrage in every profit-making transaction.[1] Consider the entrepreneur-owner-manager of, say, a small shoe factory. This person buys inputs in one set of markets at the lowest possible prices and, after combining the inputs to form finished shoes, sells the product in other markets at the highest possible prices. In a neoclassical world in which all markets were in perfectly competitive long-run equilibrium, it would be no more possible to make a profit by buying labor and leather and selling shoes than it would be to buy gold in Hong Kong and sell it in London. In such a world, the price of the leather and labor would be bid up to just equal the price of the finished shoes. In the real world, however, entrepreneurs can find arbitrage opportunities in a wide variety of markets and earn profits accordingly.

Writers of the Austrian school also link profit with the activities of entrepreneurs as innovators. In contrast to the entrepreneur as arbitrageur, taking advantage of opportunities to buy low and sell high whenever they occur, the entrepreneur as innovator creates new profit opportunities by devising a new product, production process, or marketing strategy. If successful, the entrepreneur achieves a temporary monopoly that permits pure economic profits to be earned until rival firms catch up or leap ahead with innovations of their own.

---

[1] Israel Kirzner, *Competition and Entrepreneurship* (Chicago: University of Chicago Press, 1974).

Looking Ahead

Up to this point, we have covered the basic economics of factor markets for labor, capital, and natural resources. We have also discussed the economics of profit and entrepreneurship. As pointed out at the beginning of Chapter 13, factor markets play a major role in determining the distribution of income in a market economy.

This leaves us with one remaining set of questions: the normative question of whether the market-determined distribution of income is a good or a bad one and the positive question of what can be done to change unwanted distribution of income. We will address these questions in Chapter 16.

Summary

1. **What role does interest play in credit markets and markets for capital?** The term *interest* expresses both the price paid by borrowers to lenders in credit markets and the income earned by capital as a factor of production. The interest rate is determined in credit markets. The supply of credit depends on the willingness of savers to lend. The demand for credit is composed of the demand for consumption loans plus the demand for investment loans. In the short run, supply and demand determine a lease price for the services of capital equipment. If the lease price of newly produced capital equipment (expressed as a percentage of the cost of producing the equipment) is higher than the interest rate, it will be worthwhile for firms to expand the stock of capital. As the capital stock expands, the lease price of capital equipment, other things being equal, will tend to fall. This will reduce the investment demand for credit and drive down the interest rate. In principle, the economy could reach a steady-state equilibrium in which there is no new investment. In practice, innovation constantly raises the marginal productivity of capital and, hence, the demand for capital; thus, the steady state is never reached.

2. **How can payments made at different points in time be properly compared?** Payments made at different points in time are compared using the process known as *discounting*. The discounting formula is $V_p = V_t/(1 + r)^t$, where V_p is the *present value* of the sum V_t, payable t years in the future, discounted at an annual interest rate, r.

3. **How can the theory of rent be applied to land as a factor of production?** *Pure economic rent* is the income earned by any factor of production whose supply is completely inelastic. Land is the classic example of a factor that earns a pure economic rent. The *capitalized value of a rent* determines the market price of land. Rent can also be said to be earned by other factors whose supply is perfectly inelastic, such as the special talents of athletes or performing artists.

4. **Where do profits come from in the views of various economists?** There are several theories about the nature of profits. One holds that profit is the reward that entrepreneurs earn for bearing risks. Many neoclassical economists have interpreted entrepreneurship as a fourth factor of production and viewed profits as the factor income earned by entrepreneurs. Economists of the Austrian school have seen profits as the reward entrepreneurs earn for engaging in arbitrage and innovation.

Terms for Review

- present value
- discounting
- pure economic rent
- capitalized value of a rent

Questions for Review

1. What do we mean when we say that using capital means using a roundabout method of production?

2. Under what conditions will it be worthwhile for a firm to invest in new capital equipment?

3. How is the short-run lease price for capital related to the increase in the quantity of capital in the economy as a whole?

4. Use supply and demand curves to show the difference between the pure economic rent earned by a factor of production whose supply is completely inelastic and the income earned by, say, the owner of an apartment building.

5. List three theories about the nature of profits.

Problems and Topics for Discussion

1. **Examining the lead-off case.** According to *The Wall Street Journal* story, the land tax promotes development and discourages property speculation. Use sup-

ply and demand analysis to show that the land tax promotes development in the sense of encouraging greater improvement to a given piece of property compared with a tax on the total value of land and improvements. Do you think such a tax will also discourage speculation? (Speculation, in this context, means deciding to leave a piece of land undeveloped now in the hope of selling it later at a higher price.)

2. **Farm income and pure economic rent.** In 1985, U.S. farmers earned gross revenues of $167 billion. Of this, $136 billion went to cover explicit costs of fuel, fertilizer, equipment maintenance, and so on. This left farmers with a net income of $31 billion. Is that net income best thought of as wages, rent, interest, profit, or a mixture of these?

3. **Capitalized value of an asset.** Suppose you own a professional basketball team. You are negotiating for the services of a certain college star who will soon begin a career as a professional player. You figure that having this player on your team will bring in $100,000 a year in added income from ticket sales for five years. After that the player may slow down a bit, but having him on the team will continue to bring in $50,000 in added ticket sales for another 10 years. How much will you be willing to pay (in a single, one-time payment) to get the player for your team if the interest rate is 12 percent per year?

4. **Rents earned by superstars.** Part of the income of people with unique talents can be considered a form of economic rent. Suppose you observe that a certain baseball player is paid $1 million a year. How would you distinguish the part of the player's income that is rent from the part that is a return on investment in human capital in the form of training for the sport?

5. **Christmas tree farming.** Suppose you decide to start a Christmas tree farm. You already own a suitable piece of land. You get seeds from pine cones that you gather in the woods. You plant the seeds with your own hands. Five years later, you sell the trees for $30 each. How should your revenue be divided among wages, rent, interest, and profit?

6. **Sources of labor income.** A contractor places an ad for laborers in the newspaper, offering to pay them $10 per cubic yard for removing rocks and dirt from a cellar hole. Four workers show up and start the job. Alice is a person of average build. She uses a simple shovel and bucket and manages to earn $20 a day. Bill, a giant of a man, also uses a shovel and bucket but is able to earn $50 a day. Charles uses a wheelbarrow and earns $60 a day even though he is no stronger than Alice. Donna uses a bucket and shovel too and at first earns only $20 a day. Not satisfied with this income, she takes a month off to complete a muscle-building course. When she comes back, she earns $50 a day. How should the income of each worker be classified in terms of wages, rent, interest, and profit?

Houses in the Northeast typically remain on the market for many months.

Case for Discussion
The Uneven Pace of Housing Sales

The housing market has bounced back everywhere except the Northeast. Punctured by a two-point spike in mortgage interest rates, to 11 percent or so, new home sales across the country fell 13.2 percent last May, the sharpest decline in more than 5 years. Then mortgage rates retreated. In June, according to figures the Commerce Department recently released, sales rose 3.5 percent to $92 billion. Even Texas is resurgent. Apparently betting on the turnaround in oil prices, investors are grabbing up once-languishing homes. Sales in California are healthier than they have been since 1979.

Not so in New England and many Mid-Atlantic states. Until recently, buyers there sometimes competed with sealed bids that topped the asking price. Today few people are even looking at houses to buy. Richard Palmer, regional vice president of the National Association of Realtors for New York, New Jersey, and Pennsylvania, says sales volume in some areas is 30 percent below last year's levels. Around Danbury, Connecticut, some 400 houses come on the market each month, and fewer than 150 sell. The average home near Boston takes about 75 days to sell, compared with 58 days last year.

Why the slump? Some housing experts believe prices in major Northeast markets—up 20 percent for the past five years, roughly three times the U.S. average—have finally reached their limits. "Prices look daunting to people who need mortgages," says John Tuccillo, chief economist at the National Association of Realtors. "There's still a booming market for million-dollar homes. Those in the mid-six figures have been the hardest hit."

Source: "Sticker Shock in Connecticut," *Fortune,* August 31, 1987, 9. Photo Source: Copyright © 1987 B.E. White. All rights reserved.

Questions

1. Homeowners earn an implicit lease value from the homes they occupy. How is this lease value related to the price they are willing to pay for a home?

2. Why would a rise in oil prices tend to increase prices of homes in Texas or the rate of sales of homes at given prices? Explain in terms of family incomes and implicit lease values.

3. Why would an increase in interest rates tend to lower the price of homes or slow the rate of sales of homes at given prices?

4. Why do you think slackness in housing markets is expressed partly in terms of an increase in the average length of time it takes to sell a home? Why do sellers not simply reduce the prices of their homes to the level at which they can be sold quickly?

Suggestions for Further Reading

Böhm-Bawerk, Eugen von. "The Nature of Roundabout Production." In *Contemporary Economics: Selected Readings,* 2d ed., edited by Reuben E. Slesinger, Mark Perlman, and Asher Isaacs. Boston: Allyn & Bacon, 1967.

A classic statement of the nature of capital and production by a turn-of-the-century Austrian economist.

Scitovski, Tibor. *Welfare and Competition,* rev. ed. Homewood, Ill.: Irwin, 1971.

Chapter 19 discusses capital and entrepreneurship.

16 The Problem of Poverty

After reading this chapter, you will understand . . .

- The importance factor markets have for income distribution and the problem of poverty.
- What poverty is and how it can be measured.
- What trends in poverty have been experienced in the United States in recent decades.
- How social insurance differs from public assistance.
- Why poor households are often subject to higher net tax rates at the margin than nonpoor households.
- Which poverty programs emphasize factor markets.

Before reading this chapter, make sure you know the meaning of . . .

- Taxes and transfer payments (Chapter 5)
- Human capital (Chapter 13)
- Economics of discrimination (Chapter 13)

Freeing Mothers to Work

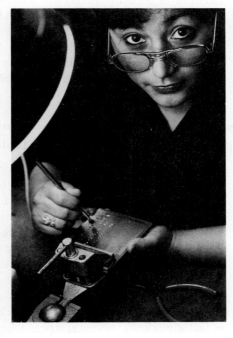

Massachusetts provides on-the-job training programs to help people get off welfare.

Donna Deshaies recently celebrated the first anniversary of her freedom—freedom from the boredom that many mothers on welfare suffer. In April, she began to work in the payroll department of Massachusetts General Hospital, a job she got with the help of the state's Employment and Training program.

Deshaies, who is 23 years old, trained for the job during a 16-week course that covered not just clerical skills but also such subjects as interviewing for a job and dressing properly for work. During her training, she continued to get her welfare check. Child care and transportation expenses were paid by the ET program.

"I wouldn't have been able to pay for my own training," she says. And even had she found tuition money, child-care expenses for her two-year-old daughter, Talana, would have been unaffordable. Today, she no longer is on welfare.

Connie Parks pays only $17.50 of the $60 weekly day-care bill for her three-year-old son, John. "If I had to pay [$60 for] day care every week, there wouldn't be any sense in working," she says. Until last October, Parks, 34, had been on welfare since another son, now 15, was born. After so many years on public assistance, she finds it somewhat hard to believe that now she is employed in the data-processing unit of Boston's Grove Hall welfare office.

Like Parks, others have been "rolled over" from welfare through ET's on-the-job training project known as supportive work and into regular, full-time employment in private industry.

The supportive work option is one of several available to ET clients. Janice Perryman chose instead to earn her high-school equivalency diploma and enter ET's 28-week Office Skills Training Program in Boston's United South End Settlements. Beyond the typing and word-processing skills that Perryman is learning, she says she is more self-assured and thus has a better relationship with her children. "Now they can ask me questions with confidence," she says.

"Before, they would say, 'She don't know.' I'm a different person, so they're different, too."

Source: Joe Davidson, "More States Now Ask Recipients of Aid to Train and Take Jobs," *The Wall Street Journal*, July 23, 1986, 1. Reprinted by permission of *The Wall Street Journal*, © Dow Jones & Company, Inc. 1986. All Rights Reserved. Photo Source: Courtesy of Public Welfare Department, Boston, MA: Hakim Raquib Photos.

THE stories of Deshaies, Parks, and Perryman draw attention to the problem of poverty, an aspect of factor markets that we have barely considered so far. Labor force participation is closely linked to poverty. The poverty rate for families with at least one worker is less than half of that for families with no workers. For families headed by women, the poverty rate in families in which the family head works is only two-fifths the rate for those in which there are no workers. At the same time, however, the problem of poverty is more than one of factor markets. In this chapter, we look at the problem of poverty from several sides.

Poverty and Income Distribution

As we emphasized in Chapter 15, factor markets not only determine how goods and services are produced; they also help determine for whom they are produced. Workers and owners of capital and natural resources are rewarded according to the productivity of the factors they contribute. Entrepreneurs earn profits or losses according to their degree of success in finding and taking advantage of new opportunities. Since people differ in skills and talents, in the amount of capital and natural resources they control, and in luck and entrepreneurial ability, their incomes also vary. Some earn nothing, while others earn millions of dollars a year.

On top of the unequal distribution of income that results from the operation of factor markets, it is necessary to take account of taxes and government transfer payments. Each year federal, state, and local governments pay out over $500 billion through a wide variety of transfer programs. Some of these transfers help equalize incomes, although cash payments to the poor account for less than 10 percent of total government transfer payments. Part of the rest goes to providing services in kind for the poor, such as the child care and training benefits mentioned in the opening case. Much of it, however, goes to middle-class and even wealthy people. As a result, even when transfer payments are taken into account, there is a great deal of income inequality. As of 1986, the poorest 20 percent of the population received less than 5 percent of all income while the richest 5 percent received more than 15 percent. Exhibit 16.1 shows how the distribution of income can be summarized in the form of a diagram called a **Lorenz curve.**

Lorenz curve
A graphic representation of the degree of inequality in an economy.

Two Views of the Nature of Poverty

Poverty obviously is something that exists at the low end of the Lorenz curve. But just how low an income must a household have in order to be considered poor? Also, is income all that matters? There are two major points of view on this subject.

Exhibit 16.1   A Lorenz Curve for the U.S. Economy

A *Lorenz curve* is a diagram that can be used to represent the degree of inequality in an economy. Such a diagram is drawn in a square, with the horizontal axis representing the percentage of the population and the vertical axis the percentage of all income earned by those at or below each population percentile. In an economy in which income was distributed equally, the poorest 20 percent of the population would earn 20 percent of all income, the poorest 40 percent would earn 40 percent of all income, and so on. In that case, the Lorenz curve would be a straight line from one corner of the box to the other. In the U.S. economy, where the poorest 20 percent of the population earns just 4.7 percent of all income while the richest 20 percent earns 42.7 percent, the Lorenz curve sags toward the lower right-hand corner of the box. The degree of inequality can be measured by the shaded area between the Lorenz curve and the line of perfect equality.

Source: Based on data from U.S. Department of Commerce, Bureau of the Census, *Statistical Abstract of the United States, 1984*, 107th ed. (Washington, D.C.: Government Printing Office, 1987), Table 733.

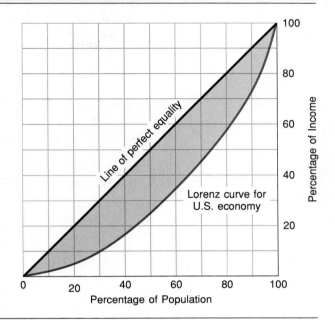

Poverty as Inadequate Income

The traditional viewpoint is that poverty means not having enough income to provide some objectively defined standard of living. People are considered poor if they cannot afford the basic necessities of life—food, clothing, and shelter. The poverty-level income may be defined in absolute terms or relative to the incomes of other members of the society. For example, it is often suggested that a poverty-level household income be defined as one that is less than half of the median income for all households. (As of 1986, the median household income was $29,458; some 20 percent of all households had cash incomes of less than half that amount.)

The view of poverty as inadequate income implies that poverty can be relieved by raising the incomes of poor families above some threshold. One example of such a threshold is that used by the U.S. government in defining and measuring poverty. The official measure begins with an economy food plan devised by the Department of Agriculture. The plan provides a balanced diet at the lowest possible cost given prevailing market prices.

By itself, a total income equal to the cost of the economy food plan is not enough to keep a family well nourished. Other needs must be met. To take those needs into account, the government sets the low-income level—the dividing line between the poor and the nonpoor—at three times the cost of the economy food plan. In 1986, the low-income level was $11,203 for a family of four. Below that level, it is assumed that the pressure of a family's needs for shelter, clothing, and other necessities tends to become so great that the family will forgo the needed food in order to get other things. It should be noted, however, that the government's 3-to-1 ratio was based on a study done in 1961. More recent surveys suggest that poor families typically spend less than a quarter of their income on food.

The view of poverty as inadequate income implies that the way to solve the problem is to replace the missing income. To do so for all poor families in the United States would cost about $50 billion per year, assuming that the process of replacing the missing income had no effect on income from other sources. That is not a large figure compared to the $500 billion or so that federal, state, and local governments spend on transfer payments each year.

Poverty as Behavioral Dependency

In recent years, the traditional view of poverty as income inadequacy has been challenged. The alternative view sees the poverty of many households as characterized not solely by low income but also by self-damaging social behaviors. This can be called the *behavioral dependency* view of poverty. The types of behavior that are seen as most self-destructive concern education, family, work, and crime:

- *Education*. One of the surest ways to avoid poverty is to attend and complete a free public high school, even a bad one. Fewer than 1 percent of all men age 20 to 64 with just a high school education are poor; for women, the figure is only 2 percent.

- *Family*. Family status is closely linked to poverty. Fully a third of people living in households headed by a woman with no husband present are poor, compared with a 6 percent poverty rate for families in which a man is the head or co-head of household. Family-related choices that bring on poverty include, for men, fathering a child without marrying the mother or contributing to the child's support; for women, bearing a child while unmarried; and for both, divorce or separation, especially when children are present.

- *Work*. Few people who take a job and hold it—even if that means starting at a minimum-wage job—remain in poverty for long. Further, jobs are usually available; unavailability of jobs is cited as a reason for not working by only 16 percent of all poor people.

- *Crime*. Poor people predominate both as criminals and as victims of crime. For example, a household with income of less than $3,000 is twice as likely to be the victim of a burglary as one with income over $25,000—and those who rob such households do not come from the affluent suburbs. Homicide is the leading cause of death among black males age 15 to 24, much of it concentrated in high-poverty neighborhoods. Drugs contribute not only to the problems of robbery and murder but also to self-destructive behaviors in the areas of education, work, and family.

What is the significance of the linkage of poverty to self-destructive behaviors? People who see poverty as a problem of behavioral dependency are sometimes accused of "blaming the victim." But they reply that such a charge misses the point, namely that for many of the poor, programs that focus on income replacement alone are inadequate unless they also find ways of encouraging poor people to take responsibility for decisions affecting their own lives and those of family members just as the nonpoor are expected to do. That, at any rate, is the thinking behind such experiments as the ET program in Massachusetts described in the opening case.

How Many Poor?

Part of the reason for the government's choice of an objective, income-based official definition of poverty was to provide a benchmark against which to measure progress toward the goal of eliminating the problem. On the basis of the official definition, the incidence of poverty fell rapidly during the decade following President Johnson's declaration of "war on poverty" in 1964. In that year, 19 percent of the population was officially classified as poor; by 1973, the figure had fallen to 11.1 percent. During the mid-1970s, however, the official poverty rate stopped falling, and in the late 1970s it began to move up. In 1983 the poverty rate peaked at 15.3 percent, its highest level since 1965. As the nation recovered from the back-to-back recessions of 1980 and 1981 to 1982, the poverty rate fell somewhat. But even by 1986, the fourth consecutive year of economic growth, the rate had fallen to only 13.6 percent—well above the levels of the 1970s.

What went wrong? A variety of answers have been proposed. Some observers blame slow economic growth. Others see the data as evidence that antipoverty programs don't work—or in fact even worsen the problem. Before examining these claims, however, we need to take a closer look at how poverty is measured.

Exhibit 16.2 compares three ways of measuring poverty. The first is the government's official measure. It is based on a household's *census income*—that is, its cash income from all sources, including wages and salaries, property income, pension benefits, social security benefits, and cash welfare benefits. It shows the pattern discussed earlier: a decline from 1964 to 1973, a flat trend during the late 1970s, and an increase after 1978.

Adjusting the Poverty Data

Many economists who study the poverty problem view the official data as an unsatisfactory mixture of market and government sources of income that in one sense overstates the extent of poverty and in another understates it. To indicate the extent of these over- and understatements, Exhibit 16.2 shows two other approaches to measuring poverty.

The approach presented in columns 2 and 3 of the table adjusts households' census income to show the effects of government programs other than cash transfers. The most important adjustment is the inclusion of **in-kind transfers**— that is, help given to poor households in the form of free or below-cost goods and services rather than of cash. Medicaid, food stamps, and housing assistance are the three largest in-kind programs. Column 2 also makes other adjustments for taxes and underreporting of income.

When poverty is measured in terms of adjusted rather than census income, the picture the official data present changes significantly. Whereas the official figures show no decline in poverty after 1973, the adjusted data indicate a continued decline through 1979. The reason for the difference is that in-kind transfers grew much faster than cash transfers during that period. From 1965 to 1981, cash transfers increased from $6.7 billion to $26.9 billion while in-kind transfers rose from just $840 million to $43.9 billion.

Clearly, if we want to measure the degree to which government programs have succeeded in reducing poverty, we should not use a measure that omits the effects of the largest and fastest-growing government programs. The continued decline of the adjusted poverty figures throughout the 1970s led some observers to conclude that the war on poverty had, for all practical purposes, been won by

In-kind transfers
Transfer payments made in the form of goods or services, such as food, housing, or medical care, rather than in cash.

Exhibit 16.2 Alternative Measures of Poverty

The U.S. government's measure of poverty includes all cash income, both earned income and cash transfer payments. It has been criticized because in one sense it overstates the problem of poverty and in another it understates it. Columns 2 and 3 of this table adjust the official data to take into account the value of in-kind transfers. Column 2 includes further adjustments for taxes paid and estimated underreporting of income. These adjustments show that after taking all aid to the poor into account, the poverty rate was lower than shown by the official measure. For some purposes, it is also useful to know how many people would be poor without government aid. Column 4 measures "pretransfer poverty" by subtracting cash transfer payments from the income of poor households. The result is a poverty percentage that is higher than the official figure.

Year		Percent of Persons		
	Official Measure (1)	Adjusted for In-Kind Transfers, Underreporting, and Taxes (2)	Adjusted for In-Kind Transfers Only (3)	Pretransfer Poverty (4)
1964	19.0	—	—	—
1965	17.3	13.4	16.8	21.3
1966	14.7	—	—	—
1967	14.2	—	—	19.4
1968	12.8	9.9	—	18.2
1969	12.1	—	—	17.7
1970	12.6	9.3	—	18.8
1971	12.5	—	—	19.6
1972	11.9	6.2	—	19.2
1973	11.1	—	—	19.0
1974	11.2	7.2	—	20.3
1975	12.3	—	—	22.0
1976	11.8	6.7	—	21.0
1977	11.6	—	—	21.0
1978	11.4	—	—	20.2
1979	11.7	6.1	9.0	20.5
1980	13.0	—	10.4	21.9
1981	14.0	—	11.7	23.1
1982	15.0	—	12.7	24.0
1983	15.3	—	13.1	24.2
1984	14.4	—	12.1	—
1985	14.0	—	11.8	—
1986	13.6	—	—	—

Source: Through 1983, unpublished data courtesy of Sheldon Danziger, University of Wisconsin–Madison, and Robert Plotnick, University of Washington. 1984 and 1985 data from U.S. Department of Commerce, *Statistical Abstract of the United States*, 107th ed. (Washington, D.C.: Government Printing Office, 1987), Table 752.

1980. But these declarations of victory turned out to be premature. After 1980 poverty rates began to rise again, even when adjusted for in-kind transfers (see column 3 of Exhibit 16.2). In order to understand what was going on, we must look at yet another approach to measuring poverty.

Pretransfer Poverty

Column 4 of Exhibit 16.2 supplies this other approach. This set of data is intended to measure not the government's success in solving the poverty problem but the size of the problem itself. To this end it adjusts households' census income by subtracting cash transfer payments. What remains is *pretransfer poverty*—a measure of the percentage of the population who would be poor if they did not receive government benefits.

Because pretransfer poverty reflects mainly income earned by households in the labor market, it is very sensitive to the growth of the economy as a whole. Between 1965 and 1969, when economic growth was strong, pretransfer poverty fell from 21.3 percent of the population to 17.7 percent. During the 1970s, when growth was slow, it rose slightly. During the severe recessions of 1974 to 1975 and 1980 to 1982, pretransfer poverty rose abruptly. It was this rise in pretransfer poverty, not any cutback in government programs, that appears to have caused the climb in the other poverty measures in the early 1980s. The 3.9-percentage-point jump in the official poverty rate between 1978 and 1983 is almost exactly matched by the 3.8 percent jump in pretransfer poverty over the same period. Although comparable data for 1984 through 1986 are not available, it is safe to say that the 1.7-percentage-point decline in the official poverty rate during those years primarily reflects a decline in pretransfer poverty.

Explaining Poverty Trends

However it is measured, the increase in poverty rates during the 1980s has become a subject of widespread debate. But the real focus of the debate is not yearly ups or downs in the official figures; rather, it is the enormous contrast between the rapid growth of government transfer payments and the persistence of poverty itself. This contrast is made clear in Exhibit 16.3.

On one side of the debate are those who see the supposed cure for poverty as part of the problem. The argument (which we will return to later in the chapter) is that federal transfer programs contain incentives that encourage people to become or remain poor in order to qualify for benefits. They do so either by reducing their work effort or by changing the structure of the family units in which they live. For example, a recent study by the National Center for Policy Analysis found that each additional $1 billion in welfare spending increases the poverty population by 250,000. The study also found that about half of the increase in the divorce rate was attributable to welfare spending and that each additional $1 billion in welfare spending therefore increased the number of households headed by women by 5,000.[1]

However, not all economists who have studied the problem agree with these findings. For example, in a survey of research on the subject Sheldon Danziger, Robert Haveman, and Robert Plotnick concluded that poverty programs appear to reduce the work effort of poor people by just 4.8 percent. This effect can account for only .5 percentage points of the 12 percent poverty rate of the mid-1970s. The authors also concluded that the impact on the living arrangements of the elderly and on the formation of households headed by women is fairly small.[2]

Despite disagreements on many points, statistical studies show that poverty trends indeed have been adversely affected by a pattern of population shifts that

---

[1] Lowell Gallaway and Richard Vedder, "Paying People to Be Poor," National Center for Policy Analysis Policy Report No. 121, February 1986.

[2] Sheldon Danziger, Robert Haveman, and Robert Plotnick, "How Income Transfer Programs Affect Work, Savings and the Income Distribution: A Critical Review" *Journal of Economic Literature* (September 1981): 975–1028.

Exhibit 16.3   Trends in Poverty and Income Transfer Programs, 1965–1986

This chart contrasts the growth of spending on means-tested transfer programs with trends in poverty. Spending is measured in constant dollars to adjust for the effects of inflation. The percentage of the population in poverty is based on the official definition. Despite the increase in the real value of transfer payments over the period shown, the percentage of the population living in poverty stopped falling during the 1970s and grew significantly in the early 1980s.

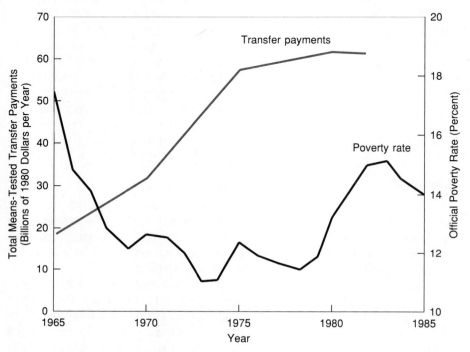

Source: Data on means-tested transfers from James Gwartney and Thomas S. McCaleb, "Have Antipoverty Programs Increased Poverty?" *Cato Journal* (Spring/Summer 1987): Table 2. Official poverty data from President's Council of Economic Advisers, (Washington, D.C.: Government Printing Office, 1987), Table B-29.

moved more people into groups with a high incidence of poverty even while poverty rates within groups have fallen. For example, households headed by women have the highest incidence of poverty of any population group, but the poverty rate for this group has been dropping. In 1969, the poverty rate for such households was 38.4 percent; by 1983, the recent peak year for poverty, it had fallen to 35.8 percent; and by 1985, it had fallen a bit more, to 33.5 percent. From the standpoint of national poverty statistics, however, the decline in poverty among households headed by women has been more than offset by the increase in their numbers. In 1970 they constituted just 8 percent of all households, a figure that had risen to more than 11 percent by 1985.

     More work needs to be done before the causes of poverty trends can be determined conclusively. However, all participants in the debate agree that it is disturbing to find that the government's efforts to eliminate poverty have not been more effective. Let's take a closer look at specific programs and policies and at ideas for making them more effective.

Helping the Poor: Transfer Strategies

The chief strategies of government aid to the poor emphasize income transfers. These transfers can be divided into two categories. The first, **social insurance,** includes programs in which transfers are made available to everyone, regardless of income, at the occurrence of a specified event such as retirement, unemployment, or disability. The second category, **public assistance,** includes programs that are available to people who meet some specified low-income standard. These programs are also known as *means-tested* programs or *welfare.*

Exhibit 16.4 lists the major income transfer programs. It classifies them as social insurance or public assistance and also according to whether their benefits are paid in cash or in kind. In addition, where possible it shows the percentage of the benefits of each program that go to poor households. This percentage is based on the pretransfer concept of poverty; thus, households that would have been poor but were raised out of poverty by the benefits they received are included.

Social insurance
Programs under which transfers are made available to everyone, regardless of income, upon the occurrence of a specified event such as retirement, unemployment, or disability.

Public assistance
Programs under which transfers are made to people who meet some specified low-income standard.

Social Security and Related Programs

The Social Security Act of 1935 set up what has become the largest single income transfer program of the U.S. government. Social security is one of the most popular, and in some ways one of the most successful, programs of the federal government. This is especially true when one views the program as a way of reducing poverty among the elderly. In 1960, families headed by elderly people had a poverty rate almost double that of nonelderly families. By 1985, the poverty rate for elderly families was lower than that for all families (12.6 percent versus 14 percent). Elderly people living alone (mainly widows) still had a higher poverty rate in 1985 than nonelderly people living alone, but the gap had greatly narrowed since 1960. These improvements in the economic status of the elderly are largely due to the fact that social security benefits increased more than twice as rapidly as the average level of wages and salaries during the second half of this period.

Despite this record, social security is the target of many criticisms. It is worth looking at some of them.

Fairness

Although social security has made a major contribution to reducing poverty among the elderly, many critics see it as unfair in certain respects. One problem concerns the type of tax used to finance it. Social security benefits are financed by a special payroll tax, half of which is deducted from employees' gross pay and half of which is paid by employers. However, most economists believe that all or most of the true incidence of the tax is on employees' wages and salaries. Because the tax is levied only on earnings below a certain threshold and on wage and salary income, lower- and middle-income households pay taxes that are higher in relation to their incomes than the taxes paid by higher-income households. Thus, the tax used to finance social security adds to income inequality, partly offsetting the effect of the benefits paid out under the program.

The distribution of benefits is also seen as unfair by critics, especially with regard to the treatment of women and minorities. One problem concerns working wives. Both working and nonworking wives receive a spouse's benefit equal

Exhibit 16.4 Major Transfer Programs of the U.S. Government

This table shows expenditures on the major U.S. transfer programs for 1965 and 1981. Estimates are also given for 1985, where possible. The programs are classified according to whether they are social insurance or public assistance and to whether benefits are paid in cash or in kind.

		Public Expenditures (Billions of Current Dollars)			
	Date Enacted	1965	1981	1985 (Selected Programs)	Percent of Expenditures Paid to Poor People
Social Insurance					
Cash benefits:					
Social security (OASDI)	1935	$16.5	$137.0	$191.1	57
Unemployment insurance	1935	2.5	18.7	16.8	22
Workers' compensation	1908	1.8	14.8		40
Veterans' disability compensation	1917	2.2	7.5	13.8	55
Railroad retirement	1937	1.1	5.2	5.4	
Black lung	1969	NE	0.9	0.9	
In-kind benefits:					
Medicare	1965	NE	38.4	66.3	60
Public Assistance (Welfare)					
Cash benefits:					
Aid to Families with Dependent Children (AFDC)	1935	1.7	12.8	8.9	94
Supplemental security income (SSI)	1972	2.7	8.5	9.2	84
Veterans' pensions	1933	1.9	4.1		55
General assistance	NA	0.4	1.5		82
In-kind benefits:					
Medicaid	1965	0.5	27.6	22.9	80
Food stamps	1964	0.04	9.7	11.5	88
Housing assistance	1937	0.3	6.6	10.7	74
Total expenditures		$31.5	$293.2		
Total expenditures as a percentage of GNP		4.6	10.0		

Source: Sheldon Danziger, Robert Haveman, and Robert Plotnick, "How Income Transfer Programs Affect Work, Savings, and the Income Distribution: A Critical Review," *Journal of Economic Literature* 19 (September 1981): Table 1. Data for 1985 are from *The Budget of the United States Government, Fiscal Year 1986.*

to 50 percent of their husbands' benefits. If a married woman earns enough to qualify for benefits in her own right, she must forgo her spouse's benefits. Thus, the social security system offers women substantially less of an incentive to work than it offers their husbands, and many working wives get no benefits in return for the social security taxes they pay.

Some observers also see the system as unfair to blacks and other minorities. Because minority-group members have shorter life expectancies than whites, they can expect to receive less, on the average, in retirement benefits. According to one calculation, a white male entering the labor market in the mid-1980s can expect to receive 74 percent more in retirement benefits than a black male earning the same wage.[3] Reforms of the system that aim to ease its financial problems by raising the retirement age above the traditional 65 are devastating to blacks given current mortality rates.

Financial Problems

For the moment, the social security system is financially sound, as the large "baby boom" generation born in the 1940s and 1950s is paying for the retirement of a much smaller previous generation. This situation will change dramatically in the future, however. Today there are about five workers paying taxes into the system for each retiree receiving benefits. By the middle of the next century, that ratio will fall to between 1.5 and 2.5 workers per retiree.[4] Given the lower figure, the social security tax would have to rise to 38 percent of the national payroll to keep the system solvent. Given the likelihood that such a tax burden would provoke a political backlash, it is small wonder that two-thirds of workers under 30 polled by the *Washington Post* believed that social security would not exist by the time they were ready to retire.[5]

Effects on Saving

A third criticism of the social security program is based on the belief that it tends to displace private saving. The program was intended to be a source of saving— workers paid taxes into a trust fund during their earning years and drew on the fund during retirement. The trust fund concept was long ago abandoned in all but name, however, and replaced by a pay-as-you-go system. The proceeds of the payroll tax are now used to pay benefits to currently retired workers; hence, no saving is involved.

Even though payroll taxes no longer represent saving from the viewpoint of the economy as a whole, they are a substitute for saving from the viewpoint of individual workers. Knowing that they will receive social security benefits upon retirement, workers feel that they can put aside less money with which to finance their own retirement.

Just how much private saving is displaced by each dollar of promised social security benefits is a matter of debate. But to the extent that there is any displacement of private saving by social security, the economy is left with less saving with which to finance investment—and with less investment, it is left with slower economic growth. This implies that today's workers will retire into a world in which income and living standards will be lower than they would have been had the social security system not promised to protect those same living standards for future beneficiaries.

Other Social Insurance Programs

The second largest social insurance program is medicaid. This adjunct to the social security program provides in-kind medical benefits to the elderly. The sources of financing and criticisms of the program parallel those of the rest of the

---

[3] The impact of social security on racial minorities is detailed in "Social Security and Race," National Center for Policy Analysis, Policy Report No. 128, June 1987.

[4] The future financing problems of social security are detailed in "Social Security: Who Gains, Who Loses?" National Center for Policy Analysis, Policy Report No. 127, May 1987.

[5] ABC/Washington Post Poll, January 11–16, 1985, reprinted in *Public Opinion* (April/May 1985): 22.

social security system. The remaining social insurance programs are smaller and, as Exhibit 16.4 shows, tend to channel a smaller percentage of their benefits to the poor. For both reasons, then, they do less to alleviate poverty.

Public Assistance

In addition to social security and other transfer programs keyed to specific events, the federal government operates a number of income-conditioned transfer programs. The most important of these are listed in Exhibit 16.4.

Aid to Families with Dependent Children

To most people, "welfare" means Aid to Families with Dependent Children (AFDC). AFDC assists in covering the costs of food, shelter, and clothing for needy dependent children, generally in single-parent households. AFDC is one of the largest of the government's cash transfer programs.

The most controversial aspect of AFDC concerns its effect on family structure. On the surface, the program appears to provide an incentive for fathers to desert their families and for women to bear large numbers of children. Despite attempts to reform the eligibility rules in many states and the addition of the AFDC-Unemployed Father program at the federal level, these incentives have not been completely eliminated. Defenders of the program correctly point out that there is no hard evidence that these incentives actually operate. As mentioned earlier, statistical studies have obtained widely varying results regarding the effects of AFDC on family structure.

Medicaid

Medical assistance to low-income people under the medicaid program is the largest in-kind transfer program. Unlike most other public assistance programs, medicaid benefits are not gradually reduced as income rises. Low-income families either qualify for full coverage or receive none at all. AFDC families qualify for medicaid in all states, and in some states families with somewhat higher incomes also are eligible.

Food Stamps

A third major public assistance program is food stamps. In some areas in which a high percentage of residents are eligible for the program, food stamps have become almost a form of currency. Although they can be spent only on food, they release money for other uses that otherwise would have been spent on food. While there is no doubt that food stamps are important to the budgets of a great many low-income families, it is not certain that they have a greater impact on nutrition than cash grants of the same value would have.

Income Transfers and Work Incentives

All income transfer programs affect the incentive to work to some extent by imposing either explicit or implicit taxes on earned income. The social security payroll tax is an example of an explicit tax. The **benefit reduction rate** built into the AFDC program is an example of an implicit tax: For each $1 of earned income in excess of $30 a month, AFDC benefits tend to fall by about $.33. Further, some transfer programs, such as medicaid, have all-or-nothing cutoff incomes that also reduce the incentive to work.

The percentage of each additional dollar of earned income that a household

Benefit reduction rate
The reduction in the benefits of a transfer program that results from a $1 increase in the beneficiary's earned income.

loses through either explicit taxes or benefit reductions can be called the **net marginal tax rate** for that household. A key principle of the economics of poverty is that marginal tax rates and benefit reduction rates are *additive* in their effects on the net marginal tax rate. For example, a family facing a 7 percent marginal tax rate for the social security payroll tax and a 33 percent benefit reduction rate under AFDC is subject to a 40 percent net marginal tax rate. If, in addition, food stamp benefits are reduced by $.20 for each dollar of added earned income, the net marginal tax rate rises to 60 percent, and so on.

"Applying Economic Ideas 16.1" shows how the effects of various programs combine to create net marginal tax rates that can exceed 100 percent for households in certain income ranges. Taxes paid by low-income families are, of course, lower than those paid by higher-income families, but when benefit reduction rates are taken into account, the net marginal tax rates for low-income families are actually higher than those for high-income ones.

The Case for a Negative Income Tax

Concern over the incentive effects of transfer programs is widely shared. Among those who view the problem of poverty in terms of income replacement, a long-standing proposal has been to "cash out" all in-kind transfers and combine them, along with all existing cash transfers, into a single program. Such a program is often referred to as a **negative income tax.** The basic idea is simple. Under a positive income tax, people pay the government an amount that varies according to how much they earn. A negative income tax puts the same principle to work in reverse: It makes the government pay individuals an amount that varies inversely with their earnings.

Exhibit 16.5 gives a schematic representation of a negative income tax. The horizontal axis of the graph measures the income a household earns; the vertical axis measures what it actually receives after payments from or to the government. The 45-degree line represents the amount of disposable income households would have if there were no tax of any kind. The negative and positive income tax schedules show their disposable income with the negative income tax program in force.

In this exhibit, the benefit received by a family with no income at all is just equal to the average low-income level, which is assumed to be $10,000. That is necessary if the scheme is to eliminate poverty as officially measured. Starting from zero earnings, benefits are reduced by $.50 for each dollar earned. When earned incomes reach a level equal to twice the low-income level, a breakeven point at which no taxes are paid and no benefits are received is reached. Beyond that point, a positive income tax schedule takes over.

The negative income tax has the advantage of maintaining work incentives for all beneficiaries. The marginal tax rate for poor families is only 50 percent. This rate presumably would result in greater work effort than would current programs, whose benefit reduction rates often approach 100 percent. The cost of the program, however, is much greater than the total amount by which the incomes of all the poor fell below the poverty line to begin with. All but the very poorest families receive more than the minimum they need to reach the low-income cutoff. Moreover, many nonpoor families—those with earned incomes in the $10,000 to $20,000 range—also receive benefits. The spillover of benefits to nonpoor families is an inevitable part of the negative income tax scheme. It cannot be avoided without lowering benefits for the poorest families or raising the net marginal tax rate to a level that would destroy work incentives.

Net marginal tax rate
The sum of the marginal tax rate for all taxes paid by a household plus the benefit reduction rates of all transfer programs from which the household benefits.

Negative income tax
A plan under which all transfer programs would be combined into a single program paying cash benefits that depend on a household's income level.

APPLYING ECONOMIC IDEAS　16.1

Net Marginal Tax Rates for a Los Angeles Family

Poor families are often subject to extremely high net marginal tax rates, as shown by the data given in the accompanying table. The data show how taxes and reductions in benefits affect the monthly disposable income of an inner-city family of four in Los Angeles at various levels of gross monthly wages. Gross monthly wages are the cost of labor to the employer and include both employer and employee contributions to social security. The data on disposable income reflect all payroll and income taxes and assume that the family makes use of the maximum city, county, state, and federal welfare benefits to which it is entitled.

Source: Arthur Laffer, "The Tightening Grip of the Poverty Trap," Cato Institute Policy Analysis No. 41, August 30, 1984. Reprinted with permission.

The net marginal tax rate is the sum of the marginal tax rates and benefit reduction rates to which the family is subject. The disincentive effects of benefit reductions and taxes reach a peak just above and below the poverty threshold ($833 a month, based on a low-income level of about $10,000 a year for a family of four). Note that as the family's gross wages increase from $700 a month to $1,200 a month, its disposable income falls from $1,423 to $1,215. This reflects loss of $385 in AFDC benefits; loss of $9 in food stamps; a reduction of $23 in the family's housing subsidy; an estimated reduction of $130 in the value of its medical benefits; an $8 increase in state income and disability insurance taxes; $68 in payroll taxes; and $85 in federal income taxes.

Monthly Gross Wages (Dollars)	Monthly Family Disposable Income (Dollars)	Change in Disposable Income (Dollars)	Net Marginal Tax Rate (Percent)
0	1,261	NA	NA
100	1,304	43	57
200	1,341	37	63
300	1,366	25	75
400	1,391	25	75
500	1,419	28	72
600	1,429	10	90
700	1,423	−5	105
800	1,418	−5	105
900	1,420	2	98
1,000	1,432	12	89
1,100	1,253	−178	278
1,200	1,215	−39	139
1,300	1,217	2	98
1,400	1,296	39	61
1,500	1,294	38	62
1,600	1,330	37	63

NA = not applicable.

Helping the Poor: Job Market Strategies

The traditional transfer strategies for helping the poor are all based on the notion that combating poverty is primarily a matter of income replacement. The implied cure is to give the poor more resources, either in cash or in kind. A

Exhibit 16.5   A Negative Income Tax

A negative income tax would replace all transfer programs with a single cash transfer based on income. This chart assumes a poverty level of $10,000 for a family of four. A family with no earned income receives $10,000 in benefits from the negative income tax. From $0 to $10,000, benefits are reduced by $.50 for each $1 of additional earned income. When earned income exceeds $20,000, benefits fall to zero and the family begins to pay income tax. Here a flat 33 percent marginal tax rate is assumed for incomes above $20,000.

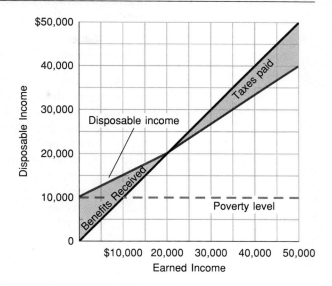

different approach to the problem of poverty is based on the belief that poverty results from a failure of factor markets to properly allocate human resources. This implies that putting wasted labor to work would make many poor households self-supporting.

In the past, there has been a tendency to see the contribution that job market strategies can make as a limited one. It has often been pointed out that a third of the poor are children and half of the adult poor are over 65, mothers with children under age 6, disabled, or unavailable to the labor market for other reasons. However, those who view poverty as partly a matter of behavioral dependency see a greater role for job market strategies in aiding the poor. They view the job market not just as an alternative to transfers as a way of replacing income but as a way of encouraging the behaviorally dependent poor to take responsibility for their own lives and to become better role models for their children. In this section, we look at both traditional and recent job market strategies for aiding the poor.

Antidiscrimination Programs

Antidiscrimination programs are one traditional job market strategy for aiding the poor. In Chapter 13, we showed that discrimination can lower the incomes of people in the disfavored group. In the absence of laws to the contrary, discrimination is likely to lead to a situation in which workers from different groups doing the same work receive different wages. Today equal-pay laws prohibit this practice.

However, as also shown in Chapter 13, equal-pay laws by themselves do not benefit all members of a disfavored group if employers' discriminatory attitudes are not changed. Instead, they tend to replace low wages with limited job opportunities. In fact, equal-pay laws by themselves can even increase the degree to which minority workers are crowded into low-paying jobs in the secondary sector of the economy. To combat this danger, the equal-pay laws are often supplemented by affirmative-action programs that aim to insure minority groups equal treatment in filling job openings as well as in terms of pay.

Public Employment

Another traditional job market strategy for aiding the poor is to have the government employ them directly. The U.S. government has experimented with various types of public employment programs for more than 50 years. Some people advocate expanding these programs to the point at which the government would become the "employer of last resort" for all people who seek jobs but cannot find them in the private sector.

However, public employment programs have their problems. One of the most frequent problems is that the jobs that the government can create most easily are service jobs that require little capital investment, such as park maintenance. Such jobs do not provide the skills and training needed to qualify people for jobs in the primary sector of the private economy. To get around this problem, some economists favor subsidies to private employers who create jobs for the poor rather than direct employment in the public sector.

Minimum-Wage Laws

Minimum-wage laws are another approach that is often seen as a poverty-fighting measure. Some jobs pay such low wages that even a full-time job held by the head of a household does not bring in enough income to raise a family above the poverty level. (At present, counting 40 hours a week for 50 weeks a year as a full-time job, a wage of more than $5 an hour, disregarding taxes, is needed for one earner to support a family of four at the official low-income level.) A simple way to raise the working poor to a more comfortable standard of living seemingly would be to legislate a higher minimum wage. The first U.S. federal minimum-wage law was passed in 1938 and required employers to pay $.25 per hour. Since then, the federal minimum wage has been raised several times. It now stands at $3.35 an hour.

Many economists doubt the effectiveness of the minimum wage as an antipoverty program, however. Although raising the minimum wage does make some low-skilled workers better off, it reduces the quantity of such workers demanded. Each increase in the minimum wage thus means that some people lose their jobs—restaurants remain open fewer hours, automated gates replace parking lot attendants, and so on. Making some low-skilled workers better off while putting others out of work does little to reduce inequality.

There are other reasons to doubt the effectiveness of the minimum wage as an antipoverty program. For one thing, according to a study by William R. Johnson and Edgar K. Browning, low-wage workers do not come mostly from low-income households.[6] Instead, over half of all workers at the minimum-wage level come from households in the top half of the national income distribution. These workers include students working part-time and living with their families, low-paid spouses in households in which both husband and wife work, and so on. At the same time, low-income households get less than 14 percent of their

---

[6]William R. Johnson and Edgar K. Browning, "The Distributional and Efficiency Effects of Increasing the Minimum Wage: A Simulation," *American Economic Review* 73 (March 1983): 204–211.

total incomes from low-wage jobs. More typically, low-income households depend on income from pensions, disability payments, welfare, and other nonwage sources.

All in all, Johnson and Browning conclude, a 22 percent increase in the minimum wage would add just two-tenths of 1 percent to the average income of households in the bottom 30 percent of the income distribution—and even that slight increase in the average masks the fact that more low-income households would be made worse off because of job losses than would gain.

Welfare, Work, and Education

At present, there is a tendency among both policymakers and researchers to place a renewed emphasis on the labor market as an ingredient in the cure for poverty. However, recent thinking on the matter goes beyond the traditional concerns of job availability and pay. Instead, the new focus is on the need to break patterns of self-destructive social behavior and build a sense of personal responsibility among the behaviorally dependent poor.

There are many variants of the new approach, some favored by liberals and others by conservatives, some tried in one state and others in another. But a common element in the new approach to welfare, work, and education is the notion that welfare should be viewed as a contract rather than as unilateral charity. In exchange for income support from the government acting in the name of "society," the recipient is expected to make an effort to achieve personal and financial independence.

The examples from the Massachusetts ET program with which this chapter opens are in many ways typical. The aim in each case is to move the aid recipient from the status of welfare client to independent participant in the labor market. However, it is recognized that simply making a job available is not enough, nor is a threat to cut off payments if a job is not taken. What is needed varies from case to case. In one instance, subsidized child care might be the key; in another, it might be a first job in a structured, supportive environment; in still another, it might be completion of a high school education. In each case there is an implicit, or often explicit, contract between the source of the aid and the recipient: "In return for the aid, I will agree to do the following . . ."

Some early experiments with "workfare" saw the concept primarily as a means of ridding the roles of "welfare cheats" who were capable of working but preferred not to. When these programs were introduced as a quick way to cut the welfare budget, the results were usually disappointing. The current tendency is to view work and education programs as investments. In the short run, what is spent on training, subsidized child care, administration, and so on may mean that there are no immediate budgetary savings. But every time a former welfare client can be brought to the point where he or she can say, "I'm a different person," the investment pays off.

Summary

1. **What is the importance of factor markets for income distribution and the problem of poverty?** Factor markets help determine for whom goods and services are produced as well as how they are produced.

Workers and owners of capital and natural resources are rewarded according to the productivity of the factors they contribute. Because skills, ability, and factor ownership are distributed unequally, income also tends to be allocated unequally in a market economy. A *Lorenz curve* is a diagram that can be used to give a graphic picture of the degree of inequality in an economy.

2. **What is poverty, and how can it be measured?** The problem of poverty is traditionally viewed as a matter of inadequate income. Currently, however, there is a tendency to recognize that self-destructive choices related to education, family, work, and crime add an element of behavioral dependency to that of income inadequacy. The U.S. government measures poverty in relation to a low-income level equal to three times the cost of an economy food plan. In measuring poverty, the government takes into account all cash income, including earned income and transfer payments, but excludes the value of *in-kind transfers*. Economists often use two other measures of poverty. One excludes all transfer payments, and the other includes the value of in-kind transfers along with cash transfers.

3. **What trends in poverty have been experienced in the United States in recent decades?** However it is measured, poverty in the United States decreased during the 1960s and 1970s and increased during the early 1980s. The increase was partly a result of the recessions of 1980 and 1981 to 1982. Another factor was demographic shifts that put a higher percentage of the population into groups, such as households headed by women with young children, with a high incidence of poverty. Still another, according to some observers, may have been undesired effects of antipoverty programs.

4. **How does social insurance differ from public assistance?** The term *social insurance* refers to transfer programs to which everyone is entitled regardless of income. Social security is the largest such program; veterans' benefits and medicare are other examples. *Public assistance* programs are those to which people are entitled only if they meet a low-income test. Aid to Families with Dependent Children is one of the largest public assistance programs that pays benefits in cash; medicaid, food stamps, and housing assistance are programs that provide benefits in kind.

5. **Why are poor households often subject to higher net tax rates at the margin than nonpoor households?** The *benefit reduction rate* of a transfer program means the amount of benefits lost per dollar increase in earned income. A household's *net marginal tax rate* is the sum of its marginal tax rate for taxes paid plus the benefit reduction rates of all transfer programs to which it is entitled. Net marginal tax rates are higher in the United States for low-income families than for high-income ones. Many economists believe that high net marginal tax rates provide a major incentive not to work. A *negative income tax* would convert all transfer programs into cash and subject them to a uniform net marginal tax rate lower than the rate currently imposed on poor families.

6. **What poverty programs emphasize factor markets?** In addition to transfer programs, there are programs whose goal is to help the poor by improving their ability to earn income and find jobs in the primary sector of the job market. Traditional job market strategies include antidiscrimination laws, public employment, and minimum-wage laws. More recent programs are based on a contractual relationship between the government and the welfare client, with an emphasis on work and education.

Terms for Review

- Lorenz curve
- in-kind transfers
- social insurance
- public assistance
- benefit reduction rate
- net marginal tax rate
- negative income tax

Questions for Review

1. What four areas of personal choices are especially important in avoiding poverty?

2. What is the shape of the Lorenz curve for an economy in which income is distributed equally? How does the Lorenz curve for the U.S. economy compare to this standard?

3. Why do economists often use measures of poverty that differ from the government's measure?

4. What has been the trend of poverty in the United States over the past 20 years as officially measured? List at least three factors that have contributed to the trend.

5. What are the largest federal transfer programs in each of the following categories: cash social insurance; in-kind social insurance; cash public assistance; and in-kind public assistance?

6. If a family pays 10 percent income tax on all earned income, loses $.25 in public housing benefits for each dollar of earned income, and loses $.20 in food stamps for each dollar of earned income, what is its net marginal tax rate?

7. List three job market strategies for helping the poor.

Problems and Topics for Discussion

1. **Examining the lead-off case.** In what ways does the Massachusetts program address the problem of its clients' inadequate income? How does it address the

problem of behavioral dependence? Discuss the following possible objection to the program: "If child care and administrative costs are considered, it costs just as much to put a mother of several young children to work at a sheltered job as it would to leave her at home receiving cash assistance."

2. **Poverty and consumer choice.** According to the official definition of poverty, a family living below the low-income level is likely to be unable to afford an adequate diet. Yet a government survey completed in 1977 showed that of families at or near the poverty line, 68 percent owned one or more cars and 12 percent owned two or more; 71 percent owned black-and-white television sets and 37 percent owned color sets; 55 percent owned clothes washers and 25 percent owned clothes dryers; and 38 percent owned air conditioners. Do you find it reasonable that families would begin to give up some food before giving up these durable goods? How does this issue bear on the fact that many families counted as poor in a given year are not poor in the previous or the following year?

3. **Cash versus in-kind transfers.** What are the relative merits of cash and in-kind transfers? Review Chapter 7, paying particular attention to the concepts of marginal utility and consumer equilibrium. Suppose that program A gives a family a $1,000 cash benefit and program B gives it $1,000 worth of goods in kind, but in proportions that are not chosen by the family itself. Which program would be likely to give the family greater utility? *Bonus question:* If you read the appendix to Chapter 7, illustrate these two programs for the case of an economy in which there are just two consumer goods: food and clothing.

4. **Social insurance versus public assistance.** Suppose an effective negative income tax was in force and that poverty had been eliminated. Would you then be willing to see social insurance programs such as social security, medicare, and unemployment compensation abolished? Why or why not?

5. **Transfer payments and the nonpoor.** Discussions of "waste" in poverty programs often focus on the fact that some benefits go to families whose incomes are above the poverty line. After reading this chapter, do you agree that it is wasteful to pay benefits to some nonpoor families? Would you favor a program that cut off all benefits exactly when the poverty line was reached? In what ways might such a program itself be wasteful? Discuss.

Case for Discussion
The New Underclass

Ken Auletta added a word to the popular vocabulary with his series of *New Yorker* articles and a book on the underclass. At first, people interested in social policy balked at the term, concerned that it would have an adverse labeling effect, stigmatizing the people in what the *Economist* recently termed America's "huge and intractable, largely black underclass."

The underclass condition is also attitudinal and behavioral.

Regrettably, I conclude that the word reflects a real and new condition with which we must come to terms. It is a condition properly described by the term "class."

Sociologist Ralf Dahrendorf defines class as a group emerging from structural changes in a society. Indeed, that's what we've seen in the U.S. over the past two decades. "Underclass" is a shorthand expression for the concentration of economic and behavioral problems among racial minorities in large, older cities.

The existence of a distinctive underclass group is an ironic result of the success, not the failure, of American social policy. The civil-rights revolution (surely not complete, but extraordinary nonetheless) has caused a bifurcation within the black and Hispanic sectors that were the focus of the civil-rights laws of the 1950s and 1960s. With opportunities opened up for upwardly mobile and educated members of these groups to move to suburbs and better-off urban neighborhoods, the people left behind in the urban ghettos are more isolated. The role models of an earlier day (a teacher, postman, civil servant) have departed. There is no reason they shouldn't. But the result is that the dangerous inner-city areas that fester in our land have become an increasingly serious social and economic problem.

We cannot easily put our social science calipers to the task of measuring the underclass. It involves more than conventional economic and demographic indicators. The underclass condition is also attitudinal and behavioral. It is often manifest in crime and vandalism, which further isolate underclass groups.

I believe this situation represents a change in kind over the past two decades, although it must always be added that we are talking about a relatively small subgroup among the poor. Not everyone who is poor is in the underclass.

Source: Richard P. Nathan, "Liberals + Conservatives = Workfare," *The Wall Street Journal*, October 16, 1986, 32. Reprinted by permission of *The Wall Street Journal*, © Dow Jones & Company, Inc. 1986. All Rights Reserved. Photo Source: UPI/Bettmann Newsphotos.

Questions

1. Do you agree that there is a subgroup of the poor that is properly and accurately described as an "underclass"? If so, how would you characterize this group?

2. To what extent is the problem of the "underclass" one of inadequate income? Behavioral dependency?

3. Give some examples of poor families and individuals who do not belong to the "underclass."

4. What policies do you think are appropriate for dealing with problems of the "underclass"?

Suggestions for Further Reading

Campbell, Colin D., ed. *Income Redistribution*. Washington, D.C.: American Enterprise Institute, 1977.

The papers in this volume consider not only practical questions but also broad philosophical issues.

Goodman, John C., and Edwin G. Dolan. *Economics of Public Policy*, 3d ed. St. Paul, Minn.: West, 1985.

Chapter 14 is devoted to the minimum wage and Chapter 15 to social security.

Murray, Charles. *Losing Ground*. New York: Basic Books, 1984.

Murray argues that antipoverty efforts over the past 20 years have made the problem of poverty worse rather than better.

Novak, Michael, et al. *The New Consensus on Family and Welfare*. Washington, D.C.: American Enterprise Institute, 1987.

This book summarizes the findings of a working seminar on the subject of behavioral dependency and poverty.

Problems of
Microeconomic Policy

Part
Five

17 Antitrust and Regulation

After reading this chapter, you will understand . . .

- The economic and social goals of antitrust laws.
- Which business practices are illegal under the antitrust laws.
- How antitrust policy has changed over time.
- Why some industries are regulated despite their inherently competitive structure.
- The effects of regulatory reform.
- Current trends in health and safety regulation.

Before reading this chapter, make sure you know the meaning of . . .

- Rent seeking (Chapter 5)
- Market structure (Chapter 9)
- Monopoly (Chapter 10)
- Oligopoly and cartel (Chapter 11)

Court Blocks Coke–Dr Pepper Merger

A federal judge blocked Coca-Cola Co.'s proposed acquisition of Dr Pepper Co., calling it a "stark, unvarnished" attempt to eliminate competition that "totally lacks any apparent redeeming feature."

The preliminary injunction issued by U.S. District Judge Gerhard Gesell in Washington, D.C., prohibits the companies from completing the $470 million transaction until a final determination by the Federal Trade Commission.

But the strongly worded decision may scuttle the entire proposal before FTC hearings begin. In his ruling, the judge said that Coca-Cola's attorneys indicated the transaction "will likely be abandoned" in the face of judicial opposition. [The merger attempt was in fact later abandoned.]

Antitrust law prevented the merger of Coca-Cola and Dr Pepper.

Besides thwarting Coca-Cola's short-term expansion plans, the decision is likely to inhibit long-term consolidation trends in the soft-drink industry and focus public attention on what Judge Gesell called "severe" and inherent barriers to new competition.

The ruling suggests that any future acquisition plans by Coca-Cola and its archrival, PepsiCo Inc. of Purchase, New York, may be illegal. Coca-Cola's "already commanding" position in the marketplace and recent efforts to increase control over its nationwide bottling network, the judge asserted, "raises an almost absolute prohibition to further enhancement of that" power by aquisitions.

The ruling represents a big victory for the FTC, which argued that Coca-Cola's bid for Dallas-based Dr Pepper and PepsiCo's earlier $380 million proposal to purchase Seven-Up Co. of St. Louis threatened to substantially reduce competition, increase chances of collusion and make it even more difficult for smaller players to gain a foothold in the industry.

PepsiCo shelved plans to acquire Seven-Up's domestic operations immediately after the FTC's initial opposition, but Coca-Cola challenged the agency in court on its bid for Dr Pepper.

397

Source: Andy Pasztor, "Coke's Plan to Buy Dr Pepper Is Blocked by U.S. Judge, Pending Decision by FTC," *The Wall Street Journal,* August 1, 1986, 3. Reprinted by permission of *The Wall Street Journal,* © Dow Jones & Company, Inc. 1986. All Rights Reserved. Photo Source: © 1987 Phyllis Woloshin.

Antitrust laws
A set of laws, including the Sherman Act and the Clayton Act, that seek to control market structure and the competitive behavior of firms.

IN earlier chapters, we discussed the issue of market performance under a variety of market structures. In this chapter, we turn our attention to government regulations that are intended to affect market performance in some way. We begin with a discussion of antitrust laws—a set of laws that seek to control the competitive behavior of firms by influencing the structure of markets. The FTC's opposition to the merger of Coca-Cola and Dr Pepper and that of PepsiCo and Seven-Up are examples of antitrust law in action. Later in the chapter, we turn to other regulatory policies that share with antitrust laws the goal of influencing the competitive behavior of firms and the performance of markets.

Antitrust Laws and Policies

Antitrust laws, which date back almost 100 years, are among the oldest government policies aimed at influencing firms' competitive behavior. There is a connection between the antitrust laws and economists' concern with the performance of concentrated markets, but that linkage is not as close as one might expect. The antitrust laws are not a simple translation into law of the economic theories discussed in earlier chapters. Their foundations were laid in the nineteenth century, before the modern theories of monopoly and oligopoly had seen the light of day. Today, as then, antitrust policy reflects broad social concerns rather than economic theory.

In the United States of the nineteenth century, people were hostile toward "trusts," as they called the large firms of their day, not because they were inefficient but because they were rich and powerful. If they were efficient as well, that made them still richer and more powerful. Consider the viewpoint reflected in this passage from an 1897 Supreme Court decision:

> [Large firms] may even temporarily, or perhaps permanently, reduce the price of the article traded in or manufactured, by reducing the expense inseparable from the running of many different companies for the same purpose. Trade or commerce under those circumstances may nevertheless be badly and unfortunately restrained by driving out of business the small dealers and worthy men whose lives have been spent therein and who might be unable to readjust themselves to their altered surroundings. Mere reduction in the price of the commodity dealt in might be dearly paid for by the ruin of such a class.[1]

The concerns of a judge who would dismiss the benefits of "mere" price reductions in favor of the interests of "small dealers and worthy men" differ markedly from the concerns of today's economists. These typically judge market performance from the standpoint of the consumer's welfare rather than the producer's. The theories of market structure and economic performance discussed

---

[1] *United States* v. *Trans-Missouri Freight Ass'n.,* 166 U.S. 323 (1897).

in the last few chapters all stress the need to promote efficiency and consumer welfare. The main purpose of antitrust laws, in this view, is to keep prices low through active competition. As long as competition makes consumers better off, economists tend not to care whether some firms—no matter how "worthy" the individuals who run them—fail to survive the contest.

The connection between the social and political goals of the antitrust laws on the one hand and their economic purposes on the other is a major theme of this chapter. In this chapter, we will try to ascertain the precise degree of overlap between the kind of antitrust policy that actually exists and the type that economic theory suggests ought to exist. Of course, opinions differ as to how large the overlap is, but the following sections will deal as much with areas of broad agreement among economists as with areas of controversy.

The Sherman Antitrust Act

The logical starting point for a description of antitrust laws is the Sherman Antitrust Act of 1890. This act forms the core of antitrust policy in the United States. It outlaws "every contract, combination in the form of a trust or otherwise, or conspiracy in restraint of commerce among the several states, or with foreign nations." It also declares that "every person who shall monopolize, or attempt to monopolize, or combine or conspire with any other person or persons, to monopolize any part of the trade or commerce among the several States, or with foreign nations, shall be deemed guilty of a misdemeanor." (In 1974, the act was amended to make violations of its provisions treated as felonies.)

Under the Sherman Act, the government can sue firms that violate its provisions and ask for any of several types of penalties. It can request fines or jail sentences. (The latter, once rare in antitrust cases, have become much more common now that violations are felonies.) It can also obtain an *injunction* (a court order that bars the offending firm from continuing the action that is in violation of the act). In extreme cases, it can ask the court to order the offending firm to be broken up into smaller units that would compete with one another.

In addition, private parties who claim injuries from violations of the Sherman Act can bring suits of their own. If they win, they can obtain damages equal to three times the value of any loss they can prove to have suffered. Private antitrust suits are quite common today.

The Clayton Act and the Federal Trade Commission Act

Antitrust officials of the federal government won some notable early victories under the Sherman Act, the most dramatic of which were the breakups of Standard Oil and American Tobacco in 1911. Nevertheless, many people felt that the Sherman Act was not enough. For one thing, the act was unclear about the status of monopolies achieved through merger. Also, people felt that the law should state more clearly the kinds of business practices that were likely to have anticompetitive effects. The outcome of these concerns was the Clayton Act of 1914, which has four major provisions:

1. It outlaws price discrimination among purchasers of goods except when such discrimination is based on the grade, quality, or quantity of the product sold or on clear differences in selling costs. Any other form of price discrimination is illegal if the effect is to reduce competition substantially or to tend to create a monopoly.

2. It forbids sellers from making *tying contracts*—contracts for the sale of a firm's products that include an agreement prohibiting the purchaser from using or dealing in a competitor's products—when the effect of such contracts is to reduce competition.

3. An antimerger section of the act forbids any firm that is engaged in commerce to acquire the shares of a competing firm or to purchase the stocks of two or more competing firms. Again, the ban is not total; it applies only when the effect is to reduce competition substantially.

4. The act outlaws *interlocking directorates*—situations in which the same person is on the boards of directors of two or more firms: (a) if the firms are competitors; (b) if they are of a certain size or larger; and (c) if reduction of competition will violate the antitrust laws. Such situations are illegal whether or not proof of a reduction of competition can be found.

In the same year that it passed the Clayton Act, Congress passed the Federal Trade Commission Act, which supplements the former. This act declares broadly that "unfair methods of competition in commerce are illegal." It leaves the question of what constitutes an unfair method to the Federal Trade Commission, which was formed by the act as an independent agency with the purpose of attacking unfair practices. (The FTC also has some regulatory functions: It protects the public against false and misleading advertisements for foods, drugs, cosmetics, and therapeutic devices.) The importance of the Federal Trade Commission Act lies less in broadening the definition of illegal business behavior than in setting up an independent antitrust agency with the power to bring court cases.

Since 1914, the Clayton Act has undergone two major amendments. One is the Robinson-Patman Act of 1936, which strengthened the law against price discrimination. The other is the Celler-Kefauver Antimerger Act of 1950, which, as the name implies, strengthened the law against mergers. We will discuss these acts shortly.

Antitrust Policy

In practice, U.S. antitrust policy is not determined by the antitrust laws alone. The laws are broadly written. Congress left the questions of what constitutes an "attempt to monopolize," a "substantial lessening of competition," and an "unfair method of competition" to the courts. The government's two major antitrust agencies—the Federal Trade Commission and the antitrust division of the Department of Justice—also have a great deal of discretion in setting the course of antitrust policy. Within the framework of the laws and prior court decisions, it is their job to decide precisely what kinds of business conduct should be viewed as anticompetitive.

In this section, we will attempt to outline the growth of antitrust policy over the years with respect to the subjects of price fixing, mergers, vertical restraints, and price discrimination.

Price fixing
Any action by two or more firms to cooperate in setting prices.

Price Fixing
Whatever else the Sherman Act may do, no one denies that it outlaws **price fixing.** Competing firms must make their pricing decisions on their own; they cannot cooperate to set prices more to their liking than those resulting from independent action. The recent tendency of the courts and antitrust officials has

been to treat price fixing as a per se violation of the law—which means that only the fact of a price-fixing agreement need be proven in order to win a conviction. It is not necessary to prove that the price-fixing attempt was successful or that the prices set were unreasonable. It also means that accused price fixers cannot defend themselves on the ground that their action might have had beneficial effects.

Besides making price fixing illegal, the law has been interpreted as applicable to other forms of cooperative conduct that might affect prices indirectly. For example, certain practices in which cartels engage, such as agreeing to restrict output or divide markets, have been treated just as severely as agreements on prices. In general, however, the law has made little headway against tacit coordination of prices. Enforcement agencies have often argued that such activities as price leadership or exchange of price information among competitors also amount to price fixing, but the courts have not always ruled against these practices.

Mergers

Not long after the passage of the Sherman Act, the question of what to do about monopolies created by mergers arose. There seemed to be a danger that competing firms could get around the law against cartels by merging into one big firm. That would have made price fixing and output restrictions matters of company policy and thus beyond the reach of the law.

In an early case that involved the merger of two railroads, the Supreme Court ruled that a merger by direct competitors was a combination in restraint of trade and, hence, a violation of the antitrust laws. However, this precedent was not always followed in later decisions, nor did the antimerger section of the Clayton Act prove very effective. Not until the Clayton Act was amended by the Celler-Kefauver Act in 1950 did control of mergers become a major part of antitrust law enforcement. After the Celler-Kefauver Act was passed, the courts and antitrust agencies moved in a direction that brought virtually any merger under scrutiny. Mergers of relatively small firms as well as those of dominant firms such as Coca-Cola and PepsiCo were challenged.

Besides opposing **horizontal mergers**—mergers of firms that compete in the same market—the government often challenged **vertical mergers**—mergers of firms with a supplier-customer relationship (such as an automaker and a spark plug manufacturer). **Conglomerate mergers**—mergers of firms in unrelated markets (for example, an oil company and a retail chain)—were also frequent government targets.

Current Policy on Mergers

While antitrust officials continue to closely scrutinize large horizontal mergers such as those described in the opening case, federal policy on mergers tends to be much less strict than it once was. The more relaxed policy on mergers stems partly from trends in economic theory. Economists are less sure that increased market concentration leads to poor performance than they were a few years ago. Also, it is recognized that mergers can add to efficiency if they cause weak management to be replaced by stronger management. (The hope that a firm's stock price will rise after its management is replaced is often the main motive behind a merger.) Finally, in markets in which international competition is strong, concentration in the U.S. market is seen as less of a threat to consumer interests. The reality of foreign competition is reflected, for example, in the

Horizontal merger
A merger between firms that compete in the same market.

Vertical merger
A merger between firms with a supplier-purchaser relationship.

Conglomerate merger
A merger between firms in unrelated markets.

government's approval of Chrysler's bid to merge with American Motors, described in the opening case of Chapter 4.

The trend toward a relatively less strict merger policy was confirmed in 1982 when the Justice Department published a new set of merger guidelines that allowed some mergers that the old ones (which had not been revised since 1968) would have challenged. Under the new guidelines, vertical and conglomerate mergers are challenged only when they are likely to result in harm to consumers.

Herfindahl index
An index of market concentration that is calculated by squaring the percentage market shares of all firms in an industry and summing the squares.

The 1982 merger guidelines used the so-called **Herfindahl index,** rather than the four-firm concentration ratio, to measure market concentration. As "Applying Economic Ideas 17.1" explains, the Herfindahl index is calculated by squaring the percentage market share of each firm and then adding those squares. In cases in which the index is 1,000 or less following the merger, the Department of Justice normally will not challenge the merger. It would be acceptable, for example, for mergers to result in an industry in which 10 firms of equal size share the market. In more concentrated markets, mergers that would result in an increase of 100 points or more in the index are likely to be challenged unless other factors indicate that the merger would have no harmful effects on consumers.

In borderline cases, antitrust authorities consider a number of factors that are likely to affect market performance, including the following:

- Mergers are more likely to be challenged in industries with homogeneous products.

- Mergers are less likely to be challenged in industries that face competition from products that are fairly close substitutes.

- Mergers are less likely to be challenged in industries in which orders are large and infrequent than in industries in which orders are small and frequent.

- Mergers are less likely to be challenged in industries in which technological change is rapid.

- Mergers are more likely to be challenged in industries in which there has been collusion among firms in the past.

In most cases, vertical and conglomerate mergers are less likely to be challenged than horizontal mergers by firms of equal size. However, several factors could cause the Justice Department to object to such mergers, including:

- The elimination of potential entrants into a market

- The creation of barriers to entry into a market

- A tendency to facilitate collusion among competitors

- The elimination of a firm that has not "played along" with tacit cooperative arrangements among firms in a market

Vertical Restraints

Like vertical mergers, vertical restraints on trade involve agreements between a supplier and a customer. They are distinct from horizontal restraints, which involve agreements between competing suppliers. Many kinds of vertical restraints have been attacked under the antitrust laws, though not always successfully. Among the kinds that have been challenged most often are resale price maintenance agreements, territorial restrictions, tying agreements, and exclusive dealing.

APPLYING ECONOMIC IDEAS 17.1

The Herfindahl Index

The Herfindahl index of market concentration is calculated by squaring the percentage market shares of all the firms in the market and summing the squares. For an industry with n competing firms, the formula is

$$H = S1^2 + S2^2 + S3^2 + \ldots + Sn^2.$$

As the examples in the accompanying table show, the index rises as a market becomes more concentrated, reaching a maximum of 10,000 under pure monopoly. The U.S. Department of Justice considers a market with an index of less than 1,000 to be "unconcentrated." A market with an index of between 1,000 and 1,800 is "moderately concentrated," and one with an index of 1,800 or more is "highly concentrated."

The chief difference between the Herfindahl index and the four-firm concentration ratio is the added weight that the Herfindahl index gives to large firms. For example, a market that contains eight firms of equal size has a four-firm concentration ratio of 50 and a Herfindahl index

of 1,250. A market that contains 1 firm with a 35 percent market share and 13 others with 5 percent each has the same four-firm concentration ratio, but it has a Herfindahl index of 1,550—much higher than in the case of equal market shares.

To calculate the Herfindahl index for a market, one needs to know the market shares of all firms in the industry. In the case of a merger, however, one needs to know only the market shares of the firms involved to calculate the *increase* in concentration that would result from the merger. Consider, for example, an actual case: the 1984 merger of Republic Steel (7.1 percent) with Jones & Laughlin (8.6 percent) to make LTV Steel (15.7 percent). This merger increased the Herfindahl index for the steel market by about 122. The formula for calculating the outcome of a merger of firms A and B to create a new firm, C, is

$$SC^2 - (SA^2 + SB^2).$$

Herfindahl Concentration Indexes for Various Industries

Industry Structure	Index
100 equal-sized firms	100
10 equal-sized firms	1,000
8 equal-sized firms	1,250
1 firm with 30 percent market share plus 7 with 10 percent each	1,600
5 equal-sized firms	2,000
1 pure monopoly	10,000

Under resale price maintenance agreements, retailers agree not to sell a good below a price set by the manufacturer. Such agreements have been held to be unlawful restraints on trade because they limit price competition among the retailers that carry a manufacturer's product. In practice, the restriction on resale price maintenance has never been watertight; some agreements that indirectly achieve the same thing have survived court tests.

Manufacturer-imposed limits on the area in which a retailer can sell also reduce competition at the retail level. Antitrust officials have viewed such limits with suspicion; but, as in the case of resale price maintenance, such restrictions have not been foolproof.

The Clayton Act outlaws tying agreements when their effect is to substantially limit competition. The Supreme Court has found that "tying arrangements serve hardly any purpose beyond the suppression of competition."[2] Among the tying agreements that have been declared illegal by the Court was one in which

---

[2] *Standard Oil Co. of California and Standard Stations Inc.* v. *U.S.*, 337 U.S. 293, 305 (1949).

IBM required buyers of its business machines also to buy IBM-brand punch cards.

In an exclusive-dealing agreement, a manufacturer obtains from a retailer a promise that the latter will not deal in products supplied by the manufacturer's competitors. Many exclusive-dealing agreements have been overturned by the courts, although the practice of exclusive dealing has survived in some industries.

Price Discrimination

In the original Clayton Act, price discrimination was listed as an illegal practice, but this section was not widely or successfully enforced for some time. Things changed in 1936, when the Clayton Act was amended by the Robinson-Patman Act, which greatly strengthened the law against price discrimination. Although the Robinson-Patman Act is complex, its basic purpose is to prevent sellers from offering different discounts to different buyers unless it can be shown that those discounts reflect cost savings or are efforts to meet competition.

Both the Federal Trade Commission and the Department of Justice can bring suits under the Robinson-Patman Act, although for practical reasons the FTC has done most of the enforcement work. Private suits for triple damages can also be brought in price discrimination cases.

The Robinson-Patman Act has been criticized by economists more than any other aspect of antitrust law. The reason is the ease with which this act can be turned from a tool for promoting competition into a means of allowing a firm to shield itself from competition by its rivals. "Applying Economic Ideas 17.2" shows what can go wrong under the Robinson-Patman Act.

Partly because of the tendency of the Robinson-Patman Act to produce bizarre results such as in the Utah Pie case, the government has sharply cut back its enforcement efforts. In 1976, the Department of Justice issued a report that favored repeal of the act, but efforts in this direction have made little headway. However, private suits are still brought under the act. Many small firms see Robinson-Patman as a weapon with which to defend themselves against competition by larger and more efficient rivals.

Antitrust Policy Today

As our discussion so far has shown, the growth of antitrust law over almost a century has been gradual. The limits of each major act were tested in cases and shaped by court decisions. From time to time, as the limits were approached Congress passed new legislation that would set off another round of cases.

There are still some who believe that the scope of antitrust law should continue to expand. They are critical of the tendency of antitrust officials to focus only on the economic effects of competition and on the interests of consumers. One critic of current trends has written that "antitrust was intended also to further a social and moral vision of America. At the core of that vision was a conviction that the past greatness, and future potential, of the country depended on the kind of character—resourceful, practical, and determined—that only competitive individualism would foster."[3] A former assistant attorney general for antitrust, John H. Shenefield, spoke of "the rich blend of American themes—diversity, opportunity, local ownership, economic liberty—that play eloquently

---

[3] Robert A. Katzman, "The Attenuation of Antitrust," *Brookings Review* (Summer 1984): 24.

APPLYING ECONOMIC IDEAS 17.2

The Utah Pie Case

In 1958 Utah Pie Company, a local bakery in Salt Lake City, built a new frozen-pie plant. The frozen-pie market in that city was growing rapidly. It more than quadrupled in size between 1958 and 1961. Through an aggressive campaign stressing low prices, Utah Pie was able to capture a full two-thirds of this market soon after building its plant.

Utah Pie's main competitors were three national food product companies—Pet Milk Company, Carnation Milk Company, and Continental Bakery Company. Nowhere else had these firms faced the kind of competition that Utah Pie was giving them. But rather than pulling out of the Salt Lake City market, they decided to fight back. By cutting prices on their own pies and making special deals with supermarkets to sell their pies under house brands, they succeeded in cutting Utah Pie's slice of the market back to 45 percent by 1961. (In absolute terms, Utah Pie's sales grew steadily throughout the period because the size of the market as a whole was growing.)

Source: Ward S. Bowman, "Restraint of Trade by the Supreme Court: The Utah Pie Case," *Yale Law Journal* 77 (1967): 70–85, and *Utah Pie* v. *Continental Baking Co.*, 386 U.S. 685 (1967).

Angered by the actions of the three outside companies, Utah Pie sued them under the Robinson-Patman Act. Its lawyers claimed that Pet, Carnation, and Continental were engaging in illegal price discrimination by selling pies at lower prices in Salt Lake City than elsewhere. When the case reached the Supreme Court, it was decided in favor of Utah Pie. In the words of the Court, Pet, Carnation, and Continental "contributed to what proved to be a deteriorating price structure over the period covered by this suit," thus harming the local firm. And that, said the Court, was just the sort of action the Robinson-Patman Act was designed to prevent.

Economist Ward Bowman has sharply criticized the decision. Initially, Bowman points out, Utah Pie had a virtual monopoly over its local market in 1958. Then Pet, Carnation, and Continental moved in, with the result of lower prices and more pies for consumers, although prices stayed high enough to give all four companies a profit. True, the three national companies did engage in price discrimination—they sold their pies more cheaply in Salt Lake City than elsewhere. But if that was a sign that something was wrong, the solution surely should have been to encourage more competition in the other markets, not less competition in Salt Lake City.

through the legislative history of the antitrust laws." A former FTC Chairman, Michael Pertschuk, sees the proper focus of antitrust policy as a "Jeffersonian preference for dispersed power."

However, these views no longer predominate. For some time, criticism of the traditional view of antitrust was largely confined to scholarly journals and university campuses. The agencies that brought antitrust cases, the lawyers who argued them, and the judges who decided them were not affected. In the 1980s, however, things have changed.

For one thing, a number of academic critics of the traditional view of antitrust have left their universities for government posts. Two pioneers in this regard, who helped set the tone of antitrust policy for the decade, were William Baxter, who headed the antitrust division of the Department of Justice during the first term of the Reagan administration, and James C. Miller III, who headed the Federal Trade Commission. Perhaps more important, several academic critics of the traditional view, including Robert Bork, Richard Posner, and Ralph Winter, have been appointed to federal judgeships.

Trends in legal education have also had an effect on the thinking of antitrust lawyers. Legal education has long stressed learning from past cases and judicial opinions. In the antitrust area, as we have pointed out, these reflect a broad range of social and political as well as economic views. Today, however, it is common for this aspect of legal training to be supplemented with formal training in economics. As a result, students of antitrust law are encouraged to focus more closely on the questions of efficiency and consumer welfare raised by the cases with which they deal.

The new generation of lawyers, judges, and antitrust officials bring to their jobs the idea that antitrust policy should be guided by economic rather than social or political values. Their views can be summarized as follows:

1. Antitrust policy should be clearly focused on consumers' welfare. The idea that antitrust laws are there to protect firms against competition and change should be set aside.

2. In judging consumer welfare, the potential benefits of any action in terms of efficiency of production or distribution should be weighed against possible anticompetitive effects.

3. The main enforcement targets should be conspiracies to fix prices or divide markets, horizontal mergers that would create very large market shares, and predatory actions aimed at harming competitors (with predation carefully distinguished from active competition).

4. Enforcement actions should not overemphasize vertical restraints that have little effect on the efficiency of economic activity; nor should they be directed at small horizontal mergers or any vertical or conglomerate merger or at price discrimination.

In setting forth a similar program for antitrust policy, Robert Bork wrote in 1978 that these are "not prescriptions for the nonenforcement of the antitrust laws, but rather for their enforcement in a way that advances, rather than retards, competition and consumer welfare."[4]

Regulation of Competitive Behavior

Antitrust policy seeks to affect the competitive behavior of firms by controlling market structure and, in some cases, proscribing specific business practices, such as price discrimination. But antitrust policy is not the only government activity whose objective is the control of competition. In many industries—transportation, finance, communications, and others—competition has long been regulated by special government agencies that share at least some of the goals of antitrust authorities. In this section, we look at this area of regulation. It is distinct from the regulation of natural monopoly, discussed in Chapter 10, in that the regulated industries we examine here have market structures that, in the absence of regulation, are oligopolistic, monopolistically competitive, and, in some cases, close to perfectly competitive.

Historical Origins

Railroads first came under regulation in the late nineteenth century, but the big surge in regulation came in the 1930s. One tends to think of the Great Depression mainly in terms of high unemployment; however, another major feature of the Depression was low prices. Between 1929 and 1933, the consumer price

---

[4] See Robert H. Bork, *The Antitrust Paradox* (New York: Basic Books, 1978), 405–406.

index dropped about 25 percent. Today most economists would explain both the high unemployment and the falling prices in macroeconomic terms, blaming them on low aggregate demand, inappropriate monetary policy, and so on. At the time, however, people tended to blame the high unemployment levels on low prices. If only prices could be raised, business leaders said, it would be possible to put more workers on the payroll.

It is not surprising that competition, which tends to keep prices in certain markets low, was not popular—in fact, too much competition was seen as a barrier to economic recovery. In 1933, Congress passed the National Recovery Act, which encouraged firms to use cartel-like methods to prop up prices. That act was declared unconstitutional by the Supreme Court, but other legislation that applied only to specific industries survived. Two of the most important industries that were regulated in order to limit competition were trucking, which was brought under the control of the Interstate Commerce Commission (ICC) in 1935, and airlines, which came under the regulation of the Civil Aeronautics Board (CAB) in 1938. As discussed in Chapter 11, agricultural marketing orders, another way of limiting competition, date from the same period.

Rate and Entry Regulation in Transportation

An examination of transportation regulation will show some typical differences between the regulation of competitive industries and that of natural monopolies. Two of these differences were a focus on control of entry by new firms and a tendency to set minimum rather than maximum prices. The traditional argument for regulation of natural monopolies was that without it prices would rise too high. In the case of airlines and trucking, the concern was that without regulation prices would fall too low. Both the ICC and the CAB were, however, given the power to set maximum as well as minimum rates.

It is generally agreed that regulation of trucking and airlines achieved the goal of raising prices and limiting the number of firms in those industries. As the years passed, however, many economists began to have second thoughts as to whether high prices and limited competition were the proper goals of government policy. With the advent of high inflation rates in the 1970s, the doubts about regulation grew stronger, and economists turned almost unanimously against the regulation of entry and the setting of minimum rates in competitive industries.

Regulation and Rent Seeking

Critics of transportation regulation tended to view this area of policy as an example of rent seeking. They saw regulation as a device that permits rival firms to form cartels, thus enabling them to raise prices above opportunity costs and earn profits in excess of those that would be possible in a more competitive environment.

Regulated Industries as Cartels

It is easy to see why this theory developed. In Chapter 11, we saw that two major drawbacks of most cartels are the inability to control competition by nonmembers and the inability to keep members from cheating on price agreements. The laws that gave the ICC and the CAB authority over trucking and airlines were directed at these problems. Both agencies became highly restrictive in terms of entry by new firms. (The CAB did not let in a single new major airline for 40 years, and the ICC was only slightly less restrictive.) Further, both agencies were granted, and used, authority to prevent carriers from cutting prices below specific minimum levels.

Indeed, the agencies' authority to set maximum as well as minimum limits on prices did not fit in well with the cartel theory of regulation. But proponents of the theory argued that both agencies were soon "captured" by the industries they regulated and, hence, did not fully utilize their power to impose maximum rates. Also, for many years trucking firms and airlines were able to use their influence to insure that most of the members of the regulatory agencies were friendly to the industry's point of view.

A number of studies at the time seemed to support the cartel theory of regulation. Many of them were based on comparisons of regulated and unregulated markets. One study, for example, showed that unregulated intrastate airline fares in California and Texas were only about half of regulated interstate fares for similar distances. Other studies compared regulated freight rates for industrial goods with those for agricultural produce, which had been exempted from regulation. Again the regulated rates seemed substantially higher.

Imperfections in the Cartels

Certain aspects of regulation did not fit conveniently with the notion that regulators acted as cartel managers aiming solely to maximize the profits of regulated firms. For example, despite the CAB's best efforts, regulated airlines were not always able to earn high profits. In the trucking industry, the major users of freight service, who should have been hurt most by high rates, rarely complained—in fact, they tended to praise regulation for bringing about a high level of service.

In trying to explain these puzzling facts, economists began to pay more attention to imperfections in the cartels that regulation allegedly had created. The most glaring of these was the fact that although airline and trucking regulations controlled *price* competition, they did not control *nonprice* competition. Both trucking firms and airlines were free to compete for customers by offering more frequent and convenient service, advertising more heavily, and engaging in active personal selling. This nonprice competition was very costly. In the case of airlines, for example, adding more flights every day meant that each flight would carry fewer passengers. Nonprice competition thus pushed up the cost per passenger so high that no matter what level of fares the CAB allowed, no more than a normal rate of return could be earned—and sometimes not even that.

As some of these effects of regulation became better understood, economists began to see that regulation could not be thought of simply in terms of a transfer of rents from users to producers. The effects of regulation were much more complicated than that. Some producers no doubt were able to earn higher profits than they otherwise would have—some of the time. But most of the rents resulting from high fares went elsewhere.

Unionized workers were one group that seemed to benefit from regulation. Controls on entry reduced competition by nonunionized firms and made it possible for teamsters and airline pilots to bargain for higher wages. (Both of these unions strongly favored regulation.) Because nonprice competition sometimes put more planes in the sky and more trucks on the road than were strictly needed, suppliers of trucks and planes may have enjoyed higher sales than they otherwise would have. Also, at least some customers were able to benefit from nonprice competition by getting a higher level of service than would have been likely without regulation. In particular, small shippers at out-of-the-way points may have benefited in that their rates did not always reflect the higher cost of their service compared to that of larger customers on heavily used routes.

Regulatory Reform

In the late 1970s, long-standing criticisms of transportation regulation began to be translated into policy. Through legislation and the appointment of reform-minded regulators, restrictions on competition were eased for passenger airlines, air freight, trucking, and intercity bus service. There was also extensive deregulation of railroad rates and a relaxation of barriers to competition between railroads and motor freight. The CAB was abolished, and a few of its former powers were granted to the Federal Aviation Administration (FAA), whose main concern is air safety. The ICC stayed in business with a reduced staff and much more limited functions. Although we focus on transportation regulation here, note that there were also significant changes in regulation of the communications and financial industries at this time.

The following results have occurred in most newly deregulated industries:

· Lower prices on the average, though not for all customers

· A greater variety of services, including many low-price, no-frills choices that were unavailable under regulation

· New entrants, mergers, and bankruptcy for a few firms that were unable to adapt to increased competition

Trucking

The case of trucking provides a particularly clear illustration of the results of deregulation. One of the first effects was a flood of new entrants into the market. In 1980, the first year of deregulation, 1,500 new firms applied for permits. By this time, the ICC had reversed its earlier policies and granted nearly all new applications. The number of applications rose to 4,600 in 1981 and 4,900 in 1982. At the same time, under the pressure of competition, many existing firms were forced into mergers or out of business. Further, the change in the number of trucking firms was only one aspect of increased competition. While new firms were entering the industry, many firms that had been restricted to narrow segments of the market branched out to compete in new regions or new types of freight.

The increased competition put downward pressure on freight rates. By 1982, the rates paid by large shippers had fallen to 75 percent of the average before deregulation.[5] There was also downward pressure on wages—the average wage paid to employees fell by 19 percent. The unionized part of the labor force was hit with widespread job losses. More than 100,000 members of the Teamsters Union lost their jobs.

In some ways, the most dramatic effects of deregulation have been on the quality and variety of services available to customers. Regulation often had been viewed as necessary for insuring good service, but the evidence does not support

---

[5] Thomas Gale Moore, "Rail and Truck Reform—The Record So Far," *Regulation* (November/December 1983): Tables 5, 6.

this view. According to one survey, 86 percent of firms that shipped freight by truck found the quality of service to be better or unchanged after deregulation; only 14 percent found it worse. Also, 47 percent found service to be prompter, while 73 percent found it to be more available.[6] Much of the improvement was due to the truckers' greater freedom to tailor their rates and service quality to individual shippers' needs.

Railroads

Regulation of the railroad industry was substantially eased by the Staggers Rail Act of 1980. Prior to that time, railroads' share of freight traffic had been falling steadily for more than half a century—from 75 percent in the 1920s to 36 percent in the late 1970s. Since passage of the Staggers Act, the rail share of freight traffic has stabilized at around 37 percent, a remarkable achievement considering the decline in rates charged by trucks, the railroads' arch-rivals, over this same period.

Railroads have been able to hold their own against deregulated trucking for two reasons: a decrease in rates charged to most shippers and an improvement in service quality. A major reason for both has been the railroads' ability under the Staggers Act to make contracts with individual shippers spelling out detailed terms of rates and service. Before regulatory reform, railroads were under pressure to offer the same rates and service to all shippers regardless of differences in shipper needs, cost of service, and so on.

Restructuring of the industry has included the abandonment of some lines and the sale of others to new "short-line" railroads. Conrail and an important group of railroads in New England have returned to financial health since passage of the Staggers Act. Both formerly operated at a loss, Conrail under government ownership and the New England railroads under protection of a bankruptcy court.

Airlines

Airlines are the third major transportation industry to experience regulatory reform in the 1980s. Since deregulation, average fares have declined and passenger volume has risen dramatically. Air travelers have a wider variety of options, ranging from ultra-discount tickets with severe restrictions on refunds and travel times to full-fare tickets with no restrictions. New entrants to the industry have offered everything from no-frills, brown-bag service to all-first-class flights. However, despite many new entries, mergers of existing carriers have left the market dominated by a relatively few "supercarriers." Also, some small communities have seen scheduled jetliner service replaced by less comfortable commuter-line service with prop planes.

The airline situation is complicated by the fact that one part of the air travel system—the airlines—was deregulated and made more competitive while two other parts—the air traffic control system and the airports—remained government monopolies. The growth in air traffic has placed great strains on air traffic control and airports, leading to increased flight delays and worries about safety. (Despite legitimate safety concerns, however, the actual safety record since 1980 is superior to that prior to deregulation.)

Industry critics are divided as to the proper remedy for the remaining problems of the airline industry. Some call for re-regulation, a return to the system that existed before 1980. This option is popular with some business travelers

---

[6] Ibid., Table 8.

who fly frequently but do not pay for their own tickets. These travelers benefited under the old regulatory system that kept ticket prices high and airports uncrowded. Others think the solution is privatization of the air traffic control and airport systems. As private agencies, the traffic controllers and airports would charge airlines for their services. Although in some cases this might mean higher prices for air travelers, there would at least be the assurance that the proceeds would be invested in improvement of facilities.

Banking

Banking regulation has also been extensively reformed in the 1980s. From a microeconomic point of view, some of the most interesting reforms have concerned consumer banking, wherein banks have been freed of many old restrictions. The results resemble those in transportation. The banking equivalent of lower prices has been higher interest rates paid to depositors. However, as in other industries, not all consumers have benefited, partly because banks have increased service charges for such items as bounced checks and made the higher interest rates subject to minimum-balance requirements. As in other industries, a much greater variety of price and service options are available than previously: ordinary checking accounts, interest-bearing NOW accounts, higher-interest money market deposit accounts with limited checking privileges, and so on.

Also as elsewhere, regulatory reform has been accompanied by structural change. Liberalized branching across state lines, enhanced activity by foreign-owned banks, and innovative methods of direct financing by corporations have intensified the competition faced by U.S. banks. Together with losses on loans to foreign governments, farmers, and energy firms, the increased competition has contributed to a higher rate of bank failures.

Telephone Service

The telephone industry is unique in that regulatory reform has, in large part, grown out of an antitrust case rather than legislation. The breakup of AT&T split off local service, which remains a local monopoly in most cases, from long-distance service, in which several companies now compete. Long-distance rates have fallen dramatically as a result, but local rates have increased in many instances. Before the AT&T breakup, it was the company's practice to charge more than cost for long-distance service and use the excess revenue to provide local service below cost to at least some classes of customers. As in other industries, regulatory reform has been accompanied by a proliferation of options available to consumers in both the long-distance and local-service markets.

But even while some industries were shedding the old regulatory frameworks, the 1970s and 1980s saw a rapid increase in regulation in the areas of health, safety, and the environment. We turn to these growing areas of regulation in the next section.

Health and Safety Regulation

Among the fastest-growing regulatory agencies in recent years have been the Occupational Safety and Health Administration (OSHA), the Consumer Product Safety Commission (CPSC), the National Highway and Traffic Safety Administration (NHTSA), and the Environmental Protection Agency (EPA). In addition, some older agencies, such as the Food and Drug Administration (FDA), have become much more active than before. These agencies are not directly concerned with prices and competition; rather, their focus is on the kinds of goods that are produced and how they are produced. Leaving environmental issues to the next chapter, in this section we will look at what economists have to say about health and safety regulation, an issue that has provoked much debate.

Normative Issues

The goal of health and safety regulation is to make the world a safer, healthier, more pleasant place in which to live. Since this is a goal that no one can argue with, why are regulations designed to achieve it a matter of debate? Part of the answer is that even when goals are agreed upon, there can be disagreements about the best ways to pursue them. Such disagreements, which belong to the realm of positive economics, will be discussed shortly. Other major sources of controversy are normative. Although almost everyone believes that health and safety are good in themselves, there are disagreements about their relationship to other worthwhile goals. Two such disagreements often threaten to overshadow any consideration of the positive economics of health and safety regulation.

Can an Economic Value Be Put on Health and Safety?

The first issue is whether one should even consider trade-offs between human health and safety on the one hand and material well-being on the other. Many supporters of strong, strictly enforced health and safety regulations argue that there is no way to measure the value of human life. Regulations, therefore, should be set without regard for economic trade-offs or cost-benefit ratios of any kind.

Others, however, do not share this view. They do not belittle the value of human life; rather, they see no point in condemning something that people do every day—and people do sacrifice their own health and safety in favor of other goals daily. They choose the convenience of car travel over the discomforts of bus travel, even though buses are known to be many times safer than cars. They take high-paying jobs in cities rather than low-paying jobs in the country, even though city air is known to be many times unhealthier than country air. They have medical checkups once a year but not twice a year or once a week because the gain in terms of health is not worth the sacrifice in terms of time and money.

Whose Values?

The second normative question remains to be answered even if one concedes that cost-benefit analysis can be reasonably applied in the areas of health and safety. That is the question of whose values should govern any trade-offs made between health and safety on the one hand and economic costs on the other. Should policy be guided by the values of the people who receive the benefits and bear the costs, or should it be deferred to the judgment of experts? In practical terms, this comes down to the question of when people should simply be warned about health and safety hazards and when they should be forced to be safe and healthy whether they want to or not. Should people simply be warned that tobacco and saccharin can be dangerous to their health, or should use of these products be banned? Should people be allowed to decide for themselves whether to buckle their seat belts, or should they be prohibited from buying cars that are not equipped with airbags or other safety devices?

Strictly speaking, economics as a science has nothing to say about these normative issues. Nevertheless, economists often strongly believe that it is reasonable to consider economic costs and benefits in health and safety decisions and to allow well-informed people to make those choices for themselves whenever possible. When such an economist discusses health and safety regulation with someone who believes in health and safety at any cost, what is likely to take place is a fight rather than a rational debate. This is unfortunate, because there are some things that economics as a science—positive economics—can contribute to the controversy over health and safety regulation.

Positive Issues

One area of positive economics on which economists and regulators should be able to agree is that of insuring that regulatory goals, once chosen, are achieved at the lowest cost. Consider the matter of giving local decision makers the greatest possible leeway in choosing the least-cost means of complying with regulation. One way to do this is to issue regulations in the form of performance standards rather than of engineering controls. *Performance standards* are rules that specify the results to be achieved, whereas *engineering controls* are rules that specify particular techniques to be used or equipment to be installed. A case in point is the regulation of worker exposure to cotton dust, the cause of the brown-lung disease that affects an estimated 150,000 workers in the textile industry. Reduced exposure can be achieved either by installing equipment that reduces cotton dust in the workplace or by requiring workers to wear personal respirators while on the job. OSHA regulations issued in 1978 took the first approach on the ground that it would be more effective. Critics have pointed out, however, that once this regulation was in place, it decreased the incentive to develop more effective and easier-to-use personal respirators. Had a standard of exposure been set, there would have been an incentive to develop better respirators.

Another issue on which positive economics can focus is that of the benefits of a proposed regulation versus its costs. For example, in 1984 the EPA issued a study that showed that banning lead in gasoline would have benefits totaling $1.8 billion. In the EPA's view, this would more than offset the cost, which it estimated at about $.02 per gallon of gasoline. Ethyl Corporation, which produced the lead additive that the EPA sought to ban, said that the agency had left out a major cost. According to Ethyl, banning lead would mean that older cars (which had been designed before lead-free gasoline was widely available) would need valve repairs much more often. In Ethyl's estimate, the cost of these repairs would be $18 billion per year, far more than the benefits. The point of this case is not that cost-benefit analysis ended the dispute over the proposed ban on leaded gasoline; rather, the point is that the grounds of the dispute were narrowed and shifted to the plane of positive economics, where some progress toward agreement might be hoped for.

Conclusions

This chapter has covered a lot of ground, from traditional antitrust policy to health and safety regulation. Everywhere it has turned, however, it has encountered one constant theme: Economists are skeptical of government attempts to improve market performance through regulation. The economic case against regulation can be stated in the form of two basic propositions.

The first proposition is that in practice regulation tends to be dominated by questions of rent seeking and income distribution rather than efficiency. In some cases, the goal may be to keep the owners of regulated firms from earning monopoly profits. In other cases it may be to prevent such firms from competing so intensely that none of them can earn a profit. The goal may be to favor one group of customers or suppliers at the expense of others. It may be to give workers higher wages than they otherwise would earn or to give them a different balance between wages and a safe workplace. Economists do not argue with any of these goals; their complaint is that regulation is an inefficient way of benefiting one group at the expense of another. Many dollars in costs are incurred for every dollar in benefits gained by those whom the regulation is intended to help.

The second proposition is that regulation is less efficient than the market as a means for making decisions and using information. Regulators fail to keep prices down because they know too little about the cost and demand conditions under which firms operate. They try to second-guess the market in deciding which firms should be allowed to serve which markets. In this way, they end up raising costs for everyone. They leave too little room for innovation and local initiatives aimed at satisfying special needs or suiting unique circumstances.

Summary

1. **What are the economic and social goals of antitrust laws?** The antitrust laws seek to control market structure and the competitive behavior of firms. They are shaped by a mix of social, political, and economic factors. To a great extent they are hostile toward large, powerful firms, whether efficient or not, and sympathetic to small, local firms. The economic concerns of antitrust law—promoting efficiency and consumer welfare—sometimes clash with social and political goals. The oldest of the antitrust laws is the Sherman Act of 1890, which outlaws combinations and conspiracies in restraint of trade and makes any attempt to monopolize a market illegal. The Clayton and Federal Trade Commission Acts of 1914 seek to control unfair trade practices. The Robinson-Patman Act of 1936 focuses on price discrimination. The Celler-Kefauver Act of 1950 controls mergers.

2. **What business practices are illegal under the antitrust laws?** Price fixing means any attempt by competing firms to cooperate in setting prices. Actions that might affect prices indirectly—such as dividing markets or restricting output—are treated as forms of price fixing. Price fixing is a felony and often results in jail sentences. Horizontal mergers involve firms that compete in the same market. Vertical mergers involve firms with a customer-supplier relationship. Conglomerate mergers involve firms in unrelated markets. All types of mergers have at times been challenged under antitrust laws. Under current antitrust guidelines, however, horizontal mergers are more likely to be challenged than vertical or conglomerate mergers.

3. **How has antitrust policy changed over time?** The traditional view of antitrust law has favored its expansion into new areas and has stressed social and political as well as economic goals. At present, this view is on the defensive. The conception prevailing today puts more emphasis on efficiency and consumer welfare. It takes a harsh view of price fixing and horizontal mergers and is less likely to challenge vertical restrictions, nonhorizontal mergers, and price discrimination.

4. **Why are some industries regulated despite their inherently competitive structure?** Many industries have been regulated even though they are not natural monopolies. Transportation industries are an example. Some economists have seen such regulation as a form of rent seeking. In effect, regulation amounts to government imposition of a cartel. The rents generated by regulatory "cartels" are shared among firms, their workers, and their customers. Efficiency does not seem to be a major reason for the regulation of such industries.

5. **What have been the effects of regulatory reform?** A great deal of regulatory reform has taken place in airlines, air freight, trucking, intercity bus service, and railroads as well as in some areas of banking, and communications. The results are lower prices, though not for all customers; increased competition, with many new entrants and some failures of established firms; and more variety in the products and services offered to consumers.

6.   What are the current trends in health and safety regulation? Regulation has been growing in the areas of health and safety at the same time that it has been decreasing in such industries as transportation, communication, and financial services. Disputes in these areas of regulation raise both normative and positive issues. The normative issues include the question of whether one can place an economic value on health and safety, as well as that of whose values should guide regulatory policy. The positive issues include finding ways to keep down the costs of regulation and to compare its costs and benefits.

Terms for Review

- antitrust laws
- price fixing
- horizontal merger
- vertical merger
- conglomerate merger
- Herfindahl index

Questions for Review

1.   What are the social and political goals of antitrust laws? In what cases do they conflict with their economic goals?

2.   List four major antitrust laws and their main provisions.

3.   What kinds of actions are viewed as forms of price fixing?

4.   Give examples of horizontal, vertical, and conglomerate mergers.

5.   Why are industries such as trucking, airlines, and taxis not viewed as natural monopolies? If they are not natural monopolies, how did they come to be regulated?

6.   What industries have been deregulated either wholly or partly since the 1970s? What have been the effects of deregulation?

7.   Give some examples of positive and normative issues in health and safety regulation.

Problems and Topics for Discussion

1.   Examining the lead-off case. What basis would there be in economic theory for believing that consumers might be harmed by a merger of Coca-Cola and Dr Pepper? (This merger would give the combined company more than 50 percent of the soft-drink market in many cities.) What economic advantages might such a merger bring? What, if any, are the noneconomic reasons for wishing to prevent such a merger?

2.   "Everyone should have the unrestricted right both to sell goods and services in any market and to withhold goods or services from sale." Are the antitrust laws consistent with this statement? Why or why not?

3.   Before 1980, the ICC limited the number of trucking firms that could serve any given route. Often the only way a new firm could get permission to serve a route was to buy the "certificate" (permit) of a firm that already served it. Some of those permits were worth hundreds of thousands of dollars. After deregulation, the value of such permits fell to zero. Why do you think this happened?

4.   How are taxis regulated in the area in which you live? Is there free entry into the market? Are minimum or maximum fares set? How easy is it to get a cab if you need one? Would you suggest any changes in regulation?

5.   In 1987, states were given the option of raising the speed limit on rural interstate highways from 55 to 65 miles per hour. The move was controversial, because it was feared that highway fatalities would increase as the result of higher speeds. How would you go about judging whether the change in the speed limit is a good idea? Discuss both positive and normative aspects of the question.

Case for Discussion

How Safe Are Reclining Chairs?

Two-year-old Joy Griffith had wandered into the living room to watch cartoons on television when she apparently became trapped between the seat and leg rest of her grandfather's brown recliner.

As she struggled to free herself, the footrest squeezed her neck. It was five minutes before Joy was discovered, and by then, doctors said, the brain damage was irreversible.

The accident was more than her father could bear. Eight months later,

Should cost matter when it comes to safety?

Charles Griffith visited her hospital crib with a $40 handgun and fired two fatal shots into the chest of the comatose child.

"I was wrong, your honor, but it wasn't my fault," Griffith later told a Florida judge who sentenced him to life in prison for first-degree murder. "I just couldn't see her suffer anymore."

In 1985, when the Consumer Product Safety Commission (CPSC) learned of the deaths of Joy and eight other children in similar accidents, it alerted furniture manufacturers and the group quickly agreed to urge modifications in the way the chairs were made and to issue warnings to customers.

"We recognized it as a responsibility of the industry," said Joe Gerard, vice president of the American Furniture Manufacturers Association. Costs "really didn't matter," he said.

But back at the CPSC, the federal agency with authority to order unsafe products off the market, agency economists also examined the chair issue, using a controversial "cost-benefit" formula that the Reagan administration has pressed all regulatory agencies to employ before undertaking action.

The results shocked some agency officials, as well as furniture manufacturers. The economists concluded the agency should not support the changes in recliners.

"It is our recommendation that nothing be done beyond mentioning [the problem] in safety alerts . . . ," wrote Warren Je Prunella, an assistant to the director of the agency's economic analysis staff, in an internal memo.

When Prunella drafted his memo, commission officials knew of nine deaths and three serious injuries in the preceding 12 years that involved children who had been entrapped in recliners, or one per year.

The costs of the hazard were simple to calculate. Figuring that each death or injury had a value of $1 million, Prunella placed "the costs" of the recliner hazard at $1 million a year.

Under the formula, that figure became the limit for what the economists believed society should have to pay to improve the product, the other side of the cost-benefit equation.

The commission had estimates that 40 million recliners were in use, so Prunella divided the $1 million by 40 million chairs and came up with an estimate of how much the repair should cost to be economically beneficial.

Prunella's answer was $2\frac{1}{2}$ cents per chair per year. Since Prunella figured each chair would last 10 years, he calculated that the repair costs could be spread over 10 years: 10 times $2\frac{1}{2}$, or 25 cents.

His conclusion: " . . . a remedial strategy that is fully effective in eliminating the hazards of entrapment will be cost effective only if it adds less than a quarter to consumers' costs."

Representatives of the American Furniture Manufacturers Association, a major industry group, had agreed two months earlier to recommend that its members install a device between the leg rest and the seat in any recliners made after October 1986. An association spokesman said he didn't know what the cost to most firms was, but that it was more than 25 cents. Despite the agency's recommendation against it, they proceeded with the modification.

Source: Bill McAllister, "Formula for Product Safety Raises Questions about Human Factor," *The Washington Post,* May 26, 1987, A19. Reprinted with permission. Photo Source: © 1987 Phyllis Woloshin.

Questions

1. Do you think that $1 million per fatal accident is a reasonable figure to use in the cost-benefit formula? To put the matter in human terms, consider the following two ways of looking at the matter:

    a. Imagine yourself standing at the door of Joy Griffith's hospital room as Charles Griffith enters the room, gun loaded. You stop Griffith and offer him a choice: He can either have $1 million or get his daughter restored to health. Which option would you expect him to take?

    b. Imagine that you are about to buy a car and that a seat belt is optional rather than required equipment. You expect to drive the car 100,000 miles before junking it. If the car has no seat belt, your chances of being killed in a car accident over that period are about 3 in 1,000. If it has a seat belt and you use it regularly, your chances of being killed over the same period are about 2 in 1,000. According to the CPSC formula, if you value your life at $1,000,000, you should be willing to pay up to $1,000 for the seat belt. What is the maximum you would actually be willing to pay?

2. Setting aside the issue of whether $1 million is the "right" value for a human life, do you agree in principle that the cost-benefit formula is the proper framework for making the reclining chair decision? Or do you, along with the manufacturers, feel that "cost doesn't really matter"? If you were a manufacturer, would you install safeguards even at a cost of more than $.25 per chair? If you were a consumer rather than a manufacturer, how much would you pay for an optional, easily installed conversion kit that would prevent entrapment accidents? More than $.25? Less?

Suggestions for Further Reading

Armentano, D. T. *Antitrust and Monopoly: Anatomy of a Policy Failure.* New York: Wiley, 1982.

A critique of antitrust laws and policies that concludes that they do more harm than good.

Bork, Robert H. *The Antitrust Paradox.* New York: Basic Books, 1978.

A modern study of antitrust laws that expresses the view that economic concerns merit more emphasis.

Crandall, Robert W., et al. *Regulating the Automobile.* Washington, D.C.: The Brookings Institution, 1986.

This study applies cost-benefit methods to the regulation of auto safety, fuel economy, and vehicle emissions.

Katzmann, Robert A. "The Attenuation of Antitrust." *Brookings Review* (Summer 1984): 23–27.

A brief, clear statement of the view that economic concerns should be balanced with broader social and political concerns in antitrust laws.

Regulation. Washington, D.C.: American Enterprise Institute.

A bimonthly journal published by the American Enterprise Institute; contains analysis and commentary on all aspects of regulation.

Viscusi, W. Kip. *Regulating Consumer Product Safety.* Washington, D.C.: American Enterprise Institute, 1984.

A study of the methods and decisions of the Consumer Product Safety Commission.

18

Externalities and Environmental Policy

After reading this chapter, you will understand . . .

- How the problem of pollution can be understood in terms of the concepts of *externalities* and *market failure*.
- How the optimal quantity of pollution can be determined.
- How a production possibility frontier can be used to examine the problem of pollution.
- How supply and demand analysis can be applied to pollution control policy.
- What problems have been encountered by pollution control policy in the case of acid rain.

Before reading this chapter, make sure you know the meaning of . . .

- Production possibility frontier (Chapters 1 and 2)
- Externalities (Chapter 5)
- Market failure and government failure (Chapter 5)
- Rent seeking (Chapter 5)

No Fishing in the Governor's Lake

At the lake next to the governor's mansion in Baton Rouge, Louisiana, "no fishing" signs have sprung up. The Department of Environmental Quality posted them. The governor's lake contains PCBs.

It isn't unusual to find contaminated water here in the state's industrial, oil-refining and petrochemical corridor. Tons of waste containing potentially toxic heavy metals and organic chemicals are generated daily, and have been for decades.

But Louisiana's water problems aren't confined to the industrial zones. In the coastal marshes, areas of heavy oil and gas production, thousands of open waste pits brim with the soup of chemicals poured into the wells during drilling.

Externalities in the form of pollution can be unpleasant and dangerous.

Some energy and petrochemical companies in Louisiana have begun to take more care in disposing of wastes. A few are spending millions to clean up their worst dumps. But much waste continues to be disposed of haphazardly.

Meanwhile unusual levels of illness are showing up in much of South Louisiana. No one can demonstrate whether any of the illness is linked to oil and gas activity or to the area's extensive water pollution, but concern is mounting. Statewide, cancer deaths are 9.1 percent higher than the national average, using the figure for white males. And ten counties in the major oil producing and refining region rank in the top 5 percent nationwide for cancer deaths per capita among white males.

IN Chapter 5, we introduced the term *externalities* to refer to effects of production or consumption that have an impact on third parties without being reflected in prices. Pollution is a leading example. As the story of the PCBs in the Louisiana governor's lake illustrates, externalities in the form of pollution are often unpleasant and dangerous. In addition, as we noted in our earlier discussion, externalities are a form of *market failure*, that is, they prevent the efficient operation of the price system. The reason is that opportunity costs in terms of the victims of pollution that the producer does not have to pay are not reflected in market prices. As a result, users of the product receive a false signal telling them to use more of the product than they should given its true opportunity costs.

In this chapter, we look at the externalities of pollution. We examine how pollution can lead to inefficient resource use and discuss policies with which prices and markets can be put to work to remedy the problems caused by pollution. We will see that while government policies have resulted in some progress against pollution, much remains to be done in order to achieve a truly efficient solution to the problem.

How Much Pollution, How Much Cleanup?

We begin with the basic issue of how much pollution, if any, should be allowed and how much pollution control should be undertaken in light of the standard of economic efficiency. Chapter 2 used a production possibility frontier as a framework for considering this matter. Such a production possibility frontier is shown in Exhibit 18.1. The horizontal axis of the graph is labeled "environmental quality" and the vertical axis "other goods."

The upper end of the frontier represents a situation in which all efforts are focused on producing material goods, with no attempt made to protect the environment. The lower end represents an uninhabited wilderness in which nothing

Exhibit 18.1 Trade-offs Faced by Environmental Policy

A production possibility frontier can be used to show the trade-offs faced by environmental policy. A move toward a better environment—for example, from point A to point B—entails an opportunity cost in terms of other goods. A move toward more other goods entails an opportunity cost in terms of environmental values.

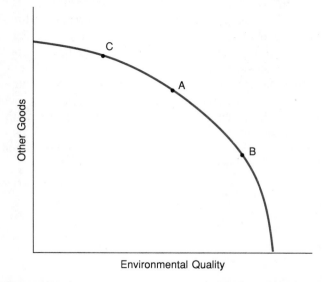

is produced and the environment is undisturbed. But these extremes are of little practical importance. Instead, we can picture ourselves somewhere along the central part of the frontier, say, at point A. From there we can devote somewhat more resources to cleaning up the environment, thus moving toward point B, or we can relax our efforts to protect the environment in favor of more production, thus moving toward point C.

How should we approach the decision of where to move along the production possibility frontier? Economists propose that we approach this problem in *marginal* terms.

Applying the Marginal Principle to Pollution

The trade-off between environmental quality and other goods involves a balancing of two kinds of marginal costs: the costs of putting up with more pollution on the one hand and those of eliminating pollution on the other.

Exhibit 18.2 represents the first of these costs—the **marginal social cost of pollution.** This means the total additional cost to all members of society of an additional unit of pollution. For each type of pollution—say, sulfur dioxide— the harm done by each additional ton of pollution to each person is summed. Presumably some people are harmed more and in different ways than others; the marginal social cost of pollution adds all of these together. As the total quantity of pollution increases, the harm done by each additional unit is also likely to increase. Hence, the curve showing the marginal social cost of pollution slopes upward.

The second factor to be taken into account is the **marginal cost of pollution abatement,** which is the cost of reducing a given type of pollution by one unit. Other things being equal, the marginal cost of pollution abatement tends to rise as the level of pollution falls. For example, in controlling automobile exhaust emissions, relatively cheap devices can cut pollution by half. Somewhat more complex and costly devices are required to cut the amount in half again to the level of 75 percent abatement. Very elaborate and costly methods must be in-

Marginal social cost of pollution
The total added cost to all members of society of an additional unit of pollution.

Marginal cost of pollution abatement
The added cost of reducing a given kind of pollution by one unit.

Exhibit 18.2   Marginal Social Cost of Pollution

The marginal social cost of pollution is the total additional cost to all members of society that results from a one-unit increase in pollution. At low pollution levels—those that are within the environment's natural absorptive capacity—the marginal social cost of pollution may be zero. As the quantity of pollution increases, the marginal social cost probably rises for most pollutants.

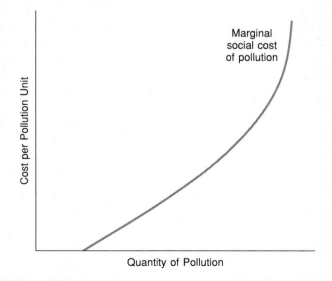

Exhibit 18.3   Marginal Cost
of Pollution Abatement

The marginal cost of pollution abatement is the added cost
of reducing pollution by one unit. The marginal cost of
eliminating pollution tends to rise as the percentage of all
pollution that is eliminated increases. This gives the marginal
cost of pollution abatement curve a downward slope.

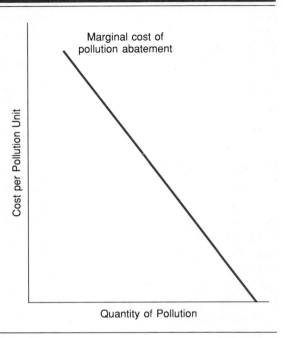

stalled to cut it in half a third time to 87.5 percent abatement. Because of this
tendency, the marginal abatement cost curve slopes downward, as in Exhibit
18.3.

The Optimal Quantity of Pollution

In Exhibit 18.4, both schedules appear in one diagram. This makes it possible to
identify the point—the intersection of the two curves—at which the marginal
cost of abatement equals the marginal social cost of pollution. As far as economics is concerned, this point represents the optimal quantity of pollution. If pollution is allowed to exceed this amount, the harm done by additional pollution will
exceed the cost of reducing it. (Such a situation corresponds to moving too far up
and to the left along the production possibility frontier in Exhibit 18.1.) However, if pollution is reduced below the optimal amount, the marginal cost of
pollution abatement will exceed the marginal social cost of pollution. The small
gain in environmental quality will be more than offset by the relatively large
decrease in the supply of resources available for other uses. (This situation corresponds to moving too far down and to the right along the production possibility
frontier in Exhibit 18.1.)

Criticisms of the Optimal Pollution Concept

To economists, the logic behind the choice of the optimal quantity of pollution is
no different than that underlying the choice of the least-cost method of producing running shoes or the choice of the optimal balance of oil and vinegar in
making a salad dressing. No one denies that cleaning up the environment entails
costs and trade-offs. Few people would advocate choosing either of the extremes—the whole world as an uninhabitable sewer or the whole world as a

Exhibit 18.4   The Optimal Quantity of Pollution

The optimal quantity of pollution is determined by the intersection of the marginal cost of pollution abatement curve and the marginal social cost of pollution curve. To the left of that point, the benefits of further reductions in pollution do not justify the high marginal cost of abatement. To the right of it, the marginal cost of abatement is less than the cost imposed on society by more pollution.

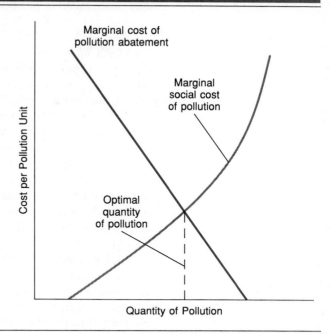

deserted wilderness. Therefore, say the economists, there must be an optimal point between the extremes.

Despite the logic of the optimal pollution concept, many critics doubt that it is a useful guide to public policy. The criticisms are of two types, some focusing on problems of measurement and some on problems of rights.

Problems of Measurement

Attempts to measure the social cost of pollution usually focus on such factors as damage to property, health costs measured in terms of medical expenses and time lost from work, and the value of wildlife and crops killed. These attempts encounter a number of problems. First, data on the costs of pollution are limited at best, and the many gaps must be filled by guesswork. Second, it is difficult to account for purely subjective costs, such as damage to natural beauty and discomforts that do not result in actual damage to health. Finally, estimates of the social costs of pollution rarely give more than the average cost figures. But the marginal cost data, which are much more difficult to obtain, are far more relevant in making pollution policy decisions.

There are also difficulties in estimating the costs of pollution abatement. One major problem is that the calculations must take into account not only the direct costs of getting rid of one form of pollution but the social costs of other forms of pollution that may result. Measurement of these costs is subject to all the problems encountered in measuring the social costs of any kind of pollution.

Data on abatement costs seem to be somewhat easier to come by. According to critics, this is a problem in itself. Studies of the costs and benefits of pollution control tend to list dollars-and-cents data on the cost side and subjective claims on the benefit side. This tends to stack the deck against pollution control. Economists often warn policymakers that the difficulty in measuring social costs of pollution does not mean that these costs are small. Even so, the fear that benefit-cost studies tend to be biased in favor of pollution has given the whole idea of an optimal quantity of pollution a bad name among environmentalists.

Problems of Rights

The optimal pollution concept also encounters a quite different criticism. This is based on the notion that environmental policy must respect certain basic rights and should not be guided by economic trade-offs alone.

The idea here is that pollution should be viewed in the same way as crimes such as theft, vandalism, or rape. Suppose a vandal breaks into a person's home and smashes a valuable statue. How should a court decide the case? Should it listen to testimony from the owner about the statue's value, then hear testimony from the vandal about the thrills of smashing it, and make its decision by weighing the vandal's marginal utility against the owner's? Most people would be outraged by such an approach. They would say that the vandal violated the owner's right to enjoy the statue and that the vandal's benefit from the smashing should count for nothing in deciding the case.

Following this line of thought, it is proposed that environmental policy, like criminal law, be guided by a notion of basic rights. This proposal would place an oil company that poisons the water supply of a Louisiana town on the same footing as an armed robber who holds up the town's banks. The list of environmental rights would include a right to clean air, a right to clean water, a right to enjoy the beauty of unspoiled wilderness areas, and so on. Some environmentalists believe that public policy should respect not only the rights of people but also the rights of other living things—for example, the rights of species to survive. In this view, benefit-cost analysis should enter into environmental policy—if at all—only in determining the least-cost way to protect these rights.

This notion of a rights-based environmental policy is not rejected by all economists. Although benefit-cost analysis continues to dominate environmental economics, there has been serious discussion of the economics of a rights-based policy, as we will see in the next section.

Economic Strategies for Pollution Control

In the last section, we looked at the issue of how much pollution should be allowed. We presented this question as a matter of choosing a point along a production possibility frontier for environmental quality versus other goods. We found that economics can offer a framework for considering the trade-offs involved but not an acceptable, dollars-and-cents answer to the question of where the optimal pollution point lies. This being the case, it seems likely that economics will continue to play only a minor role in making decisions about allowable pollution levels.

There are other issues of environmental policy, however, on which economists believe they have more to offer. These questions deal with how to achieve a given degree of pollution control once it has somehow been chosen as the proper policy goal. This issue too can be presented in terms of the production possibility frontier, as we saw in Chapter 2. Consider Exhibit 18.5. Here the economy starts out at point A, where the level of environmental quality is E_1. It decides (somehow) to move to a higher level of environmental quality, E_2. If efficient

Exhibit 18.5   Efficiency versus Optimality
in Environmental Policy

An optimal environmental policy is one that balances the
marginal social cost of pollution against the marginal cost of
pollution abatement to pick just the right point on the
production possibility frontier. An efficient policy is one that
at least gets to the frontier, even if not to the optimal point.
In this case, a move from point A to point B is efficient. A
move from A to C achieves the same improvement in
environmental quality, but it is inefficient because it results in
too great a loss of other goods. A move from A to D is even
less efficient.

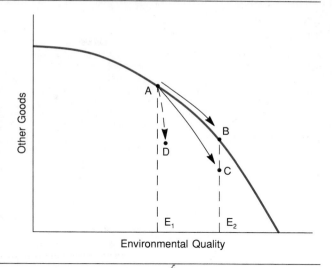

means for reaching this goal are chosen, the economy can move along the production possibility frontier from point A to point B. If inefficient means are
selected, however, the economy may end up at a point such as C, where the
environmental goal is reached but at a higher cost than necessary in terms of
other goods. Worse yet, it may end up at D, where there are no major environmental gains despite high costs.

In this section we will discuss several strategies for pollution control, focusing on the search for environmental policies that are compatible with economic
efficiency.

Supply and Demand

The tools of supply and demand analysis can be applied to the choice of pollution control policy as they can to so many other economic problems. Exhibit
18.6 sets the scene. In this figure, the curve that represents the marginal cost of
pollution abatement is given a new name—the "demand curve for pollution
opportunities." To understand why the same curve serves both purposes, we
can ask how much a firm would be willing to pay for the opportunity to dump an
additional unit of untreated waste directly into the environment. The answer is
that it would pay any sum smaller (but not larger) than the marginal cost of
pollution abatement—that is, the cost of getting rid of a marginal unit of waste
products in a nonpolluting way. Thus, the value of pollution to a firm and,
hence, its demand for opportunities to pollute, is determined by its desire to
avoid abatement costs.

Exhibit 18.6 also shows a supply curve for pollution opportunities. The
supply curve is a straight line lying right along the horizontal axis. It shows that
unlimited pollution opportunities are available without paying any price at all.
The equilibrium quantity of pollution is found where the supply and demand
curves intersect. This equilibrium occurs at a pollution level that is far above the
optimum, shown by the intersection of the demand curve with the curve representing the marginal social cost of pollution. What can be done to correct this
situation?

Exhibit 18.6 Supply and Demand
for Pollution Opportunities

The marginal cost of pollution abatement curve can also be
called the "demand curve for pollution opportunities." The
position of the supply curve for pollution opportunities
depends on how much firms must pay to discharge wastes
into the environment. If they need not pay at all, the supply
curve will coincide with the horizontal axis, as shown here,
and the equilibrium quantity of pollution will be greater than
the optimal quantity.

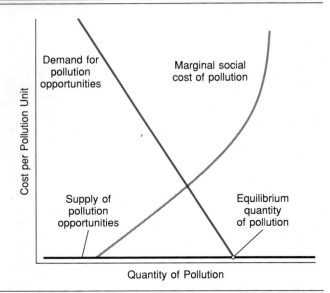

Command and Control

To date, most pollution control efforts have taken the so-called command-and-
control approach. This strategy, as embodied in the Clean Air Act, the Clean
Water Act, the National Environmental Policy Act, the Noise Control Act, and
several other laws of the 1970s, relies on engineering controls and pollution
ceilings. Often the law states that a specific pollution control method must be
used, without considering its cost compared to other equally effective methods.
In other cases a quantitative goal, such as 90 percent cleanup, is set. Sometimes,
in areas in which pollution is especially bad, new pollution sources are banned
entirely.

   The command-and-control strategy has scored some notable successes.
Oregon's Willamette River is swimmable again. Sturgeon are coming back to the
Hudson. Cleveland's Cuyahoga River no longer catches fire. Many cities can
boast of air that is cleaner than it was a decade ago. Nevertheless, the present set
of environmental laws is subject to much criticism. The complaints fall into
three groups.

   First, pollution control efforts have been less effective than desired. The
local success stories just mentioned are not mirrored in national statistics. For
example, there has been a slight reduction in phosphorus pollution of inland
lakes and rivers (phosphorus promotes algae growth) but little increase in the
dissolved oxygen needed by fish and little reduction in fecal bacteria counts. In
the air, the level of particulate pollutants has fallen a great deal, and local sulfur
dioxide concentrations have dropped. On the other hand, little progress has
been made against hydrocarbons or carbon monoxide, and nitrogen dioxide
pollution has worsened. Perhaps most worrisome of all, efforts to control local
sulfur dioxide levels through the use of giant smokestacks appear to have caused
acid rain hundreds of miles downwind. (We will return to the acid rain problem
shortly.)

   Second, environmental laws allegedly have put a brake on economic growth. Pollution control spending has drained away investment funds. Between 1972 and 1979, such spending rose from $34.5 billion to $48.5 billion in constant 1979 dollars—more than 10 percent of gross private domestic investment. (Some economists cite these expenditures as a factor in the slowdown in productivity growth that occurred between 1973 and 1981.) But direct spending is not the whole story. It is also costly to cut through the red tape involved in complying with environmental laws. In many cases, it takes two to three years to obtain the environmental permits for building a new plant, roughly doubling lead times for such construction. Of course, many new plants are built despite the red tape. When an industry needs to expand, it has no viable choice but to build new plants. However, the problem of meeting environmental standards gives firms an incentive not to replace old plants even though they may be obsolete and costly to run. This makes pollution worse, since the old plants do not use new, cleaner technology and are exempt from some of the pollution control requirements placed on new plants.

Finally, existing pollution control laws pay little attention to cost effectiveness. At the time the major laws were passed, Congress apparently expected regulators to find a safe threshold level for each type of pollutant, a level below which pollution would be harmless and above which it would be extremely dangerous. In terms of our diagrams, this threshold concept is equivalent to drawing a marginal social cost of pollution curve that is a vertical line at the maximum tolerable pollution level. If there were such a threshold, no analysis of cost effectiveness would be required to find the optimal level of pollution, since the answer would be the same regardless of the height or shape of the marginal cost of pollution abatement curve.

The prevailing view today, however, is that there are no thresholds. At least for many pollutants, cleaner is always safer. The scientific or engineering question of finding a threshold thus is replaced by the economic question of how much safety people want to pay for. Also, even when standards are set, current law pays little attention to cost effectiveness in meeting them. Requirements to use specific cleanup methods reduce the incentive to discover new, lower-cost techniques. No attempt is made to balance the marginal social cost of various kinds of pollutants, with the result that the most serious problems are not always attacked first. Further, different plants are subject to quite different cleanup standards depending on their age and location.

The high costs and uneven achievements of past policies have created pressure to cut back on pollution control efforts. Economists see this as the wrong response to the problem. Instead, for years they have argued that the cost effectiveness of pollution control can be greatly increased by using different means to achieve environmental quality. The hope of doing this lies in replacing the command-and-control approach with more flexible strategies based on market incentives. Three such market-oriented pollution control approaches are pollution charges, marketable pollution permits, and rights-based pollution control strategies.

Pollution Charges

One market-oriented strategy for controlling pollution works by shifting the pollution opportunity supply curve. It does this by imposing a charge of a fixed amount per unit of waste on all sources of a given kind of waste. Such charges are, in effect, a tax on pollution. For example, all sources of sewage might be

Exhibit 18.7   Effects of a Pollution Tax

Ideally a pollution tax could be set just high enough to reduce pollution by the optimal amount. Here the supply curve for pollution opportunities cuts the demand and marginal social cost curves at the point at which they intersect. In practice, such fine-tuning of pollution taxes would be difficult to achieve.

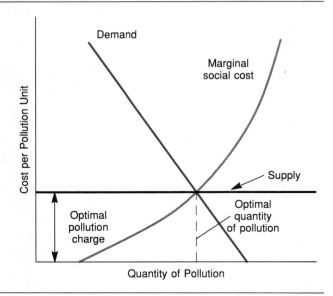

required to pay a charge of $40 per ton of sewage discharged into lakes and rivers.

Exhibit 18.7 shows that such a charge would shift the supply curve for pollution opportunities upward from its position along the horizontal axis to a position $40 higher. Polluters react to the tax by moving back along their demand curve to a new equilibrium in which there is less pollution. They do this because it pays them to use any abatement method that can remove a ton of pollutants from their wastewater for $40 or less.

By raising or lowering the amount of the charge, any desired degree of pollution control can be achieved. Ideally the charge is set so that the pollution opportunity supply curve passes through the intersection of the marginal abatement cost curve (demand curve) and the marginal social cost curve.

Of course, there are measurement problems to contend with. There is no easy way to tell just where the curves intersect and, hence, how high the residual charge should be. In the case of water pollution, the damage done is likely to vary from time to time and from place to place depending on how much dissolved oxygen is in the water, what the water temperature is, and so on. This would make it difficult to insure that the charge is always at the right level. However, advocates of pollution charges point out that their plan has advantages even if the charges are not set at exactly the correct level. In particular, a charge that was applied uniformly to all sources would exert equal pressure at the margin on all polluters. It would encourage them to eliminate pollution first from the sources that can be controlled most cheaply. Thus, it would avoid the present situation, in which some sources (for example, industrial plants and municipal sewage systems) pay high marginal costs to meet very strict standards, while other sources (for example, agricultural runoff and urban storm runoff) are almost entirely free from control.

Economists view pollution charges as an efficient means of control even when problems of measuring costs and benefits make it impossible to calculate the optimal degree of pollution control. In effect, such charges represent a means of reaching the production possibility frontier rather than staying inside it even when the optimal point on the frontier cannot be identified.

Marketable Pollution Permits

A second market-oriented approach to pollution control uses a vertical rather than a horizontal supply curve for pollution opportunities. This is the method of marketable pollution permits (see Exhibit 18.8). Like some forms of the command-and-control approach, this one begins by setting a quantitative limit on the amount of pollution allowed. Ideally this limit corresponds to the optimal quantity of pollution.

Once the limit is determined, however, command-and-control methods are avoided. Instead, a fixed number of permits are issued, each allowing the owner to emit a set quantity of a given pollutant. The permits can then be freely bought and sold. Presumably the highest bidders will be the plants with the highest marginal costs of pollution abatement. As the market for permits approaches equilibrium, each firm will move upward and to the left along its marginal cost of pollution abatement curve by selling permits or move downward and to the right along the curve by buying permits until the marginal cost of abatement is equalized for all firms. Marketable permits thus are seen as another means of achieving the goal of efficiency.

In recent years, policymakers have taken some steps in the direction of marketable pollution permits. For example, the following limited versions of the concept have been tried:

- *Bubbles.* The idea here is to treat all emissions from a given plant as a single "bubble" of pollution. Within the bubble, the plant is permitted to trade off costly control of some sources for less costly control of others. For example, a steel mill might put tighter controls on its blast furnaces to avoid more costly controls on its open-hearth furnaces.

- *Offsets.* Here the idea is to treat a whole region as a single bubble. For

---

Exhibit 18.8   Effects of Marketable
Pollution Permits

In a system using marketable pollution permits, policymakers must first decide what quantity of pollution to allow. Ideally, if they can solve the measurement problem, they will set this quantity at the level at which the marginal social cost of pollution curve intersects the demand curve for pollution opportunities (that is, the marginal cost of pollution abatement curve). Once the permits have been issued, the supply curve for pollution opportunities will be a vertical line. As the permits are traded from one firm to another, they will end up in the hands of the firms with the highest abatement costs. The effect will be to minimize the cost of attaining the target level of pollution reduction.

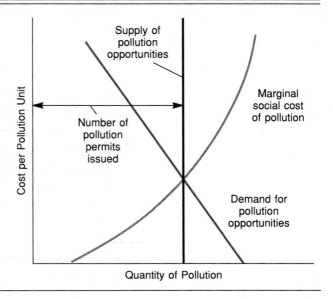

ECONOMICS IN THE NEWS   18.1

One Person's Pollution Is Another's Treasure

Ron Clark, president of Sundance Spas in Chino, California, runs the 84th fastest growing company in the United States. He manufactures fiber glass jacuzzis. But to keep on growing, Clark has to buy emission reduction credits (ERCs) that literally give him, and the others who use them, the right to pollute the air. "I spend a lot of time shopping for ERCs," he says. "For us, they are a matter of life and death."

Like pork bellies or molasses, ERCs have become a commodity. They are bought, sold, banked, and optioned within cities across the country. Perhaps as much as $500 million has been saved by the more than 100 U.S. companies that have traded them during the last decade. ERCs are created when a company in a major urban area reduces emissions below the legal ceiling—through installation of air pollution controls, production changes, or an outright shutdown.

In 1984 John Palmisano, an economist trained at the University of Maryland, started his own company to trade ERCs. Called AER★X—for air emission reduction exchange—the company is based in Washington, D.C. Palmisano, who started out at a General Electric think tank and went from there to the Environmental Protection Agency, began to develop the idea of trading emission credits in 1980. "Eventually I came to the conclusion that I was the only person who believed in this idea 100 percent,"

he says. "As a result, I decided I had to go out on my own and develop it through AER★X."

To make ERC trades, Palmisano and his staff of six approach companies with a standard spiel: "I want to talk to you about an asset you don't realize you have." To customers like Sundance's growth-minded Ron Clark, they are saviors. Were his company in the middle of Wyoming, Clark would have no problem. But in southern California the fiber glass laminating process used to make Sundance spas creates an emissions problem.

When he opened a new plant several years ago, Clark had to purchase credits for 316 pounds of organic gas per day. "I shopped long and hard and finally got them from a fiber glass job shop and a camper manufacturer in Santa Ana for about $25,000. The problem with finding ERCs is that a lot of people don't realize they are assets. There was one guy who was forced to close down because he was short $20,000 cash. What he didn't realize was that his ERCs were worth $200,000, more than enough to sell off some and still keep his business going."

Last winter, just as he was gearing up for peak production, Clark turned to AER★X to find more credits. "This latest purchase, 204 pounds per day, cost $40,000. But it was worth it. With this investment I'll be able to expand my business by about a third." Although the price seemed high to Clark, AER★X broker Josh Margolis believes the spa plant owner got a bargain. "Because credits are sold on a spot market, prices fluctuate widely. He paid about $1,100 per ton. Today reactive organic gas credits in the Los Angeles area are going for three to five times that price."

Source: Roger Rapoport, "Trading Dollars for Dirty Air," *Science 86* (July/August 1986): 75–76. Copyright © 1986 by the American Association for the Advancement of Science. Reprinted by permission.

instance, a steel mill could get permission to build a new blast furnace by paying for an offsetting reduction in pollution from a nearby electric power plant.

- *Banks.* Under this concept, a polluter that cut emissions below the level required by law could put the credit for the extra pollution control in a "bank." Such a credit could later be sold to a firm that wants to build a new plant in the region.

Experiments of this sort have been limited to date. However, as "Economics in the News 33.1" illustrates, in those instances where regulations have permitted it, the new markets in pollution permits have attracted a new breed of pollution entrepreneurs to the mutual benefit of producers and the environment.

Rights-Based Strategies

A third way of introducing market incentives into pollution control is based on the idea that people have property rights to a clean environment. From the viewpoint of owners of property rights, pollution is theft. If you use the air in and around my home as a dumping ground for your unwanted combustion products, you are stealing waste disposal services from me. If you use my living room as a reverberation chamber for noise from your truck or motorcycle, you are robbing me of my right to peace and quiet. If you leak toxic metals into my well water, you are robbing me of my health. As the owner, I should have the right to prevent you from using my property in these ways unless you negotiate with me in advance to buy my permission. If you do not, I should be able to bring civil or criminal action against you in a court of law.

The current legal system is ill equipped to deal with the kinds and sources of harm that are common in pollution cases. The law embodies concepts of proof, causation, evidence, fault, and so on that were developed for purposes other than pollution control. As a result, it is difficult for victims of pollution to win their cases. This is especially true when there are many victims of chronic, low-level pollution—a situation that many people believe is responsible for the largest share of harm done by pollution.

In recent years, many writers have addressed the issue of reforming the legal system to offer better protection of the rights of pollution victims.[1] Some experts believe that such legal reforms, rather than marketable permits or pollution charges, are the best approach to dealing with pollution from toxic substances, especially when the effects are localized and the sources identifiable. This approach might, for example, offer the best remedy for residents of some of the Louisiana communities whose wells and surface water have been poisoned by chemical wastes.

What would be the economic effect of laws that allowed property owners to protect themselves from pollution? One possible result would be the creation of a private market for pollution rights. In such a market, people would sell pollution opportunities to firms only if they were offered a high enough price to compensate them for damage done. If everyone sold pollution rights at prices equal to their marginal costs of pollution damage, the pollution market would look like the graph in Exhibit 18.9. The pollution opportunity supply curve would follow the marginal social cost curve. The equilibrium quantity of pollution would be exactly the optimal amount.

The Problem of Acid Rain: A Case Study[2]

The general principles of the economics of externalities apply to many types of pollution—pollution of surface water with sewage and farm runoff, of groundwater with toxic metals, of the air with automobile exhaust, noise pollu-

---

[1]The special issue of the *Cato Journal* listed in the suggested readings at the end of this chapter contains many useful articles and references.

[2]This section draws on Glen E. Gordon, "Acid Rain: What Is It?" *Resources* (Winter 1984): 6–8; Paul R. Portney, "Acid Rain: Making Sensible Policy," *Resources* (Winter 1984): 9–12; Peter Huber, "The I-Ching of Acid Rain," *Regulation* (September/December 1984): 15–65; Robert W. Crandall, "An Acid Test for Congress," *Regulation* (September/December 1984): 21–28.

Exhibit 18.9   Effects of a Rights-Based
Pollution Control Policy

If polluters always had to compensate the victims of pollution
for damage to person or property, a private market in
pollution opportunities would be created. Ideally the supply
curve in this market would exactly coincide with the marginal
social cost of pollution curve. The equilibrium quantity of
pollution would then equal the optimal quantity.

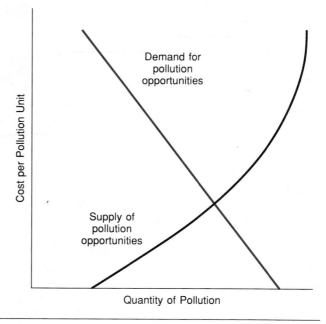

tion, and so on. In this section, we will illustrate those principles by applying
them to a specific pollution problem—acid rain. How to deal with acid rain is
one of the most controversial issues of environmental policy today. We will look
first at the chemistry of acid rain, then at the problem of measuring the costs and
benefits of control, and finally at the economics of various control strategies.

The Chemistry of Acid Rain

Rain is always slightly acidic, but there are parts of the world in which it is much
more so than in others. In Germany, Scandinavia, eastern Canada, and the
eastern United States, acidity levels 5 to 20 times that of natural rain, or even
higher, are often found. In some areas acid rain is neutralized by natural alkaline
substances in the soil, but in the eastern United States many of the areas with the
most acidic rainfall have a low tolerance for acid rain. When acid rain (as well as
acid snow, acid fog, and dry acidic particles) falls on such a region, it can
damage plants and aquatic life. There are areas of upper New York State and
New England in which trees are dying and lakes are crystal clear but devoid of
fish. Acid rain is believed to be the cause of much of this damage.

   The formation of acid rain begins with the release of sulfur dioxide and
nitrogen oxides into the air. These compounds react with oxidizing agents to
form sulfuric or nitric acid. Some of the acid created is neutralized by alkaline
substances that are also present in the air, such as limestone dust and ammonia
gas.

   Of the many sources of sulfur dioxide and nitrogen oxides, by far the largest
is coal combustion. The burning of coal is believed to release some 27 million
tons of sulfur dioxide into the air in the United States each year. About two-
thirds of this amount comes from electric utilities, especially those in the Ohio
Valley. The prevailing winds in the eastern United States blow from west to east;

thus, it is this Ohio Valley sulfur dioxide that is thought to be the source of the acid rain of New England and eastern Canada. (Although much acid rain is "exported" from the United States to Canada, some is also "imported" from industrial sources in Ontario.)

On the basis of this reading of the facts, it is proposed that sulfur dioxide emissions from coal-burning industries, especially in the Midwest, be reduced in the expectation that this will decrease the acidity of rain in the East and save eastern lakes and forests from further damage. On the surface, this seems simple enough. However, when it comes to measuring costs and benefits, determining an optimal degree of cleanup, and choosing control methods, things turn out to be far less simple.

Measuring the Costs and Benefits of Controlling Sulfur Dioxide Emissions

The basic facts of the chemistry of acid rain create a plausible case for controlling sulfur dioxide emissions. According to the logic of the economics of externalities, once the problem has been identified the next step should be to estimate the costs and benefits of reducing emissions in order to calculate the optimal degree of reduction.

The technology and economics of reducing sulfur dioxide emissions from coal-burning power plants have been studied extensively. Many of the possible methods have undergone large-scale, practical trials. As a result, dollar costs for various degrees of reduction can be calculated much more accurately than in the cases of many types of pollution. "Applying Economic Ideas 18.1" shows how a cost of pollution abatement curve can be constructed for this industry.

As is often the case, measuring the benefits of pollution abatement is more difficult than measuring the costs. In the case of acid rain, there are three major sources of uncertainty.

One concerns the transportation of sulfur dioxide from coal-burning plants in the Midwest to vulnerable areas in the East. It is known that the prevailing winds in this region blow from west to east, but at present it is not possible to say which midwestern boilers emit the sulfur that falls in a given eastern lake. Knowledge of transportation patterns is important, because the greatest control effort should be focused on the sources that cause the most harm. At the other extreme, about a third of sulfur dioxide emissions blow out over the ocean. These are thought to cause little or no harm, since the ocean contains abundant alkaline material with which to neutralize acid rain.

An even greater area of uncertainty concerns the chemistry of acid rain. There are two possible conditions under which a reduction in sulfur dioxide emissions would fail to reduce the acidity of eastern rain. One is that the formation of acid rain is limited not by the quantity of available sulfur dioxide but by the quantity of available oxidizing agents. The formation of acid rain is sometimes compared to baking a cake. Suppose each cake requires two cups of flour (sulfur dioxide) and one cup of sugar (oxidizing agents). If you have 20 cups of flour and 4 cups of sugar, you can bake only 4 cakes. A marginal reduction in your flour supply will not reduce your cake output. At present, scientists disagree as to whether it is the sulfur dioxide "flour" or the oxidizing "sugar" that limits the formation of acid rain. Thus, they are not sure whether a cutback in sulfur dioxide emissions will result in a proportional reduction in the acidity of rain. Much the same holds true for the natural alkaline materials in the air that

APPLYING ECONOMIC IDEAS   18.1

Marginal Costs of Pollution Abatement for Sulfur Dioxide

The costs of reducing sulfur dioxide emissions from coal-burning electric utilities have been studied extensively. As the accompanying chart shows, there is a hierarchy of methods—fuel switching, fuel washing, cleaner burning, and scrubbing—each more expensive than the one before. An analysis of these methods permits construction of a stair-step curve, as shown here, that approximates the theoretical negatively sloped cost of pollution abatement curves used in earlier figures.

The cheapest way of reducing sulfur dioxide emissions appears to be switching from high-sulfur to low-sulfur coal. The most serious polluters among midwestern utilities are located close to sources of high-sulfur coal, which is mined in Illinois, Ohio, and some other midwestern and Appalachian states. There are some sources of low-sulfur coal in this region and larger sources in the West. Taking into account higher transportation costs, the high price of low-sulfur coal, and the costs of converting boilers to burn a different type of coal, the cost of changing fuels is estimated at $250 per ton. It is estimated that about 6 million of the total of 27 million tons of sulfur dioxide from

coal-burning sources could be eliminated through fuel switching.

The next least expensive method of reducing emissions is to buy dirty coal and clean it before it is burned. The technology for doing this is already in use in some places. It is estimated that an additional 1.5 million tons of sulfur dioxide emissions could be abated through fuel cleaning at a cost of about $580 per ton.

Instead of cleaning the fuel—or in addition to doing so—it is possible to burn the fuel more cleanly. Several technologies for clean burning of coal have been developed, although none is yet in wide use. At present, the costs of these methods are estimated at about $800 per ton of sulfur dioxide abated. The degree of reduction that could be achieved by these methods is not known for certain.

Finally, the most expensive option is to "scrub" the stack gases that come from the boiler after the fuel is burned. Scrubbing costs about $1,000 per ton of sulfur dioxide abated—more when scrubbers are installed on existing rather than new plants. Scrubbing also creates a local environmental problem, namely the disposal of thousands of tons of sludge. It is thought that the use of scrubbing in addition to other methods could bring the total reduction of sulfur dioxide emissions to 10 million tons per year.

Source: Based on data given by Peter Huber, "The I-Ching of Acid Rain," *Regulation* (September/December 1984): 59–60.

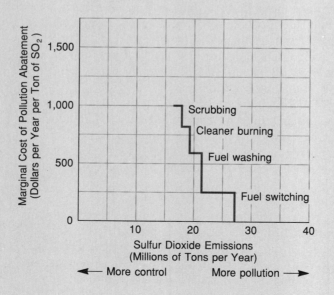

neutralize part of the acid rain before it falls. There is some evidence that variations in acid rain from time to time and place to place are associated more with
variations in levels of alkaline materials than with levels of sulfur dioxide and
nitrogen oxides. Once again, because the recipe for the "cake" is complex, the
marginal effects of changing the quantity of one ingredient are not certain.

The third uncertainty regarding the benefits of reducing sulfur dioxide
emissions concerns the dollar value of the damage done by acid rain. Even if the
chemical and biological effects of a given degree of abatement were known, they
would still have to be converted into dollar terms in order to be compared with
the costs of abatement. However, the uncertainties here are enormous. At least
six areas of potential benefit have been identified:

- *Water resources*. It is certain that excess acidity of lake and river water
  can kill fish and other aquatic life. Acid rain is a likely factor in the excess acidity of many lakes, especially in the Adirondacks. The economic
  loss in such cases would be represented by the impact of sport fishing,
  tourism, and aesthetic values.
- *Forests*. Both in Europe and the eastern United States, trees have been
  dying at unusually high rates in many of the areas in which acid rain
  falls. However, these forests have also been exposed to ozone, heavy-
  metal pollution, drought, and colder than average winters. It therefore is
  not certain how quickly the forests' health would respond to any given
  reduction in the acidity of rain.
- *Farming*. In the case of many types of pollution, crop damage is one of
  the effects that can be assigned a dollar value. However, in view of the
  heavy treatment of farmland with both acid and alkaline chemicals, it is
  difficult to sort out the effect, if any, of a change in the acidity of rain.
- *Materials*. Sulfur dioxide and other pollutants can attack a broad range
  of materials, including stone, metals, and paint. Using reasonable assumptions, it is easy to come up with figures in the hundreds of millions
  of dollars for pollution damage to materials. However, it is hard to separate the effects of acid rain from those of local pollution sources, such as
  automobile exhaust, that cause similar damage.
- *Human health*. Sulfur dioxide in the air is known to be a health hazard.
  Thus, any effort to reduce sulfur dioxide emissions presumably would
  have some health benefits. It is also possible that acid rain causes health
  problems of its own by dissolving metals from the soil that then become
  incorporated into drinking water.
- *Visibility*. The same chemicals that cause acid rain cause the summer
  haze that hangs over much of the eastern United States. Thus, any effort
  to control acid rain probably would, as a by-product, improve visibility.
  This would have an impact on tourism, property values, and aesthetic
  standards.

Striking a Balance

Our review of the costs and benefits of controlling sulfur dioxide emissions
makes it clear that the costs of abatement are considerable. The social costs of
pollution are high too, but they are much harder to measure. Where does this
leave us?

First, it is fair to say that we are nowhere close to knowing enough to determine the optimal quantity of pollution. We just don't know the point at which the curves for marginal abatement costs and marginal social costs of pollution intersect. Any decision regarding how many tons of sulfur dioxide to allow into the atmosphere will have to be made on grounds other than dollars-and-cents comparisons of costs and benefits.

Second, it must be stressed that the fact that we have better numbers for the costs of abatement than for those of the benefits does not mean that the former are larger. There is no basis in science, economics, or logic for such a conclusion. It is true that under the too-much-flour/too-little-sugar hypothesis, spending $5 billion each year to take 10 million tons of sulfur dioxide out of the air might have no benefits at all. On the other hand, it should be kept in mind that some 50 million people live in the region affected by acid rain. It would take only $100 per person per year in benefits of all types—fish, trees, crops, paint, human lungs, and clear vistas—to justify the $5 billion. Since those same people currently spend thousands of dollars apiece in an average year on recreation, food, forest products, and home maintenance, $100 doesn't look like such a big number.

In the end, then, policymakers must choose between two arguments. On the one hand, some people say, "We don't know exactly how big a problem we have, so let's study it a little more before we spend billions of dollars trying to solve it." On the other hand, there are those who say, "We can't risk not spending the money now, because by the time we're sure how much damage is being done, it will be too late." Economics can offer only limited help in deciding this matter.

Choosing an Efficient Control Strategy

Economists may sit on the sidelines while engineers and scientists dominate the debate over measurement of costs and benefits. However, once it is decided that an effort should be made to control sulfur dioxide emissions, the economists are eager to take the field and start calling the plays. "Whatever we decide to do," they say, "let's do it efficiently." Just what would an efficient strategy for acid rain control look like, and how would it compare with existing regulations and current proposals for change?

The Least-Cost Principle

Economists may disagree about a lot of things, but they concur on one principle: If we are going to reduce sulfur dioxide emissions, less costly methods of doing so are better than more costly methods assuming that the results are the same. This means starting on the lowest step of the marginal cost of abatement schedule shown in "Applying Economic Ideas 18.1" and then moving upward along it one step at a time. Two economic strategies for pollution control seem well suited to insuring that this principle will be followed. One is a pollution tax and the other a system of marketable permits.

According to the figure we have drawn, a tax of, say, $400 per ton would produce a 6-million-ton cutback, one of $1,000 per ton would produce a 10-million-ton cutback, and so on. Each plant would choose the combination of fuel switching, fuel cleaning, combustion technology, and scrubbing that was best suited to local conditions. The total cost of reaching the goal would be a minimum figure. If policymakers guessed wrong and set the tax too low, it could be raised later.

As an alternative, marketable permits could be issued that would allow a total of, say, 17 million tons of sulfur dioxide per year—10 million tons less than at present. Firms with clean boilers or nearby sources of clean coal presumably would sell some of their permits to others who could not clean up as cheaply. According to the figure, the market price of permits would rise to $1,000 per ton, equal to the height of the marginal cost curve for pollution abatement at the 17-million-ton limit. Again costs would be minimized.

If these ideas are too radical for policymakers to accept, economists have a third proposal: Set a specific emission target for each plant, but leave it up to local managers to determine the method of control to use. This would be less efficient than a pollution tax or a system of marketable permits. The reason is that plants that could clean up cheaply would have no incentive to reduce emissions by more than the minimum required amount. However, it would leave cost-cutting incentives in place for managers on a plant-by-plant basis.

Current Regulations and Rent Seeking

Unfortunately, current regulations for control of sulfur dioxide are nearly the opposite of what economists recommend. In its 1977 amendments to Section 111 of the Clean Air Act, Congress required that any newly constructed electric power plant meet the emissions limit by the most expensive available technology—namely, scrubbing. The scrubbing requirement applied regardless of how clean or dirty the plant's fuel or combustion technology was. Many old plants, including some of the dirtiest ones that burn the most sulfurous midwestern coal, were not forced to scrub. Instead, they were allowed to meet standards for local pollution by building tall smokestacks—up to 1,000 feet high—that keep the air in surrounding communities fairly clean. Unfortunately, the tall stacks put the sulfur dioxide right up where the chemical mischief that turns it into acid rain is done. They simply turned a local problem into a national one—or, more correctly, an international one, if Canada is considered.

Why did Congress choose such a seemingly irrational approach to controlling sulfur dioxide emissions? The answer appears to lie in rent-seeking behavior on the part of members of Congress and their constituents. In particular, the choice of regulations can be traced to the nature of the coalition that passed the Clean Air Act and its amendments. The coalition included these elements:

- Coal-mining interests in the high-sulfur areas of Ohio, Illinois, and elsewhere who wanted to generate rents by strengthening the demand for their product. These factions, including both mine owners and unions, were afraid that fuel switching would mean the shifting of coal production and jobs from their regions to other parts of the country.

- Industrial and political interests from eastern and midwestern states who wanted to protect rents by stopping the flight of industry to western and southern states. By focusing control efforts on newly built plants, the Clean Air Act gives old, dirty plants a few more years of life. Further, by focusing on scrubbing rather than fuel switching, the act insures that coal-burning plants in the South and West are unable to exploit the cost advantage they would otherwise be given by a location close to sources of low-sulfur coal.

- Environmentalists, who were unable to swing a majority in Congress by themselves and were willing to enter an unholy alliance on the theory that any pollution control measures were better than none.

This coalition appears to still be alive in the Congress of the mid-1980s. The case illustrates the dilemma that efforts to use political means to overcome the effects of market failures often run up against the problem of government failure. In Chapter 19, we will explore this problem in more detail.

Summary

1. **How can the problem of pollution be understood in terms of the concepts of externalities and market failure?** Pollution is an example of an externality in that it is a cost of production or consumption that falls on third parties but is not reflected in the price system. When externalities are present, market prices do not reflect opportunity costs. For this reason, there tends to be too much use of goods whose production or consumption results in pollution.

2. **How can the optimal quantity of pollution be determined?** The task of determining the optimal quantity of pollution can be approached through marginal analysis. The *marginal social cost of pollution* is the total additional cost to all members of society of an additional unit of pollution. On a graph with the horizontal axis representing the level of pollution and pollution increasing toward the right, the marginal social cost of pollution can be shown as an upward-sloping curve. The *marginal cost of pollution abatement* is the cost of reducing pollution by one unit. It is shown by a downward-sloping curve. The optimal quantity of pollution is shown by the intersection of these two curves. At that point, the marginal social cost of pollution equals the marginal cost of pollution abatement.

3. **How can a production possibility frontier be used to examine the problem of pollution?** The trade-offs that must be faced in making environmental policy can be illustrated with a production possibility frontier. The horizontal axis represents environmental quality, and the vertical axis represents all other goods and services. An optimal policy puts the economy at a point on the frontier that represents the balance between environmental quality and other goods that best suits the interests of present and future members of society. A policy can be efficient without being optimal if it puts the economy on the frontier, but at a point that has too much or too little pollution. Inefficient policies leave the economy inside the frontier.

4. **How can supply and demand analysis be applied to pollution control policy?** The marginal cost of pollution abatement curve can be viewed as a demand curve for pollution opportunities. The shape of the supply curve for pollution opportunities depends on pollution control policy. A pollution tax would result in a horizontal supply curve. A policy of marketable pollution permits would produce a vertical supply curve. A rights-based policy, under which people could collect damages from polluters through the court system, would produce a supply curve that coincided with the curve representing the marginal social cost of pollution.

5. **What problems have been encountered by pollution control policy in the case of acid rain?** The acid rain issue illustrates many of the problems of environmental policy. The costs of abatement are large and fairly well understood. The benefits of controlling acid rain via the reduction of sulfur dioxide emissions are less well understood, but they too may be considerable. There appears to be little chance of determining the optimal level of pollution. However, economists recommend that whatever the level of pollution control chosen, it should be achieved efficiently. This means that incentives should be provided to use the least-cost methods of pollution control first. Current policy for controlling sulfur dioxide emissions often results in control costs that are higher than necessary, in part because policy has been shaped as much by considerations of rent seeking as by those of improving environmental quality.

Terms for Review

- marginal social cost of pollution
- marginal cost of pollution abatement

Questions for Review

1. Provide an illustration of a good or service whose price is below opportunity cost because of pollution caused by its production. In what sense are consumers encouraged to use too much of the good? Why is this a market failure?

2. Draw a production possibility frontier to represent the trade-off between environmental quality and other goods. What is meant by a movement along this frontier? Under what conditions could the frontier shift outward?

3. Why does the marginal cost of pollution abatement curve slope downward? Why does the marginal social cost of pollution curve slope upward?

4. How does pollution control policy affect the shape of the supply curve for pollution opportunities?

5. What prevents an optimal solution to the acid rain problem? What prevents an efficient solution?

Problems and Topics for Discussion

1. **Examining the lead-off case.** Draw a production possibility frontier for "energy" and "environmental quality." How can you use this frontier to illustrate the story about pollution in Louisiana? What other uses for this frontier can you think of?

2. **An alternative graphical framework.** Review Exhibits 18.2 through 18.4. Draw a graph in which the horizontal axis measures "environmental quality" (that is, degree of pollution control) rather than "quantity of pollution." What are the shapes of the curves representing the marginal cost of pollution abatement and the marginal social cost of pollution when plotted on this new set of axes? Which version of the curves do you find easier to explain?

3. **Environmental rights.** Where do you stand on the issue of environmental rights? Do you think people (or other species) have some environmental rights that ought to be upheld regardless of the economic cost of doing so? Discuss.

4. **Revenues from pollution control taxes.** In discussing a tax as a pollution control strategy, we said nothing about what would be done with the revenues raised by the tax. These might be considerable; for example, it has been estimated that a $1,000-a-ton tax on sulfur dioxide emissions would raise some $15 billion to $20 billion. What do you think should be done with these revenues if the tax were imposed? Consider, among others, the following possibilities:

    a. Using the tax as general revenue to pay for normal government spending

    b. Returning the proceeds of the tax to the industry that pays it so that stockholders will not suffer a loss of earnings.

    c. Spending the tax only on environmental projects such as toxic waste cleanup, maintaining national parks, and so on

    d. Spending the revenue to benefit people who are hurt by pollution control measures—for example, miners of high-sulfur coal

5. **Marketable pollution permits.** Under a system of marketable pollution permits, the market value of permits could be quite high. For example, in the case of permits that limit sulfur dioxide emissions to 17 million tons per year, the permits might have a total market value of about $17 billion. Considering the permits' value, how should they be distributed to electric utilities and other coal-using firms? Should they be sold by the government? Should they be given away? If given away, should they be distributed in proportion to current pollution levels? In proportion to electricity output? According to some other rule? Consider both efficiency and fairness in answering these questions.

Case for Discussion
Chernobyl Awakens Polish Environmentalists

WROCLAW, POLAND. Nine months after the Chernobyl nuclear accident, several dozen banner-waving youths marched into the central square of the Old Town here, sat down and defiantly locked arms to face the squads of police surrounding them. Their purpose was specific: to pressure for the closing of a huge metal works that has poisoned this city's air and water supply.

The police soon moved in with truncheons and handcuffs, and two dozen of the youths were hauled off to short detentions and stiff summary fines. But the reverberations of the brief protest were lasting. Two weeks after the march in January by the Freedom and Peace organization, provincial authorities decided to close the offending industrial plant within five years.

"The Chernobyl accident awakened us to the need to take a special interest in the environmental situation here," said Marek Krukowski, 26, a participant in the demonstration. "Now we have given an example of how people can organize to do something about the pollution that is threatening their local areas."

The Chernobyl nuclear accident awakened Polish opposition.

By most accounts, Poland's pollution problems are staggering even by the low standards of Central Europe.

"More than 50 percent of Polish rivers do not meet standards of cleanliness and are practically industrial gutters. More than 50 percent of Poland's land area is strongly affected by sulphur dioxide," the national, communist-backed Patriotic Movement for National Rebirth reported last September. "Very little time is left to avert the threat of an ecological catastrophe."

In Silesia, the broad band across southern and western Poland where much heavy industry is located, life expectancy runs two years below the national average. Cancer and respiratory disease cases are reported to be more than one-third higher, largely because of the toxic fallout of air and water pollution. Lead content in the air and soil is far above international health norms.

Activists say the Wroclaw metal-works plant is a classic example of ineffective official action on the environment.

The pre–World War II mill, which produces ferrochromium composites, relies on outmoded technology with few pollution controls. The plant and its huge, open slag heap lie only 550 yards from Wroclaw's principal water reservoir. Chromium and lead levels in local water are more than 50 times above normal and smoke spewing from the plant has endangered hundreds of families living in nearby homes.

Although the mill was targeted for shutdown or renovation beginning in the early 1970s, neither has been done, largely because of repeated administrative decisions that the "economic value" of its production was too great to sacrifice, and because of pressure from industry officials to "renovate" its equipment and keep it open into the 1990s.

Source: Jackson Diehl, "Chernobyl Awakens Polish Opposition," *The Washington Post*, March 16, 1987, A13. Reprinted with permission. Photo Source: Reuters/Bettmann Newsphotos.

Questions

1. Problems of pollution in Western economies are sometimes attributed to conflict between the profit-oriented interests of private firms on the one hand and the broader public interest on the other. Government is seen as the repository of the public interest; thus, government action is perceived as the solution to the problem. Why, then, do you think there is an even worse pollution problem in Poland and other East European countries, where government owns the factories?

2. Polish authorities are reported to have decided that the "economic value" of the metal works was too great to shut the plant down. Do you think it is proper, in principle, to balance the economic value of a plant against the damage done by its pollution? Do you think the Polish decision was likely to have been based on such a balanced assessment?

Suggestions for Further Reading

The Cato Journal (Spring 1982).

This special issue is devoted to articles about rights-based strategies of environmental policy.

Mills, Edwin S. *The Economics of Environmental Quality.* New York: Norton, 1978.

A thorough treatment of environmental policies and problems from an economic viewpoint, including a historical sketch of environmental policy in the United States.

Stroup, Richard L., and John A. Baden. *Natural Resources: Bureaucratic Myths and Environmental Management.* Cambridge, Mass.: Ballinger, 1983.

The authors stress a public choice approach to environmental questions. The book devotes much discussion to problems of public land use as well as of pollution.

19 The Theory of Public Choice

After reading this chapter, you will understand . . .

- How economic theory can be applied to government.
- What role self-interest plays in the theory of public choice.
- How public expenditures are determined under direct democracy.
- How representative democracy differs from direct democracy.

Before reading this chapter, make sure you know the meaning of . . .

- Public goods (Chapter 5)
- Market failure (Chapter 5)
- Rent seeking (Chapter 5)

How the Highway Beautification Act Went by the Boards

Dilution of the Highway Beautification Act illustrates the staying power of special interests.

When the Senate voted in early 1987 on a highway-bill amendment to restore teeth in the 22-year effort to control proliferation of billboards, sharp-eyed observers had only to glance at the Senate gallery for a fair idea of the likely outcome.

Sitting in the area reserved for members' families and guests was Vernon A. Clark, chief lobbyist for the $1.2-billion-a-year outdoor-advertising industry.

Clark's favored perch, from which he watched the Senate kill the amendment offered by Senator Robert T. Stafford (R-Vt.) 57 to 40, was symbolic of the enduring political muscle that Clark and the Outdoor Advertising Association of America (OAAA) have flexed in the Capitol on behalf of the billboard industry.

More than two decades after Congress responded to a personal crusade by Lady Bird Johnson and enacted the Highway Beautification Act to control billboards along federal highways, Clark and the industry remain heavyweights on Capitol Hill.

Critics say the industry has not only frustrated the intent of the 1965 legislation, but has turned the act into its own instrument, exploiting loopholes and chipping away at the law to the point that Stafford ruefully suggested renaming it the "Billboard Protection and Compensation Act."

Leon Billings, a former Senate aide who lobbied the billboard issue on behalf of the Coalition for Scenic Beauty, says dilution of the Highway Beautification Act over the years illustrates the staying power of special interests and the fragility of underfinanced popular causes.

"This is a classic example of where a great public debate takes place . . . and then the public goes away and the special interests stay and winnow away, winnow away, and winnow away until the purpose of the program is totally perverted," he said.

Source: Tom Kenworthy, "How the Highway Beautification Act Went by the Boards," *The Washington Post*, February 24, 1984, A19. © 1984 *The Washington Post*, reprinted with permission. Photo Source: Courtesy of American Media Network, Inc.

IN Chapter 5, we introduced two theories of government, one based on the concept of market failure and the other on the notion of rent seeking. According to the first, government is to play a limited role in the economy. What the market can do well is left to the market; the government steps in only when markets produce results that are unsatisfactory in terms of efficiency or fairness. Externalities, public goods, insufficient competition, and inequitable distribution of income are among the market failures often said to justify a role for government in the economy.

However, in other chapters we have seen examples of government policies that are hard to explain in terms of the market failure theory of government. These include subsidies for the rich; transfer programs that distort the incentives of the poor; policies that restrict rather than promote competition; inefficient methods of dealing with externalities; and so on. Why do we have such programs, which arguably promote neither efficiency nor fairness? The answer can be found in the notion of rent seeking. Once the government is given the powers it needs to act against market failures, people make use of those institutions to serve their own private purposes. High on the list of these incentives is creating and protecting rents.

The theory of how people actually use government institutions to promote private ends—as opposed to the theory of how they could be used to alleviate the effects of market failures—has drawn increasing attention from economists in recent years. This area of economics has come to be known as **public choice theory.** This relatively new field received particular recognition in 1987 when its foremost practitioner, James Buchanan of George Mason University, was awarded the Nobel Memorial Prize in economics for his work (see "Who Said It? Who Did It? 19.1").

Public choice theory
The study of how people use the institutions of government in pursuit of self-interest.

Without attempting to be comprehensive, this chapter illustrates public choice theory as applied to democratic government. We begin by examining the role self-interest plays in public choice. Next, we look at how economic decisions are made in a simple majority-rule system such as a town meeting. Then we consider some of the complications introduced by representative democracy. In the course of the discussion, we examine, among other things, the basis for the frequently disproportionate power of small interest groups such as the outdoor-advertising industry.

The Self-Interest Assumption of Public Choice Theory

A basic principle of public choice theory is that people act in the same way in both public and private roles. They are the same people all day long as they eat, shop, drive cars, enter the voting booth, go to work in a government bureau, or even rise to speak on the Senate floor. In analyzing people's private choices, economists have long assumed that people act in rational pursuit of self-interest. As consumers, people are assumed to maximize utility; as entrepreneurs, they are assumed to maximize profit; and so on. Thus, public choice theorists assume that the actions people take and the choices they make in public roles are guided by self-interest as well.

Some people protest that this assumption of self-interested behavior is cynical and unrealistic, but when properly understood, it is neither. The self-interest assumption must be understood as a working hypothesis, not as an unqualified

WHO SAID IT? WHO DID IT? 19.1

James Buchanan and Public Choice Theory

James Buchanan, founder of the field of public choice theory, grew up on a farm in Murfreesboro, Tennessee. He initially mapped out a career in law and politics but eventually settled on economics. He received a doctorate in economics from the University of Chicago and taught at Florida State University, the University of Virginia, UCLA, and Virginia Polytechnic Institute. He now heads the Center for the Study of Public Choice at George Mason University.

Buchanan traces his thinking on public choice issues to an obscure dissertation written in 1896 by the Swedish economist Knut Wicksell. *The Calculus of Consent*, which Buchanan wrote in 1962 with Gordon Tullock, explains

---

Source: Quoted passages are from James Buchanan and Gordon Tullock, *The Calculus of Consent* (Ann Arbor, Mich.: University of Michigan Press, 1962), and Paula Odin, "Nobel Laureate," *George Mason Magazine*, Fall 1986, 2. Photo Source: Courtesy of the Center for the Study of Public Choice, George Mason University.

how public choice theory differs from traditional political theory. Traditional analysis, the authors write, has

> often been grounded on the implicit assumption that the representative individual seeks not to maximize his own utility, but to find the "public interest" or "common good." Moreover, a significant factor in the popular support for socialism throughout the centuries has been the underlying faith that the shift of an activity from the realm of private to that of social choice involves the replacement of the motive of private gain by that of social good.

Buchanan and his colleagues, in contrast, believe that people do not change when they move from the marketplace into the political arena. In both realms, they seek to use existing institutions to their best advantage. Any analysis of political institutions that ignores the rational pursuit of self-interest on the part of individual citizens and government officials is subject to serious error.

In his *Demand and Supply of Public Goods* (1968), Buchanan made a pioneering contribution to the positive theory of public spending. Instead of asking how much of a public good the government ought to supply, as earlier writers on public goods had done, Buchanan sought to develop a theory of the political marketplace analogous to the theory of the economic market. He strove to learn who decides, and on what basis, how much of each good and service to provide and how the costs are to be shared. Says Buchanan,

> In order to get better government policy, we'd better look not to electing better people, but to changing the structure of the rules which constrain them. The ordinary man has always had a sort of common-sense wisdom about politics and government—especially early on in the history of this country. This isn't far from what public choice distills in an informal way.

---

assertion that applies to every person in every instance. The self-interest assumption of public choice theory may be compared in this respect to the utility-maximizing hypothesis as applied to consumer choice. Using the utility-maximizing hypothesis as a tool for understanding consumer behavior does not mean denying that some people occasionally behave altruistically or that some people sometimes make choices that are inconsistent with their stated goals. Reasonable conclusions may be drawn from the utility-maximizing hypothesis, for example, the prediction that lowering the price of donuts will result in more donuts sold. But common sense must be used too. Naive application of the self-interest hypothesis might lead to the prediction that people will take money out of the collection plate when it is passed around in church rather than putting money in it; however, that prediction turns out to be false for the most part.

In the same way, the self-interest assumption is applied to public choice as a working hypothesis. For example, public choice economists do not assert that all politicians are corrupt vote sellers. Nonetheless, they notice that lobbyists like those for the outdoor-advertising industry spend a lot of money for campaign contributions, free travel, speech-making honoraria, and so on to try to influence congressional votes. (The OAAA spent more than $350,000 on contributions and honoraria from 1983 to 1985.) If these lobbyists acted rationally—another working hypothesis—they would not spend so much money year after year unless they thought they were getting something in return. When public choice economists observe that 16 out of 22 senators who received honoraria from the outdoor-advertising industry vote against billboard restrictions, they consider the result to be consistent with the self-interest hypothesis.

Public Choice in Direct Democracy

We will return to the issue of the self-interested behavior of elected representatives later in the chapter. For a first illustration of public choice theory, we will turn to the simpler case of direct democracy.

A *direct democracy* is a democracy in which the people affected by policies—taxation, public works projects, regulations, and so forth—have the right to vote in person on each policy. This form of organization is used in some government units in the United States, as in the case of traditional New England town meetings. It is often used in small not-for-profit organizations, such as clubs. It is not the predominant form of government in the United States, where people more commonly vote to elect representatives who then vote on the issues. However, examination of the case of direct democracy provides a number of insights into the workings of government that can then be modified to fit the case of representative democracy.

How Much Should Be Spent?

Public choice theory can be applied to any type of decision made by government, but to take a specific example, we will begin with the question of how much government ought to spend on provision of a public good. One way to approach the decision is through *benefit-cost analysis*. The object of such an analysis is to find out whether the benefits the public receives from a government program are great enough to justify its costs.

Exhibit 19.1 gives an example of a benefit-cost analysis for the project of providing streetlighting in a small community. Streetlighting is a public good partly because there is no way that a streetlight can illuminate an intersection for one citizen without also illuminating it for all others. Also, the cost of lighting does not depend on the number of people who use the street.

Because of the free-rider problem, it is likely that a less than optimal number of streetlights would be installed by private persons acting individually. Recognizing this potential market failure, the citizens of this community have agreed to pay for lighting the streets with public funds.

The community has only three citizens, whom we will call Smith, Jones, and Brown. All three would get some benefit from streetlights. However, they

Exhibit 19.1   Benefit-Cost Analysis of Streetlighting

This exhibit shows the costs and benefits of streetlighting in a small community inhabited by three people—Smith, Jones, and Brown. Because of where they live and how often they go out at night, benefits are not distributed equally. Smith is assumed to get 50 percent of total benefits, Jones 30 percent, and Brown 20 percent. Streetlights are assumed to cost $300 each. The efficient number of streetlights in this town is seven. Beyond that point, the added benefits of another light are less than the added cost.

(a)

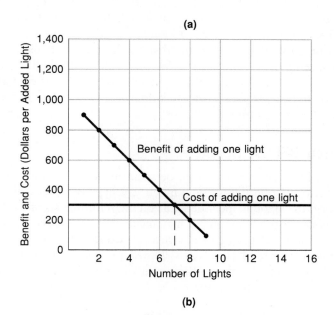

(b)

		Benefit to:		
Number of Lights	Total Benefit	Smith (50%)	Jones (30%)	Brown (20%)
1	$ 900	$ 450	$ 270	$180
2	1,700	850	510	340
3	2,400	1,200	720	480
4	3,000	1,500	900	600
5	3,500	1,750	1,050	700
6	3,900	1,950	1,170	780
7	4,200	2,100	1,260	840
8	4,400	2,200	1,320	880

would not all benefit equally because of where they live, how often they go out at night, and so on. For the sake of the example, we will assume that Smith gets 50 percent of the total benefit of the streetlights, Jones 30 percent, and Brown 20 percent.

The more lights provided, the greater the total benefits. However, the benefits are greatest with the first few lights. As more and more lights are added, each additional light adds less to the total benefit. Part b of Exhibit 19.1 shows the total benefit at various levels of lighting as well as the increase in benefits produced for each individual and for the community as a whole by adding one more light. The downward-sloping line in part a shows the benefit added by each additional light. The height of the line at various points shows the difference between successive entries in part b. For example, adding light number 2 raises total benefits from $900 to $1,700 and thus adds $800 in benefits. Part b also shows the total and marginal cost of the lighting program assuming that lights cost a constant $300 per unit.

The data given in the exhibit are all we need for a benefit-cost analysis of the streetlight program. The rule for efficient streetlighting is to add lights up to the point at which the benefits of the last light added (that is, the marginal benefit) just equal the costs of the last light (that is, the marginal cost). This means putting in seven lights. Smith gets $150 in benefits from the last light added, Jones gets $90, and Brown gets $60, for a total of $300. That is enough to justify the $300 cost of the last light. An eighth light would give them only $200 more in benefits—not enough to justify the cost.

How Much Will Be Spent?

Now that we know how much *should* be spent using the benefit-cost standard, we move on to the question of how much *will* be spent. According to public choice theory, the amount spent depends on the self-interests of citizens and on the political structure within which they make choices. We have already specified one key feature of the political structure, namely the fact that choices are made by majority vote of all citizens. Now let's look at the effect of another feature of the political structure: the way in which costs of public activities are shared among community members.

Costs Shared in Proportion to Benefits Received

First we will examine the case in which costs are shared in proportion to the benefits received. In our example, this means that for each dollar of taxes raised, Smith pays $.50, Jones $.30, and Brown $.20.

Under these conditions, the town meeting will be a model of harmony. "Should we put up, say, five lights?" asks Smith. He calculates that the fifth light will give him $250 in benefits (half of the total benefit of $500) and cost him $150 (half of the $300 cost of an extra light). Jones and Brown see that the fifth light will also give them more in benefits than their share of the cost. The vote for five lights is unanimous.

"Let's vote a sixth light," says Jones. She figures that the sixth light will bring her $120 in benefits (30 percent of the total benefit) and cost her just $90 (30 percent of the total cost). Smith and Brown make their respective calculations, and again the vote is unanimous.

"Why not a seventh light?" says Brown. His share of the $300 benefit will be $60, exactly the same as his share of the $300 cost. Indeed, why not? Smith and Jones agree.

Then the meeting falls silent. No one wants to vote another light. They all see that their personal shares of the eighth light's benefits would be smaller than their shares of its costs. They all go home, having hit the benefit-cost nail on the head.

Conclusion: In a direct democracy in which taxes are shared in exact proportion to the benefits of public programs, the most efficient amount of spending—no more and no less—will take place provided that everyone votes according to his or her own self-interest.

Costs Shared Equally

The next case we will look at is that of a direct democracy in which costs are shared equally but benefits are not. To continue our example, this means that Smith, Jones, and Brown will each pay $100 of the $300 cost of each light.

Given this distribution of benefits, the town meeting goes a bit differently. The proposal for a fifth light is still passed by a unanimous vote, but just barely. Smith is looking at $250 in benefits to offset his $100 in costs; Jones sees $150 in benefits and $100 in costs; and Brown $100 in benefits and $100 in costs. The proposal for a sixth light passes by a vote of 2 to 1. This time Brown is looking at $80 in benefits and $100 in costs. If he votes in his own self-interest (as public choice theorists assume), he will vote no—and the proposal for a seventh light will lose by a 1-to-2 vote. Smith will see $150 in benefits and $100 in costs; Jones $90 in benefits and $100 in costs; and Brown $60 in benefits and $100 in costs.

Conclusion: In a direct democracy, when the costs of a program are distributed evenly but the benefits are not, there will be a tendency to spend less than the efficient amount on each government program.

Benefits Equal, Costs Shared Unequally

Our third case assumes that the benefits of the streetlights are distributed equally but the costs are shared unequally: Smith now pays 60 percent of total taxes, while Jones and Brown pay 20 percent each.

By now the reasoning is familiar, although the results differ. Smith drops out on the vote for the fifth light, since his share of the benefits ($166) now falls short of his share of the costs ($180). Lights 6 and 7 also pass by 2-to-1 votes. Then the eighth light comes up for vote. The total benefits of light 8 are just $200—less than the cost. But Jones's and Brown's share of the benefit is $66—more than their $60 share of the cost. Thus, eight lights—one more than the efficient number—are approved.

Conclusion: In a direct democracy, when the benefits of a program are spread evenly but the costs are shared unequally, there will be a tendency to spend more than the efficient amount on each government program.

It is possible to come up with real-world examples that fit each of the three cases we have just reviewed. Highway construction can be compared with the example in which costs and benefits fall equally on each citizen, in that much of the cost of highway construction is paid for by gasoline taxes and other road use taxes. Other things being equal, this method of financing highway construction therefore would tend to move expenditures toward the optimal level.

For an example in which costs are spread equally but benefits are not, think of a town in which there are many retired people but only a few young families. Such a town is likely to be stingy with its school budget, spending less than analysis of total costs and benefits, regardless of distribution, would call for.

Finally, for an example in which benefits are spread equally but costs are shared unequally, picture a proposal to fight a war using an army of draftees. All citizens benefit from national defense, whereas the burden of the draft falls disproportionately on people who are a minority of voters. Public choice theory would predict that, other things being equal, a military draft would make a country more willing to go to war than would a system in which taxpayers' money was used to hire soldiers at a wage determined by supply and demand.

Public Choice and Rent Seeking in a Representative Democracy

Our analysis of public goods spending in a direct democracy has yielded some applications to real policy choices, but it represents only a starting point. In this section, we will expand the discussion in two ways.

First, we will consider a broader range of government decisions than public goods expenditures. Public choice theory is equally applicable to decisions regarding regulation of industry, farm price supports, residential rent control, nationalization or privatization of enterprises, the structure of the tax system—the list is practically endless. All of these decisions offer opportunities for rent seeking.

Second, we will shift our focus from direct democracy to representative democracy. In a representative democracy, citizens at large periodically vote to elect representatives to Congress, state legislators, city councils, and the like. The representatives, in turn, vote on specific issues. This two-stage voting procedure brings advantages of specialization. Citizens can go about their daily lives without having to worry about the details of thousands of government programs. But it also brings changes to the kinds of decisions the government makes.

In a representative democracy, one encounters many decisions that do not fit the patterns identified in the case of direct democracy. For example, in a direct democracy, one would not normally see programs—say, import restrictions—that benefit a small group of workers and industrialists at the expense of the broad population of consumers. Nor would one see votes for tax loopholes that excuse a small group of citizens from bearing their proportionate share of the costs of programs that benefit all citizens equally. Yet such decisions are made routinely in Congress, state legislatures, and city councils. The ability of rent seekers to obtain favorable decisions stems largely from certain features of representative democracy not found in the simpler form of government examined in the preceding section.

Lobbying, Information, and the Costs of Political Expression

We begin our discussion of representative democracy by comparing a democratic political system to a market economy. There are some superficial similarities. In a market economy, people are said to exercise "consumer sovereignty" by "voting with dollars." Similarly, politicians are said to compete in a "political marketplace" in which they use many of the same tools of advertising, promotion, and public relations that business firms use. However, there are also important differences between politics and the market.

The choices people make as voters in a representative democracy differ from the choices they make as consumers in two important ways. First, consumers "vote" every day in the marketplace, whereas they vote only at wide intervals for elected officials. Second, in the marketplace consumers can pick and choose among a wide variety of goods to suit their individual preferences, whereas in an election they must choose among candidates who offer "package deals" covering a broad range of issues. In a supermarket a shopper may choose separately what to have for breakfast, lunch, and dinner, but at election time it is not possible to choose one person as a representative for foreign policy issues, another for civil rights issues, and a third for economic issues.

However, there are channels of political expression other than voting. People who want to influence the outcome of particular legislative decisions can also engage in *lobbying*. We use this term here in a broad sense to mean any method of communicating with elected officials in order to advocate some given policy.

Like any activity in which people engage, lobbying has opportunity costs. First, people must become informed about the issues and decide what decisions they want to see made. Becoming informed takes time, at the very least. Second, they must communicate with their representatives. Expressing oneself through letters, telegrams, newspaper ads, or professional lobbyists in Washington or the state capitol costs both time and money. Few voters feel that they have enough at stake in any one issue to repay the effort of even writing a letter.

However, groups of people with shared interests are in a different situation. They can share the costs of both keeping informed and making their views known to their representatives. They can hire full-time lobbyists. As a result, their influence may be greater than would be possible if each member acted alone.

The disproportionate strength of small, well-organized groups works in favor of some high-minded groups that seek what they see as the general good of all citizens. But it also applies to groups of rent seekers who have narrow self-interests in mind. Consider the issue of airport crowding. One way to relieve airport congestion would be to charge higher fees for "general aviation"—the small planes that account for 16 percent of all flights at the nation's busiest airports. As of this writing, fees paid by general aviation account for only about 6 percent of the FAA's fund for airport improvements—far less than the share of the benefits enjoyed by general aviation. But general aviation has a strong lobby: the 270,000-member Aircraft Owners and Pilots Association. Although the AOPA's membership is only a fraction of the number of people who suffer delays on commercial flights each year, one airline executive rates the AOPA lobby as "100-to-1" more effective than that of commercial airlines and their passengers.[1]

Logrolling

As we have mentioned, in a representative democracy voters at large do not vote often and few of them meet for political purposes between elections. Representatives, on the other hand, vote on hundreds of issues every congressional session and meet daily. As a result, they routinely engage in vote trading or **logrolling,** as the practice is often called.

Logrolling
The practice of trading votes among members of a legislative body.

The idea of logrolling is simple. Each representative selects a few issues that are important to the voters in his or her home state or district. In exchange for yes votes on those issues, he or she promises to vote for issues that are important to other representatives. Trading away a vote on an issue that affects people far away in order to benefit the folks at home is a good deal for both the representative and the home-town voters.

Logrolling leads to the passage of certain kinds of programs that would never be approved in a direct democracy. These are programs that generate rents for a few people while dispersing costs widely among taxpayers or consumers in general. Consider electricity from the Hoover Dam as a case in point. Since 1937, the Hoover Dam has been generating electricity that, by federal law,

[1] See John Paul Newport, Jr., "The Big Role of Little Planes," *Fortune*, October 1, 1984, 38.

is sold to consumers in California, Nevada, and Arizona at rates that are one-fourth to one-fourteenth of commercial electric rates. The law was scheduled to expire in 1987, at which time rates would have gone up to normal market levels. But just before the 1984 elections, a bill was brought up in the Senate to extend the law for another 30 years.

The bill would directly benefit the citizens of only three states. Taxpayers in the rest of the country would have to make up for the federal revenue lost through cut-rate electricity sales from the Hoover Dam. Yet the bill passed the Senate by a vote of 64 to 34. Every senator from a state west of Missouri voted to continue the subsidy. In return for supporting their colleagues from Arizona, Nevada, and California on this issue, they could expect their colleagues' votes for subsidized water or power projects in their own states.[2]

In a political system in which each representative is elected by the voters of a small geographical area, as is the case with the U.S. Congress, logrolling tends to promote local interests at the expense of national interests, because local issues are what affect voters most. Thus, it may make sense for a representative to trade away his or her votes on weighty national issues—the budget deficit, a Supreme Court nomination, a treaty—in order to win others' votes on a narrow local issue such as a defense contract or a protective tariff that would benefit a local employer.

A variant of vote trading is the *pork barrel*. This is a bill that consists largely or entirely of a series of small, local projects (highways, post offices, harbor dredging) that produce rents for local interests at the expense of general taxpayers. Political entrepreneurs in Congress add more pork to the barrel until it commands a majority of votes and then submit the whole package as a single bill. The bill passes even though none of its components would command a majority vote or pass a benefit-cost test individually.

Pork barreling can be used to illustrate how a change in political rules could affect government spending patterns. Observers concerned about wasteful spending on projects that benefit local interests at the expense of national interests have proposed that the President be given a *line-item veto*. Under this procedure, the President could single out individual items in a bill that were thought to be especially wasteful. For example, suppose Congress passes a defense spending bill that, as often happens, directs the Pentagon to buy certain weapons that military leaders do not want. The weapons are included because they are made in the home district of some influential member of Congress. With a line-item veto, the President could delete these expenditures while allowing the rest of the military budget to go into effect. Under current rules, however, the President has the choice only of vetoing or signing the whole billion-dollar package.

Despite many examples in which logrolling leads to wasteful spending, public choice theorists are quick to point out that the practice can have its good side as well. Without vote trading, for example, federal highway funds might be spent entirely in the most populous states. Objectively viewed, logrolling is neutral. It favors neither "good" nor "bad" policy; rather, its function is to express preferences that are strongly favored by a minority and slightly opposed by a majority. These may include pork-barrel spending and special tax loopholes, but they may also include such issues as civil rights, religious freedom,

---

[2] See George F. Will, "Conservative Cowboys Head 'em Off at the Hoover Dam," *Washington Post*, August 9, 1984, A23.

and environmental protection. It is far from certain that representative government without vote trading would be better government.

The Self-Interest of Representatives

One additional difference between representative and direct democracies lies in the fact that representatives have interests of their own that do not always match those of the voters who elect them. The interest in being reelected is a leading example. Whether representatives want to promote voters' interests, fight for a cause, gain power and prestige, or simply have a job, getting reelected is a must.

But getting reelected costs money. Therefore, the representative must become a political entrepreneur. Sources of campaign contributions must be found. Lobbyists for rent-seeking special-interest groups are one of the richest sources of contributions for political candidates. Although few members of Congress would sell a vote outright, campaign contributions do buy time on representatives' crowded schedules. Further, often the side that gets the time to present its views most fully is the side that wins.

As a case in point, consider the dairy lobby. Early in the Reagan administration, officials started talking about cutting dairy subsidies. Such a move would have hurt several thousand dairy farmers but would have benefited millions of consumers and taxpayers. However, before the issue came to a vote in Congress, the dairy lobby got out its checkbook. In the next 23 months, it gave $1,343,868 to 293 members of the House of Representatives. Included in this number were 117 representatives from urban districts—those with farm populations of less than 1 percent. Of those, 72 voted with the dairy lobby and against the milk drinkers in their own districts.[3]

In a representative democracy, the voters are principals and representatives their agents. Politics is not the only case in which agents serve their principals' interests imperfectly. In Chapter 4, we discussed a similar problem—that of corporate control—in which managers as agents sometimes act contrary to the interests of their principals, the stockholders. In both cases, the agent's independence arises from the fact that a single voter, or a stockholder with only a few shares, does not find it worthwhile to monitor or communicate with the agent. Often the voters or shareholders do not find it worthwhile to cast their votes at all.

However, shareholders in a corporation have one means of keeping their agents in line that voters do not: By proxy or by selling their shares, they can transfer their votes to someone who is willing to keep informed, to fulfill the monitoring function, and to act. There is nothing comparable to a hostile takeover in the political realm. It is interesting to speculate about the operation of a political system in which the right to vote could be openly transferred.

Democracy, Market Failure, and Government Failure

Public choice theorists do not seek to praise or condemn the economic workings of government so much as they simply attempt to explain them. They believe that when the costs and benefits of programs are shared in certain ways, the government tends to make efficient decisions. When the costs and benefits are

---

[3] See Brooks Jackson and Jeffrey Birnbaum, "Dairy Lobby Obtains U.S. Subsidies with Help from Urban Legislators," *The Wall Street Journal*, November 18, 1983, 33.

shared in other ways, programs that cannot stand up to benefit-cost analysis are funded. Representative democracy, they conclude, is neither all good nor all bad.

Nonetheless, public choice theory provides grounds for caution in expanding the economic role of government. In particular, it suggests that government action to correct market failures will not necessarily improve matters. The reason is that the powers that government needs to be granted in order to deal with market failures can be—and often are—also used to serve the interests of private rent seekers. This ever-present possibility of government failure must be balanced against the losses that could result from market failure in the absence of government action. When this is done, one is often led to conclude that the market, for all its imperfections, produces better results than the government alternative.

Summary

1. **How can economic theory be applied to government?** *Public choice theory* examines how people actually use the institutions of government to promote private ends. It allows for the possibility that government programs will be used in the service of rent seeking as well as to correct market failures.

2. **What role does self-interest play in the theory of public choice?** Public choice theory seeks to explain government policies in terms of the interaction of individuals' self-interests with the rules of the political process. It assumes that people act out of self-interest in their political roles as voters, government officials, and so on just as they do in their private lives. However, the self-interest assumption is properly interpreted as a working hypothesis rather than as an absolute statement that allows no exceptions.

3. **How are public expenditures determined under direct democracy?** Under direct democracy, the level of public expenditure on any given program is determined by the way costs and benefits are distributed among voters. If costs are distributed in proportion to benefits, expenditures tend toward an efficient level. If costs are distributed evenly while benefits are not, less than an efficient amount will be spent on the program. If benefits are distributed evenly while costs are not, more than an efficient amount will be spent.

4. **How does representative democracy differ from direct democracy?** Three features of representative democracy make it possible for programs to be instituted that will benefit rent-seeking minority interests at the expense of the majority. The first is the ability of small, well-organized interest groups to share the costs of information and political expression. The second is the practice of vote trading, or *logrolling*. The third is the tendency of representatives to act in their own interests rather than in their constituents'.

Terms for Review

- public choice theory
- logrolling

Questions for Review

1. Compare the use of the assumption of self-interest in public choice theory and in consumer choice theory. Is the assumption true for every choice of every individual?

2. In a direct democracy, under what conditions will a government tend to spend more or less than can be justified in terms of benefits and costs?

3. Why do small groups of rent seekers tend to have more political influence than large groups with a moderate interest in an issue?

4. What is meant by *logrolling?*

5. How are political decisions influenced by the self-interest of representatives?

Problems and Topics for Discussion

1. **Examining the lead-off case.** The number of people who are offended by the sight of billboards presumably is greater than the number of members of the OAAA. Why, then, has the OAAA been able to block congressional action that would place tighter restrictions on billboards?

2. **Political expression.** Have you ever tried to influence the outcome of a political decision by writing to or otherwise communicating with government officials? Do you belong to any groups that try to influence legislative decisions? What lobbying actions do these groups undertake?

3. **Farm subsidies.** Review the discussion of farm subsidies in "Economics in the News 5.1" (page 116). are farmers able to obtain subsidies and price supports from the government even though there are more consumers of food than there are farmers? Why do you think subsidies are not restricted to the neediest farmers?

4. **Lobbying.** If Congress is currently in session, read news accounts of the debates on a legislative issue of your choice. Do you see any evidence that the outcome is being influenced by lobbying? By logrolling? By representatives' self-interests?

Case for Discussion

Bethel Town Meeting Considers Sewage Treatment Project

BETHEL, VERMONT. By a close vote of 198 to 179, Bethel voters last Wednesday rejected a plan to build a sewage treatment plant for the village at a local cost of $950,000.

As a result, Bethel will continue to be the only municipal polluter of the White River.

The total project cost was to be $4.4 million, with the federal and state governments picking up the balance of the tab. . . .

More than 100 more people voted last Wednesday than had voted in early August, when a slightly more expensive plan was turned down, also by a narrow margin. Some observers guessed that the extra 100 voters were those from outside the Village area, taxpayers who would have to help support the new system but would receive no direct benefit from it.

Bethel taxpayers voted against building a sewage treatment plant.

Note: In Vermont, a "village" is a built-up area of houses and streets. A "town" is a political unit that includes both a village and the surrounding rural areas. All issues—those that affect only village residents and those that affect the whole town—are decided by a majority vote of town residents.

Source: *White River Valley Herald* (Randolph, Vermont), October 4, 1984, 1. Photo Source: © 1987 Phyllis Woloshin.

Questions

1. Compare the Bethel vote to the Smith-Jones-Brown examples in the text. Which pattern does the Bethel case fit?

2. Do you think the federal policy of paying all or most of the costs of local sewage plants would, other things being equal, encourage spending of just the right amount, too much, or too little on the construction of such plants? In answering, consider the fact that much of the benefit of the Bethel sewage plant would go to people downstream in other towns and states along the White River and the Connecticut River.

3. If you were a Bethel selectman (selectmen prepare proposals to be presented at town meetings), how would you change the sewage plant proposal to increase its chances of passing?

Suggestions for Further Reading

Buchanan, James, and Gordon Tullock. *The Calculus of Consent.* Ann Arbor, Mich.: University of Michigan Press, 1962.

A classic treatment of the theory of public goods and public choice.

Hyman, David N. *Public Finance*, 2d ed. Hinsdale, Ill.: Dryden Press, 1987.

Chapters 1 through 6 cover the principles of government activity in the economy, including the supply of public goods.

The World Economy

Part Six

20 International Trade and Trade Policy

After reading this chapter, you will understand . . .

- How the principle of comparative advantage can be applied to international trade.

- How the notion of "competitiveness" is related to that of comparative advantage.

- The trend of trade policy during the post–World War II period.

- How international trade affects income distribution within each country.

- How protectionist policies can be explained in terms of public choice theory and rent seeking.

Before reading this chapter, make sure you know the meaning of . . .

- Comparative advantage (Chapter 2)

- Rent seeking (Chapter 5)

- Public choice theory (Chapter 19)

The Great Tokyo Pizza Wars

American fast food is a booming business in Japan.

In the great Tokyo pizza wars, Ernest Higa is a field commander.

Every evening from his base in western Tokyo's Ebisu area, the 34-year-old deploys 16 motor scooters that are specially designed to do battle in Tokyo's narrow streets. In just 15 months, aggressive pizza deliverymen in red, white, and blue uniforms have become a familiar sight in Tokyo's upscale neighborhoods.

"First it was just a fashion. Then all of a sudden it was a boom," says Higa, who recently opened his fourth Domino's Pizza store.

The home-delivery competition here is unlike anything a pizza entrepreneur would find in the U.S. or Europe. For one thing, no street names and a cumbersome address system make Tokyo a tough city to navigate. For another, in addition to other pizza squads there are more established rivals delivering everything from sushi to noodles to smoked eel.

But the constant battles in the Japanese fast-food market are nothing new to Higa and his family. They practically invented the idea of bringing American fast food to Japan. With frozen pizza, Pepsi-Cola, Kentucky Fried Chicken, and now Domino's Pizza to their credit, the Higas are something of a First Family of fast food here.

In addition to Ernest, there is his father, Yetsuo "Yets" Higa, a 71-year-old Hawaiian native and the family patriarch. There is his older sister, Merle, who brought frozen pizza to coffee shops in the 1960s when everyone assured her it would flop. And there is Merle's husband, Shin Ohkawara, the president and chief executive officer of Kentucky Fried Chicken Japan Ltd., with 611 outlets, the most outlets anywhere outside the U.S.

"All of the successful restaurant concepts here have come from the United States, not Europe," says Ernest Higa. "Saying you are from the U.S.A. is the best way to show you are different from the sushi shop down the road."

Source: Kathryn Graven, "Family in Japan Plays Big Role in Importing Fast Food from U.S.," *The Wall Street Journal,* March 3, 1987, 1. Reprinted by permission of *The Wall Street Journal,* © Dow Jones & Company, Inc. 1987. All Rights Reserved. Photo Source: Courtesy of Domino's Pizza International.

459

AS this example shows, there is more to the world trade picture than boatloads of the familiar Toyotas and Hondas being unloaded on U.S. shores. Services, capital, technology, management skills, and even fads are traded in addition to goods. Also, despite much handwringing in Congress and elsewhere about declining U.S. "competitiveness," U.S. firms remain in the thick of the action around the world. In the mid-1980s, real exports from the United States were running at double their 1970 level and nearly quadruple their 1960 level. Further, the activities of companies such as Domino's Pizza and Kentucky Fried Chicken do not always show up in conventional trade statistics. For example, in 1984 import-export data showed that the United States imported $56.8 billion of goods made in Japan while exporting to that country only $25.6 billion of U.S.-made goods. Yet in the same year, U.S.-based firms operating in Japan were far more successful ($43.9 billion in sales) than Japanese firms operating in the United States ($12.8 billion in sales).

In this chapter, we look at the economics and politics of international trade. We begin with a review of comparative advantage, adding a graphical presentation of that theory. Then we turn to the arena of trade policy, where "free traders" and "protectionists" battle on a thousand fronts.

The Theory of Comparative Advantage: Review and Extensions

The microeconomics of international trade begins with the concept of *comparative advantage*. In Chapter 2, we introduced this concept in discussing the division of labor within the economy of one country and showed how it can be extended to trade among countries. We will now review this theory, using first a new numerical example and then a graphical approach.

Numerical Example

For illustrative purposes, imagine a world with just two countries—Norway and Spain. Both have farms and offshore fishing grounds, but the moderate climate of Spain makes both the farms and the fishing grounds more productive. A ton of fish can be produced in Spain with 4 hours of labor and a ton of grain with 2 hours of labor. In Norway, 5 labor hours are required to produce a ton of fish and 5 labor hours to produce a ton of grain. We will consider only labor costs in this example; other costs can be assumed to be proportional to labor costs. Also, we will assume constant per-unit labor costs for all output levels.

Absolute advantage
The ability of a country to produce a good at a lower cost in terms of quantity of factor inputs than its trading partners.

Because both fish and grain require fewer labor hours to produce in Spain, Spain can be said to have an **absolute advantage** in the production of both goods. However, it is not the absolute cost differences that matter for international trade but the differences in opportunity costs between the two countries. In Norway, producing a ton of fish means forgoing the opportunity to use 5 labor hours in the fields. A ton of fish thus has an opportunity cost of 1 ton of grain there. In Spain, producing a ton of fish means giving up the opportunity to produce 2 tons of grain. In terms of opportunity costs, then, fish is cheaper in Norway than in Spain and grain is cheaper in Spain than in Norway. As we saw in Chapter 2, the country in which the opportunity cost of a good is lower is said to have a *comparative advantage* in producing that good.

Considering only labor costs, it might seem as though there is no possibility of mutually beneficial trade. Norwegians might like to get their hands on some of those cheap Spanish goods, but why would the Spanish be interested? After all, couldn't they produce everything at home more cheaply than it could be produced abroad? If so, how could they gain from trade? However, a closer analysis shows that this view is incorrect. In this case, absolute advantage turns out to be unimportant in determining patterns of trade; only comparative advantage matters.

To see that possibilities for trade between the two countries do exist, imagine that a Norwegian fishing party decides to sail into a Spanish port with a ton of its catch. Before the Norwegians' arrival, Spanish merchants in the port will be used to giving 2 tons of locally produced grain for a ton of fish. The Norwegians, before coming to Spain, will be accustomed to getting only 1 ton of Norwegian grain for each ton of Norwegian fish. Thus, any exchange ratio between 1 and 2 tons of grain per ton of fish will seem attractive to both parties. For instance, a trade of 1.5 tons of grain for a ton of fish will make both the Spanish merchants and the Norwegian fishing party better off than they would be by trading only with others from their own country.

The profits of the first boatload of traders are only the beginning of the story. The more significant benefits come as each country begins to specialize in producing the good in which it has a comparative advantage. In Norway, farmers will discover that instead of working 5 hours to raise a ton of grain from their own rocky soil, they can fish for 5 hours and trade their catch to the Spaniards for 1.5 tons of grain. In Spain, people will find that it is no longer worth their while to spend 4 hours catching a ton of fish. Instead, they can work just 3 hours in the fields, and the 1.5 tons of grain that they grow will get them a ton of fish from the Norwegians. In short, the Norwegians will find it worthwhile to specialize in fish and the Spaniards will find it advantageous to specialize in grain.

Now suppose that trade continues at the rate of 1.5 tons of grain per ton of fish until both countries have become completely specialized. Spain no longer produces any fish, and Norway no longer produces any grain. Norwegians catch 200 tons of fish, half of which are exported to Spain. The Spanish grow 500 tons of grain, 150 tons of which are exported to Norway. Exhibit 20.1 compares this situation with a nonspecialized, pre-trade situation in which each country produces some of both products. The comparison reveals three things. First, the Norwegians are better off than before; they have just as much fish to eat and 50 tons more grain than in the pre-trade equilibrium. Second, the Spanish are also better off; they have just as much grain to consume as ever—and more fish. Finally, total world output of both grain and fish has risen as a result of trade. Everyone is better off, and no one is worse off.

Graphic Presentation

The concept of comparative advantage can be illustrated graphically using a set of production possibility frontiers based on the example just given. This is done in Exhibit 20.2, which shows three production possibility frontiers.

Part a is the production possibility frontier for Spain. Given 1,000 labor hours available and a cost of 2 labor hours per ton of grain, Spain can produce up to 500 tons of grain per year if it produces no fish (point B). If it produces no grain, up to 250 tons of fish per year can be caught at 4 hours per ton of fish (point D). The combinations of grain and fish that Spain can produce are represented by the line running from D to B.

Exhibit 20.1   Effects of Trade on
Production and Consumption

This table shows production and consumption of fish and
grain in Spain, Norway, and the world as a whole before and
after trade. It is assumed that each country specializes in
the product in which it has a comparative advantage and
that fish is traded for grain at the rate of 1.5 tons of grain
per ton of fish.

	Spain	Norway	World Total
Before Trade			
Fish			
Production	75 tons	100 tons	175 tons
Consumption	75	100	175
Grain			
Production	350	100	450
Consumption	350	100	450
After Trade			
Fish			
Production	0	200	200
Consumption	100	100	200
Grain			
Production	500	0	500
Consumption	350	150	500

Part b shows the production possibility frontier for Norway. In Norway, fish and grain each take 5 labor hours per ton to produce. If Norwegians devote all their time to fishing, they can catch up to 200 tons of fish per year (point B′). If they devote all their time to farming, they can grow up to 200 tons of grain (point D′). The line between B′ and D′ represents Norway's production possibility frontier.

According to the example summarized in Exhibit 20.1, before trade begins Spain produces and consumes 350 tons of grain and 75 tons of fish. This is shown as point A on Spain's production possibility frontier. Norway is assumed to produce and consume 100 tons each of fish and grain. This is shown by point A′ on Norway's frontier.

The World Production Possibility Frontier
A production possibility frontier for the world as a whole (consisting of just these two countries in our example) can be constructed as shown in part c of Exhibit 20.2. First, assume that both countries devote all their labor to grain. That gives 500 tons of grain from Spain plus 200 from Norway, or 700 tons of grain in all (point R in part c of Exhibit 20.2). Starting from there, assume that the world output of fish is to be increased. For the sake of efficiency, it is clear that Norwegian farmers should be the first to switch to fishing, since the opportunity cost of fish is lower in Norway (1 ton of grain per ton of fish) than in Spain (2 tons of grain per ton of fish). As Norwegians switch to fishing, then, world production moves upward and to the left along the line segment RQ.

When all Norwegians have abandoned farming for fishing, the world will have arrived at point Q—500 tons of grain (all Spanish) and 200 tons of fish (all Norwegian). From that point on, the only way to get more fish is to have Spanish farmers switch to fishing. At the opportunity cost of 2 tons of grain per ton of fish, this moves the economy along the line segment QS. When all Spanish farmers are fishing, the world arrives at point S, where 450 tons of fish and no grain are produced. The production possibility frontier for the world as a whole is thus the kinked line RQS.

Exhibit 20.2   A Graphic Illustration of Comparative Advantage

This exhibit shows production possibility frontiers for Spain, Norway, and the two countries combined. Before trade, Spain produces and consumes at point A and Norway at point A′. Together these correspond to world consumption point P, which is inside the world production possibility frontier. After trade begins, Spain specializes in producing grain (point B) and trades part of the grain for fish, moving to consumption point C. Norway specializes in producing fish (point B′) and reaches consumption point C′ through trade. As a result, world efficiency is improved and point Q is attained on the world production possibility frontier.

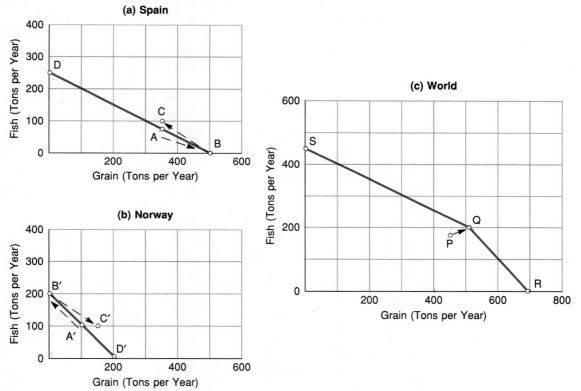

Effects of Trade

The pre-trade production point for the world as a whole lies inside the world production possibility frontier. Adding together the quantities of fish and grain from A and A′, we arrive at point P in part c of Exhibit 20.2—450 tons of grain and 175 tons of fish. This is inefficient; the world economy as a whole could produce more of both goods. To increase efficiency, both countries must specialize.

Following our earlier example, suppose that Spain shifts its production from 350 tons of grain and 75 tons of fish (point A) to 500 tons of grain and no fish (point B). It then trades the extra 150 tons of grain for 100 tons of Norwegian fish. Spain's consumption thus ends up at point C, while its production remains at B. At the same time, Norway shifts its production from A′ to B′, thus specializing entirely in fish. The extra 100 tons of fish are traded for the 150 tons of Spanish grain, moving Norwegian consumption to point C′.

As a result of specialization plus trade, then, both Spain and Norway have moved to points that lie outside their own production possibility frontiers. As they do so, the world as a whole moves from point P inside its production possibility frontier to point Q. Thus, specialization improves world efficiency, increases world production of both goods, and leaves both countries better off than they would be if they did not trade.

Comparative Advantage and "Competitiveness"

The theory of comparative advantage is easy enough to demonstrate in a simplified world in which "Spain" carries out a barter trade in just two goods with "Norway." But what about the more complex world in which we live? In closing this section, we will consider some implications of comparative advantage for the United States and the world in the 1980s and particularly for the issue of "competitiveness."

As noted at the outset of this chapter, U.S. involvement in world trade has grown greatly in recent decades. However, while U.S. exports have shown remarkable strength, imports have grown still more rapidly. By the mid-1980s, the *trade deficit*—the amount by which imports exceed exports—reached an all-time record level. This became a major cause of national concern. News reporters, editorialists, and politicians feared that the United States was no longer "competitive" in the world economy. The idea of competitiveness meant different things to different people, but at the heart of it lay a concern that foreign workers worked harder and foreign business managers had become smarter than their U.S. counterparts. "Soon the Japanese, the Koreans, and the Europeans will be better at everything than we are," people said. "Eventually we won't be able to export anything at all!"

Certainly there were some worrisome aspects of trade trends in the 1980s. However, the theory of comparative advantage casts doubt on the notion that a country can reach a point at which it imports everything and exports nothing. In fact, our Spain-Norway example and the similar U.S.-China illustration of Chapter 2 clearly show that a country always has a comparative advantage in producing something even when it has an absolute disadvantage (in terms of labor hours or other factor inputs) for all goods. In the sense of comparative advantage, then, a country must always be "competitive" in the production of some goods or services.

However, comparative advantage does not guarantee an exact match between the value of a country's exports and imports of goods and services. The numerical examples we have given, which suggest that must be the case, omit two important details. First, they leave out international financial transactions, including purchases and sales of corporate stocks, government bonds, and other securities, as well as several kinds of international banking transactions. Second, the numerical examples assume that trade takes the form of barter, whereas in practice most international trade is conducted using money as a means of payment. Let's look briefly at the implications of each of these factors for comparative advantage and competitiveness.

Financial Transactions and the Balance of Trade

International financial transactions are important because they make it possible for a country to import more goods and services than it exports, or export more than it imports, in a given year. To take a very simple case, suppose that U.S. consumers decide to buy $100 million of TV sets from Korean firms. What will the Korean firms do with the $100 million they receive? They can use it to buy airliners built in the United States, in which case U.S. and Korean trade in goods will balance. However, they can instead use it to buy U.S. government bonds or make deposits in U.S. banks. In that case, no U.S. exports will be generated in the current year to balance the imports. Of course, the Korean owners of the bonds or bank deposits have a claim on future exports from the United States; they can cash in their financial assets and spend them any time they like. But meanwhile, despite the U.S. comparative advantage in producing airliners, the U.S. trade accounts will not be balanced.

Could we say, then, that the U.S. balance-of-trade deficit in the 1980s reflects a U.S. comparative advantage in the production of financial assets? That would certainly be one way to look at it. We could also say that Korean buyers simply prefer future U.S. airliners to current ones. Either way, we should be cautious about assuming that the imbalance in merchandise trade reflects a loss of "competitiveness" in the sense of lost comparative advantage.

Exchange Rates and Competitiveness

In order to understand international trade fully, we must also take into account the fact that it is conducted in terms of money. However, there is no "world money"; each country has its own currency. Thus, before one can buy goods, services, or financial instruments from abroad, one must first visit the *foreign exchange markets*, in which one currency can be traded for another. The windows at international airports at which tourists can use their dollars to buy French francs or British pounds are a tiny part of these markets. Larger, commercial exchanges of currency are carried out through major banks in New York, London, Tokyo, and other world financial centers.

The rates at which two currencies are exchanged are determined by the forces of supply and demand. These vary substantially from day to day and from year to year. For example, in early 1986 a U.S. dollar was worth 10 French francs; two years later, it was worth only 6 French francs. As exchange rates vary, so do the prices of countries' imports and exports. For example, at 10 francs to a dollar, an American firm need spend only $6 to import a 60-franc bottle of French wine. At 6 francs to the dollar, it takes $10 to buy the same 60-franc bottle. Similarly, at 10 francs to the dollar, a French buyer would have to lay out 100,000 francs to buy a $10,000 IBM computer made in the United States. At 6 francs to the dollar, the price to the French buyer would be much less—only 60,000 francs.

We see, then, that the ability of U.S. exporters to compete in world markets—and the ability of U.S. firms to compete against imports in the home market—depends very heavily on exchange rates. In fact, the troubles U.S. exporters faced in the first half of the 1980s and the growing appetite of U.S. consumers for imported goods in that period were largely caused by a steady rise in the dollar's exchange value from 1980 to early 1985. It is not necessary to cite a lapse of management skills, technological leadership, or marketing ability in order to explain the loss of "competitiveness" of U.S. industry during this period. Indeed, the success of U.S. multinational companies with operations outside the United States—ranging from Kentucky Fried Chicken to Caterpillar Tractor—suggests that there has been no such lapse.[1]

---

[1] A study by Robert E. Lipsey and Irving B. Kravis showed that in the two decades following 1966, U.S.-based multinationals have held a steady 7.7 percent share of world exports. See "The Competitiveness and Comparative Advantage of U.S. Multinationals, 1957–1983" (National Bureau of Economic Research Working Paper No. 2051, October 1987).

Similarly, changes in "competitiveness" caused by exchange rate movements do not reflect a loss of comparative advantage. Exchange rates do affect a country's balance of trade and have a strong impact on the flow of international financial transactions. But whether exchange rates are high or low, whether there is a trade deficit or a trade surplus, the goods that a country exports still are those that it can produce at a comparatively low opportunity cost and those it imports are the ones that can be produced at a relatively low opportunity cost abroad.

A full discussion of international financial transactions and exchange rates requires an understanding of macroeconomic theory. These topics form an important part of the macroeconomics course. However, the theory of international finance and exchange rates does not undermine the validity of the microeconomic principle of comparative advantage nor the fact that international trade that follows this principle is beneficial to all countries involved.

Trade Policy and Protectionism

Up to this point, we have not mentioned government policy toward international trade. We have pictured a world in which Norwegian fishers and Spanish farmers are free to trade as dictated by comparative advantage. In practice, however, governments are deeply involved in the regulation and promotion of international trade. In this section, we examine government's role.

Trends in Post–World War II Trade

The post–World War II period as a whole has seen a broad movement toward freer trade. Several international organizations were set up after the war to promote freer trade. The International Monetary Fund was created in 1944 to maintain a stable financial climate for trade. The General Agreement on Tariffs and Trade (GATT) was founded in an attempt to prevent a return of policies of **protectionism**—policies designed to shield domestic industries from import competition—that were common in the 1930s. GATT rules permit use of taxes on imports, known as **tariffs,** but restrict their use. Under the so-called most-favored-nation principle, GATT members are supposed to charge the same tariff rates for imports from all GATT countries. A series of multinational negotiations sponsored by GATT succeeded in lowering the average rate of tariffs. Also, GATT has tried to discourage the use of **import quotas,** which are restrictions on the quantity of a good that can be imported over a given period.

In addition to the activities of GATT, the post–World War II period has seen efforts to set up regional trading blocs in several parts of the world. The best known of these is the European Economic Community, or Common Market. The aim of the Common Market was to eliminate all barriers to trade among the major European countries, eventually leading to a situation in which trade among these countries would be as free as trade among the states of the United States. The Common Market has not yet achieved this goal, but it has contributed to the growth and prosperity of Western Europe, where standards of living in most countries now are similar to those in the United States. In the fall of 1987, the United States and Canada reached an agreement in principle to establish a free-trade area between them that would in several respects share the trade goals of the European Common Market.

Protectionism
Any policy intended to shield domestic industries from import competition.

Tariff
A tax on imported goods.

Import quota
A limit on the quantity of a good that can be imported over a given period.

Protectionism: Old and New

Although the volume of world trade has increased greatly in the past four decades, protectionism is far from dead. In addition to continued use of traditional tariffs and quotas, a "new protectionism" has sprung up and imposed other restrictive mechanisms. The new protectionism focuses in part on such devices as "orderly marketing agreements" and "voluntary export restraints." These involve the use of political pressure,—usually backed by the threat of a tariff or quota—to restrain trade in a particular good. A leading example is the complex set of agreements that the United States has negotiated with textile-exporting countries. A U.S.-Japanese agreement on quotas for automobile imports in the early 1980s is another. Although these agreements are referred to as "voluntary," their effects on consumers scarcely differ from those of a traditional tariff or quota. Prices go up and losses in efficiency occur as production moves against the direction of comparative advantage.

Antidumping practices are another device of the new protectionism. A country is said to be "dumping" its goods when it sells them in a foreign market for less than the price it maintains at home or for less than the cost of producing them. Under certain provisions of U.S. law, domestic producers facing competition from imports dumped on the U.S. market can seek tariffs. Steelmakers are one group that has sought this type of protection. Free traders object to antidumping laws on two grounds. First, they point out that in times of slack world demand for a product, efficiency requires that firms temporarily sell that product at prices below average total costs. (Chapter 9 explains why this is so for domestic markets; the same holds true for international markets.) Second, they claim that "dumped" imports, like any other imports, produce benefits for consumers that must be weighed against the harm done to producers.

Finally, the new protectionism often takes the form of product standards or procurement practices that have both the intent and the effect of limiting foreign competition. U.S. firms trying to sell their products in Japan constantly complain of such barriers. For example, Japan has insisted that all electrical products be tested in Japanese laboratories, even if they have passed similar tests in the United States. (U.S. procedures permit Japanese exports to be tested in Japan.) As another example, Japan's huge telephone company has used procurement methods that have hampered the efforts of U.S. manufacturers to bid on supply contracts. These practices have been a focal point of U.S.-Japanese trade negotiations in recent years, and some progress has been made in opening Japanese markets to U.S. goods. But Japan is by no means the only offender. As "Economics in the News 20.1" points out, even the United States is not in all respects the champion of free trade it is sometimes said to be.

Despite the progress made against tariff barriers to trade, then, protectionism remains a live issue. In the remainder of this section, we will look at its origins and effects.

Income Distribution and Multiple Factors of Production

To understand the sources of protectionism, we must begin by considering the effects of trade on the distribution of income within each country. This, in turn, requires an expansion of our analysis to include more than one factor of production. A modification of the Spain-Norway example will serve this purpose.

Assume from now on that fishing requires a relatively large capital invest-

ECONOMICS IN THE NEWS   20.1

United States Not Always the Champion of Free Trade

In Sault Ste. Marie, Ontario, a Canadian shopper can buy a four-kilogram bag of white cane sugar at New Dominion Stores Ltd. for about $1.50 (U.S.).

But across the St. Marys River in Sault Ste. Marie, Michigan, a 10-pound bag (4.54 kilograms) of the same sugar sells at Norden's Foodland for $3.35, roughly double the Canadian price.

The reason is simple: protectionism. To support domestic sugar producers, the U.S. imposes stiff quotas on sugar imports, keeping the domestic wholesale price far higher than the world price. "It's a glaring discrepancy," says Francis Mansfield, director of the Sault-area Chamber of Commerce.

The current congressional debate over trade legislation rings with complaints that the United States is the last bastion of unfettered international trade in a world of protectionists. "The United States has permitted imports to gush ashore freely while not demanding comparable access abroad," asserts Senator Lloyd Bentsen, a Texas Democrat.

But the United States isn't the pure free-trader that many in Congress and business seem to think. Sugar quotas are just one example of a large array of trade barriers the United States has built to restrict imports. Indeed, significant trade barriers cover more than a quarter of all manufactured goods sold in the United States and cost U.S. consumers more than $50 billion per year, or $450 for every working man and woman.

Clothing tariffs and quotas provide a dramatic example of the high costs of U.S. protectionism. During the 1970s, the United States negotiated import quotas with all the major apparel-producing nations, and in 1983 those quotas were tightened substantially. The United States also has a tariff averaging 26 percent of the value of all clothing imports.

As a result, the cost of imported clothing here is more than double what it would be if the United States had no trade barriers, according to a recent study by the Federal Reserve Bank of New York. The study, which conservatively assumes that trade barriers don't raise the price of domestically manufactured clothes, estimates that consumers pay a tax of as much as $12 billion a year to protect the U.S. textile industry. A more comprehensive measurement, according to Prof. Gary Hufbauer of Georgetown University, puts the figure at $27 billion, or $42,200 for every job saved.

What is more, economists argue that such protectionist policies probably eliminate as many jobs in other parts of the economy as they save in the protected industry. For one thing, when consumers must pay more for clothes, they have less to spend on other items, leading to less employment in other industries. Most economists also believe that import restrictions usually result in reduced U.S. exports.

"I happen to believe there are no jobs saved in the economy as a whole" as a result of protectionist measures, says Robert Lawrence, a senior fellow at the Brookings Institution.

Some other imported products that are protected by U.S. trade barriers:

- *Book manufacturing.* The U.S. book printing industry is largely shielded from foreign competition. To be eligible for U.S. copyright protection, virtually all books and periodicals published in this country must be printed and bound here. According to Hufbauer, that restriction costs consumers an estimated $500 million each year.

- *Ceramic tiles.* Makers of ceramic floor and wall tiles are protected by tariffs that average about 25 percent of the import value. The cost to consumers, Hufbauer says, is about $116 million a year.

- *Peanuts.* To prevent imports from undermining its peanut price support program, the government has kept a strict quota on imported peanuts since 1953. The approximate annual cost to the consumer, according to Hufbauer's research: $170 million.

"I think it is probably true that we are less protectionist" than both Europe and Japan, says Lawrence. "Nonetheless, we ought not to be necessarily as self-righteous as we are."

ment per worker and farming a relatively small one. Fishing therefore is said to be capital intensive and farming labor intensive. Also assume, as before, that in the absence of trade the opportunity cost of fish will be higher in Spain than in

Norway. The theory of comparative advantage still applies regardless of the number of factors of production involved. International trade will still make it possible for total world production of both fish and grain to increase. It will still enable the quantities of both goods available in both countries to rise. Now, however, a new question arises: How will the gains from trade be distributed within each country?

To answer this question, we must look at what happens in factor markets as trade brings about increasing specialization in each country. In Norway, production shifts from farming to fishing. As grain production is phased out, large quantities of labor and relatively small quantities of capital are released. The shift in production thus creates a surplus of labor and a shortage of capital. Factor markets can return to equilibrium only when wages fall relative to the rate of return on capital. Only then will fisheries adopt more labor-intensive production methods. Meanwhile, the opposite process occurs in Spain. The shift from fishing to farming depresses the rate of return on capital and increases the wage rate. This causes Spanish workers to use more capital per worker than before.

These changes in relative factor prices determine how the gains from trade are distributed among the people of each country. Spanish workers and Norwegian boat owners will gain doubly from trade: first because trade increases the size of the pie (the total quantity of goods) and second because the shifts in factor prices give them a larger slice. For Norwegian workers and Spanish farm owners, in contrast, one of these effects works against the other. The workers and farm owners still benefit from the growth of the pie, but they get a smaller piece of it than before. They may or may not end up better off as a result of the trade.

Suppose that the comparative advantage in the pre-trade situation is large and the difference in factor intensity between the two countries is small. Norwegian workers and Spanish farm owners will still gain from trade in an absolute sense, even though they will lose ground relative to others in their own country. If conditions are less favorable, however, they can end up worse off than before trade began. Who gains and who loses depends partly on the degree of specialization of factors of production. So far we have looked at matters in terms of only two broadly defined factors of production—labor and capital. However, suppose instead that we think in terms not of labor in general but of people with farming skills and those with fishing skills and not of capital in general but of boat owners and tractor owners. It then becomes even more likely that trade will have a very uneven impact on incomes. The more specialized and less mobile the factors of production, the more factor prices will shift as a result of trade and the more likely it will be that some specific groups will be harmed by trade.

Protectionism and Rent Seeking

International competition, like other forms of competition, tends to drive wages and the returns to other factors of production toward the level of opportunity costs. Protection from foreign competition relieves the pressure and permits the protected firms and workers to earn rents, that is, profits and wages in excess of opportunity costs. Thus, the political process that results in trade restrictions can be analyzed in terms of public choice theory and the notion of rent seeking.

As a specific example, consider the quotas that were imposed on U.S. automobile imports from Japan beginning in 1981. "Applying Economic Ideas 20.1" describes those quotas and their effects. According to the research cited there, the quotas imposed large costs on U.S. consumers, substantially boosted the

Benefits and Costs of Automobile Import Quotas

The early 1980s were hard times for the U.S. auto industry. A combination of soaring gasoline prices and back-to-back recessions cut demand. Sales of fuel-hungry U.S.-built cars were especially hard hit, falling from 9 million units per year in 1978 to an average of just under 6 million units in 1980 through 1982. Meanwhile, the profits of U.S. automakers, which had averaged 14.9 percent of stockholders' equity in the 1960s and 12.5 percent in the 1970s, turned into losses in the 1980s. It took a government bailout to save Chrysler, one of Detroit's Big Three, from bankruptcy.

As the market share of foreign producers soared from around 15 percent in the mid-1970s to nearly 30 percent in the early 1980s, the automakers, the United Auto Workers union, and politicians from car-producing states joined forces to demand protection. The Reagan administration's response was an agreement with the Japanese government to hold Japanese car imports to the United States to 1.68 million units in the year beginning April 1981. This quota was extended for the next two years at the same level and for the year beginning April 1984 at a level of 1.85 million units.

The effects of the quotas were dramatic. As the economy recovered from recession in 1983 and 1984, a frantic seller's market developed. Waiting lists for popular models grew. Dealer markups of hundreds and even thousands of dollars replaced the rebates and low-interest loans of previous years. The quotas, which had been quietly accepted as a way of saving American jobs during the recession, became a subject of widespread debate.

Were the gains in terms of profits and jobs saved worth the cost of the quotas to consumers? Probably not, according to studies of the effects of the quotas.

First, it is necessary to estimate the impact of the quotas on car prices. The claims were conflicting. The auto-

Source: Robert W. Crandall, "Import Quotas and the Automobile Industry: The Costs of Protectionism," *Brookings Review* (Summer 1984): 8–16; Clifford Winston and associates, *Blind Intersection: Policy and the Automobile Industry* (Washington, D.C.: The Brookings Institution, 1987), Chapter 4.

makers themselves said that any increase in prices had resulted from consumers' switching to larger cars after fuel prices started to fall in 1982 and 1983. A study by Robert Crandall of the Brookings Institution used three different statistical approaches to separate the effects of the quotas from those of changes in the size and other features of cars sold. All three methods led to similar conclusions: In the 1981 to 1983 period, the quotas raised the prices of U.S.-made cars by about $400 per unit and those of Japanese cars by about $1,000 per unit. The total cost to U.S. consumers in 1983 was about $4.3 billion. Fred Mannering and Clifford Winston, also of Brookings, extended the study to 1984, when the effect of quotas was even stronger. In that year, they found, prices of Japanese cars were raised by 20 percent and those of U.S.-built cars by 8 percent for a total cost to consumers of $14 billion.

What were the gains to workers? Crandall estimated that for 1983 about 26,000 autoworker jobs were saved out of a base of 600,000 at a cost of $160,000 per job saved. Using a somewhat different estimation method, Mannering and Winston concluded that there was an actual loss of U.S. auto jobs as a result of the quotas, peaking at a 30,000-job loss in 1984. This job loss occurred because U.S. automakers, shielded from Japanese competition, cut output in order to raise prices and profits. However, although jobs may have been lost to the U.S. work force, the average industry wage was estimated to have risen about 10 percent as automakers shared some of their increased profits with their employees.

Mannering and Winston estimated that the quotas boosted the profits of U.S. automakers by $8.9 billion in 1984. Japanese automakers also gained: The 20 percent increase in the price of their cars more than offset the decrease in volume sold, increasing the profits of Japanese firms by an estimated $3 billion.

In effect, the quotas amounted to an international automobile cartel, organized and enforced by the U.S. and Japanese governments. The Japanese were so pleased with the results of this cartel that they decided to continue it unilaterally by limiting exports to 2.25 million cars per year after the United States withdrew from the quota agreement in 1985.

profits of both U.S. and Japanese auto companies, and resulted in wage increases for workers with either a small job gain or a small job loss. Virtually all economists who have investigated the quotas agree that the total costs to U.S. consumers exceed the gain in rents (whether in the form of profits or wages) to

U.S. firms and workers. Public choice theory suggests how this policy could have won approval in the representative democracy of the United States despite its unfavorable ratio of benefits to costs.

First, consider consumers. According to Mannering and Winston's estimates, the 20 percent increase in the prices of Japanese autos and 8 percent increase in those of U.S. autos cost consumers $14 billion in 1984 alone. However, some 77 million U.S. households owned cars that year. Thus, the cost of the quotas per car-owning household averaged less than $200 per year. According to public choice theory, benefits or costs shared widely among large numbers of people tend to have relatively little political impact.

Next, consider U.S. producers. Three major U.S. producers shared some $9 billion in rents in 1984 alone as a result of the quotas. These three ranked first, third, and eleventh in size of all U.S. corporations. Large benefits concentrated on a few visible and politically active parties tend to have more than proportionate influence in a representative democracy.

The situation with respect to workers is more complex. The United Auto Workers union strongly supported the quotas, arguing that they would save U.S. jobs. Estimates by Robert Crandall showed some gain in jobs for U.S. autoworkers, though at a very high cost per job. Unionized workers fit the pattern of a well-organized group on whom benefits are concentrated. Such a group would tend to have relatively more political clout in proportion to its size than would more numerous but less organized consumers. However, what can we make of Mannering and Winston's estimates, which showed an actual loss of U.S. jobs as a result of the quotas? If these estimates are valid, do they imply that the UAW behaved irrationally in supporting quotas? Not necessarily, because the principles of public choice also apply to internal union politics. According to the median-worker model of union behavior mentioned in Chapter 14, the least-senior workers tend to have relatively little influence on union policy. Yet it is these least-senior workers who would have borne the brunt of the layoffs estimated by Mannering and Winston. The median autoworker would support quotas in the expectation of sharing increased industry rents via higher wages.

Finally, consider the Japanese automakers. According to Mannering and Winston's estimates, the 20 percent rise in Japanese auto prices more than offset the reduction in sales of Japanese cars, leading to a $3 billion revenue gain. (This would perhaps be shared in part by Japanese autoworkers.) It is not surprising, then, that the Japanese agreed to the quotas—and even decided to continue them after they were abandoned by the United States. Why, though, should the United States have preferred quotas to a tariff increase? A 20 percent tariff would have cut Japanese sales by just as much while raising revenue for the U.S. Treasury rather than the Japanese automakers.

Again the answer is found in public choice theory. U.S. taxpayers are a large but poorly organized group. They have no effective means of lobbying for a tariff rather than a quota. The Japanese government, by comparison, maintains an effective political presence in Washington, and the Japanese auto industry, in turn, is an influential lobbying force within the Japanese political system. Thus, it is no surprise to find that the Japanese earned a generous slice of the rents generated by the quotas.

This analysis could be repeated for countless protected markets—textiles, peanuts, books, ceramic tile, or whatever. In each case, economic investigators have found that total gains to producers fall short of total costs to consumers.

Likewise in each case, however, the benefits are concentrated on compact, politically active groups while the costs are spread widely among millions of households. It is revealing that in post–World War II U.S. politics, the President—elected by all the people—has leaned toward support of free trade regardless of political party. At the same time, Congress—each member of which is elected by a narrower constituency—has inclined more often toward protectionism.

The Rhetoric of Protectionism

While protectionist policies can be explained in terms of the theory of rent seeking, advocates of such policies are often reluctant to speak the language of naked self-interest, at least in public; rather, they prefer to present their policies as consistent with the general interest. They rarely invoke positive economic analysis, which, with its benefit-cost analysis, tends to favor free trade. Instead, they more often tend to strike normative themes.

Nationalism is one such theme. Economic strength is often equated with national self-sufficiency. The desire to buy foreign goods simply because they are cheaper or better is depicted as selfish and unpatriotic. At the same time, protectionists routinely treat jobs for American workers as the only jobs that matter and ignore the damage done by protectionist policies to workers abroad. In some cases, this aspect of protectionist rhetoric borders on open racism, calling to mind the efforts of white workers in earlier times to protect their jobs from the competition of minority workers within the United States.

In other cases, rather than scorning foreign workers, the protectionists pose as their allies. Foreign workers who earn lower wages than U.S. workers are characterized as "exploited," with the implication that those workers would somehow be better off if we stopped buying the products they make. However, this proposition is hard to support in terms of positive economics. If foreign workers earn less than U.S. workers, it is not necessarily because they are exploited but because their countries are poorly endowed with human and physical capital. Injecting capital into their economies through foreign investment and adding to labor demand by importing their products is far more likely to benefit than to harm those workers.

The analogy of "leveling the playing field" is another favorite rhetorical device of protectionists. Other countries do not follow the rules of free trade. They impose tariff and nontariff barriers on our exports; therefore, we should retaliate by refusing to buy their exports. But a distinction must be drawn between the sometimes valid use of tariffs and quotas as bargaining tools through which to win freer trade and the unsupported notion that retaliatory trade restrictions are beneficial in themselves. Free traders offer an analogy of their own. Suppose, they say, that you are in a lifeboat and one of your fellow passengers shoots a hole in it. That is a stupid thing to do—but is it smart to retaliate by shooting another hole in the boat yourself?

There is no reason to expect the war of words over trade policy to end soon. There is also no indication that firms and workers will cease using the machinery of representative democracy to pursue their own economic interests, sometimes at the expense of their neighbors'. But an understanding of the economics of international trade can help in evaluating the claims made by the various participants in this ongoing debate.

Summary

1. **How can the principle of comparative advantage be applied to international trade?** A country is said to have a comparative advantage in the production of a good if it can produce it at a lower opportunity cost than its trading partner. Trade is based on the principle that if each country exports goods in which it has a comparative advantage, total world production of all goods and services can increase and boost total consumption in each trading country.

2. **How is the notion of "competitiveness" related to that of comparative advantage?** In the first half of the 1980s, U.S. imports expanded more rapidly than exports, leaving the country with a record trade deficit. Some interpreted this as a loss of "competitiveness," implying that U.S. firms were performing poorly in terms of quality and cost and that the United States was no longer capable of producing goods that other countries wanted. The principle of comparative advantage holds, however, that a country must always have some goods that can be profitably exported. The troubles of U.S. exporters in the 1980s cannot be fully understood unless international financial transactions and exchange rates are taken into account. It is these, rather than failures of U.S. workers or managers, that seem to explain much of the apparent loss of "competitiveness" in the 1980s.

3. **What has been the trend in international trade policy during the post–World War II period?** The general trend in international trade policy since World War II has been toward a reduction of traditional *tariff* and *quota* barriers to trade. However, recent years have seen increased use of new *protectionist* devices, such as orderly marketing agreements and "voluntary" quotas.

4. **How does international trade affect income distribution within each country?** In a world with two or more factors of production, trade tends to increase demand for factors that are used relatively intensively in producing export goods and to decrease demand for factors that are used relatively intensively in producing goods that compete with imported goods. Thus, although trade benefits a country as a whole, it may not benefit owners of factors that are specialized in producing import-competing goods.

5. **How can protectionist policies be understood in terms of public choice theory and rent seeking?** Because protectionist policies shield firms and factor owners from international competition, they allow rents—that is, payments in excess of opportunity costs—to be earned. Often those who benefit from these rents are small, well-organized groups that have political influence out of proportion to their numbers. Although the overall costs of protectionism tend to outweigh the benefits, the costs are spread widely among consumers, each of whom is affected less than producers by any given trade barrier.

Terms for Review

- absolute advantage
- protectionism
- tariff
- import quota

Questions for Review

1. Why are patterns of international trade determined by comparative advantage rather than by absolute advantage?

2. How do international financial transactions make it possible for a country's exports and imports not to balance?

3. How do changes in currency exchange rates affect a country's imports and exports? What does this have to do with the notion of "competitiveness"?

4. How does international trade affect the demand for factors of production within each trading country?

5. Give some examples of protectionist policies in use during the 1980s (in addition to simple tariffs and quotas).

6. Why is international trade often restricted by government policy even when the overall costs of the restrictions exceed their benefits?

Problems and Topics for Discussion

1. **Examining the lead-off case.** What does this case imply regarding the "competitiveness" of U.S. business? What are the advantages to a company of conducting its production operations abroad rather than producing at home and then exporting? Discuss this issue with regard to both a service firm such as Domino's Pizza and a manufacturing firm such as Caterpillar.

2. **A change in costs and comparative advantage.** Suppose that new, high-yield grains are introduced in Norway and that the number of labor hours needed to grow a ton of grain there is cut from 5 to 2.5 hours. What will happen to trade between Norway and

Spain? If labor hours per ton of grain in Norway fall all the way to 2, what will happen to the pattern of trade?

3. **Competitiveness.** Consider the following statement: "The United States may still be number 1, but I don't think we will be much longer. The Common Market, Japan, all areas of the world are catching up. Soon it will no longer be economical for us to produce anything." On the basis of what you have learned about the principle of comparative advantage, do you think it is possible to reach a point at which it is no longer worthwhile to produce anything—that is, a point at which it becomes economical to import all goods? Discuss.

4. **Trade bargaining.** If you were a strong supporter of free trade and in charge of U.S. international trade policy, would you cut tariffs and quotas or would you negotiate with trading partners, maintaining U.S. trade barriers unless they lowered theirs too? Discuss.

5. **Real-world trade patterns.** The simple trade theory presented in this chapter tells us that countries export goods in which they have a comparative advantage and import goods in which they do not. In practice, countries often import many of the same kinds of goods that they export. For example, France, Germany, and Italy are both importers and exporters of automobiles and the United States is both an importer and an exporter of computers. Why do you think these patterns of trade exist? Do they invalidate the principle of comparative advantage?

Case for Discussion
A Labor Leader Speaks Out on Trade Policy

The following passages are excerpted from a Washington Post *editorial by Lane Kirkland, president of the American Federation of Labor and Congress of Industrial Organizations:*

Lane Kirkland

Scores of industries, thousands of companies and millions of workers are drowning under a flood of imports generated by foreign government initiatives and Washington's neglect. The effects are felt in every sector of the economy through plant closings, farm foreclosures, bankruptcies and recession-level unemployment.

Yet President Reagan insists that "free trade and open markets . . . generate more jobs, a more productive use of a nation's resources, more rapid innovation and high standards of living both for this nation and its trading partners." But free trade doesn't exist except as an empty slogan. Not a product, commodity or service, including money, moves across any border except ours under free trade conditions.

Much of the world disavows a market economy and practices the most brutal form of protectionism: the protection of mercantile power and profit. Most trade is not open but directed—directed by governments in support of national policies and multinational corporations that move labor-intensive production to countries with the most exploitable workforces.

There is no sign of the jobs that "free trade" supposedly generates. The Labor Department reports that from 1979 through 1984, 11.5 million workers lost jobs because of plant closings or layoffs due to slack work.

Living standards have not risen. Real average weekly earnings for production workers fell by 9 percent from 1977 through 1985. Nearly half the workers displaced from manufacturing who were lucky to find jobs were forced to accept lower pay and reduced living standards.

Their loss of jobs has not brought gains to workers overseas. Too many less developed nations enjoy booms because workers are paid rock bottom subsistence wages, are forbidden to organize and bargain collectively and have no health and safety protection, no pensions, no security.

If "free trade" benefits anyone, it is manipulators who depress wages in order to inflate profits. They are absolved of guilt by the "free trade" evangelists who say that our "overpaid" workers have "priced themselves out of the market."

What is going overseas are not only jobs that sustain millions of families but the industrial capacity that sustains America. Company after company is no longer a producer but a mere relabeler and distributor of imports. And foreign label goods sold across the nation cost no less than products once made here. The only difference is that none of the money is returned as wages and payroll taxes to communities where it is spent. . . .

[Must we] accept the proposition that it is fair to allow other countries, aided by business and government, to slash American standards of living and human decency to the level that exploiters growing rich off the free trade myth praise as "competitive"? Such thinking must be resisted. The labor movement's historic mission is not to lower American standards but to raise them—and, as well, to raise the world's standards to our level.

Photo Source: Courtesy of AFL-CIO.

Questions

1. From 1982 to 1987, while the U.S. trade deficit was growing rapidly, the unemployment rate fell from 9.5 percent of the work force to below 6 percent and the total number of jobs in the U.S. economy increased by some 12 million. What might Kirkland say in response to these figures?

2. As a library project, look for data on trends in living standards of workers in such U.S. trading partners as Japan, Korea, Taiwan, and Hong Kong. Try also to find data on trends in workers' rights to form unions in these countries and on health and life expectancy standards. Does your research support Kirkland's contention that free trade has brought no gains to workers overseas?

3. Kirkland suggests that "free trade" benefits manipulators who depress wages in order to inflate profits. How, then, can it be explained that labor unions and their employers often join forces to lobby for trade restrictions? Consider the quotas on Japanese auto imports as a case in point.

Suggestions for Further Reading

Grennes, Thomas. *International Economics*. Englewood Cliffs, N.J.: Prentice-Hall, 1984.

Chapters 1 through 13 of this text cover the pure theory of international trade.

Hufbauer, Gary, et al. *Trade Protection in the United States: 31 Case Studies*. Washington, D.C.: Institute for International Economics, 1986.

The case studies in this book include sugar, textiles, steel, ceramic tile, peanuts, and many others.

Ricardo, David. *Principles of Political Economy and Taxation*. London, 1817. (Available in a modern paperback edition from Pelican Books, 1971.)

Chapter 7, "On Foreign Trade," is generally credited with being the first clear statement of the principle of comparative advantage.

21 The Soviet Economy: Central Planning and Reform

After reading this chapter, you will understand . . .

- The historical and ideological origins of the Soviet economic system.
- The key features of the Soviet economy's formal and informal structure.
- The chief accomplishments and failures of Soviet economic performance.
- Prospects for reform of the Soviet economy.

Before reading this chapter, make sure you know the meaning of . . .

- Opportunity costs (Chapter 1)
- Capitalism and socialism (Chapter 2)

Moscow Shows Off a Factory That Works

SUMY, U.S.S.R. The fate of Soviet leader Mikhail Gorbachev's economic reform drive may rest on whether others follow the lead of a factory official named Vladimir Moskolenko.

Moskolenko, a burly man with a booming voice, is deputy director of the M. V. Frunze Scientific and Industrial Conglomerate, a typically aged Soviet complex of five machine-building plants and a research institute sprawling across 20 acres of this neatly groomed northern Ukrainian company town.

Soviet factories may become more autonomous under Gorbachev's attempts at economic reform.

Moskolenko's achievements, acknowledged by his frequent invitations to confer with party boss Gorbachev's chief economic aides in Moscow, provide a measure of how far the Soviet leader's reform drive has come. They also show how far the drive has to go to realize Gorbachev's goal of transforming the national economy from one that blindly worships production figures at the expense of quality and profitability and is managed by orders dictated from above, rather than local managers' initiative.

The national spotlight fell on Moskolenko in 1985, when his plant, which makes compressors for gas pipelines, centrifuges for chemical plants and 50-ton water pumps for cooling nuclear reactors, was chosen as one of two Soviet enterprises—from a total of 48,000—to carry out a one-year experiment in broad managerial and financial autonomy. The experiment was so successful that the reforms were made permanent starting January 1, 1986.

Under a plan that Moskolenko was integral in establishing, plant officials can for the first time in Soviet industry keep part of the profits to use as they see fit. The plant pays 30 kopeks on each ruble of profit as taxes to the state, while retaining the remaining 70 percent. Full authority is granted the plant director to spend the money for plant modernization, worker bonuses and worker benefits such as housing, child care, and vacation homes.

The plant's work force, 20,000 men and women organized into brigades, has responded. At noisy shop No. 15, where vacuum pumps are made, 34-year-old Gennadi Mocholov steps back from his whirling metal lathe and says that higher bonuses have pushed his monthly pay to 400 rubles from 300 in one year. "The demands were stricter, but when the plant prospers we all gain. So we work harder," he says.

Will other enterprises do as well as the reforms spread? "I don't know," says Moskolenko, acknowledging that only 1 percent of Soviet plant directors are trained business managers with an appreciation for economics. "Our directors don't like economics. They don't understand it."

Source: Mark D'Anastasio, "Moscow Shows Off a Factory That Works," *The Wall Street Journal*, July 21, 1987. Reprinted by permission of *The Wall Street Journal*, © Dow Jones & Company, Inc. 1987. All Rights Reserved. Photo Source: © 1987 Phyllis Woloshin.

T HE Soviet economy must solve the same problems of what, how, and for whom that face the economy of the United States and that of any other country. However, different methods are used to make those decisions in the Soviet Union. Rather than relying on markets to provide information and incentives concerning such matters as how to build industrial water pumps, the Soviet economy emphasizes central planning. Under this system, the Soviet economy grew from a very backward one after World War I to an industrial giant. However, in the 1970s and 1980s, the system encountered problems that slowed its growth. In response, the new Soviet leadership headed by Mikhail Gorbachev has begun a wide-ranging discussion of reforms and, in some cases, has begun to put reforms in place.

In this chapter, we look at the Soviet economy—its history, structure, and performance. To do so is worthwhile not only because the Soviet Union is an important country; it also offers us a chance to look at nonmarket solutions to economic problems.

Origins of the Soviet Economic System

The problems of the Soviet economy and its prospects for reform cannot be understood without some knowledge of the origins of the system of central planning under which it has operated in the past. These roots can be traced back to the thinking of Karl Marx as interpreted and implemented by Vladimir Lenin, leader of the Russian revolution.

Marx's extensive writings are largely devoted to the evolution and structure of capitalism (see "Who Said It? Who Did It 2.2," page 45). Marx wanted to pave the way to revolution by showing that capitalism was headed for a breakdown, but he did not try to draw a detailed blueprint for the socialist economy that would replace it. There is little doubt, however, that he viewed the socialist economy in highly centralized terms. Private ownership of nonlabor factors of production would be abolished, and planning would replace the market as the main path to allocating resources.

Lenin was, if anything, more of a centralist than Marx himself. The secret of Lenin's political success was the highly centralized, disciplined structure of the Bolshevik (later Communist) party, which he led. It was natural for him to apply the same methods of administration to the economy. In a book he wrote just before coming into power, Lenin likened the task of running the economy to that of running the post office or any other bureaucratic agency. The important thing would be a strong party leadership that would clearly define economic goals and provide the discipline and willpower needed to carry them out. To Lenin, the details of economic calculation were relatively insignificant.

War Communism

Within months of the revolution of October 1917, the Bolsheviks were engaged in a civil war with their White Russian opponents. From the beginning of the civil war, the market economy that had grown up under the Tsarist regime was abandoned. Trade between the city and the countryside was replaced by forced requisitioning of farm products. Almost all industry was nationalized, including many small-scale businesses. Retail trade was also nationalized, although a large black market soon emerged. Industrial labor was put under semimilitary discipline, with workers sent to jobs wherever the need was most pressing. As a final blow to the market, a massive outpouring of paper money sent inflation so high that money became useless. Workers in key positions were paid in food or other goods. Party leaders proudly proclaimed that socialism had come to the Russian economy.

Either the civil war or the government's radical policies taken one at a time would have produced chaos; combined, they were a disaster. Militarily, the Bolsheviks scraped through against the White Russians and Western allies who opposed them. By 1921, however, with the war over, the economy was in sad shape. Agricultural production was down by one-third, and industrial workers had fled to the countryside in search of food. It was time for a change of direction.

The NEP

With the threat of war removed, Lenin launched his New Economic Policy, known as the NEP. It was a step backward, taken, as he put it, in order to prepare for two steps forward. Lenin had endorsed the centralist and antimarket policies of war communism, which fitted well with the views he had expressed before the revolution. Now he set those policies aside in order to get production back on its feet. Trade and small industry went back into private hands. Buying replaced forced requisitioning of farm products. Peasants once again found it worthwhile to sow their fields. Currency reform put the brake on inflation, and the money economy reappeared. The "commanding heights"—heavy industry, transportation, banking, and foreign trade—remained in government hands, while the rest of the economy returned to market principles. Planning was reduced to the issuance of "control figures," which were not directives but merely forecasts intended to help guide investment decisions.

As a tool of economic recovery, the NEP was a great success. By 1928, prewar production levels had been surpassed in both industry and agriculture. In 1924, Lenin died. Soon after, Stalin came to power. Stalin made it his first priority to take the two steps forward toward socialism that Lenin had promised.

Collectivization and the Five-Year Plan

The two steps forward taken in 1928 were the Five-Year Plan for industry and the policy of collectivization in agriculture. These steps were designed to overcome two features of the NEP that Stalin saw as serious defects. First, as long as the NEP was in force, central authorities were unable to control the direction of the market economy. Events went their own way, while the planners sat on the sidelines and gathered statistics. Second, the NEP provided no mechanism for shifting resources from agriculture to industry. The party needed such a shift in order to pursue its industry-first development strategy. Higher taxes, lower farm prices, or forced requisitioning of grain would result only in a withdrawal of effort by peasants, as had occurred during the civil war.

In industry, the Five-Year Plan was, for the first time, supposed to set the course of development in advance. Annual plans were to be drawn up in accordance with it. The intent of these plans was to assign raw materials to producers on a nonmarket basis. Above all, the Five-Year Plan envisioned a massive program of capital investment.

Industrial growth was to be financed by obtaining more farm produce. Collectivization was the technique used to insure that the needed grain moved from the country to the city. Between 1928 and 1932, some 15 million peasant households—about two-thirds of the rural population—were formed into 211,000 collective farms. On the collectives, land and livestock were owned in common and farm machinery was supplied by independent machine-tractor stations. Land was worked in common too, and a complex system of payment to farmers was set up. Party control over the peasantry was greatly strengthened. Party policy could be imposed on the collectives in a way that had never been possible while agriculture was in private hands.

Collectivization had limited success. It wreaked havoc with agricultural production. The number of livestock fell by almost half as peasants slaughtered their animals rather than turn them over to the collectives. Grain output also fell sharply, both because of the chaos caused by collectivization and because the incentive structure of the collectives themselves discouraged effort. Despite the disruption of production, however, the flow of goods from the countryside to the city increased—and that, after all, was a major goal of the policy.

The increased flow to the cities occurred partly because collectivization put the grain where party authorities could get their hands on the first share, before the rest was distributed to the peasants, and partly because there were fewer farm animals left to eat it. There were fewer people in the countryside as well. Several million died in the turmoil of collectivization and the famine of 1932 to 1934.

Emergence of the Classical Stalinist Economy

Out of the disorder of the early 1930s emerged the classical Stalinist economy. Industry, trade, banking, transportation, and foreign commerce were all nationalized. Agriculture was almost entirely collectivized. At the top of the system sat Gosplan, the state planning agency. This agency and the ruling party guided the economy with a development strategy that stressed centralization and planning.

Structure of the Soviet Economic System

The classical Soviet system of central planning established in the 1930s remains largely intact today, although it is no longer immune to criticism. Sweeping reforms are under discussion, and some are actually in the process of implementation, as we will see later in the chapter. But the problems and prospects of reforms cannot be understood without a knowledge of the key features of the system they aim to supplant. In this section, we look at the structure of the classical Soviet system.

The Central Hierarchy

According to classical Soviet doctrine, the Soviet economy functions as a single enterprise directed by a single will. At the top of the economic hierarchy are the highest political bodies of the Soviet government—the Supreme Soviet and its Council of Ministers. Under the Council of Ministers are a number of specialized agencies, including Gosplan, the Central Statistical Administration, and the State Bank. Also under the Council of Ministers is a long list of ministries in charge of specific industries, such as coal, railroads, and ferrous metallurgy. Below these ministries are numerous regional agencies that act as intermediaries between the central government and the firms at the bottom of the hierarchy.

Parallel to the government administrative structure is a Communist party hierarchy that also has major economic responsibilities. One of them is to observe, check, and report to the party leaders what is going on in firms and administrative agencies throughout the economy. A second task is to control appointments to administrative and managerial posts at all levels. A third is to mobilize and exhort the labor force to greater efforts in service of the plan. In addition to these specific responsibilities, local party officials take part in many kinds of managerial decision making at the enterprise level.

Enterprise Status

The operation of individual Soviet firms is governed by a so-called technical-industrial-financial plan. This plan, which is issued annually, is broken down into quarterly and monthly segments. Its most important component is the production plan, which states how much output is to be produced, what assortment of products is to be included, and when the output is to be delivered. Other parts of the plan set forth the quantities of labor and material inputs allotted to individual firms. A financial section sets targets for costs, wage bills, profits, use of short-term credit, and so on. In all, the plan may contain two dozen or more physical and financial targets that a particular firm must meet.

The plan is binding on the firm's management. In principle, criminal penalties can be imposed for failure to fulfill the plan, although administrative penalties, such as demotion or transfer to less desirable jobs, are more common. Positive incentives are also provided. Large bonuses are given to managers who fulfill or exceed the various parts of their plans.

Planning Procedures

The heart of the planning process is a set of material balances—summaries of the sources and uses of 200 to 300 of the most important industrial commodities—drawn up by Gosplan. The purpose of each balance is to insure that the sources (supply) and uses (demands) for each good are equal and that there will be no shortages or surpluses.

In simplified form, the process by which material balances are drawn up works something like this. As soon as Gosplan receives directives from the political authorities telling them the general rate of projected development and the most important priorities, work begins on a preliminary set of balances called "control figures." These figures show roughly how much of each good must be produced and how much must be used in each sector of the economy if the overall goals are to be met. The next step is to pass the control figures down through the planning hierarchy, where the main balances are broken down into requirements first for each region of the country and then for each firm.

When managers receive these control figures, they are supposed to suggest ways in which they can increase output or reduce inputs in order to achieve more ambitious goals. They also have a chance to complain if they think the plans exceed their output capacity or provide insufficient inputs. These responses to the control figures are sent back up through the hierarchy to Gosplan.

When the control figures are corrected on the basis of information collected from below, it is likely that the sources and uses of materials will no longer balance. The people who are in charge of carrying out the plans often will have tried to make their jobs easier by asking for reduced output targets or increased supplies of inputs. What follows is a complex process of adjustment and bargaining in which Gosplan tries to avoid material shortages without giving up overall targets. In some cases, shortages may be covered by imports or drawing down inventories. More commonly, Gosplan responds by tightening the plan—putting pressure on producers to do more with less. If the tightening process goes too far, the result will be a balance on paper only. The plan will contain concealed shortages that will emerge as it is being carried out.

The final balances are then broken down again. In addition to the crucial 200 to 300 materials that are subject to central balancing, individual ministries or regional authorities will have prepared balances on thousands of other, less important goods. When combined, these material balances become the technical-industrial-financial plans for all firms throughout the economy. This is a time-consuming process; often the final plans are not completed until the planned year is several weeks or even months underway.

Labor Planning

The planning process for one key resource needs special treatment. Allocating labor is partly a matter of how goods are to be produced and partly one of who is to do a given job. Indirectly, the decisions made on the "hows" and "whos" also affect the distribution of income.

Roughly speaking, the "how" is decided by central planners. Gosplan draws up labor balances for various kinds of work in much the same way that it establishes material balances. Basic policy on how much labor each firm is to use to meet its goals is set forth in the technical-industrial-financial plan.

The "who" of labor allocation, in contrast, is handled largely by markets. For the most part, workers are free to choose their occupation and place of work. The authorities use two methods to insure that the right number of workers is available in each sector of the economy. One is to offer large wage differentials, with premiums paid for skilled work or for work that is unattractive. The other is to influence the labor supply through education and training programs.

Individual firms exercise some control over the wages they pay. They do this both by adding bonus payments to standard wages and by deciding to which skill bracket to assign a particular worker. The overall result is a system in which variations in wages are used to insure a balance between the supply of and demand for labor. This is the most important example of the use of the market to allocate resources in the Soviet economy.

Informal Structure

The formal structure of the Soviet economy exactly fits the model of centralized socialism. Communications follow vertical paths up and down the planning hierarchy. The messages passed to enterprise managers have the force of law. Managers are rewarded or punished on the basis of the extent to which they obey the plan. Only the method of assigning particular workers to specific jobs is a major exception.

A close study of the informal structure of the Soviet economy, however, shows that central control is not absolute. A good deal of informal "horizontal" communication and exchange has always occurred among firms. Plans are not always treated as binding; sometimes they are handled as only one among a number of factors that influence managers' actions—and for a Soviet manager, the attainment of a comfortable and prosperous life is not merely a matter of obeying commands to the letter.

The Safety Factor

Soviet managers do not simply wait for plans to arrive from above and then do the best they can to fulfill them. Instead, they put a great deal of effort into insuring that they have a safety factor that will cushion them against the danger of being assigned impossible goals and then being punished for failing to achieve them.

Safety factors often take the form of large inventories of inputs or semifinished products. Inventories have always been a problem in the Soviet Union. Sometimes, when there are shortages, inventories get so low that any break in deliveries disrupts production. At other times, when a firm manages to get its hands on more of some essential material than it needs, it hoards the extra supply to guard against future shortages.

A somewhat different safety factor takes the form of concealed productive capacity. By hiding their firm's true capacity, managers hope to get an easy plan. For example, when provisional control figures come down to some textile mill, they call for an output of, say, 100,000 yards of fabric in the next year. The manager knows that this is just about all the mill can squeeze out given the inputs the control figures say will be available. However, it does not pay to let Gosplan know that. Instead, the manager complains that it will be impossible to produce more than 90,000 yards unless the labor force is increased and the firm is given a bigger allotment of synthetic yarn. The easy 90,000-yard plan provides the needed safety factor. The target will be met even if something goes wrong during the year.

Of course, the people in Gosplan know that managers always try to develop some kind of safety factor. They act on that knowledge when they are juggling their material balances to make them come out even. They do not hesitate to tighten up the plan even when they are told that it cannot be done. The whole thing develops into a type of game, which greatly increases the degree of uncertainty involved in the planning process.

Procurement

According to the formal structure of the Soviet economic system, managers of individual firms are not responsible for procuring their own raw materials, energy supplies, equipment, or other inputs. As part of the plan, each user of, say, copper tubing is given a schedule of expected deliveries. At the same time, some supplier is given a schedule of deliveries to make. In principle, the user and supplier need not even communicate with each other. The required plans are all supposed to be set up on the basis of information passed along to higher authorities.

In practice, however, managers who just wait for carloads of copper tubing to roll up to their factory gates are likely to be in trouble. Instead, they must be concerned about the possibility that their assigned supplies are behind the schedule stated in their production plans or that the suppliers are trying to tuck away a hoard of tubing as a safeguard against future demand. Managers use various means to deal with such problems. Among other things, they keep on their payrolls people who are known as "pushers." The pusher's job is to wine, dine, and wheedle suppliers in much the same way that the salespeople of a capitalist firm go after potential buyers. Of course, technical-industrial-financial plans do not allow for funds with which to hire pushers. These people must be worked in under a title such as "consulting engineer."

Sometimes all pushers have to do to get supplies moving on time is twist a few arms. Other times they may have to pay bribes. On still other occasions they may have to work out a barter deal in which one firm will come up with a hoarded carload of copper tubing in exchange for a sorely needed crate of ball bearings. All in all, the telephone lines are always busy, despite the fact that such activities are not supposed to be necessary in a centrally planned economy.

Selective Fulfillment

The plan sets not one but many targets for each enterprise. There are targets for total production, assortment of production, cost reduction, technological improvements, and many other things. Sometimes the end result of setting so many different targets is to give managers more rather than less freedom. This happens when it becomes impossible to fulfill all targets at once and managers must decide which part of the plan is most important.

The Second Economy

Up to this point, we have confined our attention to "informal" activities of officially recognized Soviet enterprises. In addition, there exists in the Soviet Union a large underground economy, called a *second economy*. This economy consists of illegal, unrecognized firms. Some of these are very small, for example, back-alley automobile repair shops. Some are remarkably large, including building contractors and consumer goods factories. Some Soviet enterprises produce for both the official economy and the second economy, using the same production equipment and work force but buying and selling through separate channels. Professionals such as doctors and dentists also may do business in both the official sector and the second economy.

Firms engaged in the second economy do not simply skirt the law as do, say, the informal procurement activities of official firms; rather, the second economy operates entirely outside the law. In fact, much of the knowledge about the informal economy comes from reports of legal proceedings against "speculators" and other economic criminals. Convictions sometimes bring the death penalty. Nonetheless, demand for the quality goods and services produced by the second economy is strong enough to induce underground entrepreneurs to take great risks and to allow them to earn substantial profits. A considerable portion of those profits is devoted to bribing local officials to look the other way. One hope of reformers is to bring the productive energies of the second economy into the light of day and, in the process, put an end to the widespread official corruption that it has fostered in the past.

Performance of the Soviet Economy

With this brief summary of Soviet economic structure as background, we turn to the question of the system's performance. Soviet leaders—and Soviet citizens as well—are proud of the fact that within a lifetime their country has been transformed from an economic backwater into one of the world's largest industrial economies. In 1917, Russia was on a level with today's less developed countries. It had only a small industrial sector set against a backdrop of vast rural poverty. Today Soviet living standards are modest compared with those in Western countries, but they are much higher than they once were. Exhibit 21.1 provides some international comparisons.

However, since the mid-1960s Soviet economic growth has slowed down. The decline is evident in both Soviet and Western growth rate estimates, as Exhibit 21.2 shows. By the early 1980s, Soviet leaders were faced with the likelihood that their economy would grow more slowly than that of the United States for a long period. This prospect has strengthened the hand of central-

Exhibit 21.1   Consumption Levels in the Soviet
Union and Selected Other Countries

This table shows consumption levels in the Soviet Union and a number of other countries. In each case, the U.S. consumption level is equal to 100. By these measures, the Soviet standard of living approaches that of Italy and Japan in some respects but remains short of the United States' in all categories.

	USSR 1976	Hungary 1973	Italy 1973	Japan 1973	West Germany 1973	United Kingdom 1973	France 1973
Total consumption	42.8	49.5	54.0	56.8	68.1	68.6	73.7
Food, beverages, tobacco	58.2	75.2	72.1	65.9	77.4	81.1	113.2
Clothing and footwear	55.9	41.2	50.8	55.2	71.7	66.3	55.3
Gross rent and fuel	17.6	27.7	40.2	36.6	59.3	56.2	65.4
Household furnishings and operations	29.7	33.8	33.7	52.8	94.6	51.3	63.2
Medical care	60.1	79.7	92.3	119.6	104.5	82.4	111.1
Transport and communications	19.4	17.9	32.5	18.4	38.4	50.4	40.8
Recreation	40.4	76.5	44.5	31.2	76.9	97.7	83.3
Education	96.7	66.9	63.0	67.6	64.6	83.7	58.7

Source: Abram Bergson and Herbert S. Levine, eds., *The Soviet Economy: Toward the Year 2000* (London: Allen & Unwin, 1983), Table 10.4.

Exhibit 21.2   Slowing Soviet Economic Growth

Soviet measures of economic output and growth differ from those used in the West, but Soviet and Western estimates agree that growth has slowed. This table shows one Soviet measure of growth of "national income produced" and one set of Western estimates, the Soviet GNP statistics as calculated by the U.S. Central Intelligence Agency. In the 1980s, for the first time, Soviet leaders face the prospect that their economy may grow more slowly than that of the United States over a prolonged period.

Period	Growth of Soviet National Income Produced (Percent per Year) (Official Data)	Growth of Soviet GNP (Percent per Year) (CIA)
1966–1970	7.7	5.2
1971–1975	5.7	3.7
1976–1980	4.3	2.7
1981–1984	3.6	2.7

Source: Courtesy of Abram Bergson.

planning critics within the Soviet Union and lies behind the current reform movement.

To see what has happened, let's look first at the sources of earlier Soviet growth and then at reasons for the slowdown.

Sources of Earlier Growth

In the past, the major source of rapid economic growth in the Soviet Union was the ability of the centrally planned economy to mobilize vast new supplies of factor inputs. In the decades just before and after World War II, the number of labor hours employed in the Soviet economy increased at a rate of 2.2 percent per year compared to only .5 percent annually in the United States. Even more impressive is the fact that the Soviet capital stock grew at a rate of 7.4 percent per year compared with just 1 percent per year in the U.S. economy. These very rapid growth rates of factor supplies more than made up for the lower efficiency of factor use in the Soviet system. The type of growth experienced by the Soviet Union, which is based mainly on expansion of inputs, is often called **extensive growth.** The type of growth experienced by the United States, which is based on better use of inputs, is called **intensive growth.**

As another comparison, in the 1950-to-1970 period, increased factor inputs accounted for almost four percentage points of Soviet economic growth while increased factor productivity accounted for the rest. In contrast, increased factor inputs are estimated to have contributed only about 1.6 percentage points to the growth of U.S. output over this period.[1]

Extensive growth is just as effective as intensive growth in adding to the economic power and prestige of a nation as a political unit, but it has some drawbacks for consumers. For example, in order to achieve a given growth rate, a much larger share of GNP has had to be shifted from consumption to investment in the Soviet Union than in the United States—something like 35 percent compared with about 15 percent. As a result, Soviet consumption per capita is only about one-third of that of the United States, even though GNP per capita is nearly half. It is also worth noting that Japan, one of the few noncommunist countries to invest as high a fraction of GNP as the Soviet Union, grew about twice as rapidly during the post–World War II period. The Japanese experience

Extensive growth
Growth that is based mainly on the use of increasing quantities of factor inputs.

Intensive growth
Growth that is based mainly on improvements in the quality of factor inputs and in the efficiency with which they are used.

---

[1] Data for the Soviet Union are from Abram Bergson and Herbert S. Levine, eds., *The Soviet Economy: Toward the Year 2000* (London: Allen & Unwin, 1983), Table 2.1. For the U.S. estimate, see Edward F. Denison, *Accounting for Slower Economic Growth* (Washington, D.C.: The Brookings Institution, 1979), Table 8.1.

shows what can be achieved when rapid growth of inputs is combined with high efficiency of factor use rather than used as a substitute for efficiency.

Explaining the Slowdown

As we have seen, Soviet economic growth slowed markedly during the 1970s. In 1979, as a result of a bad harvest, the growth rate fell to an estimated record low of .7 percent. Not only grain output but also per capita meat and milk consumption fell. However, farming was not the only problem. Industrial output, in which the Soviet Union had been a leader, grew less than 3 percent in the late 1970s. Actual declines in output were reported in such sectors as ferrous metals and cement.

The decline in Soviet growth reflects both slower growth of factor input and a slowdown in productivity. In the energy sector, the growth of investment is falling just as a shift to Siberian sources is making energy production much more capital intensive. The labor force is not expected to grow at all in the 1980s; the number of people reaching the age of 16 will barely balance a rising retirement rate. Also, population growth has been most rapid in Soviet Central Asia, the least industrialized region. In the European Soviet Union, the labor force is likely to shrink. In principle, declines in investment and the labor force could be offset by rising productivity. But when adjusted to reflect the increase in average education of the labor force, the rate of productivity growth in the Soviet Union is estimated by Western economists to have been negative in the 1970s.

Pricing and Industrial Efficiency

All of this points to a glaring lack of efficiency. Western estimates indicate that the Soviet economy gets only about half as much output per unit of input as the U.S. economy. The problem is acknowledged by Soviet economists as well, who see proper diagnosis of the sources of inefficiency as the key to designing successful reform. With regard to the industrial sector of the economy, Western and Soviet economists agree that a major source of inefficiency is the lack of a price system capable of communicating information about opportunity costs to the economy's decision makers.

Consider two functions that are performed by the price system in a capitalist economy. The first is an accounting function: Prices make it possible to add apples and oranges and come up with a total expressed in dollars' worth of fruit. The second is an allocative function: Input prices measure the opportunity cost of doing a certain thing or doing it in a particular way, and output prices measure the value of doing it.

In the Soviet economy, the price system performs the first function but not the second. Industrial and consumer goods are all given prices such that industrial accountants can turn in reports on the number of rubles' worth of output produced. The prices, however, have little to do with opportunity cost. In principle, prices are supposed to cover the accounting costs of production, but they reflect average cost rather than marginal cost concepts and typically make insufficient allowance for the opportunity cost of capital. In practice, many Soviet prices do not even cover accounting costs, necessitating huge subsidies to many enterprises.

Without knowledge of opportunity costs as reflected in a price system, Soviet planners often have trouble deciding what to produce and how to produce

APPLYING ECONOMIC IDEAS 21.1

The Great Dieselization Blunder

During the 1950s, Soviet planners were faced with a classic problem in resource allocation: how to decide what proportion of truck and tractor engines should be diesel powered and what proportion gasoline powered. The final decision was in favor of massive dieselization. It is revealing to look at the factors that influenced this major decision.

First, from a strict engineering point of view, diesels seemed attractive. They offered higher mechanical efficiency and in many ways were more technically sophisticated than gasoline engines. Second, the price of diesel fuel in the Soviet economy was low relative to that of gasoline—about 30 rubles a ton for diesel fuel versus 60 to 100 rubles for gasoline in the late 1950s. Finally, a study of Western experience showed large-scale dieselization of transportation equipment and heavy tractors.

Far from being a wise piece of economic calculation, however, the dieselization program turned out to be a great blunder. For one thing, diesels have higher initial costs. In part, then, the diesel-versus-gasoline decision is a matter of capital budgeting, in which higher initial costs must be balanced against discounted future gains. One defect in the Soviet price system is that the discount rate used by planners in such decisions is too low. Because the discount rate is, in effect, the "price" of future gains in terms of present

costs, there is a bias in favor of techniques with high initial costs. This no doubt played a part in the dieselization blunder.

Moreover, there is evidence that the official Soviet price for diesel oil was too low compared to that of gasoline in the 1950s. Thus, the price greatly underestimated the opportunity cost of using the heavier fuel. (In the United States, the refinery price of diesel fuel is not much lower than that of gasoline.)

Finally, the program failed to take into account the conditions prevailing in the Soviet economy. The kinds of crude oil available in the Soviet Union are less suitable for making diesel fuel than those available in the United States. In order to provide fuel for all the new diesel engines, refineries were given plans that they could fulfill only by letting the quality of diesel fuel decline. The oil they used to make diesel fuel should have been made into kerosene or furnace oil. Even worse, they allowed the sulfur content of diesel fuel to rise; as a result, cylinders and pistons wore out more quickly. Under these conditions, the operating cost of diesel engines turned out to be higher instead of lower than that of gasoline engines.

In the 1960s, planners realized their mistake. They reversed their decision and began a program of de-dieselization. Perhaps the correct ratio of the two kinds of engines has now been reached. If so, the discovery was made as a result not of rational economic calculation but of an expensive process of trial and error.

Source: Based on Robert W. Campbell, *The Economics of Soviet Oil and Gas*, Resources for the Future Series (Baltimore: Johns Hopkins University Press, 1968), 164–167.

it—in fact, it is impossible for them to make accurate calculations. Instead, they can use one of three methods of deciding the what and how of resource allocation. First, they can give up calculations in terms of prices and use rough rules of thumb based on engineering factors. Second, they can do profit-and-loss calculations in terms of their own imperfect prices, even though the answers will be only approximate. Third, they can imitate Western practices. As "Applying Economic Ideas 21.1" shows, however, none of these methods is foolproof.

Soviet Agriculture and Individual Incentives

Even in the heyday of Soviet industrial growth, agriculture was a serious trouble spot. While Soviet industry grew at a rate of 6.5 percent per year in the first half of the 1970s, agriculture crept ahead at only 2 percent. In 1961, then Premier Nikita Khrushchev set a target of 302 million tons of grain for 1980. In 1975, with three-quarters of Khrushchev's allotted time elapsed, output was a mere 140 million tons. That was an especially bad year, to be sure, but even the best recent years have fallen well short of the earlier goal.

The roots of Soviet agricultural problems date from the earliest days of collectivization. In the Stalin era, agriculture was a cow to be milked for the benefit of industrial development. Now that it has become a serious constraint on industrial development, it is proving difficult to reverse the effects of decades of neglect.

The heart of the Soviet agricultural system is the collective farm, or *kolkhoz*. On paper, the kolkhoz is a cooperative that is run by its members. In practice, however, the kolkhoz is part of the system of central planning. The Communist party controls the selection of collective farm managers and guides their decisions. In addition, the kolkhoz, like the industrial enterprise, is subject to a plan that sets forth inputs, outputs, production methods, capital investment projects, and countless other details.

In the 1930s, the entire structure of Soviet agriculture was aimed at a single goal: moving grain from the farm to the city. To that end, delivery targets for the kolkhoz were set not at a percentage of output but at a fixed rate per acre sown. If bad weather brought yields down, the collective farmers bore the entire burden of the shortfall. Although this might have seemed to create a strong incentive for the collective to work hard in order to avoid shortfalls, the effect was blunted by a complex and inefficient system of distributing collective income among kolkhoz members. The system left them with few incentives to contribute to the common effort.

In the Brezhnev era, from the early 1960s to the early 1980s, agricultural investment rose from less than one-sixth of total investment to almost one-third. However, without basic reform of the incentive structure of the kolkhoz, much of the investment was wasted. For example, from 1976 through 1980 agriculture received 1.8 million tractors, but the stock of tractors at work on farms rose by only 246,000. Many of the rest sat idle for lack of spare parts and maintenance.

Today the Soviet farm sector remains a backwater, with one exception: the tiny private plots on which collective farmers produce the bulk of the nation's fresh produce and much of its meat and eggs. The contrast between the stagnation of the collective farm sector and the productivity of the private plots attests to the importance of incentives—a lesson of which Soviet economists are well aware as they consider possible directions for reform.

Reforming the Soviet Economy

The Brezhnev era was a period of stagnation in economic affairs. While economists such as Abel Aganbegyan (see "Who Said It? Who Did It? 21.1") watched slowing growth rates from remote research institutes, the enterprise managers and government officials—the rent seekers of the Soviet system—enjoyed the privileges and stability. In 1985, after the short reigns of Yuri Andropov and Konstantin Chernenko, Mikhail Gorbachev came to power determined to make major strategic choices. In speech after speech, in demonstration projects, and, more recently, in laws and Central Committee resolutions, Gorbachev and his allies have pushed the cause of reform. At this writing, reform cannot yet be said to have taken hold of the Soviet economy. Many of the sweeping decrees await implementation. But certain directions that reform must take if it is to have any chance of success are clear.

WHO SAID IT? WHO DID IT? 21.1

The "New Economists" of the Soviet Union

When John Kennedy was inaugurated as president of the United States, many of the country's best and brightest "new economists" followed him to Washington. Somewhat the same thing seems to be happening in the Soviet Union of the 1980s, as that country's own "new economists" follow Communist party leader Mikhail Gorbachev to Moscow. Writing for The New York Times, *Philip Taubman provides the following sketch.*

Abel G. Aganbegyan, a key architect of Mikhail S. Gorbachev's audacious new economic program, likes to travel. "It's my passion," he said, reporting that he covers 150,000 miles a year crisscrossing the Soviet Union on Economic Missions.

His longest journey, however, was one that traversed not space but conventional thinking, bringing him to the forefront of Gorbachev's campaign of radical change to stimulate the lagging Soviet economy.

It was a 25-year journey that culminated in the adoption [in June 1987] by the Communist party's Central Committee of ideas that Aganbegyan began to espouse as an unorthodox young economist in Siberia in the early 1960s, when Nikita S. Khrushchev was the Soviet leader.

Along with a small band of like-minded economists and sociologists who challenged the tenets of Soviet ideology, Aganbegyan has seen his unconventional views supplant the established order. The Central Committee endorsed economic changes that would have been unthinkable three years ago, including a partial dismantling of centralized planning and subsidized prices, two cornerstones of the Soviet system that he has opposed.

Source: Philip Taubman, "Architect of Soviet Change," *The New York Times*, July 10, 1987. Copyright © 1987 by The New York Times Company. Reprinted by permission.

With Gorbachev as patron, Aganbegyan and his colleagues moved in the last two years into key government and academic positions, as advisers, spokesmen and an informal brain trust for the Soviet leader.

Aganbegyan, the group's dean, is 54. A portly figure of Armenian background, he has, since [1986], been secretary of the economics department of the Academy of Sciences, the elite Soviet school for fundamental research and general scientific leadership. His position there, in effect, makes him the country's senior economic thinker.

Soviet officials described him as Gorbachev's top economic adviser, the equivalent to being chairman of the White House's Council of Economic Advisers.

Other members of the brain trust include Leonid I. Abalkin, director of the Academy of Sciences' Institute of Economics, and Oleg T. Bogomolov, head of the Institute of Economics of the World Socialist System.

Another influential figure is Tatyana I. Zaslavskaya, an economic sociologist at the academy's Siberian branch in Novosibirsk. Although she holds no high Moscow post, she is highly regarded as an economist and writer and has helped promote in print the new economic views. . . .

When the Central Committee completed its work [on plans for economic reform], it was Aganbegyan who was selected to summarize the proceedings for Soviet and foreign reporters. . . . He described policies, now official party doctrine, that five or ten years ago were so far removed from the mainstream of Soviet economics they would have seemed almost heretical.

He talked about the need to cut agricultural subsidies and raise the price to produce more food. He spoke of increasing competition between enterprises to improve efficiency and quality, and of letting businesses that are failing go bankrupt.

And he remarked how the economy must eliminate central management so that market forces can be allowed to work. . . .

[Aganbegyan] clearly relishes his new role. In an interview [in 1986], he said, "Certainly there is a sense of satisfaction in seeing these ideas embraced by the leader of our country, although you shouldn't exaggerate my role."

Enterprise Independence

It is widely agreed that a major flaw in the classical Soviet system is the dependence of enterprise managers on central authorities for every detail of operations. Output, supply, investment, and choice of technology are all determined by the plan. In this stifling environment, the energy and ingenuity of individual managers have had little outlet save the task of outsmarting higher-ups in the planning hierarchy.

This reasoning lay behind experiments such as that at the Frunze complex early in the Gorbachev era. In 1987, the Supreme Soviet (the Soviet legislature) passed a law extending the reforms to industry at large. Key features of the law include the following:

- Planning is not to be ended, but in the future plans are to be confined to the most general targets. Local managers are to be able to choose production methods and negotiate contracts for supply and sale of goods within broad parameters.

- Enterprises are to become self-financing. They are to pay all costs, including those of investment, out of their revenues. If they make profits, they must be left free to determine their use within broad guidelines. If they lose money, they are to be allowed to go out of business.

- Work collectives are to be established in all enterprises within which workers will hold competitive elections to choose leaders and managers.

On paper, these reforms are certainly far reaching. There are potential problems, however. One difficulty is that in some cases the authorities who must implement the reforms are the same ones whose power and position have, in the past, rested on detailed control over local enterprises. The second problem, mentioned by manager Moskolenko in the case with which this chapter opens, is that many Soviet managers are ill trained in basic business skills. But economists tend to point to a third problem as the most serious one: the inadequacy of the Soviet price system.

Price Reform

As discussed earlier, Soviet prices do not reflect opportunity costs—not even approximately, in many cases. Left to make choices over inputs and outputs, then, Soviet managers could be expected routinely to make mistakes comparable to the "great dieselization blunder."

In addition, the irrationality of the current price system stands as a serious barrier to implementing the financial independence of enterprises. Some enterprises, such as the Frunze complex, were already profitable before they became independent simply because their high-priority output was assigned a high price. However, other enterprises produce outputs with unreasonably low prices and have required subsidies in order to stay afloat. The threat of actually cutting off the subsidies is not a credible one; yet if the subsidies continue, where is the incentive to improve performance?

Soviet economists are, of course, well aware of these problems. No less a figure than Valentin Pavlov, chairman of the Soviet state committee for prices, has spoken of the need to "overhaul the entire price system," hoping to replace it with one that will "establish a balance of supply and demand." However, price reform faces two daunting obstacles.

The first barrier is the relationship of price reform to enterprise independence. As we have seen, it is impossible to grant enterprises full independence without a reform of the price system. Yet at the same time, it is impossible to reform prices without independence of enterprises. It is one thing to know that the current set of prices fails to reflect opportunity costs and quite another to find the new, "correct" set of prices that does reflect these costs. The centrally planned economy does not provide would-be reformers with data on which to base calculations of such prices. The "correct" prices can emerge only through the interplay of supply and demand, a process of trial and error.

However, the "demand" for a good—copper tubing, diesel fuel, whatever—by a firm that is subject to strict planning targets and incentives tied to those goals has a different economic significance than the demand of an independent firm subject only to the incentive of profits. Under the profit motive, the manager balances the marginal contribution of each input against the marginal revenue earned from sale of the corresponding output. Under planning, the manager "demands" as much as possible of every input, hoping to build a safety factor that will permit plan fulfillment and knowing that cost overruns will be covered by subsidies. Thus, under central planning there always tends to be a shortage of all goods rather than a shifting pattern of shortages and surpluses that coaxes prices toward equilibrium values in a market economy.

The second obstacle to price reform is a political one and may well be even more serious. The political issue arises because reform of industrial prices cannot be isolated from that of consumer prices.

Consider that the average Soviet wage is slightly under 200 rubles a month, or about $310 at the official exchange rate. How can Soviet consumers survive on such low wages? The answer, in part, is massive subsidies to food prices, rents, utility rates, and other basics. These subsidies are not imposed just at the retail level; rather, they are built deep into the price structure, for example, through the sale of fertilizers and farm machinery below cost to collective farms. Even with the subsidies, however, the average Soviet household spends about 30 percent of its budget on food, compared to less than 20 percent in the United States. Raising food prices to the level of costs while simultaneously raising costs by removing subsidies to farm inputs could cause widespread unrest. In neighboring Poland, for example, proposed increases in food prices had to be canceled after a wave of protests, strikes, and riots.

Liberating Small-Scale Enterprise

The thorny problems of enterprise independence and price reform make it unlikely that economic reform of large-scale industry will yield quick returns. Plunging ahead means risking wrenching price adjustments, plant closings, and unemployment; moving cautiously means retaining many of the inefficiencies of central planning. But there is another area of economic reform in which quick returns are not out of the question: the liberation of small-scale enterprise in services, light industry, and, above all, agriculture.

This road to reform has been a hallmark of Chinese policy under the leadership of Deng Xiaoping (see "Perspective 21.1"). Soviet reformers, who closely watch the Chinese example, have made some moves in the same direction themselves.

In May 1987, the Soviet government issued a far-reaching law on "individual labor"—the favorite Soviet euphemism for small-scale capitalism. In effect, the law brings much of the second economy into the open. Workers in some 40 categories, ranging from repair workers and plumbers to hairdressers and fast-food cooks, will be able, under the law, to receive business licenses. In addition to individual or family businesses, which may not use hired labor, a new law governing cooperative enterprises was also issued. Early applicants for cooperative licenses included a dating service in Latvia, three publishing cooperatives in Moscow, and another cooperative in Moscow producing ballet shoes.

PERSPECTIVE   21.1

Reforming the Chinese Economy

After World War II, Mao Zedong led China into the camp of revolutionary communism. For an economic system, Mao turned to the obvious model: the Soviet Union. By the mid-1950s, most of the basic features of the Soviet economic system had been transplanted to China—state ownership, central planning, collectivized agriculture, and so on.

Today, in place of slogans like "Unlimited Loyalty to Mao Zedong Thought," a Chinese worker is likely to find something like "Time Is Money and Efficiency Is Life" posted on the factory wall.

Today's top Chinese leader, Deng Xiaoping, was hounded as a "capitalist roader" in the Mao era. The Red Brigades who pinned that label on him seem to have been right, for under Deng China has undertaken the most far-reaching reform of a Soviet-type economy ever attempted—and the outcome, at least in some respects, looks a lot like capitalism.

Deng's reforms started in the countryside, where four-fifths of China's 1 billion people live. Collectivization was largely scrapped, and villagers were given the right to produce what they wanted for whatever markets they could find. The result has been a steady rise in average income—an increase estimated at 66 percent between 1980 and 1985.

Small-scale trade and services were the next targets of reform. Chinese neighborhoods are now dotted with hole-in-the-wall noodle shops, repair shops, and other small businesses. Many of the proprietors were sent to hard labor in the countryside during the Mao era. Now, operating on profit margins of a few pennies per bowl of noodles, they can afford formerly undreamed-of luxuries such as television sets, motorcycles, and refrigerators.

Now Deng's reformers are tackling the biggest challenge of all: large-scale industry. Firms are to be cut loose from the planners' apron strings to find their own markets and supply sources. They are supposed to sink or swim on the basis of their managers' profit-making skills. Some of the newly liberated plants are working wonders. Entering into partnerships with foreign investors, they are turning out Honda motorcycles, Jeeps, and soft drinks for long waiting lists of eager buyers.

But the capitalist road is proving to be a bumpy one in some ways. The government has not yet come to grips with two big problems: prices and unemployment. Most industrial prices are still set by the state, often at levels that are far removed from opportunity costs. As a result, some firms that produce much-needed goods are starved for funds because their output is underpriced. Meanwhile, others grow rich turning out products that command high official prices but cannot be sold. Then there are factories whose plants are so obsolete and whose labor forces are so bloated that they have no hope of making a profit at any realistic price. The government has yet to face up to the problem of what to do with the oversupply of workers. Forced unemployment is still out of the question. Thus, there are cases in which workers show up every day and collect a day's pay even though their factories haven't received an order for months.

Recently China's economy has been growing at 8 percent per year. Deng aims to quadruple output by the year 2000. But China is still one of the poorest countries in the world, with a per capita income of under $400 a year. The capitalist road will not be short—but then, to borrow one of Mao's favorite slogans, "A Journey of a Thousand Miles Begins with a Single Step."

There is great interest in cooperative and individual enterprises, but some of these have faced official obstacles. For example, when it sought operating space, the ballet shoe cooperative was at first offered only basement quarters that the Ministry of Health refused to license.[2] Some observers expect the new undertakings to fare better in the Baltic states, Georgia, and Armenia, where there is an established entrepreneurial tradition, than in Russia, where traditions of collectivism are strong.

The potential for individual enterprise is perhaps greatest in farming. The long-established system of private plots, where 30 percent of the nation's meat,

---

[2] See Celestine Bohlen, "Soviets Get Right to Sell Services," *Washington Post*, May 1, 1987, A25.

milk, and eggs are produced on 4 percent of the land, provides a precedent. Now Gorbachev, who was the party official in charge of agriculture from 1978 to 1985, has called for expansion of the private plot system. In some areas, production on the private plots has declined as young people have moved to the city. One current idea is to lease the vacant plots to city dwellers for part-time farming.

A much more sweeping idea, though as yet not widely implemented, is family "contract farming." Under this system, contract farmers would lease land from a collective farm, receive wide latitude in shopping for supplies and equipment, and live on profits from crop sales. Such a scheme would resemble the system of long-term leases that has revitalized Chinese agriculture in recent years. However, anything remotely as radical as the Chinese system would face strong opposition in the Soviet Union as an ideological innovation.

Outlook

What, on balance, is the outlook for Soviet economic reform? Certainly much better at this writing than five years ago. By 1987, reform was beginning to move from rhetoric and isolated experiments to general application. However, major obstacles of both a technical and political nature remain.

The faults of the Soviet system have been obvious to Western economists—and, for that matter, to Soviet economists—for many years. Yet it must be recognized that from the viewpoint of Soviet leaders the system's virtues have by and large outweighed those faults. For all its inefficiencies, central control of the whole economy has made it possible to focus resources on key goals such as military power and the space program. No less important for political stability, the same central control has made it possible to reward loyal members of the party elite with access to special stores, hospitals, and resorts closed to the Soviet citizenry at large. Thus, even if the system is weak when measured in terms of technological progress and economic growth, this does not mean that it is bound to collapse. As long as forward momentum is maintained, there is no reason why the Soviet economy cannot exist forever in a state that is 5 years behind the West in technology and 20 years behind in living standards. A crisis—falling output rather than a mere slowdown, unemployment (currently unknown), or inflation (almost unknown)—might force more rapid change. Short of a crisis, the reform process seems certain to be a long one.

Summary

1. **What are the historical and ideological origins of the Soviet economic system?** The origins of the Soviet economic system are found first in Marxist-Leninist ideology and second in the experience of the first years of Soviet rule. After the 1917 revolution, an attempt to abolish the market economy all at once (war communism) was followed by a temporary restoration of the market (the New Economic Policy). The main features of what is now known as the Soviet-type economy—central planning plus collectivization of agriculture—were established around 1928. They were designed to achieve the government's goals of complete political control of the economy and rapid, industry-first economic growth. The combination of planning plus collectivization proved effective.

2. **What are the key features of the Soviet economy's formal and informal structures?** In its formal structure, the Soviet economy is a fully centralized hierarchy. Enterprises receive plans that specify inputs and outputs along with many other targets. These plans are legally binding on firms. In practice, managers of

Soviet firms have room to maneuver in fulfilling their plans. They bargain for safety factors, use initiative in procuring scarce inputs, and fulfill plans selectively. There is also a large underground sector, or "second economy," that produces both goods and services.

3. **What have been the chief accomplishments and failures of Soviet economic performance?** The greatest achievement of the Soviet economy has been rapid growth. However, that growth has slowed since the beginning of the 1970s. The need to switch from a strategy of *extensive growth* to one of *intensive growth* has focused attention on the inefficiencies of Soviet industry and agriculture. The shortcomings of the system can be traced in part to a lack of an adequate system of prices.

4. **What are the prospects for reform of the Soviet economic system?** Economic reform is a subject of wide discussion in the Soviet Union today, and some steps have been taken to implement reforms. Key features of reform efforts include greater independence for enterprises, price reform, and liberation of small-scale private enterprise in light industry, services, and agriculture. However, reform efforts still face major technical and political obstacles.

Terms for Review

- extensive growth
- intensive growth

Questions for Review

1. When did the main features of the Soviet economic system take shape? What was the New Economic Policy?

2. What is the balance between managerial coordination and market coordination in the formal structure of the Soviet economy? In its informal structure?

3. What is the difference between extensive and intensive growth? How does this difference bear on the slowdown in Soviet economic growth?

4. What are the shortcomings of the Soviet price system?

5. How are enterprise independence and price reform related?

6. What role might small-scale private enterprise play in the Soviet economy of the future?

Problems and Topics for Discussion

1. **Examining the lead-off case.** How does the example of the Frunze complex illustrate the importance of enterprise independence as an element of reform? What obstacles might be encountered in duplicating the success of this enterprise on a wide scale?

2. **Money in the Soviet economy.** During the period of war communism in the Soviet Union, some leaders proposed that money be abolished as part of the transition to a centralized economy. Money was restored during the NEP, however, and no further attempt was made to abolish it. Why does even a centrally planned economy find it hard to get along without money?

3. **Externalities and central planning.** In what ways do you think a centrally planned economy might be better equipped than a capitalist economy to deal with the problem of pollution? In what ways might it be less equipped?

4. **Soviet and Chinese reforms.** If you were a member of the Soviet leadership, what lessons could you learn from the Chinese economic reforms?

5. **Progress of Soviet reform.** As of this writing, the reform process in the Soviet Union is just beginning and its prospects are far from clear. Look through newspapers and magazines in your library for news of recent Soviet economic policies. Has the system traveled any of the paths of reform mentioned in this chapter? Discuss.

Case for Discussion
Nails, Carpenters, and Central Planning

In a small city in the Soviet Union, there was once a factory whose business was to produce nails for use in the construction trade. In a certain year, the plant was given the task of producing x tons of nails in a variety of sizes based on the needs of Soviet carpenters. Before the planned year was far underway, the factory manager realized that he could not achieve his target for total output if he kept to the planned assortment of sizes. Experience had taught him that the authorities were much more interested in the total output than in the size breakdown, so he

Soviet carpenters suffer as factory managers struggle to meet output targets.

Photo Source: © 1987 Phyllis Woloshin.

came up with a clever strategy: He gave up making little nails, which were a bother to produce and weighed hardly anything, and concentrated on enormous spikes. In that year, he turned out far more than x tons of output and was lavishly rewarded for surpassing his quota.

Naturally, the long-suffering Soviet carpenters complained. They had no way to fasten together anything smaller than two railroad ties. A smart planning official hit on a solution. When the plan was issued the following year, the total output target for the factory was stated not in tons but in number of nails. The reader can guess how the factory manager responded. He gave up entirely on huge spikes, which used up far too much hard-to-procure steel. Instead, he concentrated on producing the tiniest pins and brads, which used hardly any metal and counted millions to the ton.

Naturally, the long-suffering Soviet carpenters complained. . . .

Questions

1. How does this anecdote illustrate the informal exercise of enterprise independence under the classic Soviet central planning system?

2. Suppose that instead of being given a plan target, the manager of the nail factory in question was told to maximize his plant's profit. However, suppose too that the price of nails is set at the same number of rubles per ton, disregarding the fact that more worker-hours (and the same amount of steel) are required to make a ton of small nails than a ton of large ones. How does your answer to this question bear on the relationship between managerial independence and price reform?

3. Suppose you are chairman of the Soviet state committee for prices. What recommendation would you make regarding the best way to establish the "correct" relative prices for different sizes of nails?

Suggestions for Further Reading

Bergson, Abram, and Herbert S. Levine, eds. *The Soviet Economy: Toward the Year 2000*. London: Allen & Unwin, 1983.

Contains a series of papers by leading Western experts on the Soviet economy that discuss all aspects of the Soviet system.

Johnson, Gale, and Karen McConnell. *Prospects for Soviet Agriculture in the 1980s*. Bloomington, Ind.: Indiana University Press, 1985.

A comprehensive discussion of the problems of and prospects for Soviet agriculture.

U.S. Congress, Joint Economic Committee.

The Joint Economic Committee publishes many reports on the Soviet and other centrally planned economies.

Appendix
Careers in Economics*

The General Value of an Economics Degree

In describing the qualities essential to being a good economist, John Maynard Keynes, himself a master at the profession, remarked:

> He must study the present in the light of the past for the purpose of the future.
> No part of man's nature or his institutions must lie entirely outside his regard.[1]

As you begin the study of economics, you will quickly become aware of the breadth to which Keynes refers. There seem to be no limits to the reaches of economic inquiry. Your first exam may include a question that applies to today's newspaper headlines. At the same time, economics is very much a part of your everyday life. A discussion with a local merchant concerning the price of an item may lead you to conclude that an understanding of economics is a matter of common sense. However, economics is not a subject to be left to common sense alone, since what is "common sense" to one person may well be "nonsense" to another.

The trained economist is a valuable and respected member of many organizations, be they private businesses, public utilities, governments, or colleges and universities. The career opportunities open to an economist are limited only by the resourcefulness of employers and employees. The following two sections will show you how an economics major can prepare you for a wide variety of careers in economics and will also briefly comment on the employment outlook for economists between 1987 and 1995. Every effort has been made to provide you, the beginning economics student, with the latest information concerning career opportunities in economics. Major assistance was provided by the National As-

---

*This appendix was written by Keith D. Evans, chairman of the Department of Economics at California State University, Northridge. It was prepared with the cooperation of the National Association of Business Economists and the Society of Government Economists.

[1] John Maynard Keynes, *Essays in Biography*, ed. Geoffrey Keynes (New York: Norton, 1963).

sociation of Business Economists (NABE) through its secretary-treasurer, David L. Williams. In addition, the attitudes, opinions, and experiences of successful, currently employed business and government economists were solicited by means of a questionnaire sent to a significant number of randomly selected members of the NABE and the Society of Government Economists. (This will be referred to below as the *Dryden questionnaire* to distinguish it from the NABE publications used.)

Even if your career interests lie in other directions, the analytical training emphasized in an economics major generally can make you more adaptable to changing employment opportunities after graduation. As one member of the NABE puts it, "Some theoretical micro and macro concepts proved useful; however, more often than not my training in analyzing and researching subjects was used." Further, there are definite benefits in having a thorough understanding of how our private enterprise economy works and a basis for comparing it with centrally planned economies. Often people report that in their first career jobs they literally got lost in a maze—they had no sense of where they fit in and how their jobs pertained to a larger picture. A background in economics can ease that shock. The analytical training, with specific applications to real-life situations, makes it easier to come to grips with the events of the world around us.

One respondent to the Dryden questionnaire put it this way: "My work in economics prepared me well for career advancement and flexibility because of the emphasis my economics study placed on cause-and-effect relationships, on the link between incentives and resultant actions, all of which have helped me develop a rational and productive way of generating results-oriented thinking." Another replied that the most useful part of his training in economics was "flexibility, perspective, and ability to deal with intangibles and uncertainty." Still another successful career economist reflected on the importance of his economics degree as follows: "It taught me the ability to think and to reason."

You cannot possibly learn all you will need to know in four years of college; but in pursuing a degree in economics, you can learn how to think better. With that ability, your opportunities are immensely varied and exciting.

Career Opportunities Available to an Economics Major

It is not enough to tell yourself that you will study economics because in doing so you will learn how to think better and thinking better is essential to a career as an economist. Choosing a course of study in college is more likely to lead to a successful career if you discover which subjects interest you and in which you do well. Thus, it follows that if you enjoy and do well in courses in economics and business administration, you will very likely enjoy a career as an economist.

But what are your opportunities as an economics major? What type of work might you actually do as an economist? In general—and depending on the amount of education you ultimately receive—your future lies in one of three areas—working in one of a wide variety of positions in private business; serving in a local, state, or national government agency; and teaching economics at the college and university level. In fact, many economists combine their primary work in one of these fields with part-time work in another. It is not unusual for a business economist to teach part time or for a professor to also be a consultant to business or government.

Economics as an academic subject goes back more than 150 years. In practical terms, economists found that their theories increasingly influenced federal government decisions as the Depression of the 1930s occupied worldwide attention. It was not until after World War II, however, that private businesses began to realize the extent to which economic theory might be applied in solving business problems and formulating business policies. Despite this relatively late start, about 23,000 of the people identified as economists by the Bureau of Labor Statistics in 1984 work in private business.[2] They are employed by manufacturing firms, banks, insurance companies, securities and investment companies, economic research firms, management consulting firms, and others.

Business organizations that are large enough to warrant having their own economists employ them directly. Smaller firms hire the services of economic consultants as needed. Regardless of their size, all businesses are aware that government policies and subsequent actions have economic effects. A major function of the business economist, therefore, is to analyze and interpret government policies in light of their effects on the economy in general and the specific firm in particular.

According to the same 1984 Bureau of Labor Statistics report, another 15,000 economists are employed by government agencies, including a wide range of federal agencies. In addition, approximately 22,000 hold economics and marketing faculty positions at colleges and universities.

Certainly the primary function of the business economist is to apply economic theory to problems faced by the firm. This requires the ability to understand the economic implications of events taking place throughout the world; to project how those events might affect the firm; to prepare guidelines for decision makers in the organization; and to communicate concepts, principles, and conclusions in a clear, effective, and concise manner.

In a booklet entitled *Careers in Business Economics*, the National Association of Business Economists stresses that business economists follow no set patterns. The most successful, established economists have high job mobility because their ability to interpret national and international events in light of their economic impact on a particular sector of business makes them especially adaptable to changing business requirements.

Following are descriptions of the activities of several kinds of business economists based on *Careers in Business Economics*.

Bank Economist

> The primary function of our bank's economics department is to analyze how changes in economic and financial market conditions affect the banking business and to suggest—to the extent possible—appropriate strategies and policies to protect or enhance the bank's earnings. Obviously, this is an assignment of tall order and presents great challenges as well as opportunities.[3]

An essential analytical tool that the *bank economist* must develop is the macroeconomic forecast. Such a forecast forms the basis for anticipating changes in the bank's volume of business—primarily its loans and investments. Even more important for the bank economist is a firm grasp of the underlying forces that determine interest rates. Changes in interest rates directly affect the spread be-

[2] U.S. Department of Labor, Bureau of Labor Statistics, *Occupational Outlook Handbook*, 1986–1987 ed. (Washington, D.C.: Government Printing Office, April 1986), 102.

[3] National Association of Business Economists, *Careers in Business Economics* (Cleveland, Ohio, 1986), 10.

tween the yields the bank earns on its investments and the cost of acquiring investment funds. Hence, the profitability of a bank's operations hinges on correctly anticipating interest rate changes.

A bank also manages and invests money for customers through its trust department. Thus, the bank economist's expertise can be highly valuable, since sound investment strategies depend on expert judgment of economic and financial trends. In addition, the bank economist represents the bank in interviews with financial reporters and is likely to be quoted in newspapers and magazines. Further, the bank economist may write newsletters for the bank and make numerous presentations both within and outside. Hence, good communication skills are essential.

As you can see, the bank economist's job responsibilities are very important. The bank economist constantly interacts with high-level managers and is often a member of the senior management team.

Consulting Economist

The following quote from *Careers in Business Economics* indicates the nature of the duties performed by the *consulting economist:*

> Within our firm, we conduct research and advise clients of developments affecting financial institutions, trends in economic activity, and interest rates in money and capital markets—with special emphasis on the monetary policy of the Federal Reserve. The firm has carried out a number of assignments—including the preparation of estimates of the cost of capital for public utilities, assessments of the impact of alternative tax measures on the volume of investment, the impact of research and development expenditures on technology and innovation in American industry, the economic cost of restrictions on a range of imports, excise taxes and the demand for distilled spirits, monetary policy and the housing sector, and the economic benefits of lease financing.[4]

Like a bank economist, a consulting economist may also do macroeconomic forecasting. The results of research done by consulting economists are usually given to their clients as private reports. Some of the findings of economics consulting firms, however, are made public in the form of reports, congressional testimony, and publications in professional journals.

Industrial Economist

An *industrial economist* employed by a large, widely diversified manufacturing company writes:

> The most important part of my job is meeting with our management committee every month to discuss economic and political developments in the countries where we have operations, and the likely impact of such developments on our businesses. Preparation for these meetings involves maintaining contacts with a large number of economists, business analysts, and academic experts around the world. This means that I'm usually on an airplane about four out of every five weeks and am physically out of the office about 60 percent of the time.[5]

The industrial economist also does macroeconomic forecasting, but on an international level. It is common for industrial economists to participate in pre-

---

[4] Ibid., 13.
[5] Ibid., 17.

paring forecasts of their firms' operations for as much as 10 years in advance. Some industrial economists also engage in "structural analysis," which involves "the basic econometric analysis of the relationships among various businesses with a variety of external series as well as internal data, such as advertising expense, research and development programs, capital expenditures, and so on. The results are used to evaluate strategic plans of individual businesses, to determine the relative impacts of various external policy changes, and to determine strategies for improving profitability."[6]

Like the bank economist, the industrial economist usually represents his or her firm in interviews requested by the news media, might prepare a newsletter, and may make numerous presentations to groups outside the company.

Government Economist

The *government economist* may perform essentially the same tasks as business economists as far as forecasting the outcome of economic conditions is concerned. However, the emphasis may be on formulating policy rather than reacting to policy changes, since the government agency can be in a position to initiate economic changes. The government economist may be called upon to do research on major policy issues, draft speeches for legislators and government officials, and help determine the purpose and scope of congressional hearings.

Academic Economist

The *academic economist* concentrates on the understanding and improvement of economic theory. In teaching theory, he or she stresses how economies function and how a knowledge of economics applies to decision making by business and government as well as individuals. In addition, the academic economist may devote some time to research, writing, and consulting with business firms, government agencies, or private individuals.

Advice from Practicing Economists

The Dryden questionnaire asked members of the National Association of Business Economists and the Society of Government Economists to reflect on the value of their college education and to offer advice for people just beginning the study of economics. Of those whose major was economics, more than two-thirds from each group reported that their college studies had been very useful to them in their first full-time jobs. From the vantage point of their ultimate careers, more than half felt that their college education was useful in performing the duties of their present occupations. What courses did they feel had such lasting value? Both business and government economists most frequently mentioned courses in microeconomic and macroeconomic theory, econometrics (the application of statistical techniques to obtain quantitative estimates of relationships suggested by economic analysis), money and banking, forecasting, and international economics and courses that provided specific applications of economic theory to the decision-making process or to public policy.

---

[6]Ibid.

Respondents also emphasized the importance of courses involving economic and business applications of statistics and accounting, as well as the study of related business institutions, especially financial ones. Important too were courses on using and programming computers. Mathematics courses were emphasized as having been helpful. Along with the references to applied statistics, there was continual mention of such courses as analytical geometry, calculus, and linear algebra.

One necessary skill for an economist, whether academic, business, or government, cannot be overemphasized: the ability to make the results of one's work understandable to a wide range of people. To be useful, economic analyses and forecasts must be understood by those who make the decisions for the business or government agency involved. Therefore, an economist must be able to write and speak clearly and to state sophisticated economic ideas in a way that people with little economic knowledge can understand. Recognizing this need to make their work clear and usable for others, both government and business economists placed high value on courses that improved their written and oral communication skills.

The NABE advises potential business economists to strive to be generalists rather than specialists. Its *Careers in Business Economics* booklet recommends some familiarity with as many of the major fields of economics and business administration as possible. In addition to the areas mentioned by the Dryden questionnaire respondents, economics and business administration deal with economic and business history, national income and public finance, business cycles and government stabilization policies, corporate finance and industrial organization, marketing and consumer behavior, labor and collective bargaining, purchasing and personnel policies, and economic development and comparative economic systems.

Some respondents to the Dryden questionnaire had not majored in economics at the undergraduate level. Many of them said they had benefited from the broad-based liberal arts education they acquired before earning advanced degrees in economics or business. It was generally agreed, however, that any liberal arts major would be well advised, considering the current job market, to take courses in economics, accounting, statistics, and computer science.

Interestingly, in the last three to four years many major corporations have begun to look increasingly favorably on candidates who have earned an undergraduate liberal arts degree, especially if they have done well at universities that are held in high academic regard at least regionally, if not nationally. Such individuals, however, are expected to have taken relevant courses in economics and applied statistics, as well as business courses such as accounting fundamentals and principles of finance. Moreover, business and government recruiters have become increasingly insistent that students be exposed to a variety of "hands-on" computer applications, ideally including some programming. All of the fields of economics profiled earlier require extensive use of computers.

June Hillman, associate director of the Office of Career Planning and Placement at California State University, Northridge, summarized this recent change in attitude on the part of recruiters as follows: "Recruiters are tending to be attracted to the well-educated university graduate with some business-related courses and work experience rather than the specific, vocationally oriented majors. This continues to be a trend in recruiting criteria."[7]

For further support of the recent change in attitude by many recruiters

---

[7] Interview given September 30, 1987.

toward liberal arts graduates, refer to the references at the end of the *Study Guide* career section.

It should be added that the guidelines presented here must be taken in the spirit in which they have been given—as suggestions from practicing economists. When you are planning your particular course of study to fulfill the requirements of your college or university and to satisfy your unique interests, you cannot expect these guidelines to replace the need for personal faculty advisement.

How important is an advanced degree? For an academic economist, it is a must. A master's degree is the minimum qualification for teaching at the community college level, and a Ph.D. is required for most university teaching. Eighty percent of the government economists who responded to the Dryden questionnaire indicated that they consider an advanced degree very important, and 11 percent consider one moderately important. Of that number, 56 percent specified a Ph.D. while an additional 25 percent emphasized a master's degree. The business economists surveyed placed less importance on an advanced degree. Only 57 percent rated it as very important, and 25 percent considered it moderately important. Those responses were much more evenly distributed regarding which advanced degree is more important. Almost 30 percent favored the M.B.A., while another 30 percent suggested pursuing either an M.A. or an M.S. degree in economics or business administration. Only 35 percent considered a doctorate essential.

These differences undoubtedly reflect the attitudes of various employers in different businesses and government agencies. Again they are presented here as guidelines that can be one source of help to you as you make your own career decisions.

Employment Outlook for Economists, 1987–1995

Before launching into some "fearless forecasts" for the employment outlook for economists in the 1990s, *caveat emptor:* Let the buyer, whether of tangible goods or intangible ideas, beware. Keeping in mind this recognition that all forecasts are fallible, let's look at the current thought regarding the employment outlook for economists in the decade ahead.

The U.S. Department of Labor offers the following job outlook for economists:

> Employment of economists is expected to grow about as fast as the average for all occupations through the mid-1990's. Most job openings will result from the need to replace experienced economists who transfer to other occupations, retire, or leave the labor force for other reasons.
>
> Overall, economists are likely to have more favorable job prospects than most other social scientists. Opportunities should be best in manufacturing, financial services, advertising agencies, research organizations, and consulting firms, reflecting the complexity of the domestic and international economies and increased reliance on quantitative methods of analyzing business trends, forecasting sales, and planning purchasing and production. The continued need for economic analyses by lawyers, accountants, engineers, health service administrators, urban and regional planners, environmental scientists, and others will also increase the number of jobs for economists.[8]

---

[8] U.S. Department of Labor, *Occupational Outlook Handbook*, 103.

The U.S. Department of Labor projects little change in the employment of economists in the federal government. Average growth is expected in the employment of economists in state and local government.[9]

The National Association of Business Economists agrees that job prospects are by far the brightest for various types of business economists. Besides the reasons given in the above quoted passage, the NABE points out that more and more firms are becoming aware of the contribution that business economists can make in day-to-day decision making. This greater awareness is due partly to the growing number of middle and top managers who have master's degrees in business or similar training that equips them to understand and utilize the professional work of economists.[10]

> Finally, the career of business economics is increasingly recognized as one of the routes to top management. In recent years, business economists have become presidents or senior officers of banks, insurance companies, trade associations, investment houses, and industrial companies. Although not all business economists are capable or even desirous of advancing to a top management position, it is clear that economics is a business function of central importance and thus can be a pathway to the top.[11]

Because of the relative difficulty of obtaining satisfactory employment in an academic setting, many people who might otherwise have directed themselves toward a career in higher education are now accepting nonacademic jobs. That puts graduates with bachelor's degrees in a position of competing not only with others of similar academic background and level but also with candidates who have more advanced degrees. However, through the mid-1990s graduates with bachelor's degrees in economics should compete well if they have training in applied mathematics, statistics, and computer use.

These indicators are in harmony with the comments of several respondents to the Dryden questionnaire, who believe that the best preparation for many of today's careers in economics begins with an undergraduate degree in economics and continues with acquisition of an M.B.A.

---

[9] Ibid.

[10] National Association of Business Economists, *Careers in Business Economics*, 28.

[11] Ibid.

Dictionary of Economic Terms

Absolute advantage
The ability of a country to produce a good at a lower cost in terms of quantity of factor inputs than its trading partners.

Accounting profit
Total revenue minus explicit costs.

Antitrust laws
A set of laws, including the Sherman Act and the Clayton Act, that seek to control market structure and the competitive behavior of firms.

Arbitrage
The activity of earning a profit by buying something at a low price in one market and reselling it at a higher price in another.

Assets
All the things to which a firm or household holds legal claim.

Balance sheet
A financial statement showing a firm's or household's assets, liabilities, and net worth.

Barrier to entry
Any factor that prevents a new firm in a market from competing on an equal footing with existing ones.

Benefit reduction rate
The reduction in the benefits of a transfer program that results from a $1 increase in the beneficiary's earned income.

Bilateral monopoly
A market situation in which both the buyer and the seller have some monopoly or monopsony power and neither behaves as a price taker.

Bond
A promise, given in return for borrowed funds, to make a fixed annual or semiannual payment over a set number of years plus a larger final payment equal to the amount borrowed.

Budget line
A line showing the various combinations of goods and services that can be purchased at given prices within a given budget.

Capital
All means of production that are created by people, including tools, industrial equipment, and structures.

Capitalism
An economic system in which control of business firms rests with the owners of capital.

Capitalized value of a rent
The sum that would earn annual interest equal to the annual rent if it were invested at the current market rate of interest.

Cartel
A group of producers that jointly maximize profits by fixing prices and limiting output.

Change in demand
A change in the quantity of a good that buyers are willing and able to purchase that results from a change in some condition other than the price of that good; a shift in the demand curve.

Change in quantity demanded
A change in the quantity of a good that buyers are willing and able to purchase that results from a change in the good's price, other things being equal; a movement from one point to another along a demand curve.

Change in quantity supplied
A change in the quantity of a good that producers are willing and able to sell that results from a change in the good's price, other things being equal; a movement along a supply curve.

Change in supply
A change in the quantity of a good that producers are willing and able to sell that results from a change in some condition other than the good's price; a shift in the supply curve.

Common property
Property to which all members of a community have open access.

Common stock
A certificate of part ownership in a corporation that gives the owner a vote in the selection of the firm's directors and the right to a share of dividends, if any.

Comparative advantage
The ability to produce a good or service at a lower opportunity cost than another person or country.

Complements
A pair of goods for which an increase in the price of one results in a decrease in demand for the other.

Concentration ratio
The percentage of all sales that is accounted for by the four or eight largest firms in a market.

Conditional forecast
A prediction of future economic events, usually stated in the form "If A, then B, other things being equal."

Conglomerate merger
A merger between firms in unrelated markets.

Constant returns to scale
A situation in which there are neither economies nor diseconomies of scale.

Consumer equilibrium
A state of affairs in which a consumer cannot increase the total utility gained from a given budget by spending less on one good and more on another.

Consumer sovereignty
A system under which consumers determine which goods and services will be produced by means of what they decide to buy or not to buy.

Consumer surplus
The difference between the maximum that a consumer would be willing to pay for a unit of a good and the amount that he or she actually pays.

Contestable market
A market in which barriers to entry and exit are low.

Corporation
A firm that takes the form of an independent legal entity with ownership divided into equal shares and each owner's liability limited to his or her investment in the firm.

Craft union
A union of skilled workers who all practice the same trade.

Cross-elasticity of demand
The ratio of the percentage change in the demand for a good to a given percentage change in the price of some other good, other things being equal.

Cross-subsidization
The practice of setting prices that cover total costs on the average by charging some customers more than the cost of their services while charging other customers less than that cost.

Deadweight loss
A loss of consumer or producer surplus that is not balanced by a gain to someone else.

Demand curve
A graphic representation of the relationship between the price of a good and the quantity of it that buyers demand.

Direct financing
The process of raising investment funds directly from savers.

Discounting
The procedure by which the present value of a sum payable in the future is calculated.

Diseconomies of scale
A situation in which long-run average cost increases as output increases.

Dynamic efficiency
The ability of an economy to increase consumer satisfaction through growth and innovation.

Economic efficiency
A state of affairs in which it is not possible, by changing the pattern of either distribution or production, to satisfy one person's wants more fully without causing some other person's wants to be satisfied less fully.

Economic planning
Systematic government intervention in the economy with the goal of improving coordination, efficiency, and growth.

Economic rent
Any payment to a factor of production in excess of its opportunity costs.

Economics
The study of the choices people make and the actions they take in order to make the best use of scarce resources in meeting their wants.

Economies of scale
A situation in which long-run average cost decreases as output increases.

Efficiency in distribution
A situation in which it is not possible, by redistributing existing supplies of goods and services, to satisfy one person's wants more fully without causing some other person's wants to be satisfied less fully.

Efficiency in production
A situation in which it is not possible, given available technology and factors of production, to produce more of one good or service without forgoing the opportunity to produce some of another good or service.

Efficiency wage theory
The theory that wages higher than the minimum necessary to attract qualified workers can raise productivity and hence increase profit.

Elastic demand
A situation in which quantity demanded changes by a larger percentage than price and total revenue therefore increases as price decreases.

Elasticity
A measure of the responsiveness of quantity demanded or supplied to changes in the price of a good or in other economic conditions.

Entrepreneurship
The process of looking for new possibilities—making use of new ways of doing things, being alert to new opportunities, and overcoming old limits.

Equilibrium
A condition in which buyers' and sellers' plans exactly mesh in the marketplace so that the quantity supplied exactly equals the quantity demanded at a given price.

Excess burden of a tax
The part of the economic burden of a tax that takes the form of consumer surplus and producer that is lost because the tax reduces the equilibrium quantity sold.

Excess quantity demanded (shortage)
A condition in which the quantity of a good demanded at a given price exceeds the quantity supplied.

Excess quantity supplied (surplus)
A condition in which the quantity of a good supplied at a given price exceeds the quantity demanded.

Explicit costs
Opportunity costs that take the form of payments to outside suppliers, workers, and others who do not share in the firm's ownership.

Extensive growth
Growth that is based mainly on the use of increasing quantities of factor inputs.

Externality
An effect of producing or consuming a good whose impact on third parties other than buyers and sellers of the good is not reflected in prices.

Factor markets
The markets in which the factors of production—labor, capital, and natural resources—are bought and sold.

Factors of production
The basic inputs of labor, capital, and natural resources used in producing all goods and services.

Financial intermediaries
Financial firms, including banks, savings and loan associations, insurance companies, pension funds, and mutual funds, that gather funds from net savers and provide funds to net borrowers.

Financial markets
Markets through which borrowers obtain funds from savers.

Fixed inputs
Inputs that cannot be easily increased or decreased in a short time.

Goods
All things that people value.

Government purchases
See Government purchases of goods and services.

Government purchases of goods and services
Purchases of finished goods by government plus the cost of hiring the services of government employees and contractors.

Gross national product (GNP)
A measure of the economy's total output of goods and services.

Herfindahl index
An index of market concentration that is calculated by squaring the percentage market shares of all firms in an industry and summing the squares.

Horizontal merger
A merger between firms that compete in the same market.

Human capital
Capital in the form of learned abilities that have been acquired through formal training or education or through on-the-job experience.

Implicit costs
Opportunity costs of using resources owned by the firm or contributed by its owners.

Import quota
A limit on the quantity of a good that can be imported over a given period.

Income effect
The part of the change in quantity demanded of a good whose price has fallen that is caused by the increase in real income resulting from the price change.

Income elasticity of demand
The ratio of the percentage change in the demand for a good to a given percentage change in consumer income, other things being equal.

Indifference curve
A graphic representation of an indifference set.

Indifference map
A selection of indifference curves for a single consumer and pair of goods.

Indifference set
A set of consumption choices of which each yields the same utility so that no member of the set is preferred to any other.

Indirect financing
The process of raising investment funds via financial intermediaries.

Industrial union
A union of all the workers in an industry, including both skilled and unskilled workers in all trades.

Inelastic demand
A situation in which quantity demanded changes by a smaller percentage than price and total revenue therefore decreases as price decreases.

Inferior good
A good for which an increase in consumer income results in a decrease in demand.

Inflation
A sustained increase in the average prices of all goods and services.

In-kind transfers
Transfer payments made in the form of goods or services, such as food, housing, or medical care, rather than in cash.

Intensive growth
Growth that is based mainly on improvements in the quality of factor inputs and in the efficiency with which they are used.

Inventory
Stocks of a finished good awaiting sale or use.

Investment
The act of increasing the economy's stock of capital, that is, its stock of means of production made by people.

Isoquant
See Isoquantity line.

Isoquantity line
A line showing the different

combinations of variable inputs that can be used to produce a given amount of output.

Labor
The contributions to production made by people working with their minds and muscles.

Law of demand
The principle that, other things being equal, the quantity of a good demanded by buyers tends to rise as the price of the good falls and to fall as its price rises.

Law of diminishing returns
The principle that as one variable input is increased with all others remaining fixed, a point will be reached beyond which the marginal physical product of the variable input will begin to decrease.

Liabilities
All the legal claims against a firm by nonowners or against a household by nonmembers.

Limit pricing
The practice by the dominant firm in a market of charging less than the short-run profit-maximizing price in order to limit the likelihood of new competitors' entry.

Logrolling
The practice of trading votes among members of a legislative body.

Long run
A time horizon that is long enough to permit changes in both fixed and variable inputs.

Lorenz curve
A graphic representation of the degree of inequality in an economy.

Macroeconomics
The branch of economics that deals with large-scale economic phenomena, particularly inflation, unemployment, and economic growth.

Managerial coordination
A means of coordinating economic activity that uses directives from managers to subordinates.

Marginal-average rule
The rule that marginal cost must equal average cost when average cost is at its minimum.

Marginal cost
The increase in cost required to raise the output of some good or service by one unit.

Marginal cost of pollution abatement
The added cost of reducing a given kind of pollution by one unit.

Marginal factor cost
The amount by which a firm's total factor cost must increase in order for the firm to obtain an additional unit of that factor of production.

Marginal physical product
The increase in output, expressed in physical units, produced by each added unit of one variable input, other things being equal.

Marginal productivity theory of distribution
A theory of the distribution of income according to which each factor of production receives a payment equal to its marginal revenue product.

Marginal rate of substitution
The rate at which one good can be substituted for another with no gain or loss in satisfaction.

Marginal revenue
The amount by which total revenue increases as a result of a one-unit increase in quantity sold.

Marginal revenue product
The change in revenue that results from the sale of the output produced by one additional unit of a factor of production.

Marginal social cost of pollution
The total added cost to all members of society of an additional unit of pollution.

Marginal utility
The amount of added utility gained from a one-unit increase in consumption of a good, other things being equal.

Market
Any arrangement that people have for trading with one another.

Market concentration
The degree to which a market is dominated by a few large firms.

Market coordination
A means of coordinating economic activity that uses the price system to transmit information and provide incentives.

Market failure
An instance in which a market fails to meet accepted standards of efficiency or fairness in performing its functions of transmitting information, providing incentives, and distributing income.

Marketing
The process of finding out what customers want and channeling a flow of goods and services to meet those wants.

Market structure
The key traits of a market, including the number and size of firms, the extent to which the products of various firms are different or similar, and the ease of entry and exit.

Merit good
A good to which all citizens are entitled regardless of ability to pay.

Microeconomics
The branch of economics that deals with the choices and actions of small economic units—households, business firms, and government units.

Minimum efficient scale
The output level at which economies of scale cease.

Model
A simplified representation of the way in which facts are related.

Monopolistic competition
A market structure in which there are many small firms, a differentiated product, and easy entry and exit.

Monopoly
A market structure in which there is only one firm selling a unique product and protected from the entry of rivals.

Monopsony
A situation in which there is only a single buyer in a market.

Natural monopoly
An industry in which average total costs are kept to a minimum by having just one producer serve the entire market.

Natural resources
Anything that can be used as a productive input in its natural state, such as farmland, building sites, forests, and mineral deposits.

Negative income tax
A plan under which all transfer programs would be combined into a single program paying cash benefits that depend on a household's income level.

Net marginal tax rate
The sum of the marginal tax rate for all taxes paid by a household plus the benefit reduction rates of all transfer programs from which the household benefits.

Net worth (owners' equity)
A firm's or household's assets minus its liabilities.

Nominal
In economics, a term that refers to data that have not been adjusted for the effects of inflation.

Normal good
A good for which an increase in consumer income results in an increase in demand.

Normal profit
A term sometimes used to describe the opportunity cost of capital.

Normative economics
The part of economics devoted to making judgments about which economic policies or conditions are good or bad.

Oligopolistic interdependence
In an oligopolistic market, the need to pay close attention to the actions of rival firms when making price or production decisions.

Oligopoly
A market structure in which there are a few firms, at least some of which are large in relation to the size of the market.

Opportunity cost
The cost of a good or service measured in terms of the lost opportunity to pursue the best alternative activity with the same time or resources.

Owners' equity
See Net worth.

Parity-price ratio
The ratio of an index of prices that farmers receive to an index of prices that they pay.

Partnership
An association of two or more people who operate a business as co-owners by voluntary legal agreement.

Perfect competition
A market structure that is characterized by a large number of small firms, a homogeneous product, and freedom of entry and exit.

Perfectly elastic demand
A situation in which the demand curve is a horizontal line.

Perfectly inelastic demand
A situation in which the demand curve is a vertical line.

Positive economics
The part of economics concerned with statements about facts and the relationships among them.

Present value
The present value of a sum, V_t, payable t years in the future, discounted at r percent interest, is the sum V_p that if invested today at r percent interest would grow to the value V_t in t years; the present value formula is $V_p = V_t/(1 + r)^t$.

Price discrimination
The practice of charging different prices for various units of a single product when the price differences are not justified by differences in cost.

Price elasticity of demand
The ratio of the percentage change in the quantity demanded of a good to a given percentage change in its price, other things being equal.

Price elasticity of supply
The ratio of the percentage change in quantity supplied to a given percentage change in the price of a good, other things being equal.

Price fixing
Any action by two or more firms to cooperate in setting prices.

Price leadership
In an oligopoly, a situation in which increases or decreases in price by one dominant firm, known as the *price leader*, are matched by all or most of the other firms in the market.

Price taker
A firm that sells its outputs at prices that are determined by forces beyond its control.

Primary financial markets
Markets in which newly issued stocks, bonds, and other securities are sold.

Principle of diminishing marginal utility
The principle that the greater the consumption of some good, the smaller the increase in utility from a one-unit increase in consumption of that good.

Privatization
The turning over of government functions to the private sector.

Producer surplus
The difference between what producers receive for a unit of a good and the minimum they would be willing to accept.

Production possibility frontier
A graph showing the possible

combinations of goods that can be produced in an economy given the available factors of production and technology.

Protectionism
Any policy intended to shield domestic industries from import competition.

Public assistance
Programs under which transfers are made to people who meet some specified low-income standard.

Public choice theory
The study of how people use the institutions of government in pursuit of self-interest.

Public good
A good or service that (1) cannot be provided for one person without also being provided for others and (2) once provided for one person can be provided for others at zero added cost.

Pure economic profit
The sum that remains when both explicit and implicit costs are subtracted from total revenue.

Pure economic rent
The income earned by any factor of production whose supply is perfectly inelastic.

Rate of return
A firm's accounting profit expressed as a percentage of its net worth.

Rational choice
Purposeful choice directed systematically toward the achievement of objectives given the alternatives and constraints of the situation.

Real
In economics, a term that refers to data that have been adjusted for the effects of inflation.

Regulation
Government intervention in the market for the purpose of influencing the production and

distribution of particular goods and services.

Rent seeking
The activity of obtaining and defending rents.

Revenue
Price times quantity sold.

Scarcity
A situation in which there is not enough of a resource to meet all of everyone's wants.

Secondary financial markets
Markets in which previously issued bonds, stocks, and other securities are traded among investors.

Services
The valued acts that people perform for one another.

Shortage
See Excess quantity demanded.

Short run
A time horizon within which output can be adjusted only by changing the amounts of variable inputs used while fixed inputs remain unchanged.

Social insurance
Programs under which transfers are made available to everyone, regardless of income, upon the occurrence of a specified event such as retirement, unemployment, or disability.

Socialism
An economic system in which firms are owned and controlled by the people who work in them or by the government acting in their name.

Sole proprietorship
A firm that is owned and usually operated by one person, who receives all the profits and is responsible for all of the firm's liabilities.

Static efficiency
The ability of an economy to get the greatest degree of consumer

satisfaction from given resources and technology.

Substitutes
A pair of goods for which an increase in the price of one causes an increase in demand for the other.

Substitution effect
The part of the increase in quantity demanded of a good whose price has fallen that is caused by substitution of the good that is now relatively cheaper for others that are now relatively more costly.

Supply curve
A graphic representation of the relationship between the price of a good and the quantity of it supplied.

Surplus
See Excess quantity supplied.

Tariff
A tax on imported goods.

Tax incidence
The issue of who bears the economic burden of a tax.

Total physical product
Total output of a firm measured in physical units.

Transaction costs
Incidental costs to buyers and sellers of making a transaction, including the costs of gathering information, making decisions, carrying out trades, writing contracts, and making payments.

Transfer payments
Payments by government to individuals that are not made in return for goods and services currently supplied.

Transitivity
The principle that if A is preferred to B and B is preferred to C, A must be preferred to C.

Unemployment rate
The percentage of people in the labor force who are not working but are actively looking for work.

Unit elastic demand
A situation in which price and quantity demanded change by the same percentage and total revenue therefore remains unchanged as price changes.

Utility
The pleasure, satisfaction, or need fulfillment that people get from the consumption of goods and services.

Value of marginal product
Marginal physical product times the product's per-unit price.

Variable inputs
Inputs that can be easily varied within a short time in order to increase or decrease output.

Vertical merger
A merger between firms with a supplier-purchaser relationship.

Index*

---

*Words appearing in boldface type are glossary terms defined in text. The boldface page numbers indicate the pages on which the key terms are defined.